SIXTH EDITION

MACROECONOMICS

Roger A. Arnold

California State University
San Marcos

THOMSON
＊
SOUTH-WESTERN

Australia · Canada · Mexico · Singapore · Spain · United Kingdom · United States

To
Sheila, David,
and Daniel

Macroeconomics, 6e
by Roger A. Arnold

Editor-in-Chief:
Jack W. Calhoun

Vice President, Team Director:
Michael P. Roche

Publisher of Economics:
Michael B. Mercier

Acquisitions Editor:
Michael W. Worls

Developmental Editor:
Jennifer E. Baker

Executive Marketing Manager:
Lisa L. Lysne

Production Editor:
Starratt E. Alexander

Manufacturing Coordinator:
Sandee Milewksi

Production House and Compositor:
Lachina Publishing Services, Inc.

Printer:
Quebecor World Versailles

Sr. Design Project Manager:
Michelle Kunkler

Cover and Internal Designer:
a small design studio, Cincinnati

Cover Images:
© Paul Hardy/Corbis and
© PhotoDisc, Inc.

Photography Manager:
John Hill

Photo Researcher:
Seidel Associates

Library of Congress Control Number:
2002115318

ISBN: 0-324-16358-1

Brief Contents

AN INTRODUCTION TO ECONOMICS

PART 1 Economics: The Science of Scarcity

MACROECONOMICS

PART 2 Macroeconomic Fundamentals

PART 3 Macroeconomic Stability, Instability, and Fiscal Policy

PART 4 Money, the Economy, and Monetary Policy

PART 5 Expectations and Growth

THE WORLD ECONOMY

PART 6 International Economics: Theory and Policy

Contents

AN INTRODUCTION TO ECONOMICS

PART 1 Economics: The Science of Scarcity

FEATURES

Economics in Popular Culture: Why Anna Kournikova and Venus Williams Are Not in College 9

Economics in the World: Why Is the Extended Family Customary in India and Not in the United States? 12

Economics in Everyday Life: A Small Private College in Boston Goes Coed 16

MACROECONOMICS

PART 2 Macroeconomic Fundamentals

F E A T U R E S

Economics in Popular Culture: Who Earned More as President: John F. Kennedy or George W. Bush? 137

Economics in Popular Culture: Economics at the Movies 138

Economics in Technology: The Internet, Information, and Frictional Unemployment 144

Economics in the World: What Explains the Increasing Percentage of Women in the Labor Force? 147

F E A T U R E S

Economics in the World: Underground Economies 157

Economics in Everyday Life: The O.J. Trial, Divorce, Crime, and September 11th 159

Economics in Everyday Life: Does the State of the Economy Influence How People Vote? 169

PART 3 Macroeconomic Stability, Instability, and Fiscal Policy

More on Government Spending and Taxes: Beyond Fiscal Policy 275

FEATURES

Economics in Everyday Life: Two Plumbers on New Year's Eve and Progressive Taxation 278

Economics in The World: Taxes, Smuggling, and Gangs with Machetes 280

Economics in Everyday Life: Special Interests Dressed in Fiscal-Policy and Public-Goods Clothing 283

PART 4   Money, the Economy, and Monetary Policy

Money and Banking 293

FEATURES

Economics in The World: English and Money 297

Economics in Popular Culture: Would Chris Rock Be Funny in a Barter Economy? 298

Economics in Everyday Life: Is Money the Best Gift? 301

Economics in Popular Culture: Economics on the Yellow Brick Road 302

The Federal Reserve System 314

FEATURES

Economics in Everyday Life: Federal Reserve District Banks and the U.S. Attorney General 319

Money and the Economy 328

FEATURES

Economics in The World: Money and Inflation 332

Economics in Popular Culture: The California Gold Rush, or an Apple for $72 335

Economics in Everyday Life: Grade Inflation: It's All Relative 345

FEATURES

Monetary Policy 356

PART 5 Expectations and Growth

FEATURES

Expectations Theory and the Economy 380

FEATURES

Economic Growth: Resources, Technology, and Ideas 400

THE WORLD ECONOMY

PART 6 International Economics: Theory And Policy

F E A T U R E S

Economics in Everyday Life: Dividing Up the Work 422

Economics in The World: Immigration and Wages 430

F E A T U R E S

Economics in Everyday Life: The Nobel Prize in Economics and Foreign Exchange Markets 452

Economics in Everyday Life: Back to the Futures 457

To the Instructor

Nobel laureate James Buchanan once wrote, "a natural economist is one who more or less unconsciously thinks like an economist."[1] But how does an economist think? Buchanan said "an economist . . . views human beings as self interested, utility-maximizing agents, basically independent one from another, and for whom social interchange is initiated and exists simply as a preferred alternative to isolated action."[2] In other words, if we were to tell a natural economist that "human beings are self interested, utility-maximizing agents, basically independent one from another, and for whom social interchange is initiated and exists simply as a preferred alternative to isolated action," we would expect to hear back, "But I never thought things were any different."

Buchanan went on to say that there aren't many natural economists in the world. (Three that he mentioned were Gordon Tullock, Gary Becker, and Armen Alchian.) Those of us who have spent years in the economics profession know that Buchanan is right: there aren't many natural economists. Natural economists are probably no more common than natural-born singers, natural-born baseball players, or natural-born mathematicians.

But just because there are not many natural economists, it doesn't follow that people can't learn how to think about economics naturally. What the phrase "thinking about economics naturally" means to me is to think about economics in an easy, flowing, even effortless way.

To explain what I mean here, consider the difference between Jones and Smith. Jones is a natural-born baseball player. When he is up at bat, he holds the bat correctly, swings correctly, even has just the right snap in his hips. No one had to teach him how to do this, he just does it. Go figure.

On the other hand, Smith is not a natural-born baseball player. It has taken him hours of work to learn how to hold the bat and to swing correctly. But, alas, he has practiced long enough, and he has come to understand the "logic" and "science" of hitting, such that now it comes fairly easily (flowingly) to him. If one didn't know better, one might even say it comes rather "naturally" to him.

Batting coaches can't take individuals who aren't natural-born baseball players and turn them into ones. But they can take individuals who aren't natural-born baseball players and teach them how to play baseball naturally. (Not every Major Leaguer is a natural-born baseball player, but all Major Leaguers play baseball naturally.)

UNDERSTANDING THE LOGIC OF ECONOMICS

If we teach economics as a list of topics (unemployment today, theory of the firm tomorrow), we aren't teaching economics. What we are doing is taking our students on a journey through the "encyclopedia of economics." The best they will ever be able to do is spout back the facts and figures of certain topics—and some of them can do this quite well. But this isn't economics. Economics is a "way of thinking," as as almost everyone has been saying for 50 years now. But it is more than just a way of thinking: it is a way of thinking that is built upon a certain logic. Understand the logic, and you understand how economists think, and you will do economics naturally; don't understand the logic, and you don't understand how economists think, and any economics you do will be forced; it will be hit and miss.

Every economics principles book you pick up today looks like an encyclopedia. Each topic has its "15 minutes of fame" before the next topic arrives on the scene. But if we are to teach economics (and not just take the student on an encyclopedic journey), we have to make sure we say certain things as we pass from one topic to another. We have to take all 101 economic topics and show students how each of the 101 topics can be unraveled—and ultimately understood—using just a few simple economic concepts.

---

1. James M. Buchanan, "The Qualities of a Natural Economist," *Democracy and Public Choice*, ed. Charles Rowley (Oxford: Basil Blackwell Ltd., 1987), p. 9.
2. Ibid.

GETTING A LOT WITH A LITTLE

It has been said that good science is concerned with explaining or predicting behavior as economically as possible. What "economically as possible" means in this context is "with as little as possible." In good science we get a lot from a little.

Getting a lot from a little also holds for the Chinese language. To paraphrase Rudolf Flesch, it is a simple language that conveys a lot.[3] Roughly, whereas English speakers might say, "A dog is an animal," Chinese speakers are much more likely to say something tantamount to "Dog: animal." According to Flesch, Chinese is a language of "full words" (words that have a lot of meaning) and not many "empty words" (words that only connect words that have a lot of meaning) whereas English has many more empty words.

If you think of good science and the Chinese language, there is a similarity. Both are concerned with "getting a lot from a little."

To me, some economics principles books come closer to the "good science–Chinese language" end of the spectrum than others—and that is the part of the spectrum I think one ought to aim for. In other words, while some economics principles books keep to the basics, emphasize the concepts, and develop a reasonable and memorable theme, others do a little of everything, too often take detours, and leave their readers with a feeling of "What just happened here?"

FIVE THEMES

My objective in writing this book was to get as close to the "good science–Chinese language" end of the spectrum as possible. I wanted to keep things simple (without losing meaning), focus on key concepts that can be used repeatedly, and help students learn the logic of economics. If I could do this, I knew students would then have a chance at doing economics naturally.

How did I set out to meet my objective? First, by focusing on theory or model building. Economists use theories or models to organize their thoughts and study the world. The sooner the student learns this, and then goes on to learn how and why it is done, the better.

Second, by focusing on, and repeating as often as possible, the key concepts in economics. The key concepts are the "full words" of the language we call economics.

Third, by emphasizing what Henry Hazlitt thought was one of the key points in economics: the difference between primary and secondary consequences. In other words, by showing, repeatedly, that economic actions have consequences—some further removed from the initial action than others.

Fourth, by pointing out that economists have a certain "model of human behavior" that is implicit in almost all their theories.

Fifth, by softly playing a common tune throughout the text: that economics is about gifts, exchanges, and transfers. Stated differently, there are only three ways to gain in multi-person relationships: by giving or getting a gift (both the gift-giver and gift-recipient gain utility), by exchanging something of lesser value for something of greater value, or by transferring something from others to yourself.

---

3. Rudolf Flesch, *How to Write, Speak, and Think More Effectively* (New York: Penguin Books, 1951).

WHAT PROFESSORS AND STUDENTS HAVE TO SAY

Over the past five editions of this book I have heard from many economics professors and students. Overwhelmingly, they tell me that "the book works." Professors will sometimes add, "Of course, students don't always read as much as we would like them to, but, for the most part, they like reading your book and they read more of it than many other books we have assigned in the past."

Students will often say, "I thought economics was going to be boring. I learned differently. I liked all the applications in the book and, believe it or not, I now look at the world differently than I did before."

It is the last part of this statement—"I now look at the world differently than I did before"—that tells me the student is beginning to understand that economics is more than a list of topics, that it is a "way of thinking" that she is beginning to understand and utilize.

Let me end with a question that I once put to Gary Becker. I once asked him what one or two questions he would ask someone if he wanted to know whether or not the person thinks like an economist. Here is what he had to say:

> *I was recently in Moscow and I was asked by the Vice Dean of Moscow State University to interview some of their students who would come to the University of Chicago to do graduate work. I only had an hour to interview six students so I had to be very quick. I was told what courses they had had, and so I decided to ask them one or two microeconomic questions. My questions were simple economic questions: First, What determines a shortage in a competitive market? Second, What does your answer imply about black market prices? The answers are that a shortage is caused by preventing prices from equilibrating, and black market prices would tend to exceed what market prices would be in a competitive market because supply is restricted. Some [of the students] did quite well and some did not do well. But those would be two of the questions I would ask and there is nothing fancy about them. But the way they answered told me if someone had learned by rote, or had learned to think like an economist.[4]*

As I wrote this book, I always tried to keep Gary Becker's words in mind. Whenever I had written something that I thought the student could only "learn" by memorizing, I decided to delete it and start again. I'd ask myself, "How would a natural economist process the material at hand? What is it that the natural economist thinks that makes this material easy for him?" Then, I'd start to write again. Usually, what followed was some simple economic concept, some example, or some obvious link between the topic before me and some earlier topic. I hope I have asked the right questions and rewritten enough times so that your students will find the economics before them clear, simple, and appealing—almost natural.

---

4. This comes from an interview I conducted with Gary Becker in 1992. The full interview was published in Roger A. Arnold, *Economics*, 2nd ed. (St. Paul, Minnesota: West Publishing Company, 1992).

KEY CONTENT CHANGES

Here are some of the major things that are new to the Sixth Edition of *Economics*.

General Updates and Changes

- Chapter Road Maps at the beginning of each chapter
- Discussion of behavioral economics
- Discussion of corporate scandals
- Discussion of the politics of fiscal policy
- More applications in the *Supply and Demand: Practice* chapter
- Discussion of the Taylor rule in monetary policy
- A new feature, *A Reader Asks*
- More applications of game theory
- More graphs and tables within text
- Cleaner, easier discussion of elasticity
- Better organization of production and costs
- More emphasis on economic thinking and greater discussion of key economic concepts
- New and updated material in the four applications features—*Economics in Everyday Life, Economics in the World, Economics in Popular Culture,* and *Economics in Technology*

ORGANIZATION OF THE SIXTH EDITION

Section I: An Introduction to Economics

Section I presents the "economic way of thinking" to students. Specifically, it introduces key concepts in economics (opportunity cost, efficiency, costs and benefits, deciding at the margin, unintended effects, and more), explains the uses and abuses of theory and theorizing, focuses on two key economic activities—producing and trading—and generally develops one of the key economic frameworks of analysis in economics—supply and demand.

Section II: Macroeconomics

Students start off learning about macroeconomic measurements, then proceed to discuss various schools of macroeconomic thought (Classical, Keynesian, New Classical, Monetarist, New Keynesian) within the context of key economic phenomena—business cycles, inflation, deflation, economic growth, and more. Both fiscal and monetary policy are extensively discussed, as is expectations theory.

Section III: Microeconomics

The theme of the microeconomics part of the book, from the first edition to the sixth, is that microeconomics is about objectives, constraints, and choices. What is the objective of the individual consumer? What constraints does she face? How does she make her choices? What is the objective of the firm? What constraints does it face? How does it make its choices?

Specifically, students start off learning about marginal utility analysis and elasticity, proceed to a discussion of the firm and various market structures, and then turn to a thorough discussion of resource markets and microeconomic policies.

Section IV: The World Economy

In this section of the book students learn the details of international trade theory and international finance theory. Specifically, they learn why countries trade, how exchange rates are established, the effects of tariffs and quotas, and more.

THE STRUCTURE OF EACH CHAPTER

Each chapter of *Economics* contains the following features and pedagogical devices:
- Opening photo and vignette
- Chapter Road Map
- Margin Definitions
- http:// margin links
- Interspersed Questions and Answers
- Thinking Like an Economist
- Applications Features (*Economics in Everyday Life, Economics in Popular Culture, Economics in the World,* and *Economics in Technology*)
- Self-Tests
- A Reader Asks
- Chapter Summary
- Questions and Problems
- Working with Numbers and Graphs
- Internet Activities
- Economic Connections to You

Each of these features and pedagogical devices is described in words and visually in the *Student Learning Guide* that follows this preface.

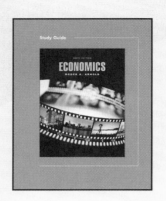

Study Guide

Each chapter explains, reviews, and tests for the important facts, concepts, and diagrams found in corresponding chapters of this book. Chapter parts include a chapter outline, multiple-choice questions, problems and exercises, and a self-test. The Study Guide is also available in microeconomic and macroeconomic splits.

Economics Study Guide   ISBN: 0-324-16364-9
Macroeconomics Study Guide   ISBN: 0-324-16360-6
Microeconomics Study Guide   ISBN: 0-324-16361-4

Practice Tests

Each practice test allows students to test their knowledge of the chapter material before they take the assigned test in class. ISBN: 0-324-16366-5

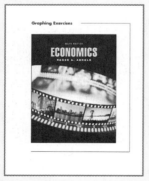

Graphing Exercises in *Economics*

For the introductory economics student, the many graphs in economics may initially seem overwhelming. It takes time and practice to master the "language" of graphs. Graphing Exercises in *Economics* provides you with the practice you need to shorten the time it takes for you to master this language. There are graphing exercises for 17 different topics, including supply and demand, the production possibilities frontier, perfect competition, monopoly, factor markets, and aggregate demand and aggregate supply. ISBN: 0-324-26119-5

Arnold Xtra!

Complimentary access to the Arnold Xtra! Web Site (**http://arnoldxtra.swcollege.com**) is included with every new copy of the textbook.* This site offers a robust set of online multimedia learning tools, including the following.

▣ Diagnostic Pretests
These innovative quizzes offer students diagnostic self-assessment of their comprehension of each chapter and an individualized plan for directed study based on the areas in which they are found to have a weaker understanding.

▣ Technology Road Map
Each chapter's Technology Road Map gives step-by-step instructions associated with each learning objective to guide students systematically through all the activities that will deepen their understanding of that particular concept.

▣ The Graphing Workshop
The Graphing Workshop is a one-stop learning resource for help in mastering the language of graphs, which is one of the more difficult aspects of an economics course for many students. It enables students to explore important economic concepts through a unique learning system made up of tutorials, interactive drawing tools, and exercises that teach how to interpret, reproduce, and explain graphs.

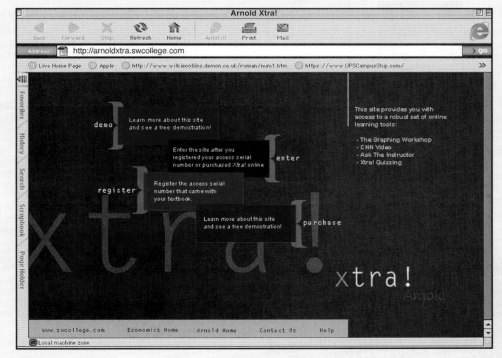

▣ CNN Online
CNN video segments bring the "real world" right to students' desktops. The accompanying CNN video exercises help to illustrate how economics is an important part of their daily lives, and help them learn the material by applying it to current events.

▣ Xtra! Quizzing
Students can create and take randomly generated quizzes on whichever chapters they wish to test themselves, offering them endless practice for exams.

▣ Economic Applications
(e-con @pps) EconNews Online, EconDebate Online, EconData Online, and EconLinks Online features help to deepen students' understanding of theoretical concepts through hands-on exploration and analysis of the latest economic news stories, policy debates, and data.

---

*Students with a used textbook can purchase access to Xtra! online at *http://arnold.swcollege.com*.

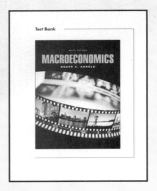

Test Bank

The Test Bank has been revised by Peggy Crane of Southwestern College in San Diego. The Test Bank consists of multiple-choice, true-false, and essay questions. There are more than 4,500 questions in the test bank.

Macroeconomics Test Bank   ISBN: 0-324-16372-X
Microeconomics Test Bank   ISBN: 0-324-16373-8

ExamView Testing Software

ExamView—Computerized Testing Software contains all of the questions in the printed test banks. ExamView is an easy-to-use test creation software compatible with Microsoft Windows. Instructors can add or edit questions, instructions, and answers, and select questions by previewing them on the screen, selecting them randomly, or selecting them by number. Instructors can also create and administer quizzes online, whether over the Internet, a local area network (LAN), or a wide area network (WAN).

ExamView for *Macroeconomics*   ISBN: 0-324-16355-X
ExamView for *Microeconomics*   ISBN: 0-324-16352-5

Instructor's Manual

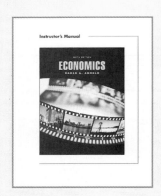

The Instructor's Manual has been revised by Philip Sprunger of Lycoming College. The Instructor's Manual offers detailed lecture assistance, including an overview of each chapter, a list of chapter objectives, key terms, a detailed chapter outline with lecture notes, answers to end-of-chapter questions, and more. ISBN: 0-324-16374-6

Transparency Acetates

More than 150 full color transparencies of key exhibits in the text are available for classroom use.

Macroeconomics Acetates ISBN: 0-324-16299-5
Microeconomics Acetates ISBN: 0-324-16298-7

Microsoft PowerPoint® Presentation Slides

These slides include all exhibits from the textbook. They are available for downloading under "Teaching Resources" at the Arnold Web site **http://arnold.swcollege.com**. ISBN: 0-324-14778-3

Turner Learning/CNN Economics Video with Integration Guide

Professors can bring the real world into the classroom by using the Turner Learning/CNN Economics Video. This video provides current stories of economic interest. The accompanying integration guide provides a summary and discussion questions for each clip. The video is produced in cooperation with Turner Learning Inc. Contact your South-Western/Thomson Learning sales representative for ordering information. ISBN: 0-324-14778-3

Instructor's Resource CD-ROM

Get quick access to all instructor ancillaries from your desktop. This easy-to-use CD lets you review, edit, and copy exactly what you need in the format you want. ISBN: 0-324-16297-9

FOR STUDENTS AND INSTRUCTORS

The Wall Street Journal Edition

The Wall Street Journal is synonymous with the latest word on business, economics, and public policy. *Economics, 6e* makes it easy for students to apply economic concepts to this authoritative publication, and for you to bring the most up-to-date, real-world events into your classroom. For a nominal additional cost, *Economics, 6e* can be packaged with a card entitling students to a 15-week subscription to both the print and online versions of *The Wall Street Journal*. Instructors who have at least seven students activate their subscriptions will automatically receive their own free subscription. Contact your South-Western/Thomson Learning sales representative for package pricing and ordering information.

InfoTrac College Edition

An InfoTrac College Edition 4-month subscription card is automatically packaged free with new copies of this text. With InfoTrac College Edition, journals like *Business Week, Fortune,* and *Forbes* are just a click away! InfoTrac College Edition provides students with anytime, anywhere access to 20 years' worth of full-text articles (*more than 10 million!*) from nearly *4,000* scholarly and popular sources! In addition to receiving the latest business news as reported in the popular business press, students also have access to many other journals, among them those that are particularly valuable to the economics discipline—including the *Economist (US), American Economist, Economic Review,* and *Quarterly Journal of Economics.* For more information on InfoTrac College Edition, visit **http://infotrac/thomsonlearning.com/index.html**.

TextChoice: Economic Issues and Activities

TextChoice is the home of Thomson Learning's online digital content. TextChoice provides the fastest, easiest way for you to create your own learning materials. South-Western's Economic Issues and Activities content database includes a wide variety of high-interest, current event/policy applications as well as classroom activities that are designed specifically to enhance introductory economics courses. Choose just one reading, or many—even add your own material—to create an accompaniment to the textbook that is perfectly customized to your course. Contact your South-Western/Thomson Learning sales representative for more information.

The Arnold *Economics* Web Site

http://arnold.swcollege.com provides instructors and students with updates to the text, teaching and learning resources, and the opportunity to communicate with the author. All Internet addresses in the text are found at this site and are updated regularly.

South-Western Economics Resource Center

A unique, rich and robust online resource for economics instructors and students. **http://economics.swcollege.com** provides customer service and product information, teaching and learning tips and tools, information about careers in economics, access to all of our text-supporting Web sites, and other cutting-edge educational resources such as our highly regarded EconNews, EconDebate, EconData, and EconLinks Online features.

WebTutor™ on WebCT and on Blackboard

Online learning is growing at a rapid pace. Whether instructors are looking to offer courses at a distance, or to offer a web-enhanced classroom, WebTutor provides instructors with text-specific content that interacts in the two leading higher education course management systems—WebCT and Blackboard. WebTutor is a turnkey solution for instructors who want to begin using technology like WebCT or Blackboard, but do not have web-ready content available or do not want to be burdened with developing their own content. South-Western offers two levels of WebTutor—WebTutor and WebTutor Advantage.

WebTutor—An interactive study guide, WebTutor uses the Internet to turn everyone in your class into a front-row student. WebTutor offers quizzing, concept concept review, flashcards, discussion forums, and more. Instructor tools are also provided to assist communication between students and faculty.

WebTutor Advantage—WebTutor Advantage is more than just an interactive study guide because it delivers innovative learning aids that actively engage students. Its benefits include automatic and immediate feedback from quizzes; interactive, multimedia-rich explanation of concepts, such as Flash-animated graphing tutorials and graphing exercises that use an online graph-drawing tool; streaming video applications; online exercises; flashcards; and greater interaction and involvement through online discussion forums. Powerful instructor tools are also provided to assist communication and collaboration between students and faculty.

For more information and a demo of what WebTutor can do for your classes, visit **http://webtutor.swcollege.com**.

IN APPRECIATION

First Edition Reviewers

Paul Seidenstat
Temple University, Pennsylvania

Shahram Shafiee
North Harris County College, Texas

Alan Sleeman
Western Washington University

John Sondey
University of Idaho

Robert W. Thomas
Iowa State University

Richard L. Tontz
California State University, Northridge

Roger Trenary
Kansas State University

Bruce Vanderporten
Loyola University, Illinois

Thomas Weiss
University of Kansas

Richard O. Welch
University of Texas at San Antonio

Donald A. Wells
University of Arizona

John Wight
University of Richmond, Virginia

Thomas Wyrick
Southwest Missouri State University

Second Edition Reviewers

Scott Bloom
North Dakota State University

Thomas Carroll
University of Nevada, Las Vegas

Larry Cox
Southwest Missouri State University

Diane Cunningham
Los Angeles Valley College

Emit Deal
Macon College

Michael Fabritius
University of Mary Hardin Baylor

Frederick Fagal
Marywood College

Ralph Fowler
Diablo Valley College

Bob Gilette
Texas A&M University

Lynn Gillette
Indiana University, Indianapolis

Simon Hakim
Temple University

Lewis Karstensson
University of Nevada, Las Vegas

Abraham Kidane
California State University, Dominguez Hills

W. Barbara Killen
University of Minnesota

J. David Lages
Southwest Missouri State University

Anthony Lee
Austin Community College

Marjory Mabery
Delaware County Community College

Bernard Malamud
University of Nevada, Las Vegas

Michael Marlow
California Polytechnic State University, San Luis Obispo

Phil J. McLewin
Ramapo College of New Jersey

Tina Quinn
Arkansas State University

Terry Ridgway
University of Nevada, Las Vegas

Paul Snoonian
University of Lowell

Paul Taube
Pan American University

Roger Trenary
Kansas State University

Charles Van Eaton
Hillsdale College

Mark Wheeler
Bowling Green State University

Thomas Wyrick
Southwest Missouri State University

Third Edition Reviewers

Carlos Aguilar
University of Texas, El Paso

Rebecca Ann Benakis
New Mexico State University

Scott Bloom
North Dakota State University

Howard Erdman
Southwest Texas Junior College

Arthur Friedberg
Mohawk Valley Community College

Nancy A. Jianakoplos
Colorado State University

Lewis Karstensson
University of Nevada, Las Vegas

Rose Kilburn
Modesto Junior College

Ruby P. Kishan
Southeastern Community College

Duane Kline
Southeastern Community College

Charles A. Roberts
Western Kentucky University

Bill Robinson
University of Nevada, Las Vegas

Susan C. Stephenson
Drake University

Charles Van Eaton
Hillsdale College

Richard O. Welch
The University of Texas at San Antonio

Calla Wiemer
University of Hawaii at Manoa

I would like to thank Peggy Crane of Southwestern College, who revised the Test Bank, Philip Sprunger of Lycoming College, who revised the Instructor's Manual, and Guillermo Cruz of the College of the Canyons who revised the Internet Activities and http:// links that are in each chapter.

I would also like to thank Robert W. Brown, a friend and colleague in the Economics Department at California State University San Marcos. Our long and detailed talks have helped focus my thinking, some of the benefits of which I hope have spilled over into this book.

I owe a deep debt of gratitude to all the fine and creative people I worked with at South-Western College Publishing. These persons include Jack Calhoun, Editor-in-Chief; Mike Roche, Vice-President/Publisher; Mike Worls, Acquisitions Editor; Jennifer Baker, Developmental Editor; Starratt Alexander, Production Editor; Lisa Lysne, Executive Marketing Manager for Economics; Michelle Kunkler, Senior Design Project Manager; and Sandee Milewski, Manufacturing Coordinator. I would also like to thank Barbara Sheridan, copy-editor, of Sheridan Publications Services, who not only did a masterful job of copyediting the book but also made numerous suggestions on how to improve the presentation.

My deepest debt of gratitude goes to my wife, Sheila, and to my two sons, David, twelve years old, and Daniel, fifteen years old. They make all my days happy ones.

Roger A. Arnold

Student Learning Guide

Before you begin your study of economics, it is important to know something about the road you are about to travel. That's what this preface is about. Let me suggest how you should read and study this book to get the most out of it. You will find the road to learning economics less bumpy if you know something about the structure of each chapter and about the pedagogical devices used throughout the text.

Chapter Structure and Pedagogy

ch.2

ECONOMIC ACTIVITIES: PRODUCING AND TRADING

■ **Opening Photo and Vignette**

Each chapter opens with a photo and short vignette. Look at the photo and read the vignette (it will take no more than 15 seconds to do both) to get an idea of what the chapter is about.

■ **Chapter Road Map**

Reading an economics textbook for the first time is similar to driving to a place you haven't been before: It's easy to get lost. Sometimes a simple road map helps. Each chapter of this book opens with a chapter road map. By reading the opening paragraphs and consulting the chapter road map, you will have a good idea of where your journey through the chapter will take you.

Besides looking at the road map before you start to read the chapter, take another look at it when you have completed the chapter, and also here and there along the way. Referring back to it now and again will help you put the material you are reading into usable form. You will see how what you are currently reading relates to something you read earlier in the chapter, and you will realize how what you are reading now will be connected with something you will soon read about.

■ **Interspersed Questions and Answers**

As you are reading, you may have some questions. This feature tries to anticipate the questions you might have. It then answers those questions. These questions and answers are placed at natural stopping places in each chapter.

■ **Self-Tests**

Frequent feedback plays an important role in learning new material, so Self-Tests are included throughout the chapters. The answers to the Self-Tests are at the end of the book. Don't skip over a Self-Test because you are in a hurry. Stop, take the test, and then check your answers. If you don't answer a question correctly, go back and reread the relevant material so that you can answer it correctly.

Self-Test

1. Identify what will happen to the price level and Real GDP (in the short run) as a result of each of the following:
   a. SRAS rises
   b. SRAS falls
   c. AD rises
   d. AD falls
   e. AD rises by more than SRAS rises
   f. AD falls by less than SRAS falls
2. Explain Exhibit 11 in your own words.

LONG-RUN AGGREGATE SUPPLY

In this section, we discuss long-run aggregate supply and draw a long-run aggregate supply (LRAS) curve. We also discuss long-run equilibrium and explain how it differs from short-run equilibrium.

exhibit 12

A Summary Exhibit of AD and SRAS

GOING FROM THE SHORT RUN TO THE LONG RUN

Graphically, short-run equilibrium is at the intersection of the AD curve and the (upward-sloping) SRAS curve. As an earlier section explains, economists give

Economy in the Short Run

Self-Test

◼ Margin Definitions

The first time you study economics, you have a lot to learn: language, concepts, theories, and ways of thinking. This feature helps you learn the language of economics. All key economics terms and their definitions are in the margins of the text. To more effectively learn and understand these definitions, you may find it useful to first read them and then to re-state them in your own words.

◼ http://

This Internet feature is placed in the margins of the text. It points you to a Web site address where you can find information that relates to the discussion of the material in the text. You can use this feature to enhance your understanding of the chapter, as a starting point for research, or just to check out some interesting, real-world applications of economics.

◼ Thinking Like an Economist

Most economics instructors believe that a primary goal of this course is to teach you how economists think. There's more to thinking like an economist than knowing the concepts and technical tools of analysis. There's a special way of looking at situations, events, decisions, and behavior. Pay attention to this feature—it will give you unique insight into the economist's mind, allowing you to see how interesting issues are approached from an economic perspective.

Budget Deficit
Government expenditures greater than tax revenues.

Budget Surplus
Tax revenues greater than government expenditures.

Balanced Budget
Government expenditures equal to tax revenues.

Expansionary Fiscal Policy
Increases in government expenditures and/or decreases in taxes to achieve particular economic goals.

Contractionary Fiscal Policy
Decreases in government expenditures and/or increases in taxes to achieve particular economic goals.

Discretionary Fiscal Policy
Deliberate changes of government expenditures and/or taxes to achieve particular economic goals.

Automatic Fiscal Policy
Changes in government expenditures that a...

expenditures and tax revenues. If expenditures are greater than tax revenues, a **budget deficit** exists. If tax revenues are greater than expenditures, a **budget surplus** exists. If expenditures equal tax revenues, a **balanced budget** exists.

SOME RELEVANT FISCAL POLICY TERMS
Notice in our definition of fiscal policy that we use the term *government expenditures* instead of *government purchases*, the term you are familiar with from earlier chapters. Government expenditures—which is sometimes simply called *government spending*—is not the same as *government purchases*. Government expenditures is the sum of government purchases and (government) transfer payments.[1]

Expansionary fiscal policy refers to increases in government expenditures and/or decreases in taxes to achieve macroeconomic goals. **Contractionary fiscal policy** refers to decreases in government expenditures and/or increases in taxes to achieve these goals.

Expansionary fiscal policy: Government expenditures up and/or taxes down
Contractionary fiscal policy: Government expenditures down and/or taxes up

When changes in government expenditures and taxes are brought about deliberately through government actions, fiscal policy is said to be *discretionary*. For example, if Congress decides to increase government spending by, say, $10 billion in an attempt to lower the unemployment rate, this is an act of **discretionary fiscal policy**. In contrast, a change in either government expenditures or taxes that occurs automatically in response to economic events is referred to as **automatic fiscal policy**. To illustrate, suppose Real GDP in the economy turns down, causing more people to become unemployed. As a result, more people automatically receive unemployment benefits. These added unemployment benefits automatically boost government spending.

---

around the existing quantity of money between various individuals and firms but do not change the total.

Self-Test (*Answers to Self-Test questions are in the Self-Test Appendix.*)

1. Why (not how) did money evolve out of a barter economy?
2. If individuals remove funds from their checkable deposits and transfer them to their money market accounts, will M1 fall and M2 rise? Explain your answer.
3. How does money reduce the transaction costs of making trades?

HOW BANKING DEVELOPED

Just as money evolved, so did banking. This section discusses the origins of banking. The discussion will shed some light on and aid in understanding modern banking.

THE EARLY BANKERS
Our money today is easy to carry and transport. But money was not always so portable. For example, when money was principally gold coins, carrying it about was neither easy nor safe. First, gold is heavy. Second, a person transporting thousands of gold coins can easily draw the attention of thieves. But storing gold ... be risky. Most individuals turned to their local goldsmith for ... was already equipped with safe storage facilities. Goldsmiths ... ...nkers. They took in other people's gold and stored it for them. ...what th...'d deposited gold, goldsmiths issued receipts called ...

http://
Go to *http://www.frbsf.org/currency/civilwar/show.html*. Why aren't living persons portrayed on U.S. money? What do you think explains the reason postage stamps were used as a substitute for coins during the Civil War? What is a greenback?

http://
Go to *http://www.jpmchase.com*. Under the "About the firm" menu, select "History" and then "JPMorgan." When was J. P. Morgan founded? Who were the customers of J. P. Morgan? What effect did the Glass-Steagall Act have on J. P. Morgan? Do you think large companies use banks the same way today as they did 100 years ago?

---

of labor. You will see in the next chapter that the flexible wages and prices position taken by these economists has not gone unchallenged.

The following table summarizes how a self-regulating economy works for three possible states of the economy.

State of the Economy	What Happens If the Economy Is Self-Regulating?
Recessionary gap (Real GDP < Natural Real GDP)	Wages fall and *SRAS* curve shifts to the right until Real GDP = Natural Real GDP.
Inflationary gap (Real GDP > Natural Real GDP)	Wages rise and *SRAS* curve shifts to the left until Real GDP = Natural Real GDP.
Long-run equilibrium (Real GDP = Natural Real GDP)	No change in wages and no change in SRAS.

THINKING LIKE AN ECONOMIST

Like other scientists, economists are often interested in knowing whether the phenomena they are studying have a natural resting place. For example, the natural resting place for a ball thrown high into the air is the ground. Gravity pulls the ball downward. Where is the natural resting place for a competitive market? It is where the quantity demanded of a good equals the quantity supplied of the good. Markets are "at rest" when they are in equilibrium.

Macroeconomists want to know if the economy has a natural resting place. Some economists think it does. They think the natural resting place for the economy is where Natural Real GDP is being produced and the natural unemployment rate exists. Economists who believe that the economy can eliminate both recessionary and inflationary gaps smoothly and quickly by itself, and thus return to its natural state, use the analogy of a person's normal body temperature, which is ...

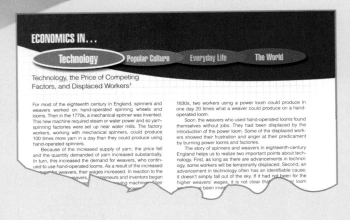

Applications Features

Read the features in each chapter titled *Economics in Everyday Life, Economics in Popular Culture, Economics in the World,* and *Economics in Technology*. Often, students gloss over these features because they think they are irrelevant to the discussion in the main body of the text. Nothing could be further from the truth. These features often apply the tools, concepts, and theories discussed in the main body of the text. Without these applications, economics may initially seem dry and abstract. To dispel the notion that economics is simply about inflation, unemployment, costs of production, profit, economic growth, monetary and fiscal policy, and so on, I have included these applications features to show you some of the interesting, everyday things that economics is about. Economics, as I hope you will soon learn, is about many more things than you have ever imagined.

A Reader Asks

Have you ever wanted to ask an instructor a question you thought you might get into trouble for asking? Suppose you're learning about supply and demand in economics and you really want to ask, "How will supply and demand help me?" But you don't ask the question because you think the professor will take offense.

Or suppose you want to ask a very practical question, such as, "How much do economists earn?" or "Is an economics degree respected in the marketplace?" Here, you may not ask the question because you think it isn't quite academic enough.

In the feature *A Reader Asks*, I answer some of the pointed and basic questions that real readers have on their minds.

Graphs and Exhibits

Take your time with the diagrams. An introductory course in economics is full of diagrams, and they are central to communicating economic material. The sooner you learn to "think diagrammatically," the more quickly and thoroughly you will learn economics. The way you learn to think in diagrams is to work with them. Read the caption, identify the curves that are mentioned in the text, explain to yourself what they mean when they shift right and left, and so on. Every diagram tells a story; you need to find out what the story is.

Graphs

I've carefully used consistent colors, shaded arrows to show movement, multistep formats, and boxed explanations to make it easy for you to visually interpret important economic concepts at a glance.

■ A Closer Look

For many students, the difficult part of economics is seeing how all the topics and concepts fit together. Use these special diagrams to more easily understand how the separate pieces of the puzzle fit together to form a cohesive picture of complex interrelationships. Flow diagrams and other unifying devices are used to help you identify cause-effect relationships and clarify the connections between concepts.

Chapter Summary

■ Chapter Summary

Each chapter ends with a detailed and categorized summary of the main topics in the chapter. The summary is a useful refresher before class and a good starting point for studying.

■ Questions and Problems

Each chapter ends with numerous questions and problems. Be sure to answer all the questions at the end of each chapter. You never really know how well you have learned economics until someone calls upon you to answer a question. If we can't use what we have read and studied to answer a question, we have to wonder if we learned anything in the first place.

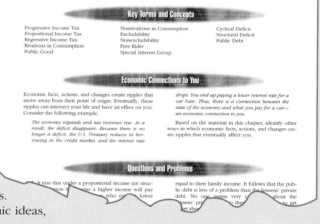

■ Working with Numbers and Graphs

Each chapter ends with a few numerical and graphical problems. When you are able to numerically and graphically analyze economic ideas, you will solidify your conceptual understanding.

■ Key Terms and Concepts

A list of key terms concludes each chapter. If you can define all these terms, you have a good head start on studying.

■ Economic Connections to You

Economic Connections to You is a short feature at the end of the chapter. Economic Connections to You requires you to identify how economic facts, actions, and changes (discussed in the chapter) affect you. This feature challenges you to apply your newly acquired economic analysis skills.

■ Internet Activities

Each chapter ends with Web activities, helping you broaden your understanding of the chapter by applying what you've learned to interpreting economic data on the Internet.

Arnold Xtra!

You are probably already aware that you have your own unique learning style—the way you digest information the best. You may learn by reading information, hearing it, seeing it, having hands-on experiences, and so on. Each of these learning styles requires different tools for the most effective delivery of information, and so a textbook alone may not offer you the optimal way to learn. Luckily, today's technology can offer an exciting array of tools to support and extend the textbook in order to reach out to a variety of students like yourself, each of whom has different needs in terms of how they learn best.

To this end, you'll find that complimentary access to the Arnold Xtra! Web site (**http://arnoldxtra.swcollege.com**) is included with every new copy of this textbook. Arnold Xtra! provides you with a comprehensive set of online multimedia learning tools that will help you gain a deeper and richer understanding of the material on many different levels—not just reading the text, but also seeing, hearing, and doing.

Here is a tour through some of the features that you will find in Arnold Xtra!

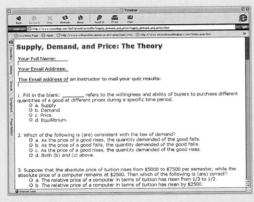

DIAGNOSTIC PRETESTS

These innovative quizzes offer diagnostic self-assessment and an individualized plan for directed study of each chapter. Start each chapter by taking the pretest to assess your understanding of key chapter learning objectives. If you answer a question incorrectly, Xtra! will link you to a Technology Road Map (see below) that will guide you systematically through a variety of learning tools to eliminate confusion and solidify your understanding.

TECHNOLOGY ROAD MAPS

You can also begin studying each chapter by using the Technology Road Map feature. Each chapter's Technology Road Map functions as a central navigational tool and complete e-learning guide to all the Xtra! resources that are available to enhance comprehension of the chapter's main ideas. Step-by-step instructions associated with each chapter learning objective guide you systematically through all available text and multimedia tools to deepen your understanding of that particular concept.

THE GRAPHING WORKSHOP

The Graphing Workshop is your one-stop learning resource for help in mastering the language of graphs, one of the more difficult aspects of economics for many students. It enables you to explore important economic concepts through a unique learning system made up of tutorials, interactive tools, and exercises that teach how to interpret, reproduce, and explain graphs:

► **Grasp It!** Java-powered graphs allow you to grasp key economics graphing concepts through hands-on interaction with a "live" graph.
► **See It!** Animated graphing tutorials provide step-by-step graphical presentations and audio explanations.
► **Try It!** Interactive graphing exercises encourage you to practice manipulating and interpreting graphs with hands-on Java graphing tools. You can check your work online.
► **Apply It!** Interactive graphing assignments challenge you to apply what you have learned by creating your own graphs from scratch to analyze a specific scenario. Answers can be printed and/or e-mailed to your instructor for grading.

CNN ONLINE

CNN video segments bring the "real world" to your desktop. The accompanying CNN Video exercises help to illustrate how economics is an important part of your daily life and help you learn the material by applying it to current events.

ASK THE INSTRUCTOR

Via streaming video, difficult concepts from each chapter are explained and illustrated. These video clips are extremely helpful review and clarification tools if you have trouble understanding an in-class lecture or are a visual learner.

XTRA! QUIZZING

You can practice for tests, midterms, and finals by creating and taking as many randomly generated quizzes as you like on whichever chapters you wish to test yourself.

ECONOMIC APPLICATIONS (E-CON @PPS)

EconNews Online, EconDebate Online, EconData Online and EconLinks Online features help to deepen your understanding of theoretical concepts through hands-on exploration and analysis of the latest economic news stories, policy debates, and data.

ch.1

WHAT ECONOMICS IS ABOUT

Economists look at the world and ask questions. Their questions give us insights into the economic way of thinking. For example, an economist might look at a college student and ask: What are the benefits and costs to this student of attending college? Thus, the economic way of thinking considers both benefits and costs, and not only one or the other. You will learn much more about the economic way of thinking in this chapter and throughout the book.

Chapter Road Map

Reading an economics textbook for the first time is similar to driving to a place you haven't been to before: it's easy to get lost. Following a simple road map makes it less likely you will get lost driving; referring to an economics road map makes it less likely you will get lost studying economics.

Each chapter in this text begins with a road map. By reading these opening paragraphs and consulting the chapter road map, you will have a good idea of where your journey through the chapter will take you.

This chapter starts with a basic question: What is economics? *An economist might answer this question by giving a formal dictionary-like definition of economics or by discussing the* economic way of thinking. *In this chapter, we both define economics and outline the details of the economic way of thinking—thinking in terms of (1) various categories of economics, (2) key concepts in economics, and (3) building and testing theories.*

DEFINITIONS OF ECONOMICS

Economics has been defined in various ways in its more than 200 year history. However, some definitions of economics are familiar to almost all economists. We identify three of these definitions in this section, and then give the definition of economics that we use in this text.

The economist Alfred Marshall (1824–1924) was Professor of Political Economy at the University of Cambridge (in England) from 1885 to 1908. Marshall's major work, *Principles of Economics* (first published in 1890), was the most influential economics treatise of its time and has been called the "Bible of British Economics." In the first few lines of the book, Marshall wrote: "Political economy or economics is a study of mankind in the ordinary business of life; it examines that part of individual and social action which is most closely connected with the attainment and with the use of the material requisites of well being." He then said that economics is "on the one side a study of wealth; and on the other, and more important side, a part of the study of man." In short, according to Marshall, economics is the study of mankind in the ordinary business of life; it is the study of wealth and of man.

Lionel Robbins (1898–1984), who taught economics at both Oxford University and the London School of Economics, put forth one of the most widely cited definitions of economics. In his book *The Nature and Significance of Economic Science,* Robbins wrote, "Economics is the science which studies human behavior as a relationship between ends and scarce means which have alternative uses."

Milton Friedman (b. 1912), the 1976 winner of the Nobel Prize in Economics, proposed a similar definition of economics in his work *Price Theory*. Friedman wrote, "Economics is the science of how a particular society solves its economic problems." He then said, "an economic problem exists whenever scarce means are used to satisfy alternative ends."

Ask a noneconomist what economics is and he or she will probably answer that it has something to do with business and wealth. So Marshall's definition of economics accords most closely with the a noneconomist's concept of economics. The Robbins and Friedman definitions both stress the relationship between *ends* and *means*. This relationship naturally leads us to a discussion of scarcity.

Scarcity is the condition in which our wants are greater than the limited resources available to satisfy them. Our wants are *infinite;* our resources are *finite*. That's scarcity. To define scarcity in terms of ends and means, we can say that our ends are *infinite* and the means available to satisfy those ends are *finite*.

Many economists say that if scarcity didn't exist, neither would economics. In other words, if our wants weren't greater than the limited resources available to satisfy them, there would be no field of study called economics. This is similar to saying that if matter and motion didn't exist, neither would physics, or that if living things didn't exist, neither would biology. For this reason, we define **economics** in this text as the *science of scarcity*. More completely, *economics is the science of how individuals and societies deal with the fact that wants (or ends) are greater than the limited resources (or means) available to satisfy those wants*.

Scarcity
The condition in which our wants are greater than the limited resources available to satisfy those wants.

Economics
The science of scarcity: the science of how individuals and societies deal with the fact that wants are greater than the limited resources available to satisfy those wants.

ECONOMIC CATEGORIES

Economics is sometimes broken down into different categories, according to the type of questions economists ask. Four common economic categories are positive economics, normative economics, microeconomics, and macroeconomics.

POSITIVE AND NORMATIVE ECONOMICS

Positive economics attempts to determine *what is.* **Normative economics** addresses *what should be*. Essentially, positive economics deals with cause-effect relationships that can be tested. Normative economics deals with value judgments and opinions that cannot be tested.

Positive Economics
The study of "what is" in economic matters.

Normative Economics
The study of "what should be" in economic matters.

Many topics in economics can be discussed within both a positive and a normative framework. Consider a proposed cut in federal income taxes. An economist practicing positive economics would want to know the *effect* of a cut in income taxes. For example, she may want to know how a tax cut will affect the unemployment rate, economic growth, inflation, and so on. An economist practicing normative economics would address issues that directly or indirectly relate to whether the federal income tax *should* be cut. For example, she may say that federal income taxes should be cut because the income tax burden on many taxpayers is currently high.

This book mainly deals with positive economics. For the most part, we discuss the economic world as it is, not the way someone might think it should be. As you read, you should keep two points in mind. First, although we have taken pains to keep our discussion within the boundaries of positive economics, at times we may operate perilously close to the normative border. If, here and there, we drop a value judgment into the discussion, recognize it for what it is. You should not accept as true something that we simply state as an opinion.

Second, keep in mind that no matter what your normative objectives are, positive economics can shed some light on how they might be accomplished. For example, suppose you believe that absolute poverty should be eliminated and the unemployment rate should be lowered. No doubt you have ideas as to how these goals can be accomplished. But are they correct? For example, will a greater redistribution of income eliminate absolute poverty? Will lowering taxes lower the unemployment rate? There is no guarantee that the means you think will bring about certain ends will do so. This is where sound positive economics can help. It helps us see what is. As someone once said: It is not enough to want to do good, it is important also to know how to do good.

MICROECONOMICS AND MACROECONOMICS

It has been said that the tools of microeconomics are microscopes, and the tools of macroeconomics are telescopes. Macroeconomics stands back from the trees in order to see the forest. Microeconomics gets up close and examines the tree itself, its bark, its limbs, and the soil in which it grows. **Microeconomics** is the branch of economics that deals with human behavior and choices as they relate to relatively small units—an individual, a firm, an industry, a single market. **Macroeconomics** is the branch of economics that deals with human behavior and choices as they relate to an entire economy. In microeconomics, economists discuss a single price; in macroeconomics, they discuss the price level. Microeconomics deals with the demand for a particular good or service; macroeconomics deals with aggregate, or total, demand for goods and services. Microeconomics examines how a tax change affects a single firm's output; macroeconomics looks at how a tax change affects an entire economy's output.

Microeconomists and macroeconomists ask different types of questions. A microeconomist might be interested in answering such questions as:

- How does a market work?
- What level of output does a firm produce?
- What price does a firm charge for the good it produces?
- How does a consumer determine how much of a good he will buy?
- Can government policy affect business behavior?
- Can government policy affect consumer behavior?

On the other hand, a macroeconomist might be interested in answering such questions as:

- How does the economy work?
- Why is the unemployment rate sometimes high and sometimes low?
- What causes inflation?
- Why do some national economies grow faster than other national economies?

Microeconomics
The branch of economics that deals with human behavior and choices as they relate to relatively small units—an individual, a firm, an industry, a single market.

Macroeconomics
The branch of economics that deals with human behavior and choices as they relate to highly aggregate markets (such as the goods and services market) or to the entire economy.

- What might cause interest rates to be low one year and high the next?
- How do changes in the money supply affect the economy?
- How do changes in government spending and taxes affect the economy?

Self-Test *(Answers to Self-Test questions are in the Self-Test Appendix.)*

1. Scarcity is the condition of finite resources. True or false? Explain your answer.
2. How are the Friedman and Robbins definitions of economics similar?
3. What is the difference between positive and normative economics? What is the difference between macroeconomics and microeconomics?

KEY CONCEPTS IN ECONOMICS

You can think of the key concepts in economics as tools that the economist keeps in a tool bag. Just as a carpenter uses tools (saw, hammer, screwdriver) to build a house, an economist uses tools to analyze or discuss something of interest. Most of the tools in the economist's tool bag are unique to economics—you won't find them in the sociologist's, historian's, or psychologist's tool bags. A few tools, though, are not unique to economics. The first nine concepts we discuss in this section are used principally by economists; the last two concepts are used by both economists and others.

THINKING IN TERMS OF SCARCITY AND ITS EFFECTS

Recall that *scarcity* is the condition in which our wants are greater than the limited resources available to satisfy them. But what are our wants? Our wants include anything that provides **utility** or satisfaction. In economics, something that provides utility or satisfaction is called a **good.** Something that provides **disutility** or dissatisfaction is called a **bad.** For example, for most people pollution is a bad. Basically, people want goods and they don't want bads.

A good can be either tangible or intangible. For example, a car is a tangible good; friendship is an intangible good. Goods do not just appear before us when we snap our fingers. It takes resources to produce goods. (Sometimes resources are referred to as *inputs* or *factors of production*.)

Generally, economists divide resources into four broad categories: land, labor, capital, and entrepreneurship. **Land** includes natural resources, such as minerals, forests, water, and unimproved land. For example, oil, wood, and animals fall into this category. (Sometimes economists refer to this category simply as *natural resources*.)

Labor consists of the physical and mental talents people contribute to the production process. For example, a person building a house is using his or her own labor.

Capital consists of produced goods that can be used as inputs for further production. Factories, machinery, tools, computers, and buildings are examples of capital. One country might have more capital than another. This means that it has more factories, machinery, tools, and so on.

Entrepreneurship refers to the particular talent that some people have for organizing the resources of land, labor, and capital to produce goods, seek new business opportunities, and develop new ways of doing things.

Scarcity and the Need for a Rationing Device

How does scarcity affect your life? Imagine you are considering buying a T-shirt for $10 at the university bookstore. The T-shirt has a price of $10 because of scarcity. There is a scarcity of T-shirts because people want more T-shirts than there are T-shirts available. And as long as there is a scarcity of anything, there is a need for a rationing device. Dollar price is a **rationing device.** If you are

Utility
The satisfaction one receives from a good.

Good
Anything from which individuals receive utility or satisfaction.

Disutility
The dissatisfaction one receives from a bad.

Bad
Anything from which individuals receive disutility or dissatisfaction.

Land
All natural resources, such as minerals, forests, water, and unimproved land.

Labor
The physical and mental talents people contribute to the production process.

Capital
Produced goods that can be used as inputs for further production, such as factories, machinery, tools, computers, and buildings.

Entrepreneurship
The particular talent that some people have for organizing the resources of land, labor, and capital to produce goods, seek new business opportunities, and develop new ways of doing things.

Rationing Device
A means for deciding who gets what of available resources and goods.

willing and able to pay the price, the T-shirt is yours. If you are either unwilling or unable to pay the price, the T-shirt will not become yours.

If scarcity didn't exist, there would be no need for a rationing device and people wouldn't pay dollar prices for resources and goods. In every transaction—buying a T-shirt at the university bookstore, buying food in a grocery store, or buying a new computer—scarcity plays a role.

Scarcity and Competition

Do you see much competition in the world today? Are people competing for jobs? Are states and cities competing for businesses? Are students competing for grades? The answer to all these questions is yes. The economist wants to know why this competition exists and what form it takes. First, the economist concludes, *competition exists because of scarcity*. If there were enough resources to satisfy all our seemingly unlimited wants, people would not have to compete for the available but limited resources.

Second, the economist sees that competition takes the form of people trying to get more of the rationing device. If dollar price is the rationing device, people will compete to earn dollars. Look at your own case. You are a college student working for a degree. One reason (but perhaps not the only reason) you are attending college is to earn a higher income after graduation. But why do you want a higher income? You want it because it will allow you to satisfy more of your wants.

Suppose muscular strength (measured by lifting weights) were the rationing device instead of dollar price. People with more muscular strength would receive more resources and goods than people with less muscular strength would receive. In this situation, people would compete for muscular strength. The lesson is simple: *Whatever the rationing device, people will compete for it.*

THINKING IN TERMS OF OPPORTUNITY COST

Opportunity Cost
The most highly valued opportunity or alternative forfeited when a choice is made.

As noted earlier, people have to make choices because scarcity exists. Because our seemingly unlimited wants push up against limited resources, some wants must go unsatisfied. We must therefore choose which wants we will satisfy and which we will not. The most highly valued opportunity or alternative forfeited when a choice is made is known as **opportunity cost.** Every time you make a choice, you incur an opportunity cost. For example, you have chosen to read this chapter. In making this choice, you denied yourself the benefits of doing something else. You could have watched television, e-mailed a friend, taken a nap, eaten a pizza, read a novel, shopped for a new computer, and so on. Whatever you would have chosen to do had you decided not to read this chapter is the opportunity cost of your reading this chapter. For example, if you would have watched television had you chosen not to read this chapter—if this was your next best alternative—then the opportunity cost of reading this chapter is watching television.

Opportunity Cost and Behavior

Economists think about people's behavior in terms of opportunity cost. Specifically, they believe that a change in opportunity cost will change a person's behavior. For example, consider Bill, who is a sophomore at the University of Kansas. He attends classes Monday through Thursday of every week. Every time he chooses to go to class he gives up the opportunity to do something else, such as the opportunity to earn $8 an hour working at a job. The opportunity cost of Bill spending an hour in class is $8.

Now let's raise the opportunity cost of attending class. On Tuesday, we offer Bill $70 to cut his economics class. He knows that if he attends his economics class he will forfeit $70. What will Bill do? An economist would predict that as the opportunity cost of attending class increases relative to the benefits of attending class, Bill is less likely to attend class.

This is how economists think about behavior, whether it is Bill's or your own. *The higher the opportunity cost of doing something, the less likely it will be done.* This is part of the economic way of thinking.

Before you continue, look at Exhibit 1, which summarizes some of the things about scarcity, choice, and opportunity cost up to this point.

There Is No Such Thing as a Free Lunch

Economists are fond of saying that *there is no such thing as a free lunch*. This catchy phrase expresses the idea that opportunity costs are incurred when choices are made. Perhaps this is an obvious point, but consider how often people mistakenly assume there *is* a free lunch. For example, some parents think education is free because they do not pay tuition for their children to attend public elementary school. Sorry, but there is no such thing as a free lunch. Free implies no sacrifice, no opportunities forfeited, which is not true in regard to elementary school education. Resources that could be used for other things are used to provide elementary school education.

Consider the people who speak about free medical care, free housing, free bridges ("there is no charge to cross it"), and free parks. None of these are actually free. The resources that provide medical care, housing, bridges, and parks could have been used in other ways.

THINKING IN TERMS OF COSTS AND BENEFITS

If it is possible to eliminate air pollution completely, should all air pollution be eliminated? If your answer is yes, then you are probably focusing on the *benefits* of eliminating air pollution. For example, one benefit might be healthier individuals. Certainly individuals who do not breathe polluted air have fewer lung disorders than people who do breathe polluted air.

But benefits rarely come without costs. The economist reminds us that while there are benefits to eliminating pollution, there are costs too. To illustrate, one way to eliminate all car pollution tomorrow is to pass a law stating that anyone caught driving a car will go to prison for 40 years. With such a law in place, and enforced, very few people would drive cars and all car pollution would be a thing of the past. Presto! Cleaner air! However, many people would think that the cost of obtaining that cleaner air is too high. Someone might say, "I want cleaner air, but not if I have to completely give up driving my car. How will I get to work?"

What distinguishes the economist from the noneconomist is that the economist thinks in terms of *both* costs and benefits. Often, the noneconomist thinks

exhibit 1

Scarcity and Related Concepts

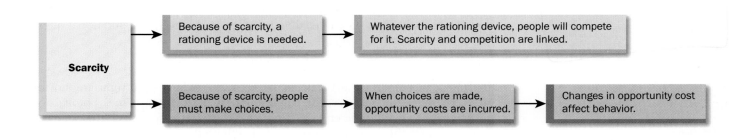

in terms of either one or the other. There are benefits from studying, but there are costs too. There are benefits to coming to class, but there are costs too. There are costs to getting up early each morning and exercising, but let's not forget that there are benefits too.

THINKING IN TERMS OF DECISIONS MADE AT THE MARGIN

It is late at night and you have already studied three hours for your biology test tomorrow. You look at the clock and wonder if you should study another hour. How would you summarize your thinking process? What question or questions do you ask yourself to decide whether or not to study another hour?

Perhaps without knowing it, you think in terms of the costs and benefits of further study. You probably realize that there are certain benefits from studying an additional hour (you may be able to raise your grade a few points), but that there are costs too (you will get less sleep or have less time to watch television or talk on the phone with a friend). Thinking in terms of costs and benefits, though, doesn't tell us *how* you think in terms of costs and benefits. For example, when deciding what to do, do you look at the total costs and total benefits of the proposed action or do you look at something less than the total costs and benefits? According to economists, for most decisions you think in terms of *additional,* or *marginal,* costs and benefits, not *total* costs and benefits. That's because most decisions deal with making a small, or additional, change.

To illustrate, suppose you just finished eating a hamburger and drinking a soda for lunch. You are still a little hungry and are considering whether or not to order another hamburger. An economist would say that in deciding whether or not to order another hamburger, you will compare the additional benefits of the additional hamburger to the additional costs of the additional hamburger. In economics, the word "marginal" is a synonym for "additional." So we say that you will compare the marginal benefits of the (next) hamburger to the marginal costs of the (next) hamburger. If the marginal benefits are greater than the marginal costs, you obviously expect a net (marginal) benefit to ordering the next hamburger, and therefore you order the next hamburger. If, however, the marginal costs of the hamburger are greater than the marginal benefits, you obviously expect a net (marginal) cost to ordering the next hamburger, and therefore you do not order the next hamburger.

What you don't consider when making this decision are the total benefits and total costs of hamburgers. That's because the benefits and costs connected with the first hamburger (the one you have already eaten) are no longer relevant to the current decision. You are not deciding between eating two hamburgers and eating no hamburgers; your decision is whether to eat a second hamburger after you have already eaten a first hamburger.

According to economists, when individuals make decisions by comparing marginal benefits to marginal costs, they are making **decisions at the margin.** The President of the United States makes a decision at the margin when deciding whether or not to talk another 10 minutes with the Speaker of the House of Representatives, the employee makes a decision at the margin when deciding whether or not to work two hours overtime, and the college professor makes a decision at the margin when deciding whether or not to add an additional question to the final exam.

Decisions at the Margin
Decision making characterized by weighing additional (marginal) benefits of a change against the additional (marginal) costs of a change with respect to current conditions.

THINKING IN TERMS OF EFFICIENCY

Suppose you are studying for an economics test. What is the right amount of time to study? In economics, the "right amount" of anything is the "optimal" or "efficient" amount and the efficient amount is the amount for which the marginal benefits equal the marginal costs. Stated differently, you have achieved **efficiency** when the marginal benefits equal the marginal costs.

To illustrate, suppose for the first hour of studying, the marginal benefits (MB) are greater than the marginal costs (MC):

Efficiency
Exists when marginal benefits equal marginal costs.

Why Anna Kournikova and Venus Williams Are Not in College

Anna Kournikova and Venus Williams are well-known tennis players. Kournikova was born in 1981; Williams, in 1980. Many of the persons who were born in 1980 and 1981 are today sitting in college classrooms learning accounting, biology, economics, or history. But Anna Kournikova and Venus Williams are not sitting in college classrooms. Instead, they are playing tennis on courts around the world.

Why aren't Anna and Venus in college? Not because they can't pay the tuition; both tennis stars have more than enough money to pay the tuition charged at most colleges. Also, either tennis player would likely be admitted to one or more colleges. Anna and Venus are not in college because it is more expensive for them to attend college than it is for most 18 to 25 year olds to attend college.

To understand, think of what it costs you to attend college. If you pay $1,000 tuition a semester for eight semesters, the full tuition amounts to $8,000. However, $8,000 is not the full cost of your attending college because if you were not a student, you could be earning income working at a job. For example, you could be working at a full-time job earning $25,000 annually. Certainly this $25,000, or at least part of it if you are currently working part-time, is forfeited because you attend college. It is part of the cost of your attending college.

Thus, the *tuition cost* may be the same for everyone who attends your college, but the *opportunity cost* is not. Some people have higher opportunity costs of attending college than others do. Both Anna Kournikova and Venus Williams have extremely high opportunity costs of attending college.

Each would have to give up hundreds of thousands of dollars in tennis prize money, endorsements, and so on if she were to attend college on a full-time basis.

This discussion illustrates two related points made in this chapter. First, *the higher the opportunity cost of doing something, the less likely it will be done.* The opportunity cost of attending college is higher for Anna and Venus than it (probably) is for you, and that is why you are in college and Anna and Venus are not.

Second, according to economists, *individuals think and act in terms of costs and benefits and only undertake actions if they expect the benefits to outweigh the costs.* Both Anna and Venus likely see certain benefits to attending college—just as you see certain benefits to attending college. However, those benefits are insufficient for Anna and Venus to attend college because benefits are not all that matter. Costs matter too. For Anna and Venus, the costs of attending college are much higher than the benefits, and so they choose not to attend college. In your case, the benefits are higher than the costs, and so you have decided to attend college.

$$MB \text{ studying first hour} > MC \text{ studying first hour}$$

Given this condition, you will certainly study for the first hour. After all, it is worthwhile: the additional benefits are greater than the additional costs, so there is a net benefit to studying.

Suppose for the second hour of studying, the marginal benefits are still greater than the marginal costs:

$$MB \text{ studying second hour} > MC \text{ studying second hour}$$

You will study for the second hour because the additional benefits are still greater than the additional costs. In other words, it is worthwhile studying the second hour. In fact, you will continue to study as long as the marginal benefits are greater than the marginal costs. Exhibit 2 graphically illustrates this discussion.

The marginal benefit (*MB*) curve of studying is downward sloping because we have assumed that the benefits of studying for the first hour are greater than the benefits of studying for the second hour and so on. The marginal cost (*MC*)

exhibit 2

Efficiency

MB = marginal benefits and MC = marginal costs. In the exhibit, the MB curve of studying is downward sloping and the MC curve of studying is upward sloping. As long as $MB > MC$, the person will study. The person stops studying when $MB = MC$. This is where efficiency is achieved.

curve of studying is upward sloping because we assume that it costs a person more (in terms of goods forfeited) to study the second hour than the first, more to study the third than the second, and so on. (If we assume the additional costs of studying are constant over time, the MC curve is horizontal.)

In the exhibit, the marginal benefits of studying equal the marginal costs at three hours. So three hours is the efficient length of time to study in this situation. At less than three hours, the marginal benefits of studying are greater than the marginal costs, and so at all these hours there are net benefits from studying. At more than three hours, the marginal costs of studying are greater than the marginal benefits, and so it wouldn't be worthwhile to study beyond three hours.

THINKING IN TERMS OF UNINTENDED EFFECTS

Has anything turned out different from what you intended? No doubt, you can provide numerous examples. Economists think in terms of unintended effects. Consider an example. Andres, 16 years old, currently works after school at a grocery store. He earns $5.50 an hour. Suppose the state legislature passes a law specifying that the minimum dollar wage a person can be paid to do a job is $6.50 an hour. The legislators' intention in passing the law is to help people like Andres earn more income.

Will the $6.50 an hour legislation have the intended effect? Perhaps not. The manager of the grocery store may not find it worthwhile to continue employing Andres if she has to pay him $6.50 an hour. In other words, Andres may have a job at $5.50 an hour, but not at $6.50 an hour. If the law specifies that no one will earn less than $6.50 an hour and the manager of the grocery store decides to fire Andres rather than pay this amount, then an unintended effect of the $6.50 an hour legislation is Andres losing his job.

As another example, let's analyze mandatory seatbelt laws to see if they have any unintended effects. Many states have laws that require drivers to wear seatbelts. The intended effect is to reduce the number of car fatalities by making it more likely drivers will survive an accident.

Could these laws have an unintended effect? Some economists think so. They look at accident fatalities in terms of this equation:

Total number of fatalities = Number of accidents × Fatalities per accident

For example, if there are 200,000 accidents and 0.10 fatalities per accident, the total number of fatalities is 20,000.

The objective of a mandatory seatbelt program is to reduce the total number of fatalities by reducing the fatalities per accident. Many studies have found that wearing seatbelts does just this. If you are in an accident, you have a better chance of not being killed if you are wearing a seatbelt.

Let's assume that with seatbelts, there are 0.08 instead of 0.10 fatalities per accident. If there are still 200,000 accidents, this means that the total number of fatalities falls from 20,000 to 16,000. Thus, there is a drop in the total number of fatalities if fatalities per accident are reduced and the number of accidents is constant.

Number of Accidents	Fatalities per Accident	Total Number of Fatalities
200,000	0.10	20,000
200,000	0.08	16,000

However, some economists wonder if the number of accidents stays constant. Specifically, they suggest that seatbelts may have an unintended effect: *The number of accidents may increase.* This happens because wearing seatbelts may make drivers feel safer. Feeling safer may cause them to take chances that they wouldn't ordinarily take—such as driving faster or more aggressively or concentrating less on their driving and more on the music on the radio. For example, if the number of accidents rises to 250,000, then the total number of fatalities is 20,000.

Number of Accidents	Fatalities per Accident	Total Number of Fatalities
200,000	0.10	20,000
250,000	0.08	20,000

We conclude the following: If a mandatory seatbelt law reduces the number of fatalities (intended effect) but increases the number of accidents (unintended effect), it may, contrary to popular belief, not reduce the total number of fatalities. In fact, some economic studies show just this.

What does all this mean for you? You may be safer if you know that this unintended effect exists and you adjust accordingly. To be specific, when you wear your seatbelt, your chances of getting hurt in a car accident are less than if you don't wear your seatbelt. But if this added sense of protection causes you to drive less carefully than you would otherwise, then you could unintentionally offset the measure of protection your seatbelt provides. To reduce the probability of hurting yourself and others in a car accident, *the best policy is to wear a seatbelt and to drive as carefully as you would if you weren't wearing a seatbelt*. Knowing about the unintended effect of wearing your seatbelt could save your life.

THINKING IN TERMS OF WHAT DOLLARS BUY

Alexis, who just graduated from college, tells her grandfather, Bud, that she will earn $36,000 a year in her new job. Bud is both shocked and delighted. He says, "When I first went to work, back in 1924, I earned only $2,000 a year. Alexis, you're rich earning $36,000 a year. That's 18 times more than I earned."

Bud compares Alexis's income ($36,000) to his own ($2,000) and concludes that Alexis is rich because she will earn 18 times more than he earned. But something is amiss here. Intuitively, we know that $36,000 today is much different than $36,000 in 1924. What makes it different, of course, is that prices are higher today than they were in 1924.

According to economists, dollar income is not as important as what the dollar income buys. Although $36,000 is 18 times greater than $2,000, does it buy 18 times as many goods and services? It could, but only if prices are the same for the person with the $36,000 income as for the person with the $2,000 income. It doesn't buy 18 times as many goods and services if prices are different.

http://

Go to *http://www.nhtsa.dot.gov*, and select "Traffic Safety/Occupant Issues." Under "Crash Information," select "Economics of Crashes." Then, click "the Economic Impact of Motor Vehicle Crashes, 2000" and, finally, "Summary." What is the average cost to society of a fatality? of a critical injury accident? How is the cost of a fatality estimated? Seatbelts and other safety devices can protect drivers and passengers enough to change a fatal crash into a critical injury accident. Are these forms of protection economically justifiable according to the NHTSA?

Why Is the Extended Family Customary in India and Not in the United States?

People in different countries have different customs and traditions. In India, the extended family is customary. When a man and woman marry, they move in with one or the other's parents. Later, should they have children, they continue to live with the parents. Often, three generations live together under one roof. In contrast, the extended family is not customary in the United States today.

Why is the extended family customary in India and not in the United States? Some people may answer that it is because Indians are more "family oriented" than Americans or because Indians have a longer tradition of the extended family than Americans do. But these are not answers. "Family oriented" simply describes the extended family; it does not explain it. And saying that Indians have a longer tradition of the extended family than Americans does not answer the question of *why* they have a longer tradition.

Let's look at the issue from an economic perspective. An economist would say that several generations of a family are more likely to live together under one roof if it is more costly for the average family member to be independent of the others. Stated differently, the more costly it is to "go it alone," the less likely one will live alone and the more likely one will live with family members.

The per capita income (total income divided by population) is lower in India than in the United States. The average American is more than 18 times richer than the average Indian. In 1999, the per capita income in India was $1,800 and the per capita income in the United States was $33,900.[1]

Now the poorer a person is, the less likely he or she can make it alone. The average newlywed couple in India cannot afford to rent an apartment or buy a home. In fact, it has been estimated that nearly 40 percent of the Indian population is too poor to even afford an adequate diet. Given the poverty in India, the extended family may simply be a means of survival. After all, it is cheaper to house and feed four people under one roof than four people living separately.

In addition, the Indian government does not provide a retirement program comparable to Social Security. Company retirement benefits are also much less common in India than in the United States. Not having Social Security and retirement benefits forces an old person to be more dependent on others than he or she would be otherwise. Adult children in their forties and fifties are more likely to live with their aged parents if their aged parents cannot survive on their own.

In some ways, the extended family in India is simply the Indian form of Social Security. In the United States, Social Security works by having the working generation pay for the retired generation, in return for having the upcoming working generation pay for them when they retire. In India, adult children take care of their aged parents in return for having their children take care of them when they become aged.

In summary, people often talk about customs and traditions as if they cannot be explained. It's always been this way; who knows why? To an economist, there is often an economic explanation for a custom or tradition.

To illustrate, let's suppose the same goods were produced in 1924 as today, but the average price of these goods in 1924 was $40 and the average price of these goods today is $1,000. With an income of $2,000 in 1924, Bud would have been able to buy 50 units of goods in a year ($2,000 income ÷ $40 average price = 50 units of goods). With an income of $36,000 today, Alexis would be able to buy 36 units of goods ($36,000 income ÷ $1,000 average price = 36 units of goods). In other words, although Bud earned a smaller dollar income than Alexis will earn, he was able to buy more units of goods than Alexis will be able to buy with her larger dollar income.

THINKING IN TERMS OF EQUILIBRIUM

People sometimes think in terms of natural resting places. For example, suppose you call up a friend and ask him how he is doing today. He tells you he is sick. "Do you have a fever?" you ask. He says that he has a fever; his temperature is 103.4 degrees.

---

1. The dollar amounts are based on purchasing power parity exchange rates.

Now suppose someone asks you to assign a probability to your friend's body temperature staying at 103.4 degrees for the next two weeks. Would you assign a 100 percent probability, a 75 percent probability, or some much smaller probability? Most people would assign a very tiny probability of your friend's temperature remaining at 103.4 degrees for the next two weeks. Most people would think one of the following two options is more likely: (1) The temperature will rise so high that it kills the person (and therefore it no longer makes much sense to speak of a body temperature) or (2) the temperature will fall until it is close to the normal body temperature of 98.6 degrees.

The normal body temperature of 98.6 degrees is often thought of as a natural resting place in that for living human beings, any temperature higher or lower than 98.6 degrees is a temporary temperature. A person's temperature always seems to settle back down or back up to 98.6 degrees.

Economists tend to think that many economic phenomena have natural resting places. These natural resting places are often called **equilibrium.** One way to think of equilibrium is as a place where economic forces are driving things. To illustrate, let's consider an example.

Equilibrium
Equilibrium means "at rest"; it is descriptive of a natural resting place.

Suppose Smith has a single painting that he wants to sell. He suggests a price of $5,000 for the painting, and at that price, three people say they are willing to buy it. How does he decide to whom he will sell the painting? Will he draw names out of a hat? Will he have the three people draw straws? Most likely he will ask the three people to offer him a higher price for the painting. At $6,000, two people still want to buy the painting, but at $6,500, only one person wants to buy the painting. In other words, the bidding activity of the buyers has moved the price of the painting to its natural resting place or to an equilibrium price of $6,500.

Economists are well known for analyzing economic phenomena in terms of equilibrium. First, they will try to identify whether or not equilibrium exists. Second, if equilibrium exists, they will then proceed to determine how that equilibrium should be specified. They then sometimes proceed to ask, What can change equilibrium? We will have much more to say about this latter question in Chapter 3.

THINKING IN TERMS OF THE *CETERIS PARIBUS* ASSUMPTION

Wilson has eaten regular ice cream for years, and for years his weight has been 170 pounds. One day Wilson decides he wants to lose some weight. With this in mind, he buys a new fat-free ice cream at the grocery store. The fat-free ice cream has half the calories of regular ice cream.

Wilson eats the fat-free ice cream for the next few months. He then weighs himself and finds that he has gained two pounds. Does this mean that fat-free ice cream causes people to gain weight and regular ice cream does not? The answer is no. But why, then, did Wilson gain weight when he substituted fat-free ice cream for regular ice cream? Perhaps Wilson ate three times as much fat-free ice cream as regular ice cream. Or perhaps during the time he was eating fat-free ice cream, he wasn't exercising, and during the time he was eating regular ice cream, he was exercising. In other words, a number of factors—such as eating more ice cream or exercising less—may have offset the weight loss that Wilson would have experienced had these factors not changed.

Now suppose you want to make the point that Wilson would have lost weight by substituting fat-free ice cream for regular ice cream had these other factors not changed. What would you say? A scientist would say, "If Wilson has been eating regular ice cream and his weight has stabilized at 170 pounds, then substituting fat-free ice cream for regular ice cream will lead to a decline in weight, *ceteris paribus*."

The term **ceteris paribus** means *all other things held constant* or *nothing else changes*. In our ice cream example, if nothing else changes—such as how much ice cream Wilson eats, how much exercise he gets, and so on—then substituting fat-free ice cream for regular ice cream will result in weight loss. This is

Ceteris Paribus
A Latin term meaning "all other things held constant."

based on the theory that a reduction in calorie consumption will result in weight loss and an increase in calorie consumption will result in weight gain.

Using the *ceteris paribus* assumption is important because, with it, we can clearly designate what we believe is the correct relationship between two variables. In the ice cream example, we can designate the correct relationship between calorie intake and weight gain.

Economists don't often talk about ice cream, but they will often make use of the *ceteris paribus* assumption. An economist might say, "If the price of a good decreases, the quantity demanded or consumed of that good increases, *ceteris paribus*." For example, if the price of Pepsi-Cola decreases, people will buy more Pepsi-Cola, assuming that nothing else changes.

The use of the *ceteris paribus* assumption is so prevalent in economics it has even inspired humor: How many economists does it take to change a light bulb? Eight. One to change the bulb and seven to hold everything else constant.

Q & A

Q: Why would economists want to assume that when the price of Pepsi-Cola falls, nothing else changes? Don't other things change in the real world? Why assume things that we know are not true?

A: Economists do not specify *ceteris paribus* because they want to say something false about the world. They specify it because they want to clearly define what they believe to be the real-world relationship between two variables. Look at it this way. If you drop a ball off the roof of a house, it will fall to the ground unless someone catches it. This statement is true, and probably everyone would willingly accept it as true. But here is another true statement: If you drop a ball off the roof of a house, it will fall to the ground, *ceteris paribus*. In fact, the two statements are identical in meaning. This is because adding the phrase "unless someone catches it" in the first sentence is the same as saying "*ceteris paribus*" in the second sentence. If one statement is acceptable to us, the other should be too.

THINKING IN TERMS OF THE DIFFERENCE BETWEEN ASSOCIATION AND CAUSATION

Association is one thing, causation is another. A problem arises when we confuse the two. Two events are associated if they are linked or connected in some way. For example, suppose you wash your car at 10:00 A.M. and at 10:30 A.M. it starts to rain. Because it rains shortly after you wash your car, the two events are associated (linked, connected) in time. Does it follow that the first event (your washing the car) caused the second event (the rain)? The answer is no. Association is not causation. If *A* occurs before *B,* it does not necessarily follow that *A* is the cause and *B* the effect.

In the car-rain example, it is obvious that association was not causation. But consider a case where this is not so apparent. Suppose Jones tells you that the U.S. trade deficit grew larger in January and 11 months later economic activity had turned down. She then states that the first event (the growing trade deficit) caused the second event (the downturn in economic activity). You may be tempted to accept this as truth. But, of course, a simple statement of cause and effect is not enough to establish cause and effect. Without any evidence, we can't be certain that we haven't stumbled onto a disguised version of the car-rain example.

Q & A

Q: James broke a mirror on Wednesday and has been having bad luck ever since. He thinks that breaking the mirror caused his bad luck. Is this an example where association is not causation?

A: Yes, it is. In fact, most superstitions are nothing more than people incorrectly assuming that association is (necessarily) causation.

http://

At *http://cnn.com*, you will find a number of news articles. How many of these articles are related to economics? Read carefully.

THINKING IN TERMS OF THE DIFFERENCE BETWEEN THE GROUP AND THE INDIVIDUAL

Some people will say that what is good or true for the individual is necessarily good or true for the group. Fact is, what is good for the individual may be good for the group, but not necessarily. For example, John stands up at a soccer game and sees the game better. Does it follow that if everyone stands up at the soccer game, everyone will see better? No. Mary moves to the suburbs because she dislikes crowds in the city. Does it follow that if everyone moves from the city to the suburbs for the same reason as Mary, everyone will be better off? No. Andres does his holiday shopping early so he can beat the crowds. Does it follow that if everyone does his holiday shopping early, everyone can beat the crowds? No.

People who believe that what is good for the individual is also good for the group are said to believe in the **fallacy of composition.** Economists do not believe in the fallacy of composition.

Consider two economic examples where the fallacy may appear. Some people argue that tariffs benefit certain industries by protecting them from foreign competition. They then conclude that because tariffs benefit some industries, the economy as a whole benefits from tariffs. This is not true though.

Or consider the fact that some people have limited wants for particular goods. Does it follow that society has limited wants for all goods? Not at all. To argue otherwise is to commit the fallacy of composition.

Fallacy of Composition
The erroneous view that what is good or true for the individual is necessarily good or true for the group.

Self-Test

1. How does competition arise out of scarcity?

2. Give an example to illustrate how a change in opportunity cost can affect behavior.

3. There are both costs and benefits of studying. If you continue to study (say, for a test) as long as the marginal benefits of studying are greater than the marginal costs and stop studying when the two are equal, will your action be consistent with having maximized the net benefits of studying? Explain your answer.

4. Give an example to illustrate how a politician running for office can mislead the electorate by implying that association is causation.

5. Your economics instructor says, "If the price of going to the movies goes down, people will go to the movies more often." A student in class says, "Not if the quality of the movies goes down." Who is right, the economics instructor or the student?

ECONOMISTS BUILD AND TEST THEORIES

An important component of the economic way of thinking is theorizing or building theories or models to explain and predict real-world events. This section discusses the nature and uses of theory.

WHAT IS A THEORY?

Almost everyone, including you, builds and tests theories or models on a regular basis. (In this text, the words *theory* and *model* are used interchangeably.) Perhaps you thought only scientists and other people who have high-level mathematics at their fingertips built and tested theories. However, theory building and testing is not the domain of only the highly educated and mathematically proficient. Almost everyone builds and test theories.

People build theories any time they do not know the answer to a question. Someone asks, "Why is the crime rate higher in the United States than in Belgium?" Or, "Why did Aaron's girlfriend break up with him?" Or, "Why does Professor Avalos give easier final exams than Professor Shaw even though they teach the same subject?" If you don't know the answer to a question, you are likely to build a theory so you can provide an answer.

A Small Private College in Boston Goes Coed

Economics is not just found in the boardrooms of companies, in the government buildings in Washington, D.C., or in a textbook. Economics is all around you—every day. You can find economics in a college class or a local coffee bar or while driving on a freeway or doing your homework.

To find economics in everyday places, you have to look below the surface. Let's consider Emmanuel College, a small private college in Boston, Massachusetts. As you read about Emmanuel, look for some of the topics discussed in this chapter—scarcity, rationing devices, costs and benefits, and so on. See if you can find any economics below the surface.

Emmanuel College was founded in 1919 by the Sisters of Notre Dame de Namur. From its founding in 1919 through the year 2000, Emmanuel College admitted only women. Like many women's colleges founded in the eighteenth, nineteenth, and early twentieth centuries, Emmanuel College was founded to give women the education that was being denied to them by men-only schools.

In 2000, Emmanuel decided to change its women-only policy. Beginning in fall 2001, it would begin to admit men to the college. Emmanuel decided to admit men partly because of the declining number of applicants. In 1999, only 572 women applied to the college and 160 were admitted.

As soon as Emmanuel College went coed, the number of applicants increased. In 2002, 1,607 students applied and 320 students were admitted. Certainly some of the increase in applicants (from 572 to 1,607) was due to men becoming part of the applicant pool. However, the number of women applicants also increased.

Where's the economics in this story about Emmanuel College? Did you notice any economic concepts lying below the surface? If you didn't, think about it for a few minutes, then read on.

First, let's consider scarcity and its effects. Because scarcity exists, a rationing device is needed. The rationing device used by Emmanuel College prior to 2001 was that a person had to (1) have certain grades, (2) be able to pay the tuition, and (3) be a woman. In 2001, the rationing device changed: it was no longer necessary to be a woman. Thus, for a large subset of the population, the male population, the rationing device used by Emmanuel became less restrictive. (We assume that as Emmanuel changed from a women-only college to a coed college, it did not raise tuition or change the grade point average or SAT scores necessary for admission.)

The question is: *Why* did Emmanuel make its rationing device less restrictive? Might the *restrictiveness* of a rationing device have something to do with the *degree* of scarcity? Think of goods lying along a spectrum, with some of the goods being relatively more scarce than others. An economist would predict that the rationing device used to allocate relatively more scarce goods would be more restrictive than the rationing device used to allocate relatively less scarce goods. Does this prediction apply to Emmanuel? Yes. The declining applicant pool signaled to the college that it was becoming a relatively less scarce (albeit still scarce) good. In response, its rationing device (for purposes of admission) became less restrictive.

Now, let's consider the fact that more women applied to Emmanuel after it became coed. Does this fact have anything to do with the costs and benefits of attending Emmanuel? A quick, and perhaps wrong, answer is that the benefits to women of attending Emmanuel increased after the college became coed. This might be a wrong answer because it is an incomplete answer. While it is certainly possible that the benefits of Emmanuel increased for *some* women after the college became coed, the costs probably increased for other women. In fact, this is exactly what happened. Some women were angry with Emmanuel for changing its women-only policy. Their preference was to attend a women-only college.

So as a result of Emmanuel's change in policy, we surmise that the benefits of attending Emmanuel increased for some women and that the costs increased for other women. Do we know the overall result? Because the number of women applicants increased with the change to the coed policy, we conclude that women who received higher benefits outnumbered those who incurred higher costs.

Theory
An abstract representation of the real world designed with the intent to better understand that world.

Abstract
The process (used in building a theory) of focusing on a limited number of variables to explain or predict an event.

What exactly is a theory? To an economist, a **theory** is an abstract representation of the world. In this context, **abstract** means to omit certain variables or factors when trying to explain or understand something. For example, suppose you were to draw a map for a friend, showing him how to get from his house to your house. Would you draw a map that showed every single thing your friend would see on the trip from his house to yours, or would you simply draw the main roads and one or two landmarks? If you'd do the latter, you would be abstracting from reality; you would be omitting certain things.

You would abstract for two reasons. First, to get your friend from his house to yours, you don't need to include everything on your map. Simply noting main roads may be enough. Second, if you did note everything on your map, your friend might get confused. Giving too much detail could be as bad as giving too little.

When economists build a theory or model, they do the same thing you do when you draw a map. They abstract from reality; they leave out certain things. They focus on the major factors or variables that they believe will explain the phenomenon they are trying to understand.

Suppose a criminologist's objective is to explain why some people turn to crime. Before actually building the theory, he considers a number of variables that may explain why some people become criminals. These variables include (1) the ease of getting a gun, (2) parental childrearing practices, (3) the neighborhood a person grew up in, (4) whether a person was abused as a child, (5) family education, (6) the type of friends a person has, (7) a person's IQ, (8) climate, and (9) a person's diet.

The criminologist may think that some of these variables greatly affect the chance that a person will become a criminal, some affect it only slightly, and others do not affect it at all. For example, a person's diet may have only a 0.0001 percent effect on the person becoming a criminal. But whether or not a person was abused as a child may have a 30 percent effect.

A theory emphasizes only those variables that the theorist believes are the main or critical variables that explain an activity or event. Thus, if the criminologist in our example thinks that parental childrearing practices and family education are likely to explain much more about criminal behavior than the other variables, then his (abstract) theory will focus on these two variables and will ignore the other variables.

All theories are abstractions from reality. But it doesn't follow that (abstract) theories cannot explain reality. The objective in theory building is to ignore those variables that are essentially irrelevant to the case at hand, so that it becomes easier to isolate the important variables that the untrained observer would probably miss.

In the course of reading this text, you will come across numerous theories. Some of these theories are explained in words, and others are graphically represented. For example, Chapter 3 presents the theory of supply and demand. First, the parts of the theory are explained. Then the theory is represented graphically in terms of a supply curve and a demand curve.

BUILDING AND TESTING A THEORY

The same basic procedure for building and testing a theory is used in all scientific work, whether the discipline is biology, chemistry, or economics. Exhibit 3 summarizes the approach outlined next.

1. **Decide what it is you want to explain or predict.** For example, you may want to explain or predict interest rates, the exchange rate between the U.S. dollar and the Japanese yen, or another concept.

2. **Identify the variables that you believe are important to what you want to explain or predict.** Variables are magnitudes that can change. For example, price is a variable. One day the price of a good may be $10, and a week later it may be $12. An economist who wants to explain or predict the buying behavior of consumers may build his "theory of buying behavior" on the variable price.

3. **State the assumptions of the theory.** An assumption is a critical or key element of a theory. It is a statement that one supposes to be true. The difference between an assumption and a fact is that a fact represents objective truth. It is a fact that you are reading this book at this moment; no one doubts

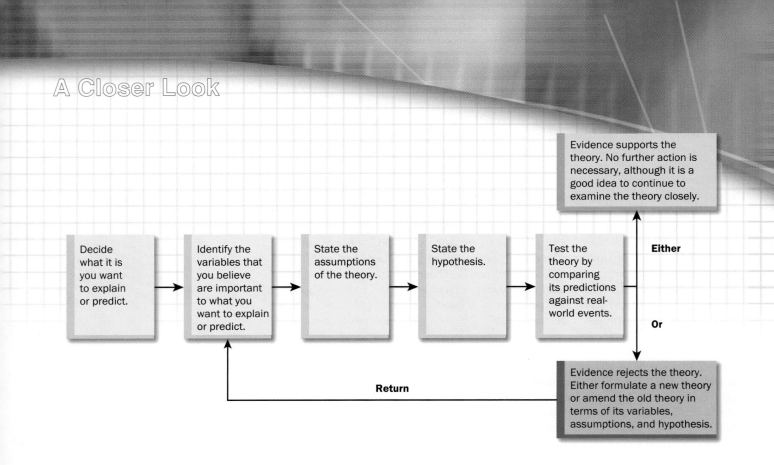

Evidence supports the theory. No further action is necessary, although it is a good idea to continue to examine the theory closely.

Decide what it is you want to explain or predict.

Identify the variables that you believe are important to what you want to explain or predict.

State the assumptions of the theory.

State the hypothesis.

Test the theory by comparing its predictions against real-world events.

Either

Or

Return

Evidence rejects the theory. Either formulate a new theory or amend the old theory in terms of its variables, assumptions, and hypothesis.

exhibit 3

Building and Testing a Theory

this. With an assumption, objective truth does not necessarily exist; there is room for doubt. An economist may make the assumption that the owners of business firms have only one motive—to earn as much profit as possible. But, of course, this may not be the truth. The owners of business firms may not be motivated only by profits, or they may not be motivated by profits at all. The next section discusses the importance of realistic assumptions in building and testing a theory.

4. **State the hypothesis.** A hypothesis is a conditional statement specifying how two variables are related. Typically, hypotheses follow the "if-then" form. For example, if you smoke cigarettes, then you will increase your probability of getting lung cancer. In effect, the hypothesis is a prediction of what will happen to one thing (e.g., to your lungs) when something else changes (you smoke cigarettes).

5. **Test the theory by comparing its predictions against real-world events.** Suppose an economist's theory predicts that as taxes are raised, there will be less saving in the economy. To test this theory, we look at the data on saving to see if the evidence *supports* the theory that produced that specific prediction.

6. **If the evidence supports the theory, then no further action is necessary, although it is a good idea to continue to examine the theory closely.** Suppose a theory predicts that orange prices will rise within two weeks of a cold snap in Florida. If this actually happens, then the evidence supports the theory.

7. **If the evidence rejects the theory, then either formulate a new theory or amend the old theory in terms of its variables, assumptions, and hypothesis.** For example, suppose a theory predicts that interest rates will

rise within two months of an increase in the amount of money in circulation. If this does not happen, then it is time to either formulate a new theory or amend the old theory.

Q & A

Q: In the preceding point 5, the phrase "supports the theory" was used instead of "proves the theory." Why not say "we look at the data to see if the evidence proves the theory" instead of "we look at the data to see if the evidence supports the theory"?

A: The following example explains why. Suppose a theory predicts that all swans are white. Researchers go out into the field and record the color of all the swans they see. Every swan they see is white. The evidence does not prove the theory is correct because there may be swans that are not white that the researchers did not see. How can the researchers be certain they saw all the swans? Thus, it is more accurate to say that the evidence supports the theory than to say it proves the theory.

HOW DO WE JUDGE THEORIES?

We judge theories by how well they predict. Some people forget this and try to judge a theory by its assumptions. They say that some economic theories are based on unrealistic assumptions. For example, economists assume that business firms try to maximize profits. Do all business firms try to do this every second of every day? Probably not; yet they might do it often enough to make it seem as if they do it all the time.

Economist Milton Friedman argues that the relevant question to ask about the assumptions of a theory is not whether they are descriptively "realistic," for they never are, but whether they are "sufficiently good approximations for the purpose in hand." And this question can be answered only by seeing whether the theory works, which means whether it yields sufficiently accurate predictions.

To illustrate, Friedman cites Newton's law of falling bodies, which assumes, unrealistically, that bodies fall in a vacuum. Does the theory predict well, even though it is based on an unrealistic assumption? For many falling bodies, such as a rubber ball dropped off a roof, it does. Friedman would argue that the theory is useful because it predicts well for numerous falling bodies, even though in the real world bodies do not always fall in a vacuum. We could say that for many falling bodies it is *as if* they were falling in a vacuum. Friedman would say that the assumption of a vacuum is a "sufficiently good approximation for the purpose in hand."

Friedman's position can be summarized as follows: If the theory works, if the evidence supports the theory, then it is a good and useful theory and the assumptions of the theory, no matter what anyone might think of them, are a sufficiently good approximation for the purpose in hand. Some economists accept Friedman's position, along with all its implications. Other economists, many of them well respected, do not. As you will soon find out, there are not only numerous theories in economics but also numerous debates.

WHAT TO ASK A THEORIST

Physicists, chemists, and economists aren't the only persons who build and test theories. Historians, sociologists, anthropologists, and many others build and test theories. In fact, as suggested earlier in this section, almost everyone builds theories (although not everyone tests theories).

Any time you listen to someone expound upon his or her theory, you should always ask a key question: *If your theory is correct, what do you predict we will see in the world?*

To illustrate, let's consider a very simple example. Suppose your history professor comes to class each day clean-shaven and dressed in slacks, shirt, tie, and sports jacket. One day he comes to class unshaven and dressed in jeans and a somewhat wrinkled T-shirt. The difference in appearance is obvious. You turn to your friend who sits next to you in class and ask, "What do you think explains the difference in appearance and dress?"

Notice what you have asked: a question that does not have an obvious answer. Such questions are ripe for theory building. Your friend proposes an explanation. He says, "I think the professor forgot to set his alarm clock last night. He got up late this morning and didn't have time to shave or to dress the way he usually does. He just threw on the first clothes he found and rushed to class."

Your friend has advanced a theory of sorts. He has implicitly assumed that the professor wants to shave and dress in slacks, shirt, tie, and sports jacket but that some unusual event prevented him from doing so today.

Somehow, you don't think your friend's theory is correct. Instead, you think your history professor has decided to make a life change of some sort. He has decided to look more casual, to take life a little easier, to be less formal. You tell your friend what you think explains your professor's new behavior.

You, like your friend, have advanced a theory of sorts. Whose theory, if either, is correct? Now is the time for you to ask your friend, and your friend to ask you, *If your theory is correct, what do you predict we will see in the world?*

Your friend's answer should be, "If my theory is correct, then the next time the professor comes to class, he will be clean shaven and dressed in his old way—slacks, shirt, tie, and sports jacket."

Your answer should be, "If my theory is correct, then the next time the professor comes to class, he will be unshaven and dressed as he is today—in jeans, T-shirt, and so on."

The question—If your theory is correct, what do you predict we will see in the world?—gives us a way to figure out who might be closer to the truth when people disagree. It minimizes talk and maximizes the chances of establishing who is correct and who is incorrect.

Self-Test

1. What is the purpose of building a theory?
2. How might a theory of the economy differ from a description of the economy?
3. Why is it important to test a theory? Why not simply accept a theory if it "sounds right"?

A Reader Asks...

What's in Store for an Economics Major?

This is my first course in economics. The material is interesting and I have given some thought to majoring in economics. Please tell me something about the major and about job prospects for an economics graduate. What courses do economics majors take? What is the starting salary of economics majors? Do the people who run large companies think highly of people who have majored in economics?

If you major in economics, you will certainly not be alone. Economics is one of the top three majors at Harvard, Brown, Yale, University of California at Berkeley, Princeton, Columbia, Cornell, Dartmouth, and Stanford. The popularity of economics is probably based on two major reasons. First, many people find economics an interesting course of study. Second, what you learn in an economics course is relevant and applicable to the real world.

Do executives who run successful companies think highly of economics majors? Well, a *BusinessWeek* survey found that economics was the second favorite undergraduate major of chief executive officers (CEOs) of major corporations. Engineering was their favorite undergraduate major.

An economics major usually takes a wide variety of economic courses, starting with introductory courses—principles of microeconomics and principles of macroeconomics—and then studying intermediate microeconomics and intermediate macroeconomics. Upper-division electives usually include such courses as public finance, international economics, law and economics, managerial economics, labor economics, health economics, money and banking, environmental economics, and more.

According to a College Placement Council survey, the average starting salary for economics majors exceeded all other majors within the business and social sciences. It was $40,776 in 2001. Also, according to the Economics and Statistics Administration of the U.S. Department of Justice, economics undergraduates have relatively higher average annual salaries than students who have majored in other fields. Specifically, of 14 different majors, economics majors ranked third. Only persons with bachelor's degrees in engineering or agriculture/forestry had higher average annual salaries.

Chapter Summary

Definitions of Economics

- Alfred Marshall said, "Political economy or economics is a study of mankind in the ordinary business of life."
- Lionel Robbins said, "Economics is the science which studies human behavior as a relationship between ends and scarce means which have alternative uses."
- Milton Friedman said, "Economics is the science of how a particular society solves its economic problems." He added, "an economic problem exists whenever scarce means are used to satisfy alternative ends."
- In this book, economics is defined as the science of scarcity. More completely, economics is the science of how individuals and societies deal with the fact that wants are greater than the limited resources available to satisfy those wants.

Economic Categories

- Positive economics attempts to determine what is; normative economics addresses what should be.
- Microeconomics deals with human behavior and choices as they relate to relatively small units—an individual, a firm, an industry, a single market. Macroeconomics deals with human behavior and choices as they relate to an entire economy.

Goods, Bads, and Resources

- A good is anything that gives a person utility or satisfaction.
- A bad is anything that gives a person disutility or dissatisfaction.
- Economists divide resources into four categories: land, labor, capital, and entrepreneurship.
- Land includes natural resources, such as minerals, forests, water, and unimproved land.
- Labor refers to the physical and mental talents that people contribute to the production process.
- Capital consists of produced goods that can be used as inputs for further production, such as machinery, tools, computers, trucks, buildings, and factories.

- Entrepreneurship refers to the particular talent that some people have for organizing the resources of land, labor, and capital to produce goods, seek new business opportunities, and develop new ways of doing things.

Scarcity

- Scarcity is the condition in which our wants are greater than the limited resources available to satisfy them. Scarcity implies choice. In a world of limited resources, we must choose which wants will be satisfied and which will go unsatisfied.
- Because of scarcity, there is a need for a rationing device. A rationing device is a means of deciding who gets what quantities of the available resources and goods.
- Scarcity implies competition. If there were enough resources to satisfy all our seemingly unlimited wants, people would not have to compete for the available but limited resources.

Opportunity Cost

- Every time a person makes a choice, he or she incurs an opportunity cost. Opportunity cost is the most highly valued opportunity or alternative forfeited when a choice is made. The higher the opportunity cost of doing something, the less likely it will be done.

Costs and Benefits

- What distinguishes the economist from the noneconomist is that the economist thinks in terms of *both* costs and benefits. Asked what the benefits of taking a walk may be, an economist will also mention the costs to taking a walk. Asked what the costs of studying are, an economist will also point out the benefits of studying.

Decisions Made at the Margin

- Marginal benefits and costs are not the same as total benefits and costs. When deciding whether to talk on the phone one more minute, an individual would not consider the total benefits and total costs of speaking on the phone. Instead, the individual would compare only the marginal benefits (additional benefits) of talking on the phone one more minute to the marginal costs (additional costs) of talking on the phone one more minute.

Efficiency

*   As long as the marginal benefits of an activity are greater than its marginal costs, a person gains by continuing to do the activity—whether the activity is studying, running, eating, or watching television. All the net benefits possible from an activity are achieved when the marginal benefits of the activity equal its marginal costs. Efficiency exists at this point.

Unintended Effects

*   Economists often think in terms of causes and effects. Effects may include both intended effects and unintended effects. Economists want to denote both types of effects when speaking of effects in general.

Dollar Income and What Dollars Buy

*   According to economists, you have more information when you know what a specific dollar income can buy in terms of goods and services than if you simply know the dollar income. A $4,000 annual income may sound like a low income today, but was it always a low income? Was it a low income in 1936? To answer this question, we need some idea of what prices were in 1936 relative to what they are today. Lower prices in 1936 can make a $4,000 income in 1936 comparable to a much higher dollar income today.

Equilibrium

*   Equilibrium means "at rest." Many natural and economic phenomena move toward equilibrium. Economists will often ask if equilibrium exists for a given phenomenon. If equilibrium does not exist, then the economist will try to identify the condition that must exist before equilibrium ("at rest") is achieved.

Ceteris Paribus

*   *Ceteris paribus* is a Latin term that means "all other things held constant." *Ceteris paribus* is used to designate what we believe is the correct relationship between two variables.

Association and Causation

*   Association is one thing, causation is another. Simply because two events are associated (in time, for example), it does not necessarily follow that one is the cause and the other is the effect.

The Fallacy of Composition

*   The fallacy of composition is the erroneous view that what is good or true for the individual is necessarily good or true for the group.

Theory

*   Economists build theories in order to explain and predict real-world events. Theories are necessarily abstractions from, as opposed to descriptions of, the real world.
*   All theories abstract from reality; they focus on the critical variables that the theorist believes explain and predict the phenomenon at hand.
*   The steps in building and testing a theory are:
    1. Decide what it is you want to explain or predict.
    2. Identify the variables that you believe are important to what you want to explain or predict.
    3. State the assumptions of the theory.
    4. State the hypothesis.
    5. Test the theory by comparing its predictions against real-world events.
    6. If the evidence supports the theory, then no further action is necessary, although it is a good idea to continue to examine the theory closely.
    7. If the evidence rejects the theory, then either formulate an entirely new theory or amend the old theory in terms of its variables, assumptions, and hypothesis.
*   Economists commonly judge a theory according to how well it predicts, not according to the degree of realism of its assumptions.

Key Terms and Concepts

Scarcity
Economics
Positive Economics
Normative Economics
Microeconomics
Macroeconomics
Utility
Good

Disutility
Bad
Land
Labor
Capital
Entrepreneurship
Rationing Device
Opportunity Cost

Decisions at the Margin
Efficiency
Equilibrium
Ceteris Paribus
Fallacy of Composition
Theory
Abstract

implicit
v.
explicit costs

A stone, thrown into a lake, creates ripples. The ripples move away from where the stone entered the lake. Similarly, economic facts, actions, and changes create ripples that move away from their point of origin. Eventually, these ripples can intersect your life and have an effect on you. Consider the following example.

Scarcity, an economic fact, creates a need for a rationing device. The major rationing device in our society is money, or dollar, price. This means that you need money before you can satisfy many of *your wants. Attending college helps you obtain money because college students, on average, earn higher dollar incomes than people who do not attend college. Thus, there is a connection between scarcity and your attending college—an economic connection to you.*

Based on the material in this chapter, identify other ways in which economic facts, actions, and changes create ripples that eventually affect you.

1. What is the similarity between the Robbins and Friedman definitions of economics?
2. The United States is considered a rich country because Americans can choose from an abundance of goods and services. How can there be scarcity in a land of abundance?
3. Give two examples for each of the following: (a) an intangible good, (b) a tangible good, (c) a bad.
4. What is the difference between the resource labor and the resource entrepreneurship?
5. Explain the link between scarcity and each of the following: (a) choice, (b) opportunity cost, (c) the need for a rationing device, (d) competition.
6. Is it possible for a person to incur an opportunity cost without spending any money? Explain.
7. Discuss the opportunity costs of attending college for four years. Is college more or less costly than you thought it was? Explain.
8. Explain the relationship between changes in opportunity cost and changes in behavior.
9. Smith says that we should eliminate all pollution in the world. Jones disagrees. Who is more likely to be an economist, Smith or Jones? Explain your answer.
10. A layperson says that a proposed government project simply costs too much and therefore shouldn't be undertaken. How might an economist's evaluation be different?
11. Economists say that individuals make decisions at the margin. What does this mean?
12. How would an economist go about defining the efficient amount of time spent playing tennis?
13. A change in X will lead to a change in Y; the predicted change is desirable, so we should change X. Do you agree or disagree? Explain.
14. Smith lives in country A and earns $40,000 a year; Jones lives in country B and earns $50,000 a year. Will Jones be able to buy more goods and services than Smith?
15. Suppose the price of an ounce of gold is $300 in New York and $375 in London. Do you think the difference in gold prices is indicative of equilibrium? Explain your answer.
16. Why would economists assume "all other things are constant," or "nothing else changes," when, in reality, some other things may change?
17. Give three examples that illustrate that association is not causation.
18. Give three examples that illustrate the fallacy of composition.
19. Which of the following statements would Milton Friedman agree with and why?

    Statement 1: The theory does not work because its assumptions are false.

    Statement 2: The assumptions are false because the theory does not work.
20. Why do economists prefer to say that the evidence supports the theory instead of that the evidence proves the theory is correct?
21. Theories are abstractions from reality. What does this mean?

1. Go to *http://www.whitehouse.gov*. Under West Wing connections, Policies in Focus, select "Economy & Budget." Select and read a press briefing or release that has something to do with the economy. What is the content of the briefing or release?

2. Go to *http://www.yahoo.com*. Click on "advanced search" and then key "sci.econ" in the Search box. Select Usenet in the adjacent box and click "Search." A list of titles will appear. These are writings submitted to a group that discusses economics. Select one of the submissions with an interesting title.

   a. What is the author discussing? Is it a microeconomic or a macroeconomic issue?

   b. Does the author state a hypothesis and then test his or her case scientifically? Or does the author just present an opinion?

   c. Is the author writing from the perspective of positive or normative economics?

   d. Based on what you know so far, do you agree or disagree with the author?

3. Go to *http://netec.wustl.edu/JokEc.html*. Pick a joke that doesn't make sense to you and write it down so you won't forget it. At the end of the class, reread the joke and see if you get it now. How many of the jokes are based on economists always having more than one answer or having answers that are not usable in the real world?

Log on to the Arnold Xtra! Web site now (*http://arnoldxtra.swcollege.com*) for additional learning resources such as practice quizzes, help with graphing, video clips, and current event applications.

WORKING WITH DIAGRAMS

A picture is worth a thousand words. With this familiar saying in mind, economists construct their diagrams or graphs. With a few lines and a few points, much can be conveyed.

TWO-VARIABLE DIAGRAMS

Most of the diagrams in this book represent the relationship between two variables. For example, suppose our two variables of interest are *consumption* and *income.* We want to show how consumption changes as income changes. Suppose we collect the data in Table 1. By simply looking at the data in the first two columns, we can see that as income rises (column 1), consumption rises (column 2). Suppose we want to show the relationship between income and consumption on a graph. We could place *income* on the horizontal axis, as in Exhibit 1, and *consumption* on the vertical axis. Point *A* represents income of $0 and consumption of $60, point *B* represents income of $100 and consumption of $120, and so on. If we draw a straight line through the various points we have plotted, we have a picture of the relationship between income and consumption, based on the data we collected.

Notice that our line in Exhibit 1 slopes upward from left to right. Thus, as income rises, so does consumption. For example, as you move from point *A* to *B,* income rises from $0 to $100 and consumption rises from $60 to $120. The line in Exhibit 1 also shows that as income falls, so does consumption. For example, as you move from point *C* to *B,* income falls from $200 to $100 and consumption falls from $180 to $120. When two variables—such as consumption and income—change in the same way, they are said to be **directly related.**

Now let's take a look at the data in Table 2. Our two variables are *price of compact discs (CDs)* and *quantity demanded of CDs.* By simply looking at the data in the first two columns, we see that as price falls (column 1), quantity demanded rises (column 2). Suppose we want to plot these data. We could place *price* (of CDs) on the vertical axis, as in Exhibit 2, and *quantity demanded* (of CDs) on the horizontal axis. Point *A* represents a price of $20 and a quantity demanded of 100, point *B* represents a price of $18 and a quantity demanded of

exhibit 1

A Two-Variable Diagram Representing a Direct Relationship
In this exhibit, we have plotted the data in Table 1 and then connected the points with a straight line. The data represent a direct relationship: as one variable (say, income) rises, the other variable (consumption) rises too.

The variables income and consumption are directly related.

table 1

(1) When Income Is:	(2) Consumption Is:	(3) Point
$ 0	$ 60	A
100	120	B
200	180	C
300	240	D
400	300	E
500	360	F

table 2

(1) When the Price of CDs Is:	(2) Quantity Demanded of CDs Is:	(3) Point
$20	100	A
18	120	B
16	140	C
14	160	D
12	180	E

exhibit 2

A Two-Variable Diagram Representing an Inverse Relationship
In this exhibit, we have plotted the data in Table 2 and then connected the points with a straight line. The data represent an inverse relationship: as one variable (price) falls, the other variable (quantity demanded) rises.

120, and so on. If we draw a straight line through the various points we have plotted, we have a picture of the relationship between price and quantity demanded, based on the data in Table 2.

Notice that as price falls, quantity demanded rises. For example, as price falls from $20 to $18, quantity demanded rises from 100 to 120. Also as price rises, quantity demanded falls. For example, when price rises from $12 to $14, quantity demanded falls from 180 to 160.

When two variables—such as price and quantity demanded—change in opposite ways, they are said to be **inversely related.**

As you have seen so far, variables may be directly related (when one increases, the other also increases), or they may be inversely related (when one increases, the other decreases). Variables can also be **independent** of each other. This condition exists if as one variable changes, the other does not.

In Exhibit 3a, as the X variable rises, the Y variable remains the same (at 20). Obviously, the X and Y variables are independent of each other: as one changes, the other does not.

In Exhibit 3b, as the Y variable rises, the X variable remains the same (at 30). Again, we conclude that the X and Y variables are independent of each other: as one changes, the other does not.

SLOPE OF A LINE

It is often important not only to know *how* two variables are related but also to know *how much* one variable changes as the other variables changes. To find

exhibit 3

Two Diagrams Representing Independence between Two Variables
In (a) and (b), the variables X and Y are independent: as one changes, the other does not.

out, we need only calculate the slope of the line. The **slope** is the ratio of the change in the variable on the vertical axis to the change in the variable on the horizontal axis. For example, if Y is on the vertical axis and X on the horizontal axis, the slope is equal to $\Delta Y/\Delta X$. (The symbol "Δ" means "change in.")

$$\text{Slope} = \frac{\Delta Y}{\Delta X}$$

Exhibit 4 shows four lines. In each case we have calculated the slope. After studying (a)–(d), see if you can calculate the slope in each case.

THE SLOPE OF A CURVE

Economic graphs use both straight lines and curves. The slope of a curve is not constant throughout as it is for a straight line. The slope of a curve varies from one point to another.

Calculating the slope of a curve at a given point requires two steps, as illustrated for point A in Exhibit 5. First, draw a line tangent to the curve at the point (a tangent line is one that just touches the curve but does not cross it). Second,

exhibit 4

Calculating Slopes
The slope of a line is the ratio of the change in the variable on the vertical axis to the change in the variable on the horizontal axis. In (a)–(d), we have calculated the slope.

exhibit 5

Calculating the Slope of a Curve at a Particular Point
The slope of the curve at point *A* is +0.67. This is calculated by drawing a line tangent to the curve at point *A* and then determining the slope of the line.

exhibit 6

The 45° Line
Any point on the 45° line is equidistant from both axes. For example, point *A* is the same distance from the vertical axis as it is from the horizontal axis.

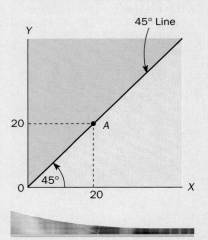

pick any two points on the tangent line and determine the slope. In Exhibit 5 the slope of the line between points *B* and *C* is +0.67. It follows that the slope of the curve at point *A* (and only at point *A*) is +0.67.

THE 45° LINE

Economists sometimes use a *45° line* to represent data. This is a straight line that bisects the right angle formed by the intersection of the vertical and horizontal axes (see Exhibit 6). As a result, the 45° line divides the space enclosed by the two axes into *two equal parts*. We have illustrated this by shading the two equal parts in different colors. The major characteristic of the 45° line is that any point that lies on it is equidistant from both the horizontal and vertical axes. For example, point *A* is exactly as far from the horizontal axis as it is from the vertical axis. It follows that point *A* represents as much *X* as it does *Y*. Specifically, in the exhibit, point *A* represents 20 units of *X* and 20 units of *Y*.

PIE CHARTS

In numerous places in this text, you will come across a *pie chart*. A pie chart is a convenient way to represent the different parts of something that when added together equal the whole. Suppose we consider a typical 24-hour weekday for Charles Myers. On a typical weekday, Charles spends 8 hours sleeping, 4 hours taking classes at the university, 4 hours working at his part-time job, 2 hours doing homework, 1 hour eating, 2 hours watching television, and 3 hours doing nothing in particular (we'll call it "hanging around"). It is easy to represent the breakdown of a typical weekday for Charles in pie chart form, as shown in Exhibit 7. Pie charts give a quick visual message as to rough percentage breakdowns and relative relationships. For example, in Exhibit 7 it is easy to see that Charles spends twice as much time working as doing homework.

BAR GRAPHS

The *bar graph* is another visual aid that economists use to convey relative relationships. For example, suppose we wanted to represent the gross domestic

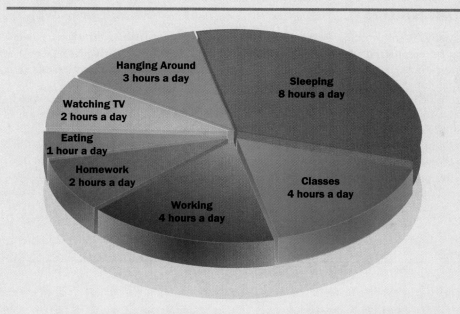

exhibit 7

A Pie Chart
The breakdown of activities for Charles Myers during a typical 24-hour weekday is represented in pie chart form.

product for the United States in different years. The **gross domestic product (GDP)** is the value of the entire output produced annually within a country's borders. A bar graph can show the actual GDP for each year and can also provide a quick picture of the relative relationships between the GDP in different years. For example, it is easy to see in Exhibit 8 that the GDP in 1990 was more than double what it was in 1980.

Gross Domestic Product (GDP)
The value of the entire output produced annually within a country's borders.

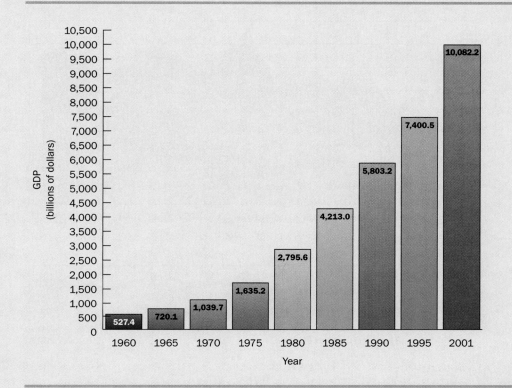

exhibit 8

A Bar Graph
U.S. gross domestic product for different years is illustrated in bar graph form.

Source: Bureau of Economic Analysis

LINE GRAPHS

Sometimes information is best and most easily displayed in a *line graph*. Line graphs are particularly useful for illustrating changes in a variable over some time period. Suppose we want to illustrate the variations in average points per game for a college basketball team in different years. As you can see from Exhibit 9a, the basketball team has been on a roller coaster during the years 1989–2002. Perhaps the message transmitted here is that the team's performance has not been consistent from one year to the next.

Suppose we plot the data in Exhibit 9a again, except this time we use a different measurement scale on the vertical axis. As you can see in (b), the variation in the performance of the basketball team appears much less pronounced than in (a). In fact, we could choose some scale such that if we were to plot the data, we would end up with close to a straight line. Our point is simple: Data plotted

exhibit 9

The Two Line Graphs Plot the Same Data

In (a) we plotted the average number of points per game for a college basketball team in different years. The variation between the years is pronounced. In (b) we plotted the same data as in (a), but the variation in the performance of the team appears much less pronounced than in (a).

Year	Average Number of Points per Game
1989	50
1990	40
1991	59
1992	51
1993	60
1994	50
1995	75
1996	63
1997	60
1998	71
1999	61
2000	55
2001	70
2002	64

Data plotted here are the same as in (b). Looks different, doesn't it?

(a)

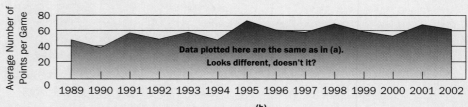

Data plotted here are the same as in (a). Looks different, doesn't it?

(b)

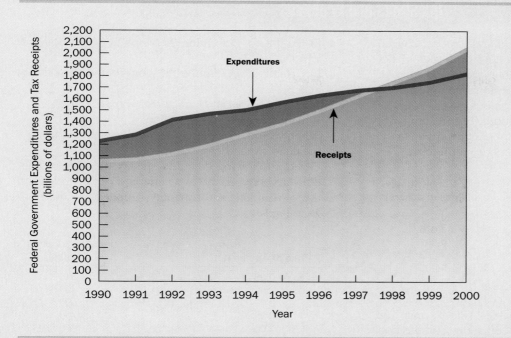

exhibit 10

Federal Government Expenditures and Tax Receipts, 1990–2000
Federal government expenditures and tax receipts are shown in line graph form for the period 1990–2000.

Source: Bureau of Economic Analysis

in line graph form may convey different messages depending on the measurement scale used.

Sometimes economists show two line graphs on the same axes. Usually, they do this to draw attention to either (1) the *relationship* between the two variables or (2) the *difference* between the two variables. In Exhibit 10, the line graphs show the variation and trend in federal government outlays and tax receipts for the years 1990–2000 and draw attention to what has been happening to the "gap" between the two.

Appendix Summary

- Two variables are directly related if one variable rises as the other rises.
- An upward-sloping line (left to right) represents two variables that are directly related.
- Two variables are inversely related if one variable rises as the other falls.
- A downward-sloping line (left to right) represents two variables that are inversely related.
- Two variables are independent if one variable rises as the other remains constant.
- The slope of a line is the ratio of the change in the variable on the vertical axis to the change in the variable on the horizontal axis.

- To determine the slope of a curve at a point, draw a line tangent to the curve at the point and then determine the slope of the tangent line.
- Any point on a 45° line is equidistant from the two axes.
- A pie chart is a convenient way to represent the different parts of something that when added together equal the whole. A pie chart visually shows rough percentage breakdowns and relative relationships.
- A bar graph is a convenient way to represent relative relationships.
- Line graphs are particularly useful for illustrating changes in a variable over some time period.

1. What type of relationship would you expect between the following: (a) sales of hot dogs and sales of hot dog buns, (b) the price of winter coats and sales of winter coats, (c) the price of personal computers and the production of personal computers, (d) sales of toothbrushes and sales of cat food, (e) the number of children in a family and the number of toys in a family.

2. Represent the following data in bar graph form.

Year	U.S. Money Supply (billions of dollars)
1997	1,067
1998	1,075
1999	1,097
2000	1,103
2001	1,135

3. Plot the following data and specify the type of relationship between the two variables. (Place "price" on the vertical axis and "quantity demanded" on the horizontal axis.)

Price of Apples ($)	Quantity Demanded of Apples
0.25	1,000
0.50	800
0.70	700
0.95	500
1.00	400
1.10	350

4. In Exhibit 4a, determine the slope between points B and C.
5. In Exhibit 4b, determine the slope between points A and B.
6. What is the special characteristic of a 45° line?
7. What is the slope of a 45° line?
8. When would it be preferable to illustrate data using a pie chart instead of a bar graph?
9. Plot the following data and specify the type of relationship between the two variables. (Place "price" on the vertical axis and "quantity supplied" on the horizontal axis.)

Price of Apples ($)	Quantity Supplied of Apples
0.25	350
0.50	400
0.70	500
0.95	700
1.00	800
1.10	1,000

Log on to the Arnold Xtra! Web site now (*http://arnoldxtra.swcollege.com*) for additional learning resources such as practice quizzes, help with graphing, video clips, and current event applications.

Appendix B

SHOULD YOU MAJOR IN ECONOMICS?

You are probably reading this textbook as part of your first college course in economics. You may be taking this course because you need it to satisfy the requirements in your major. For example, economics courses are sometimes required for students who plan to major in business, history, liberal studies, social science, or computer science. Of course, you may also be taking this course because you plan to major in economics.

If you are like many college students, you may complain that there is just not enough information available to students about the various majors at a college or university. For example, students who major in business sometimes say they are not quite certain what a business major is all about, but then they go on to add that majoring in business is a safe bet. "After all," they comment, "you are pretty sure of getting a job if you have a business degree. That's not always the case with other degrees."

Many college students choose their majors based on their high school courses. History majors sometimes say that they decided to major in history because they "liked history in high school." Similarly, chemistry, biology, and math majors say they chose chemistry, biology, or math as a college major because they liked studying chemistry, biology, or math in high school. In addition, if a student had a hard time with chemistry in high school and found it boring, then he doesn't usually want to major in chemistry in college. If a student found both math and economics easy and interesting in high school, then she is likely to major in math or economics.

Students also often look to the dollars at the end of the college degree. A student may enjoy history and want to learn more history in college but tell herself that she will earn a higher starting salary after graduation if she majors in computer science or engineering.

Thus, when choosing a major, students often consider (1) how much they enjoy studying a particular subject, (2) what they would like to see themselves doing in the future, and (3) income prospects.

Different people may weight these three factors differently. But no matter what weights you put on each of the factors, it is always better to have more information than less information, *ceteris paribus*. (We note *"ceteris paribus"* because it is not necessarily better having more information than less information if you have to pay more for the additional information than the additional information is worth. Who wants to pay $10 for a piece of information that only provides $1 in benefits?)

We believe this appendix is a fairly low-cost way of providing you with more information about an economics major than you currently have. We start by dispelling some of the misinformation you might possess about an economics major. Stated bluntly, some things that people think about an economics major and about a career in economics are just not true. For example, some people think that economics majors almost never study social relationships; instead, they only study such things as inflation, interest rates, and unemployment. Not true.

Economics majors study some of the same things that sociologists, historians, psychologists, and political scientists study. We also provide you with some information about the major that you may not have.

Next, we tell you the specifics of the economics major—what courses you study if you are an economics major, how many courses you are likely to have to take, and more.

Finally, we tell you something about a career in economics. Okay, so you have opted to become an economics major. But the day will come when you have your degree in hand. What's next? What is your starting salary likely to be? What will you be doing? Are you going to be happy doing what economists do? (If you never thought economics was about happiness, you already have some misinformation about economics. Contrary to what most laypeople think, economics is not just about money. It is about happiness too.)

FIVE MYTHS ABOUT ECONOMICS AND AN ECONOMICS MAJOR

Myth 1: Economics is all mathematics and statistics. Some students choose not to major in economics because they think economics is all mathematics and statistics. Math and statistics are used in economics, but at the undergraduate degree level, the math and statistics are certainly not overwhelming. Economics majors are usually required to take one statistics course and one math course (usually an introductory calculus course). Even students who say, "Math isn't my subject" are sometimes happy with the amount of math they need in economics. Fact is, at the undergraduate level at many colleges and universities, economics is not a very math-intensive course of study. There are many diagrams in economics, but there is not a large amount of math.

A proviso: The amount of math in the economics curriculum varies across colleges and universities. Some economics departments do not require their students to learn much math or statistics, but others do. Speaking for the majority of departments, we still hold to our original point that there isn't really that much math or statistics in economics at the undergraduate level. The graduate level is a different story.

Myth 2: Economics is only about inflation, interest rates, unemployment and other such things. If you study economics at college and then go on to become a practicing economist, no doubt people will ask you certain questions when they learn your chosen profession. Here are some of the questions they ask:

- Do you think the economy is going to pick up?
- Do you think the economy is going to slow down?
- What stocks would you recommend?
- Do you think interest rates are going to fall?
- Do you think interest rates are going to rise?
- What do you think about buying bonds right now? Is it a good idea?

People ask these kinds of questions because most people believe that economists only study stocks, bonds, interest rates, inflation, unemployment, and so on. Well, economists do study these things. But these topics are only a tiny part of what economists study. It is not hard to find many economists today, both inside and outside academia, who spend most of their time studying anything but inflation, unemployment, stocks, bonds, and so on.

As we hinted at earlier, much of what economists study may surprise you. There are economists who use their economic tools and methods to study crime, marriage, divorce, sex, obesity, addiction, sports, voting behavior, bureaucracies, presidential elections, and much more. In short, today's economics is not your grandfather's economics. Many more topics are studied today in economics than were studied in your grandfather's time.

Myth 3: People become economists only if they want to "make money."
Awhile back we asked a few well-respected and well-known economists what got them interested in economics. Here is what some of them had to say:[1]

Gary Becker, the 1992 winner of the Nobel Prize in Economics, said: "I got interested [in economics] when I was an undergraduate in college. I came into college with a strong interest in mathematics, and at the same time with a strong commitment to do something to help society. I learned in the first economics course I took that economics could deal rigorously, à la mathematics, with social problems. That stimulated me because in economics I saw that I could combine both the mathematics and my desire to do something to help society."

Vernon Smith, the 2002 winner of the Nobel Prize in Economics, said: "My father's influence started me in science and engineering at Cal Tech, but my mother, who was active in socialist politics, probably accounts for the great interest I found in economics when I took my first introductory course."

Alice Rivlin, an economist and former member of the Federal Reserve Board, said: "My interest in economics grew out of concern for improving public policy, both domestic and international. I was a teenager in the tremendously idealistic period after World War II when it seemed terribly important to get nations working together to solve the world's problems peacefully."

Allan Meltzer said: "Economics is a social science. At its best it is concerned with ways (1) to improve well being by allowing individuals the freedom to achieve their personal aims or goals and (2) to harmonize their individual interests. I find working on such issues challenging, and progress is personally rewarding."

Robert Solow, the 1987 winner of the Nobel Prize in Economics, said: "I grew up in the 1930s and it was very hard not to be interested in economics. If you were a high school student in the 1930s, you were conscious of the fact that our economy was in deep trouble and no one knew what to do about it."

Charles Plosser said: "I was an engineer as an undergraduate with little knowledge of economics. I went to the University of Chicago Graduate School of Business to get an MBA and there became fascinated with economics. I was impressed with the seriousness with which economics was viewed as a way of organizing one's thoughts about the world to address interesting questions and problems."

Walter Williams said: "I was a major in sociology in 1963 and I concluded that it was not very rigorous. Over the summer I was reading a book by W.E.B. DuBois, *Black Reconstruction,* and somewhere in the book it said something along the lines that blacks could not melt into the mainstream of American society until they understood economics, and that was something that got me interested in economics."

Murray Weidenbaum said: "A specific professor got me interested in economics. He was very prescient: He correctly noted that while lawyers dominated the policy-making process up until then (the 1940s), in the future economics would be an important tool for developing public policy. And he was right."

Irma Adelman said: "I hesitate to say because it sounds arrogant. My reason [for getting into economics] was that I wanted to benefit humanity. And my perception at the time was that economic problems were the most important problems that humanity has to face. That is what got me into economics and into economic development."

Lester Thurow said: "[I got interested in economics because of] the belief, some would see it as naïve belief, that economics was a profession where it would be possible to help make the world better."

Myth 4: Economics wasn't very interesting in high school, so it's not going to be very interesting in college. A typical high school economics course emphasizes consumer economics and spends much time discussing this topic. Students learn about credit cards, mortgage loans, budgets, buying insurance,

---

1. See various interviews in Roger A. Arnold, *Economics, 2d edition* (St. Paul, Minnesota: West Publishing Company, 1992).

renting an apartment, and other such things. These are important topics because not knowing the "ins and outs" of such things can make your life much harder. Still, many students come away from a high school economics course thinking that economics is always and everywhere about consumer topics.

However, a high school economics course and a college economics course are usually as different as day and night. Simply leaf through this book and look at the variety of topics covered compared to the topics you might have covered in your high school economics course. Go on to look at texts used in other economics courses—courses that range from law and economics to history of economic thought to international economics to sports economics—and you will see what we mean.

Myth 5: Economics is a lot like business, but business is more marketable. Although business and economics have some common topics, much that one learns in economics is not taught in business and much that one learns in business is not taught in economics. The area of intersection between business and economics is not large.

Still, many people think otherwise. And so thinking that business and economics are "pretty much the same thing," they often choose to major in the subject they believe has greater marketability—which they believe is business.

Well, consider the following:

1. A few years ago *BusinessWeek* magazine asked the chief executive officers (CEOs) of major companies what they thought was the best undergraduate degree. Their first choice was engineering. Their second choice was economics. Economics scored higher than business administration.

2. The National Association of Colleges and Employers undertook a survey in the summer of 2001 in which they identified the starting salary offers in different disciplines. The starting salary in economics/finance was $40,776. The starting salary in business administration was 7.7 percent lower at $37,844.

WHAT AWAITS YOU AS AN ECONOMICS MAJOR?

If you become an economics major, what courses will you take? What are you going to study?

At the lower-division level, economics majors must take both the principles of macroeconomics course and the principles of microeconomics course. They usually also take a statistics course and a math course (usually calculus).

At the upper-division level, they must take intermediate microeconomics and intermediate macroeconomics, along with a certain number of electives. Some of the elective courses include: (1) money and banking, (2) law and economics, (3) history of economic thought, (4) public finance, (5) labor economics, (6) international economics, (7) antitrust and regulation, (8) health economics, (9) economics of development, (10) urban and regional economics, (11) econometrics, (12) mathematical economics, (13) environmental economics, (14) public choice, (15) global managerial economics, (16) economic approach to politics and sociology, (17) sports economics, and many more courses. Most economics majors take between 12 and 15 economics courses.

One of the attractive things about studying economics is that you will acquire many of the skills employers highly value. First, you will have the quantitative skills that are important in many business and government positions. Second, you will acquire the writing skills necessary in almost all lines of work. Third, and perhaps most importantly, you will develop the thinking skills that almost all employers agree are critical to success.

A study published in the 1998 edition of the *Journal of Economic Education* ranked economics majors as having the highest average scores on the Law School

Admission Test (LSAT). Also, consider the words of the Royal Economic Society: "One of the things that makes economics graduates so employable is that the subject teaches you to think in a careful and precise way. The fundamental economic issue is how society decides to allocate its resources: how the costs and benefits of a course of action can be evaluated and compared, and how appropriate choices can be made. A degree in economics gives a training in decision making principles, providing a skill applicable in a very wide range of careers."

Keep in mind, too, that economics is one of the most popular majors at some of the most respected universities in the country. As of this writing, economics is the top major at Harvard, Princeton, Columbia, Stanford, University of Pennsylvania, and University of Chicago. It is the second most popular major at Brown, Yale, and the University of California at Berkeley. It is the third most popular major at Cornell and Dartmouth.

WHAT DO ECONOMISTS DO?

Employment for economists is projected to grow between 21 and 35 percent between 2000 and 2010. According to the *Occupational Outlook Handbook:*

Opportunities for economists should be best in private industry, especially in research, testing, and consulting firms, as more companies contract out for economic research services. The growing complexity of the global economy, competition, and increased reliance on quantitative methods for analyzing the current value of future funds, business trends, sales, and purchasing should spur demand for economists. The growing need for economic analyses in virtually every industry should result in additional jobs for economists.

Today, economists work in many varied fields. Here are some of the fields and some of the positions economists hold in those fields:

Education
College Professor
Researcher
High School Teacher

Journalism
Researcher
Industry Analyst
Economic Analyst

Accounting
Analyst
Auditor
Researcher
Consultant

General Business
Chief Executive Officer
Business Analyst
Marketing Analyst
Business Forecaster
Competitive Analyst

Government
Researcher
Analyst
Speechwriter
Forecaster

Financial Services
Business Journalist
International Analyst
Newsletter Editor
Broker
Investment Banker

Banking
Credit Analyst
Loan Officer
Investment Analyst
Financial Manager

Other
Business Consultant
Independent Forecaster
Freelance Analyst
Think Tank Analyst
Entrepreneur

Economists do a myriad of things. For example, in business, economists often analyze economic conditions, make forecasts, offer strategic planning initiatives, collect and analyze data, predict exchange rate movements, and review regulatory policies, among other things. In government, economists collect and analyze data, analyze international economic situations, research monetary conditions, advise on policy, and much more. As private consultants, economists work with accountants, business executives, government officials, educators, financial firms, labor unions, state and local governments, and others.

Median annual earnings of economists were $64,830 in 2000. The middle 50 percent earned between $47,370 and $87,890. The lowest 10 percent earned less than $35,690, and the highest 10 percent earned more than $114,580.

PLACES TO FIND MORE INFORMATION

If you are interested in an economics major and perhaps a career in economics, here are some places where you can go and some people you can speak with to acquire more information:

- To learn about the economics curriculum, we urge you to speak with the economics professors at your college or university. Ask them what courses you would have to take as an economics major. Ask them what elective courses are available. In addition, ask them why they chose to study economics. What is it about economics that interested them?
- For more information about salaries and what economists do, you may want to visit the *Occupational Outlook Handbook* Web site at *http://www.bls.gov/oco/*.
- For starting salary information, you may want to visit the National Association of Colleges and Employers Web site at *http://www.naceweb.org/*.
- To see a list of famous people who have majored in economics, go to *http://www.marietta.edu/~ema/econ/famous.html*.

CONCLUDING REMARKS

Choosing a major is a big decision and therefore should not be made too quickly and without much thought. In this short appendix, we have provided you with some information about an economics major and a career in economics. Economics may not be for everyone (in fact, economists would say that if it were, many of the benefits of specialization would be lost), but it may be right for you. It is a major where many of today's most marketable skills are acquired—the skills of good writing, quantitative analysis, and thinking. It is a major in which professors and students daily ask and answer some very interesting and relevant questions. It is a major that is highly regarded by employers. It may just be the right major for you. Give it some thought.

Log on to the Arnold Xtra! Web site now (*http://arnoldxtra.swcollege.com*) for additional learning resources such as practice quizzes, help with graphing, video clips, and current event applications.

ECONOMIC ACTIVITIES: PRODUCING AND TRADING

Producing and trading activities occur frequently in everyone's life. People produce goods and services—books, cars, houses, sociology lectures, and so on. People trade money for goods and trade their labor services for money. Most people take their producing and trading activities for granted and rarely study them carefully. In this chapter, we put these two major economic activities—producing and trading— under the microscope. You may be surprised to see what pops up.

Most of our activities involve giving, producing, trading, and transferring. Although economists are interested in all these activities, their primary concerns are producing and trading, the subject matter of this chapter. In analyzing various aspects of production, economists look at (1) individuals and firms producing goods and (2) economies producing goods. In analyzing trade, economists look at (1) trades that affect only the traders and (2) trades that affect the traders and third parties too. Economists also examine some general trade topics—the reason for trading, how the benefits of trade are measured, and how potential trades can be turned into actual trades.

THE PRODUCTION POSSIBILITIES FRONTIER

In order to analyze the various aspects of production, economists find it helpful to define a model or framework in which to examine production. This section introduces and discusses such a framework—the *production possibilities frontier.*

PRODUCING GOOD GRADES IN COLLEGE

When we think of producing goods, we usually think of goods such as cars, computers, furniture, and so on. That is, we think of goods that are produced by business firms. But individuals produce things every day. For example, college students sometimes work at producing "good grades" in their courses. They use both labor and time to produce good grades.

To illustrate, suppose you are taking two courses this semester, sociology and economics. Because you have a part-time job and many other responsibilities, you decide you can spend only 6 hours a week studying these two subjects. If you study economics for 4 hours, you have 2 hours to study sociology; if you study economics for 5 hours, you have 1 hour to study sociology.

Now let's suppose that the more time you spend studying economics, the higher the grade you will earn in economics; the less time you spend studying economics, the lower the grade you will earn. The same holds for sociology.

Exhibit 1a shows the combination of grades you can earn with 6 hours of study. For example, if you study sociology for 6 hours and economics for 0 hours, you will get a 90 in sociology and a 60 in economics. In Exhibit 1b, this combination of grades is identified by point *A*.

(1) Hours Spent Studying Sociology	(2) Grade in Sociology	(3) Hours Spent Studying Economics	(4) Grade in Economics	(5) Point in Part (b)
6	90	0	60	A
5	85	1	65	B
4	80	2	70	C
3	75	3	75	D
2	70	4	80	E
1	65	5	85	F
0	60	6	90	G

(a)

(b)

exhibit 1

Production Possibilities Frontier for Grades
Part (a) shows the different combinations of grades that can be earned in sociology and economics by studying 6 hours per week. The data in columns (2) and (4) of part (a) are plotted as points *A–G* in part (b). Connecting points *A–G* in (b) gives us a production possibilities frontier for grades.

Now look again at the table in part (a). If you study sociology for 5 hours and economics for 1 hour, you will get an 85 in sociology and a 65 in economics. This combination of grades is identified by point *B* in the graph in part (b).

In part (a), we have continued listing the possible combinations of grades based on the number of hours spent studying each subject. In part (b), we have continued to plot and identify the combinations. After all the combinations were plotted and identified, we drew a line connecting the points. This line is called a **production possibilities frontier (PPF).**[1] It gives us the combination of grades in economics and sociology that you will earn if you study a given period of time.

After a production possibilities frontier has been identified, you must identify where on that frontier you will be. Will you choose to be at point *A, B, C, D, E, F,* or *G*? Of course, no matter which point you choose, you will incur a **trade-off.** The nature of a tradeoff is that you get more of one thing but less of something else. If you choose point *A* over point *B,* you will get a higher sociology grade (90 instead of 85) but a lower economics grade (60 instead of 65).

Production Possibilities Frontier (PPF)
Represents the possible combinations of two goods that can be produced in a certain period of time, under the conditions of a given state of technology and fully employed resources.

Tradeoff
More of one good means less of another good.

THINKING LIKE AN ECONOMIST

According to the economist, the world is full of tradeoffs. We are regularly faced with the fact that more of one thing means less of something else. More time at work means less time at home. More reading means less time watching television. A higher grade in economics may mean a slightly lower grade in sociology. Recognizing that the world is full of tradeoffs is really no more than recognizing that we incur opportunity costs when we make choices. And why do we make choices? Scarcity.

THE ECONOMY'S PPF

Just as there is a production possibilities frontier for an individual, there is a PPF for an economy. This section discusses the straight-line PPF and the bowed-outward PPF, two possibilities for an economy's PPF.

The Straight-Line PPF: Constant Opportunity Costs

Assume three things: (1) Only two goods can be produced in an economy, computers and television sets. (2) The opportunity cost of 1 television set is 1 computer. (3) As more of one good is produced, the opportunity cost between television sets and computers is constant.

In Exhibit 2a, we have identified six combinations of computers and television sets that can be produced in an economy. For example, combination *A* is 50,000 computers and 0 television sets, combination *B* is 40,000 computers and 10,000 television sets, and so on. We plotted these six combinations of computers and television sets in Exhibit 2b. Each combination represents a different point. For example, the combination of 50,000 computers and 0 television sets is represented by point *A*. As discussed earlier, the line that connects points *A–F* is the production possibilities frontier.

The production possibilities frontier is a straight line because the opportunity cost of producing computers and television sets is constant. For example, if the economy were to move from point *A* to *B,* or from *B* to *C,* and so on, the opportunity cost of each good would remain constant at 1 for 1. To illustrate, at point *A,* 50,000 computers and 0 television sets are produced. At *B,* 40,000 computers and 10,000 television sets are produced.

Point *A:* 50,000 computers, 0 television sets
Point *B:* 40,000 computers, 10,000 television sets

---

1. If we were talking about the production of two goods—such as computers and television sets—instead of the "production" of sociology and economics grades, we would define a production possibilities frontier a little more completely, such as: represents the possible combinations of two goods that can be produced in a certain period of time, under the conditions of a given state of technology and fully employed resources.

Combination	Computers	and	Television Sets	Point in
	(number of units per year)			Part (b)
A	50,000	and	0	A
B	40,000	and	10,000	B
C	30,000	and	20,000	C
D	20,000	and	30,000	D
E	10,000	and	40,000	E
F	0	and	50,000	F

(a)

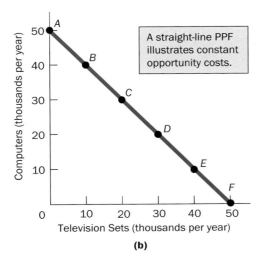

(b)

exhibit 2

Production Possibilities Frontier (Constant Opportunity Costs)
The economy can produce any of the six combinations of computers and television sets in part (a). We have plotted these combinations in part (b). The production possibilities frontier in part (b) is a straight line because the opportunity cost of producing either good is constant: for *every* 1 computer not produced, 1 television set is produced.

We conclude that for every 10,000 computers not produced, 10,000 television sets are produced—a ratio of 1 to 1. The opportunity cost—1 computer for 1 television set—that exists between points *A* and *B* also exists between points *B* and *C*, *C* and *D*, *D* and *E*, and *E* and *F*. In other words, opportunity cost is constant at 1 computer for 1 television set.

The Bowed-Outward (Concave-Downward) PPF: Increasing Opportunity Costs

Assume two things: (1) Only two goods can be produced in an economy, computers and television sets. (2) As more of one good is produced, the opportunity cost between computers and television sets changes.

In Exhibit 3a, we have identified four combinations of computers and television sets that can be produced in an economy. For example, combination *A* is 50,000 computers and 0 television sets, combination *B* is 40,000 computers and 20,000 television sets, and so on. We plotted these four combinations of computers and television sets in Exhibit 3b. Each combination represents a different point. The curved line that connects points *A–D* is the production possibilities frontier.

In this case, the production possibilities frontier is bowed outward (concave downward) because the opportunity cost of television sets increases as more sets are produced. To illustrate, let's start at point *A*, where the economy is producing 50,000 computers and 0 television sets, and move to point *B*, where the economy is producing 40,000 computers and 20,000 television sets.

Point *A*: 50,000 computers, 0 television sets
Point *B*: 40,000 computers, 20,000 television sets

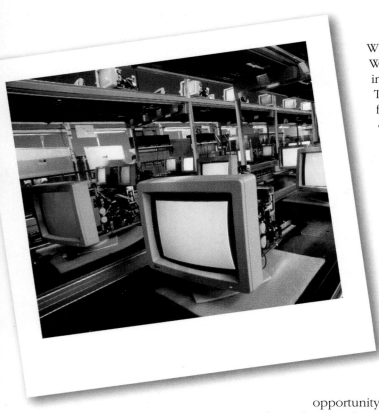

What is the opportunity cost of a television set over this range? We see that 20,000 more television sets are produced by moving from point *A* to *B* but at the cost of only 10,000 computers. This means for every 1 television set produced, ½ computer is forfeited. Thus, the opportunity cost of 1 television set is ½ computer.

Now let's move from point *B*, where the economy is producing 40,000 computers and 20,000 television sets, to point *C,* where the economy is producing 25,000 computers and 40,000 television sets.

> Point *B:* 40,000 computers, 20,000 television sets
> Point *C:* 25,000 computers, 40,000 television sets

What is the opportunity cost of a television set over this range? In this case, 20,000 more television sets are produced by moving from point *B* to *C but at the cost of 15,000 computers.* This means for every 1 television set produced, ¾ computer is forfeited. Thus, the opportunity cost of 1 television set is ¾ computer.

What statement can we make about the opportunity costs of producing television sets? Obviously, as the economy produces more television sets, the opportunity cost of producing television sets increases. This gives us the bowed-outward production possibilities frontier in Exhibit 3b.

---

exhibit 3

Production Possibilities Frontier (Changing Opportunity Costs)
The economy can produce any of the four combinations of computers and television sets in part (a). We have plotted these combinations in part (b). The production possibilities frontier in part (b) is bowed outward because the opportunity cost of producing television sets increases as more television sets are produced.

Combination	Computers	and	Television Sets	Point in Part (b)
	(number of units per year)			
A	50,000	and	0	A
B	40,000	and	20,000	B
C	25,000	and	40,000	C
D	0	and	60,000	D

(a)

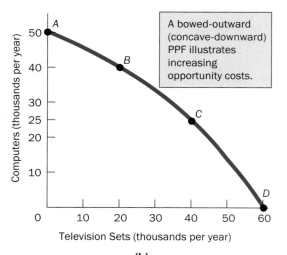

A bowed-outward (concave-downward) PPF illustrates increasing opportunity costs.

(b)

A Closer Look

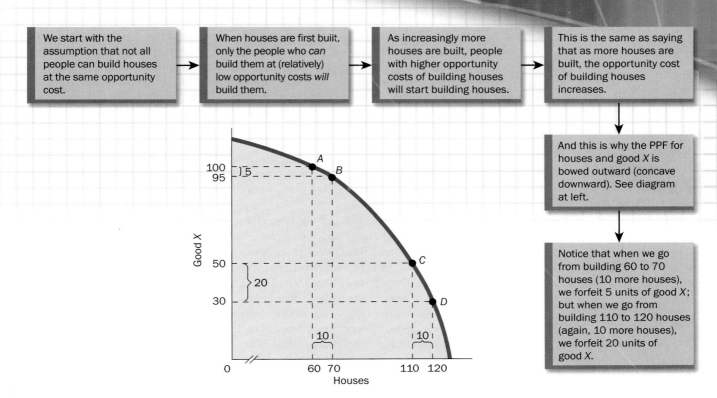

We start with the assumption that not all people can build houses at the same opportunity cost.

When houses are first built, only the people who *can* build them at (relatively) low opportunity costs *will* build them.

As increasingly more houses are built, people with higher opportunity costs of building houses will start building houses.

This is the same as saying that as more houses are built, the opportunity cost of building houses increases.

And this is why the PPF for houses and good *X* is bowed outward (concave downward). See diagram at left.

Notice that when we go from building 60 to 70 houses (10 more houses), we forfeit 5 units of good *X*; but when we go from building 110 to 120 houses (again, 10 more houses), we forfeit 20 units of good *X*.

LAW OF INCREASING OPPORTUNITY COSTS

We know that the shape of the production possibilities frontier depends on whether opportunity costs (1) are constant or (2) increase as more of a good is produced. In Exhibit 2b, the production possibilities frontier is a straight line; in Exhibit 3b, it is bowed outward. In the real world, most production possibilities frontiers are bowed outward. This means that for most goods, the opportunity costs increase as more of the good is produced. This is referred to as the **law of increasing opportunity costs.**

But why (for most goods) do the opportunity costs increase as more of the good is produced? The answer is because people have varying abilities. For example, some people are better suited to building houses than other people are. When a construction company first starts building houses, it employs the people who are most skilled at house building. The most skilled persons can build houses at lower opportunity costs than others can. But as the construction company builds more houses, it finds that it has already employed the most skilled builders, so it must employ those who are less skilled at house building. These people build houses at higher opportunity costs. Where three skilled house builders could build a house in a month, as many as seven unskilled builders may be required to build it in the same length of time. Exhibit 4 summarizes the points in this section.

THREE ECONOMIC CONCEPTS WITHIN A PPF FRAMEWORK

The PPF framework is useful for illustrating and working with economic concepts. This section looks at the economic concepts of efficiency, unemployed resources, economic growth, and an advance in technology.

exhibit 4

A Summary Statement about Increasing Opportunity Costs and a Production Possibilities Frontier That Is Bowed Outward (Concave Downward)
Many of the points about increasing opportunity costs and a production possibilities frontier that is bowed outward are summarized here.

Law of Increasing Opportunity Costs
As more of a good is produced, the opportunity costs of producing that good increase.

Efficiency

Chapter 1 discusses efficiency in terms of the right amount of something. For example, you may recall the discussion of the efficient length of time to study for an economics test. In that example, efficiency is considered in terms of an individual's actions and choices.

Economists also consider **efficiency** in terms of an economy. For example, economists often say that an economy is *efficient* if it is producing the maximum output with given resources and technology. In Exhibit 5, points *A, B, C, D,* and *E* are all efficient points. Notice that all these points lie *on* the production possibilities frontier. In other words, we are getting the most (in terms of output) from what we have (in terms of available resources and technology).

It follows that an economy is exhibiting **inefficiency** if it is producing less than the maximum output with given resources and technology. In Exhibit 5, point *F* is an inefficient point. It lies *below* the production possibilities frontier; it is below the outer limit of what is possible. In other words, we could do better with what we have.

Consider another way of viewing efficiency and inefficiency. Start at efficient point *A* in Exhibit 5 and move to efficient point *B*. We go from producing 55,000 television sets and 5,000 cars to producing fewer television sets (50,000) and more cars (15,000). Now move from point *B* back to point *A*. We go from producing 50,000 television sets and 15,000 cars to producing more television sets (55,000) and fewer cars (5,000). Notice that if we start at an efficient point—such as *A* or *B*—it is impossible to produce more of one good without producing less of another good. We can move from *A* to *B* and produce more cars but not without producing fewer television sets. *Efficiency implies that gains are impossible in one area without losses in another.* Another way to state this is that efficiency implies a *tradeoff*—before more of one good can be obtained, some of another good has to be given up. A movement between any two points on the PPF in Exhibit 5 implies a tradeoff. For example, if we move from *D* to *C*, we get 7,000 more television sets but must give up 10,000 cars.

Efficiency
In terms of production, the condition where the maximum output is produced with given resources and technology. Efficiency implies the impossibility of gains in one area without losses in another.

Inefficiency
In terms of production, the condition where less than the maximum output is produced with given resources and technology. Inefficiency implies the possibility of gains in one area without losses in another.

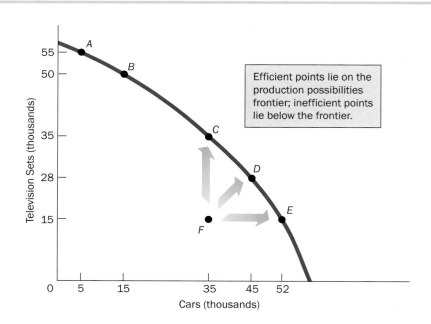

exhibit 5

Efficiency, Inefficiency, and Unemployed Resources within a PPF Framework

Points *A, B, C, D,* and *E* are efficient points. They lie on the production possibilities frontier. It is *impossible* to move away from these points and get more of one good without getting less of another good. Point *F* is an inefficient point. It lies below the production possibilities frontier. It is *possible* to move away from this point and get more of (at least) one good and no less of another. At efficient points, all resources are being used in the production of goods. At inefficient points, some resources are not being used to produce goods; that is, there are some unemployed resources.

Efficient points lie on the production possibilities frontier; inefficient points lie below the frontier.

This is common sense. If efficiency exists, we already are getting the most we can out of what we have. Therefore, we cannot do better in one area (getting more of one good) without necessarily doing worse in another (getting less of another good).

Now consider inefficient point *F*, a point at which the economy is not producing the maximum output with given resources and technology. Move from point *F* to point *C*. We produce more television sets and no fewer cars. What if we move from *F* to *D*? We produce more television sets and more cars. Finally, if we move from *F* to *E*, we produce more cars and no fewer television sets. Thus, moving from *F* can give us more of at least one good and no less of another good. (Moving from *F* to *D*, we produced more of both goods.) *Inefficiency implies that gains are possible in one area without losses in another.* This is also common sense. If inefficiency exists, we are not getting the most out of what we have. Therefore, we can do better in one area without necessarily doing worse in another.

Q & A

Q: Suppose we move from point *F* to point *B* in Exhibit 5. More television sets are produced but fewer cars—in other words, more of one good but less of another. Doesn't this mean *F* is an efficient point although it was labeled an inefficient point?

A: Efficiency implies that gains are *impossible* in one area without losses in another. Point *F* does not fit this definition. We could move from *F* to *C, D,* or *E*—all these moves are *possible*—and get gains in one area without getting losses in another. It follows that *F* is an inefficient point. Simply because a move from *F* to *B* brings gains in one area and losses in another, it does not necessarily follow that a move from *F* to some other point would always bring the same results. As long as it is possible to move from *F* to some point and get gains in one area without getting losses in another, then *F* is an inefficient point.

Unemployed Resources

When the economy exhibits inefficiency, it is not producing the maximum output with the available resources and technology. One reason may be that the economy is not using all its resources—that is, some of its resources are unemployed, as at point *F* in Exhibit 5.

When the economy exhibits efficiency, it is producing the maximum output with the available resources and technology. This means it is using all its resources to produce goods—all its resources are employed, none are unemployed. At the efficient points *A–E* in Exhibit 5, there are no unemployed resources.

Economic Growth

Economic growth refers to the increased productive capabilities of an economy. It is illustrated by a shift outward in the production possibilities frontier. Two major factors that affect economic growth are an increase in the quantity of resources and an advance in technology.

With an increase in the quantity of resources (say, through a new discovery of resources), it is possible to produce a greater quantity of output. In Exhibit 6, an increase in the quantity of resources makes it possible to produce both more military goods and more civilian goods. Thus, the PPF shifts outward from PPF₁ to PPF₂.

Technology refers to the body of skills and knowledge concerning the use of resources in production. An advance in technology commonly refers to the ability to produce more output with a fixed quantity of resources or the ability to produce the same output with a smaller quantity of resources.

Suppose there is an advance in technology such that more military goods and more civilian goods can be produced with the same quantity of resources. As a result, the PPF in Exhibit 6 shifts outward from PPF₁ to PPF₂. The outcome is the same as when the quantity of resources is increased.

Technology
The body of skills and knowledge concerning the use of resources in production. An advance in technology commonly refers to the ability to produce more output with a fixed amount of resources or the ability to produce the same output with fewer resources.

exhibit 6

Economic Growth within a PPF Framework
An increase in resources or an advance in technology can increase the production capabilities of an economy, leading to economic growth and a shift outward in the production possibilities frontier.

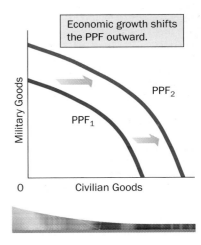

Technology   Popular Culture   Everyday Life   The World

Can Technology on the Farm Affect the Number of Lawyers in the City?

There is no doubt that an advance in technology affects the industry in which it is developed and used. For example, a technological advance in the car industry will increase the output of cars; a technological advance in the house-building industry will increase the output of houses.

But can a technological advance in one industry have ripple effects beyond the industry in which it is developed and used? With this question in mind, let's start with a fact. The United States had 32.1 million farmers in 1910, 30.5 million farmers in 1940, 9.7 million farmers in 1970, and about 4.8 million farmers in 2000. Farmers accounted for 34.9 percent of the U.S. population in 1910, 23.2 percent in 1940, 4.8 percent in 1970, and only 1.9 percent in 2000. Where did all the farmers go and why did they leave farming?

Many farmers left farming because farming has experienced major technological advances during this century. Where farmers once farmed with minimal capital equipment, today they use computers, tractors, pesticides, cellular phones, and much more. As a result, more food can be produced with fewer farmers.

Because fewer farmers were needed to produce food, many farmers left the farms and entered the manufacturing and service industries. In other words, people who were once farmers (or whose parents and grandparents were farmers) began to produce cars, airplanes, television sets, and computers. They became attorneys, accountants, and police officers.

What should we learn from this? First, a technological advance in one sector of the economy may make it possible to produce goods in another sector of the economy. Technological advances in agriculture made it possible for fewer farmers to produce more food, thus releasing some farmers to produce other things. In other words, there may be more services in the world in part because of agriculture's technological advances.

Second, technological advances may affect the composition of employment. The technological advances in agriculture resulted in (1) a smaller percentage of people working in rural areas on farms and (2) a larger percentage of people working in manufacturing and services in the cities and suburbs. (Is the growth of the suburbs in the last 50 years due in part to technological advances on farms?)

Self-Test *(Answers to Self-Test questions are in the Self-Test Appendix.)*

1. What does a straight-line production possibilities frontier (PPF) represent? What does a bowed-outward PPF represent?

2. Would you expect to see more intense political battles in a growing economy or in a stagnant economy, *ceteris paribus*? Why? (Hint: Think in terms of the PPF.)

3. A politician says, "If you elect me, we can get more of everything we want." Under what condition(s) is the politician telling the truth?

4. In an economy there is only one combination of goods that is efficient. True or false? Explain your answer.

TRADE OR EXCHANGE

Trade (Exchange)
The process of giving up one thing for something else.

Trade or **exchange** is the process of giving up one thing for something else. Usually, money is traded for goods and services. Trade is all around us; we are involved with it every day. Few of us, however, have considered the full extent of trade.

THE PURPOSE OF TRADE

Why do people trade? Why do they exchange things? They do so in order to make themselves better off. When a person voluntarily trades $100 for a jacket, she is saying "I prefer to have the jacket instead of the $100." And, of course, when the seller of the jacket voluntarily sells the jacket for $100, he is saying, "I prefer to have the $100 instead of the jacket." In short, through trade or exchange, each person gives up something he or she values less for something he or she values more.

PERIODS RELEVANT TO TRADE
Three time periods are relevant to the trading process.

Before the Trade
Before a trade is made, a person is said to be in the **ex ante** position. For example, suppose Ramona has the opportunity to trade what she has, $2,000, for something she does not have, a big screen television set. In the ex ante position, she will think that she will be better off with either (1) the television set or (2) $2,000 worth of other goods. If she believes she will be better off with the television set than with $2,000 worth of other goods, she will make the trade. Individuals will make a trade only if they believe ex ante (before) the trade that the trade will make them better off.

Ex Ante
Phrase that means "before," as in before a trade.

At the Point of Trade
Suppose Ramona now gives $2,000 to the person in possession of the television set. Does Ramona still believe she will be better off with the television set than with the $2,000? Of course she does. Her action testifies to this fact.

After the Trade
After a trade is made, a person is said to be in the **ex post** position. Suppose two days have passed. Does Ramona still feel the same way about the trade as she did before the trade and at the point of trade? Maybe, maybe not. She may look back on the trade and regret it. She may say that if she had it to do over again, she would not trade the $2,000 for the big screen television set. In general, though, people expect a trade to make them better off, and usually the trade meets their expectations. But there are no guarantees that a trade will meet expectations because no one in the real world can see the future.

Ex Post
Phrase that means "after," as in after a trade.

MEASURING THE BENEFITS OF TRADES
Economists determine the benefits of a trade by examining the trade in terms of both the consumer's or buyer's point of view and the producer's or seller's point of view. They then use these two points of view to analyze various trading situations.

Thinking of Trade from the Consumer's or Buyer's Point of View
Suppose you would be willing to pay a maximum of $10 to see a new movie release. But at the movie theater, you are charged only $7. The difference between the maximum price you are willing and able to pay to see the movie and the price you actually pay is **consumers' surplus.** In this case, consumers' surplus is $3.

Consumers' Surplus (CS)
The difference between the maximum price a buyer is willing and able to pay for a good or service and the price actually paid. CS = Maximum buying price − Price paid.

Consumers' surplus = Maximum buying price − Price paid

Obviously, a buyer prefers a large consumers' surplus to a small consumers' surplus. You would have preferred to pay only $6 for the movie and obtain $4 worth of consumers' surplus.

Thinking of Trade from the Producer's or Seller's Point of View
Now consider the seller. Suppose the minimum price the owner of the theater would have accepted for admission is $5. But she doesn't sell tickets for $5; she

ECONOMICS IN...

The World   Popular Culture   Technology   Everyday Life

What Do Blue Jeans and Rock 'n' Roll Have to Do with the Fall of the Berlin Wall?

The Berlin Wall once stood as the symbol of communism and the Cold War. Today, the Berlin Wall is gone and the Cold War is over. What happened? Was the military strength of the United States too much for the former Soviet Union to cope with continually? Some people think this is exactly what happened. Other people think that blue jeans and rock music had more to do with the decline of the Soviet Union and the demise of communism in Eastern Europe than did the military might of the United States.

Tension may develop between political parties in the United States because each party wants to be at a different point on the production possibilities frontier. Only through economic growth will that tension subside and then only for a while. Some economists and political scientists believe that one reason for the downfall of communism in the Soviet Union and Eastern Europe was the political tension that developed between government leaders and the majority of the people.

Consider the PPF framework shown in Exhibit 7a. Suppose the majority of the people in the Soviet Union wanted to be at point 1, producing C_1 consumer goods (blue jeans and

rock music) and M_1 military goods. The government leaders, however, wanted to be at point 2, producing C_2 consumer goods and M_2 military goods. The majority of the people wanted more consumer goods than the government wanted to produce, and the government wanted more military goods than the people wanted to produce.

Is there any evidence that this scenario actually took place in the Soviet Union? Many Soviet scholars think it did. Even Soviet leaders admitted this. In May 1990, Eduard Shevardnadze, the Soviet foreign minister at the time, said that the Kremlin's emphasis on military goods and a large army was contrary to what the majority of the people wanted.[2]

Furthermore, numerous accounts of life in the former Soviet Union suggest that the majority of the people were not satisfied with the quality or quantity of consumer goods they were able to purchase. People complained of continual food shortages, shoddy products, telephone service that often broke down, and much much more.

To get an idea of Soviet economic priorities, consider that in 1980, 12.9 percent of all expenditures were for the military.

---

exhibit 7

The Collapse of the Former Soviet Union within a PPF Framework
In (a) we have hypothesized that the majority of the people in the former Soviet Union wanted to be at point 1 on the production possibilities frontier and that government leaders wanted to be at point 2. Given the difference between the points, we would expect some tension between the people and the government leaders. It is possible for the people to get more of what they want (consumer goods) through economic growth, as shown in (b). Through economic growth, it is possible to move from point 2 on PPF$_1$ to point 3 on PPF$_2$, bringing the people closer to their preferred amount of consumer goods (C_1). Without economic growth, the tension between the two groups may build and become "explosive."

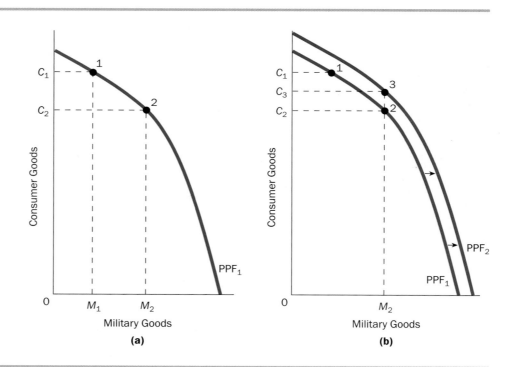

(a)   (b)

---

2. See Walter Friedenberg, "Shevardnadze Warns of Explosion," *Washington Times*, sec. A, 7 May 1990. p. 1.

In contrast, the percentage of total military expenditures in most other countries was between 2 and 6 percent. It was 5.3 percent in the United States, for example. As for consumer goods, in the Soviet Union at the end of the 1980s, there were approximately 330 television sets for every 1,000 persons and 12 telephones for every 100 persons. In the United States, there were 815 television sets for every 1,000 persons and 51 telephones for every 100 persons.

As long as the Soviet Union experienced some economic growth and all the growth didn't go to the military, it was possible to alleviate some of the tension between the people and the government leaders. For example, suppose economic growth shifted the production possibilities frontier outward from PPF_1 to PPF_2 as shown in Exhibit 7b. In this case, the Soviet Union could maintain military goods production at M_2, while increasing consumer goods production to C_3, which is closer to the amount of consumer goods, C_1, that the majority of the people wanted.

But there is reason to believe that the Soviet Union didn't experience much economic growth. On February 17, 1988, Soviet leader Mikhail Gorbachev told the Central Committee of the Communist Party that the Soviet economy had not grown in 20 years.[3] In other words, it is possible that for 20 years there was constant tension between the people and the government leaders. Couldn't this lead to an "explosion" of sorts?

Some political scientists and economists believe that the popular revolt against communism that took place in the late 1980s and early 1990s was just this explosion. The Berlin Wall, once the symbol of communism for many, began to crack, metaphorically speaking. Then it came crumbling down, literally.

The bigger lesson to learn can be expressed in terms of the production possibilities frontier. A country that locates itself at a point on the production possibilities frontier where the majority of people do not want it to be is likely to experience greater political instability than a country that does not.

charges \$7. The difference between the price paid for the ticket and the minimum price the seller would be willing and able to sell the ticket for is **producers' (or sellers') surplus.** For this trade, the producers' surplus is \$2.

Producers' (or sellers') surplus = Price received − Minimum selling price

A seller prefers a large producers' surplus. The seller would have preferred to sell the movie ticket for \$8 and receive \$3 worth of producers' surplus.

Will a Policy Make You Better Off or Worse Off?

Many different policies and laws are put into effect by governments and organizations each year. For example, the federal government may change its tariff policy and place a tariff (tax) on certain imported goods. Or it could subsidize the production of wheat, corn, or sugar. HMOs (health maintenance organizations) may institute a policy in which they will pay for only some of the medicines you may need. The state legislators in your state may increase or decrease the tuition at a state-supported college or university. The federal government may block a merger between two major companies that produce and sell office supplies. When you hear about a new policy or law, you may naturally wonder "How does this affect me? Will I be better off or worse off?"

To answer these questions, you need to remember that you do many things. You buy goods, you sell goods, you may work for a company, you may own your own business. In other words, you wear many hats. One day you wear the hat of a buyer, the next day, that of a seller. On any given day, you may wear both the hat of an employee and the hat of a buyer. As a buyer, there is an easy way to figure out how a policy will affect you. Simply ask, "As a result of the policy, will my consumers' surplus rise, fall, or stay the same?" If it will rise, then as a buyer, the policy will make you better off. If it will fall, then you will be worse off. If it will stay the same, then your situation will be unchanged. Later

---

3. Communique on the Plenary Session of the Central Committee of the Communist Party of the Soviet Union, *Pravda* and *Izvestiya*, 18 February 1988. Some economists think that Gorbachev's statement was slightly exaggerated. It is likely that the former Soviet economy experienced some growth, but not much. Even with economic growth, if the population grew faster than the economy, per capita consumer goods would decline.

Terms of Trade
How much of one thing is given up for how much of something else.

Transaction Costs
The costs associated with the time and effort needed to search out, negotiate, and consummate an exchange.

chapters show how the concept of consumers' surplus can be used to determine how a given policy or change in policy will affect an individual.

Trade and the Terms of Trade

Suppose Emilio walks into a bookstore and browses through a few of the best-sellers. Minutes later he walks to the counter with a book, takes $30 out of his wallet (the price of the book), gives it to the cashier, and walks out. Away from the store, he thinks, "They charged too much for the book; I've been taken."

Given Emilio's thoughts and accepting that he is currently in the ex post position, is it correct to assume that he now regrets the trade that he made only moments earlier? The answer may be yes. But probably, Emilio is simply expressing his discontent over paying as much for the book as he did. He would rather have paid less for the book and received more consumers' surplus, as would any buyer.

This example illustrates the difference between trade and the terms of trade. *Trade* refers to the process whereby "things" (money, goods, services, and so on) are given up in order to obtain something else. The **terms of trade** refer to *how much* of one thing is given up for *how much* of something else. For example, if $30 is traded for a best-selling book, the terms of trade are 1 bestseller for $30. If the price of a loaf of bread is $2.50, the terms of trade are 1 loaf of bread for $2.50. Buyers and sellers can always think of more advantageous terms of exchange. Buyers prefer lower prices, sellers prefer higher prices.

Knowing the difference between trade and the terms of trade prevents us from believing that someone has been harmed by an exchange when the person claims to have been "taken" or "ripped off." Many times, the person is expressing his or her desire to have paid less (if a buyer) or to be paid more (if a seller) for the good or service that was exchanged.

COSTS OF TRADES

As always, economists consider both benefits and costs. They want to determine what costs are involved in a trade and whether the costs may prevent a trade from taking place.

Unexploited Trades

Suppose Smith wants to buy a red 1965 Ford Mustang in excellent condition. The maximum price she is willing and able to pay for the Mustang is $30,000. Also suppose that Jones owns a red 1965 Ford Mustang in excellent condition. The minimum price he is willing and able to sell the Mustang for is $23,000. Obviously, Smith's maximum buying price ($30,000) is greater than Jones's minimum selling price ($23,000), so a potential trade or exchange exists.

Will the potential trade between Smith and Jones become an actual exchange? The answer to this question may depend on the transaction costs. **Transaction costs** are the costs associated with the time and effort needed to search out, negotiate, and consummate a trade. To illustrate, neither Smith nor Jones may know that the other exists. Suppose Smith lives in Roanoke, Virginia, and Jones lives 40 miles away in Blacksburg, Virginia. Each needs to find the other, which may take time and money. Perhaps Smith can put an ad in the local Blacksburg newspaper stating that she is searching for a 1965 Ford Mustang in mint condition. Alternatively, Jones can put an ad in the local Roanoke newspaper stating that he has a 1965 Ford Mustang to sell. The ad may or may not be seen by the relevant party and then acted upon. Our point is a simple one: Transaction costs sometimes keep potential trades from turning into actual trades.

Consider another example. Suppose Kurt hates to shop for clothes because shopping takes too much time. He has to get in his car, drive to the mall, park the car, walk into the mall, look in different stores, try on different clothes, pay for the items, get back in his car, and drive home. Suppose Kurt spends an average of 2 hours when he shops and he estimates that an hour of his time is worth $30. It follows, then, that Kurt incurs $60 worth of transaction costs when he buys clothes. Usually, he is not willing to incur the transaction costs necessary to buy a pair of trousers or a shirt.

Now, suppose we ask Kurt if he would be more willing to buy clothes if shopping were easier. Suppose, we say, the transaction costs associated with buying clothes could be lowered from $60 to less than $10. At lower transaction costs, Kurt says that he would be willing to shop more often.

How can transaction costs be lowered? Both people and computers can help lower the transaction costs of trades. For example, real estate brokers lower the transaction costs of selling and buying a house. Jim has a house to sell but doesn't know how to find a buyer. Karen wants to buy a house but doesn't know how to find a seller. Enter the real estate broker, who brings buyers and sellers together. In so doing, she lowers the transaction costs of buying and selling a house.

As another example, consider e-commerce on the Internet. Ursula can buy a book by getting in her car, driving to a bookstore, getting out of her car, walking into the bookstore, looking at the books on the shelves, taking a book to the cashier, paying for it, leaving the store, getting back in her car, and returning home. Or, Ursula can buy a book over the Internet. She can click on one of the online booksellers, search for the book by title, read a short description of the book, and then click on 1-Click Buying. Buying on the Internet has lower transaction costs than shopping at a store because online buying requires less time and effort. Before online book buying and selling, were there potential book purchases and sales that weren't being turned into actual book purchases and sales? There is some evidence that there were.

Turning Potential Trades into Actual Trades

Some people are always looking for ways to earn a profit. Can what you have learned about exchange and transaction costs help you earn money? It would seem that one way to earn a profit is to turn potential trades into actual trades by lowering transaction costs. Consider the following example. Buyer Smith is willing to pay a maximum price of $400 for good X; Seller Jones is willing to accept a minimum price of $200 for good X. Currently, the transaction costs of the exchange are $500, evenly split between Buyer Smith and Seller Jones.

Buyer Smith thinks, "Even if I pay the lowest possible price for good X, $200, I will still have to pay $250 in transaction costs, bringing my total to $450. The maximum price I am willing to pay for good X is $400, so I will not make this purchase."

Seller Jones thinks, "Even if I receive the highest possible price for good X, $400, I will still have to pay $250 in transaction costs, leaving me with only $150. The minimum price I am willing to accept for good X is $200, so I will not make this sale."

This potential trade will not become an actual trade, unless someone can lower the transaction costs. One role of an entrepreneur is to try *to turn potential trades into actual trades by lowering transaction costs.* Suppose Entrepreneur Brown can lower the transaction costs for Buyer Smith and Seller Jones to $10 each, asking $60 from each person for services rendered. Also, Entrepreneur Brown negotiates the price of good X at $300. Will the potential exchange become an actual exchange?

Buyer Smith thinks, "I am willing to pay a maximum of $400 for good X. If I purchase good X through Entrepreneur Brown, I will pay $300 to Seller Jones, $10 in transaction costs, and $60 to Brown. This is a total of $370, leaving me with a consumers' surplus of $30. It is worthwhile for me to purchase good X."

Seller Jones thinks, "I am willing to sell good X for a minimum of $200. If I sell good X through Entrepreneur Brown, I will receive $300 from Buyer Smith and will have to pay $10 in transaction costs and $60 to Brown. That will leave me with $230, or $30 worth of sellers' surplus. It is worthwhile for me to sell good *X*."

Thus, an entrepreneur can earn a profit by finding a way to lower transaction costs. As a result, a potential exchange turns into an actual exchange.

TRADES AND THIRD-PARTY EFFECTS

Consider two trades. In the first, Harriet pays 80 cents to Taylor for a pack of chewing gum. In this trade, both Harriet and Taylor are made better off (they wouldn't have traded otherwise) and no one is made worse off.

In the second trade, Bob pays $4 to George for a pack of cigarettes. Bob takes a cigarette, lights it, and smokes it. It happens that he is near Caroline when he smokes the cigarette, and she begins to cough because she is sensitive to cigarette smoke. In this trade, both Bob, who buys the cigarettes, and George, who sells the cigarettes, are made better off. But Caroline, who had nothing to do with the trade, is made worse off. In this exchange, a third party, Caroline, is adversely affected by the exchange between George and Bob.

These examples show that some trades affect only the parties involved in the exchange, and some trades have *third-party effects* (someone other than the parties involved in the exchange is affected). In the cigarette example, the third-party effect was negative; there was an adverse effect on Caroline, the third party. Sometimes economists call adverse third party effects *negative externalities*. A later chapter discusses this topic in detail.

Self-Test

1. The maximum price a buyer is willing and able to pay for a good is $100,000. The minimum price a seller is willing to accept for the good is $89,000. The price paid for the good is $92,000. What is the producers' surplus? What is the consumers' surplus?

2. What are transaction costs? Are the transaction costs of buying a house likely to be greater or less than those of buying a car? Explain your answer.

3. "I bought a computer and I feel ripped off," Cynthia says. Does it follow that in the ex post position Cynthia regrets having purchased the computer? Explain your answer.

4. Give an example of a trade without third-party effects. Next, give an example of a trade with third-party effects.

PRODUCTION, TRADE, AND SPECIALIZATION

The first section of this chapter discusses production; the second section discusses trade. From these two sections, you might conclude that production and trade are unrelated activities. However, they are not: Before you can trade, you need to produce something. This section ties production and trade together and also shows how the benefits one receives from trade can be affected by how one produces.

PRODUCING AND TRADING

To show how a change in production can benefit traders, we eliminate anything and everything extraneous to the process. Thus, we eliminate money and consider a barter, or moneyless, economy.

In this economy, there are two individuals, Elizabeth and Brian. They live near each other and each engages in two activities: baking bread and growing apples. Let's suppose that within a certain period of time, Elizabeth can produce 20 loaves of bread and no apples, or 10 loaves of bread and 10 apples, or no bread and 20 apples. In other words, three points on Elizabeth's production pos-

Under socialism, there is more government control over who gets what goods. For example, within a socialist economic system there may be a redistribution of funds from Smith to Jones. Or perhaps goods are given to Jones even though he is unable to pay the prices of these goods.

THINKING LIKE AN ECONOMIST   *The layperson looks at countries and sees differences. For example, people speak French in France and English in the United States; the crime rate is higher in the United States than Belgium; and so on. The economist knows that there are some things that are the same for all countries. The United States has to decide what goods to produce, and China has to decide what goods to produce. The United States has to decide how goods will be produced, and Brazil has to decide how goods will be produced. The United States has to deal with scarcity and its effects, and so do South Korea, Pakistan, India, and Canada.*

TRADE AND PRICES

Capitalism and socialism have different views of trade and prices. We outline these differences in the following paragraphs.

Trade

Consider an ordinary, everyday exchange of $100 for some clothes. Under capitalism, it is generally assumed that both the buyer and seller of the clothes benefit from the trade or else they would not have entered into it. Under socialism, the view often expressed is that one person in a trade is being made better off at the expense of the other person. In this example, perhaps the clothes seller took advantage of the buyer by charging too much money for the clothes.

Prices

When we buy something in a market—whether it is a car, a house, or a loaf of bread—we pay a price. Prices are a common market phenomenon. Under capitalism, price (1) rations goods and services, (2) conveys information, and (3) serves as an incentive to respond to information.

As discussed in Chapter 1, price is a rationing device. Those people who are willing and able to pay the price of a good, obtain the good; those persons who are either unwilling or unable to pay, do not obtain the good. In a world of scarcity, where people's wants outstrip the resources available to satisfy those wants, some type of rationing device is necessary. It may be price, first-come-first-served, brute force, or something else. For capitalist thinkers, there needs to be some way of determining who gets what of the available resources, goods, and services. Price serves this purpose.

Now consider an example to see how price can convey information and serve as an incentive to respond to information. Suppose Tom buys a dozen oranges each week for 40 cents an orange. One day, a devastating freeze hits the Florida orange groves and destroys half the orange crop. As a result, there are fewer oranges in the world and price rises to 60 cents an orange. Tom notices the higher price of oranges and wonders what caused the price to rise. He does not know about the freeze, and even if he did, he might not connect the freeze with a reduced supply of oranges and higher orange prices. Nevertheless, Tom responds to the higher price of oranges by reducing his weekly purchase from 12 oranges to 8 oranges.

Let's consider the role price has played in this example. First, through an increase in price, the "information" of the freeze was conveyed to buyers. Specifically, price has transmitted information on the relative scarcity of a good. The higher price of oranges is saying "There has been a cold spell in Florida resulting in fewer oranges. The gap between people's wants for oranges and the amount of oranges available to satisfy those wants has widened."

Second, by rising, price has provided Tom with an incentive to reduce the quantity of oranges he consumes. Tom responds to the information of the increased relative scarcity of oranges, even without knowing about Florida weather conditions.

Under socialism, price is viewed as being set by greedy businesses with vast economic power. Perhaps because of this, socialists usually stand ready to "control" price. For example, under socialism it is not uncommon to pass a law making it illegal to charge more than a certain price for, say, gasoline or rental homes. It is also not uncommon to pass a law that makes it illegal to pay less than a certain dollar wage to a worker.

By passing laws that make it illegal to charge more than a certain price for certain goods and services, socialists seek to reduce some of the economic power that they believe sellers have over consumers. By passing laws that make it illegal to pay less than a certain wage to workers, socialists seek to reduce some of the economic power that they believe the owners of businesses have over workers.

Self-Test

1. What are the three economic questions that deal with production that every society must answer?

2. How is trade viewed in a capitalist economic system?

3. What does an economic system have to do with where on its PPF the economy operates?

A Reader Asks...

How Will Economics Help Me If I Am a History Major?

I'm a history major taking my first course in economics. But quite frankly, I don't see how economics will be of much use in my study of history. Any thoughts on the subject?

Economics often plays a major role in historical events. For example, the feature "What Do Blue Jeans and Rock 'n' Roll Have to Do With the Fall of the Berlin Wall?" discusses the collapse of the Soviet Union—certainly a historical event. But was that historical event based in part on economics? Did the low economic growth of the Soviet Union contribute to its collapse? Did the ratio of civilian goods to military goods play a role in the collapse?

There are many other places where understanding economics may help you understand a historical event or period. If, as a historian, you study the Great Depression, you will need to know something about the stock market, tariffs, and more. If you study the California Gold Rush, you will need to know about supply, demand, and prices. If you study the history of prisoner-of-war camps, you will need to know about how and why people trade

and about money. If you study the Boston Tea Party, you will need to know about government grants of monopoly and about taxes.

Economics can also be useful in another way. Suppose you learn in your economics course what can and cannot cause inflation. We'll say you learn that X can cause inflation and that Y cannot. Then one day you read an article in which a historian says that Y caused the high inflation in a certain country and that the high inflation led to a public outcry, which was then met with stiff government reprisals. Without an understanding of economics, you might be willing to accept what the historian has written. But with your understanding of economics, you know that events could not have happened as the historian reports because Y, which the historian claims caused the high inflation, could not have caused the high inflation.

In conclusion, a good understanding of economics will not only help you understand key historical events but also help you discern inaccuracies in recorded history.

An Economy's Production Possibilities Frontier

- An economy's production possibilities frontier (PPF) represents the possible combinations of two goods that the economy can produce in a certain period of time, under the conditions of a given state of technology and fully employed resources.

Increasing and Constant Opportunity Costs

- A straight-line PPF represents constant opportunity costs: increased production of one good comes at constant opportunity costs.
- A bowed-outward (concave-downward) PPF represents the law of increasing opportunity costs: increased production of one good comes at increased opportunity costs.

Efficiency and Inefficiency

- All points on the PPF are efficient points; all points below the PPF are inefficient.
- Efficiency implies that gains are impossible in one area without losses in another. Inefficiency implies that gains are possible in one area without losses in another.
- When the economy is efficient, it is employing all its resources. When the economy is inefficient, some resources are unemployed.

Economic Growth and the PPF

- Economic growth is illustrated by a shift outward in the PPF. Two major factors that affect economic growth are an increase in the quantity of resources and an advance in technology.

Trade or Exchange

- People trade in order to make themselves better off. Exchange is a utility-increasing activity.
- The three time periods relevant to the trading process are (1) the ex ante period, which is the time before the trade is made; (2) the point of trade; and (3) the ex post period, which is the time after the trade has been made.
- There is a difference between trade and the terms of trade. Trade refers to the act of giving up one thing for something else. For example, a person may trade money for a car. The terms of trade refer to *how much* of one thing is traded for *how much* of something else. For example, how much money ($25,000? $30,000?) is traded for one car.

Consumers' Surplus and Producers' Surplus

- Consumers' surplus is the difference between the maximum price buyers are willing and able to pay for a good and the price actually paid for the good.

- Producers' surplus is the difference between the price sellers receive for a good and the minimum price for which they would have sold the good.
- The more consumers' surplus that buyers receive, the better off they are. The more producers' surplus that sellers receive, the better off they are.

Transaction Costs

- Transaction costs are the costs associated with the time and effort needed to search out, negotiate, and consummate a trade. Some potential exchanges are not realized because of high transaction costs. Lowering transaction costs can turn a potential exchange into an actual exchange.
- One role of an entrepreneur is to try to lower transaction costs.

Comparative Advantage and Specialization

- Individuals can make themselves better off by specializing in the production of the good in which they have a comparative advantage and then trading some of that good for other goods. A person has a comparative advantage in the production of a good if he or she can produce the good at a lower opportunity cost than another person can.

Economic Systems

- An economic system refers to the way in which a society decides to answer key economic questions—in particular those questions that relate to production and trade.
- There are two major economic systems: the capitalist (or market) economic system and the socialist economic system.
- One of the key differences between capitalism and socialism is how decisions are made with respect to where on the PPF the economy will operate. Under capitalism, the market (buyers and sellers) largely determines at which point on the PPF the economy will operate. Under socialism, government plays a large role in determining at which point on the PPF the economy will operate.
- Three economic questions that relate to production that every society must answer are: (1) What goods will be produced? (2) How will the goods be produced? (3) For whom will the goods be produced?
- Under capitalism, price (1) rations goods and services, (2) conveys information, and (3) serves as an incentive to respond to information. Under socialism, price is viewed as being set by greedy businesses with vast economic power.

Production Possibilities Frontier (PPF)
Tradeoff
Law of Increasing Opportunity Costs
Efficiency

Inefficiency
Technology
Trade (Exchange)
Ex Ante
Ex Post
Consumers' Surplus (CS)

Producers' (Sellers') Surplus (PS)
Terms of Trade
Transaction Costs
Comparative Advantage
Economic System
Mixed Capitalism

Economic facts, actions, and changes create ripples that move away from their point of origin. Eventually, these ripples can intersect your life and have an effect on you. Consider the following example.

A country "decides" where on its PPF to locate. If a country decides to produce relatively many consumer goods and relatively few other types of goods (say, military goods), its citizens will be affected in two ways. First, a majority of the population will probably work in the sector of the economy that produces consumer goods. Second, people will likely have a wide variety of consumer goods and services from which to choose. If

a country decides to produce more military goods than consumer goods, the majority of the population will probably work in the military goods sector of the economy and its people will likely have little choice of consumer goods and services. Thus, there is a connection between where your country locates on its PPF and your desires as a consumer and worker—an economic connection to you.

Based on the material in this chapter, identify other ways in which economic facts, actions, and changes create ripples that eventually affect you.

1. Describe how each of the following would affect the U.S. production possibilities frontier: (a) an increase in the number of illegal aliens entering the country; (b) a war; (c) the discovery of a new oil field; (d) a decrease in the unemployment rate; (e) a law that requires individuals to enter lines of work for which they are not suited.

2. Explain how the following can be represented in a PPF framework: the finiteness of resources implicit in the scarcity condition; choice; and opportunity cost.

3. What condition must hold for the production possibilities frontier to be bowed outward (concave downward)? to be a straight line?

4. Give an example to illustrate each of the following: (a) constant opportunity costs; (b) increasing opportunity costs.

5. Why are most production possibilities frontiers for goods bowed outward, or concave downward?

6. Within a PPF framework, explain each of the following: (a) a disagreement between a person who favors more domestic welfare spending and one who favors more national defense spending; (b) an increase in the population; (c) a technological change that makes resources less specialized.

7. Some people have said that during the Cold War the Central Intelligence Agency (CIA) regularly estimated (a) the total quantity of output produced in the Soviet Union and (b) the total quantity of civilian goods produced in the Soviet Union. Of what interest would these data, or the information that might be deduced from them, be to the CIA? (Hint: Think in terms of the PPF.)

8. Suppose a nation's PPF shifts inward as its population grows. What happens, on average, to the material standard of living of the people? Explain your answer.

9. "A nation may be able to live beyond its means, but the world cannot." Do you agree or disagree? Explain your answer.

10. Use the PPF framework to explain something in your everyday life that was not mentioned in the chapter.

11. Describe the three time periods relevant to the trading process.

12. Are all exchanges or trades beneficial to both parties in the ex post position? Explain your answer.

13. If Donovan agrees to trade $50 for a painting, what can we say about the utility he gets from the $50 compared with the utility he expects to get from the painting?

14. A person who benefits from a trade can be disgruntled over the terms of trade. Do you agree or disagree? Explain your answer.

15. Explain how an economist might use the concepts of consumers' surplus and producers' surplus.

16. Buyers would rather pay lower prices for the goods they buy and sellers would rather receive higher prices for the goods they sell. Why?

17. Give an example of a negative third-party effect (negative externality).

18. A capitalist would be much less likely to support controls on prices and wages than would a socialist. Why?

19. Some people argue that capitalism and socialism are usually evaluated only on economic grounds, where capitalism has a clear advantage. But in order to evaluate the two economic systems evenhandedly, other factors should be considered as well—justice, fairness, the happiness of people living under both systems, the crime rate, the standard of living of those at the bottom of the economic ladder, and much more. Do you think this is the proper way to proceed? Why or why not?

20. The *convergence hypothesis,* first proposed by a Soviet economist, suggests that over time the capitalist economies will become increasingly socialistic and the socialist economies will become increasingly capitalistic. Do you believe the convergence hypothesis has merit? What real-world evidence can you cite to prove or disprove the hypothesis?

Working with Numbers and Graphs

1. Xavier is willing and able to pay up to $40 for a good that he buys for $22. Keri is willing and able to sell the good to Xavier for no less than $21. What does consumers' surplus equal? What does producers' (sellers') surplus equal?

2. Tina can produce any of the following combinations of goods X and Y: (a) $100X$ and $0Y$, (b) $50X$ and $25Y$, and (c) $0X$ and $50Y$. David can produce any of the following combinations of goods X and Y: (a) $50X$ and $0Y$, (b) $25X$ and $40Y$, and (c) $0X$ and $80Y$. Who has a comparative advantage in the production of good X? of good Y? Explain your answer.

3. Using the data in Problem 2, prove that both Tina and David can be made better off through specialization and trade.

4. Exhibit 6 represents an advance in technology that made it possible to produce more of both military and civilian goods. Represent an advance in technology that makes it possible to produce more of only civilian goods. Does this indirectly make it possible to produce more military goods? Explain your answer.

5. In the following figure, which graph depicts a technological breakthrough in the production of good X only?

6. In the preceding figure, which graph depicts a change in the PPF that is a likely consequence of war?

7. If PPF_2 in the following graph is the relevant production possibilities frontier, then which points are unattainable? Explain your answer.

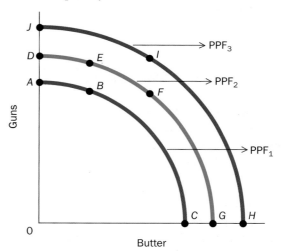

8. If PPF_1 in the figure above is the relevant production possibilities frontier, then which point(s) represent efficiency? Explain your answer.

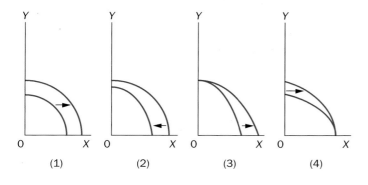

(1) (2) (3) (4)

1. Go to *http://stats.bls.gov*. Select "Economy at a Glance." What is the current unemployment rate?

2. Go to *http://www.stls.frb.org/fred*. FRED is the economic database of the Federal Reserve. Under Data Categories, click on "Business/Fiscal" and then on "Capacity Utilization: Manufacturing—Percent of Capacity—1948.1." This number represents the percentage of our total manufacturing capacity being used. What is that percentage today?

3. Click "Back" and select "Total Industrial Production Index." What is the value for 1940.01 (January 1940)? What is the value for today? If this value represents production in the economy, where is the PPF for 1940 in relation to the PPF today?

Log on to the Arnold Xtra! Web site now (*http://arnoldxtra.swcollege.com*) for additional learning resources such as practice quizzes, help with graphing, video clips, and current event applications.

ch.3

SUPPLY AND DEMAND: THEORY

Thomas Carlyle, the historian and philosopher, said: "It is easy to train economists. Just teach a parrot to say Supply and Demand." In a way, Carlyle was right—economists do mention "supply and demand" often. But they do it for a reason. Supply and demand are powerful forces, forces that together explain much of what goes on in the world. Economists use supply and demand to explain why there are shortages, why prices rise and fall, and even why an auctioneer calls out certain prices.

This chapter is about markets. A market exists anytime people come together to trade. Every market has two sides—a buying (demand) side and a selling (supply) side. We discuss both sides of a market in this chapter. We look first at demand—define what it is, identify the law of demand, and discuss those factors that can change demand. Then we discuss supply in a similar way. Finally, we put supply and demand together and discuss how the prices and quantities of goods in a market are determined.

DEMAND

The word **demand** has a precise meaning in economics. It refers to (1) the willingness and ability of buyers to purchase different quantities of a good (2) at different prices (3) during a specific time period (per day, week, and so on).[1] For example, we can express part of John's demand for magazines by saying that he is willing and able to buy 10 magazines a month at $4 per magazine and that he is willing and able to buy 15 magazines a month at $3 per magazine.

Remember this important point about demand: Unless *both* willingness and ability to buy are present, a person is not a buyer and *there is no demand*. For example, Josie may be willing to buy a computer but be unable to pay the price; Tanya may be able to buy but be unwilling. Neither Josie nor Tanya demands a computer.

Q & A   **Q:** If a person is willing and able to buy a particular car at $40,000, will she actually make this purchase?

A: Not necessarily. Willingness and ability to buy refer to the buyer, but both a buyer and a seller are required for a trade to be made. A person may be willing and able to buy a particular car for $40,000, but that car may not currently exist, or it may exist but the seller may not be willing to sell it for $40,000.

THE LAW OF DEMAND

Will people buy more units of a good at lower prices than at higher prices? For example, will people buy more personal computers at $1,000 per computer than at $4,000 per computer? If your answer is yes, you instinctively understand the law of demand. The **law of demand** states that as the price of a good rises, the quantity demanded of the good falls, and as the price of a good falls, the quantity demanded of the good rises, *ceteris paribus*. Simply put, the law of demand states that the price of a good and the quantity demanded of the good are inversely related, *ceteris paribus*:

$$P\uparrow Q_d\downarrow$$
$$P\downarrow Q_d\uparrow \text{ ceteris paribus}$$

where P = price and Q_d = quantity demanded.

Quantity demanded is the *number of units* of a good that individuals are willing and able to buy at a particular price during some time period. For example, suppose individuals are willing and able to buy 100 TV dinners per week at the price of $4 per unit. Therefore, 100 units is the quantity demanded of TV dinners at $4.

Law of Demand
As the price of a good rises, the quantity demanded of the good falls, and as the price of a good falls, the quantity demanded of the good rises, *ceteris paribus*.

THINKING LIKE AN ECONOMIST   *When Bill says, "The more income a person has, the more expensive cars (Porsches, Corvettes) he will buy," he is not thinking like an economist. An economist knows that the ability to buy something does not necessarily imply the willingness to buy it. After all, Bill Gates, the billionaire cofounder of Microsoft, Inc., has the ability to buy many things that he chooses not to buy.*

ABSOLUTE PRICE AND RELATIVE PRICE

In economics, there are absolute (or money) prices and relative prices. The **absolute price** of a good is the price of the good in money terms. For example, the absolute price of a car may be $30,000. The **relative price** of a good is the

Absolute (Money) Price
The price of a good in money terms.

Relative Price
The price of a good in terms of another good.

---

1. Demand takes into account *services* as well as goods. Goods are tangible and include such things as shirts, books, and television sets. Services are intangible and include such things as dental care, medical care, and an economics lecture. To simplify the discussion, we refer only to *goods*.

price of the good *in terms of another good.* For example, suppose the absolute price of a car is $30,000 and the absolute price of a computer is $2,000. The relative price of a car—that is, the price of a car in terms of computers—is 15 computers. A person gives up the opportunity to buy 15 computers when he or she buys a car.

For this example, the relative price of a car is computed as follows:

$$\text{Relative price of a car (in terms of computers)} = \frac{\text{Absolute price of a car}}{\text{Absolute price of a computer}}$$
$$= \frac{\$30,000}{\$2,000}$$
$$= 15$$

Thus, the relative price of a car in this example is 15 computers.

Now let's compute the relative price of a computer, that is, the price of a computer in terms of a car:

$$\text{Relative price of a computer (in terms of cars)} = \frac{\text{Absolute price of a computer}}{\text{Absolute price of a car}}$$
$$= \frac{\$2,000}{\$30,000}$$
$$= 1/15$$

Thus, the relative price of a computer in this example is $\frac{1}{15}$ of a car. A person gives up the opportunity to buy $\frac{1}{15}$ of a car when he or she buys a computer.

Now consider this question: What happens to the relative price of a good if its absolute price rises and nothing else changes? For example, if the absolute price of a car rises from $30,000 to $40,000 what happens to the relative price of a car? Obviously, it rises from 15 computers to 20 computers. In short, if the absolute price of a good rises and nothing else changes, then the relative price of the good rises too.

Knowing the difference between absolute price and relative price can help you understand some important economic concepts. In the next section, relative price is used in the explanation of why price and quantity demanded are inversely related.

WHY QUANTITY DEMANDED GOES DOWN AS PRICE GOES UP

The law of demand states that price and quantity demanded are inversely related, but it does not say why they are inversely related. We identify two reasons. The first reason is that *people substitute lower-priced goods for higher-priced goods.*

Often many goods serve the same purpose. Many different goods will satisfy hunger, and many different drinks will satisfy thirst. For example, both orange juice and grapefruit juice will satisfy thirst. Suppose that on Monday, the price of orange juice equals the price of grapefruit juice. Then on Tuesday, the price of orange juice rises. As a result, some people will choose to buy less of the relatively higher-priced orange juice and more of the relatively lower-priced grapefruit juice. In other words, a rise in the price of orange juice will lead to a decrease in the quantity demanded of orange juice.

The second reason for the inverse relationship between price and quantity demanded has to do with the **law of diminishing marginal utility,** which states that for a given time period, the marginal (additional) utility or satisfaction gained by consuming equal successive units of a good will decline as the amount consumed increases. For example, you may receive more utility or satisfaction from eating your first hamburger at lunch than from eating your second

Law of Diminishing Marginal Utility
For a given time period, the marginal (additional) utility or satisfaction gained by consuming equal successive units of a good will decline as the amount consumed increases.

and, if you continue on, more utility from your second hamburger than from your third.

What does this have to do with the law of demand? Economists state that the more utility you receive from a unit of a good, the higher price you are willing to pay for it; the less utility you receive from a unit of a good, the lower price you are willing to pay for it. According to the law of diminishing marginal utility, individuals obtain less utility from additional units of a good. It follows that they will only buy larger quantities of a good at lower prices. And this is the law of demand.

FOUR WAYS TO REPRESENT THE LAW OF DEMAND: WORDS, SYMBOLS, NUMBERS, CURVE

The law of demand can be expressed in four ways:

1. In words: "As price rises, quantity demanded falls . . ."
2. In symbols: $P\uparrow Q_d\downarrow$. . .
3. In terms of a demand schedule
4. In terms of a demand curve

A **demand schedule** is the numerical representation of the law of demand. A demand schedule for good X is illustrated in Exhibit 1a.

In Exhibit 1b, the four price-quantity combinations in part (a) are plotted and the points connected, giving us a (downward-sloping) demand curve. A (downward-sloping) **demand curve** is the graphical representation of the inverse relationship between price and quantity demanded specified by the law of demand. In short, the demand curve is a picture of the law of demand.

Demand Schedule
The numerical tabulation of the quantity demanded of a good at different prices.

(Downward-sloping) Demand Curve
The graphical representation of the law of demand.

INDIVIDUAL DEMAND CURVE AND MARKET DEMAND CURVE

An individual demand curve represents the price-quantity combinations of a particular good for a *single buyer*. For example, a demand curve could show Jones's demand for CDs. A market demand curve represents the price-quantity combinations of a particular good for *all buyers*. In this case, the demand curve would show all buyers' demand for CDs.

Exhibit 2 shows how a market demand curve can be derived by "adding" individual demand curves. The demand schedules for Jones, Smith, and other buyers are shown in part (a). The market demand schedule is obtained by adding the quantities demanded at each price. For example, at $12, the quantities demanded are 4 units for Jones, 5 units for Smith, and 100 units for other buyers. Thus, a total of 109 units are demanded at $12. In (b) the data points for the demand schedules are plotted and "added" to produce a market demand

Demand Schedule for Good X

Price (dollars)	Quantity Demanded	Point in Part (b)
4	10	A
3	20	B
2	30	C
1	40	D

(a)

(b)

exhibit 1

Demand Schedule and Demand Curve

Part (a) shows a demand schedule for good X. Part (b) shows a demand curve, obtained by plotting the different price-quantity combinations in part (a) and connecting the points. On a demand curve, the price (in dollars) represents price per unit of the good. The quantity demanded, on the horizontal axis, is always relevant for a specific time period (a week, a month, and so on).

	Quantity Demanded			
Price	Jones	Smith	Other Buyers	All Buyers
$15	1	2	20	23
14	2	3	45	50
13	3	4	70	77
12	4 +	5 +	100 =	109
11	5 +	6 +	130 =	141
10	6	7	160	173

(a)

(b)

Deriving a Market Demand Schedule and a Market Demand Curve

Part (a) shows four demand schedules combined into one table. The market demand schedule is derived by adding the quantities demanded at each price. In (b), the data points from the demand schedules are plotted to show how a market demand curve is derived. Only two points on the market demand curve are noted.

curve. The market demand curve could also be drawn directly from the market demand schedule.

CHANGES IN DEMAND MEAN SHIFTS IN DEMAND CURVES

Suppose that currently a specific demand exists for oranges, computers, houses, and cars. Will the demand for each of these goods be the same next year as it is today? If your answer is "Maybe not," then you instinctively understand that the demand for any good can change. Saying the demand for a good can change is the same as saying the demand for a good can increase or decrease.

What does it mean if the demand for a good *increases*? It means that buyers are willing and able to buy *more* of the good at all prices. For example, suppose that in January individuals are willing and able to buy 600 pairs of blue jeans at $60 each and that in February they are willing to buy 900 pairs of blue jeans at $60 each. An increase in demand shifts the entire demand curve to the right, as shown in Exhibit 3a.

The demand for a good *decreases* if people are willing and able to buy *less* of the good at all prices. For example, suppose that in January individuals are willing and able to buy 600 pairs of blue jeans at $60 each and that in February they are willing to buy 300 pairs of blue jeans at $60 each. A decrease in demand shifts the entire demand curve to the left, as shown in Exhibit 3b.

WHAT FACTORS CAUSE THE DEMAND CURVE TO SHIFT?

We know the demand for any good can change. But *why* would the demand change? For example, if the demand for blue jeans is higher in February than in January, what happened to cause the demand for blue jeans to rise? What caused

exhibit 3

Shifts in the Demand Curve
(a) The demand curve shifts rightward from D_1 to D_2. This represents an increase in demand for blue jeans: At each price the quantity demanded is greater than before. For example, the quantity demanded at $60 increases from 600 units to 900 units. (b) The demand curve shifts leftward from D_1 to D_2. This represents a decrease in demand for blue jeans: At each price the quantity demanded is less. For example, the quantity demanded at $60 declines from 600 units to 300 units.

people to want to buy more blue jeans at each and every price? The factors that can change demand include (1) income, (2) preferences, (3) prices of related goods, (4) number of buyers, and (5) expectations of future price.

Income

As a person's income changes (increases or decreases), his or her demand for a particular good may rise, fall, or remain constant.

For example, suppose that Jack's income rises. As a consequence, his demand for CDs rises. For Jack, CDs are a *normal good*. A **normal good** is one in which as income rises, demand for the good rises; and as income falls, demand for the good falls.

> **Normal Good**
> A good the demand for which rises (falls) as income rises (falls).

$$Income\uparrow + Demand\uparrow = Normal\ good$$
$$Income\downarrow + Demand\downarrow = Normal\ good$$

Now suppose Marie's income rises. As a consequence, her demand for canned baked beans falls. For Marie, canned banked beans are an *inferior good*. An **inferior good** is one in which as income rises, demand for the good falls, and as income falls, demand for the good rises.

> **Inferior Good**
> A good the demand for which falls (rises) as income rises (falls).

$$Income\uparrow + Demand\downarrow = Inferior\ good$$
$$Income\downarrow + Demand\uparrow = Inferior\ good$$

Finally, suppose George's income rises, and his demand for toothpaste neither rises nor falls. For George, toothpaste is neither a normal good nor an inferior good. Instead, it is a *neutral good*. A **neutral good** is one in which as income rises or falls, the demand for the good does not change.

> **Neutral Good**
> A good the demand for which does not change as income rises or falls.

Preferences

People's preferences affect the amount of a good they are willing to buy at a particular price. A change in preferences in favor of a good shifts the demand curve rightward. A change in preferences away from the good shifts the demand curve leftward. For example, if people begin to favor Tom Clancy novels to a greater degree than previously, the demand for Clancy novels increases and the demand curve shifts rightward.

Why Does Mickey Mouse Charge Such Goofy Prices?

The Walt Disney Company operates two major theme parks in the United States, Disneyland in California and Disney World in Florida. Every year millions of people visit each site. The ticket price for visiting Disneyland or Disney World differs depending on how many days a person visits the theme park. For example, in the past, Disneyland sold one-, two-, and three-day passports (tickets). On the day we checked, the price of a one-day passport was $38, the price of a two-day passport was $68, and the price of a three-day passport was $95.

How are the prices for one-, two-, and three-day passports related? If we take the price of a one-day passport ($38) and double it, we get $76. But Disneyland doesn't charge visitors $76 for visiting two days; it charges $68. Why does Disneyland charge less than double the price of a one-day passport for a two-day passport? Similarly, triple the price of a one-day passport is $114. But Disneyland doesn't charge $114 for a three-day passport; it charges $95. Why does Disneyland charge less than triple the price of a one-day passport for a three-day passport?

Disneyland is effectively telling a visitor that if she wants to visit the theme park for one day, she has to pay $38. But if she wants to visit the theme park for two days, the second day will only cost her $30 more, not $38 more. And if she wants to visit the theme park for three days, the third day will only cost her $27 more, not $38 more. In short, for a three-day passport, Disneyland charges $38 for the first day, $30 for the second day, and $27 for the third day, for a grand total of $95.

Why does Disneyland charge less for the second day than the first day? Why does it charge less for the third day than the second day?

An economic concept, the *law of diminishing marginal utility,* is the reason behind Disneyland's pricing scheme. The law of diminishing marginal utility states that as a person consumes additional units of a good, eventually the utility from each additional unit of the good decreases. Assuming the law of diminishing marginal utility holds for Disneyland, individuals will get more utility from the first day at Disneyland than the second day and more utility from the second day than the third day. The less utility or satisfaction a person gets from something, the lower the dollar amount he is willing to pay for it. Thus, a person would not be willing to pay as much for the second day at Disneyland as the first, and he would not be willing to pay as much for the third day as the second. Disneyland knows this and therefore prices its one-, two-, and three-day passports accordingly.

Substitutes
Two goods that satisfy similar needs or desires. If two goods are substitutes, the demand for one rises as the price of the other rises (or the demand for one falls as the price of the other falls).

Complements
Two goods that are used jointly in consumption. If two goods are complements, the demand for one rises as the price of the other falls (or the demand for one falls as the price of the other rises).

Prices of Related Goods

There are two types of related goods: substitutes and complements. Two goods are **substitutes** if they satisfy similar needs or desires. For many people Coca-Cola and Pepsi-Cola are substitutes. If two goods are substitutes, as the price of one rises (falls), the demand for the other rises (falls). For instance, higher Coca-Cola prices will increase the demand for Pepsi-Cola as people substitute Pepsi for the higher-priced Coke (Exhibit 4a). Other examples of substitutes are coffee and tea, corn chips and potato chips, two brands of margarine, and foreign and domestic cars.

If $P_X\uparrow$ and $D_Y\uparrow$ then X and Y are substitutes.
If $P_X\downarrow$ and $D_Y\downarrow$ then X and Y are substitutes.

Two goods are **complements** if they are consumed jointly. For example, tennis rackets and tennis balls are used together to play tennis. If two goods are complements, as the price of one rises (falls), the demand for the other falls (rises).

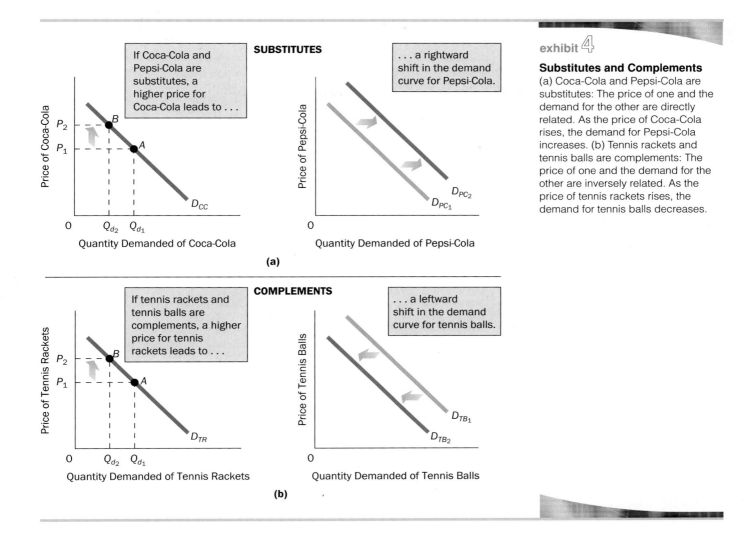

exhibit 4

Substitutes and Complements
(a) Coca-Cola and Pepsi-Cola are substitutes: The price of one and the demand for the other are directly related. As the price of Coca-Cola rises, the demand for Pepsi-Cola increases. (b) Tennis rackets and tennis balls are complements: The price of one and the demand for the other are inversely related. As the price of tennis rackets rises, the demand for tennis balls decreases.

For example, higher tennis racket prices will decrease the demand for tennis balls, as Exhibit 4b shows. Other examples of complements are cars and tires, light bulbs and lamps, and golf clubs and golf balls.

If $P_A\uparrow$ and $D_B\downarrow$ then A and B are complements.
If $P_A\downarrow$ and $D_B\uparrow$ then A and B are complements.

Number of Buyers
The demand for a good in a particular market area is related to the number of buyers in the area: More buyers, higher demand; fewer buyers, lower demand. The number of buyers may increase owing to a higher birthrate, increased immigration, the migration of people from one region of the country to another, and so on. The number of buyers may decrease owing to a higher death rate, war, the migration of people from one region of the country to another, and so on.

Expectations of Future Price
Buyers who expect the price of a good to be higher next month may buy the good now—thus increasing the current demand for the good. Buyers who expect the price of a good to be lower next month may wait until next month to buy the good—thus decreasing the current demand for the good.

For example, suppose that you are planning to buy a house. One day you hear that house prices are expected to go down in a few months. Consequently, you decide to hold off your purchase of a house for a few months. Alternatively, if you hear that prices are expected to rise in a few months, you might go ahead and purchase a house now.

A CHANGE IN DEMAND VERSUS A CHANGE IN QUANTITY DEMANDED

A *change (increase or decrease) in demand* refers to a *shift* in the demand curve, as illustrated in Exhibit 5a.

Change in demand = Shift in demand curve

For example, saying that the demand for apples has increased is the same as saying that the demand curve for apples has shifted rightward. The factors that can change demand (shift the demand curve) include income, preferences, prices of related goods, number of buyers, and expectations of future price.

A *change in quantity demanded* refers to a *movement* along a demand curve, as shown in Exhibit 5b.

Change in quantity demanded = A movement from one point to another point
on the same demand curve

Own Price
The price of a good. For example, if the price of oranges is $1, this is (its) own price.

The *only* factor that can *directly* cause a change in the quantity demanded of a good is a change in the price of the good—that is, its **own price.** For example, a change in the price of computers brings about a change in the quantity demanded of computers. A change in the price of lamps brings about a change in the quantity demanded of lamps.

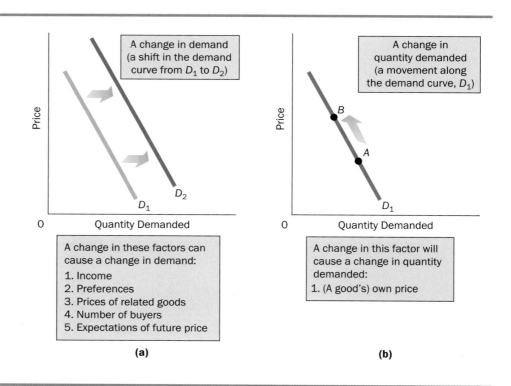

exhibit 5

A Change in Demand versus a Change in Quantity Demanded
(a) A change in demand refers to a shift in the demand curve. A change in demand can be brought about by a number of factors (see the exhibit and text). (b) A change in quantity demanded refers to a movement along a given demand curve. A change in quantity demanded is brought about only by a change in (a good's) own price.

A change in demand
(a shift in the demand
curve from D_1 to D_2)

A change in
quantity demanded
(a movement along
the demand curve, D_1)

Price

Price

D_2

D_1

B

A

D_1

0   Quantity Demanded

0   Quantity Demanded

A change in these factors can cause a change in demand:
1. Income
2. Preferences
3. Prices of related goods
4. Number of buyers
5. Expectations of future price

A change in this factor will cause a change in quantity demanded:
1. (A good's) own price

(a)

(b)

Does the Law of Demand Explain Obesity?

An accepted definition of obesity is that a person is considered obese if his weight in pounds exceeds 4.25 percent of the square of his height in inches. For example, suppose a person weighs 200 pounds and is 5 feet tall. The person's height in inches is 60; the square of 60 is 3,600. Because 200 (weight in pounds) is 5.5 percent of 3,600 (square of height in inches), the person is obese.

Steven Landsburg, an economist and a contributing columnist to the magazine *Slate*, reports that 21.1 percent of the people in Georgia are obese according to this definition. Ten years earlier, only 9.5 percent of Georgians were obese (using the same definition of obesity). Landsburg asks the question: Why are we getting so fat?[2]

The rise of obesity in Georgia is mirrored across the country, says Landsburg. He reports that obesity has been rising in every age group, in every race, in both males and females, and in every state. In 1991, a little over 12 percent of the people in the country were obese; in 1999, almost 20 percent were.

How does Landsburg explain the rise in obesity? He partly explains it using the law of demand. The law of demand states that as the price of something falls, the quantity demanded of it rises, *ceteris paribus*. So, if the quantity demanded of obesity has risen in recent years, has the price of obesity fallen to bring this about? Landsburg argues that in the 1990s, drugs were developed that reduce cholesterol and increase life expectancy. In other words, these drugs decrease two of the many undesirable consequences of obesity—high cholesterol and shorter life expectancy. Thus, these drugs have reduced the price of obesity. As a result, the quantity demanded of obesity has risen.

It is important to distinguish between a change in demand (shift in the demand curve) and a change in quantity demanded (movement along a demand curve), as the next section illustrates.

MEALS AT RESTAURANTS AND THE LAW OF DEMAND

Your friend says, "I've noticed that the price of dining out at restaurants has gone up. I've also noticed that more people are eating at restaurants. But the law of demand predicts the opposite. It states that if the price of a good rises, less of that good will be consumed. Obviously, the law of demand must be wrong."

Suppose we accept as truth that the price of dining out at restaurants has gone up and that more people are eating at restaurants. Does it follow that the law of demand does not hold? Not at all. The inverse relationship between price and quantity demanded holds, *ceteris paribus*. What your friend has observed is a case where all other things were not constant.

To illustrate, consider Exhibit 6a. Your friend may initially have observed two points, *A* and *B,* where *B* represents a higher price and a greater consumption of meals than *A*. From this he concluded that people buy more restaurant meals at higher prices than at lower prices. Your friend sees the demand curve as sloping upward, as in Exhibit 6b.

However, the 14 million meals consumed at point *B are not the result of a higher price but of a higher demand curve,* as in Exhibit 6c. The consumption of meals has increased from 10 million to 14 million because the demand curve has shifted rightward from D_1 to D_2 (owing perhaps to a rise in incomes or a change in preferences), not because price has increased from $10 to $15 (as your friend mistakenly thought was the case).

---

2. Steven Landsburg, "Why Are We Getting So Fat?" *Slate*, 1 May 2001.

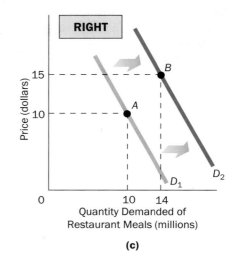

(a) (b) (c)

Quantity Demanded of Restaurant Meals (millions)

exhibit 6

The Law of Demand Holds
Your friend initially observes the equivalent of points *A* and *B* in (a). He believes that higher restaurant prices cause people to buy more restaurant meals. That is, he thinks (b) is the accurate representation of buying behavior. He is mistaken, however. People buy more restaurant meals because the demand curve for restaurant meals has shifted rightward, as in (c).

Supply
The willingness and ability of sellers to produce and offer to sell different quantities of a good at different prices during a specific time period.

Law of Supply
As the price of a good rises, the quantity supplied of the good rises, and as the price of a good falls, the quantity supplied of the good falls, ceteris paribus.

(Upward-sloping) Supply Curve
The graphical representation of the law of supply.

Self-Test *(Answers to Self-Test questions are in the Self-Test Appendix.)*

1. As Sandi's income rises, her demand for popcorn rises. As Mark's income falls, his demand for prepaid telephone cards rises. What kinds of goods are popcorn and telephone cards for the people who demand each?

2. Why are demand curves downward-sloping?

3. Give an example that illustrates how to derive a market demand curve.

4. What factors can change demand? What factors can change quantity demanded?

SUPPLY

Just as the word *demand* has a specific meaning in economics, so does the word *supply*. **Supply** refers to (1) the willingness and ability of sellers to produce and offer to sell different quantities of a good (2) at different prices (3) during a specific time period (per day, week, and so on).

THE LAW OF SUPPLY

The **law of supply** states that as the price of a good rises, the quantity supplied of the good rises, and as the price of a good falls, the quantity supplied of the good falls, *ceteris paribus*. Simply put, the price of a good and the quantity supplied of the good are directly related, *ceteris paribus*. (Quantity supplied is the number of units of a good sellers are willing and able to produce and offer to sell at a particular price.) The (upward-sloping) **supply curve** is the graphical representation of the law of supply (see Exhibit 7).

The law of supply can be summarized as follows:

$$P\uparrow Q_s\uparrow$$
$$P\downarrow Q_s\downarrow \text{ } ceteris \text{ } paribus$$

where P = price and Q_s = quantity supplied.

The law of supply holds for the production of most goods. It does not hold when there is no time to produce more units of a good. For example, suppose a theater in Atlanta is sold out for tonight's play. Even if ticket prices increased from $30 to $40, there would be no additional seats in the theater. There is no time to produce more seats. The supply curve for theater seats is illustrated in Exhibit 8a. It is fixed at the number of seats in the theater, 500.[3]

The law of supply also does not hold for goods that cannot be produced over any period of time. For example, the violinmaker Antonio Stradivari died in 1737. A rise in the price of Stradivarius violins does not affect the number of Stradivarius violins supplied, as Exhibit 8b illustrates.

Q & A

Q: According to the law of supply, price and quantity supplied are directly related. The upward-sloping supply curve is the graphical representation of this law. But then, what do the vertical supply curves in Exhibit 8 represent? It can't be the law of supply.

A: They represent an independent relationship between price and quantity supplied.

WHY MOST SUPPLY CURVES ARE UPWARD-SLOPING

The reason why most supply curves are upward-sloping involves the law of diminishing marginal returns, which is discussed in a later chapter. For now, we say that an upward-sloping supply curve reflects the fact that under certain conditions, a higher price is an incentive to producers to produce more of a good. The incentive is in the form of higher profits. For example, if the price of books rises, book companies will earn higher profits per book, assuming all other things (for example, per-unit costs) are held constant. The expectation of higher profits encourages the companies to increase the quantity of books they supply to the market.

Generally though, costs do not remain constant as more of a good is provided because of the law of increasing opportunity costs. As discussed in Chapter 2, the law states that increased production of a good comes at increased opportunity costs. Thus, an upward-sloping supply curve reflects the fact that costs rise when more units of a good are produced, so a higher price is necessary to elicit more output.

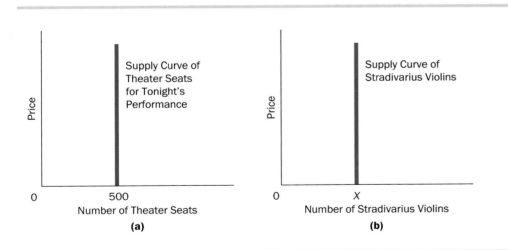

---

3. The vertical supply curve is said to be *perfectly inelastic*.

THE MARKET SUPPLY CURVE

An individual supply curve represents the price-quantity combinations for a single seller. The market supply curve represents the price-quantity combinations for all sellers of a particular good. Exhibit 9 shows how a market supply curve can be derived by "adding" individual supply curves. In (a), a **supply schedule,** the numerical tabulation of the quantity supplied of a good at different prices, is given for Brown, Alberts, and other suppliers. The market supply schedule is obtained by adding the quantities supplied at each price, *ceteris paribus.* For example, at $11, the quantities supplied are 2 units for Brown, 3 units for Alberts, and 98 units for other suppliers. Thus, a total of 103 units are supplied at $11. In (b), the data points for the supply schedules are plotted and "added" to produce a market supply curve. The market supply curve could also be drawn directly from the market supply schedule.

CHANGES IN SUPPLY MEAN SHIFTS IN SUPPLY CURVES

Just as demand can change, so can supply. The supply of a good can rise or fall. What does it mean if the supply of a good *increases*? It means that suppliers are willing and able to produce and offer to sell *more* of the good at all prices. For example, suppose that in January sellers are willing and able to produce and offer for sale 600 shirts at $25 each and that in February they are willing and able to produce and sell 900 shirts at $25 each. An increase in supply shifts the entire supply curve to the right, as shown in Exhibit 10a.

The supply of a good *decreases* if sellers are willing and able to produce and offer to sell *less* of the good at all prices. For example, suppose that in January sellers are willing and able to produce and offer for sale 600 shirts at $25 each

Supply Schedule
The numerical tabulation of the quantity supplied of a good at different prices.

exhibit 9

Deriving a Market Supply Schedule and a Market Supply Curve
Part (a) shows four supply schedules combined into one table. The market supply schedule is derived by adding the quantities supplied at each price. In (b), the data points from the supply schedules are plotted to show how a market supply curve is derived. Only two points on the market supply curve are noted.

	Quantity Supplied			
Price	Brown	Alberts	Other Suppliers	All Suppliers
$10	1	2	96	99
11	2 +	3 +	98 =	103
12	3 +	4 +	102 =	109
13	4	5	106	115
14	5	6	108	119
15	6	7	110	123

(a)

(b)

(a)

Quantity Supplied of Shirts

(b)

Quantity Supplied of Shirts

exhibit 10

Shifts in the Supply Curve
(a) The supply curve shifts rightward from S_1 to S_2. This represents an increase in the supply of shirts: At each price the quantity supplied of shirts is greater. For example, the quantity supplied at $25 increases from 600 shirts to 900 shirts. (b) The supply curve shifts leftward from S_1 to S_2. This represents a decrease in the supply of shirts: At each price the quantity supplied of shirts is less. For example, the quantity supplied at $25 decreases from 600 shirts to 300 shirts.

and that in February they are willing and able to produce and sell only 300 shirts at $25 each. A decrease in supply shifts the entire supply curve to the left, as shown in Exhibit 10b.

WHAT FACTORS CAUSE THE SUPPLY CURVE TO SHIFT?

We know the supply of any good can change. But what causes supply to change? What causes supply curves to shift? The factors that can change supply include (1) prices of relevant resources, (2) technology, (3) number of sellers, (4) expectations of future price, (5) taxes and subsidies, and (6) government restrictions.

Prices of Relevant Resources

Resources are needed to produce goods. For example, wood is needed to produce doors. If the price of wood falls, it becomes less costly to produce doors. How will door producers respond? Will they produce more doors, the same number of doors, or fewer doors? With lower costs and prices unchanged, the profit from producing and selling doors has increased; as a result, there is an increased incentive to produce doors. Door producers will produce and offer to sell more doors at each and every price. Thus, the supply of doors will increase and the supply curve of doors will shift rightward. If the price of wood rises, it becomes more costly to produce doors. Consequently, the supply of doors will decrease and the supply curve of doors will shift leftward.

Technology

In Chapter 2, technology is defined as the body of skills and knowledge concerning the use of resources in production. Also, an advance in technology refers to the ability to produce more output with a fixed amount of resources, thus reducing per-unit production costs. To illustrate, suppose it currently takes $100 to produce 40 units of a good. The per-unit cost is therefore $2.50. If an advance in technology makes it possible to produce 50 units at a cost of $100, then the per-unit cost falls to $2.00.

If per-unit production costs decline, we expect the quantity supplied of a good to increase. Why? The reason is that lower per-unit costs increase profitability and therefore provide producers with an incentive to produce more. For

Go to *http://stats.bls.gov/ppi/home.htm*. Under "Economic News Releases," select "PPI News Release (TXT)," and then choose Table 2. The PPI measures prices of the resources (inputs) used in production. Try to find resources whose prices have risen more than 10 percent in the past year. What consumer products will be affected by this resource price increase? What will happen to the supply of these products? Answer the same questions for a resource whose price has fallen more than 10 percent.

example, if corn growers develop a way to grow more corn using the same amount of water and other resources, it follows that per-unit production costs will fall, profitability will increase, and growers will want to grow and sell more corn at each price. The supply curve of corn will shift rightward.

Number of Sellers

If more sellers begin producing a particular good, perhaps because of high profits, the supply curve will shift rightward. If some sellers stop producing a particular good, perhaps because of losses, the supply curve will shift leftward.

Expectations of Future Price

If the price of a good is expected to be higher in the future, producers may hold back some of the product today (if possible; for example, perishables cannot be held back). Then, they will have more to sell at the higher future price. Therefore, the current supply curve will shift leftward. For example, if oil producers expect the price of oil to be higher next year, some may hold oil off the market this year to be able to sell it next year. Similarly, if they expect the price of oil to be lower next year, they might pump more oil this year than previously planned.

Taxes and Subsidies

Some taxes increase per-unit costs. Suppose a shoe manufacturer must pay a $2 tax per pair of shoes produced. This tax leads to a leftward shift in the supply curve, indicating that the manufacturer wants to produce and offer to sell fewer pairs of shoes at each price. If the tax is eliminated, the supply curve shifts rightward.

Subsidies have the opposite effect. Suppose the government subsidizes the production of corn by paying corn farmers $2 for every bushel of corn they produce. Because of the subsidy, the quantity supplied of corn is greater at each price and the supply curve of corn shifts rightward. Removal of the subsidy shifts the supply curve of corn leftward. A rough rule of thumb is that we get more of what we subsidize and less of what we tax.

(Production) Subsidy
A monetary payment by government to a producer of a good or service.

Government Restrictions

Sometimes government acts to reduce supply. Consider a U.S. import quota on Japanese television sets. An import quota, or quantitative restriction on foreign goods, reduces the supply of Japanese television sets. It shifts the supply curve leftward. The elimination of the import quota allows the supply of Japanese television sets in the United States to shift rightward.

Licensure has a similar effect. With licensure, individuals must meet certain requirements before they can legally carry out a task. For example, owner-operators of day-care centers must meet certain requirements before they are allowed to sell their services. No doubt this reduces the number of day-care centers and shifts the supply curve of day-care centers leftward.

A CHANGE IN SUPPLY VERSUS A CHANGE IN QUANTITY SUPPLIED

A *change in supply* refers to a *shift* in the supply curve, as illustrated in Exhibit 11a. For example, saying that the supply of oranges has increased is the same as saying that the supply curve for oranges has shifted rightward. The factors that can change supply (shift the supply curve) include prices of relevant resources, technology, number of sellers, expectations of future price, taxes and subsidies, and government restrictions.

A *change in quantity supplied* refers to a *movement* along a supply curve as in Exhibit 11b. The *only* factor that can *directly* cause a change in the quantity supplied of a good is a change in the price of the good, or own price.

exhibit 11

A Change in Supply versus a Change in Quantity Supplied
(a) A change in supply refers to a shift in the supply curve. A change in supply can be brought about by a number of factors (see the exhibit and text). (b) A change in quantity supplied refers to a movement along a given supply curve. A change in quantity supplied is brought about only by a change in (a good's) own price.

Left panel (a): S_1, S_2; Price (vertical axis), Quantity Supplied (horizontal axis); 0

A change in supply (a shift in the supply curve from S_1 to S_2)

A change in these factors can cause a change in supply:
1. Prices of relevant resources
2. Technology
3. Number of sellers
4. Expectations of future price
5. Taxes and subsidies
6. Government restrictions

(a)

Right panel (b): S_1; Price (vertical axis), Quantity Supplied (horizontal axis); 0; points A and B

A change in quantity supplied (a movement along the supply curve, S_1)

A change in this factor will cause a change in quantity supplied:
1. (A good's) own price

(b)

Self-Test

1. What would the supply curve for houses (in a given city) look like for a time period of (a) the next 10 hours and (b) the next 3 months?
2. What happens to the supply curve if each of the following occurs?
   a. There is a decrease in the number of sellers.
   b. A per-unit tax is placed on the production of a good.
   c. The price of a relevant resource falls.
3. Why do most supply curves slope upward?

THE MARKET: PUTTING SUPPLY AND DEMAND TOGETHER

In this section, we put supply and demand together and discuss the market. The purpose of the discussion is to gain some understanding about how prices are determined. Have you ever wondered why the price, say, of a car is $25,000? Why isn't the price $20,000 or $40,000?

SUPPLY AND DEMAND AT WORK AT AN AUCTION

Imagine you are at an auction where bushels of corn are bought and sold. At this auction, the auctioneer will adjust the corn price to sell all the corn offered for sale. The supply curve of corn is vertical, as in Exhibit 12. It intersects the horizontal axis at 40,000 bushels; that is, quantity supplied is 40,000 bushels. The demand curve for corn is downward-sloping. Furthermore, suppose each potential buyer of corn is sitting in front of a computer that immediately registers the

exhibit 12

Supply and Demand at Work at an Auction

Q_d = quantity demanded; Q_s = quantity supplied. The auctioneer calls out different prices, and buyers record how much they are willing and able to buy. At prices of $6.00, $5.00, and $4.00, quantity supplied is greater than quantity demanded. At prices of $1.25 and $2.25, quantity demanded is greater than quantity supplied. At a price of $3.10, quantity demanded equals quantity supplied.

number of bushels he or she wants to buy. For example, if Nancy Bernstein wants to buy 5,000 bushels of corn, she simply keys "5,000" into her computer. The auction begins. (Follow along in Exhibit 12 as we relay what is happening at the auction.) The auctioneer calls out the price:

- **$6.00.** The potential buyers think for a second, and then each registers the number of bushels he or she is willing and able to buy at that price. The total is 10,000 bushels, which is the quantity demanded of corn at $6.00. The auctioneer, realizing that 30,000 bushels of corn (40,000 − 10,000 = 30,000) will go unsold at this price, decides to lower the price per bushel to:
- **$5.00.** The quantity demanded increases to 20,000 bushels, but still the quantity supplied of corn at this price is greater than the quantity demanded. The auctioneer calls out:
- **$4.00.** The quantity demanded increases to 30,000 bushels, but the quantity supplied at $4.00 is still greater than the quantity demanded. The auctioneer drops the price down to:
- **$1.25.** At this price, the quantity demanded jumps to 60,000 bushels, but that is 20,000 bushels more than the quantity supplied. The auctioneer calls out a higher price:
- **$2.25.** The quantity demanded drops to 50,000 bushels, but buyers still want to buy more corn at this price than there is corn to be sold. The auctioneer calls out:
- **$3.10.** At this price, the quantity demanded of corn is 40,000 bushels and the quantity supplied of corn is 40,000 bushels. The auction stops. The 40,000 bushels of corn are bought and sold at $3.10 per bushel.

THE LANGUAGE OF SUPPLY AND DEMAND: A FEW IMPORTANT TERMS

If quantity supplied is greater than quantity demanded, a **surplus** or **excess supply** exists. If quantity demanded is greater than quantity supplied, a **shortage** or **excess demand** exists. In Exhibit 12, a surplus exists at $6.00, $5.00, and $4.00. A shortage exists at $1.25 and $2.25. The price at which quantity demanded equals quantity supplied is the **equilibrium price** or **market-clearing price.** In our example, $3.10 is the equilibrium price. The quantity that corresponds to the equilibrium price is the **equilibrium quantity.** In our example, it is 40,000 bushels of corn. Any price at which quantity demanded is not equal to quantity supplied is a **disequilibrium price.**

Surplus (Excess Supply)
A condition in which quantity supplied is greater than quantity demanded. Surpluses occur only at prices above equilibrium price.

Shortage (Excess Demand)
A condition in which quantity demanded is greater than quantity supplied. Shortages occur only at prices below equilibrium price.

Equilibrium Price (Market-Clearing Price)
The price at which quantity demanded of the good equals quantity supplied.

Equilibrium Quantity
The quantity that corresponds to equilibrium price. The quantity at which the amount of the good that buyers are willing and able to buy equals the amount that sellers are willing and able to sell, and both equal the amount actually bought and sold.

Disequilibrium Price
A price other than equilibrium price. A price at which quantity demanded does not equal quantity supplied.

ECONOMICS IN...

Everyday Life • **Popular Culture** • **Technology** • **The World**

The Stock Market and the Housing Market

On August 29, 2002, at 10:00 A.M., the price of a share of IBM stock was $76.81. A few seconds later, the price had risen to $77.05. Obviously, the stock market is a market that equilibrates quickly. If demand rises at the current equilibrium price, initially there is a shortage of the stock. The price is bid up and there is no longer a shortage. All this happens in seconds.

Now consider a house offered for sale in any city in the country. It is not uncommon for the sale price of a house to remain the same even though the house does not sell for months. For example, a person offers to sell her house for $400,000. One month passes, no sale; two months pass, no sale; three months pass, no sale; and so on. Ten months later, the house has still not sold and the price is still $400,000.

Is $400,000 the equilibrium price of the house? Obviously not. At equilibrium price, quantity supplied equals quantity demanded. In this case at equilibrium price, there would be a buyer for the house and a seller of the house.

However, at a price of $400,000, there is a seller of the house but no buyer. There is no doubt that the price of $400,000 is above equilibrium price. At $400,000, there is a surplus in the market; equilibrium has not been achieved.

Some people may be tempted to argue that supply and demand are at work in the stock market but not in the housing market. A better explanation, though, is that not all markets equilibrate at the same speed. While it may take only seconds for the stock market to go from surplus or shortage to equilibrium, it may take months for the housing market to do so.

A market that exhibits either a surplus ($Q_s > Q_d$) or a shortage ($Q_d > Q_s$) is said to be in **disequilibrium.** A market in which quantity demanded equals quantity supplied ($Q_d = Q_s$) is said to be in **equilibrium.** Equilibrium is identified by the letter E in Exhibit 12.

Q & A

Q: Some people use the words *shortage* and *scarcity* as synonyms. Do they refer to the same thing?

A: No. Scarcity is the condition where wants are greater than the resources available to satisfy them. Shortage is the condition where quantity demanded is greater than quantity supplied. A shortage occurs at any disequilibrium price that is below equilibrium price (for example, $2.25 in Exhibit 12). Scarcity occurs at all prices. Even at equilibrium price ($3.10 in Exhibit 12), where quantity demanded equals quantity supplied, scarcity exists.

MOVING TO EQUILIBRIUM: WHAT HAPPENS TO PRICE WHEN THERE IS A SURPLUS OR A SHORTAGE?

What did the auctioneer do when the price was $6.00 and there was a surplus of corn? He lowered the price. What did the auctioneer do when the price was $2.25 and there was a shortage of corn? He raised the price. The behavior of the auctioneer can be summarized this way: If a surplus exists, lower price; if a shortage exists, raise price. This is how the auctioneer moved the corn market into equilibrium.

Not all markets have auctioneers. (When was the last time you saw an auctioneer in the grocery store?) But many markets act *as if* an auctioneer were calling

Disequilibrium
A state of either surplus or shortage in a market.

Equilibrium
Equilibrium means "at rest." Equilibrium in a market is the price-quantity combination from which there is no tendency for buyers or sellers to move away. Graphically, equilibrium is the intersection point of the supply and demand curves.

out higher and lower prices until equilibrium price is reached. In many real-world auctioneerless markets, prices fall when there is a surplus and rise when there is a shortage. Why?

Why Does Price Fall When There Is a Surplus?

In Exhibit 13, there is a surplus at a price of $15: quantity supplied (150 units) is greater than quantity demanded (50 units). Suppliers will not be able to sell all they had hoped to sell at $15. As a result, their inventories will grow beyond the level they hold in preparation for demand changes. Sellers will want to reduce their inventories. Some will lower prices to do so, some will cut back on production, others will do a little of both. As shown in the exhibit, there is a tendency for price and output to fall until equilibrium is achieved.

Why Does Price Rise When There Is a Shortage?

In Exhibit 13, there is a shortage at a price of $5: quantity demanded (150 units) is greater than quantity supplied (50 units). Buyers will not be able to buy all they had hoped to buy at $5. Some buyers will bid up the price to get sellers to sell to them instead of to other buyers. Some sellers, seeing buyers clamor for the goods, will realize that they can raise the price on the goods they have for sale. Higher prices will also call forth added output. Thus, there is a tendency for price and output to rise until equilibrium is achieved.

Q & A

Q: In Exhibit 13, the horizontal axis is labeled "Quantity." In earlier exhibits in this chapter, either "Quantity Demanded" or "Quantity Supplied" was on the horizontal axis, depending on whether we were discussing demand or supply. Why are we switching to "Quantity"?

http://

Go to *http://www.century21.com*. Select "Property Search." Set the state to California, and key in San Diego as the city. Under Property Type, select "Resale—Single Family Detached." Select two bathrooms and four bedrooms. Click "Find Properties." What are the prices of the properties? How attractive are the ones under $200,000? Click back and redo the search by changing the state to Alabama and the city to Birmingham. How do the prices compare? How can supply and demand explain the differences in dollar amounts between San Diego and Birmingham?

exhibit 13

Moving to Equilibrium
If there is a surplus, sellers' inventories rise above the level they hold in preparation for demand changes. Sellers will want to reduce their inventories. As a result, price and output fall until equilibrium is achieved. If there is a shortage, some buyers will bid up price to get sellers to sell to them instead of to other buyers. Some sellers will realize they can raise the price on the goods they have for sale. Higher prices will call forth added output. Price and output rise until equilibrium is achieved. (Note: Recall that price, on the vertical axis, is price per unit of the good, and quantity, on the horizontal axis, is for a specific time period. In this text, we do not specify this on the axes themselves, but consider it to be understood.

Price	Q_s	Q_d	Condition
$15	150	50	Surplus
10	100	100	Equilibrium
5	50	150	Shortage

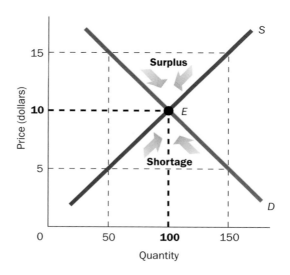

A: If we are discussing only demand, as in Exhibit 1, we put "Quantity Demanded" on the axis. If we are discussing only supply, as in Exhibit 7, we put "Quantity Supplied" on the axis. But when we discuss both demand and supply, as in Exhibit 13, we put "Quantity" on the axis, which is understood as the shortened version of "Quantity Demanded and Supplied."

MOVING TO EQUILIBRIUM: MAXIMUM AND MINIMUM PRICES

The discussion of surpluses illustrates how a market moves to equilibrium, but there is another way to show this. Exhibit 14 shows the market for good X. Look at the first unit of good X. What is the *maximum price buyers would be willing to pay* for it? The answer is $70. This can be seen by following the dotted line up from the first unit of the good to the demand curve. What is the *minimum price sellers need to receive before they would be willing to sell* this unit of good X? It is $10. This can be seen by following the dotted line up from the first unit to the supply curve. Because the maximum buying price is greater than the minimum selling price, the first unit of good X will be exchanged.

What about the second unit? Here the maximum price buyers are willing to pay is $60, and the minimum price sellers need to receive is $20. The second unit of good X will be exchanged. In fact, exchange will occur as long as the maximum buying price is greater than the minimum selling price. The exhibit shows that a total of four units of good X will be exchanged. The fifth unit will not be exchanged because the maximum buying price ($30) is less than the minimum selling price ($50).

In the process just described, buyers and sellers trade money for goods as long as both benefit from the trade. The market converges on a quantity of 4 units of good X and a price of $40 per unit. This is equilibrium. In other words, *mutually beneficial trade drives the market to equilibrium.*

Units of Good X	Maximum Buying Price	Minimum Selling Price	Result
1st	$70	$10	Exchange
2nd	60	20	Exchange
3rd	50	30	Exchange
4th	40	40	Exchange
5th	30	50	No Exchange

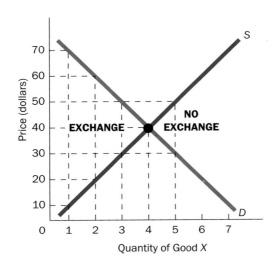

exhibit 14

Moving to Equilibrium in Terms of Maximum and Minimum Prices
As long as the maximum buying price is greater than the minimum selling price, an exchange will occur. This condition is met for units 1–4. The market converges on equilibrium through a process of mutually beneficial exchanges.

Q: It appears that in equilibrium the maximum buying price and the minimum selling price are the same. Is this correct?

A: Yes. In Exhibit 14, at the equilibrium quantity (4 units), the maximum buying price and the minimum selling price are the same—$40.

VIEWING EQUILIBRIUM IN TERMS OF CONSUMERS' AND PRODUCERS' SURPLUS

Chapter 2 discusses the key economic concepts of consumers' surplus and producers' surplus. This section looks at how these concepts are related to equilibrium.

In Exhibit 15a, consumers' surplus is represented by the shaded triangle. This triangle includes the area under the demand curve and above the equilibrium price. Recall that the definition of consumers' surplus is the highest price buyers are willing to pay minus the price they pay. For example, the window in (a) shows that buyers are willing to pay as high as $7 for the 50th unit, but only pay $5. Thus, the consumers' surplus on the 50th unit of the good is $2. If we add the consumers' surplus on each unit of the good between and including the first and the 100th (100 units being the equilibrium quantity), we obtain the shaded consumers' surplus triangle.

In Exhibit 15b, producers' surplus is represented by the shaded triangle. This triangle includes the area above the supply curve and under the equilibrium price. Keep in mind the definition of producers' surplus—the price received by the seller minus the lowest price the seller would accept for the good. For example, the window in (b) shows that sellers would have sold the 50th unit for as low as $3 but actually sold it for $5. Thus, the producers' surplus on the 50th unit of the good is $2. If we add the producers' surplus on each unit of the good between and including the first and the 100th, we obtain the shaded producers' surplus triangle.

Now consider consumers' surplus and producers' surplus at the equilibrium quantity. Exhibit 16 shows that consumers' surplus at equilibrium is equal to areas $A + B + C + D$, and producers' surplus at equilibrium is equal to areas $E + F + G + H$. At any other exchangeable quantity, such as at 25, 50, or 75 units, both consumers' surplus and producers' surplus are less. For example, at 25 units, consumers' surplus is equal to area A and producers' surplus is equal to

exhibit 15

Consumers' and Producers' Surplus

(a) Consumers' surplus. As the shaded area indicates, the difference between the maximum or highest amount buyers would be willing to pay and the price they actually pay is consumers' surplus. (b) Producers' surplus. As the shaded area indicates, the difference between the price sellers receive for the good and the minimum or lowest price they would be willing to sell the good for is producers' surplus.

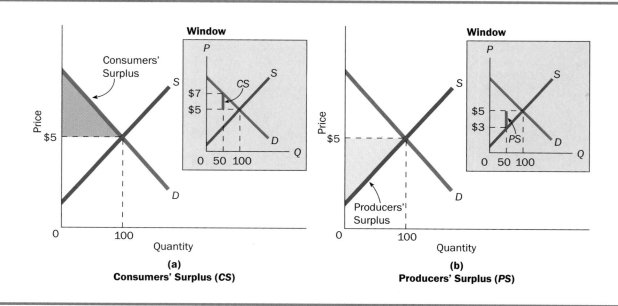

(a)
Consumers' Surplus (CS)

(b)
Producers' Surplus (PS)

Quantity (units)	Consumers' Surplus	Producers' Surplus
25	A	E
50	A + B	E + F
75	A + B + C	E + F + G
100 (Equilibrium)	A + B + C + D	E + F + G + H

(a)

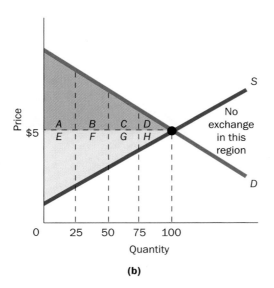

(b)

area E. At 50 units, consumers' surplus is equal to areas A + B and producers' surplus is equal to areas E + F.

Is there a special property to equilibrium? At equilibrium, both consumers' surplus and producers' surplus are maximized. In short, the sum of consumers' and producers' surplus is maximized.

WHAT CAN CHANGE EQUILIBRIUM PRICE AND QUANTITY?

Equilibrium price and quantity are determined by supply and demand. Whenever demand changes or supply changes or both change, equilibrium price and quantity change. Exhibit 17 illustrates eight different cases where this occurs. Cases (a)–(d) illustrate the four basic changes in supply and demand, where either supply or demand changes. Cases (e)–(h) illustrate changes in both supply and demand.

- (a) Demand rises (the demand curve shifts rightward), and supply is constant (the supply curve does not move). Equilibrium price rises, equilibrium quantity rises.
- (b) Demand falls, supply is constant. Equilibrium price falls, equilibrium quantity falls.
- (c) Supply rises, demand is constant. Equilibrium price falls, equilibrium quantity rises.
- (d) Supply falls, demand is constant. Equilibrium price rises, equilibrium quantity falls.
- (e) Demand rises and supply falls by an equal amount. Equilibrium price rises, equilibrium quantity is constant.
- (f) Demand falls and supply rises by an equal amount. Equilibrium price falls, equilibrium quantity is constant.

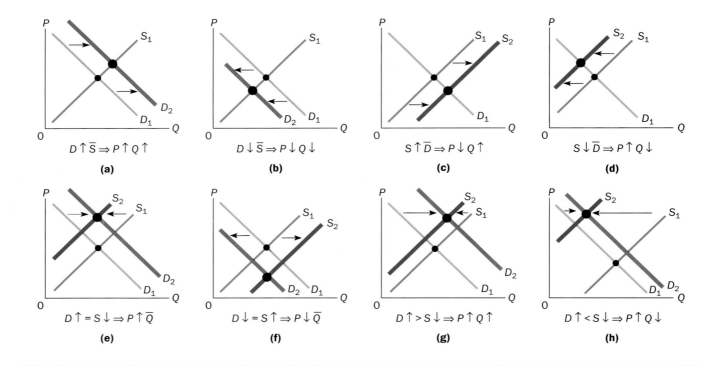

exhibit 17

Equilibrium Price and Quantity Effects of Supply Curve Shifts and Demand Curve Shifts

The exhibit illustrates the effects on equilibrium price and quantity of a change in demand, a change in supply, or a change in both. Below each diagram the condition leading to the effects is noted, using the following symbols: (1) a bar over a letter means *constant* (thus, $\bar{S}$ means that supply is constant); (2) a downward-pointing arrow ($\downarrow$) indicates a fall; (3) an upward-pointing arrow ($\uparrow$) indicates a rise. A rise (fall) in demand is the same as a rightward (leftward) shift in the demand curve. A rise (fall) in supply is the same as a rightward (leftward) shift in the supply curve.

- (g) Demand rises by a greater amount than supply falls. Equilibrium price and quantity rise.
- (h) Demand rises by a lesser amount than supply falls. Equilibrium price rises, equilibrium quantity falls.

Self-Test

1. When a person goes to the grocery store to buy food, there is no auctioneer calling out prices for bread, milk, and other items. Therefore, supply and demand cannot be operative. Do you agree or disagree? Explain your answer.

2. The price of a given-quality personal computer is lower today than it was five years ago. Is this necessarily the result of a lower demand for computers? Explain your answer.

3. What is the effect on equilibrium price and quantity of the following?
   a. A decrease in demand that is greater than the increase in supply
   b. An increase in supply
   c. A decrease in supply that is greater than the increase in demand
   d. A decrease in demand

PRICE CONTROLS

Because scarcity exists, there is a need for a rationing device—such as dollar price. But price is not always permitted to be a rationing device. Sometimes price is controlled. There are two types of price controls: price ceilings and price floors. In the discussion of price controls, the word *price* is used in the generic sense. It refers to the price of an apple, for example, the price of labor (wage), the price of credit (interest rate), and so on.

PRICE CEILING: DEFINITION AND EFFECTS

A **price ceiling** is a government-mandated maximum price above which legal trades cannot be made. For example, suppose the government mandates that the maximum price at which good X can be bought and sold is $8. It follows that $8 is a price ceiling. If $8 is below the equilibrium price of good X, as in Exhibit 18, any or all of the following effects may arise.[4]

Shortages

At the $12 equilibrium price in Exhibit 18, the quantity demanded of good X (150) is equal to the quantity supplied (150). At the $8 price ceiling, a shortage exists. The quantity demanded (190) is greater than the quantity supplied (100). When a shortage exists, there is a tendency for price and output to rise to equilibrium. But when a price ceiling exists, this tendency cannot be realized because it is unlawful to trade at the equilibrium price.

Fewer Exchanges

At the equilibrium price, 150 units of good X are bought and sold. At the price ceiling in Exhibit 18, 100 units of good X are bought and sold. (Buyers would prefer to buy 190 units, but only 100 are supplied.) We conclude that price ceilings cause fewer exchanges to be made.

Nonprice Rationing Devices

If the equilibrium price of $12 fully rationed good X before the price ceiling was imposed, it follows that a (lower) price of $8 can only partly ration this good. In short, price ceilings prevent price from rising to the level sufficient to ration goods fully. But if price is responsible for only part of the rationing, what accounts for the rest? The answer is some other (nonprice) rationing device, such as first-come-first-served (FCFS).

Price Ceiling
A government-mandated maximum price above which legal trades cannot be made.

exhibit 18

A Price Ceiling
The price ceiling is $8 and the equilibrium price $12. At $12, quantity demanded = quantity supplied. At $8, quantity demanded > quantity supplied. (Recall that price, on the vertical axis, always represents price per unit. Quantity, on the horizontal axis, always holds for a specific time period.)

---

4. If a price ceiling is above the equilibrium price (say, $8 is the price ceiling and $4 is the equilibrium price), it has no effects. Usually, however, a price ceiling is below the equilibrium price. The price ceilings discussed here hold for a particular market structure and not necessarily for all market structures. The relevant market structure is usually referred to as a perfectly competitive market, a price-taker market, or a perfect market. In this market, there are enough buyers and sellers so that no single buyer can influence price.

In Exhibit 18, 100 units of good X will be sold at $8 although buyers are willing to buy 190 units at this price. What happens? Possibly, good X will be sold on an FCFS basis for $8 per unit. In other words, to buy good X, a person must not only pay $8 per unit but also be one of the first people in line.

Buying and Selling at a Prohibited Price

Buyers and sellers may regularly circumvent a price ceiling by making their exchanges "under the table." For example, some buyers may offer some sellers more than $8 per unit for good X. No doubt some sellers will accept the offers. But why would some buyers offer more than $8 per unit when they can buy good X for $8? The answer is because not all buyers can buy the amount of good X they want at $8. As Exhibit 18 shows, there is a shortage. Buyers are willing to buy 190 units at $8, but sellers are willing to sell only 100 units. In short, 90 fewer units will be sold than buyers would like to buy. Some buyers will go unsatisfied. How, then, does any one buyer make it more likely that sellers will sell to him or her instead of to someone else? The answer is by offering to pay a higher price. Because it is illegal to pay a higher price, the transaction must be made "under the table."

Tie-in Sales

Tie-in Sale
A sale whereby one good can be purchased only if another good is also purchased.

In Exhibit 18, the maximum price buyers would be willing and able to pay per unit for 100 units of good X is $18. (This is the price on the demand curve at a quantity of 100 units.) The maximum legal price, however, is $8. This difference between two prices often prompts a **tie-in sale,** a sale whereby one good can be purchased only if another good is also purchased. For example, if Ralph's Gas Station sells gasoline to customers only if they buy a car wash, the two goods are linked together in a tie-in sale.

Suppose that the sellers of good X in Exhibit 18 also sell good Y. They might offer to sell buyers good X at $8 only if the buyers agree to buy good Y at, say, $10. We choose $10 as the price for good Y because that is the difference between the maximum per-unit price buyers are willing and able to pay for 100 units of good X (specifically, $18) and the maximum legal price ($8).

In New York City and other communities with rent-control laws, tie-in sales sometimes result from rent ceilings on apartments. Occasionally, in order to rent an apartment, an individual must agree to buy the furniture in the apartment.

THINKING LIKE AN ECONOMIST   *Economists think in terms of unintended effects. For example, a price ceiling policy intended to lower prices for the poor may cause shortages, the use of nonprice rationing devices, illegal market transactions, and tie-in sales. When we consider both the price ceiling and its effects, it is not clear that the poor have been helped. The economist knows that wanting to do good (for others) is not sufficient. It is important to know how to do good too.*

DO BUYERS PREFER LOWER PRICES TO HIGHER PRICES?

"Of course," someone might say, "buyers prefer lower prices to higher prices. What buyer would want to pay a higher price for anything?" But wait a minute. Price ceilings are often lower than equilibrium prices. Does it follow that buyers prefer price ceilings to equilibrium prices? Not necessarily. Price ceilings have effects that equilibrium prices do not: shortages, use of first-come-first-served as a rationing device, tie-in sales, and so on. A buyer could prefer to pay a higher price (an equilibrium price) than to pay a lower price and have to deal with the effects of a price ceiling. All we can say for certain is that buyers prefer lower prices to higher prices, *ceteris paribus*. As in many cases, the *ceteris paribus* condition makes all the difference.

PRICE FLOOR: DEFINITION AND EFFECTS

A **price floor** is a government-mandated minimum price below which legal trades cannot be made. For example, suppose the government mandates that the minimum price at which good X can be sold is $20. It follows that $20 is a price floor (see Exhibit 19). If the price floor is above the equilibrium price, the following two effects arise.[5]

Surpluses

At the $15 equilibrium price in Exhibit 19, the quantity demanded of good X (130) is equal to the quantity supplied (130). At the $20 price floor, a surplus exists. The quantity supplied (180) is greater than the quantity demanded (90). A surplus is usually a temporary state of affairs. When a surplus exists, there is a tendency for price and output to fall to equilibrium. But when a price floor exists, this tendency cannot be realized because it is unlawful to trade at the equilibrium price.

Fewer Exchanges

At the equilibrium price in Exhibit 19, 130 units of good X are bought and sold. At the price floor, 90 units are bought and sold. (Sellers want to sell 180 units, but buyers buy only 90.) We conclude that price floors cause fewer exchanges to be made.

Self-Test

1. Do buyers prefer lower prices to higher prices?

2. "When there are long-lasting shortages, there are long lines of people waiting to buy goods. It follows that the shortages cause the long lines." Do you agree or disagree? Explain your answer.

3. Who might argue for a price ceiling? a price floor?

Price Floor
A government-mandated minimum price below which legal trades cannot be made.

exhibit 19

A Price Floor
The price floor is $20 and the equilibrium price is $15. At $15, quantity demanded = quantity supplied. At $20, quantity supplied > quantity demanded.

---

5. If a price floor is below the equilibrium price (say, $20 is the price floor and $25 is the equilibrium price), it has no effects. Usually, however, a price floor is above the equilibrium price. As with price ceilings, the price floor effects discussed here hold for a perfectly competitive market. See footnote 4.

Some things are interesting but not useful. Other things are useful but not interesting. For example, supply and demand are interesting, but not useful. Learning how to fix a car is useful, but not particularly interesting. Am I wrong? Have I missed something? Is knowledge of supply and demand useful? If it is, what can you do with it?

A knowledge of supply and demand can be used both to explain and to predict. Let's look at prediction first. Suppose you learn that the federal government is going to impose a quota on imported television sets. What will happen when the quota is imposed? With your knowledge of supply and demand, you can predict that the price of television sets will rise. In other words, you can use your knowledge of supply and demand to predict what will happen. Stated differently, you can use your knowledge of supply and demand to see into the future. Isn't the ability to see into the future useful?

Supply and demand also allows you to develop richer and fuller explanations of events. To illustrate, suppose there is a shortage of apples in country *X*. The cause of

the shortage, someone says, is that apple growers in the country are simply growing too few apples. Well, of course, it is true that apple growers are growing "too few" apples as compared to the number of apples consumers want to buy. But does this explanation completely account for the shortage of apples? Your knowledge of supply and demand will prompt you to ask *why* apple growers are growing too few apples. When you understand that quantity supplied is related to price, you understand that apple growers will grow more apples if the price of apples is higher. What is keeping the price of apples down? Could it be a price ceiling? Without a price ceiling, the price of apples would rise, and apple growers would grow (and offer to sell) more apples. The shortage of apples will vanish.

In other words, without a knowledge of supply and demand you may have been content to explain the shortage of apples by saying that apple growers are growing too few apples. With your knowledge of supply and demand, you delve deeper into why apple growers are growing too few apples.

Chapter Summary

Demand

- The law of demand states that as the price of a good rises, the quantity demanded of the good falls, and as the price of a good falls, the quantity demanded of the good rises, *ceteris paribus*. The law of demand holds that price and quantity demanded are inversely related.
- Quantity demanded is the total number of units of a good that buyers are willing and able to buy at a particular price.
- A (downward-sloping) demand curve is the graphical representation of the law of demand.
- Factors that can change demand and cause the demand curve to shift include income, preferences, prices of related goods (substitutes and complements), number of buyers, and expectations of future price.
- The only factor that can directly cause a change in the quantity demanded of a good is a change in the good's own price.

Absolute Price and Relative Price

- The absolute price of a good is the price of the good in money terms.
- The relative price of a good is the price of the good in terms of another good.

Supply

- The law of supply states that as the price of a good rises, the quantity supplied of the good rises, and as the price of a good falls, the quantity supplied of the good falls, *ceteris paribus*. The law of supply asserts that price and quantity supplied are directly related.
- The law of supply does not hold when there is no time to produce more units of a good or when goods cannot be produced at all (over any period of time).
- The upward-sloping supply curve is the graphical representation of the law of supply. More generally, a supply curve (no matter how it slopes) represents the relationship between price and quantity supplied.

- Factors that can change supply and cause the supply curve to shift include prices of relevant resources, technology, number of sellers, expectations of future price, taxes and subsidies, and government restrictions.
- The only factor that can directly cause a change in the quantity supplied of a good is a change in the good's own price.

The Market
- Demand and supply together establish equilibrium price and quantity.
- A surplus exists in a market if, at some price, quantity supplied is greater than quantity demanded. A shortage exists if, at some price, quantity demanded is greater than quantity supplied.
- Mutually beneficial trade between buyers and sellers drives the market to equilibrium.
- The sum of consumers' surplus and producers' surplus is maximized at equilibrium.

Price Ceilings
- A price ceiling is a government-mandated maximum price. If a price ceiling is below the equilibrium price, some or all of the following effects arise: shortages, fewer exchanges, nonprice rationing devices, buying and selling at prohibited prices, and tie-in sales.
- Consumers do not necessarily prefer (lower) price ceilings to (higher) equilibrium prices. They may prefer higher prices and none of the effects of price ceilings to lower prices and some of the effects of price ceilings. All we can say for sure is that consumers prefer lower prices to higher prices, *ceteris paribus*.

Price Floors
- A price floor is a government-mandated minimum price. If a price floor is above the equilibrium price, the following effects arise: surpluses and fewer exchanges.

Key Terms and Concepts

Demand	Neutral Good	Shortage (Excess Demand)
Law of Demand	Substitutes	Equilibrium Price (Market-Clearing
Absolute (Money) Price	Complements	Price)
Relative Price	Own Price	Equilibrium Quantity
Law of Diminishing Marginal	Supply	Disequilibrium Price
Utility	Law of Supply	Disequilibrium
Demand Schedule	Supply Curve	Equilibrium
Demand Curve	Supply Schedule	Price Ceiling
Normal Good	Subsidy	Tie-in Sale
Inferior Good	Surplus (Excess Supply)	Price Floor

Economic Connections to You

Economic facts, actions, and changes create ripples that move away from their point of origin. Eventually, these ripples can intersect your life and have an effect on you. Consider the following example.

An economic change, such as a change in supply due to the price of a relevant resource, can raise or lower the price of a good. The price of one meg of RAM, a key component of a computer, fell from $2,867 in 1982 to $36 in 1996. Thus, it became cheaper for firms to produce computers. This increased the sup-

ply of computers and, in turn, lowered the price of computers. As a result, more universities, high schools, and individuals could afford to buy computers. Thus, there is a connection between the price change of a relevant resource and your access to a computer—an economic connection to you.

Based on the material in this chapter, identify other ways in which economic facts, actions, and changes create ripples that eventually affect you.

1. True or false? As the price of oranges rises, the demand for oranges falls, *ceteris paribus*. Explain your answer.
2. "The price of a bushel of wheat, which was $3.00 last month, is $3.70 today. The demand curve for wheat must have shifted rightward between last month and today." Discuss.
3. "Some goods are bought largely because they have 'snob appeal.' For example, the residents of Beverly Hills gain prestige by buying expensive items. In fact, they won't buy some items unless they are expensive. The law of demand, which holds that people buy more at lower prices than higher prices, obviously doesn't hold for the residents of Beverly Hills. The following rules apply in Beverly Hills: high prices, buy; low prices, don't buy." Discuss.
4. "The price of T-shirts keeps rising and rising, and people keep buying more and more. T-shirts must have an upward-sloping demand curve." Identify the error.
5. Predict what would happen to the equilibrium price of marijuana if it were legalized.
6. Compare the ratings for television shows with prices for goods. How are ratings like prices? How are ratings different from prices? (Hint: How does rising demand for a particular television show manifest itself?)
7. Do you think the law of demand holds for criminal activity? Do potential criminals "buy" less (more) crime, the higher (lower) the "price" of crime, *ceteris paribus*? Explain your answer.
8. Many movie theaters charge a lower admission price for the first show on weekday afternoons than for a weeknight or weekend show. Explain why.
9. A Dell computer is a substitute for a Compaq computer. What happens to the demand for Compaqs and the quantity demanded of Dells as the price of a Dell falls?
10. Describe how each of the following will affect the demand for personal computers: (a) a rise in incomes (assuming computers are a normal good); (b) a lower expected price for computers; (c) cheaper software; (d) computers become simpler to operate.
11. Describe how each of the following will affect the supply of personal computers: (a) a rise in wage rates; (b) an increase in the number of sellers of computers; (c) a tax placed on the production of computers; (d) a subsidy placed on the production of computers.
12. The law of demand specifies an inverse relationship between price and quantity demanded, *ceteris paribus*. Is the "price" in the law of demand absolute price or relative price? Explain your answer.
13. Use the law of diminishing marginal utility to explain why demand curves slope downward.
14. Explain how the market moves to equilibrium in terms of shortages and surpluses and in terms of maximum buying prices and minimum selling prices.
15. Identify what happens to equilibrium price and quantity in each of the following cases:
    a. Demand rises and supply is constant
    b. Demand falls and supply is constant
    c. Supply rises and demand is constant
    d. Supply falls and demand is constant
    e. Demand rises by the same amount that supply falls
    f. Demand falls by the same amount that supply rises
    g. Demand falls by less than supply rises
    h. Demand rises by more than supply rises
    i. Demand rises by less than supply rises
    j. Demand falls by more than supply falls
    k. Demand falls by less than supply falls
16. Many of the proponents of price ceilings argue that government-mandated maximum prices simply reduce producers' profits and do not affect the quantity supplied of a good on the market. What must the supply curve look like before a price ceiling does not affect quantity supplied?

1. If the absolute price of good X is $10 and the absolute price of good Y is $14, then what is (a) the relative price of good X in terms of good Y and (b) the relative price of good Y in terms of good X?
2. Price is $10, quantity supplied is 50 units, and quantity demanded is 100 units. For every $1 rise in price, quantity supplied rises by 5 units and quantity demanded falls by 5 units. What is the equilibrium price and quantity?
3. Draw a diagram that shows a larger increase in demand than the decrease in supply.
4. Draw a diagram that shows a smaller increase in supply than the increase in demand.

5. At equilibrium in the following figure, what area(s) does consumers' surplus equal? producers' surplus?

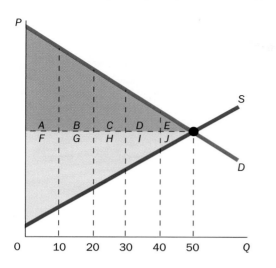

6. At what quantity in the preceding figure is the maximum buying price equal to the minimum selling price?
7. Diagrammatically explain why there are no exchanges in the area where the supply curve is above the demand curve.
8. In the following figure, can the movement from point 1 to point 2 be explained by a combination of an increase in the price of a substitute and a decrease in the price of nonlabor resources? Explain your answer.

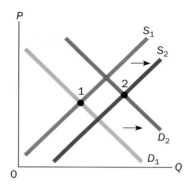

9. The demand curve is downward-sloping, the supply curve is upward-sloping, and the equilibrium quantity is 50 units. Show on a graph that the difference between the maximum buying price and minimum selling price is greater at 25 units than at 33 units.
10. Diagrammatically show and explain why a price ceiling that is above the equilibrium price will not prompt a tie-in sale.

Internet Activities

Go to *http://w3.access.gpo.gov/eop/* and make sure that the button next to the 2002 Economic Report is clicked. In the Search box, key "B-60" and then click "SUBMIT." From the results, find Table B-60, "Consumer Price Indexes for Major Expenditure Classes," and click the "TXT" icon. Assume the numbers listed are the generic prices for the goods. Also, a food number of 100 last year and of 120 this year means that food prices have risen by 20 percent.

1. Did the price of housing rise in 2001? Draw two different supply and demand diagrams that could account for the change in the price of housing. If the number of houses sold increased, which of your diagrams more likely represents the market?
2. Assume the number of houses sold increased and we know the costs of production rose as well. Draw a supply and demand diagram that shows the changes in both supply and demand that are necessary to explain the data.
3. Which is rising faster, the price of housing or the price of transportation? Are housing and transportation substitutes? (If I work where houses are expensive, can I lower my housing costs by driving from somewhere else? Can I cut my driving costs by living closer to work?) If they are substitutes, what do you think will happen in the housing and transportation markets in the future?
4. What is happening to the price of medical care relative to other goods and services? Are there substitutes for medical care? What is the likely impact on other markets (specify which markets) of the rising costs of medical care?

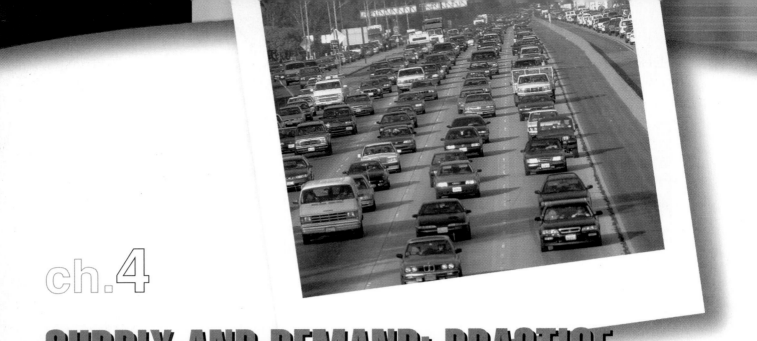

ch.4

SUPPLY AND DEMAND: PRACTICE

The last chapter presented the theory of supply and demand. You learned about demand, supply, the law of demand, the law of supply, the factors that can change demand, the factors that can change supply, and so on. The theory of supply and demand is of little use if you cannot apply it. This chapter applies that theory to explain such things as gold prices, gas prices, health care, getting a seat at a Las Vegas show, being admitted to college, traffic congestion on a freeway, and much more.

Chapter Road Map

Most of what economists do is explain and predict.

For example, they might explain why interest rates went up,

why house prices went down, or why economic growth wasn't as rapid in

one decade as in another. They might predict what will happen to the federal budget

in the next few years, at what rate the price level will rise over the next year, or if the unemploy-

ment rate will rise or fall.

To assist them in their explanations and predictions, economists use theories. One theory widely used

by economists to explain and predict is the theory of supply and demand.

Each of the 21 applications in this chapter asks a specific question and each uses the theory of supply and demand to

either explain something or predict something. As you read the applications, ask yourself two questions: (1) What question is

being asked and answered? (2) Is the theory of supply and demand being used to explain something or to predict something?

The first thought many economists have about any question is to ask themselves how it fits into the notion of supply and demand. . . . I am a supply-and-demand economist. When I come across something, I ask myself what is being transferred here and where does the supply come from and where does the demand come from.[1]

—Robert Solow
Winner of the 1987 Nobel Prize in Economics

APPLICATION 1: WHY DO COLLEGES USE GPAs, ACTs, AND SATs FOR PURPOSES OF ADMISSION?

At many colleges and universities, a student pays part of the price of his or her education (by way of tuition payments) and taxpayers and private donors pay part (by way of tax payments and charitable donations, respectively). Thus, the tuition that students pay to attend colleges and universities is usually less than the equilibrium tuition. To illustrate, suppose a student pays tuition T_1 at a given college or university. As shown in Exhibit 1, T_1 is below the equilibrium tuition, T_E. At T_1, the number of students who want to attend the university (N_1) is greater than the number of openings at the university (N_2); that is, quantity demanded is greater than quantity supplied. The university receives more applications for admission than there are places available. Something has to be done. But what?

The college or university is likely to ration its available space by a combination of money price and some other nonprice rationing devices. The student must pay the tuition, T_1, *and* meet the standards of the nonprice rationing devices. Colleges and universities usually use such things as GPAs (grade point averages), ACT scores, and SAT scores as rationing devices.

THINKING LIKE AN ECONOMIST

The layperson sees a university that requires a GPA of 3.8 and an SAT score of 1100 or better for admission. An economist sees a rationing device. The economist then

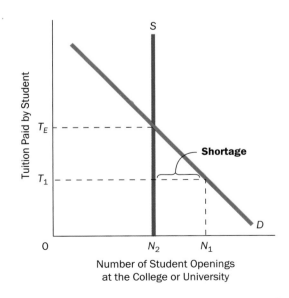

exhibit 1

College and University Admissions

If the college or university charges T_1 in tuition (when T_E is the equilibrium tuition), a shortage will be generated. The college or university will then use some nonprice rationing device, such as GPAs, ACTs, and SATs, as admission criteria.

1. Interview with Robert Solow. The entire interview is in *Economics* by Roger A. Arnold (St. Paul, Minnesota: West Publishing Company, 1992).

goes on to ask why this particular nonprice rationing device is being used. He reasons that there would be no need for a nonprice rationing device if (dollar) price were fully rationing the good or service.

Self-Test *(Answers to Self-Test questions are in the Self-Test Appendix.)*

1. Suppose the demand rises for admission to a university but both the tuition and the number of openings in the entering class remain the same. Will this affect the admission standards of the university? Explain your answer.

2. Administrators and faculty at state colleges and universities often say that their standards of admission are independent of whether there is a shortage or surplus of openings at the university. Do you think this is true? Do you think that faculty and administrators ignore surpluses and shortages of openings when setting admission standards? Explain your answer.

APPLICATION 2: CAN PREJUDICE AFFECT WAGES?

Suppose there are three groups of people, *A, B,* and *C.* The members of group *A* are always employers and the members of groups *B* and *C* are always employees. The employers in group *A* have no hiring preference for either group of employees. Let's assume that there are 100 members of group *B* and 100 members of group *C* and that the members of groups *B* and *C* are equally productive workers. Because the workers in groups *B* and *C* are equally productive and because employers show no preference for hiring one group of workers over the other, the demand for group B workers is the same as the demand for group *C* workers. As Exhibit 2a and b show, when the demand for and supply of *B* and *C* workers is the same, each *B* and *C* worker receives a wage rate of W_1.

Now suppose some (but not all) employers in group *A* become prejudiced against the members of group *B.* Let's call this subset of employers the *discriminator employers.*

The discriminator employers do not want to hire group *B* workers. As a result, the demand for *B* workers falls, and as shown in Exhibit 2c, the demand curve for *B* workers shifts leftward from D_{B_1} to D_{B_2}. For a given supply curve (S_{B_1}), the wage rate for *B* workers falls. Thus, apparently, employer prejudice results in lower wages for the group at which the prejudice is directed.

However, some economists point out that the story may not end here. They argue that in competitive product markets, the discriminator employers might be forced out of business by the nondiscriminator employers. Why might this happen?

exhibit 2

Employer Prejudice and Wages
Group *A* consists of employers, and groups *B* and *C* consist of equally productive workers. Part (a) shows the market for *B* workers. Part (b) shows the market for *C* workers. In each market the equilibrium wage rate is W_1. Later, some employers become prejudiced against *B* workers and no longer hire *B* workers. As a result, the demand curve for *B* workers shifts leftward from D_{B_1} to D_{B_2}, as shown in (c). The wage rate in the market for *B* workers falls from W_1 to W_2. Now, nondiscriminator employers may hire more *B* workers because *B* workers are as productive as *C* workers but work at a lower wage rate. As a result, the labor costs of the nondiscriminator employers fall. Nondiscriminator employers are able to lower their prices and, thus, force their discriminator competitors out of business. The prejudice that discriminator employers expressed toward *B* workers may eventually adversely affect these employers.

(a)

(b)

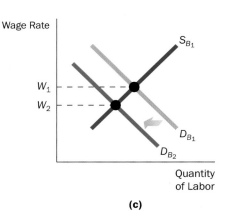

(c)

Let's look at how the prejudice of some employers might affect the nondiscriminator employers. The nondiscriminator employers realize that B and C workers are equally productive, but that it costs less to hire B workers than it does to hire C workers. So, nondiscriminator employers start to hire more B workers, and as a result, their labor costs decline. The nondiscriminator employers can now lower the price of their product and, thus, force their prejudiced competitors out of business. In other words, the prejudice that discriminator employers earlier expressed in the labor market might eventually adversely affect them.

Self-Test

1. If B workers are more productive than C workers, will the demand for B workers be greater than, less than, or the same as the demand for C workers?

2. How can a discriminator employer be hurt by his discriminatory actions?

APPLICATION 3: WHAT WILL HAPPEN TO THE PRICE OF MARIJUANA IF THE PURCHASE AND SALE OF MARIJUANA ARE LEGALIZED?

In the United States, the purchase or sale of marijuana is unlawful. However, there is still a demand for and supply of marijuana. There is also an equilibrium price of marijuana. Let's say that price is P_1.

Suppose that beginning tomorrow, the purchase and sale of marijuana become legal. Would P_1 rise, fall, or remain the same?

The answer, of course, depends on what we think will happen to the demand for and supply of marijuana. If the purchase and sale of marijuana are legal, then some people currently producing corn and wheat might choose instead to produce and sell marijuana. So, the supply of marijuana would rise. If nothing else changes, the price of marijuana would fall.

But something else is likely to change. If marijuana consumption is no longer illegal, then the number of people who want to buy and consume marijuana will likely rise. In other words, there will be more buyers of marijuana. This will increase the demand for marijuana.

Thus, decriminalizing the purchase and sale of marijuana is likely to shift both the marijuana demand and supply curves to the right. If the demand curve shifts to the right by the same amount as the supply curve shifts to the right, the price of marijuana will not change. If the demand curve shifts to the right by more than the supply curve shifts to the right, the price of marijuana will rise. If the supply curve shifts to the right by more than the demand curve shifts to the right, the price of marijuana will fall.

Q & A **Q:** So the price of marijuana may stay the same, rise, or fall, depending on how much the demand for marijuana rises relative to how much the supply of marijuana rises. But what will happen to the equilibrium quantity of marijuana? Will it rise, fall, or stay the same?

A: It will rise. If demand and supply rise, the new equilibrium quantity will be greater than the old equilibrium quantity. Draw it and see.

Self-Test

1. What will happen to the price of marijuana if the supply of increases by more than the demand for it?

2. What will happen to the quantity of marijuana (purchased and sold) if the demand for marijuana rises by more than the supply of marijuana falls?

APPLICATION 4: THE MINIMUM WAGE LAW

Recall that a price floor is a legislated minimum price below which trades cannot legally be made. The *minimum wage* is a price floor—a government-mandated minimum price for labor. It affects the market for unskilled labor. In Exhibit 3, the minimum wage is W_M and the equilibrium wage is W_E. At the equilibrium wage, N_1 workers are employed. At the higher minimum wage, N_3 workers want to work but only N_2 actually do work. There is a surplus of workers equal to $N_3 - N_2$ in this unskilled labor market. In addition, fewer workers are working at the minimum wage (N_2) than at the equilibrium wage (N_1). Overall, the effects of the minimum wage are (1) a surplus of unskilled workers and (2) fewer workers employed.

Suppose two economists decide to test the theory that as the minimum wage rises some unskilled workers will lose their jobs. They look at the number of unskilled workers before and after the minimum wage is raised, and, surprisingly, they find that the number of unskilled workers is the same. Do you think this is sufficient evidence to say that an increase in the minimum wage does not cause some workers to lose their jobs?

We'll leave that question hanging while we consider whether or not the economists have adequately tested their theory. Suppose instead of focusing on the number of people who lose their jobs, they look at the people who keep their jobs but have their hours reduced as a result of the higher minimum wage.

Let's look at an example. Suppose a local hardware store currently employs David and Francesca to work after school cleaning up and stocking the store. The owner of the store pays each of them the minimum wage of, say, $5.15 an hour. Then, the minimum wage is raised to $6.75 an hour. Will either David or

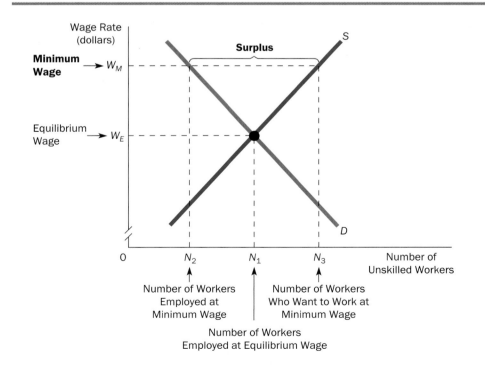

exhibit 3

Effects of the Minimum Wage
At a minimum wage of W_M an hour, there is a surplus of workers, and fewer workers are employed than would be at the equilibrium wage, W_E.

Francesca lose their jobs as a result? Not necessarily. Instead, the owner of the store could reduce the number of hours he employs the two workers. For example, instead of having each of them work 20 hours a week, he might ask each to work only 14 hours a week.[2]

Now, let's reconsider our original question: Has the higher minimum wage eliminated jobs? In a way, no. It has, however, reduced the number of hours a person works in a job. (Of course, if we define a job as including both a particular task and a certain number of hours completing that task, then the minimum wage increase has eliminated "part" of the job.) This discussion argues for changing the label on the horizontal axis in Exhibit 3 from "Number of Unskilled Workers" to "Number of Unskilled Labor Hours."

Q & A

Q: Isn't the minimum wage necessary to guarantee everybody a decent wage? If the minimum wage didn't exist, wouldn't employers hire workers for next to nothing?

A: Employers may want to hire workers for "next to nothing," but the wages workers receive depend on the demand for and supply of labor. In other words, employers do not set wages at whatever level they like. In a competitive market setting, the forces of supply and demand determine equilibrium wages.

As to the minimum wage guaranteeing a decent wage, suppose Johnny Bates, a 17-year-old in Chicago, finds that his labor is worth $5.00 an hour to employers. If the government mandates that Johnny must be paid $6.00 an hour ($1.00 more an hour than he's currently worth to employers), no employer will hire him. So the minimum wage does not guarantee Johnny a decent wage; in fact, it may guarantee him no wage.

THINKING LIKE AN ECONOMIST

In economics, some questions relate to "direction" and some to "magnitude." For example, suppose someone asks, "If the demand for labor is downward-sloping and the labor market is competitive, how will a minimum wage (above the equilibrium wage) affect employment?" This person is asking a question that relates to the direction of the change in employment. Usually, these types of questions can be answered by applying a theory. Applying the theory of demand, an economist might say, "At higher wages, the quantity demanded of labor, or the employment level, will be lower than at lower wages." The word "lower" speaks to the directional change in employment.

Now suppose someone asks, "How much will employment decline?" This person is asking a question that relates to magnitude. Usually, questions that deal with magnitude can be answered only through some kind of empirical (data-collecting and analyzing) work. In other words, we would have to collect employment figures at the equilibrium wage and at the minimum wage and then find the difference.

Self-Test

1. When the labor supply curve is upward-sloping, a minimum wage law that sets the wage rate above its equilibrium level creates a surplus of labor. If the labor supply curve is vertical, does a surplus of labor still occur? Explain your answer.

2. Someone says that an increase in the minimum wage will not cause firms to hire fewer workers. What is this person assuming?

---

2. Our two economists need to find data that relate not only to how many, if any, people lose their jobs as a result of the higher minimum wage, but also how many people who keep their jobs end up working fewer hours.

APPLICATION 5: PRICE CEILING
IN THE KIDNEY MARKET

Just as there are people who want to buy houses, computers, and books, there are people who want to buy kidneys. These people have kidney failure and either will die without a new kidney or will have to endure years of costly and painful dialysis. This demand for kidneys is shown as D_K in Exhibit 4.

The supply of kidneys is shown as S_K in Exhibit 4. Notice that at $0 price, the quantity supplied of kidneys is 350. These kidneys are from people who donate their kidneys to others, asking nothing in return. They may donate their kidneys upon their death or may donate one of their two kidneys while living. We have drawn the supply curve as upward-sloping because we assume that some people who today are unwilling to donate a kidney for $0 might be willing to do so for some positive dollar amount. Specifically, we assume that as the price of a kidney rises, the quantity supplied of kidneys will rise.

If there were a free market in kidneys, the price of a kidney would be P_1 in Exhibit 4. At this price, 1,000 kidneys would be purchased and sold—1,000 kidney transplants would occur.

Today, there is no free market in kidneys. Buying or selling kidneys is illegal at any dollar amount. In essence, then, there is a price ceiling in the kidney market and the ceiling is set at $0. What is the effect of this price ceiling?

If the demand curve for kidneys and the supply curve of kidneys intersected at $0, there would be neither a surplus nor a shortage of kidneys. But there is evidence that the demand and supply curves do not intersect at $0; they look more like those shown in Exhibit 4. In other words, there is a shortage of kidneys at $0: the quantity supplied of kidneys is 350 and the quantity demanded is 1,500. (Although these are not the actual numbers of kidneys demanded and supplied at $0, they are representative of the current situation in the kidney market.)

The last chapter describes the possible effects of a price ceiling set below equilibrium price: shortages, nonprice rationing devices, fewer exchanges, tie-in sales, and buying and selling at prohibited prices (in other words, illegal trades). Are any of these effects occurring in the kidney market?

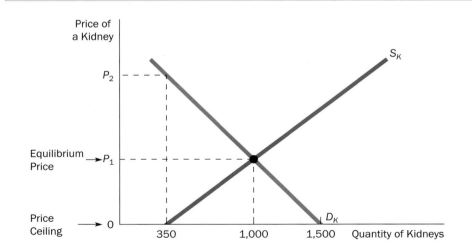

exhibit 4

The Market for Kidneys
We have identified the demand for kidneys as D_K and the supply of kidneys as S_K. Given the demand for and supply of kidneys, the equilibrium price of a kidney is P_1. It does not follow, though, that simply because there is an equilibrium price, people will be allowed to trade at this price. Today, it is unlawful to buy and sell kidneys at any positive price. In short, there is a price ceiling in the kidney market and the ceiling is $0. At the price ceiling, there is a shortage of kidneys, a nonprice rationing device for kidneys (first-come-first-served), fewer kidney transplants (than there would be at P_1), and illegal purchases and sales of kidneys.

First, there is evidence of a shortage. In almost every country in the world, there are more people on national lists who want a kidney than there are kidneys available. Some of these people die waiting for a kidney.

Second, as just indicated, the nonprice rationing device used in the kidney market is (largely) first-come-first-served. A person who wants a kidney registers on a national waiting list. How long one waits is a function of how far down the list one's name appears.

Third, there are fewer exchanges; not everyone who needs a kidney gets a kidney. With a price ceiling of $0, only 350 kidneys are supplied. All these kidneys are from people who freely donate their kidneys. If P_1 were permitted, some people who are unwilling to supply a kidney (at $0) would be willing to do so. In short, monetary payment would provide the incentive for some people to supply a kidney. At P_1, 1,000 kidneys are demanded and supplied, so more people would get kidney transplants when the price of a kidney is P_1 (1,000 in total) than when the price of a kidney is $0 (350 in total). More transplants, of course, means fewer people die waiting for a kidney.

Fourth, kidneys are bought and sold at prohibited prices. People buy and sell kidneys today; they just do so illegally. There are stories of people who need kidneys paying between $25,000 and $200,000 for a kidney.

Some people argue that a free market in kidneys would be wrong. Such a system would place the poor at a disadvantage. Think of it: A rich person who needed a kidney could buy the kidney he needed, but a poor person could not. The rich person would get a second chance at life, the poor person would not. No one particularly enjoys contemplating this stark reality.

But consider another stark reality. If it is unlawful to pay someone for a kidney, fewer kidneys will be forthcoming. In other words, the quantity supplied of kidneys is less at $0 than at, say, $20,000. Fewer kidneys supplied means, in turn, fewer kidney transplants. And fewer kidney transplants means more people will die from kidney failure.

Q & A

Q: Do economists have to analyze the price of *everything?* A price for a house is all right, but a price for a kidney is unsettling.

A: Economists simply (1) determine whether an equilibrium price exists and then (2) identify the effects of the equilibrium price (a) being the legal price and (b) not being the legal price. In the kidney market, whether we like it or not, there exists an equilibrium price for kidneys. But just because it exists, it doesn't follow that people will be allowed to legally trade at this price. The economist identifies the pricing effects in two different settings. In one setting, the legal price is not the equilibrium price; in the other setting, the legal price is the equilibrium price. That's the extent of the economist's work.

Self-Test

1. A shortage of kidneys for transplants is a consequence of the price of a kidney being below equilibrium price. Do you agree or disagree? Explain your answer.

2. Suppose the price ceiling in the kidney market is $0. Will there be a shortage of kidneys? Explain your answer.

APPLICATION 6: CRISIS IN THE ELECTRICITY MARKET

In 2001, some California residents and businesses endured electricity blackouts; they had to do without electricity for one or two hours a day. During these hours, they couldn't run air conditioners, turn on lights, watch television, and so on.

In economic terms, a blackout is simply a shortage—the quantity demanded of a good or service is greater than the quantity supplied of the good or service.

During the blackouts in California, Californians wanted to buy more electricity than there was electricity available.

But why was there a shortage of electricity? Why were there blackouts? The answer has to do with supply, demand, and price.

In California, as in other states, some companies are power distributors and other companies are power generators. A power generator generates electricity. It then sells the electricity it has generated to a power distributor, which in turn sells the electricity to consumers.

Essentially, there are two electricity markets in California. The first market, shown in Exhibit 5a, is the retail electricity market. The demand for retail electricity comes from individuals and businesses. The supply of this electricity comes from the power distributors.

The second market, shown in Exhibit 5b, is the wholesale electricity market. The demand for wholesale electricity comes from the power distributors, and the supply of this electricity comes from the power generators.

Let's suppose that both markets are currently at point 1 in parts (a) and (b). In this case, power distributors buy electricity in the wholesale electricity market for P_1 and then turn around and sell it in the retail electricity market for P_1. For example, they might buy electricity for 10 cents a kilowatt hour and sell it for 10 cents a kilowatt hour. (If you want the power distributors to sell electricity for a price a few cents more than the price they pay for the electricity, it does not change the analysis.)

Now suppose a state law is passed that places a price ceiling on retail electricity but not on wholesale electricity. For example, let's say the price ceiling on retail electricity is set at P_1 (in Exhibit 5a) and the price of wholesale electricity is

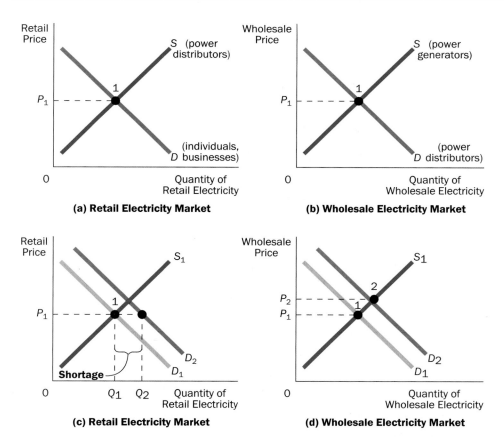

(a) Retail Electricity Market

(b) Wholesale Electricity Market

(c) Retail Electricity Market

(d) Wholesale Electricity Market

exhibit 5

Supply, Demand, and the Electricity Market
Part (a) shows the retail electricity market; part (b) shows the wholesale electricity market. The demand for electricity in the retail market comes from individuals and businesses; the supply comes from power distributors. The demand for electricity in the wholesale market comes from power distributors; the supply comes from power generators.

In 1996, the California legislature passed a law that set a ceiling on the retail price of electricity but allowed the wholesale price of electricity to be determined by supply and demand. What happens if demand for electricity rises in the retail market, as shown in (c)? Increased demand in the retail market causes increased demand in the wholesale market, as shown in (d). The wholesale price of electricity rises to P_2, but the retail price is prevented by law from rising. As a result, there is a shortage of electricity in the retail market. Shortages show up as blackouts.

determined by the forces of supply and demand. In essence, the retail electricity market is a controlled market, and the wholesale electricity market is a free market. To a large degree, this is exactly the situation in California because of a state law passed in 1996.

No problems ensue, of course, as long as the demand and supply curves remain as they are in parts (a) and (b). But suppose they change, as they did in California.

Suppose the demand for retail electricity rises from D_1 to D_2, as shown in part (c). A higher demand for retail electricity (coming from individuals and businesses) will cause power distributors to demand more generated electricity in the wholesale electricity market. So demand in that market rises from D_1 to D_2, as shown in part (d). As a result, the wholesale price of electricity rises to P_2.

Now power distributors must pay P_2 for the electricity they buy—but they must continue to sell electricity in the retail market at the price ceiling, P_1. At P_1 in the retail market, quantity demanded of electricity (Q_2) is greater than quantity supplied (Q_1); in other words, there is a shortage of electricity. Shortages of electricity are manifested as blackouts.

In reality, rising demand in the retail and wholesale electricity markets wasn't the only change in California. Supply changed, too. Supply changed because natural gas prices increased fourfold in 2000. Many of the power plants that generate electricity are fueled by natural gas. The increase in natural gas prices made generating electricity more expensive and shifted the supply curve of electricity (in the wholesale electricity market) to the left. As a result, the wholesale price of electricity was driven up even further.

Daniel McFadden, who won the Nobel Prize in Economics in 2000, summed up the electricity crisis in California: "The source of the [electricity] crisis was rigid regulation of retail prices in the face of rapid increases in wholesale prices driven by increased fuel prices and increased demand in the national electricity market."[3]

Self-Test

1. Retail and wholesale electricity markets are in equilibrium, as shown in Exhibit 5a and b. In addition, there is a price ceiling in the retail market, set at P_1, but no price ceiling in the wholesale market. Finally, fuel costs rise, causing the supply of electricity in the wholesale market to shift left. What happens to the wholesale price of electricity? What happens to the supply of electricity in the retail market? Is there a shortage, surplus, or equilibrium in the retail market? Explain your answer.

2. In our discussion, there was a price ceiling in the retail electricity market but not in the wholesale market. Suppose there had been. Specifically, suppose the price ceiling had been set at P_1 in both markets (shown in Exhibit 5a and b). Would this have averted the blackouts?

APPLICATION 7: IF GOLD PRICES ARE THE SAME EVERYWHERE, THEN WHY AREN'T HOUSE PRICES?

The price of an ounce of gold is the same everywhere in the world. For example, the price of an ounce of gold is the same in London as it is in New York City. House prices are not the same everywhere, though. For example, the median price of a house in Los Angeles, California, is higher than the median price of a house in Dubuque, Iowa. Why are gold prices the same everywhere while house prices are different?

To answer the question, let's look at what would happen if gold prices were not the same everywhere in the world. Let's assume the price of an ounce of

---

3. Daniel McFadden, "California Needs Deregulation Done Right," *Wall Street Journal,* 13 February 2001.

gold is $250 in London and $300 in New York City. What happens? Obviously this difference in prices for the same good presents a profit opportunity. People will buy gold in London for $250 an ounce, ship it to New York City, and sell it for $300 an ounce. If we ignore the costs of transporting the gold, a $50 profit per ounce is earned. When an opportunity exists for profit—by buying low and selling high—individuals are quick to try to capture the profit.

As gold is moved from London to New York in search of profit, the supply of gold in London will fall and the supply of gold in New York will rise. A falling gold supply in London will push up the price of gold (from $250), and a rising gold supply in New York will push down the price of gold (from $300). As the London gold price rises and the New York gold price falls, a point will eventually be reached where the two prices are the same. When the London price and New York price for gold are the same, profit cannot be earned by moving gold from London to New York. In short, any difference in the price of gold in various locations will quickly be eliminated by changes in the supply of gold in the various locations.

Can the same hold for houses? If the price of a house in Los Angeles is higher than the price of a house in Dubuque, is it possible to move houses and land from Dubuque to Los Angeles? Of course not. We can't pick up a house and its lot in Dubuque and move them to Los Angeles, in the process reducing the supply of houses and land in Dubuque and increasing the supply of houses and land in Los Angeles. Because the supply of houses and land cannot be reshuffled the way the supply of gold can be, we expect differences in house prices in various locations but not differences in gold prices.

Self-Test

1. What causes the price of gold to be the same in New York and London?

2. The price of a Toyota Camry is nearly the same in Miami as it is in Dallas. Why?

APPLICATION 8: GAS PRICES AFTER THE ATTACK ON THE WORLD TRADE CENTER AND THE PENTAGON

On September 11, 2001, terrorists hijacked commercial jets and flew them into the twin towers of the World Trade Center in New York City and into the Pentagon in Washington, D.C. Another hijacked jet crashed in rural Pennsylvania.

Hours after the attack, gas prices at some gas stations across the country began to rise. For example, one station in Oklahoma City raised the price of a gallon of unleaded gas from $1.68 to $5.00. A station in North Dakota raised its price of unleaded gas from $1.76 a gallon to $3.29 a gallon. A station in Illinois increased gas prices from an average of $1.88 a gallon to $4.00 a gallon.

Many people claimed that these gas stations were trying to cheat the public. Customers called Consumer Hot Lines and reported the higher prices. State officials, including the governors of many states, were fast to respond. Gas station owners were threatened with fines or lawsuits if they didn't bring gas prices back down. Prices were down in two days.

Let's consider two economic questions relevant to this incident: Why did gas prices at some stations rise? Why did prices soon return to "normal" (pre-terrorist attack) levels?

Prices might have risen because some gas station owners mistakenly thought that as a result of the terrorist attack, the demand for gas had increased and the supply of gas would soon decrease. Recall that expectation of future price is one factor that can change the current demand for a good. A gas station owner may have reasoned this way: Because of the terrorist attack, some Americans may expect a higher price for gas in the future. If they expect a higher future price, they will increase the current demand for gas. If the current demand for gas rises, price will rise.

Expectation of future price can also change the supply of a good. Again, a gas station owner could have reasoned this way: The terrorist attack may cause (my) gas suppliers to expect a higher price for gas in the future. If they expect a higher future price, they will prefer to sell gas later instead of now. The current supply of gas will fall. If the current supply of gas falls, price will rise.

Thus, expecting higher demand and lower supply, some gas station owners posted higher gas prices.

But were their expectations correct? We think not. Keep in mind that when some gas station owners were raising gas prices, many others were not. It was not uncommon for one station to be selling gas at $4.00 a gallon while a station across the street was selling gas at $1.88 a gallon. What would you think if you were the gas station owner who had posted the $4.00-a-gallon price? Would you think that people were going to see your higher price and come to your station? Or would you think that maybe your price was too high? Would you realize that the demand for gas hadn't increased and that the supply of gas wasn't likely to decrease?

If you're greedy—and no one accused the gas station owners in question of being anything but greedy—you wouldn't want to lose business by posting a price that was too high.

Some people argue that prices returned to "normal" levels because gas station owners were threatened with fines and lawsuits. But even without consumer complaints and the threat of fines and lawsuits, these gas station owners would have lowered prices to previous levels. Not lowering prices would have invited economic loss. If you think supply and demand have changed and most of the world (in the form of your competitors) is telling you that it hasn't, then your misperception of reality may be costly to you.

In the end, real supply and demand determined the price of gas, not the demand and supply some gas station owners imagined.

Q & A

Q: Can you give another example of a seller who thinks the equilibrium price of a good is higher than it actually is?

A: Consider a person who decides to sell her house. Suppose the equilibrium price for houses similar to hers is $200,000. If the house seller does not know this, she may post a price of $250,000, thinking it is the equilibrium price. With time, though, she will learn that her price of $250,000 is too high. At her price, there is a surplus of her house: there is one seller and no buyers. Eventually, she will drop the price until the house sells.

This example is really the same as the gas station example. In that example, gas station owners thought equilibrium prices were higher than they were. In time, the gas station owners learned. In the house example, the house seller thinks the equilibrium price is higher than it is. In time, she will learn.

The lesson here is a simple one: Prices are not always at their equilibrium levels, but they are always *moving toward* their equilibrium levels.

Self-Test

1. Carl argues that higher prices are caused by greed, not supply and demand (demand rises or supply falls). What might be wrong with the greed explanation of higher prices?

2. Recall from the last chapter that demand changes if income, preferences, prices of related goods, number of buyers, or expectations of future price change. Which factor is particularly relevant during a disaster? Explain your answer.

APPLICATION 9: HEALTH CARE AND THE RIGHT TO SUE YOUR HMO

A discussion of renters, landlords, and eviction notices is relevant to the right to sue an HMO. So, we begin with an analysis of two laws related to eviction of a renter. Under law 1, a renter has 30 days to vacate an apartment after being served with an eviction notice. Under law 2, the renter has 90 days to evacuate.

Landlords will find it less expensive to rent apartments under law 1 than under law 2. Under law 1, the most money a landlord can lose after serving an eviction notice is 30 days' rent. Under law 2, a landlord can lose 90 days' rent. Obviously, losing 90 days' rent is more costly than losing 30 days' rent.

A different supply curve of apartments exists under each law. The supply curve under law 1 (S_1 in Exhibit 6) will lie to the right of the supply curve under law 2 (S_2 in the exhibit). Again, that's because it is less expensive to supply apartments under law 1 than under law 2.

If the supply curve is different under the two laws, the equilibrium rent will be different too. As shown in Exhibit 6, the supply curve under law 1 lies to the right of the supply curve under law 2, so the equilibrium rent will be lower under law 1 (R_1) than under law 2 (R_2).

In conclusion, under law 1, a renter pays lower rent (good) and has fewer days to vacate the apartment (bad). Under law 2, a renter pays a higher rent (bad) and has more days to vacate the apartment (good). Who pays for the additional days to vacate the apartment under law 2? The renter pays for these additional days by paying higher rent.

Now let's turn from apartments to health care. You may frequently hear people complain about their health maintenance organizations (HMOs). The complaints are diverse and wide-ranging. One common complaint is that patients cannot sue their HMOs in state and federal courts for denial of benefits and poor-quality care.

Some people argue that patients should have the right to sue their HMOs. Let's consider two settings: one in which patients cannot sue their HMOs and one in which patients can sue.

An HMO's liability cost is lower if patients cannot sue than if they can sue. A difference in liability costs will be reflected in different supply curves. To illustrate,

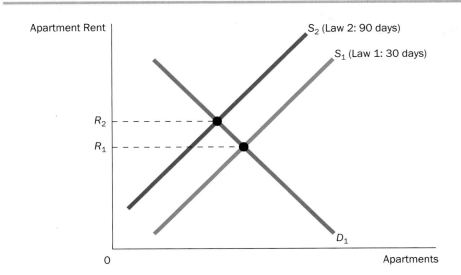

exhibit 6

Apartment Rent and the Law
Under law 1, a renter has 30 days to leave an apartment after receiving an eviction notice from his or her landlord. Under law 2, a renter has 90 days to leave an apartment after receiving an eviction notice from his or her landlord. The cost to the landlord of renting an apartment is higher under law 2 than law 1, and so the supply curve of apartments under law 1 lies to the right of the supply curve of apartments under law 2. Different supply curves mean different rents. Apartment rent is higher under law 2 (R_2) than under law 1 (R_1).

recall that any single point on a supply curve is the minimum price sellers need to receive before they would be willing and able to sell that particular unit of a good.

Suppose when patients cannot sue, an HMO is willing and able to provide health care to John for $300 a month. If patients can sue, is the HMO still willing and able to provide health care to John for $300 a month? Not likely. Because of the higher liability cost due to the patient's ability to sue, the HMO is no longer willing and able to provide health care to John for $300 month. It will, however, be willing and able to provide health care to John for, say, $350 a month.

Saying a seller's minimum price for providing a good or service rises is the same as saying the seller's supply curve has shifted upward and to the left. In other words, the supply curve of HMO-provided health care will shift upward and to the left if patients have the right to sue. This is the same way the supply curve of apartments moved in Exhibit 6.

Will a difference in supply curves affect the price patients pay for their HMO-provided health care coverage? Yes. One effect of moving from a setting where patients do not have the right to sue to one where patients do have the right to sue is that patients will have to pay more for their HMO-provided health care coverage.

Economists don't determine whether patients having the right to sue is good or bad or right or wrong. Economists use their tools (in this instance, supply and demand) to point out that things people want, such as the right to sue their HMOs, often come with price tags. Individuals must decide whether the price they pay is worth what they receive in return.

Self-Test

1. Economists often say, "There is no such thing as a free lunch." How is this saying related to patients moving from a system where they cannot sue their HMOs to one where they can?

2. A professor tells her students that they can have an extra week to complete their research papers. Under what condition are the students made better off with the extra week? Can you think of a case where the students would actually be made worse off by the extra week?

APPLICATION 10: DO YOU PAY FOR THINGS EVEN WHEN THERE IS NO EXPLICIT PRICE? OR, DO YOU PAY FOR GOOD WEATHER?

Some places in the country are considered to have better weather than other places have. For example, most people would say the weather in San Diego, California, is better than the weather in Fargo, North Dakota. Often, a person in San Diego will say, "You can't beat the weather today. And the good thing about it is that you don't have to pay a thing for it. It's free."

In one sense, the San Diegan is correct: There is no weather market. Specifically, no one comes around and asks San Diegans to pay a certain dollar amount for the weather on a given day.

But in another sense, the San Diegan is incorrect. Fact is, San Diegans indirectly pay for their good weather. How do they pay? To enjoy the weather in San Diego on a regular basis, you have to live in San Diego—you have to have housing. There is a demand for housing in San Diego, just as there is a demand for housing in other places. Is the demand for housing in San Diego higher than it would be if the weather were not so good? Without the good weather, living in San Diego would not be as pleasurable and, therefore, the demand to live there would be lower. In short, the demand for housing in San Diego is higher because San Diego enjoys good weather. It follows that the price of housing is higher too. Thus, San Diegans indirectly pay for their good weather because they pay higher housing prices than they would if San Diego had bad weather.

Was our representative San Diegan right when he said the good weather was free?

Self-Test

1. Give an example to illustrate that someone may "pay" for clean air in much the same way that she "pays" for good weather.

2. If people pay for good weather, who ultimately receives the "good-weather payment"?

APPLICATION 11: PAYING ALL PROFESSORS THE SAME SALARY

In college, you take various courses. You may take courses in accounting, economics, English, and history. From your perspective, the professors in the courses may do much the same work. Each professor regularly comes to class, lectures and leads discussions, holds office hours, gives tests and exams, grades those tests and exams, and so on. Does it follow, then, that all professors of equal experience ought to be paid the same salary? In other words, if a professor in computer science with 10 years of experience earns $100,000 a year, should a professor in history with 10 years of experience earn $100,000 a year too? If your answer is yes, then what might the effects of such a policy be?

Let's again turn to supply and demand for an answer. Exhibit 7a shows the market for accounting professors; Exhibit 7b, the market for history professors. In each market there is a demand for and supply of professors. However, the equilibrium wage in the accounting market (W_A) is higher than the equilibrium wage in the history market (W_H).

exhibit 7

Paying Professors the Same Salary

Suppose the market supply and demand conditions are as shown in (a) for accounting professors and as shown in (b) for history professors. Consequently, the equilibrium wage in the two markets would be different. As shown, the equilibrium wage for accounting professors (W_A) is higher than the equilibrium wage for history professors (W_H). What happens if both accounting and history professors are paid W_A? A surplus of history professors appears. What happens if both accounting and history professors are paid W_H? A shortage of accounting professors appears. Paying all college professors the same salary when there are differences in demand and supply creates shortages and surpluses.

(a) Market for Accounting Professors

(b) Market for History Professors

Go to *http://www.colorado.edu/pba/fcq*, and click "By college, subject, and course number." Next, select "College of Arts and Sciences," and then "Economics." Look at the course evaluations for Econ 1000, which show actual student evaluations received by professors. Do some professors get higher grades from their students than other professors do? Do some professors expect less work? Are some more accessible than others? What impact do you think publishing this information will have on the quality of teaching? How might it affect the amount of work professors require of their students?

If accounting and history professors are each paid their respective equilibrium wage, neither market will be in shortage or surplus. But pay both professors the same wage when their equilibrium wages are different, and shortages or surpluses will appear.

For example, suppose both accounting and history professors are paid the higher wage, W_A. The accounting market remains in equilibrium, but a surplus appears in the history market. There will be more historians who want to work at colleges (N_2) than colleges will hire (N_3).

Or suppose both accounting and history professors are paid the lower wage, W_H. The history market remains in equilibrium, but a shortage appears in the accounting market. Colleges will want to hire more accountants (N_2) than will be willing to work at the colleges (N_3).

Sitting in class, you may think that while the supply-and-demand analysis of the accounting and history markets is interesting, it does not affect you. What does it matter if your professors are paid the same or not?

But look at the number of professors hired in each market at the equilibrium wage and at the disequilibrium wage. In the accounting market, when the wage is W_A, N_1 accounting professors are hired. At W_H, only N_3 are hired because N_3 is the number of accounting professors who are willing and able to work at W_H. N_3 is less than N_1.

In the history market, when the wage is W_H, N_1 history professors are hired. At W_A, N_3 are hired because N_3 is the number of history professors colleges are willing and able to hire at W_A. N_3 is less than N_1.

In short, more professors are working at colleges teaching students when professors are paid equilibrium wages than when they are paid disequilibrium wages. So, how professors are paid affects the student-to-faculty ratio. Instead of 40 students per faculty member at disequilibrium wages, we might have 30 students per faculty member at equilibrium wages.

Self-Test

1. Suppose the supply of biology and computer science professors is the same but the demand for computer scientists is greater than the demand for biologists. Furthermore, suppose both biologists and computer scientists are paid the same wage. If a shortage exists in both fields, in which field is the shortage greater? Explain your answer.

2. Under what condition might an economist propose that all college professors (irrespective of their field) be paid the same?

APPLICATION 12: ARE NEW CAR COMPANIES HURT BY THE USED CAR MARKET?

New car dealers sometimes complain that the used car market hurts them. They argue that the demand for new cars would be higher if the used car market did not exist. How so? Consider Shelly, who just bought a new car. She plans to keep the car for six years, after which time she will sell it on the used car market. The person who buys Shelly's used car might have bought a new car instead had the used car market not existed. In other words, without the used car market, there would be more buyers for new cars, and therefore the demand for new cars would be higher.

But new car dealers may overlook an important fact. People may have stronger preferences for a new car if a used car market exists than if it does not exist. To illustrate, suppose we ask Shelly two questions. First, "What is the maximum price you would pay for a new Honda Accord if you *could not sell* the car at a later date (in other words, if there is no used car market)?" Let's assume she answers $20,000. Second, "What is the maximum price you would pay for a new Honda Accord if you *could sell* the car at a later date (in other words, if the used car market exists)?" If her answer is more than $20,000—say, $23,000—then her demand for a new car is higher when the used car market exists than when it does not exist.

Is Shelly's maximum price for a Honda Accord likely to be higher with the used car market than without it? We think so. The ability to sell something purchased earlier is valuable to people, and they are willing to pay for this option.

In conclusion, the existence of the used car market implies (1) fewer buyers for new cars and (2) a stronger preference for new cars. Fewer buyers for new cars means a *lower demand* for new cars, but a stronger preference for new cars means a *higher demand* for new cars. Which variable affects demand more? We do not know. But certainly it is possible for the two variables to cancel each other out so that on net, the demand for new cars is the same with the used car market as without it.

Self-Test

1. Suppose a company is building new houses in an undeveloped area of a community. The local government imposes a special tax on the buyers of these new homes, the revenues of which will be used for road construction in and around the new development. The people who buy the new houses complain that no one else has to pay a special tax for road construction, so why should they? There is little doubt that they believe they pay the full tax, but do they? Explain your answer.

2. Some companies offer rebates on the goods they sell. For example, they may advertise a good for, say, $40, but then offer a $10 rebate for buying the good. They argue that this effectively reduces the price to $30 (after the rebate). Are there similarities between rebates and being able to sell your old car on the used car market?

APPLICATION 13: SUPPLY AND DEMAND ON A FREEWAY

What does a traffic jam on a busy freeway in any large city have to do with supply and demand? Actually, it has quite a bit to do with supply and demand. Look at it this way: There is a demand for driving on the freeway and a supply of freeway space. The supply of freeway space is fixed (freeways do not expand and contract over a day, week, or month). The demand, however, fluctuates. It is higher at some times than at other times. For example, we would expect the demand for driving on the freeway to be higher at 8 A.M. (rush hour) than at 11 P.M. But even though the demand may vary, the money price for driving on the freeway is always the same—zero. A zero money price means that motorists do not pay tolls to drive on the freeway.

Exhibit 8 shows two demand curves for driving on the freeway: $D_{8A.M.}$ and $D_{11P.M.}$. We have assumed the demand at 8 A.M. is greater than at 11 P.M. We have also assumed that at $D_{11P.M.}$ and zero money price the freeway market clears: Quantity demanded of freeway space equals quantity supplied of freeway space. At the higher demand, $D_{8A.M.}$, however, this is not the case. At zero money price, a shortage of freeway space exists: Quantity demanded of freeway space is greater than quantity supplied of freeway space. The shortage appears in the form of freeway congestion, bumper-to-bumper traffic. One way to eliminate the shortage is through an increase in the money price of driving on the freeway at 8 A.M. For example, as Exhibit 8 shows, a toll of 70 cents would clear the freeway market at 8 A.M.

exhibit 8

Freeway Congestion and Supply and Demand
The demand for driving on the freeway is higher at 8 A.M. than at 11 P.M. At zero money price and $D_{11P.M.}$, the freeway market clears. At zero money price and $D_{8A.M.}$, there is a shortage of freeway space, which shows up as freeway congestion. At a price (toll) of 70 cents, the shortage is eliminated and freeway congestion disappears.

At 8 A.M. and $0 price, there is freeway congestion.

If charging different prices (tolls) at different times of the day on freeways sounds like an unusual idea, consider how Miami Beach hotels price their rooms. They charge different prices for their rooms at different times of the year. During the winter months when the demand for vacationing in Miami Beach is high, the hotels charge higher prices than when the demand is (relatively) low. If different prices were charged for freeway space at different times of the day, freeway space would be rationed the same way Miami Beach hotel rooms are rationed.

Before we leave this topic, let's consider the three alternatives usually proposed for freeway congestion. Some people propose tolls, some propose building more freeways, and others propose encouraging carpooling. Tolls deal with the congestion problem by adjusting price to its equilibrium level, as shown in Exhibit 8. Building more freeways deals with the problem by increasing supply. In Exhibit 8, it would be necessary to shift the supply curve of freeway space to the right so there is no longer any shortage of space at 8 A.M. More carpooling deals with the problem by decreasing demand. Two people in one car takes up less space on a freeway than two people in two cars. In Exhibit 8, if through carpooling the demand at 8 A.M. begins to look like the demand at 11 P.M., then there is no longer a shortage of freeway space at 8 A.M.

THINKING LIKE AN ECONOMIST

The economist knows that when there are buyers and sellers of anything (bread, cars, or freeway space), only three conditions are possible—equilibrium, shortage, or surplus. When the economist sees traffic congestion, the first thing that comes to mind is that there is a shortage of road space. Buy why is there a shortage? The economist knows that shortages occur at prices below equilibrium price. In other words, price is too low.

Self-Test

1. In Exhibit 8, at what price is there a surplus of freeway space at 8 A.M.?

2. If the driving population increases in an area and the supply of freeway space remains constant, what will happen to freeway congestion? Explain your answer.

APPLICATION 14: WHAT DOES PRICE HAVE TO DO WITH GETTING TO CLASS ON TIME?

Class starts at 10 o'clock in the morning. At 10:09, Pam Ferrario walks in late. She apologizes to the instructor, saying, "I've been on campus for 20 minutes, but I couldn't find a parking space." Her classmates nod, knowing full well what she is talking about. Here at the university, especially between the hours of 8 A.M. and 2 P.M., parking spaces are hard to find.

This scene is replayed every day at many universities and colleges across the country. Students are late for class because on many days there isn't a parking space to be found. Why can't students find parking spaces? The immediate answer is because there is a shortage of parking spaces. But why is there a shortage of parking spaces? There is a shortage of parking spaces for the same reason there is any shortage: the equilibrium price is not being charged.

Who pays for the shortage of parking spaces? The students pay—not in money, but in time. Because students know parking spaces on campus are hard to find, they often leave home or work sooner than they would if there were no shortages. Or like Pam Ferrario, they pay by being late to class.

Are there alternatives to the *pay-in-time* and *pay-in-being-late-to-class* schemes for rationing campus parking spots? Some economists have suggested a *pay-in-price* scheme. For example, the university could install meters in the parking lot and raise the fee high enough so that between the hours of 8 A.M. and 2 P.M., the quantity demanded for parking spaces equals the quantity supplied.

Such suggestions are sometimes criticized on the basis that students must pay the fee, no matter how high, in order to attend classes. But that's not exactly true. Parking off campus and using public transportation are sometimes alternatives. But this is not really the main point. The issue isn't paying or not paying, but choosing *how* to pay—in dollar price, time, or being late for class.

Some economists have taken the pay-in-price scheme further and have argued that parking spots should be auctioned on a yearly basis. In other words, a student would rent a parking spot for a year. This way the student would always know that a parking spot would be open when he or she arrived at the campus. People who parked in someone else's spot would be ticketed by campus police.

Additionally, under this scheme, a student who rented a parking spot and chose not to use it between certain hours of the day could rent it to someone else during this period. So we would expect to see notices like this on campus billboards:

PARKING SPOT FOR RENT
Near Arts Building and Student Union. Ideal for liberal arts students. Available on a 2–12 hour basis between 12 noon and 12 midnight. Rate: 50 cents per hour. Call 555-3564.

THINKING LIKE AN
ECONOMIST
The economist knows that just because someone doesn't pay a price in money terms, it doesn't mean there is no price to pay. People can pay for something in time. In fact, when money prices are below equilibrium levels, individuals usually pay in terms of something else (such as time).

Self-Test

1. If a person pays for something in terms of time, he or she is really paying in terms of money. Do you agree or disagree? Explain your answer.

2. Suppose at the price of $1 a day for parking, quantity supplied is equal to quantity demanded. What happens if the demand for parking rises more than the supply of parking and the price of parking is kept constant at $1 a day?

APPLICATION 15: AISLE SEATS ON COMMERCIAL AIRPLANES

You may have noticed that there are the same number of aisle seats as there are middle seats on commercial airplanes. For example, if there are 50 aisle seats, there are 50 middle seats too. Thus, the supply curve for aisle seats and middle seats is the same (a vertical line at 50 seats). But demand is not the same for the two types of seats because most people prefer aisle seats. So, the demand curve for aisle seats is to the right of the demand curve for middle seats.

What effect will this preference have on price? Well, if the demand for aisle seats is higher than the demand for middle seats but the supply of both types of seats is the same, then the equilibrium price will be higher for aisle seats than for middle seats. For example, suppose the equilibrium price for a middle seat is $100. Then, the equilibrium price for an aisle seat will be, perhaps, $145.

But airlines charge the same price for aisle and middle seats. In other words, if they are charging the equilibrium price for the middle seat, then they must be charging a below-equilibrium price for the aisle seat. At a below-equilibrium price, there will be a shortage of aisle seats. More people will want aisle seats (say, 80) than there are aisle seats available (say, 50). Suppose you are one of the 80 people who wants an aisle seat. How can you be one of the 50 people to get one? One way is to be one of the first 50 people to ask for an aisle seat. In other words, aisle seats are likely to be rationed by first-come-first-served. The people who are first to check in at the airport get the aisle seats (no flyer ever asks for a middle seat); the latecomers get the middle seats.

This analysis raises some additional questions for you to think about: If the equilibrium price for an aisle seat is higher than the equilibrium price for a middle seat, then why don't the airlines charge higher prices for aisle seats than for middle seats? Why not fully ration all seats by dollar price instead of rationing aisle seats partly by dollar price and partly by first-come-first-served?

THINKING LIKE AN ECONOMIST

The economist knows that it is often possible to break one market into submarkets. For example, the market for seats on an airplane can be broken into three submarkets: one for window seats, one for aisle seats, and one for middle seats. If the demand and supply conditions in these submarkets are not identical, then neither will be the equilibrium price. When airlines sell all seats for the same price, one or more submarkets will be out of equilibrium. Economists look for the consequences of disequilibria in markets.

Self-Test

1. Southwest Airlines is one of the few airlines that will not reserve seats for customers. In other words, buying a ticket on Southwest permits one to enter the airplane, but once on the airplane, it is up to the customer to locate a seat. Will the lines of people waiting to board a Southwest Airlines flight be longer than, shorter than, or the same length as the lines of people waiting to board airline flights where reserved seats are permitted?

2. There are two flights, A and B. The demand for aisle seats on flight A is greater than the demand for aisle seats on flight B, but the demand for middle seats on both flights is the same. If the same price is charged for an aisle seat and a middle seat and that price equals the equilibrium price for middle seats, then on which flight will the rationing device first-come-first-served be more extensively employed?

3. How is the discussion about seats on a commercial airline similar to the discussion of paying all professors the same wage?

APPLICATION 16: 10 O'CLOCK CLASSES IN COLLEGE

A situation similar to aisle seats on an airplane occurs for some university and college classes. Suppose an economics class is offered in the same classroom at 10 o'clock in the morning and at 8 o'clock at night. Most students would prefer the 10 A.M. class to the 8 P.M. class. Notice in Exhibit 9 that the supply of seats in the class is the same at each time but the demand to occupy those seats is not. Because the demand is greater for the 10 A.M. class than for the 8 P.M. class, the equilibrium price for the 10 A.M. class is higher than the equilibrium price for the 8 P.M. class.

But the university or college charges the same tuition no matter what time students choose to take the class. The university doesn't charge students a higher tuition if they enroll in 10 A.M. classes than if they enroll in 8 P.M. classes.

Suppose a tuition of T_1 is charged for all classes and T_1 is the equilibrium tuition for 8 P.M. classes (see Exhibit 9). It follows that T_1 is below the equilibrium tuition for 10 A.M. classes. At T_1, the quantity demanded of seats for 10 o'clock classes will be greater than the quantity supplied; more students will want the 10 o'clock class than there is space available.

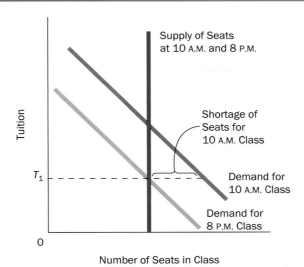

exhibit 9

The Supply and Demand for College Classes at Different Times

A given class is offered at two times, 10 A.M. and 8 P.M. The supply of seats in the classroom is the same at both times; however, the student demand for the 10 o'clock class is higher than the demand for the 8 o'clock class. The university charges the same tuition, T_1, regardless of which class a student takes. At this tuition, there is a shortage of seats for the 10 o'clock class. Seats are likely to be rationed on a first-come-first-served (first to register) basis or on seniority (seniors take precedence over juniors, etc.).

How will the university allocate the available seats? It may do it the same way that airlines ration aisle seats, that is, on a first-come-first-served basis. Those students who are first to register get the 10 A.M. class; the latecomers have to take the 8 P.M. class. Or the university could ration these "high demand classes" by giving their upperclass students (seniors) first priority.

THINKING LIKE AN ECONOMIST *The layperson sees students clamoring to get 10 A.M. classes and concludes that the demand is high for classes at this time. He then wonders why the university doesn't schedule more 10 A.M. classes. The economist knows that what the layperson sees is as much an effect of price as of demand. The demand for 10 A.M. classes may be high, but the quantity demanded may not be if the price is high enough. In fact, even though the demand for various classes at various times may be different, there is some set of prices that will make the quantity demanded of each class the same.*

Self-Test

1. Suppose college students are given two options. With option *A,* the price a student pays for a class is always the equilibrium price. For example, if the equilibrium price to take Economics 101 is $600 at 10 A.M. and is $400 at 4 P.M., then students pay more for the 10 A.M. class than they do for the 4 P.M. class. With option *B,* the price a student pays for a class is the same regardless of the time the class is taken. When given the choice between options *A* and *B,* many students would say they prefer option *B* to *A.* Is this the case for you? If so, why would this be your choice?

2. How is the analysis of the 10 o'clock class similar to the analysis of aisle seats on commercial airplanes?

APPLICATION 17: TIPPING AT A LAS VEGAS SHOW

Most of the big hotel-casinos in Las Vegas have elaborate entertainment shows. To get a good seat at many (but not all) Las Vegas shows, you have to tip (in advance) the person who seats you. Tourists in Las Vegas usually complain, "I don't know why I have to pay that guy $20 to walk me to my seat. It's ridiculous." But is it?

In Las Vegas, all tickets for the same show sell for the same price (unlike tickets for a Broadway play, baseball game, or symphony concert). Buying a ticket to a Las Vegas show guarantees a seat, but it could be *any* seat in the house. It could be a good seat up front or a bad seat way in the back.

The show, therefore, has two markets: a market for good seats and a market for bad seats.[4] In each market there is a demand for and a supply of seats. The bad seats market is shown in Exhibit 10a, the good seats market in Exhibit 10b.

Normally, different market conditions (different demand and supply curves) would bring about different equilibrium prices. The hotel-casino, however, sells all tickets for the same price, say $50. This is the equilibrium price in the bad seats market, but as the exhibit shows, it is a below-equilibrium price in the good seats market. The result is a shortage of good seats.

How are the "too few" good seats rationed? They are rationed by price, but in an unusual way. As the exhibit shows, the equilibrium price for a good seat is $70: $50 is paid to the hotel-casino that sells you the ticket and $20 is paid as a tip to the person who seats you at the show. In other words, the tip is equal to the difference between the equilibrium price for a good seat and the admission price for the show (which is equal to the equilibrium price of a bad seat).

Tip for a good seat = Equibrium price of a good seat
− Admission price to the show

An interesting question to ask is: Why don't the hotel-casinos sell tickets to their shows the same way a ticket to a baseball game or a Broadway play is sold? Broadway plays and baseball games have reserved seating, and you pay a higher price for a better seat. Why not do the same in Las Vegas? Don't the owner-operators of the hotel-casinos in Las Vegas realize they are losing $20 on each good seat? Why don't they capture this $20 instead of letting their employees get it?

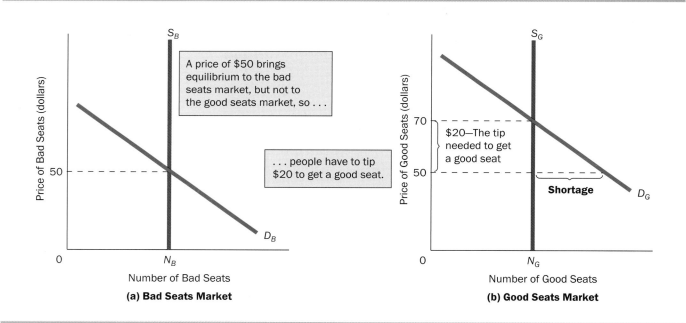

exhibit 10

Good and Bad Seats at a Las Vegas Show
If demand and supply conditions are different in the good seats and bad seats markets but the same price is charged in both markets, then at least one market is in disequilibrium. We have assumed the bad seats market is in equilibrium at $50, but at this price, there is a shortage in the good seats market. To get a good seat a customer must pay a tip equal to the difference between the equilibrium price for a good seat and the $50 admission price to the show.

A price of $50 brings equilibrium to the bad seats market, but not to the good seats market, so . . .

. . . people have to tip $20 to get a good seat.

$20—The tip needed to get a good seat

Shortage

(a) Bad Seats Market

(b) Good Seats Market

4. A person can see the show from a "bad" or "not-so-good" seat; but it is not so easy or comfortable to see the show from a bad seat as from a good seat.

118 Part 1 Economics: The Science of Scarcity

As odd as it may sound, Las Vegas hotel-casino owner-operators may want the price of a good seat to be too low (below equilibrium). If it is, it will generate a shortage of good seats, which will result in people trying to get the good seats in numerous ways. Many people visiting Las Vegas, who are unfamiliar with how things work, may think that the way to get a good seat for a show is to arrive at the show door early. The showroom is usually just off the casino. If enough people think they can get a good seat by being one of the first in line, long lines of people will be waiting in the casino for the showroom doors to open. Interestingly enough, people waiting in line near blackjack tables, roulette wheels, and hundreds of slot machines can do only one thing: gamble. It is very common to see people playing slot machines while standing in line for a show. The hotel-casinos, in other words, may deliberately price good show seats too low, knowing that this will lead to long lines of people with time to gamble. What the hotel-casino loses on the show may be more than made up for at the slot machines.

 THINKING LIKE AN ECONOMIST

At first glance, it looks as if the hotel-casino loses revenue when it chooses not to set equilibrium prices for the various submarkets of seats at a show. For example, when the equilibrium price of a good seat is $70 and the equilibrium price of a bad seat is $50, then the hotel-casino loses $20 on each good seat if it charges $50 for all seats. The first reaction may be to ask, "Why would the hotel-casino forfeit $20 per good seat?" The layperson might answer this question by saying that the hotel-casino simply made a mistake, or that it doesn't know what the equilibrium price is for various seats, or something along these lines. The economist wonders: Is there a good, solid economic reason for the hotel-casinos to forfeit income? The answer is yes if by forfeiting income in one area the hotel-casinos more than compensate for it in another. The reaction of the economist is not to say the hotel-casino has made a mistake, but to ask what the hotel-casino knows that she doesn't.

Self-Test

1. At a Broadway show, good seats fetch higher prices than not-so-good seats. A seat up front may cost $150, while a seat in the back of the playhouse might sell for less than half this amount. Why doesn't Broadway price its tickets the same way that Las Vegas prices its tickets?

2. What does the tip for a good seat depend upon?

APPLICATION 18: WHAT IS THE PRICE OF AN "A"?

The law of demand doesn't operate just on goods with explicit prices. Unpopular teachers sometimes try to increase class enrollment by raising the average grade of the students in their courses, thereby reducing the price of the course to the student.
—Richard Posner, *Economic Analysis of the Law*

At many universities and colleges, students can take a given course from any one of several professors. For example, Francine may be able to take English 101 from Professor Brown or Professor Lawson. Now suppose that both Professor Brown and Professor Lawson are considered good instructors, but students consider

Professor Lawson slightly better than Professor Brown. For example, on a scale of 1 to 10, Professor Brown gets an 8 and Professor Lawson gets a 10. Will Francine necessarily take the course from Professor Lawson instead of Professor Brown? No. Professor Brown may "compensate" for a relatively lesser reputation by lowering the price of the course to the student. For example, Professor Brown may lower the time it takes a student in his class to get a good grade. To illustrate, suppose that the average student has to work seven hours a week to get an "A" in Professor Lawson's class, but only six hours a week to get an "A" in Professor Brown's class. The demand (of students) to get into Lawson's class may be higher than the demand to get into Brown's class (because Lawson is considered a better instructor, she is, in some sense, a "higher-quality" good). However, the price of an "A" in Brown's class is certainly lower than in Lawson's class. (See Exhibit 11.)

Is it possible for the same number of students to want to be in each of the two professors' classes? It certainly is, as Exhibit 11 shows. Quantity demanded of seats in class (1 seat = 1 student) is 30 in both Brown's class and Lawson's class.

THINKING LIKE AN ECONOMIST

The economist knows that low demand and low price can generate the same quantity demanded as high demand and high price. In fact, low demand and low price can generate an even greater quantity demanded than that generated by high demand and high price. For example, suppose students choose professor A over professor B for a given course. Does it follow that the demand is greater for professor A than for professor B? Not necessarily, says the economist. Professor A may simply charge a much lower price for a good grade than professor B charges. In fact, the demand for professor B may be higher than the demand for professor A, but professor B charges such a high price for a good grade relative to professor A that more students want to take professor A's class.

Self-Test

1. If more people want to read romance novels than classic novels, it holds that the demand for romance novels is greater than the demand for classic novels. Do you agree or disagree? Explain your answer.

2. Popularity is a function of demand, not price. Do you agree or disagree? Explain your answer.

exhibit 11

The Price of an "A"
Both Brown and Lawson are good professors, but students perceive Lawson as slightly better than Brown. The demand (by students) to be in Lawson's class is greater than the demand to be in Brown's class. However, Brown charges a lower price for an "A" than does Lawson. At the prices that each charges, the same number of students want to be in Brown's class (30) as want to be in Lawson's class (30).

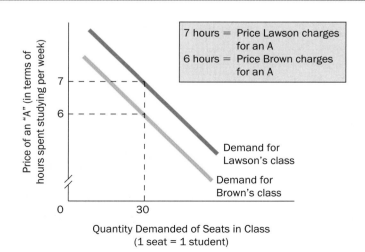

APPLICATION 19: WHY ARE SPEEDING TICKETS SO EXPENSIVE? OR, TWO WAYS TO GET THE SAME PRICE

Drivers usually speed more often than they get caught for speeding. For example, Jenny may drive over the speed limit 40 times a year, but only get caught once every two years. The price for speeding is equal to the price of a speeding ticket times the probability of getting caught. For example, if there is a 1 in 20 chance of being caught for speeding and the price of a speeding ticket is $200, then the price for speeding is not $200, but $\frac{1}{20}$ of $200, or $10.

Price of speeding = Speeding ticket price $\times$ Probability of getting caught for speeding

Suppose a police force has six police officers whose job is to apprehend speeders. With six officers working each day, the probability of a speeder being caught for speeding is, say, 5 percent (1 in 20 chance). We would expect that the lower the price of speeding, the more people will speed. Suppose the data look like this:

Speeding Ticket	Probability of Getting Caught for Speeding	Price of Speeding (Speeding Ticket $\times$ Probability of Getting Caught)	Number of People Who Will Speed
$200	5 percent (0.05)	$10.00	100
$100	5 percent	$ 5.00	200
$ 50	5 percent	$ 2.50	400

According to these data, if a speeding ticket is set at $100, the price of speeding is $5 and 200 people will speed. What is the cost to taxpayers of apprehending speeders?[5] It is the sum of the cost per day of hiring the six police officers. If each police officer is paid $200 a day, then the daily cost is $1,200.

Now suppose the taxpayers decide they want to cut costs in half by reducing the number of police officers from six to three. However, they don't want any more people to speed than have been speeding. They think more people are likely to speed if there are fewer officers patrolling. Let's say that with only three officers patrolling, the probability of being caught for speeding falls from 5 percent to 2.5 percent. If this is the case, then at the current price for a speeding ticket ($100), the price of speeding falls to $2.50. We know from the data that if the price of speeding is $2.50, 400 people will speed.

How can the taxpayers cut the police force, reduce costs, and make sure that no more people speed each day? They can increase the price of a speeding ticket. For example, if the price of a speeding ticket is raised to $200, and the probability of getting caught for speeding is 2.5 percent, the price of speeding is $5. This is the same price of speeding as when the ticket price was $100 and the probability of getting caught was 5 percent.

$200 speeding ticket and 2.5 percent chance of being caught = $5
$100 speeding ticket and 5 percent chance of being caught = $5

It follows that the same number of people will speed (200) at the $200 ticket price and a 2.5 percent probability of getting caught as were speeding at the $100 ticket price and 5 percent probability of getting caught. But police costs will be lower ($600 instead of $1,200) with three officers and a $200 ticket price than with six officers and a $100 ticket price.

So, why are speeding tickets so expensive? By charging a high price to speeders who get caught, taxpayers can reduce police costs without increasing the number of speeders.

---

5. Of the 200 speeders, 5 percent (10 of them) will be caught for speeding.

The economist knows that there is often more than one way to achieve a particular outcome. For example, there are at least two ways to reduce the number of speeders. One way is to increase the number of police officers, which increases the number of speeders apprehended. As the probability of being apprehended for speeding rises, there will be fewer speeders. Another way is to increase the price of a speeding ticket. As the price of a speeding ticket rises, the quantity consumed of "speeding" by speeders will decline.

Self-Test

1. A friend calls you on the telephone and tells you to be careful driving to work today because there is a "speed trap" near 12th Street and Georges Avenue. If you drive slower near the "speed trap" than you usually do, what does this tell you about your behavior and the price of speeding tickets?

2. If police officers receive an increase in their income, do you think the price of a speeding ticket is likely to fall, rise, or stay the same? Explain your answer.

APPLICATION 20: WILL A SELF-INTERESTED, PROFIT-SEEKING OIL PRODUCER CONSERVE OIL FOR THE FUTURE?

Tex Baldwin is an oil producer; he pumps crude oil from under his property and sells it to refineries. It costs him $10 to extract one barrel of oil and he sells each barrel for $15. At this $15 price, he pumps and sells 1 million barrels of crude oil each year. In other words, at $15 per barrel, quantity supplied is 1 million barrels.

One day Tex reads a report indicating that in five years oil will be relatively more scarce than it is today; as a result, the price of oil will rise to $30 a barrel. Tex can continue to pump and sell oil today or he can leave the oil in the ground and pump and sell it in five years. Tex Baldwin is interested in maximizing his profits. Do you predict he will pump and sell now or pump and sell in five years?

Let's analyze Tex's situation. If he pumps and sells oil today, he earns a profit of $5 per barrel; if he pumps and sells oil five years from now, he will earn a profit of $20 per barrel.[6] Of course, if he leaves the oil in the ground, he cannot earn interest on the $5 profit per barrel. Suppose he can earn 5 percent interest on every $1 he saves. Thus, a profit of $5 a barrel today will return approximately $6.40 in five years. Comparing $6.40 a barrel with $20 a barrel, Tex realizes that he will maximize his profits by leaving the oil in the ground.

Instead of reducing the quantity of oil he supplies to the market from 1 million barrels to nothing, Tex decides to cut back to supplying 100,000 barrels. He needs some income to meet his annual financial obligations.

Before Tex expected the price of oil to rise, he supplied 1 million barrels of oil to the market; afterward, he supplied 100,000 barrels. This is how we define a decrease in the supply of oil: less oil supplied at a given price. In other words, as the expected price of oil increased, the current supply of oil decreased.

From a societal perspective, it is interesting that Tex, who only wants to maximize his profits, ends up conserving a resource (oil) that is expected to become relatively more scarce in the future. In fact, because of his desire for profit, oil in the future will likely be relatively less scarce than initially expected (after all, Tex is saving oil for the future). The individual's desire for profit does not necessarily conflict with society's need to conserve resources.

---

6. We are assuming that the cost of extracting oil is not higher in five years than it is today.

The layperson often thinks that greed, self-interest, or the desire for profit could never be a motivation behind conservation. The economist knows this is not true. When the expected price of a resource is higher than the current price, the resource owner may simply conserve (hold on to) the resource today and wait to sell it in the future. In short, the economist knows that greedy, self-interested, profit-seekers care not only about current prices but also about future prices.

Self-Test

1. Suppose there is oil under a 100 square mile area in Texas that no one owns. Since the area belongs to no one, anyone who wants to drill for the oil can do so freely. The difference between this case and the case discussed in the application is that Tex owned the land in the application but no one owns this land. Is oil (under the ground) that is owned by someone more or less likely to be conserved than oil (under the ground) that is owned by no one? Explain your answer.

2. Suppose Tex Baldwin expects to die in a year. Is he more or less likely to conserve oil for the future? Does it matter to your answer whether Tex has children or not?

APPLICATION 21: WHERE WILL PEOPLE BUY RELATIVELY MORE APPLES?

Apples grow in the state of Washington and do not grow in New York City. In which place, Washington or New York City, would you predict that relatively more high-quality apples are consumed, *ceteris paribus?* The layperson's prediction is usually, "Washington—because people in Washington have greater access to high-quality apples."

Is this the same prediction and explanation an economist would offer? To see, let's consider the matter carefully. Suppose that both high-quality and medium-quality apples are grown in the state of Washington. Their absolute or money prices are 10 cents and 5 cents, respectively. It follows that the relative price of a high-quality apple is 2 medium-quality apples.

Now suppose the cost of transporting apples to New York City is 5 cents per apple, irrespective of quality. In New York City, therefore, the price of a high-quality apple is 15 cents and the price of a medium-quality apple is 10 cents. It follows that the relative price of a high-quality apple is 1.5 medium-quality apples. In short, although the absolute prices of both types of apples is higher in New York City than in Washington, the relative price of high-quality apples is lower in New York City than in Washington.

An economist would predict that relatively more high-quality apples will be eaten where high-quality apples are relatively cheaper. This is in New York City.

Q & A

Q: Is there a difference between New Yorkers buying *relatively more* high-quality apples and New Yorkers buying *more* high-quality apples?

A: Yes. *More* indicates a larger absolute number; *relatively more* indicates a greater percentage. For example, New Yorkers may be buying relatively more high-quality apples than Washingtonians, but they are still buying fewer high-quality apples.

Let's say that Washingtonians buy 10,000 high-quality apples and 30,000 medium-quality apples, and New Yorkers buy 5,000 high-quality apples and 7,500 medium-quality apples. Washingtonians buy *more* high-quality apples, but New Yorkers buy *relatively more* high-quality apples. Of the 12,500 apples that New Yorkers buy, 40 percent are high-quality apples; of the 40,000 apples that Washingtonians buy, 25 percent are high-quality apples.

When is a change not a change? To answer this question, consider two goods, X and Y. The price of X is $40 and the price of Y is $80. At these absolute prices, if a person purchases one unit of Y, she gives up the opportunity to buy two units of X. Now suppose the prices of X and Y double: X is now $80 and Y is $160. Are these changes in absolute prices really a change? Some people would say yes; after all, X went from $40 to $80 and Y went from $80 to $160. But other people would say no because at the higher absolute prices a person still gives up two units of X to purchase one unit of Y.

According to economists, equal percentage changes in absolute prices do not constitute a meaningful change. A meaningful change is one that causes peoples' behavior to change. According to economists, only relative changes (such as a change in the relative price of a good) can do this.

A Reader Asks...
How Do I Find My Own Supply-and-Demand Applications?

I can understand an economist's applications of supply and demand, but I don't know how to apply supply and demand myself. How do I find my own supply-and-demand applications?

You can proceed in several ways, two of which we discuss here. First, you can heed the words of Robert Solow, "I am a supply-and-demand economist. When I come across something, I ask myself what is being transferred here and where does the supply come from and where does the demand come from."

We can reformulate what Solow has said into a single question: Is trade involved? This is the relevant supply-and-demand question because supply and demand are about trade. In other words, when you observe something, simply ask: Is this about trade? If you are driving on a freeway, ask: Is driving on a freeway about trade? Specifically, is something being "bought" and "sold"? If so, what? If you are applying to college, ask: Is this about trade? What is being bought and sold?

A second way to proceed is to look for surpluses and shortages around you. Surpluses and shortages are manifestations of market disequilibrium. If you find them, you can be fairly sure that supply and demand are rele-

vant. If you are sitting in a classroom with empty seats, ask: Is there a surplus or shortage here? In this case, of course, there is a surplus, which should lead you to think about price. Surpluses exist when prices are too high. Why is the price too high? If you observe more people applying to a particular college than the college will admit, ask: Is there a surplus or shortage here? In this case there is a shortage, which again should lead you to think about price. Shortages exist when prices are too low. Why is price too low?

The key to finding your own supply-and-demand applications is to (1) observe things around you and then (2) ask questions about the things you observe. If you are sitting in a restaurant eating a meal, ask questions about what you observe. Is trade involved here? Yes. Is the restaurant filled to capacity and is there a line of people waiting to get in? Yes. Are there more people who want to eat at this restaurant than there are spaces to accommodate them? Yes. Is there a shortage here? Yes. Why do shortages exist? Prices are too low. Why doesn't the restaurant raise its prices and eliminate the shortage?

The process isn't that hard, is it?

Chapter Summary

Why Do Colleges Use GPAs, ACTs, and SATs for Purposes of Admission?
- Colleges and universities charging students less than the equilibrium tuition for admission create a shortage of spaces at the colleges or universities. Consequently, colleges and universities have to impose

some nonprice rationing device, such as GPAs or ACT or SAT scores.

Can Prejudice Affect Wages?
- Prejudice directed by employers toward a group of employees can lower the demand for and the wages

of these employees. If these lower-wage employees are as productive as the higher-wage employees who have not felt the effects of prejudice, then nondiscriminator employers can lower their costs by hiring the lower-wage employees. Nondiscriminator employers are then able to underprice discriminator employers.

Legalization of Marijuana

* If the purchase and sale of marijuana are legalized, the price of marijuana may rise, fall, or remain the same. The price will depend on whether the demand for marijuana rises by more than, less than, or equal to the rise in the supply of marijuana.

The Minimum Wage

* A minimum wage (above equilibrium wage) reduces the number of unskilled workers working or reduces the number of unskilled labor hours purchased by employers.

Price Ceiling in the Kidney Market

* Currently, there is a price ceiling in the kidney market, and the price is set at $0. Many of the effects of a price ceiling (shortages, fewer exchanges, and so on) are seen in the kidney market.

Crisis in the Electricity Market

* A shortage of electricity is likely to result in a setting where (1) prices in the wholesale electricity market rise due to increased demand and higher generating costs and (2) prices in the retail electricity market are controlled.

Gold Prices and House Prices

* Gold prices are the same everywhere in the world, but house prices are not. When the price of a good is higher in one location than in another location and that good can be moved from the lower-priced location to the higher-priced location, then the price of the good will end up being the same in both locations. Obviously, if the good cannot be moved from the lower-priced location to the higher-priced location, then the price of the good will not end up being the same in both locations.

Gas Prices

* After the September 11 attack on the World Trade Center and the Pentagon, gas prices at some gas stations increased. A few days later, prices were back down to pre-attack levels. Did the prices fall to normal levels because gas station owners were threatened with fines and lawsuits or because supply and demand hadn't changed in a way to justify the higher prices? We think it the latter. Although some gas station owners raised prices, other gas station owners held prices constant. Obviously, the gas sta-

tion owners who raised prices would have lost considerable business if they had kept gas prices at significantly higher levels than the levels elsewhere.

Health Care and the Right to Sue an HMO

* The supply curve of HMO-provided health care will shift upward and to the left if patients have the right to sue. As a result, patients will pay more for their HMO-provided health care coverage when they have the right to sue than when they do not have the right to sue.

Do You Pay for Good Weather?

* If good weather gives people utility, then the demand for and the price of housing will be higher in a city with good weather than in a city with bad weather. Conclusion: People who buy houses in good-weather locations indirectly pay for the good weather.

Paying All Professors the Same Salary

* Suppose the equilibrium wage rate as determined by supply and demand conditions is higher, say, for a biology professor than for a history professor. If both professors are paid the equilibrium wage in biology, then there will be a surplus of history professors. If both professors are paid the equilibrium wage in history, then there will be a shortage of biology professors.

Are New Car Companies Hurt by the Used Car Market?

* The demand for new cars is as high as it is (and prices of new cars are as high as they are) because the buyer of a new car can sell the car (later) as a used car. In other words, what a buyer of a car anticipates he can do as the seller of the car influences how high his demand will be and how high a price he will pay.

Supply and Demand on a Freeway

* The effect of a disequilibrium price for driving on a freeway is a traffic jam. If the price to drive on a freeway is $0 and at this price the quantity demanded of freeway space is greater than the quantity supplied, then there will be a shortage of freeway space that will manifest itself as freeway congestion.

What Does Price Have to Do with Getting to Class on Time?

* If price doesn't fully ration campus parking spots, something will. The rationing device may be first-come-first-served, which often prompts students to leave for campus at earlier times than they would if price rationed parking spots.

Aisle Seats on Commercial Airplanes

* If the supply for two goods is the same but the demand is different, then charging the same price for the two goods means that equilibrium is not achieved for at least one of the goods. If equilibrium is not

achieved, then there is either a shortage or a surplus. In the commercial airplanes application, there was a shortage of aisle seats. This prompted a nonprice rationing device: first-come-first-served.

10 O'Clock Classes in College

- Colleges usually charge the same tuition for a class no matter when the class is taken. The supply of seats in the class may be the same at each time, but the demand for the class may be different at different times. Thus at least for some classes, the quantity demanded of seats (in the class) will be greater than the quantity supplied. Thus, some nonprice rationing device will have to be used to achieve equilibrium.

Tipping at a Las Vegas Show

- A disequilibrium price for good seats in a Las Vegas showroom gives rise to an unusual rationing device. The price of a good seat is equal to (1) the price of admission to the showroom, which is equivalent to the price of a bad seat; plus (2) a tip equal to the difference between the equilibrium price for a good seat and the admission price. In other words, there are two components to the price of a good seat.

What Is the Price of an "A"?

- The law of demand can explain how a difference in the price of earning an "A" in two different classes could explain the difference in the quantity demanded of each class. The lower the price, the greater the quantity demanded, *ceteris paribus*.

Why Are Speeding Tickets So Expensive?

- The law of demand and an understanding of two ways to approximate the same price of speeding can explain the rationale for high-priced speeding tickets.
- Price of speeding = Speeding ticket price × Probability of getting caught for speeding. It follows that there are two ways to raise the price of speeding: (1) raise the price of a speeding ticket, or (2) raise the probability of getting caught for speeding. In addition, a higher price for a speeding ticket and a lower probability of getting caught can give us the same price for speeding as a lower price for a speeding ticket and a higher probability of getting caught.

Will a Self-Interested, Profit-Seeking Oilman Conserve Oil for the Future?

- An expected price can affect current behavior and change both current supply and future supply. Specifically, if an oil producer believes the expected price of oil will be sufficiently higher than the current price, he may decrease the amount of oil that he currently supplies to the market and increase the amount of oil that he supplies to the market in the future.

Where Will People Buy Relatively More Apples?

- Economists predict that relatively more is purchased of goods that are relatively lower priced, *ceteris paribus*. Thus, New Yorkers will buy relatively more high-quality apples than Washingtonians, even though the absolute price of high-quality apples is higher in New York City than in Washington.

Economic Connections to You

Economic facts, actions, and changes create ripples that move away from their point of origin. Eventually, these ripples can intersect your life and have an effect on you. In this chapter, we have given numerous examples of how demand, supply, and price could affect you. For example, if a below-equilibrium price is charged to park in a parking lot, you may end up wasting time looking for a place to park. Use what you have learned in this chapter to come up with your (original) application of supply, demand, and price.

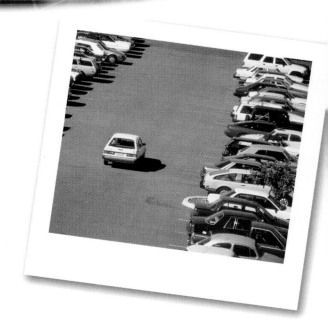

1. Harvard, Stanford, and Yale all charge relatively high tuition. Still, each uses ACT and SAT scores as admission criteria. Are charging a relatively high tuition and using standardized test scores (as admission criteria) inconsistent? Explain your answer.

2. Suppose the purchase and sale of marijuana are legalized and the price of marijuana falls. What explains the lower price of marijuana?

3. The minimum wage in year 1 is $1 higher than the equilibrium wage. In year 2, the minimum wage is increased so that it is $2 above the equilibrium wage. We observe that the same number of people are working at the minimum wage in year 2 as in year 1. Does it follow that an increase in the minimum wage does not cause some workers to lose their jobs? Explain your answer.

4. Explain how prejudiced employers can be hurt by their own prejudice.

5. In our discussion of the kidney market, we represent the demand curve for kidneys as downward-sloping and the supply curve of kidneys as upward-sloping. At the end of the discussion we state, "If it is unlawful to pay someone for a kidney, fewer kidneys will be forthcoming. In other words, the quantity supplied of kidneys is less at $0 than at, say, $20,000. Fewer kidneys supplied means, in turn, fewer kidney transplants." Would there be fewer kidney transplants if the supply curve of kidneys is vertical? Explain your answer.

6. Explain how a price ceiling in the retail electricity market can lead to blackouts.

7. What do the applications about freeway congestion, campus parking, 10 o'clock classes, and Las Vegas showrooms have in common?

8. Why might Las Vegas hotel-casinos choose not to charge the equilibrium price for the good seats in their showrooms?

9. Do you think there is likely to be a bigger price difference between candy bars in different locations or between cars in different locations? Explain your answer.

10. Economics has been called the "dismal science" because it sometimes "tells us" that things are true when we would prefer they were false. For example, although there are no free lunches, might we prefer that there were? Was there anything in this chapter that you learned was true that you would have preferred to be false? If so, identify it. Then explain why you would have preferred it to be false.

11. In the discussion of health care and the right to sue your HMO, we state, "Saying a seller's minimum price for providing a good or service rises, is the same as saying the seller's supply curve has shifted upward and to the left." Does it follow that if a seller's minimum price falls, the supply curve shifts downward and to the right? Explain your answer.

12. Application 10 explains that even though no one directly and explicitly pays for good weather ("Here is $100 for the good weather"), still it is possible to pay for good weather indirectly, such as through housing prices. Identify three other things (besides good weather) that you believe people pay for indirectly.

13. If the equilibrium wage for economics professors is higher than the equilibrium wage for history professors, which professors (do you think) are more likely to argue that all professors should be paid the same? Explain your answer.

14. Application 12 suggests that the used car market may not hurt companies that build and sell new cars. Do you think that the used housing market may not hurt companies that build and sell new houses? Explain your answer.

15. Suppose there exists a costless way to charge drivers on the freeway. Under this costless system, tolls on the freeway would be adjusted according to traffic conditions. For example, when traffic is usually heavy, such as from 6:30 A.M. to 9:00 A.M. on a weekday, the toll to drive on the freeway would be higher than the toll would be when traffic is light. In other words, freeway tolls would be used to equate the demand for freeway space and the supply of freeway space. Would you be in favor of such a system to replace our current (largely, zero-price) system? Explain your answer.

16. Wilson walks into his economics class 10 minutes late because he couldn't find a place to park. Because of his tardiness, he doesn't hear the professor tell the class there will be a quiz at the next class session. At the next class session, Wilson is unprepared for the quiz and ends up failing it.
   a. Might Wilson's failing the quiz have anything to do with the price of parking? Explain your answer.
   b. Suppose Wilson says to his professor: "If this university had set equilibrium prices for parking, I wouldn't have been late to class, and therefore, I would have heard about the upcoming quiz, studied for it, and probably passed it. It's not my fault I failed the quiz. It's the university's fault for not setting the equilibrium price for parking." What would you say if you were the professor?

17. University A charges more for a class for which there is high demand than for a class for which there is low demand. University B charges the same for all classes. All other things being equal between the two universities, which university would you prefer to attend? Explain your answer.

1. The price to drive on a freeway is $0 at all times of the day. This price establishes equilibrium at 3 A.M. but is too low to establish equilibrium at 5 P.M. There is a shortage of freeway space at 5 P.M.
   a. Graphically show and explain how carpooling may eliminate the shortage.
   b. Graphically show and explain how building more freeways may eliminate the shortage.
2. Diagrammatically show and explain why there is a shortage of classroom space for some college classes and a surplus for others.
3. Smith has been trying to sell his house for six months, but so far, there are no buyers. Draw the market for Smith's house.

4. According to students, Professor Smith teaches a better economics class than Professor Jones. Everything else between the two professors is the same—how they grade, the number of assignments they give, the time they teach their classes, and so on.
   a. Draw the student demand to get into Professor Smith's class in relation to the student demand to get into Professor Jones's class.
   b. If the same dollar tuition is charged for both classes, whose class is more likely to have a shortage of seats? Explain your answer.

1. Go to *http://www.usatoday.com* and select and read any story in the newspaper. What was the story about? Put the central idea of the story into economic terms or diagrams if it is possible to do so.
2. Go to *http://www.dailynews.yahoo.com* and select and read any current news item. What was the news item about? Put the central idea of the news item into economic terms or diagrams, if it is possible to do so.
3. Go to *http://www.forbes.com* and select and read any story. What was the story about? Put the central idea

of the story into economic terms or diagrams, if it is possible to do so.
4. Go to *http://www.economist.com* and select and read any story. What was the story about? Put the central idea of the story into economic terms or diagrams, if it is possible to do so.
5. Go to *http://www.businessweek.com* and select and read any story. What was the story about? Put the central idea of the story into economic terms or diagrams, if it is possible to do so.

Log on to the Arnold Xtra! Web site now (*http://arnoldxtra.swcollege.com*) for additional learning resources such as practice quizzes, help with graphing, video clips, and current event applications.

ch.5

MACROECONOMIC MEASUREMENTS, PART I: PRICES AND UNEMPLOYMENT

Government economists often collect and analyze the latest economic data. Their analysis includes computing important economic measurements such as the inflation rate and the unemployment rate. Our elected representatives and certain government officials then use these measurements in formulating economic policy. The structure, content, and timing of that economic policy will often affect you in your roles as buyer, seller, taxpayer, and employee.

Chapter Road Map

A doctor often takes your temperature and blood pressure and, in some cases, may order a few tests. The doctor uses these measurements to learn about the condition of your body.

In a way, economists are the physicians of the economy. They often want to take the "temperature" or "blood pressure" of the economy. Their objective in taking such measurements is to find out how the economy is doing. Is it well and healthy? Is it getting sick?

This chapter and the next explain four of the measurements economists use to find out how the economy is doing. In this chapter, we discuss how economists measure prices and the unemployment rate. In the next chapter, we discuss how economists measure the dollar size of the economy and economic growth.

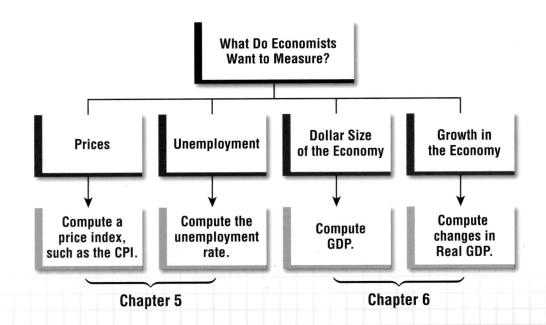

MEASURING PRICES

Before we can measure prices, we need to know what "price" means in macroeconomics. Price in macroeconomics does not usually refer to a single price, such as the price of cars or the price of computers. Price in macroeconomics usually refers to an *aggregate price,* a *price level,* a *price index,* or an *average price.*

For example, suppose there are only two goods in the economy, books and pens. Books are priced at $10 each and pens at $1 each. Without considering the quantity of each good, the *average price* in this tiny economy is $5.50. When economists talk about *price stability,* they are referring to the average price, price level, or price index remaining constant.

MEASURING PRICES USING THE CPI

The **price level** is a weighted average of the prices of all goods and services. Economists measure the price level by constructing a **price index.** One major price index is the **consumer price index (CPI).**

The CPI is calculated by the Bureau of Labor Statistics through its sampling of thousands of households and businesses. When a news report says that the "cost of living" increased by, say, 7 percent, it is usually referring to the CPI.[1]

The CPI is based on a representative group of goods and services purchased by a typical household. This representative group of goods is called the *market basket.* To simplify, let's say that the market basket is made up of only three goods instead of the many goods it actually contains. Our market basket will consist of 10 pens, 5 shirts, and 3 pairs of shoes.

To calculate the CPI, we must first calculate the total dollar expenditure of the market basket in two years: the current year and the base year. The **base year** is a benchmark year that serves as a basis of comparison for prices in other years.

In Exhibit 1, we multiply the quantity of each good in the market basket (column 1) by its current-year price (column 2) to compute the current-year expenditure on each good (column 3). By adding the dollar amounts in column 3, the total dollar expenditure on the market basket in the current year is obtained. This amount is $167.

Price Level
The weighted average of the prices of all goods and services.

Price Index
A measure of the price level.

Consumer Price Index (CPI)
A widely cited index number for the price level; the weighted average of prices of a specific set of goods and services purchased by a typical household.

Base Year
The year chosen as a point of reference or basis of comparison for prices in other years; a benchmark year.

exhibit 1

Computing the Consumer Price Index
The exhibit uses hypothetical data to show how the CPI is computed. To find the "total dollar expenditure on market basket in current year," we multiply the quantities of goods in the market basket times their current-year prices and add these products. This gives us $167. To find the "total dollar expenditure on market basket in base year," we multiply the quantities of goods in the market basket times their base-year prices and add these products. This gives us $67. We then divide $167 by $67 and multiply the quotient times 100.

(1) Market Basket		(2) Current-Year Prices (per item)		(3) Current-Year Expenditures	(1A) Market Basket		(2A) Base-Year Prices (per item)		(3A) Base-Year Expenditures
10 pens	×	$ .70	=	$ 7.00	10 pens	×	$ .20	=	$ 2.00
5 shirts	×	14.00	=	70.00	5 shirts	×	7.00	=	35.00
3 pairs of shoes	×	30.00	=	90.00	3 pairs of shoes	×	10.00	=	30.00
				$167.00					**$67.00**
				Total dollar expenditure on market basket in current year					Total dollar expenditure on market basket in base year

$$CPI = \left(\frac{\text{Total dollar expenditure on market basket in current year}}{\text{Total dollar expenditure on market basket in base year}} \right) \times 100$$

$$= \left(\frac{\$167}{\$67} \right) \times 100$$

$$= 249$$

---

1. Although changes in the CPI are often used to compute the change in the "cost of living," one's cost of living usually involves more than is measured by the CPI. For example, the CPI does not include income taxes, yet income taxes are a part of most people's cost of living.

Go to *http://www.bls.gov/cpi/*. Under "Economic News Releases," click on "Consumer Price Index (TXT)," and then on "Table 1." Find the most recent CPI numbers for (1) All Items, (2) Transportation, (3) Medical Care, (4) Tuition, and (5) Personal Computers. Have prices risen in all these categories since the base year? In which category have prices risen the fastest? How much faster is this price rise than the rise in the All Items category? Based on what you learned in Chapters 3 and 4, how do you think consumers will react to these price changes?

To find the total expenditure on the market basket in the base year, we multiply the quantity of each good in the market basket (column 1A) times its base-year price (column 2A) and then add these products (column 3A). This gives us $67.

To find the CPI, we use the formula:

$$CPI = \frac{\text{Total dollar expenditure on market basket in current year}}{\text{Total dollar expenditure on market basket in base year}} \times 100$$

The consumer price index for the United States for the years 1913 to 2002 is shown in Exhibit 2.

Q: What are some of the goods and services in the market basket?

A: The market basket includes eight major categories of goods and services: food and beverages, housing, apparel, transportation, medical care, recreation, education and communication, and other goods and services. Some examples of these goods and services are breakfast cereal, milk, coffee, bedroom furniture, men's shirts, women's dresses, jewelry, new vehicles, airline fares, gasoline, prescription drugs, cable television, sports equipment, college tuition, postage, and haircuts.

Q: What is the base year and what does the CPI in the base year equal?

A: The base year is a year that is chosen as a point of reference or basis of comparison for prices in other years. In the base year, the base year and the current year are the same year. The numerator (total dollar expenditure on market basket in current year) is the same as the denominator (total dollar expenditure on market basket in base year). Dividing the numerator ($67 in our example in Exhibit 1) by the denominator ($67) gives us 1. When we multiply 1 times 100, we get 100. The CPI in the base year is 100.

exhibit 2

CPI, 1913–2002
The CPI for 2002 is for May 2002.

Source: The data were reported at the Web site for the U.S. Department of Labor, Bureau of Labor Statistics. Site address: http://stats.bls.gov/cpi/home.htm

Year	CPI	Year	CPI	Year	CPI	Year	CPI
1913	9.9	1936	13.9	1959	29.1	1982	96.5
1914	10.0	1937	14.4	1960	29.6	1983	99.6
1915	10.1	1938	14.1	1961	29.9	1984	103.9
1916	10.9	1939	13.9	1962	30.2	1985	107.6
1917	12.8	1940	14.0	1963	30.6	1986	109.6
1918	15.1	1941	14.7	1964	31.0	1987	113.6
1919	17.3	1942	16.3	1965	31.5	1988	118.3
1920	20.0	1943	17.3	1966	32.4	1989	124.0
1921	17.9	1944	17.6	1967	33.4	1990	130.7
1922	16.8	1945	18.0	1968	34.8	1991	136.2
1923	17.1	1946	19.5	1969	36.7	1992	140.3
1924	17.1	1947	22.3	1970	38.8	1993	144.5
1925	17.5	1948	24.1	1971	40.5	1994	148.2
1926	17.7	1949	23.8	1972	41.8	1995	152.4
1927	17.4	1950	24.1	1973	44.4	1996	156.9
1928	17.1	1951	26.0	1974	49.3	1997	160.5
1929	17.1	1952	26.5	1975	53.8	1998	163.0
1930	16.7	1953	26.7	1976	56.9	1999	166.6
1931	15.2	1954	26.9	1977	60.6	2000	172.2
1932	13.7	1955	26.8	1978	65.2	2001	177.1
1933	13.0	1956	27.2	1979	72.6	2002	179.8
1934	13.4	1957	28.1	1980	82.4		
1935	13.7	1958	28.9	1981	90.9		

CALCULATING THE PERCENTAGE CHANGE IN PRICES (AS MEASURED BY THE CPI) OVER ONE YEAR OR SEVERAL YEARS

To find the percentage change in prices between any two years, we use the following formula:

$$\text{Percentage change in prices} = \left(\frac{\text{CPI}_{\text{later year}} - \text{CPI}_{\text{earlier year}}}{\text{CPI}_{\text{earlier year}}} \right) \times 100$$

For example, Exhibit 2 shows that the CPI in 1990 was 130.7 and the CPI in 2000 was 172.2. What was the percentage change in prices over this period of time? It was 31.75 percent ([(172.2 − 130.7) ÷ 130.7] × 100 = 31.75). This means that from 1990 to 2000, prices increased 31.75 percent.

Inflation is an increase in the price level and is usually measured on an annual basis. The *inflation rate* is the positive percentage change in the price level on an annual basis. For example, the inflation rate for 2000 is the percentage change in prices from the end of December 1999 through the end of December 2000. Although we do not show these data in a table, the CPI in December 1999 was 168.9; the CPI in December 2000 was 174.6. This means the inflation rate in 2000 was approximately 3.4 percent. Exhibit 3 shows the inflation rates for selected countries in 2000.

Inflation
An increase in the price level.

Q & A

Q: Earlier it was stated that the CPI in the base year is 100, but there is no year in Exhibit 2 where the CPI is 100. Does this mean that there is no base year?

A: The base year for the CPI is the period 1982–84. Look at the CPI in each of the years 1982, 1983, and 1984. If we add the CPIs for the three years and divide by 3, we get 100: (96.5 + 99.6 + 103.9) ÷ 3 = 100.

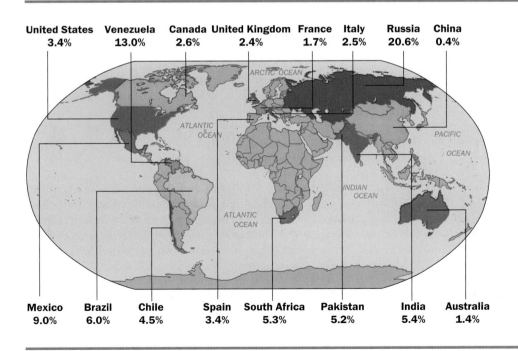

| United States 3.4% | Venezuela 13.0% | Canada 2.6% | United Kingdom 2.4% | France 1.7% | Italy 2.5% | Russia 20.6% | China 0.4% |

| Mexico 9.0% | Brazil 6.0% | Chile 4.5% | Spain 3.4% | South Africa 5.3% | Pakistan 5.2% | India 5.4% | Australia 1.4% |

exhibit 3

Inflation Rates, 2000, Selected Countries

Source: CIA World Factbook, 2001.

ARE YOU BEATING (CPI) INFLATION OR IS INFLATION BEATING YOU?

When you know the inflation rate, you can find out whether your income is (1) keeping up with, (2) not keeping up with, or (3) more than keeping up with inflation. How you are doing depends on whether your income is rising by (1) the same percentage as, (2) a lesser percentage than, or (3) a greater percentage than the inflation rate, respectively. Another way to look at this is to compute and compare your real income for different years. **Real income** is a person's **nominal income** (or money income) adjusted for any change in prices. Real income is computed as follows:

$$\text{Real income} = \left(\frac{\text{Nominal income}}{\text{CPI}}\right) \times 100$$

Case 1. Keeping Up with Inflation: Real Income Stays Constant
Jim earns $50,000 in year 1 and $55,000 in year 2. The CPI is 100 in year 1 and 110 in year 2. Jim's income has risen by 10 percent [(($55,000 − $50,000)/$50,000) × 100 = 10], and the inflation rate is 10 percent [((110 − 100)/100) × 100 = 10]. Jim's income has risen by the same percentage as the inflation rate, so he has kept up with inflation. This is evident when we see that Jim's real income is the same in the two years. In year 1, it is $50,000, and in year 2, it is $50,000 too.

Real income year 1 = ($50,000/100) × 100 = $50,000
Real income year 2 = ($55,000/110) × 100 = $50,000

Case 2. Not Keeping Up with Inflation: Real Income Falls
Karen earns $50,000 in year 1 and $52,000 in year 2. The CPI is 100 in year 1 and 110 in year 2. Karen's income has risen by 4 percent, and the inflation rate is 10 percent. Her income has risen by a lesser percentage than the inflation rate, so she has not kept up with inflation. Karen's real income has fallen from $50,000 in year 1 to $47,273 in year 2.

Real income year 1 = ($50,000/100) × 100 = $50,000
Real income year 2 = ($52,000/110) × 100 = $47,273

Case 3. More Than Keeping Up with Inflation: Real Income Rises
Carl earns $50,000 in year 1 and $60,000 in year 2. The CPI is 100 in year 1 and 110 in year 2. Carl's income has risen by 20 percent, and the inflation rate is 10 percent. His income has risen by a greater percentage than the inflation rate, so he has more than kept up with inflation. Carl's real income has risen from $50,000 in year 1 to $54,545 in year 2.

Real income year 1 = ($50,000/100) × 100 = $50,000
Real income year 2 = ($60,000/110) × 100 = $54,545

THINKING LIKE AN ECONOMIST *Comparing one thing with something else can be extremely useful. For example, in each of these three cases, we compared the percentage change in a person's nominal income with the inflation rate. Through this comparison, we learned something that we could not have learned by looking at either factor alone: how a person fared under inflation. Making comparisons is part of the economic way of thinking.*

HOW IS THE CPI USED?
The CPI is used (1) as an economic indicator, (2) to find the real value of an economic variable, and (3) to adjust certain income payments.

We have already seen how CPI is used as an economic indicator. Essentially, it is used to measure the inflation rate. The inflation rate, in turn, is often used by policymakers to determine the success of government economic policy. For example, suppose the government wants to lower the nation's inflation rate. With this in mind, it undertakes policies X and Y. Two years later, it uses the CPI to measure the inflation rate over the past two years. If the inflation rate has not fallen, the government knows that its policies to lower the inflation rate have been unsuccessful.

We have also seen how the CPI can be used to find the real value of an economic variable. We used the CPI to turn nominal income into real income. The CPI can also be used to turn, say, nominal consumption expenditures into real consumption expenditures or nominal government spending into real government spending.

Finally, the CPI is often used to adjust certain income (and other dollar) payments. For example, consider the employer who adjusts her employees' incomes by the inflation rate. In other words, if the inflation rate is 3 percent, then all employees receive a salary that is 3 percent higher than last year's salary. Also, the CPI is used to adjust the payments received by Social Security beneficiaries, military and Federal Civil Service retirees, and so on.

THE SUBSTITUTION BIAS IN FIXED-WEIGHTED MEASURES

Look at Exhibit 1 where the CPI was first calculated. Notice that the market basket in both the current year and the base year is the same: 10 pens, 5 shirts, and 3 pairs of shoes. In the base year the person bought 10 pens, 5 shirts, and 3 pairs of shoes, and even though the prices of all three of these items increased, she continued to buy the *same quantity* of each. This is like saying that Michael purchased two pounds of beef a week in 1995, and even though the price of beef increased between, say, 1995 and 1999, he continued to buy two pounds of beef a week. In reality, what Michael is likely to have done is *substitute*, say, chicken for beef *if the price of beef increased relatively more than the price of chicken during the time period in question*. In other words, Michael's buying behavior is likely to have responded to changes in *relative prices*.

Any price index that uses fixed quantities of goods, and therefore does not reflect the fact that people might substitute one good for another as the price of one good rises relative to another, is called a *fixed-weighted price index*. All fixed-weighted price measures have a *substitution bias*—they do not regularly account for the substitutions that individuals are likely to make. As a result of the substitution bias, a fixed-weighted price index can overstate the "cost of living."

For many years, economists criticized the use of the CPI (a fixed-weighted price index), largely because the expenditure weights of the various goods and services in the market basket were changed only once a decade.[2] This meant that the market basket used to measure the CPI was the same for a decade or longer even though substitutions were taking place during this time. Recently, the Bureau of Labor Statistics decided to update the expenditure weights of the market basket (used to compute the CPI) every two years.

Q & A   **Q:** What does it mean to say that a fixed-weighted price index can overstate the cost of living?

A: To answer the question, let's again focus on a fixed-weighted price index. If the fixed-weighted price index is 102 in year 1 and 110 in year 2, some people would loosely say that

---

2. The "expenditure weights" refer to the quantities of each good in the market basket. For example, the expenditure weight for pens in our market basket in Exhibit 1 is "10."

there has been a rise in the cost of living. In this context, a rise in the cost of living means that it takes more money in year 2 to purchase the same bundle of goods that was purchased in year 1. But this implicitly assumes that one's standard of living is obtained in only one way: *by purchasing a constant, or fixed, bundle of goods*. In reality this probably isn't true. Different bundles of goods may represent equivalent standards of living. For example, bundle *A*, which consists of two pounds of beef, one loaf of bread, and three boxes of Frosted Flakes cereal, may be equivalent to bundle *B*, which consists of two pounds of chicken, one loaf of bread, and three boxes of Honey Nut Cheerios.

Now let's get back to the question asked. Suppose (1) bundles *A* and *B* represent equivalent standards of living; (2) a buyer is currently purchasing bundle *A*, which costs $100 over some time period; (3) the cost of purchasing bundle *A* rises to $120, prompting the buyer to substitute bundle *B* for *A*; and (4) bundle *B* costs $100.

Has the cost of living increased for this person? If we base our answer on purchasing a fixed bundle of goods—bundle *A*—the answer is yes because the price of purchasing bundle *A* has risen from $100 to $120. But if we allow for substitutions (of bundles) and bundles *A* and *B* represent equivalent standards of living, then the answer is no because the cost of buying an equivalent bundle remains constant at $100. Many economists believe that allowing for substitutions is the only justifiable way of measuring the cost of living. Any method that does not allow for substitutions can result in overstating the change in the cost of living.

A CHAIN-WEIGHTED PRICE INDEX

What is the alternative to a fixed-weighted measure? One answer is a *chain-weighted measure* (officially this is referred to as a *chain-type annual-weighted measure*). A chain-weighted measure does not have the substitution bias of a fixed-weighted measure. It allows for substitutions. The chain-weighted price index is today the featured measure of prices used by government statisticians.

To illustrate how a chain-weighted price index is computed, first look at the following data.

Goods	Quantities in Year 1	Prices in Year 1	Quantities in Year 2	Prices in Year 2
Apples	40	50¢	30	90¢
Oranges	20	60¢	30	70¢

The chain-weighted price index for the first year is 100 (just as it was 100 for the CPI in the base year). To calculate a chain-weighted price index for year 2, we use the following formula:

$$\text{Chain-weighted price index}_{\text{year 2}} =$$

$$\sqrt{\frac{\text{Total dollar expenditure on year 1 quantities at year 2 prices}}{\text{Total dollar expenditure on year 1 quantities at year 1 prices}} \times \frac{\text{Total dollar expenditure on year 2 quantities at year 2 prices}}{\text{Total dollar expenditure on year 2 quantities at year 1 prices}}} \times 100$$

Carrying out the arithmetic, we have:

$$\sqrt{\frac{(40 \times 90¢) + (20 \times 70¢)}{(40 \times 50¢) + (20 \times 60¢)} \times \frac{(30 \times 90¢) + (30 \times 70¢)}{(30 \times 50¢) + (30 \times 60¢)}} \times 100 = 151$$

ANOTHER PRICE INDEX: GDP DEFLATOR

We have discussed two price indices so far: the CPI and the chain-weighted price index. There is another price index that is often cited—the *GDP deflator* (sometimes called the *implicit price deflator*). As you know, the CPI is based on a representative group of goods and services (the market basket) purchased by a typical household. Obviously, there are more goods and services produced in

ECONOMICS IN...

Popular Culture Technology Everyday Life The World

Who Earned More as President: John F. Kennedy or George W. Bush?

You know how to compute the CPI and how to use it to find the percentage change in prices between years. We can do something else with the CPI. We can use it to find out who earned more as president—John F. Kennedy or George W. Bush.

John F. Kennedy was president in 1961; his annual salary that year was $100,000. George W. Bush was president in 2002; his annual salary that year was $400,000. It seems clear that Bush earned more as president than Kennedy did.

But wait; have we considered everything? No. The dollars Kennedy was paid as president had greater purchasing power than the dollars Bush was paid as president. One dollar in 1961 bought more goods and services than one dollar in 2002 did. To accurately compare their salaries, we need to convert Kennedy's 1961 salary of $100,000 into 2002 dollars.

Kennedy's salary in 2002 dollars

$$= \$100,000 \times \left(\frac{179.8}{29.9} \right)$$

$$= \$601,337$$

So, in 2002 dollars, Kennedy earned $601,337; Bush, of course, earned $400,000 in 2002.

an economy than find their way into the market basket. The GDP deflator, unlike the CPI, is based on all goods and services produced in an economy. In other words, it is a broader measure of prices than the CPI.

CONVERTING DOLLARS FROM ONE YEAR TO ANOTHER

Suppose someone says to you, "Back in 1952, I had an annual salary of $6,000 a year. That sure isn't much these days." Of course, the person is right in one sense: an annual salary of $6,000 doesn't buy much these days. But was $6,000 a good salary back in 1952? It certainly could have been because prices in 1952 weren't as high as they are today. For example, the CPI was 26.5 in 1952 and it was 179.8 in 2002. In other words, one of the things that make a salary "good" or "not so good" is what the salary can buy.

Now suppose someone tells you that a $6,000 salary in 1952 is the same as a $40,709 salary today. Would you then better understand the 1952 $6,000 salary? Of course you would because you understand what it means to earn $40,709 today. Economists convert a past salary into a salary today by using this formula:

$$\text{Salary in today's (current) dollars} = \text{Salary}_{\text{earlier year}} \times \left(\frac{\text{CPI}_{\text{current year}}}{\text{CPI}_{\text{earlier year}}} \right)$$

Assume the CPI today is the same as the most recent CPI in Exhibit 2 (which is the CPI for 2002). Using the formula, we get:

$$\text{Salary in 2002 dollars} = \$6,000 \times \frac{179.8}{26.5}$$

$$= \$40,709$$

In other words, earning a $6,000 salary in 1952 is the same as earning a salary of $40,709 in 2002.

Macroeconomic Measurements, Part I: Prices and Unemployment **Chapter 5**

ECONOMICS IN...

Economics at the Movies

Some movies do better at the box office than other movies. For example, *Shrek,* a movie released in 2001, earned higher gross receipts than *Rush Hour 2,* another movie released in 2001. *Shrek* had domestic gross receipts of $267 million and *Rush Hour 2* had domestic gross receipts of $226 million.

As of June 2002, the following list ranks the all-time top 10 movies in the United States in terms of gross receipts:

1. *Titanic* (1997)
2. *Star Wars* (1977)
3. *E.T.* (1982)
4. *Star Wars: The Phantom Menace* (1999)
5. *Spider-Man* (2002)
6. *Jurassic Park* (1993)
7. *Forrest Gump* (1994)
8. *Harry Potter and the Sorcerer's Stone* (2001)
9. *The Lion King* (1994)
10. *The Lord of the Rings: The Fellowship of the Ring* (2001)

Titanic, first on this list, earned gross receipts in the United States of $600 million, and *Star Wars,* in second place, earned $461 million. Comparing these two dollar amounts, it is easy to conclude that *Titanic* did better at the box office than *Star Wars* did.

But notice that *Titanic* was released in 1997 and *Star Wars* was released 20 years earlier in 1977. In other words,

the receipts for *Titanic* are in 1997 dollars and those for *Star Wars* are in 1977 dollars. To accurately compare the receipts of the two movies, we need to put them on an even footing. To do this, we need to change each movie's receipts into today's dollars.

In today's (2002) dollars, *Titanic* earned $672 million and *Star Wars* earned $1.3 billion. Thus, when we convert the gross receipts to today's dollars, we find that *Star Wars* did better at the box office than *Titanic* did.

In today's dollars, here are the top 10 movies of all times in terms of domestic gross receipts:

1. *Gone with the Wind* (1939)
2. *Star Wars* (1977)
3. *The Sound of Music* (1965)
4. *E.T.* (1982)
5. *Titanic* (1997)
6. *The Ten Commandments* (1956)
7. *Jaws* (1975)
8. *Doctor Zhivago* (1965)
9. *The Jungle Book* (1967)
10. *Snow White and the Seven Dwarfs* (1937)

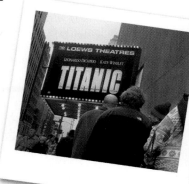

$$\frac{143.2 - 132.5}{132.5} \times 100 = 8.08\%$$

Self-Test *(Answers to Self-Test questions are in the Self-Test Appendix.)*

1. Explain how the CPI is calculated.
2. If the CPI in year 1 is 132.5 and the CPI in year 2 is 143.2, what is the inflation rate?
3. In year 1, your annual income is $45,000 and the CPI is 143.6; in year 2, your annual income is $51,232 and the CPI is 150.7. Has your real income risen, fallen, or remained constant? Explain your answer.
4. What is the difference between a fixed-weighted price index and a chain-weighted price index?

(handwritten:) $\frac{45,000}{143.6} \times 100 = 31,337.05$ $\frac{51,232}{150.7} \times 100 = 33,996.02$ risen income   % △ 7   % △ inflation

MEASURING UNEMPLOYMENT

Every month, the government surveys thousands of households to gather information about labor market activities. It uses the information from the survey to derive the number of Americans unemployed.

WHO ARE THE UNEMPLOYED?

The total population of the United States can be divided into two broad groups (Exhibit 4). One group consists of persons who are (1) under 16 years of age, (2) in the armed forces, or (3) institutionalized—that is, they are in a prison, mental institution, or home for the aged. The second group, which consists of all others in the total population, is called the *civilian noninstitutional population.*

The civilian noninstitutional population, in turn, can be divided into two groups: persons *not in the labor force* and persons in the *civilian labor force.* In April 2001, the civilian noninstitutional population in the United States consisted of 211,348,000 persons, 69,592,000 not in the labor force and 141,756,000 in the civilian labor force.

> Civilian noninstitutional population = Persons not in the labor force
> + Persons in the civilian labor force

Those persons not in the labor force are neither working nor looking for work. For example, people who are retired, who are engaged in own-home housework, or who choose not to work fall into this category.

Persons in the civilian labor force fall into one of two categories: *employed* or *unemployed.* In April 2001, 135,354,000 persons in the United States were employed and 6,402,000 persons were unemployed.

> Civilian labor force = Employed persons + Unemployed persons

A person is employed if any one of the following conditions is relevant:

1. Did at least one hour of work as a paid employee during the survey week.
2. Worked in his or her own business or profession.
3. Worked at least 15 hours per week as an unpaid worker on a family-owned farm or business.
4. Was temporarily absent from work for reasons of illness, vacation, strike, or bad weather.

A person is unemployed if any one of the following conditions is relevant:

1. Did not work during the survey week, has actively looked for work within the past four weeks, and is currently available for work.
2. Is waiting to be called back to a job from which he or she has been laid off.
3. Is waiting to report to a job within 30 days.

http://

Go to *http://www.bls.gov/cps/.* Under "Economic News Releases," click on "Employment Situation Summary (TXT)," and then on "Table B-2. Average." How many hours a week does the average goods-producing worker work? How many overtime hours a week does the average manufacturing worker work? Why might companies pay overtime rather than hire more workers? Do service workers work an average of more or less than 40 hours per week? What do you think explains the difference in hours worked between service workers and goods-producing workers?

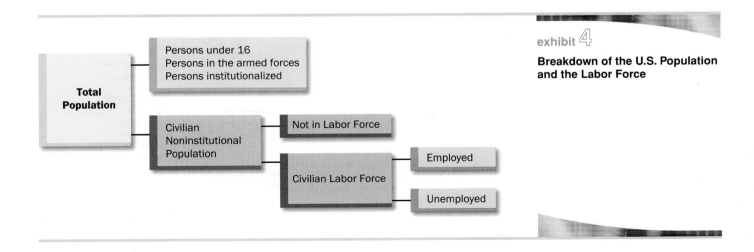

exhibit 4

Breakdown of the U.S. Population and the Labor Force

THE UNEMPLOYMENT AND EMPLOYMENT RATES

Unemployment Rate
The percentage of the civilian labor force that is unemployed: Unemployment rate = Number of unemployed persons/Civilian labor force.

The **unemployment rate** is the percentage of the civilian labor force that is unemployed. It is equal to the number of unemployed persons divided by the civilian labor force.

$$\text{Unemployment rate } (U) = \frac{\text{Number of unemployed persons}}{\text{Civilian labor force}}$$

The average annual unemployment rate in the United States during the 1990s was 5.7 percent. Exhibit 5 shows the computation of the unemployment rate in April 2001. Exhibit 6 shows the unemployment rate for selected countries in 2000.

Employment Rate
The percentage of the civilian noninstitutional population that is employed: Employment rate = Number of employed persons/Civilian noninstitutional population.

The **employment rate** (sometimes referred to as the *employment/population ratio*) is the percentage of the civilian noninstitutional population that is employed. It is equal to the number of employed persons divided by the civilian noninstitutional population:

$$\text{Employment rate } (E) = \frac{\text{Number of employed persons}}{\text{Civilian noninstitutional population}}$$

In April 2001, the employment rate was 64.0 percent in the United States.

Labor Force Participation Rate
The percentage of the civilian noninstitutional population that is in the civilian labor force: Labor force participation rate = Civilian labor force/Civilian noninstitutional population.

Finally, the **labor force participation rate** (LFPR) is the percentage of the civilian noninstitutional population that is in the civilian labor force.

$$\text{Labor force participation rate (LFPR)} = \frac{\text{Civilian labor force}}{\text{Civilian noninstitutional population}}$$

In April 2001, the labor force participation rate was 67.1 percent in the United States.

Q & A

Q: If the unemployment rate is 10 percent, does it follow that the employment rate is 90 percent?

A: No. The unemployment rate and the employment rate have different denominators. The denominator in the unemployment rate is the *civilian labor force;* the denominator in the employment rate is the *civilian noninstitutional population.* Thus, the two rates are percentages of different totals.

---

exhibit 5

Computation of the U.S. Unemployment Rate in April 2001

		Description
Civilian noninstitutional population	211,348,000	(total population excluding those under 16, members of the armed forces, and persons in institutions)
− Not in labor force	−69,592,000	(retired persons, persons doing own-home housework, and persons who choose not to work)
Civilian labor force	141,756,000	(civilian noninstitutional population minus those not in labor force)
− Employed	−135,354,000	(individuals with jobs)
Unemployed	6,402,000	(individuals without a job and actively searching)

$$\text{Unemployment Rate} = \frac{6,402,000}{141,756,000} = 4.5\%$$

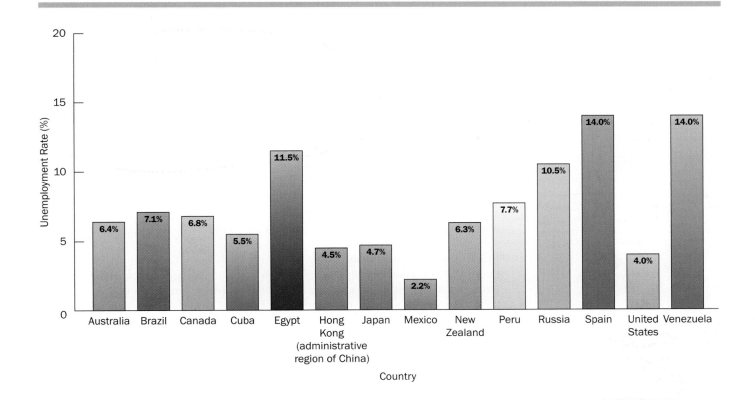

exhibit 6

Unemployment Rate, 2000, Selected Countries

Source: CIA World Factbook, 2001.

REASONS FOR UNEMPLOYMENT

Usually, we think of an unemployed person as someone who has been fired or laid off from his or her job. Certainly some unemployed persons fit this description, but not all of them do. According to the Bureau of Labor Statistics, an unemployed person may fall into one of four categories.

1. **Job loser.** This is a person who was employed in the civilian labor force and was either fired or laid off. Most unemployed persons fall into this category. In September 2001, 51.5 percent of all unemployed persons fell into this category.

2. **Job leaver.** This is a person employed in the civilian labor force who quits his or her job. For example, if Jim quit his job with company *X* and is looking for a better job, then he is a job leaver. In September 2001, 11.5 percent of all unemployed persons fell into this category.

3. **Reentrant.** This is a person who was previously employed, hasn't worked for some time, and is currently reentering the labor force. In September 2001, 30.2 percent of all unemployed persons fell into this category.

4. **New entrant.** This is a person who has never held a full-time job for two weeks or longer and is now in the civilian labor force looking for a job. In September 2001, 6.8 percent of all unemployed persons fell into this category.

Unemployed persons = Job losers + Job leavers + Reentrants + New entrants

DISCOURAGED WORKERS

Suppose Adam is fired from his job at company *A* in September. He looks for a job for about six months. During this time he is considered an unemployed person and is counted in the unemployment rate. At the end of the sixth month, Adam is very discouraged; he doesn't think he will ever find a job, and so he stops looking. A few weeks pass and he continues not to look for a job. Is Adam still considered an unemployed person? The answer is no. Remember, to be an unemployed person you have to meet certain conditions, one of which is that you have to be actively looking for work. But Adam isn't actively looking for work, and he isn't waiting to be called back to a job or to report to a job. So Adam isn't unemployed. Since Adam is not unemployed, he does not get counted in the unemployment rate. The Bureau of Labor Statistics considers Adam a *discouraged worker*. You may think that for all practical purposes, a discouraged worker is the same as an unemployed person (because neither has a job). But they aren't the same for calculating the unemployment rate. The unemployed person gets counted and the discouraged worker does not.

Some economists think that because discouraged workers are not considered unemployed, the unemployment rate is biased downward. Consequently, it doesn't really give us a good fix on the "real unemployment problem" in society.

TYPES OF UNEMPLOYMENT

This section describes a few types of unemployment.

Frictional Unemployment

Every day, demand conditions change in some markets, causing qualified individuals with transferable skills to leave some jobs and move to others. To illustrate, suppose there are two computer firms, *A* and *B*. For some reason, the demand falls for firm *A*'s computers and the demand rises for firm *B*'s computers. Consequently, firm *A* produces fewer computers. With fewer computers being produced, firm *A* doesn't need as many employees, so it fires some employees. On the other hand, firm *B* produces more computers. With more computers being produced, firm *B* hires additional employees. The employees fired from firm *A* have skills that they can transfer to firm *B*—after all, both firms produce computers. However, it takes time for people to transfer from one firm to another. During this time, they are said to be frictionally unemployed.

The unemployment owing to the natural "frictions" of the economy, which is caused by changing market conditions and is represented by qualified individuals with transferable skills who change jobs, is called **frictional unemployment.** We use the symbol U_F to designate the frictional unemployment rate, which is the percentage of the labor force that is frictionally unemployed.

In a dynamic, changing economy like ours, there will always be frictional unemployment. Many economists believe that the basic cause of frictional unemployment is imperfect or incomplete information, which prevents individuals from leaving one job and finding another instantly.

Consider the situation where there are 1,000 job vacancies and 1,000 persons with the qualifications to fill the jobs. Will there be some unemployment? It is likely that there will be because not every one of the 1,000 job seekers will know where an available job is, nor will all employers give the job to the first applicant who knocks on the door (employers don't know if "better" applicants are around the corner). Matching qualified workers with jobs takes time.

Structural Unemployment

Structural unemployment is unemployment due to structural changes in the economy that eliminate some jobs and create others for which the unemployed are unqualified. Most economists argue that structural unemployment is largely the consequence of automation (labor-saving devices) and long-lasting shifts in demand. The major difference between the frictionally unemployed and the structurally unemployed is that the latter do not have transferable skills. Their choice is between prolonged unemployment and retraining. For example, suppose there is a pool of unemployed automobile workers and a rising demand for computer analysts. If the automobile workers do not currently have the skills necessary to become computer analysts, they are structurally unemployed. We use the symbol U_S to designate the structural unemployment rate, which is the percentage of the labor force that is structurally unemployed.

Frictional Unemployment
Unemployment due to the natural "frictions" of the economy, which is caused by changing market conditions and is represented by qualified individuals with transferable skills who change jobs.

Structural Unemployment
Unemployment due to structural changes in the economy that eliminate some jobs and create others for which the unemployed are unqualified.

Natural Unemployment

Adding the frictional unemployment rate and the structural unemployment rate gives the **natural unemployment** rate (or natural rate of unemployment). We use the symbol U_N to designate the natural unemployment rate. Currently, most economists estimate the natural unemployment rate at between 4 and 6.5 percent.

$$\text{Natural unemployment rate } (U_N) = \text{Frictional unemployment rate } (U_F)$$
$$+ \text{ Structural unemployment rate } (U_S)$$

WHAT IS FULL EMPLOYMENT?

What do you think of when you hear the term **full employment?** Most people think full employment means that the actual or reported unemployment rate is zero. But a dynamic, changing economy can never have full employment of this type due to the frictional and structural changes that continually occur. In fact, it is natural for some unemployment to exist—some natural unemployment, that is. For this reason, economists *do not* equate full employment with a zero unemployment rate. Instead, for economists, *full employment exists when the economy is operating at its natural unemployment rate.* For example, if the natural unemployment rate is 5 percent, then full employment exists when the unemployment rate (in the economy) is 5 percent.

Q & A   **Q:** In other words, the economy can be operating at full employment and some people will be unemployed. Is this correct?

A: Yes, that is correct.

CYCLICAL UNEMPLOYMENT

The unemployment rate that exists in the economy is not always the natural rate. The difference between the existing unemployment rate and the natural unemployment rate is the **cyclical unemployment rate** (U_C).

$$\text{Cyclical unemployment rate } (U_C) = \text{ Unemployment rate } (U)$$
$$- \text{ Natural unemployment rate } (U_N)$$

When the unemployment rate (U) that exists in the economy is greater than the natural unemployment rate (U_N), the cyclical unemployment rate (U_C) is positive. For example, if $U = 8$ percent and $U_N = 5$ percent, then $U_C = 3$ percent. When the unemployment rate that exists in the economy is less than the natural unemployment rate, the cyclical unemployment rate is negative. For example, if $U = 4$ percent and $U_N = 5$ percent, then $U_C = -1$ percent.

Self-Test

1. What is the major difference between a person who is frictionally unemployed and one who is structurally unemployed?

2. If the cyclical unemployment rate is positive, what does this imply?

JOB SEARCH THEORY

Suppose there are six million unemployed persons and all of them are currently looking for jobs. Will each of them take the first job he or she is offered? How do unemployed persons searching for jobs conduct their search? In this section, we try to answer these questions.

The Internet, Information, and Frictional Unemployment

Consider Frank, an accountant who lives in Seattle. The company he works for has just posted its worst earnings in the past two decades. The company has decided to cut back its work force and has fired Frank.

If Frank has transferable skills, and we assume he does, then Frank is currently frictionally unemployed. He will be frictionally unemployed for as long as it takes him to locate another job.

How long do you think this will be? The answer depends on two things. First, it depends on how much time and effort Frank devotes to finding another job. He will probably locate a new job faster if he devotes eight hours each day to searching than if he devotes only one hour every third day. Second, how long Frank stays frictionally unemployed will depend on how easy or difficult it is for him to acquire information that relates to available jobs.

Let's consider how a technological change—the availability of the Internet—has affected acquiring information about available jobs. Before the availability of the Internet, Frank would have to (1) send letters to prospective employees,

(2) check the want ads in hundreds of newspapers across the country, (3) contact an employment agency, (4) call friends who may or may not know of any job openings, and so on. Frank could easily spend a week or two finding appropriate job openings.

Today, because the Internet is available, Frank can simply go online and search the available jobs listed at sites like Monster.com or Headhunters.com. For example, on August 24, 2002, we went to Monster.com and keyed in "Accountant." In less than a second, we had a list of 5,000 job openings for accountants across the country. Then we narrowed the search to job openings for accountants in Seattle, Frank's home. Thirty-four job openings for accountants were listed.

The Internet allows a person who is frictionally unemployed to more easily and quickly acquire the information needed to locate a job. As a result of individuals being able to more easily and quickly acquire information, the time they stay frictionally unemployed drops. In other words, a case can be made that the Internet has lowered the frictional unemployment rate.

THE SEARCH FOR JOBS

The economic theory of job search maintains that individuals consider *both the costs and the benefits of searching for a job* and that they will search until the additional costs and additional benefits are equal. In practice, this translates into job searchers comparing wages offered with reservation wages.

The Wage Offer Curve

Most job searchers do not accept the first job they are offered because they cannot be sure that a better job is not waiting around the corner. In economic terms, job searchers do not possess complete information about job opportunities.

Consider 1,000 individuals searching for jobs. To simplify the analysis, let's assume that each individual compares the jobs he or she is offered only in terms of wages offered (W_O). If we were to plot the wage offers of each of the 1,000 individuals, we would no doubt find that some individuals received their highest wage offer with their first job offer, some received their highest wage offer with their tenth job offer, and many fell between the two extremes. On average, we would expect wage offers to increase (up to a point) as the job search period is extended. The wage offer curve in Exhibit 7a illustrates this pattern.

The Reservation Wage Curve

Individuals searching for jobs realize that the search is costly to them. Most of the cost consists of the wages they could have been earning had they accepted the last offer and not extended the search. For this reason, each job searcher has some notion of a wage offer that is good enough to accept without extending

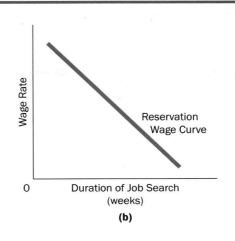

exhibit 7

The Wage Offer and Reservation Wage Curves
(a) The wage offer curve. On average, wages increase (up to a point) with search time. (b) The reservation wage curve. As search time passes, an individual's reservation wage tends to decrease.

the search. The lowest wage a person will accept at any time in the job search process is called that person's **reservation wage** (W_R).

As search time passes, an individual's reservation wage tends to decrease for several reasons. First, individuals searching for jobs usually start out optimistic and often overestimate their market worth to employers. As time passes, they gain information about themselves and the labor market and they become more realistic. Second, long periods of unemployment decrease savings accounts and put pressure on the job searchers to return to work. Third, unemployment benefits do not extend indefinitely. The relationship between the reservation wage and search time is illustrated by the reservation wage curve in Exhibit 7b.

The Optimal Search Time

When does a job searcher stop searching? The answer is when he or she receives a wage offer that (at minimum) equals his or her reservation wage. To put it differently, if the wage offer (W_O) is less than the reservation wage (W_R), the individual continues to search. The job searcher stops searching when $W_O = W_R$. Exhibit 8 represents the process. In the exhibit, the optimal search time is 11 weeks, which is the length of time it takes until W_O equals W_R. Before 11 weeks have passed, $W_R > W_O$, and the job searcher continues to search because he has not received a wage offer high enough to stop him from searching further. In short, he evaluates his wage offers as being too low. As time passes, however, wage offers rise (on average), and the reservation wage falls. Eventually, the two are equal. At this point, the job search ends. In 2000, the *mean* duration of unemployment (mean optimal search time) was approximately 13 weeks; the *median* duration of unemployment was approximately 6 weeks.

THINKING LIKE AN
ECONOMIST

When economists explain and predict behavior, they are usually comparing things. For example, in job search theory, wages offered are compared with reservation wages to explain and predict how long a person searches for a job. In the theory of supply and demand, the quantity demanded of a good is compared with the quantity supplied of the good to see if the market is in equilibrium. In the theory of opportunity cost, what one is doing is compared with what one could be doing to determine cost. When discussing wages, economists assume that people are more interested in their real wages—their money wages compared with the price level—than in their money wages alone.

This emphasis on comparing things illustrates that having a reference point is important to find out where we are or how we are doing. Jones doesn't know

Reservation Wage
The lowest wage a person will accept at any time in the job search process.

http://

Go to *http://jobsinthemoney.com/.* Under "Search Jobs," key "Business and Economics" in the box labeled "Keywords." Then select "Find Finance Jobs." Do you think the Internet affects the costs or benefits of job search? How will the use of these sites affect the length of a job search? Do you think that Taco Bell lists its job openings on the Internet? Explain your answer. What does your answer imply about how the Internet affects the job search for different categories of workers?

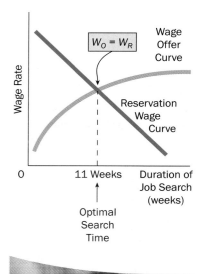

exhibit 8

Optimal Search Time
Job searchers search for jobs until the wage offer (W_O) equals the reservation wage (W_R). In the diagram, this occurs at 11 weeks.

whether or not a wage offer of $2,000 a month is good until she knows her opportunity costs. Smith doesn't know whether or not his increase in salary is an improvement until he measures the percentage increase in his salary against the percentage increase in the price level. So, when economists compare things, they are acting on the knowledge that a reference point is often necessary to tell us how we stand.

OPTIMAL SEARCH TIME AND THE UNEMPLOYMENT RATE

Why do economists consider how people search for jobs? Because job search time influences the unemployment rate. In fact, the longer the optimal search time, the higher the unemployment rate.

Optimal search time ↑ → Unemployment rate ↑
Optimal search time ↓ → Unemployment rate ↓

A simple numerical example illustrates this relationship. Suppose the civilian labor force is composed of 100 individuals and there are 10 unemployed persons. It follows that the unemployment rate is 10 percent. Now consider two cases.

In Case 1, the optimal search time is one week, and each week 10 persons become unemployed. In Case 2, the optimal search time is two weeks, and each week 10 persons become unemployed. Thus, the only difference between Case 1 and Case 2 is that the optimal search time is longer in Case 2. Does an increase in the optimal search time increase the unemployment rate?

Exhibit 9 can help answer this question. Consider Case 1. In week 1, there are 10 persons unemployed, so the unemployment rate is 10 percent. In week 2 10 persons accept job offers (recall that the optimal search time is one week) and 10 persons become unemployed. We subtract 10 persons from and add 10 persons to the number of unemployed at the end of week 1. Thus, in week 2 there are 10 persons unemployed and the unemployment rate is 10 percent. In week 3, 10 persons accept job offers and 10 persons become unemployed. We subtract 10 persons from and add 10 persons to the number of unemployed persons at the end of week 2. Thus in week 3, there are 10 persons unemployed in week 3 and the unemployment rate is 10 percent.

Now consider Case 2, where the optimal search time is two weeks. Beginning in week 1, there are 10 persons unemployed, so the unemployment rate is 10 percent. In week 2, 10 persons are added to the ranks of the unemployed but none of the previously unemployed accepts a job offer (recall that the optimal search time is two weeks). It follows that 20 persons are unemployed in week 2

exhibit 9

Optimal Search Time and the Unemployment Rate
Starting with a civilian labor force of 100 persons and 10 unemployed persons, we consider two cases: Case 1, where the optimal search time is one week and each week 10 persons become unemployed, and Case 2, where the optimal search time is two weeks and each week 10 persons become unemployed. As optimal search time increases, so does the unemployment rate—from 10 percent in Case 1 to 20 percent in Case 2.

Case 1: Optimal Search Time = 1 Week

	Week 1	Week 2	Week 3
Unemployed persons	10	$10 - 10 + 10 = 10$	$10 - 10 + 10 = 10$
Unemployment rate	$\frac{10}{100} = 10\%$	$\frac{10}{100} = 10\%$	$\frac{10}{100} = 10\%$

Case 2: Optimal Search Time = 2 Weeks

	Week 1	Week 2	Week 3
Unemployed persons	10	$10 + 10 = 20$	$20 - 10 + 10 = 20$
Unemployment rate	$\frac{10}{100} = 10\%$	$\frac{20}{100} = 20\%$	$\frac{20}{100} = 20\%$

ECONOMICS IN...

The World   Popular Culture   Technology   Everyday Life

What Explains the Increasing Percentage of Women in the Labor Force?

The Bureau of Labor Statistics, a federal government agency, reports that in 1948 in the United States, 31 percent of all women 20 years old and older were working in the labor force. In 2001, that percentage had risen to 60 percent. In fact, in the years from 1948 to 1999, the percentage of women in the labor force has steadily increased. While it was 31 percent in 1948, it was 40.7 percent in 1967, 51.3 percent in 1980, and 59.5 percent in 1996.

The same trend is visible in many other countries. In Australia in 1984, 52.8 percent of the adult female population worked in the labor force and in 1994 the percentage had increased to 63.4 percent. During the same time period, the percentage rose from 62.7 percent to 80.0 percent in Iceland, from 33.2 percent to 44.1 percent in Spain, and from 57.2 to 62.1 percent in Japan.

What explains the steady percentage increase of women in the work force over the last half of the twentieth century? One explanation is that the "work culture" has changed during this time period. Whereas once it was widely accepted that a woman's place was primarily in the home, this view has changed over time. Often, in the United States in particular, the women's movement and feminism are given credit for this change in attitude.

There is, however, another explanation—one that has nothing to do with a changing culture but is purely economic in nature. It is interesting to note that women have joined the work force in record numbers at the same time that it has become monetarily more advantageous to join the work force.

To illustrate, let's consider life at the end of the nineteenth century. In 1895, the average worker had to work 260 hours to earn enough money to buy a one-speed bicycle, 24 hours to earn enough to buy a cushioned chair, and 44 hours to earn enough to buy a 100-piece dinner set. More than 100 years later, in 2000, the average worker had to work only 7.2 hours to earn enough money to buy a one-speed bicycle, only 2.0 hours to earn enough to buy a cushioned chair, and

only 3.6 hours to earn enough to buy a 100-piece dinner set. In other words, the average worker did not have to work as many hours in 2000 as in 1895 to buy the same goods. This conclusion also holds for goods other than bicycles, cushioned chairs, and dinner sets. In fact, it holds for many if not most goods. Here are a few:[3]

Time Needed for the Average Worker to Earn the Purchase Price of Various Goods

Good	Time to Earn in 1895 (hours)	Time to Earn in 2000 (hours)
One-speed bicycle	260	7.2
Cushioned office chair	24	2
100-piece dinner set	44	3.6
Hairbrush	16	2
Cane rocking chair	8	1.6
Solid gold locket	28	6
Encyclopaedia Britannica	140	33.8
Steinway piano	2,400	1,107.6

When the average worker has to work only 7.2 hours to earn enough money to buy a bicycle, as compared to 260 hours, it follows that it is much more advantageous to work. Stated differently, using bicycles as our good, one hour of work in 1895 got the average worker 1/260 of a bicycle; but in 2000, it got the average worker about 1/7 of a bicycle. In other words, the hourly pay (in terms of bicycles) was much higher in 2000 than in 1895.

Economists would predict that more people would want to work the higher the wage rate for working (in terms of goods). In other words, the greater the benefits from working, the more people would choose to work. And this is exactly what we see. As the wage rate for working (in terms of bicycles, office chairs, dinner sets) has increased, women have joined the labor force in record numbers.

and that the unemployment rate is 20 percent. In week 3, 10 persons accept job offers (the two weeks optimal search time has passed) and 10 persons become unemployed. We therefore subtract 10 persons from and add 10 persons to the number of unemployed at the end of week 2. The number of persons unemployed in week 3 is 20, and the unemployment rate is 20 percent. Our conclusion is that as the optimal search time increases, the unemployment rate increases.

---

3. The data here are from Brad de Long, an economics professor at the University of California, Berkeley, in his work-in-progress *The Economic History of the Twentieth Century: Slouching Towards Utopia*. The work can be found at *http://j-bradford-delong .net/Index.html*.

Self-Test

1. Suppose unemployment benefits increase. How is this likely to affect the optimal search time and the unemployment rate? Explain your answer.

2. A person says, "I don't think of the costs and benefits of searching for a job. I simply search for as long as it takes to get a job." Comment.

A Reader Asks...
Where Do I Learn the Specifics of Jobs and Wages?

I'm a math major and I'll graduate from college in about a year. Is there a way for me to find out how much mathematicians earn and what types of jobs they perform?

No matter what your major is, you can learn about jobs and wages from the *Occupational Outlook Handbook.* The *Handbook* is on the Bureau of Labor Statistics Web site at *http://stats.bls.gov/emp/*.

According to the *Handbook,* mathematicians usually work as part of a team that includes economists, engineers, computer scientists, physicists, and others. In 1998, mathematicians held about 14,000 jobs. In addition, about 20,000 persons held faculty positions in mathematics at colleges and universities.

Many nonfaculty mathematicians work for the federal and state governments. The biggest employer of mathematicians in the federal government is the Department of Defense. In the private sector, major employers include research and testing services, educational services, security and commodity exchanges, and manage-

ment and public relations services. In manufacturing, the pharmaceutical industry is the primary employer. Some mathematicians also work for banks, insurance companies, and public utilities.

Median annual earnings of mathematicians were $49,120 in 1998. The middle 50 percent earned between $33,420 and $77,300. The lowest 10 percent had earnings of less than $25,150, while the top 10 percent earned more than $101,990.

Finally, according to a 1999 survey by the National Association of Colleges and Employers, starting salary offers averaged about $37,300 a year for mathematics graduates with a bachelor's degree and $42,000 for those with a master's degree. Doctoral degree candidates averaged $58,900. The average annual salary in 1999 for mathematicians employed by the federal government in supervisory, nonsupervisory, and managerial positions was $69,000, for mathematics statisticians it was $69,000, and for cryptoanalysts it was $61,100.

Chapter Summary

Measuring Prices

- One major price index is the consumer price index (CPI).

- $$CPI = \left(\frac{\text{Total dollar expenditure on market basket in current year}}{\text{Total dollar expenditure on market basket in base year}} \right) \times 100$$

- $$\frac{\text{Percentage}}{\text{change in prices}} = \left(\frac{CPI_{\text{later year}} - CPI_{\text{earlier year}}}{CPI_{\text{earlier year}}} \right) \times 100$$

- Inflation is an increase in the price level or price index.

- $$\text{Real income} = \left(\frac{\text{Nominal income}}{CPI} \right) \times 100$$

Unemployment and Employment

- $$\text{Unemployment rate } (U) = \frac{\text{Number of unemployed persons}}{\text{Civilian labor force}}$$

- $$\text{Employment rate } (E) = \frac{\text{Number of employed persons}}{\text{Civilian noninstitutional population}}$$

- An unemployed person may be a job loser, a job leaver, a reentrant, or a new entrant.

- The unemployment rate may be biased downward because discouraged workers are not considered unemployed.

- Frictional unemployment, due to the natural "frictions" of the economy, is caused by changing market conditions and is represented by qualified individuals with transferable skills who change jobs.

- Structural unemployment is due to structural changes in the economy that eliminate some jobs and create others for which the unemployed are unqualified.

- Natural unemployment is caused by frictional and structural factors in the economy. The natural unemployment rate equals the sum of the frictional unemployment rate and the structural unemployment rate.

- Full employment is the condition that exists when the unemployment rate is equal to the natural unemployment rate.
- The cyclical unemployment rate is the difference between the existing unemployment rate and the natural unemployment rate.

The Job Search Process

- The economic theory of job search maintains that individuals consider both the costs and benefits of searching for a job and that they search until the additional costs and additional benefits of the job search are equal. In practice, this means they search until they receive a wage offer that is equal to their reservation wage.
- The optimal search time is the time it takes until the wage offer equals the reservation wage. If the optimal search time increases, the unemployment rate increases; if the optimal search time decreases, the unemployment rate decreases.

Key Terms and Concepts

Price Level	Nominal Income	Natural Unemployment
Price Index	Unemployment Rate	Full Employment
Consumer Price Index (CPI)	Employment Rate	Cyclical Unemployment Rate
Base Year	Labor Force Participation Rate	Reservation Wage
Inflation	Frictional Unemployment	
Real Income	Structural Unemployment	

Economic Connections to You

Economic facts, actions, and changes create ripples that move away from their point of origin. Eventually, these ripples can intersect your life and have an effect on you. Consider the following example.

The wage offer curve can be converted to an after-tax wage offer curve. All we do is subtract taxes from wage offers. For example, if the wage offer is $10 an hour and the taxes per hour are $2, then the after-tax wage offer is $8 an hour. The job search ends when the after-tax wage offer equals the reservation wage.

With this as background, suppose that income tax rates rise while you are searching for a job. As a result, *your after-tax wage offers fall, or the after-tax offer curve shifts downward. (Draw this.) As a result, your after-tax wage offer curve crosses your reservation wage curve to the right of where it would have had taxes not risen. In other words, your optimal search time rises and you stay unemployed for a longer period of time. Thus, there is a connection between a rise in income tax rates and how long it takes you to find a job—an economic connection to you.*

Based on the material in this chapter, identify other ways in which economic facts, actions, and changes create ripples that eventually affect you.

Questions and Problems

1. What does the CPI in the base year equal? Explain your answer.
2. What is the difference between a fixed-weighted price index and a chain-weighted price index?
3. Show that if the percentage rise in prices is equal to the percentage rise in nominal income, then one's real income does not change.
4. What does it mean if the expenditure weights of the market basket used to compute the CPI are changed?
5. How does structural unemployment differ from frictional unemployment?
6. What does it mean to say that the country is operating at full employment?

7. What is "natural" about natural unemployment?

8. What is the difference between the employment rate and the labor force participation rate?

9. If the unemployment rate is 4 percent, it does not follow that the employment rate is 96 percent. Explain why.

10. What criteria must be met in order for a person to be characterized as unemployed?

11. What is the difference between a job leaver and a reentrant?

12. How is a discouraged worker different from an unemployed worker?

13. Prove that as optimal search time rises, the unemployment rate rises.

14. Optimal search time will change if the wage offer curve shifts, the reservation wage curve shifts, or both curves shift. Name three factors that you think can change each curve. In each case, specify the directional change in the curve and the effect on the optimal search time. Give reasons for the factors you choose and the directional changes you specify.

Working with Numbers and Graphs

1. Suppose there are 60 million people employed, 10 million unemployed, and 30 million not in the labor force. What does the civilian noninstitutional population equal?

2. Suppose there are 100 million people in the civilian labor force and 90 million people employed. How many people are unemployed? What is the unemployment rate?

3. Change the current-year prices in Exhibit 1 to $1 for pens, $28 for shirts, and $32 for a pair of shoes. What is the CPI for the current year based on these prices?

4. Jim earned an annual salary of $5,000 in 1913. What is this equivalent to in 1999 dollars? (Use Exhibit 2 to find the CPI in the years mentioned.)

5. A house cost $10,000 in 1954. What is this equivalent to in 1998 dollars? (Use Exhibit 2 to find the CPI in the years mentioned.)

6. In year 1, 20 units of X and 40 units of Y are produced and the per-unit price of each is $2 and $4, respectively. In year 2, 30 units of X and 50 units of Y are produced and the per-unit price of each is $3 and $6, respectively. Compute the chain-weighted price index in year 2.

7. Using the following data, compute (a) the unemployment rate, (b) the employment rate, and (c) the labor force participation rate.
Civilian noninstitutional population = 200 million
Number of employed persons = 126 million
Number of unemployed persons = 8 million

8. Based on the following data, compute (a) the structural unemployment rate, (b) the cyclical unemployment rate, and (c) the unemployment rate.
Frictional unemployment rate = 2 percent
Natural unemployment rate = 5 percent
Civilian labor force = 100 million
Number of employed persons = 82 million

9. Using Exhibit 2, compute the percentage change in prices between (a) 1953 and 1967, (b) 1976 and 1986, and (c) 1990 and 1999.

10. Assume the market basket contains 10X, 20Y, and 45Z. The current-year prices for goods X, Y, and Z are $1, $4, and $6, respectively. The base-year prices are $1, $3, and $5, respectively. What is the CPI in the current year?

11. If the CPI is 150 and nominal income is $100,000, what does real income equal?

12. Diagrammatically show what happens to the optimal search time if unemployment benefits rise. Explain your answer.

Internet Activities

1. Go to *http://www.odci.gov*. Under "Library & Reference," click on the "World Factbook" and select "Country Listing." Click on Angola, Belize, Brazil, India, and Spain to find the inflation rate for each country. (The inflation rate is in the Economy category.)

   a. Do inflation rates vary between these countries?

   b. Is there any relationship between the population of a country and its inflation rate? Do you think population is independent of the inflation rate?

2. Go to *http://www.bls.gov/cpi/*. Click on "Tables Created by BLS" and select "Annual Percent Changes from 1913 to Present." Calculate the annual inflation rate for the following years: 1917 (compare December 1916 to December 1917), 1930 (compare December 1929 to December 1930), 1974, and 1980. Calculate the change in prices between 1920 and 1940 and between 1990 and 1998.

   a. Has inflation always been present in the United States?

b. Do you think that inflation has ever been high enough in the United States to be considered a major economic problem? How high do you think the inflation rate has to rise before it becomes a major national problem?

c. Do you consider the 1990s to be a period of high inflation, low inflation, or price stability?

3. Go to *http://www.bls.gov/cps/*. Under "Tables Created by BLS," click "Employment Status" and select the following table: "Employment status of the civilian noninstitutional population by age, sex, and race (<u>TXT</u>)."

a. How many people are unemployed? What is the unemployment rate? What is the unemployment rate for men over 20? for women over 20? Go back and click on the "Employment status of the civil-

ian population 25 years and over by educational attainment."

b. What is the unemployment rate for those persons with less than a high school diploma? for college graduates?

c. What is the participation rate for those persons with less than a high school diploma? for college graduates?

d. What do you conclude about the work life of someone without a high school diploma?

4. Go to *http://www.bls.gov/cpi/*. Under "Get Detailed Statistics," select "Inflation Calculator." If the price of breakfast in 1914 was $0.25, how much is this in today's dollars?

ch.6

MACROECONOMIC MEASUREMENTS, PART II: GDP AND REAL GDP

Many thousands of goods and services are produced each day in the United States. How do we measure all this economic activity? One of the principal ways is to compute GDP, or gross domestic product. GDP is one of the most important economic measurements used by economists.

The two principal measures of macroeconomic activity are gross domestic product (GDP) and Real GDP. Stated differently, GDP and Real GDP are macroeconomic measures used to gauge macroeconomic activity. Often economists equate changes in macroeconomic activity with changes in either GDP or Real GDP.

   The chapter begins with a discussion of GDP—its definition, the three ways to compute it, its limitations, and the difference between GDP and another macroeconomic measure (GNP). We then define and discuss Real GDP and explain how Real GDP is computed and its role in both economic growth and business cycle activity. Here and there, we identify the other macroeconomic measures shown below that are also used to gauge macroeconomic activity.

GROSS DOMESTIC PRODUCT

In any given year, people in the United States produce goods and services. They produce television sets, books, pencil sharpeners, tape recorders, attorney services, haircuts, and much more. Have you ever wondered what the total dollar value of all those goods and services is? In 2000, it was $9.8 trillion. In other words, in 2000, people living and working in the United States produced $9.8 trillion worth of goods and services. That dollar amount—$9.8 trillion—is what economists call the gross domestic product. Simply put, **gross domestic product (GDP)** is the *total market value of all final goods and services produced annually within a country's borders.*

THREE WAYS TO COMPUTE GDP

Consider a simple economy in which one good is produced and sold. Bob finds a seed and plants it. Sometime later an orange tree appears. Bob pays Harry $5 in wages to pick and box the oranges. Next, Bob sells the oranges to Jim for $8. Jim turns the oranges into orange juice and sells the orange juice to Caroline for $10. Caroline drinks the juice. What is the GDP in this simple economy? Is it $5, $13, $10, $18, or some other dollar amount?

Economists use three approaches to compute GDP—the expenditure approach, the income approach, and the value-added approach. The following paragraphs describe each approach in terms of our simple economy.

Expenditure Approach

To compute GDP using the expenditure approach, add the amount of money spent by buyers on *final goods and services.* The words "final goods and services" are important in computing GDP because not all goods are final goods. Some goods are *intermediate goods.*

A **final good** (or service) is a good in the hands of the final user or ultimate consumer. Think of buyers standing in line, one after another. The first buyer in our simple economy was Jim. He bought oranges from Bob. The second buyer was Caroline, who bought orange juice from Jim.

Caroline is the final buyer in this economy; she is the final user, the ultimate consumer. No buyer comes after her. The good that she buys is the final good. In other words, the orange juice is the final good.

So, then, what are the oranges? Aren't they a final good too? No, the oranges are an *intermediate good.* An **intermediate good** is an input in the production of a final good. In other words, the oranges were used to produce orange juice (the final good).

So, what does GDP equal if we use the expenditure approach to compute it? Again, it is the dollar amount spent by buyers for final goods and services. In our simple economy, there is only one buyer (Caroline) who spends $10 on one final good (orange juice). Thus, GDP in our tiny economy is $10.

Q & A

Q: *Why* are expenditures on only final goods counted when computing GDP? Why aren't the expenditures on both final goods *and* intermediate goods counted?

A: If we count expenditures on both final goods and intermediate goods, we would be *double counting.* **Double counting** refers to counting a good more than once when computing GDP. To illustrate, if we count both Caroline's purchase of the orange juice ($10) and Jim's purchase of the oranges ($8), we count the purchase of the oranges *twice*—once when the oranges are purchased by Jim and once when the oranges are in the orange juice.

Consider another example. Some of the intermediate goods used to make a book are glue, ink, and paper. In one sense, *a book is simply another name for glue, ink, and paper together.* In equation form, book = glue + ink + paper. Now, when computing GDP, if we count the purchase of the book *and* the purchases of glue, ink, and paper, we are counting what is on the left side of the equal sign in the equation (that is, the book) and then adding it

Gross Domestic Product (GDP)
The total market value of all final goods and services produced annually within a country's borders.

Final Good
A good in the hands of its final user.

Intermediate Good
A good that is an input in the production of a final good.

Double Counting
Counting a good more than once when computing GDP.

to what is on the right side of the equal sign in the equation (that is, glue + ink + paper). That would be like saying 2 = 1 + 1 and counting both the 2 and the 1 + 1 to give us a total of 4. Counting the "2" is enough; adding the "2" and the "1 + 1" is double counting.

Income Approach

In our simple economy, income consists of wages and profits.[1] To compute GDP using the income approach, simply find the sum of all the wages and profits.

First, Harry earns $5 in wages.

Second, Bob's profit is $3: (1) Bob pays $5 to Harry, so the $5 is a cost to Bob; (2) Bob receives $8 for the oranges he sells to Jim; (3) $8 in revenue minus $5 in costs leaves Bob with $3 profit.

Third, Jim's profit is $2: (1) Jim pays $8 to Bob for the oranges, so the $8 is a cost to Jim; (2) Jim receives $10 for the orange juice he sells to Caroline; (3) $10 in revenue minus $8 in costs leaves Jim with $2 profit.

In our simple economy, the sum of Harry's wages, Bob's profit, and Jim's profit is $10. So GDP is equal to $10.

Value-Added Approach

In our tiny economy, orange juice is sold for, or has a market value of, $10. How much of the $10 market value is attributable to Jim? Stated differently, how much of the $10 market value is *valued added* by Jim? If your intuition tells you $2, then your intuition is correct. **Value added** is the dollar value contributed to a final good at each stage of production. That is, it is the difference between the dollar value of the output the producer sells and the dollar value of the intermediate goods the producer buys.

Value Added
The dollar value contributed to a final good at each stage of production.

To compute GDP using the value-added approach, find the sum of the values added at all the stages of production. Bob buys no intermediate goods (he simply found a seed, planted it, and then hired Harry to pick and box oranges), but he sells the oranges to Jim for $8. In other words, valued added at this stage of production is $8.

Jim takes the oranges (an intermediate good he buys from Bob for $8) and turns them into orange juice that he sells to Caroline for $10. Value added at this stage of production is $2.

The sum of the values added at all (two) stages of production is $10, so GDP is equal to $10.

WHAT IS THE DIFFERENCE BETWEEN GDP AND GNP?

GNP, which stands for *gross national product,* is an economic measure much like GDP. **Gross national product (GNP)** is the total market value of all final goods and services produced annually by citizens of a country. Although GDP and GNP are similar, there is an important difference. GDP measures the production of goods and services in the physical area of a country, no matter by whom the goods and services are produced. GNP measures the production of goods and services by the citizens of a country, no matter where in the world they reside.

Gross National Product (GNP)
The total market value of all final goods and services produced annually by the citizens of a country.

For example, if a Mexican citizen lives in the United States and produces cars, the total market value of these cars is counted in GDP because the Mexican citizen produced the cars in the United States. But the value of the cars would not be counted in GNP because the Mexican citizen is not a U.S. citizen.

On the other hand, if a U.S. citizen produces cars in France, the total market value of these cars is not counted in GDP because the cars were not produced in the United States. However, the value of the cars would be counted in GNP because the cars were produced by a U.S. citizen.

Go to *http://www.eaglebarter.com*. Examine the site. Do you need money to make a trade? Do you have to trade with one person at a time or can you set up multiperson exchanges? Would these transactions be counted in GDP? Would these transactions be possible without the Internet?

---

1. Later in the chapter, you will learn that in a large economy, such as the U.S. economy, income consists of more than wages and profits. To simplify the explanation, we have defined a tiny economy where only wages and profits exist.

In short, for GDP, geography matters, not citizenship. For GNP, citizenship matters, not geography.

WHAT GDP OMITS

Some exchanges that take place in an economy are not included in GDP. As the following paragraphs indicate, these trades range from sales of used cars to illegal drug deals.

Certain Nonmarket Goods and Services

If a family hires a person through the classified section of the newspaper to cook and clean, the service is counted in GDP. If family members perform the same tasks, however, their services are not counted in GDP. The difference is that, in the first case, a service is actually bought and sold for a price in a market setting, and in the other, it is not.

Some nonmarket goods are included in GDP. For example, the market value of food produced on a farm and consumed by the farm family is estimated, and this imputed value is part of GDP.

Underground Activities, Both Legal and Illegal

The underground economy consists of unreported exchanges that take place outside the normal recorded market channels. Some underground activities involve illegal goods (such as cocaine), and others involve legal goods and tax evasion.

Illegal goods and services are not counted in GDP because no record exists of such transactions. There are no written records of illegal drug sales, illegal gambling, and illegal prostitution. Neither are there written records of some legal activities that individuals want to keep from government notice. For example, a gardener might agree to do some gardening work only on the condition that he is paid in cash. Obviously, it is not illegal for a person to buy or sell gardening services, but still the transaction might not be recorded if one or both parties do not want it to be. Why might the gardener want to be paid in cash? Perhaps he doesn't want to pay taxes on the income received—an objective more easily accomplished if there is no written record of the income being generated.

Sales of Used Goods

GDP measures *current production* (that is, occurring during the current year). A used car sale, for example, does not enter into the current-year statistics because the car was counted when it was originally produced.

Financial Transactions

The trading of stocks and bonds is not counted in GDP because it does not represent the production of new assets, but simply the trading of existing assets (the exchange of stocks or bonds for money).

Government Transfer Payments

Transfer Payment
A payment to a person that is not made in return for goods and services currently supplied.

A **transfer payment** is a payment to a person that is not made in return for goods and services currently supplied. Government transfer payments—such as Social Security benefits and veterans' benefits—are not counted in GDP because they do not represent payments to individuals for *current production*.

Leisure

Leisure is a good, in much the same way that cars, houses, and shoes are goods. New cars, houses, and shoes are counted in GDP, but leisure is not because it is too difficult to quantify. The length of the workweek has fallen in the United States over the past years, indicating that the leisure time individuals have to consume has increased. But GDP computations do not take this into account.

ECONOMICS IN...

The World   Popular Culture   Technology   Everyday Life

Underground Economies

Suppose the U.S. GDP is $9 trillion in a given year. Does it follow that the $9 trillion figure captures all the goods and services produced in that year in the United States? You already know that it does not. For example, it doesn't include all the unreported exchanges that take place outside the normal recorded market channels. In other words, it doesn't take into account the economic activity in the *underground economy.*

Economists sometimes try to estimate the underground economies of different countries. This is somewhat difficult to do because they are trying to estimate something that is not visible.

One economist who has attempted the task is Friedrich Schneider of the Johannes Kepler University of Linz (in Austria). One of the ways that Schneider estimates the size of the underground economy in a given country is by identifying the amount of cash in the economy. After all, if you didn't want anyone to know you had engaged in a certain transac-

tion, wouldn't you make the transaction using cash instead of a check or credit card? Wouldn't you then need to have more cash on hand?

Suppose that in a given city, individuals usually hold $25 in cash for every $100 they have in a checking account. Then, all of a sudden, the demand to hold cash rises to $40 for every $100 in a checking account. There could be any of a number of reasons that explain the rise in the cash-to-checking-account ratio, but Schneider thinks one reason is that some people are holding more cash because they want to engage in more unreported—underground—activities.

Using the currency-demand approach to estimating the size of underground economies, as well as several other approaches, too, Schneider computed the underground economy as a percentage of GDP for several countries. See Exhibit 1.

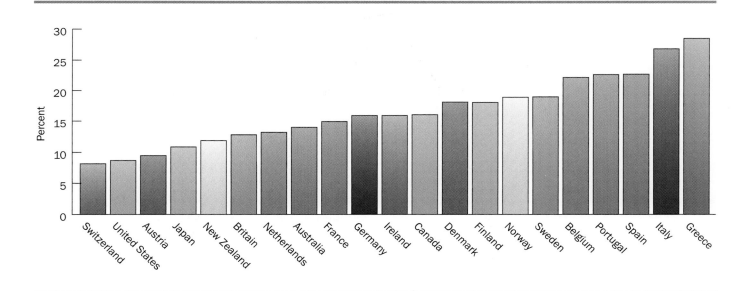

exhibit 1

The Underground Economy as a Percentage of GDP, Selected Countries, 1999

Source: Friedrich Schneider, Johannes Kepler University of Linz.

GDP IS NOT ADJUSTED FOR BADS GENERATED IN THE PRODUCTION OF GOODS

Economic growth often comes with certain *bads*. For example, producing cars, furniture, and steel often generates air and water pollution—considered bads by most people. (Remember from Chapter 1 that a bad is anything from which individuals receive disutility.) GDP counts the goods and services, but it does not net out the air and water pollution. Thus, some economists argue that GDP overstates our overall economic welfare.

PER CAPITA GDP

If we divide a country's GDP by the population in the country, we get *per capita GDP*. For example, if a country has a GDP of $2,000 billion and its population is 100 million, GDP per capita is $20,000.

IS EITHER GDP OR PER CAPITA GDP A MEASURE OF HAPPINESS OR WELL-BEING?

Are the people in a country with a higher GDP or higher per capita GDP better off or happier than the people in a country with a lower GDP or lower per capita GDP? We cannot answer that question because well-being and happiness are subjective. A person with more goods may be happier than a person with fewer goods, but possibly not. The person with fewer goods, but a lot of leisure, little air pollution, and a relaxed way of life may be much happier than the person with many goods, little leisure, and a polluted, stressful environment.

We make this point to warn against reading too much into GDP figures. GDP figures are useful for obtaining an estimate of the productive capabilities of an economy, but they do not necessarily measure happiness or well-being.

Self-Test *(Answers to Self-Test questions are in the Self-Test Appendix.)*

1. Give an example that illustrates the difference between the U.S. GDP and the U.S. GNP.

2. Suppose the GDP for a country is $0. Does this mean that there was no productive activity in the country? Explain your answer.

http://

Go to *http://www.bea.doc.gov/bea/dn1 .htm*. Under "*Time Series Estimates,*" click "Select data from the full set of NIPA Tables," and then select "list of Selected NIPA Tables." Under Section 1—National Income and Product," choose "Table 1.1 Gross Domestic Product (A)(Q)." Between 1959 and today, how many times did personal consumption expenditures fall? How many times did total gross private domestic investment rise? Which is the larger dollar amount, consumption or investment? Which do you think is more important to watch to explain the economic condition of the country? Explain your answer.

THE EXPENDITURE APPROACH TO COMPUTING GDP FOR A REAL-WORLD ECONOMY

The last section explains the expenditure, income, and value-added approaches to computing GDP for a simple economy. This simple economy consisted of one person producing oranges, one person producing orange juice, and one person buying orange juice. Obviously, the U.S. economy is much more complex than this tiny economy is.

This section explains how the expenditure approach is used to compute GDP in a real-world economy like the U.S. economy. The next section explains how the income approach is used.

EXPENDITURES IN A REAL-WORLD ECONOMY

Economists often talk about four sectors of the economy: (1) household sector, (2) business sector, (3) government sector, and (4) foreign sector. Economic actors in these sectors buy goods and services; in other words, they spend. The expendi-

ECONOMICS IN...

Everyday Life · Popular Culture · Technology · The World

The O.J. Trial, Divorce, Crime, and September 11th

What do divorce, crime, the O.J. Simpson trial, and September 11th have in common? Each has something to do with GDP.

Divorce

Think of a world in which there is no divorce and of a world in which divorce exists. In which world is GDP higher? All other things being equal, GDP is higher in the world in which divorce exists. That's because divorce stimulates spending. When couples get divorced, they have to pay lawyer's fees and have to spend money to set up separate households.

Crime

Think of a world in which there are no burglaries and of a world in which burglaries exist. In which world is GDP higher? All other things being equal, GDP is higher in the world in which burglaries exist. That's because people will produce and buy locks, alarm systems, and other security devices when burglaries exist but won't have to produce and buy these items when there are no burglaries.

The O.J. Simpson Trial

In 1994, O.J. Simpson was accused of killing his ex-wife, Nicole Brown Simpson, and a friend of hers, Ronald Goldman. The O.J. Simpson trial ran for much of 1995. On March 22, 1995, the *Wall Street Journal* printed an article titled "GDP of O.J. Trial Outruns the Total, of, Say, Grenada."

Certainly during the trial, there was a mini-O.J. economy. For example, O.J. Simpson paid lawyers, DNA specialists, private investigators, paralegals, and jury consultants. His legal fees alone were $20,000 a day. Also, people sold O.J. statuettes (for more than $3,000), rooms at hotels near the courthouse where the case was being tried, books about the trial, and much more. At one point, O.J. Simpson sold prepaid phone cards. Each card came with a certificate of authenticity signed by Simpson and one of his attorneys. Simpson's voice, recorded from jail, greeted users of the phone cards: "Hi, this is O.J. Thanks for using the Juice Line. I'd like to thank all my fans for their support."

The *Wall Street Journal* estimated that the O.J. economy, or the O.J. GDP, was probably close to $200 million. However, whether or not the O.J. GDP added to the nation's GDP is debatable. It could simply be that more O.J.-related spending was offset by less spending elsewhere in the economy.

September 11th

Think of the expenditure components of GDP: consumption, investment, government purchases, and net exports. Net exports, of course, equal exports minus imports.

Soon after the terrorist attacks of September 11th, the United Nations predicted that Asia's GDP would fall. Here was the reasoning: The terrorist attacks would cause Americans to reduce their spending. Not only would they buy fewer domestic-produced goods, but they would buy fewer foreign-produced goods too. In other words, countries like Hong Kong, Singapore, Japan, Malaysia, and the Philippines would sell fewer exports to the United States. A decline in, say, Singapore exports to the United States, all other things being equal, reduces Singapore's GDP.

---

tures of the sectors are called, respectively, (1) *consumption;* (2) gross private domestic investment, or simply *investment;* (3) government consumption expenditures and gross investment, or simply *government purchases;* and (4) *net exports.*

Consumption

Consumption (*C*) includes (1) spending on durable goods, (2) spending on nondurable goods, and (3) spending on services. Durable goods are goods that are expected to last for more than three years, such as refrigerators, ovens, or cars. Nondurable goods are goods that are not expected to last for more than three years, such as food. Services are intangible items such as lawn care, car repair, and entertainment.

Consumption
The sum of spending on durable goods, nondurable goods, and services.

Investment
The sum of all purchases of newly produced capital goods, changes in business inventories, and purchases of new residential housing.

Inventory Investment
Changes in the stock of unsold goods.

Fixed Investment
Business purchases of capital goods, such as machinery and factories, and purchases of new residential housing.

Government Purchases
Federal, state, and local government purchases of goods and services and gross investment in highways, bridges, and so on.

Government Transfer Payments
Payments to persons that are not made in return for goods and services currently supplied.

Imports
Total domestic (U.S.) spending on foreign goods.

Exports
Total foreign spending on domestic (U.S.) goods.

Net Exports
Exports minus imports.

Investment

Investment (I) is the sum of (1) the purchases of newly produced capital goods, (2) changes in business inventories, sometimes referred to as **inventory investment,** and (3) purchases of new residential housing.[2] The sum of the purchases of newly produced capital goods and the purchases of new residential housing is often referred to as **fixed investment.** In other words, investment = fixed investment + inventory investment. Fixed investment is the larger of the two components of investment.

Government Purchases

Government purchases (G) include federal, state, and local government purchases of goods and services and gross investment in highways, bridges, and so on. **Government transfer payments,** which are payments to persons that are not made in return for goods and services currently supplied, are not included in government purchases. Social Security benefits and welfare payments are two examples of transfer payments; neither is a payment for current productive efforts.

Net Exports

People, firms, and governments in the United States sometimes purchase foreign-produced goods. These purchases are referred to as **imports** (IM). Foreign residents, firms, and governments sometimes purchase U.S.-produced goods. These purchases are referred to as **exports** (EX). If imports are subtracted from exports, we are left with **net exports** (NX).

$$NX = EX - IM$$

Q & A

Q: If imports are greater than exports, then why don't we subtract exports from imports and call the difference "net imports"?

A: It is simply customary to subtract imports from exports, regardless of which is greater, and to speak of the difference as net exports. If exports are greater than imports, then net exports are positive; if imports are greater than exports, then net exports are negative.

COMPUTING GDP USING THE EXPENDITURE APPROACH

The expenditure approach to computing GDP sums the purchases of final goods and services made by the four sectors of the economy. See Exhibit 2. This may give you reason to pause because our earlier definition of GDP did not mention *purchases* of final goods and services. Rather, we defined GDP as the total market value of all final goods and services *produced* annually within a nation's borders.

The discrepancy is cleared up quickly when we note that national income accountants (those persons who compute GDP for the government) assume that anything that is produced but not sold to consumers is "bought" by the firm that produced it. In other words, if a car is produced but not sold, it goes into business inventory and is consider to be "purchased" by the firm that produced it. Thus, we can compute GDP by summing the purchases made by the four sectors of the economy. GDP equals consumption (C) plus investment (I) plus government purchases (G) plus net exports ($EX - IM$) (See Exhibit 3).[3]

$$GDP = C + I + G + (EX - IM)$$

---

2. For purposes of computing GDP, the purchases of new residential housing (although undertaken by members of the household sector) are considered investment.

3. Another way to write this equation is: GDP = $C + I + G + NX$ because $NX = EX - IM$.

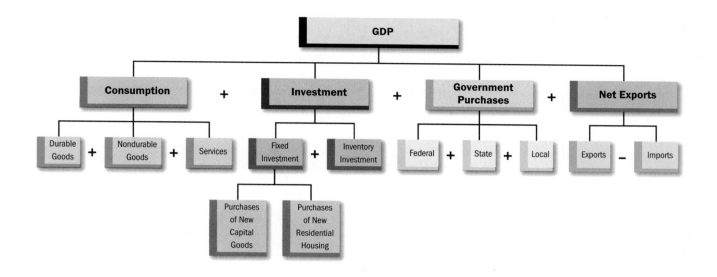

AN EASY WAY TO SEE THAT GDP $= C + I + G + (EX - IM)$

When American households buy goods and services, some of those goods and services are produced in the United States and some are produced in foreign countries. For example, let's say that American households spent $3,000 billion this year and that $2,500 billion went for U.S.-produced goods and $500 billion went for foreign-produced goods. We can write the total consumption by households as the sum of two components—consumption on U.S. goods (C_{US}) and consumption on foreign goods (C_F):

$$C = C_{US} + C_F$$

The same holds for U.S. business firms. In other words, if total investment spending is $700 billion, some of this may be for U.S.-produced goods (I_{US}) and some may be for foreign-produced goods (I_F). Thus, with respect to investment, we have

$$I = I_{US} + I_F$$

exhibit 2

The Expenditure Approach to Computing GDP

The expenditure components of GDP are consumption, investment, government purchases, and net exports. The exhibit shows what is included in each of these components.

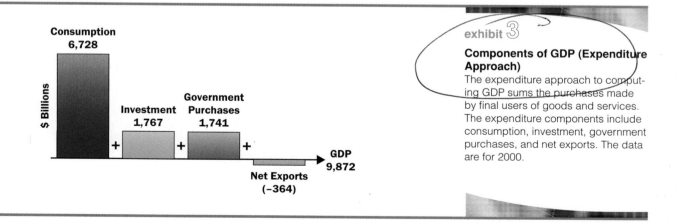

exhibit 3

Components of GDP (Expenditure Approach)

The expenditure approach to computing GDP sums the purchases made by final users of goods and services. The expenditure components include consumption, investment, government purchases, and net exports. The data are for 2000.

And for government, we have government purchases of U.S. goods and services (G_{US}) and government purchases of foreign goods and services (G_F). So,

$$G = G_{US} + G_F$$

Now when economists compute GDP they are interested in the spending on U.S. goods and services, not foreign goods and services. This means they have to subtract any spending on imports from consumption, investment, and government purchases. And then they have to add foreign spending on U.S. goods, which is included in exports (EX). We have

$$\begin{align} GDP &= \text{Total spending on U.S. goods and services} \\ &= (C - C_F) + (I - I_F) + (G - G_F) + EX \end{align} \tag{1}$$

Rearranging equation (1) gives

$$GDP = C + I + G + EX - (C_F + I_F + G_F) \tag{2}$$

Now the sum of the spending on foreign goods and services is simply $C_F + I_F + G_F$, another name for which is imports (IM). In other words,

$$C_F + I_F + G_F = IM$$

If we substitute this equation into (2), we get

$$GDP = C + I + G + (EX - IM) \tag{3}$$

 Q: What country in the world has the largest GDP?

A: In 2000, the United States had a larger GDP than any country in the world. It was followed by (in order) China, Japan, India, Germany, France, United Kingdom, Italy, Brazil, and Mexico.

Q: I thought India and China were relatively poor countries. Why would they be among the countries with the largest GDP?

A: A large GDP and a large per capita GDP are two different things. Big countries (in terms of population) tend to have a relatively large GDP because there is more economic activity, say, in a country of 1 billion people than in a country of 20 million people. But just because a country's GDP is large, it doesn't follow that its per capita GDP is large. For example, while India is the fourth largest economy in the world, Indians have a per capita GDP that ranks them in 136th place. Similarly, while China is the second largest economy in the world, the Chinese have a per capita GDP that ranks them in 88th place.

THE INCOME APPROACH TO COMPUTING GDP FOR A REAL-WORLD ECONOMY

Now let's look at how the income approach is used to compute GDP for a real-world economy. The two approaches should give us the same dollar figure for GDP. (Remember our simple orange juice economy?) Exhibit 4—a circular flow diagram of the economy—shows that in a simple economy, GDP computed by summing the purchases of the four sectors of the economy is equal to GDP computed by summing the income earned by the different resources.

Now let's examine the two steps involved in computing GDP using the income approach. First, we must compute national income. Second, we must adjust national income for certain things. The end result is GDP.

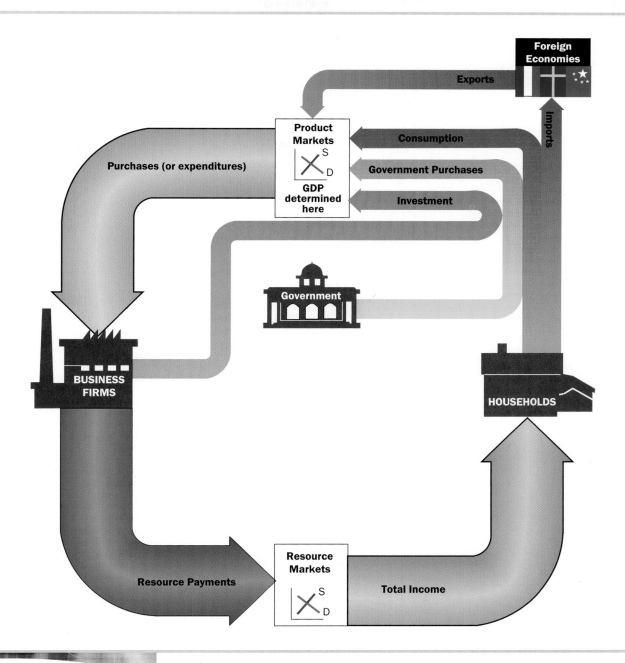

exhibit 4

The Circular Flow: Total Purchases (Expenditures) Equal Total Income in a Simple Economy
The exhibit shows an economy with four sectors: Households, Business Firms, Government, and Foreign Economies. Each sector purchases goods and services. The sum of these purchases is GDP [GDP = $C + I + G + (EX - IM)$].

The purchases (expenditures) made in product markets flow to business firms (purple arrow). Business firms then use these monies to buy resources in resource markets (dark blue arrow). In other words, these monies flow to the owners (suppliers) of land, labor, capital, and entrepreneurship. The sum of these resource payments is total income (light blue arrow), which flows to households. In this simple economy, where some things have been ignored, total purchases (expenditures) equal total income. Because total purchases (expenditures) equal GDP and total purchases equal total income, it follows that GDP equals total income.

National Income

Total income earned by U.S. citizens and businesses, no matter where they reside or are located. National income is the sum of the payments to resources (land, labor, capital, and entrepreneurship). National income = compensation of employees + proprietors' income + corporate profits + rental income of persons + net interest.

COMPUTING NATIONAL INCOME

National income is the sum of five components: (1) compensation of employees, (2) proprietors' income, (3) corporate profits, (4) rental income of persons, and (5) net interest. We discuss the details of each in the following paragraphs.

Compensation of Employees

Compensation of employees consists of wages and salaries paid to employees plus employers' contributions to Social Security and employee benefit plans plus the monetary value of fringe benefits, tips, and paid vacations. Compensation of employees is the largest component of national income.

Proprietors' Income

Proprietors' income includes all forms of income earned by self-employed individuals and the owners of unincorporated businesses, including unincorporated farmers. Included in farm income is an estimate of the value of the food grown and consumed on farms.

Corporate Profits

Corporate profits include all the income earned by the stockholders of corporations. Some of the profits are paid to stockholders in the form of dividends, some are kept within the firm to finance investments (these are called *undistributed profits* or *retained earnings*), and some are used to pay corporate profits taxes. (The portion of corporate profits used to pay corporate profits taxes is counted as income "earned" by households even though households do not receive the income.)

Rental Income (of Persons)

Rental income is the income received by individuals for the use of their nonmonetary assets (land, houses, offices). It also includes returns to individuals who hold copyrights and patents. Finally, it includes an imputed value to owner-occupied houses. For example, someone may own the house she lives in, and therefore not pay any rent, but for purposes of national income accounting, a rental value is imputed. In short, home ownership is viewed as a business that produces a service that is sold to the owner of the business.

Net Interest

Net interest is the interest income received by U.S. households and government minus the interest they paid out.

National Income

We can summarize national income and its components as follows:

$$
\begin{aligned}
\text{National income} = \ &\text{Compensation of employees} \\
&+ \text{Proprietors' income} \\
&+ \text{Corporate profits} \\
&+ \text{Rental income} \\
&+ \text{Net interest}
\end{aligned}
$$

http://

Go to *http://www.bea.gov/bea/dn1.htm*. Under "*Time Series Estimates*," click on "Select data from the full set of NIPA Tables," and then select "list of Selected NIPA Tables." Under "Section 1—National Income and Product," choose "Table 1.14 National Income by Type of Income (A)(Q)." In 1959, what percentage of national income was corporate profits? What is the percentage today? In 1959, what percentage of national income was nonfarm proprietors' income? What is this percentage today?

FROM NATIONAL INCOME TO GDP: MAKING SOME ADJUSTMENTS

After computing national income, you might think that there is nothing else to do—that national income should equal GDP. That's because we naturally think that every dollar spent is someone's income.

But when we check the actual figures for national income and GDP, we find that they are not equal. In other words, not every dollar spent is someone else's income. For example, if Jones spends $10 to buy a book, $9.50 of the $10 might end up in the seller's pocket as income, but 50 cents of the $10 might go for taxes.

With this in mind, the income approach to computing GDP requires us to add certain things to national income and to subtract certain things from national income. The following equation and Exhibit 5 identify exactly what must be added to and subtracted from national income to compute GDP. Keep the equation and exhibit in mind as you continue to read.

GDP = National income
      − Income earned from the rest of the world
      + Income earned by the rest of the world
      + Indirect business taxes
      + Capital consumption allowance
      + Statistical discrepancy

Income Earned from the Rest of the World, Income Earned by the Rest of the World

Consider that when we compute national income, we include the income earned by U.S. citizens who work and live in other countries, but we do not include the income earned by foreigners who work and live in the United States. If we want to compute GDP (rather than GNP), we have to adjust for both these incomes. We do so by (1) subtracting from national income the income earned from the rest of the world (this is income U.S. citizens living abroad earned by producing and selling goods) and (2) adding to national income the income earned by the rest of the world (this is income non-U.S. citizens earned by producing and selling goods in the United States).

Indirect Business Taxes

The main items that comprise indirect business taxes are excise taxes, sales taxes, and property taxes. These taxes are not part of national income because they are not considered a payment to any resource (land, labor, and so on). You should think of them as "monies collected by government" and not as payment to land, labor, capital, or entrepreneurship.

These indirect taxes are included in purchases of goods and services (you pay a sales tax when you buy most goods) and so are included when the expenditure approach is used to compute GDP. Therefore, we must add indirect business taxes to national income.

exhibit 5

The Income Approach to Computing GDP
The exhibit identifies the components of national income and the adjustments necessary to compute GDP using the income approach.

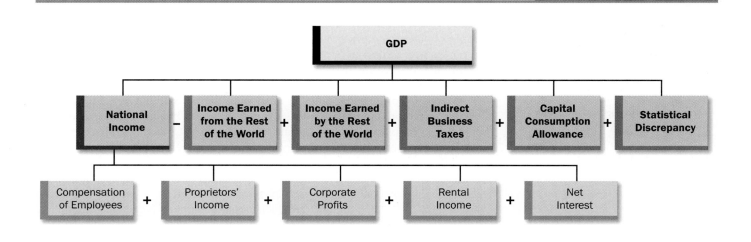

Capital Consumption Allowance

Some capital goods are used up in the production process through natural wear, obsolescence, or accidental destruction (for example, the machinery that breaks down and cannot be repaired). The cost to replace these capital goods is called the **capital consumption allowance,** or **depreciation.** We add the capital consumption allowance, or depreciation, to national income because we want a measure of all the income earned in the economy. National income, by itself, doesn't include the income payments implicit in the capital consumption allowance.

Statistical Discrepancy

GDP and national income are computed using different sets of data. Hence, statistical discrepancies or pure computational errors often occur and must be accounted for in the national income accounts.

OTHER NATIONAL INCOME ACCOUNTING MEASUREMENTS

Besides gross domestic product (GDP) and national income, three other national income accounting measures are important. They are net domestic product, personal income, and disposable income. The five measures—gross domestic product, national income, net domestic product, personal income, and disposable income—are often used interchangeably to measure the output produced and income earned in an economy.

NET DOMESTIC PRODUCT

If we use the expenditure approach to compute GDP, we add consumption, investment, government purchases, and net exports. Investment (or, more specifically, gross private domestic investment) includes fixed investment and inventory investment. Some of the fixed investment, however, is used to replace worn-out or obsolete capital goods. It is not used for the production of new goods. In short, gross private domestic investment contains within it the capital consumption allowance. If we subtract the capital consumption allowance from GDP, we are left with **net domestic product (NDP).** NDP measures the total value of new goods available in the economy in a given year after worn-out capital goods have been replaced.

> Net domestic product (NDP) = GDP − Capital consumption allowance

PERSONAL INCOME

Not all income earned is received, and not all income received is earned. An example of "income earned but not received" is undistributed profits. Undistributed profits are earned by stockholders but not received by them. Instead, the undistributed profits are usually reinvested by the corporation. An example of "income received but not earned" is Social Security benefits.

  Personal income is the amount of income that individuals actually receive. It is equal to national income minus such major earned-but-not-received items as undistributed corporate profits, social insurance taxes (Social Security contributions), and corporate profits taxes, plus transfer payments (which are received but not earned).

> Personal Income = National income
> − Undistributed corporate profits
> − Social insurance taxes
> − Corporate profits taxes
> + Transfer payments

Capital Consumption Allowance (Depreciation)
The estimated amount of capital goods used up in production through natural wear, obsolescence, and accidental destruction.

Net Domestic Product (NDP)
GDP minus the capital consumption allowance.

Personal Income
The amount of income that individuals actually receive. It is equal to national income minus undistributed corporate profits, social insurance taxes, and corporate profits taxes, plus transfer payments.

DISPOSABLE INCOME

The portion of personal income that can be used for consumption or saving is referred to as disposable personal income or simply **disposable income.** It is equal to personal income minus personal taxes (especially income taxes). Sometimes disposable income is referred to as spendable income, take-home pay, or after-tax income.

$$\text{Disposable income} = \text{Personal income} - \text{Personal taxes}$$

Self-Test

1. Describe the expenditure approach to computing GDP in a real-world economy.

2. Will GDP be smaller than the sum of consumption, investment, and government purchases if net exports are negative? Explain your answer.

3. If GDP is $400 billion, and the country's population is 100 million, does it follow that each individual in the country has $40,000 worth of goods and services?

REAL GDP

This section defines Real GDP, shows how to compute it, and then explains how it is used to measure economic growth.

WHY WE NEED REAL GDP

In 1999, U.S. GDP was $9,268 billion. One year later, in 2000, GDP was $9,872 billion. Although you know GDP was higher in 2000 than in 1999, do you know *the reason why* GDP was higher in 2000 than in 1999?

As you think about your answer, let's look at GDP in a one-good economy. Suppose 10 units of this good are produced and each unit is sold for $10, so GDP in the economy is $100.

$$\text{GDP} = \$10 \times 10 \text{ units} = \$100$$

Now suppose GDP rises from $100 to $250. What caused it to rise? It could be because price increased from $10 to $25:

$$\text{GDP} = \boxed{\$25} \times 10 \text{ units} = \$250$$

Or, it could be because quantity of output produced increased from 10 units to 25 units:

$$\text{GDP} = \$10 \times \boxed{25 \text{ units}} = \$250$$

Or, it could be because price increased to $12.50 and quantity increased to 20 units:

$$\text{GDP} = \boxed{\$12.50} \times \boxed{20 \text{ units}} = \$250$$

To gauge the health of the economy, economists want to know the *reason* for an increase in GDP. If GDP increased simply because price increased, then the economy is not growing. For an economy to grow, more output must be produced.

Because an increase in GDP can be due in part to simply an increase in price, a more meaningful measure is Real GDP. **Real GDP** is GDP adjusted for price changes.

COMPUTING REAL GDP

One way to compute Real GDP is to find the value of the output for the different years in terms of the same prices, the prices that existed in the base year. Let's look again at our one-good economy. Consider the following data.

Year	Price of Good X	Quantity Produced of Good X (units)	GDP
1	$10	100	$10 × 100 = **$1,000**
2	$12	120	$12 × 120 = **$1,440**
3	$14	140	$14 × 140 = **$1,960**

The data show *why* GDP is higher in subsequent years: GDP is higher because both price and quantity have increased. In other words, GDP rises because both price *and* quantity rise. Suppose we want to separate the part of GDP that is higher because quantity is higher from the part of GDP that is higher because price is higher. What we want then is Real GDP because Real GDP is the part of GDP that is higher because quantity (of output) is higher.

To compute Real GDP for any year, we simply multiply the quantity of the good produced in a given year by the price in the base year. Suppose we choose year 1 as the base year. So, to compute Real GDP in year 2, we simply multiply the quantity of the good produced in year 2 by the price of the good in year 1. To find Real GDP in year 3, we simply multiply the quantity of the good produced in year 3 by the price of the good in year 1.

Year	Price of Good X	Quantity Produced of Good X (units)	GDP	Real GDP
1 (Base Year)	$10	100	$10 × 100 = **$1,000**	$10 × 100 = **$1,000**
2	$12	120	$12 × 120 = **$1,440**	$10 × 120 = **$1,200**
3	$14	140	$14 × 140 = **$1,960**	$10 × 140 = **$1,400**

THE GENERAL EQUATION FOR REAL GDP

In the real world, there is more than one good and more than one price. The general equation used to compute Real GDP is:

$$\text{Real GDP} = \Sigma \, (\text{Base-year prices} \times \text{Current-year quantities})$$

Σ is the Greek capital letter *sigma*. Here it stands for *summation*. Thus, Real GDP is "the sum of all the current-year quantities times their base-year prices."

IF YOU KNOW THE PRICE INDEX AND GDP FOR A YEAR, CAN YOU COMPUTE REAL GDP?

The last chapter explains how to change nominal income into real income. For example, if nominal income is, say, $50,000 in a given year and the CPI is, say, 120 in the same year, then real income is $41,677 [Real income = (Nominal income/CPI) × 100].

We can convert GDP into Real GDP much the same way. However, instead of using the CPI as our price index, we use the chain-weighted price index.

$$\text{Real GDP} = \left(\frac{\text{GDP}}{\text{Chain-weighted price index}} \right) \times 100$$

To illustrate, GDP in 2000 was $9,872. The chain-weighted price index in that year was 107. It follows that Real GDP was $9,226 billion.

ECONOMICS IN...

Does the State of the Economy Influence How People Vote?

A presidential election is held in the United States every four years. There are usually two major presidential candidates (one from the Democratic party and one from the Republican party) and a number of third-party candidates. In the months before the presidential election, journalists follow the two major candidates across the country and record their every action and word. Not only is what they say about the issues reported, but every misstep, scandal, and piece of gossip is reported as well. Then, on election day, the voters go to the polls and elect or reelect a president.

After the results are in, news commentators analyze why the voters voted the way they did. Some commentators may say that the people voted for X over Y because X has a better foreign policy and people are worried about foreign affairs these days. Some commentators may say that the people voted for X over Y because X is more self-confident, more personable, or more charismatic. Commentators often present many different reasons to explain why the voters voted the way they did.

But suppose none of these reasons really matter. Suppose the only thing that determines how people vote is the state of the economy prior to the election. If the economy is good, then they vote for the incumbent or the incumbent's party. If the economy is bad, then they vote for the challenger.

Some economists have developed models suggesting that only economic variables influence how people vote. One model, the Fair Model, was developed by Ray Fair, an economist at Yale University. The equation he has developed to predict the outcome of presidential elections is:

$$V = 0.423 + 0.0070g_3 - 0.0072p_{15} + 0.0091_n$$

In the equation, V equals the Democratic share of the two-party presidential vote; g_3 equals the growth rate of per capita Real GDP in the three quarters prior to the election; p_{15} equals the growth rate of the GDP deflator in the 15 quarters prior to the election; n equals the number of quarters in the 15 quarters mentioned in which the growth rate of per capita Real GDP is greater than a 3.2 percent annual rate.

Fair's model has not always predicted accurately in the past, but it does have a fairly significant success rate. Thus, the state of the economy—as measured by per capita Real GDP, and so on—seems to matter to how people vote.

WHAT DOES IT MEAN IF REAL GDP IS HIGHER IN ONE YEAR THAN IN ANOTHER YEAR?

If GDP is, say, $400 billion in year 1 and $500 billion in year 2, we cannot be sure why it has increased. Obviously, GDP can rise from one year to the next if: (1) prices rise and output remains constant; (2) output rises and prices remain constant; or (3) prices and output rise.

However, if Real GDP is, say, $300 billion in year 1 and $350 billion in year 2, we *know* why it has increased. Real GDP rises only if output rises. In other words, Real GDP rises only if more goods and services are produced.

REAL GDP, ECONOMIC GROWTH, AND BUSINESS CYCLES

Suppose there are two countries, A and B. In country A, Real GDP grows by 3 percent each year. In country B, Real GDP is the same each year: if Real GDP was $400 billion last year, it is $400 billion in the current year, and it will be $400 billion next year. In which of the two countries would you prefer to live, *ceteris paribus*?

Now consider another situation. Again suppose there are two countries, A and B. In country A, Real GDP takes a roller coaster ride: it alternates between rising and falling. It rises for some months, then falls, then rises again, then falls, and so on. In country *B,* Real GDP simply rises year after year. In which of the two countries would you prefer to live, *ceteris paribus?*

If you chose one country over the other in each of these two cases, then you are implicitly saying that Real GDP matters to you. One of the reasons economists study Real GDP is simply because Real GDP matters to you and others. In other words, because Real GDP is important to you, it is important to economists too.

Economists study two major macroeconomic topics that have to do with Real GDP. One topic is *economic growth;* the other is *business cycles.*

Economic Growth

Economic Growth
Increases in Real GDP.

Annual **economic growth** has occurred if Real GDP in one year is higher than Real GDP in the previous year. For example, if Real GDP is $6,000 billion in one year and $6,500 billion in the next, the economy has witnessed economic growth. The growth rate is equal to the (positive) percentage change in Real GDP. The growth rate is computed using the following formula:

Business Cycle
Recurrent swings (up and down) in Real GDP.

$$\text{Percentage change in Real GDP} = \left(\frac{\text{Real GDP}_{\text{later year}} - \text{Real GDP}_{\text{earlier year}}}{\text{Real GDP}_{\text{earlier year}}} \right) \times 100$$

Exhibit 6 shows U.S. Real GDP for the period 1960–2002. Exhibit 7 shows the annual growth rate in U.S. Real GDP for each year during the period 1990–2001.

The "Ups and Downs" in the Economy, or the Business Cycle

If Real GDP is on a roller coaster—rising and falling and rising and falling—the economy is said to be incurring a **business cycle.** Economists usually talk about four or five phases of the business cycle. We identify five phases below and in Exhibit 8.

1. **Peak.** At the *peak* of the business cycle, Real GDP is at a temporary high. In Exhibit 8, Real GDP is at a temporary high at Q_1.

exhibit 6

U.S. Real GDP, 1960–2002
Generally, Real GDP has been on an upward path during the period 1960–2002. However, there are declines in Real GDP in some years. For example, see 1974–1975 and 1981–1982.

Source: Bureau of Economic Analysis

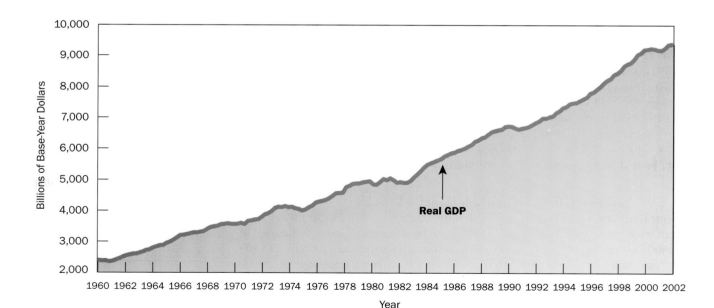

2. **Contraction.** This represents a decline in Real GDP. According to the standard definition of *recession,* two consecutive quarter declines in Real GDP constitute a recession.
3. **Trough.** The low point in Real GDP, just before it begins to turn up, is called the *trough* of the business cycle.
4. **Recovery.** The *recovery* is the period when Real GDP is rising. It begins at the trough and ends at the initial peak. The recovery in Exhibit 8 extends from the trough until Real GDP is again at Q_1.
5. **Expansion.** The *expansion* refers to increases in Real GDP beyond the recovery. In Exhibit 8, it refers to increases in Real GDP above Q_1.

An entire business cycle is measured from peak to peak. The typical business cycle is approximately four to five years, although a few have been shorter and some have been longer.

NBER and Recessions

In the contraction stage of the business cycle, we state that the "standard" definition of a recession is two consecutive quarter declines in Real GDP. This is not, however, the only definition of a recession.

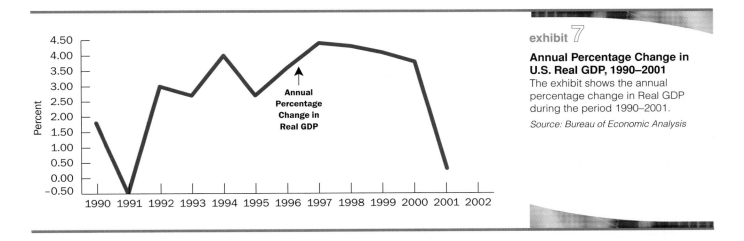

exhibit 7

Annual Percentage Change in U.S. Real GDP, 1990–2001
The exhibit shows the annual percentage change in Real GDP during the period 1990–2001.

Source: Bureau of Economic Analysis

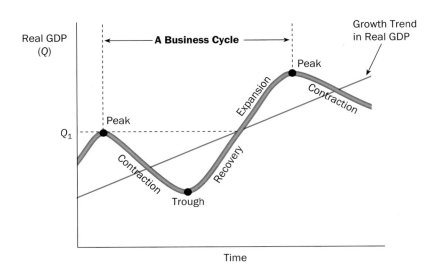

exhibit 8

The Phases of the Business Cycle
The phases of a business cycle include the peak, contraction, trough, recovery, and expansion. A business cycle is measured from peak to peak.

On November 26, 2001, the National Bureau of Economic Research, which dates the business cycle, issued a press release. The first paragraph read:

> The NBER's Business Cycle Dating Committee has determined that a peak in business activity occurred in the U.S. economy in March 2001. A peak marks the end of an expansion and the beginning of a recession. The determination of a peak date in March is thus a determination that the expansion that began in March 1991 ended in March 2001 and a recession began. The expansion lasted exactly 10 years, the longest in the NBER's chronology.

According to this statement, the U.S. economy entered a recession in March 2001. That's because according to the NBER "a peak marks the end of an expansion and the beginning of a recession" and March 2001 was dated by the NBER as the peak of the business cycle. In other words, the U.S. economy was in a recession even though Real GDP had not declined for two consecutive quarters.

The NBER definition of a recession is different from the standard definition of a recession. According to the NBER, " a recession is a significant decline in activity spread across the economy, lasting more than a few months, visible in industrial production, employment, real income, and wholesale-retail trade."

WHAT LIES AHEAD

Much of what we discuss in upcoming chapters relates to what you have learned in this chapter and the previous chapter. In the previous chapter, you learned about prices and unemployment. Much of what we discuss in upcoming chapters relates to changes in the price level and changes in the unemployment rate.

In this chapter, you learned about GDP and Real GDP. You also learned that Real GDP is relevant to the study of economic growth and business cycles. Much of what we discuss in upcoming chapters involves these two topics.

In summary, upcoming chapters discuss: (1) changes in the price level, (2) changes in the unemployment rate, (3) economic growth, and (4) the ups and downs of Real GDP, or business cycles.

Self-Test

1. Suppose GDP is $6,039 billion in year 1 and $6,245 billion in year 2. What has caused the rise in GDP?

2. Suppose Real GDP is $5,233 billion in year 1 and $5,267 billion in year 2. What has caused the rise in Real GDP?

3. Can an economy be faced with endless business cycles and still have its Real GDP grow over time? Explain your answer.

A Reader Asks...

Where Can I Find the Most Recent Economic Data?

I've been learning about the CPI, GDP, the components of GDP, national income, and so on. Where can I find the most recent data on these economic variables and others?

Your best bet for finding recent economic data is the Internet. The Federal Reserve District Bank of St. Louis Web site at *http://research.stlouisfed.org/html* is a good place to start. Once at the site, click on "FRED," which is an economic time-series database (a database in which economic information is available for comparison over various time periods). After you click on "FRED," a list of categories will appear on the screen. If you are interested in price data, click on "Consumer Price Indexes." If you are interested in GDP, Real GDP, national income (and most of the topics in this chapter), then click on "Gross

Domestic Product and Components." If you are interested in unemployment and employment, click on "Employment and Population." Clicking on a category will send you to a list of data tables. Look at these tables to decide what you are interested in viewing.

Another good Web site you may want to go to is Economagic.com at *http://www.economagic.com/*. If you click on the "Most Requested Series" at this site, you will find data on prices, GDP, Real GDP, and so on.

If you are interested in business cycle data, go to the National Bureau of Economic Research Web site at *http://www.nber.org/* and click on "Business Cycle Dates."

Finally, here is a short list of other Web sites where you can find economic data:

- Economics Statistics Briefing Room at *http://www.whitehouse.gov/fsbr/esbr.html*
- Bureau of Economic Analysis at *http://www.bea.doc.gov/*
- Bureau of Labor Statistics at *http://stats.bls.gov/*
- Congressional Budget Office at *http://www.cbo.gov/*
- U.S. Census Bureau at *http://www.census.gov/*

Chapter Summary

Gross Domestic Product

- Gross domestic product (GDP) is the total market value of all final goods and services produced annually within a country's borders. Gross national product (GNP) is the total market value of all final goods and services produced annually by citizens of a country.
- Any one of the following can be used to compute GDP: (1) expenditure approach, (2) income approach, or (3) valued-added approach.
- To avoid the problem of double counting, only final goods and services are counted in GDP.
- GDP omits certain nonmarket goods and services, both legal and illegal underground activities, the sale of used goods, financial transactions, transfer payments, and leisure (even though leisure is a good). Finally, GDP is not adjusted for the bads (such as pollution) that sometimes accompany production.

Expenditures

- The expenditures on U.S. goods and services include consumption; gross private domestic investment, or investment; government consumption expenditures and gross investment, or government purchases; and net exports (exports − imports).
- Consumption includes spending on durable goods, nondurable goods, and services.
- Investment includes purchases of newly produced capital goods (fixed investment), changes in business inventories (inventory investment), and purchases of new residential housing (also fixed investment).
- Government purchases include federal, state, and local government purchases of goods and services and gross investment in highways, bridges, and so on. Government purchases do not include transfer payments.
- Net exports equal the total foreign spending on domestic goods (exports) minus the total domestic spending on foreign goods (imports).

Computing GDP

- Using the expenditure approach, GDP = $C + I + G + (EX - IM)$. In other words, GDP equals consumption plus investment plus government purchases plus net exports.
- Using the income approach, GDP = National income − income earned from the rest of the world + income earned by the rest of the world + indirect business taxes + capital consumption allowance + statistical discrepancy.

Measures Other Than GDP

- Net domestic product (NDP) equals gross domestic product (GDP) minus the capital consumption allowance.

    NDP = GDP − Capital consumption allowance

- National income equals the sum of resource, or factor, payments.
  National income = Compensation of employees
  + Proprietors' income
  + Corporate profits
  + Rental income
  + Net interest
- Personal income equals national income minus undistributed corporate profits, social insurance taxes, and corporate profits taxes, plus transfer payments.
  Personal Income = National income
  − Undistributed corporate profits
  − Social insurance taxes
  − Corporate profits taxes
  + Transfer payments
- Disposable Income = Personal income − Personal taxes.

Real GDP

- Real GDP is GDP adjusted for price changes. It is GDP in base-year dollars.

- Real GDP $= \left(\dfrac{\text{GDP}}{\text{Chain-weighted price index}} \right) \times 100$

Economic Growth and Business Cycles

- Annual economic growth has occurred if Real GDP in one year is higher than Real GDP in the previous year.
- There are five phases to the business cycle: peak, contraction, trough, recovery, and expansion. A complete business cycle is measured from peak to peak.

Key Terms and Concepts

Gross Domestic Product (GDP)
Final Good
Intermediate Good
Double Counting
Value Added
Gross National Product (GNP)
Transfer Payment
Consumption
Investment

Inventory Investment
Fixed Investment
Government Purchases
Government Transfer Payments
Imports
Exports
Net Exports
National Income

Capital Consumption Allowance
  (Depreciation)
Net Domestic Product (NDP)
Personal Income
Disposable Income
Real GDP
Economic Growth
Business Cycle

Economic Connections to You

Economic facts, actions, and changes create ripples that move away from their point of origin. Eventually, these ripples can intersect your life and have an effect on you. Consider the following example.

When Real GDP has declined for two consecutive quarters, the economy is in the recession phase of the business cycle, according to the standard definition of a recession. In a recession, the unemployment rate is relatively high and it is difficult to find a good job. If you will be graduating from college and searching for your first post-college job in three months, a recession will make your search more difficult. Thus, there is a connection between the level and direction in Real GDP and your ability to find a good job—an economic connection to you.

Based on the material in this chapter, identify other ways in which economic facts, actions, and changes create ripples that eventually affect you.

Questions and Problems

1. "I just heard on the news that GDP is higher this year than it was last year. This means that we're better off this year than last year." Comment.

2. Which of the following are included in the calculation of this year's GDP? (a) Twelve-year-old Johnny mowing his family's lawn; (b) Dave Malone buying a used car; (c) Barbara Wilson buying a bond issued by General Motors; (d) Ed Ferguson's receipt of a Social Security payment; (e) the illegal drug transaction at the corner of Elm and Fifth.

3. Discuss the problems you see in comparing the GDPs of two countries, say, the United States and the People's Republic of China.

4. The manuscript for this book was keyed by the author. Had he hired someone to do the keying, GDP would have been higher than it was. What other activities would increase GDP if they were done differently? What activities would decrease GDP if they were done differently?

5. What is the difference between GDP and GNP?

6. Why does GDP omit the sales of used goods? of financial transactions? of government transfer payments?

7. A business firm produces a good this year that it doesn't sell. As a result, the good is added to the firm's inventory. How does this inventory good find its way into GDP?

8. Economists prefer to compare Real GDP figures for different years instead of comparing GDP figures. Why?

9. What is the difference between a recovery and an expansion?

10. Define each of the following terms:
    a. Contraction
    b. Business cycle
    c. Trough
    d. Disposable income
    e. Net domestic product

11. Explain why GDP can be computed either by measuring spending or by measuring income.

12. Corporate profits taxes are considered to be a payment to a resource, but sales taxes are not. Why the difference?

13. Does the expenditure approach to computing GDP measure U.S. spending on all goods, U.S. spending on only U.S. goods, or U.S. and foreign spending on only U.S. goods? Explain your answer.

14. In the first quarter of the year, Real GDP was $400 billion; in the second quarter, it was $398 billion; in the third quarter, it was $399 billion; and in the fourth quarter, it was $395 billion. Has there been a recession? Explain your answer.

Working with Numbers and Graphs

1. Net exports are −$114 billion and exports are $857 billion. What are imports?

2. Consumption spending is $3,708 billion, spending on nondurable goods is $1,215 billion, and spending on services is $2,041 billion. What does spending on durable goods equal?

3. Inventory investment is $62 billion and (total) investment is $1,122 billion. What does fixed investment equal?

4. In year 1, the prices of goods X, Y, and Z are $2, $4, and $6 per unit, respectively. In year 2, the prices of goods X, Y, and Z are $3, $4, and $7, respectively. In year 2, twice as many units of each good are produced as in year 1. In year 1, 20 units of X, 40 units of Y, and 60 units of Z are produced. If year 1 is the base year, what does Real GDP equal in year 2?

5. Nondurable goods spending = $400 million, durable goods spending = $300 million, new residential housing spending = $200 million, and spending on services = $500 million. What does consumption equal?

6. According to the circular flow diagram in Exhibit 4, consumption spending flows into U.S. product markets but import spending does not. But U.S. households buy imported goods in U.S. markets, don't they? Explain.

7. How would you redraw the circular flow diagram in Exhibit 4 if you wanted to show (1) taxes that firms and households pay to government and (2) transfer payments that government makes to households?

8. National income = $500 billion, income earned from the rest of the world = $10 billion, income earned by the rest of the world = $12 billion, indirect business taxes = $2 billion, capital consumption allowance = $1 billion, and GDP = $525 billion. What does the statistical discrepancy equal?

9. GDP = $100 billion, NDP = $95 billion, and investment = $33 billion. What does the capital consumption allowance equal?

10. If Real GDP in year 1 is $487 billion and it is $498 billion in year 2, what is the economic growth rate equal to?

11. If the chain-weighted price index is 132 and GDP is $8,655 billion, what does Real GDP equal?

12. If the chain-weighted price index is 143 and Real GDP is $4,322 billion, what does GDP equal?

13. The following figure shows a business cycle. Identify each of the following as a phase of the business cycle:
    a. Point A
    b. Between point A and point B
    c. Point B
    d. Between point B and point C
    e. Point D

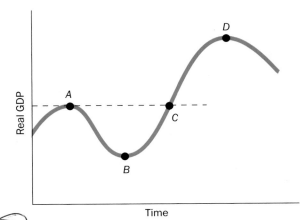

14. Using the following data, calculate: (a) gross domestic product (GDP); (b) net domestic product (NDP);

(c) national income (NI); (d) personal income (PI). All numbers are in billions of dollars. (e) disposable income

Consumption	$1,149.5
Investment	400.3
Government purchases	425.3
Net exports	89.1
Capital consumption allowance	303.8
Indirect business taxes	213.3
Statistical discrepancy	4.4
Social Security insurance taxes	216.5
Transfer payments	405.6

Undistributed profits	91.0
Corporate profits taxes	77.7
Personal taxes	340.0
Dividends	0.0
Compensation of employees	800.0
Income earned from the rest of the world	50.0
Income earned by the rest of the world	56.0
Proprietors' income	400.0
Rental income	145.0
Net interest	23.0

Internet Activities

1. Go to *http://www.nber.org*. Under Data, click on "Business Cycle Dates." This is a table of business cycles from 1854 to the present.

   a. How long was the longest expansion between 1949 and 1970? Between 1971 and today?

   b. How many expansions of 36 months or longer occurred between 1854 and 1960? How many expansions were during wars? How many expansions of 36 months or longer have occurred since 1961? How many of these expansions are connected to wars?

   c. How long was the average expansion before World War II? How long was the average contraction before World War II? How long was the average expansion after World War II? How long was the average contraction after World War II?

   d. When was the longest expansion in history? When was the second longest?

2. Go to *http://www.bea.gov*. Under "BEA's economic accounts," click on "GDP and related data." Now locate "*Time series estimates*" and select "Current-dollar and "real" GDP." This table contains both GDP and Real GDP data. Although the chain-weighted data are not presented in the table, the GDP and Real GDP data can be used to compute them. Answer the following questions:

   a. What year is currently being used as the base year for calculating Real GDP?

   b. What is the chain-weighted price index for 1996?

   c. What is the chain-weighted price index for 2001?

   d. Could you calculate the inflation rate (approximate) with the above indexes? If so, how? If not, why not?

Log on to the Arnold Xtra! Web site now (*http://arnoldxtra.swcollege.com*) for additional learning resources such as practice quizzes, help with graphing, video clips, and current event applications.

ch.7

AGGREGATE DEMAND AND AGGREGATE SUPPLY

Businesses make decisions based on what is happening in the economy today and on what they expect will happen in the economy in the future. For example, their profitability is based in part on the wages they must pay their employees, the prices of their nonlabor inputs, the productivity of their workers, and business taxes. If they want to expand in the future, they must consider all these things and also try to predict their future sales. If they trade overseas, they must worry about exchange rates and foreign real national income. The decisions that businesses make, in turn, affect their employees, their communities, and in many cases the entire U.S. economy.

Chapter Road Map

Economists ask questions, and then develop theories to answer their questions. To answer questions about why prices rise and fall, economists use the theory of supply and demand. To answer questions about the rise and fall of the price level and Real GDP, economists often use the theory of aggregate demand and aggregate supply. We explain changes in the price level and Real GDP in the short run using aggregate demand and short-run aggregate supply. We explain changes in the price level and Real GDP in the long run using aggregate demand and long-run aggregate supply.

This chapter focuses on aggregate demand and short-run aggregate supply. First, we define aggregate demand and discuss those factors that can change it. Second, we define short-run aggregate supply and discuss those factors that can change it. Finally, we put aggregate demand and short-run aggregate supply together and discuss changes in the price level and Real GDP in the short run.

THE TWO SIDES TO AN ECONOMY

Just as there are two sides to a market, a buying side (demand) and a selling side (supply), there are two sides to an economy. There is a demand side and a supply side. The demand in an economy is referred to as *aggregate demand (AD)*; the supply in an economy is referred to as *aggregate supply (AS)*.

Macroeconomists often use the *AD-AS* framework of analysis to discuss the price level, GDP, Real GDP, unemployment, economic growth, and other major macroeconomic topics. In other words, all these topics can be and are discussed within the same framework. Discussing so many important economic topics within one framework, or with the same tools of analysis, often makes things easier for the student who is just beginning to study macroeconomics. The *AD-AS* framework has three parts: (1) aggregate demand (*AD*), (2) short-run aggregate supply (*SRAS*), and (3) long-run aggregate supply (*LRAS*).

AGGREGATE DEMAND

Recall from the last chapter that people, firms, and governments buy U.S. goods and services. **Aggregate demand** refers to the quantity demanded of these (U.S.) goods and services, or the quantity demanded of (U.S.) Real GDP, at various price levels, *ceteris paribus*. For example, the following whole set of data represents aggregate demand:

Aggregate Demand

Price Index	Quantity Demanded of Goods and Services (Quantity Demanded of Real GDP)
100	$1,200 billion worth of goods and services
110	$1,000 billion worth of goods and services
120	$ 800 billion worth of goods and services

An **aggregate demand *(AD)* curve** is the graphical representation of aggregate demand. An *AD* curve is drawn in Exhibit 1. Notice that it is downward-sloping, indicating an inverse relationship between the price level (*P*) and the quantity demanded of Real GDP (*Q*): as the price level rises, the quantity demanded of Real GDP falls, and as the price level falls, the quantity demanded of Real GDP rises, *ceteris paribus*.

Q: If an *AD* curve is the graphical representation of the inverse relationship between the price level and the quantity demanded of Real GDP, then why not label the horizontal axis in Exhibit 1 "Quantity Demanded of Real GDP" instead of "Real GDP"?

A: In economics, it is customary to label the horizontal axis "Real GDP." It is understood that when aggregate demand is being discussed, the relationship specified is between the price level and the quantity demanded of Real GDP. When aggregate supply is being discussed, the relationship specified is between the price level and the quantity supplied of Real GDP.

WHY DOES THE AGGREGATE DEMAND CURVE SLOPE DOWNWARD?

Asking why the *AD* curve slopes downward is the same as asking why there is an inverse relationship between the price level and the quantity demanded of Real GDP. This inverse relationship, and the resulting downward slope of the *AD* curve, is explained by the real balance effect, the interest rate effect, and the international trade effect.

Real Balance Effect

The **real balance effect** states that the inverse relationship between the price level and the quantity demanded of Real GDP is established through changes in the value of **monetary wealth,** or money holdings.

Aggregate Demand
The quantity demanded of all goods and services (Real GDP) at different price levels, *ceteris paribus*.

Aggregate Demand (*AD*) Curve
A curve that shows the quantity demanded of all goods and services (Real GDP) at different price levels, *ceteris paribus*.

Real Balance Effect
The change in the purchasing power of dollar-denominated assets that results from a change in the price level.

Monetary Wealth
The value of a person's monetary assets. Wealth, as distinguished from monetary wealth, refers to the value of all assets owned, both monetary and nonmonetary. In short, a person's wealth equals his or her monetary wealth (such as $1,000 cash) plus nonmonetary wealth (a car or a house).

exhibit 1

The Aggregate Demand Curve
The aggregate demand curve is downward-sloping, specifying an inverse relationship between the price level and the quantity demanded of Real GDP.

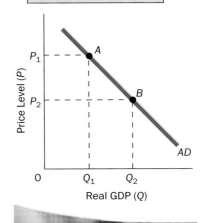

Aggregate Demand Curve
The price level and quantity demanded of Real GDP are inversely related.

Purchasing Power
The quantity of goods and services that can be purchased with a unit of money. Purchasing power and the price level are inversely related: As the price level goes up (down), purchasing power goes down (up).

To illustrate, consider a person who has $50,000 in cash. Suppose the price level falls. As this happens, the **purchasing power** of the person's $50,000 rises. That is, the $50,000, which once could buy 100 television sets at $500 each, can now buy 125 sets at $400 each. An increase in the purchasing power of the person's $50,000 is identical to saying that his monetary wealth has increased. (After all, isn't the $50,000 more valuable when it can buy more than when it can buy less?) And as he becomes wealthier, he buys more goods.

In summary, a fall in the price level causes purchasing power to rise, which increases a person's monetary wealth. As people become wealthier, the quantity demanded of Real GDP rises.

Suppose the price level rises. As this happens, the purchasing power of the $50,000 falls. That is, the $50,000, which once could buy 100 television sets at $500 each, can now buy 80 sets at $625 each. A decrease in the purchasing power of the person's $50,000 is identical to saying that his monetary wealth has decreased. And as he becomes less wealthy, he buys fewer goods.

In summary, a rise in the price level causes purchasing power to fall, which decreases a person's monetary wealth. As people become less wealthy, the quantity demanded of Real GDP falls.

Interest Rate Effect

Interest Rate Effect
The changes in household and business buying as the interest rate changes (which, in turn, is a reflection of a change in the demand for, or supply of, credit brought on by price level changes).

The **interest rate effect** states that the inverse relationship between the price level and the quantity demanded of Real GDP is established through changes in household and business spending that is sensitive to changes in interest rates.

Let's consider a person who buys a fixed bundle of goods (food, clothing, and shelter) each week. Suppose the price level falls, increasing the purchasing power of the person's money. With more purchasing power (per dollar), she can purchase her fixed bundle of goods with less money. What does she do with (part of) this increase in her monetary wealth? She saves it. In terms of simple supply-and-demand analysis, the supply of credit increases. Subsequently, the price of credit, which is the interest rate, drops. As the interest rate drops, households and businesses borrow more, so they end up buying more goods. Thus, the quantity demanded of Real GDP rises.

Now suppose the price level rises, decreasing the purchasing power of the person's money. With less purchasing power (per dollar), she cannot purchase her fixed bundle of goods with the same amount of money. If she wants to continue to buy the fixed bundle of goods, she will need to acquire more money. In an effort to acquire more money, she goes to a bank and requests a loan. In terms of simple supply-and-demand analysis, the demand for credit increases. Subsequently, the interest rate rises. As the interest rate rises, households borrow less to finance, say, automobile purchases, and firms borrow less to finance new capital goods spending. Thus, the quantity demanded of Real GDP falls.

International Trade Effect

International Trade Effect
The change in foreign sector spending as the price level changes.

The **international trade effect** states that the inverse relationship between the price level and the quantity demanded of Real GDP is established through foreign sector spending, which includes U.S. spending on foreign goods (imports) and foreign spending on U.S. goods (exports).

Suppose the price level in the United States falls. As this happens, U.S. goods become relatively cheaper than foreign goods. As a result, both Americans and foreigners buy more U.S. goods. The quantity demanded of (U.S.) Real GDP rises.

Suppose the price level in the United States rises. As this happens, U.S. goods become relatively more expensive than foreign goods. As a result, both Americans and foreigners buy fewer U.S. goods. The quantity demanded of (U.S.) Real GDP falls.

For a review of the three effects—real balance, interest rate, and international trade—see Exhibit 2.

Type of Effect	How It Works	Graphical Representation of What Happens

exhibit 2

Why the Aggregate Demand Curve Is Downward-Sloping
This exhibit outlines the three effects that explain why the *AD* curve is downward-sloping. Each effect relates to a change in the price level (*P*) leading to a change in the quantity demanded of Real GDP (*Q*).

Real Balance Effect

Price level falls → purchasing power rises → monetary wealth rises → **buy more goods.**

Price level rises → purchasing power falls → monetary wealth falls → **buy fewer goods.**

Interest Rate Effect

Price level falls → purchasing power rises → less money needed to buy fixed bundle of goods → save more → supply of credit rises → interest rate falls → businesses and households borrow more at lower interest rate → **buy more goods.**

Price level rises → purchasing power falls → borrow money in order to continue to buy fixed bundle of goods → demand for credit rises → interest rate rises → businesses and households borrow less at higher interest rate → **buy fewer goods.**

International Trade Effect

Price level in U.S. falls relative to foreign price levels → U.S. goods relatively less expensive than foreign goods → both Americans and foreigners **buy more U.S. goods.**

Price level in U.S. rises relative to foreign price levels → U.S. goods relatively more expensive than foreign goods → both Americans and foreigners **buy fewer U.S. goods.**

A CHANGE IN THE QUANTITY DEMANDED OF REAL GDP VERSUS A CHANGE IN AGGREGATE DEMAND

Chapter 3 explains the difference between a change in quantity demanded and a change in demand. Similarly, there is a difference between a change in the quantity demanded of Real GDP and a change in aggregate demand.

We know that a change in the quantity demanded of Real GDP is brought about by a change in the price level. As the price level falls, the quantity demanded of Real GDP rises, *ceteris paribus*. In Exhibit 3a, a change in the quantity demanded of Real GDP is represented as a movement from one point (A) on AD_1 to another point (B) on AD_1.

A change in aggregate demand is represented in Exhibit 3b as a shift in the aggregate demand curve from AD_1 to AD_2. Notice that with a shift in the aggregate demand curve, the quantity demanded of Real GDP changes even though the price level remains constant. For example, at a price level (index number) of 150, the quantity demanded of Real GDP on AD_1 in Exhibit 3b is $1,000 billion. But at the same price level (150), the quantity demanded of Real GDP on AD_2 is $1,500 billion.

exhibit 3

A Change in the Quantity Demanded of Real GDP versus a Change in Aggregate Demand

(a) A change in the quantity demanded of Real GDP is graphically represented as a movement from one point, *A*, on AD_1 to another point, *B*, on AD_1. A change in the quantity demanded of Real GDP is the result of a change in the price level. (b) A change in aggregate demand is graphically represented as a shift in the aggregate demand curve from AD_1 to AD_2.

THINKING LIKE AN ECONOMIST

Economists deal with curves—demand curves, supply curves, aggregate demand curves, and so on. An economist looks at a curve and asks: (1) What can move us from one point on the curve to another point on the same curve and (2) what can shift the curve? In economics, only one factor can move us from one point on a curve to another point on the same curve: A change in the factor that is identified on the vertical axis. For example, only a change in the price level can move the economy from one point on a given AD curve to another point on the same AD curve. In contrast, a shift in a curve can often be brought about by many factors.

(a)

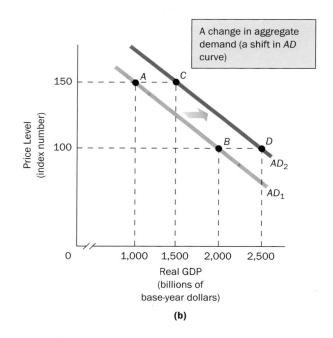

(b)

CHANGES IN AGGREGATE DEMAND

What can change aggregate demand? In other words, what can cause aggregate demand to rise and what can cause it to fall?

The simple answer is that aggregate demand changes when the spending on U.S. goods and services changes. If spending increases at a given price level, aggregate demand rises; if spending decreases at a given price level, aggregate demand falls. For example, suppose the price level in the economy is represented by the consumer price index and the index is currently 164 (CPI = 164). At this price level, U.S. residents, firms, and governments, along with foreigners, foreign firms, and foreign governments, want to buy, say, $5,000 billion worth of U.S. goods and services. Then something changes and, all of a sudden, they want to buy $6,000 billion worth of U.S. goods and services. Now before you conclude that they want to buy more goods and services because the prices of goods and services have fallen, keep in mind that we haven't lowered the price level. The price level is still represented by the CPI and it is still 164. In other words, all these people, firms, and governments want to buy more U.S. goods even though the prices of the goods and services have not changed.

When individuals, firms, and governments want to buy more U.S. goods and services, even though the prices of these goods have not changed, then we say that aggregate demand has increased. As a result, the *AD* curve shifts to the right. Of course, when individuals, firms, and governments want to buy fewer U.S. goods and services at a given price level, then we say that aggregate demand has decreased. As a result, the *AD* curve shifts to the left.

Let's look again at Exhibit 3b, which shows a change in aggregate demand (a shift in the *AD* curve). At point *A,* the price level is 150 and total expenditures on U.S. goods and services is $1,000 billion. At point *C,* the price level is still 150 but total expenditures on U.S. goods and services has increased to $1,500 billion. Why has aggregate demand moved from point *A* to point *C*; that is, what has caused the increase in total expenditures? To find out, we have to look at the components of total expenditures.

HOW SPENDING COMPONENTS AFFECT AGGREGATE DEMAND

The last chapter identifies four major spending components—consumption, investment, government purchases, and net exports. Now suppose that $C = \$100$, $I = \$100$, $G = \$100$, $EX = \$50$, and $IM = \$15$. If $EX = \$50$ and $IM = \$15$, it follows that net exports (NX) equal the difference, or $35.

Using these dollar figures, we calculate that $335 is spent on U.S. goods and services. We get this dollar amount by finding the sum of consumption, investment, government purchases, and net exports.

Total Expenditures on U.S. goods and services = $C + I + G + (EX - IM)$

Obviously, this dollar amount will go up if (1) C rises, (2) I rises, (3) G rises, (4) EX rises, or (5) IM falls. In other words, a rise in consumption, investment, government purchases, or exports, or a fall in imports will raise spending on U.S. goods and services:

$C\uparrow$, $I\uparrow$, $G\uparrow$, $EX\uparrow$, $IM\downarrow \rightarrow$ Total expenditures on U.S. goods and services $\uparrow$

Because an increase in exports or a decrease in imports results in an increase in net exports, this relationship can be written as:

$C\uparrow$, $I\uparrow$, $G\uparrow$, $NX\uparrow \rightarrow$ Total expenditures on U.S. goods and services $\uparrow$

Now what will cause spending on U.S. goods to go down? Obviously, it will decline if (1) *C* falls, (2) *I* falls, (3) *G* falls, (4) *EX* falls, or (5) *IM* rises:

$$C\downarrow, I\downarrow, G\downarrow, EX\downarrow, IM\uparrow \rightarrow \text{Total expenditures on U.S. goods and services} \downarrow$$

Because a decrease in exports or an increase in imports results in a decrease in net exports, this relationship can be written as:

$$C\downarrow, I\downarrow, G\downarrow, NX\downarrow \rightarrow \text{Total expenditures on U.S. goods and services} \downarrow$$

Because we now know what causes total expenditures on U.S. goods and services to change, we can relate the components of spending to (U.S.) aggregate demand. If, *at a given price level,* consumption, investment, government purchases, or net exports rise, aggregate demand will rise and the *AD* curve will shift to the right. If, *at a given price level,* consumption, investment, government purchases, or net exports fall, aggregate demand will fall and the *AD* curve will shift to the left. We can write these relationships as:

If, at a given price level, $C\uparrow$, $I\uparrow$, $G\uparrow$, or $NX\uparrow$, then $AD\uparrow$
If, at a given price level, $C\downarrow$, $I\downarrow$, $G\downarrow$, or $NX\downarrow$, then $AD\downarrow$

The flow charts in Exhibit 4 show how changes in spending components affect aggregate demand.

FACTORS THAT CAN CHANGE *C, I, G,* AND *NX* (*EX* − *IM*), AND THEREFORE CAN CHANGE *AD*

What can change aggregate demand (*AD*) in the economy? You know that the answer is a change in consumption, investment, government purchases, or net exports (exports minus imports). So, for example, if someone asks you why *AD* increased, you may say because consumption (*C*) increased.

But suppose the person then asks, "But what caused consumption to increase?" In other words, your answer to one question simply leads to another question. If a change in consumption changes aggregate demand, what changes consumption? The same question can be asked about changes in investment, government purchases, and net exports (which means exports and imports). For

http://

Go to *http://www.bea.doc.gov/bea/dn1 .htm.* Under "*Time Series Estimates,*" click "Select data from the full set of NIPA Tables," and then select "list of Selected NIPA Tables." Under "Section 1—National Income and Product," choose "Table 1.1 Gross Domestic Product (A)(Q)." Find the two most recent years, and write down the values of GDP, *C, I, G, EX,* and *IM* for each year. What was the percentage change in GDP between the two years? Which component of GDP do you think was the most responsible for the change in GDP? Explain your answer.

exhibit 4

Changes in Aggregate Demand
The flow charts show how aggregate demand changes given changes in various spending components.
C = Consumption, *I* = Investment, *G* = Government purchases, *NX* = Net exports, *EX* = Exports, *IM* = Imports. Keep in mind that *NX* = *EX* − *IM*.

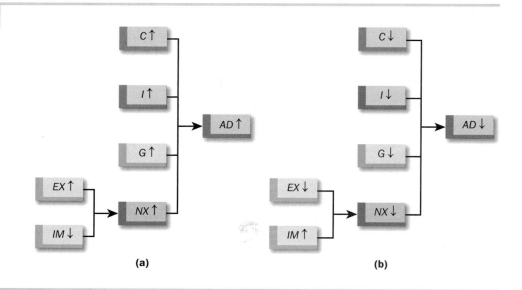

example, if aggregate demand increased because investment increased, then what caused investment to increase?

This section looks at some of the (many) factors that can change consumption, investment, and net exports. A later chapter considers the factors that can change government purchases.

Consumption

Four factors that can affect consumption are wealth, expectations about future prices and income, the interest rate, and income taxes.

1. **Wealth.** Individuals consume not only on the basis of their present income but also on the basis of their **wealth.** Consider two individuals, each receiving an income of $50,000 a year. One has $75,000 in the bank, and the other has no assets at all. Which would you expect to spend more of her income on consumption goods this year? We would expect the person with the $75,000 in the bank to consume more. Greater wealth makes individuals feel financially more secure and thus more willing to spend. Increases in wealth lead to increases in consumption. If consumption increases, then aggregate demand rises and the *AD* curve shifts to the right. What will happen if wealth decreases? Decreases in wealth lead to a fall in consumption, which leads to a fall in aggregate demand. Consequently, the *AD* curve shifts to the left.

Wealth
The value of all assets owned, both monetary and nonmonetary.

$$\text{Wealth} \uparrow \rightarrow C \uparrow \rightarrow AD \uparrow$$
$$\text{Wealth} \downarrow \rightarrow C \downarrow \rightarrow AD \downarrow$$

2. **Expectations about future prices and income.** If individuals expect higher prices in the future, they increase current consumption expenditures in order to buy goods at the lower current prices. This increase in consumption leads to an increase in aggregate demand. If individuals expect lower prices in the future, they decrease current consumption expenditures. This reduction in consumption leads to a decrease in aggregate demand.

Similarly, expectation of a higher future income increases consumption, which leads to an increase in aggregate demand. Expectation of a lower future income decreases consumption, which leads to a decrease in aggregate demand.

$$\text{Expect higher future prices} \rightarrow C \uparrow \rightarrow AD \uparrow$$
$$\text{Expect lower future prices} \rightarrow C \downarrow \rightarrow AD \downarrow$$

$$\text{Expect higher future income} \rightarrow C \uparrow \rightarrow AD \uparrow$$
$$\text{Expect lower future income} \rightarrow C \downarrow \rightarrow AD \downarrow$$

3. **Interest rate.** Current empirical work shows that spending on consumer durables is sensitive to the interest rate. Many of these items are financed by borrowing, so an increase in the interest rate increases the monthly payment amounts linked to their purchase and thereby reduces their consumption. This reduction in consumption leads to a decline in aggregate demand. Alternatively, a decrease in the interest rate reduces monthly payment amounts linked to the purchase of durable goods and thereby increases their consumption. This increase in consumption leads to an increase in aggregate demand.

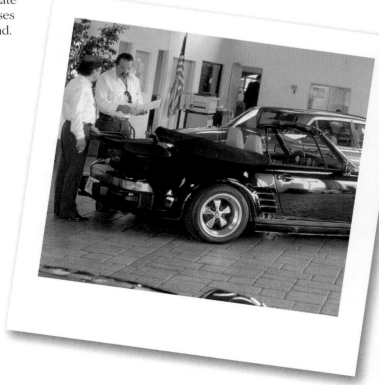

$$\text{Interest rate} \uparrow \rightarrow C \downarrow \rightarrow AD \downarrow$$
$$\text{Interest rate} \downarrow \rightarrow C \uparrow \rightarrow AD \uparrow$$

4. **Income Taxes.** Let's consider personal income taxes, the tax a person pays on the income he earns. As income taxes rise, disposable income decreases. When people have less take-home pay to spend, consumption falls. Consequently, aggregate demand decreases. A decrease in income taxes has the opposite effect; it raises disposable income. When people have more take-home pay to spend, consumption rises and aggregate demand increases.

$$\text{Income taxes} \uparrow \rightarrow C \downarrow \rightarrow AD \downarrow$$
$$\text{Income taxes} \downarrow \rightarrow C \uparrow \rightarrow AD \uparrow$$

Investment

Three factors that can change investment are the interest rate, expectations about future sales, and business taxes.

1. **Interest rate.** Changes in interest rates affect business decisions. As the interest rate rises, the cost of a given investment project rises, and businesses invest less. As investment decreases, aggregate demand decreases. On the other hand, as the interest rate falls, the cost of a given investment project falls, and businesses invest more. Consequently, aggregate demand increases.

$$\text{Interest rate} \uparrow \rightarrow I \downarrow \rightarrow AD \downarrow$$
$$\text{Interest rate} \downarrow \rightarrow I \uparrow \rightarrow AD \uparrow$$

2. **Expectations about future sales.** Businesses invest because they expect to sell the goods they produce. If businesses become optimistic about future sales, investment spending grows and aggregate demand increases. If businesses become pessimistic about future sales, investment spending contracts and aggregate demand decreases.

$$\text{Businesses become optimistic about future sales} \rightarrow I \uparrow \rightarrow AD \uparrow$$
$$\text{Businesses become pessimistic about future sales} \rightarrow I \downarrow \rightarrow AD \downarrow$$

3. **Business taxes.** Businesses naturally consider expected after-tax profits when making their investment decisions. An increase in business taxes lowers expected profitability. With less profit expected, businesses invest less. As investment spending declines, aggregate demand declines. A decrease in business taxes, on the other hand, raises expected profitability and investment spending. This increases aggregate demand.

$$\text{Business Taxes} \uparrow \rightarrow I \downarrow \rightarrow AD \downarrow$$
$$\text{Business Taxes} \downarrow \rightarrow I \uparrow \rightarrow AD \uparrow$$

Net Exports

Two factors that can change net exports are foreign real national income and the exchange rate.

1. **Foreign real national income.** Just as Americans earn a national income, so do people in other countries. There is a foreign national income. By adjusting this foreign national income for price changes, we obtain foreign real national income. As foreign real national income rises, foreigners buy more U.S. goods and services. Thus, U.S. exports (*EX*) rise. As exports rise, net exports rise, *ceteris paribus.* As net exports rise, aggregate demand increases.

This process works in reverse too. As foreign real national income falls, foreigners buy fewer U.S. goods and exports fall. This lowers net exports, which reduces aggregate demand.

$$\text{Foreign real national income} \uparrow \rightarrow \text{U.S. exports} \uparrow \rightarrow AD \uparrow$$
$$\text{Foreign real national income} \downarrow \rightarrow \text{U.S. exports} \downarrow \rightarrow AD \downarrow$$

2. **Exchange rate.** The **exchange rate** is the price of one currency in terms of another currency; for example, $1.50 = £1. A currency has **appreciated** in value if more of a foreign currency is needed to buy it. A currency has **depreciated** in value if more of it is needed to buy a foreign currency. For example, a movement in the exchange rate from $1.50 = £1 to $1.80 = £1 means that more dollars are needed to buy one pound and the pound has appreciated. And because more dollars are needed to buy one pound, the dollar has depreciated.

A depreciation in a nation's currency makes foreign goods more expensive. Consider an English coat that is priced at £200 when the exchange rate is $1 = £1. To buy the English coat for £200, an American has to pay $200, or $1 for every £1. Now suppose the dollar depreciates to $2 = £1. The American has to pay $400 for the coat. This process is symmetrical, so an appreciation in a nation's currency makes foreign goods cheaper. For example, if the exchange rate goes from $1 = £1 to $0.80 = £1, the English coat will cost the American only $160 ($0.80 per pound times £200 = $160).

The depreciation and appreciation of the U.S. dollar affect net exports. As the dollar depreciates, foreign goods become more expensive, Americans cut back on imported goods, and foreigners (whose currency has appreciated) increase their purchases of U.S. exported goods. If exports rise and imports fall, net exports increase and aggregate demand increases.

As the dollar appreciates, foreign goods become cheaper, Americans increase their purchases of imported goods, and foreigners (whose currency has depreciated) cut back on their purchases of U.S. exported goods. If exports fall and imports rise, net exports decrease, thus lowering aggregate demand.

Dollar depreciates →U.S. exports↑and U.S. imports↓→U.S. net exports↑→*AD*↑
Dollar appreciates →U.S. exports↓and U.S. imports↑→U.S. net exports↓→*AD*↓

See Exhibit 5 for a summary of the factors that change aggregate demand.

Exchange Rate
The price of one currency in terms of another currency.

Appreciation
An increase in the value of one currency relative to other currencies.

Depreciation
A decrease in the value of one currency relative to other currencies.

CAN A CHANGE IN THE MONEY SUPPLY CHANGE AGGREGATE DEMAND?
Changes in such factors as interest rates, business taxes, exchange rates, and so on can change aggregate demand (indirectly) by directly changing consumption, investment, and net exports. What about the money supply? Can a change in the money supply lead to a change in aggregate demand?

Suppose the money supply rises from, say, $1,000 billion to $1,080 billion. Will this result in an increase in aggregate demand? Most economists would say that it does, but they differ as to how the change in the money supply affects aggregate demand. One way to explain the effect is as follows: (1) A change in the money supply affects interest rates. (2) A change in interest rates changes consumption and investment (see our earlier discussion). (3) A change in consumption and investment affects aggregate demand. Therefore, a change in the money supply was a catalyst in a process that ended with a change in aggregate demand. (We will have much more to say about the money supply and interest rates in later chapters.)

Self-Test *(Answers to Self-Test questions are in the Self-Test Appendix.)*

1. Explain the real balance effect.
2. Explain what happens to the *AD* curve if the dollar appreciates relative to other currencies.
3. Explain what happens to the *AD* curve if personal income taxes decline.

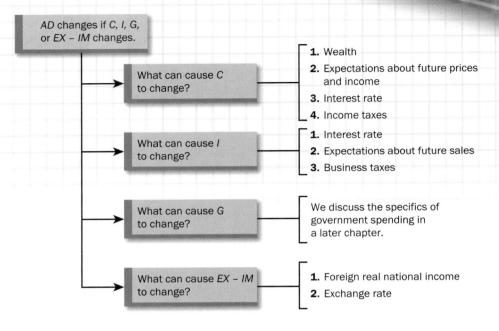

AD changes if C, I, G, or EX – IM changes.

What can cause C to change?
1. Wealth
2. Expectations about future prices and income
3. Interest rate
4. Income taxes

What can cause I to change?
1. Interest rate
2. Expectations about future sales
3. Business taxes

What can cause G to change?
We discuss the specifics of government spending in a later chapter.

What can cause EX – IM to change?
1. Foreign real national income
2. Exchange rate

exhibit 5

Factors That Change Aggregate Demand
Aggregate demand (AD) changes whenever consumption (C), investment (I), government purchases (G), or net exports (EX – IM) change. The factors that can affect C, I, and EX – IM, thereby indirectly affecting aggregate demand, are listed.

Aggregate Supply
The quantity supplied of all goods and services (Real GDP) at different price levels, *ceteris paribus*.

Short-Run Aggregate Supply (SRAS) Curve
A curve that shows the quantity supplied of all goods and services (Real GDP) at different price levels, *ceteris paribus*.

SHORT-RUN AGGREGATE SUPPLY

Aggregate demand is one side of the economy; aggregate supply is the other side. **Aggregate supply** refers to the quantity supplied of all goods and services (Real GDP) at various price levels, *ceteris paribus*. Aggregate supply includes both short-run aggregate supply (SRAS) and long-run aggregate supply (LRAS). Short-run aggregate supply is discussed in this section.

SHORT-RUN AGGREGATE SUPPLY CURVE: WHAT IT IS AND WHY IT IS UPWARD-SLOPING

A **short-run aggregate supply (SRAS) curve** is illustrated in Exhibit 6. It shows the quantity supplied of all goods and services (Real GDP or output) at different price levels, *ceteris paribus*. Notice that the SRAS curve is upward-sloping: as the price level rises, firms increase the quantity supplied of goods and services; as the price level drops, firms decrease the quantity supplied of goods and services. Why is the SRAS curve upward-sloping? Economists have put forth a few explanations, which we discuss next.

Sticky Wages

Some economists believe that wages are sticky or inflexible. This may be because wages are "locked in" for a few years due to labor contracts entered into by workers and management. For example, management and labor may agree to lock in wages for the next one to three years. Both labor and management may see this as in their best interest. Management has some idea what its labor costs will be during the time of the contract, and workers may have a sense of security knowing that their wages can't be lowered. Alternatively, wages may be sticky because of certain social conventions or perceived notions of fairness. Whatever the specific reason for sticky wages, let's see how it provides an explanation of an upward-sloping SRAS curve.

Firms pay *nominal wages* (for example, $30 an hour), but they often base their decision on how many workers to hire on real wages. *Real wages* are nominal wages divided by the price level.

$$\text{Real wage} = \frac{\text{Nominal wage}}{\text{Price level}}$$

Let's suppose the nominal wage is $30 an hour and the price level as measured by a price index is 1.50.[1] The real wage is therefore $20.

The quantity supplied of labor is directly related to the real wage: as the real wage rises, the quantity supplied of labor rises; as the real wage falls, the quantity supplied of labor falls. In short, more individuals are willing to work, and current workers are willing to work more, at higher than at lower real wages.

The quantity demanded of labor is inversely related to the real wage: as the real wage rises, the quantity demanded of labor falls; as the real wage falls, the quantity demanded of labor rises. Firms will employ more workers the cheaper it is to hire them.

With this as background, suppose that a firm has agreed to pay its workers $30 an hour for the next three years. When it agreed to this nominal wage, it thought the price index would remain at 1.50 and that the real wage would stay at $20. Now suppose the price index falls to 1.25. When the price level falls to an index of 1.25, the real wage rises to $24 ($30/1.25). This is a higher real wage than the firm expected when it agreed to lock in nominal wages at $30 an hour for the next three years. Because labor costs are a major part of a firm's overall costs, the firm finds that its real costs have risen. It responds to higher costs by cutting back its output and hiring less labor.

In conclusion, if wages are sticky, a decrease in the price level will result in a decrease in output. This is what an upward-sloping *SRAS* curve would predict: as the price level falls, the quantity supplied of goods and services declines.

Sticky Prices

Some prices in an economy adjust very quickly, others do not. For example, stock prices usually adjust in seconds or minutes. If the demand rises for a stock, its price rises almost immediately; if the demand falls, its price falls almost immediately. On the other hand, magazine prices, restaurant meal prices, and so on do not adjust as quickly as do stock prices. In fact, some prices appear to be sticky (inflexible) over some period of time. Economists reason that some prices are sticky because there are costs to changing prices, called **menu costs.**[2] Menu costs usually include such things as the cost of printing new catalogs with new prices (for a catalog company), the cost of printing a new menu (for a restaurant), and the cost of changing price tags (for many firms).

What is the sticky-price explanation for an upward-sloping *SRAS* curve? Suppose firms have set their prices based on the price level in the economy remaining constant. Then, suppose the demand for goods in the economy falls. Some firms reduce their prices accordingly, but many may not. Because some firms lower their prices, the overall price level drops.

The firms that do not adjust their prices may hold off adjusting prices because of their menu costs and because they may not yet be able to figure out whether the decline in demand in the economy is temporary or permanent. For example, put yourself in the shoes of the owner of a catalog company. You have just spent thousands of dollars printing catalogs. Then, demand in the economy drops. You

exhibit 6

The Short-Run Aggregate Supply Curve
The short-run aggregate supply curve is upward-sloping, specifying a direct relationship between the price level and the quantity supplied of Real GDP.

> **Short-Run Aggregate Supply Curve**
> The price level and quantity supplied of Real GDP are directly related.

Menu Costs
The costs of changing prices.

---

1. Alternatively, you can view the price index as 1.50 times 100, or 150. In this case, the formula for the real wage would change to Real wage = (Nominal wage/Price level) × 100.

2. Although it sounds as if menu costs might apply only to businesses that print menus (such as restaurants), this is not the case. Menu costs are the costs of changing prices and can apply to any kind of firm.

may be unsure whether this drop in demand will be permanent or whether it will somehow be reversed in a few weeks. If it does reverse, then it would be better to hold off and not incur the costs of changing the catalog prices.

There is a problem, however. Because some firms have not lowered prices in the face of falling demand, they will not be able to sell the same level of output they did at the higher demand. In other words, their sales will decline, which will cause them to cut back on the output they produce.

In conclusion, if some prices are sticky, a decline in the price level is linked with a decrease in output, which is illustrative of an upward-sloping *SRAS* curve.

Producer Misperceptions

An earlier chapter discusses the difference between absolute price and relative price. The absolute price of a good is the dollar price of a good, such as $200 for a television set. The relative price of a good is the price of the good in terms of another good. Economists generally agree that producers will produce more output as the relative price of their good rises and produce less output as the relative price of their good falls.

To illustrate, suppose Jones produces and sells good X. The current absolute price of good X is $100, and the price level as measured by a price index is 1.00. Given these data, Jones produces 1,000 units of good X each week.

Now suppose prices in the economy rise by 10 percent (the price index is now 1.10). Also, the price of good X rises by $10 to $110, or by 10 percent. Jones knows his selling price has risen, and he knows that prices in the economy are higher than they were previously, but he doesn't yet know *how much* higher. In other words, he knows the price level has risen, but he doesn't know it has risen by 10 percent. The producer-misperception explanation of the upward-sloping *SRAS* curve assumes that Jones will *underestimate the change in the price level*. In other words, while Jones knows that his price has risen by 10 percent, he mistakenly believes that the price level has risen by, say, 5 percent.

Because Jones believes his price has risen by a greater percentage than the price level, it follows that he believes that the relative price of the good he produces and sells has increased. As a result, he produces more of it. If Jones is the representative producer in the economy (all producers act the way Jones does), then all producers will do as Jones has done and produce more output.

In conclusion, if producers misperceive relative price changes (in the way we have identified), then a higher price level will bring about an increase in output, which is illustrative of an upward-sloping *SRAS* curve.

Worker Misperceptions

Just as producers may misperceive relative price changes, workers may misperceive real wage changes. To illustrate, suppose the nominal wage is $30 an hour and the price level as measured by a price index is 1.50. It follows that the real wage is $20. Now suppose the nominal wage falls to $25 and the price level falls to 1.25. The real wage is still $20 ($25/1.25 = $20) but workers may not know this. They will know their nominal wage has fallen, and they may know the price level is lower, but they may not know initially *how much* lower the price level is. For example, suppose they mistakenly believe the price level has fallen from 1.50 to 1.39. They will then think that their real wage has actually fallen from $20 ($30/1.50) to $17.98 ($25/1.39). In response to (the misperceived) falling real wage, workers may reduce the quantity of labor they are willing to supply. With fewer workers (resources), firms will end up producing less.

In conclusion, if workers misperceive real wage changes, then a fall in the price level will bring about a decline in output, which is illustrative of an upward-sloping *SRAS* curve.

WHAT PUTS THE "SHORT RUN" IN *SRAS?*

According to most macroeconomists, the *SRAS* curve slopes upward because of sticky wages, sticky prices, producers' misperceptions, or workers' misperceptions. No matter which explanation of the upward-sloping *SRAS* curve we accept, though, things are likely to change over time. Wages will not be sticky forever (labor contracts will expire), prices won't be sticky forever (firms will eventually adjust their prices or suffer the consequences), producers will figure out that they misperceived relative price changes, and workers will figure out that they misperceived real wage changes. It is only for a period of time—identified as the short run—that these issues are likely to be relevant.

SHIFTS IN THE SHORT-RUN AGGREGATE SUPPLY CURVE

The factors that can shift the short-run aggregate supply curve include wage rates, prices of nonlabor inputs, productivity, and supply shocks.

Wage Rates

Changes in wage rates have a major impact on the position of the *SRAS* curve because wage costs are usually a firm's major cost item. The impact of a rise or fall in equilibrium wage rates can be understood in terms of the following equation:

$$\text{Profit per unit} = \text{Price per unit} - \text{Cost per unit}$$

Higher wage rates mean higher costs and, at constant prices, translate into lower profits and a reduction in the number of goods managers of firms will want to produce. Lower wage rates mean lower costs and, at constant prices, translate into higher profits and an increase in the number of goods managers will decide to produce.

The impact of higher and lower equilibrium wages is shown in Exhibit 7. At the given price level, P_1 on $SRAS_1$, the quantity supplied of Real GDP is Q_1. When higher wage rates are introduced, a firm's profits at a given price level decrease. Consequently, the firm reduces production. In the diagram, this corresponds to moving from Q_1 to Q_2, which at the given price level is point *B*. Point *B* represents

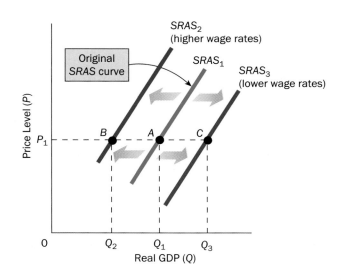

exhibit 7

Wage Rates and a Shift in the Short-Run Aggregate Supply Curve
A rise in wage rates shifts the short-run aggregate supply curve leftward. A fall in wage rates shifts the short-run aggregate supply curve rightward.

a point on a new aggregate supply curve ($SRAS_2$). Thus, a rise in equilibrium wage rates leads to a leftward shift in the aggregate supply curve. The steps are simply reversed for a fall in equilibrium wage rates.

Prices of Nonlabor Inputs

There are other inputs to the production process besides labor. Changes in their prices affect the *SRAS* curve in the same way as changes in wage rates do. An increase in the price of a nonlabor input (say, oil) shifts the *SRAS* curve leftward; a decrease in the price of a nonlabor input shifts the *SRAS* curve rightward.

Productivity

Productivity describes the output produced per unit of input employed over some period of time. While various inputs can become more productive, let's consider the input labor. An increase in labor productivity means businesses will produce more output with the same amount of labor. This causes the *SRAS* curve to shift rightward. A decrease in labor productivity means businesses will produce less output with the same amount of labor. This causes the *SRAS* curve to shift leftward. A host of factors lead to increased labor productivity, including a more educated labor force, a larger stock of capital goods, and technological advancements.

Supply Shocks

Major natural or institutional changes on the supply side of the economy that affect aggregate supply are referred to as supply shocks. Bad weather that wipes out a large part of the midwestern wheat crop would be considered a supply shock. So would a major cutback in the supply of oil coming to the United States from the Middle East, a change in (marginal) tax rates, or a change in regulatory rules.

Supply shocks are of two varieties. *Adverse supply shocks* (such as the examples just given) shift the *SRAS* curve leftward, and *beneficial supply shocks* shift it rightward. Examples of the latter include a major oil discovery and unusually good weather leading to increased production of a food staple. These supply shocks are reflected in resource or input prices.

Exhibit 8 summarizes the factors that affect short-run aggregate supply.

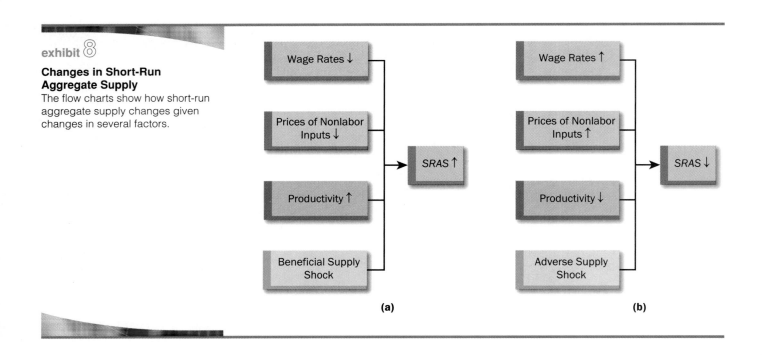

exhibit 8

Changes in Short-Run Aggregate Supply
The flow charts show how short-run aggregate supply changes given changes in several factors.

Self-Test

1. If wage rates decline, explain what happens to the short-run aggregate supply (SRAS) curve.

2. Give an example of an increase in labor productivity.

PUTTING *AD* AND *SRAS* TOGETHER: SHORT-RUN EQUILIBRIUM

In this section, we put aggregate demand and short-run aggregate supply together to achieve short-run equilibrium in the economy. Aggregate demand and short-run aggregate supply determine the price level, Real GDP, and the unemployment rate in the short run.

HOW SHORT-RUN EQUILIBRIUM IN THE ECONOMY IS ACHIEVED

Exhibit 9 shows an aggregate demand (*AD*) curve and a short-run aggregate supply (*SRAS*) curve. We consider the quantity demanded of Real GDP and the quantity supplied of Real GDP at three different price levels: P_1, P_2, and P_E.

At P_1, the quantity supplied of Real GDP (Q_2) is greater than the quantity demanded (Q_1). There is a surplus of goods. As a result, the price level drops, firms decrease output, and consumers increase consumption. Why do consumers increase consumption as the price level drops? (Hint: Think of the real balance, the interest rate, and the international trade effects.)

At P_2, the quantity supplied of Real GDP (Q_1) is less than the quantity demanded (Q_2). There is a shortage of goods. As a result, the price level rises, firms increase output, and consumers decrease consumption.

In instances of both surplus and shortage, economic forces are moving the economy toward *E*, where the quantity demanded of Real GDP equals the (short-run)

exhibit 9

Short-Run Equilibrium
At P_1, the quantity supplied of Real GDP is greater than the quantity demanded. As a result, the price level falls and firms decrease output. At P_2, the quantity demanded of Real GDP is greater than the quantity supplied. As a result, the price level rises and firms increase output. Short-run equilibrium occurs at point *E*, where the quantity demanded of Real GDP equals the (short-run) quantity supplied. This is at the intersection of the aggregate demand (*AD*) curve and the short-run aggregate supply (*SRAS*) curve. (Note: Although real-world *AD* and *SRAS* curves can, and likely do, have some curvature to them, we have drawn both as straight lines. This does not affect the analysis. Whenever the analysis is not disturbed, we follow suit throughout this text.)

quantity supplied of Real GDP. This is the point of **short-run equilibrium.** P_E is the short-run equilibrium price level; Q_E is the short-run equilibrium Real GDP.

A change in aggregate demand or short-run aggregate supply or both will obviously affect the price level and/or Real GDP. For example, an increase in aggregate demand raises the equilibrium price level and, in the short run, Real GDP (Exhibit 10a). An increase in short-run aggregate supply lowers the equilibrium price level and raises Real GDP (Exhibit 10b). A decrease in short-run aggregate supply raises the equilibrium price level and lowers Real GDP (Exhibit 10c).

THE UNEMPLOYMENT RATE IN THE SHORT RUN

When a change occurs in aggregate demand, short-run aggregate supply, or both, the price level and Real GDP are not the only economic variables affected. Because Real GDP changes, the unemployment rate can also change.

Changes in Real GDP and Changes in the Unemployment Rate

There is always some unemployment in the economy. And no matter what the unemployment rate (U) is—5 percent, 6 percent, or whatever—some Real GDP (Q) is being produced at that particular unemployment rate.

All other things held constant, we expect a higher Real GDP level to be associated with a lower unemployment rate and a lower Real GDP level to be associated with a higher unemployment rate. In other words, Real GDP and the unemployment rate are inversely related: as one goes up, the other goes down.

But why? The reason is that more workers are needed to produce more output and fewer workers are needed to produce less output, *ceteris paribus*. Since more workers are needed to produce more output (more Real GDP), fewer people remain unemployed and the unemployment rate drops, *ceteris paribus*. Since fewer workers are needed to produce less output, more people are unemployed and the unemployment rate rises, *ceteris paribus*.

Ceteris Paribus Makes All the Difference in the Relationship between Real GDP and the Unemployment Rate

Do the data substantiate the inverse relationship between Real GDP and the unemployment rate? In 1997, Real GDP was $8,159 billion and the unemployment rate was 4.9 percent. In 1998, Real GDP had risen to $8,508 billion and the

exhibit 10

Changes in Short-Run Equilibrium in the Economy
(a) An increase in aggregate demand increases the price level and Real GDP. (b) An increase in short-run aggregate supply decreases the price level and increases Real GDP. (c) A decrease in short-run aggregate supply increases the price level and decreases Real GDP.

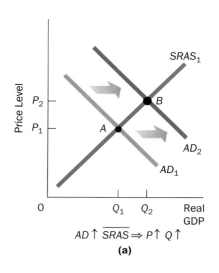

$AD \uparrow \ \overline{SRAS} \Rightarrow P \uparrow \ Q \uparrow$

(a)

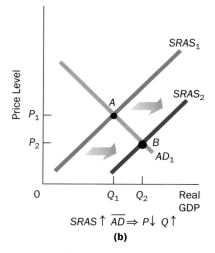

$SRAS \uparrow \ \overline{AD} \Rightarrow P \downarrow \ Q \uparrow$

(b)

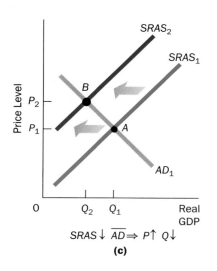

$SRAS \downarrow \ \overline{AD} \Rightarrow P \uparrow \ Q \downarrow$

(c)

ECONOMICS IN...

Aggregate Demand, the Great Depression, and Scrabble

Economist Christina Romer writes, "At the broadest conceptual level, the Great Depression in the United States can be analyzed quite well with the simple aggregate supply-aggregate demand model familiar to introductory economics students. Between 1929 and 1933, a series of shocks caused aggregate demand to decline repeatedly in the United States. [In other words, the *AD* curve repeatedly shifted to the left.] These declines in aggregate demand moved the economy down along an upward-sloping aggregate supply curve. The net result was both progressively worsening unemployment and deflation."[3]

Certainly a fall in aggregate demand can cause a rise in unemployment and a fall in prices. But can a repeated fall in aggregate demand lead to anything else? In an indirect way, it can. In fact, if it weren't for falling aggregate demand and the ensuing Great Depression, we might not have one of the more popular games people play—Scrabble.

The story of Scrabble is an interesting one. Scrabble was invented by Alfred M. Butts of Poughkeepsie, New York. Before Butts invented Scrabble he was an architect. Because of the Great Depression, Butts lost his job and couldn't find another. Wondering what to do with his time, he started analyzing different board games. He found that every game fell into one of three categories: number games, such as dice and bingo; move games, such as chess and checkers; and word games, such as anagrams.

Alfred Butts set out to create a board game that would combine chance and skill. He combined features of anagrams and crossword puzzles and called his game "Criss Cross Word." The first boards of his Criss Cross Word game were hand drawn with his architectural drafting equipment. In time, Butts's game was purchased and renamed "Scrabble."

unemployment rate had fallen to 4.5 percent. Obviously, these data support the inverse relationship between Real GDP and the unemployment rate.

But here are some data that do not. In 1991, Real GDP was $6,676 billion and the unemployment rate was 6.8 percent. In 1992, Real GDP had risen to $6,880 billion and the unemployment rate had risen to 7.5 percent.

Conclusion: The 1997–1998 data support the inverse relationship between Real GDP and the unemployment rate, but the 1991–1992 data do not. What explains these inconsistent findings?

Recall that the inverse relationship between Real GDP and the unemployment rate is conditioned upon *ceteris paribus,* or nothing else changing. If some other things do change, it may appear as if the inverse relationship between Real GDP and the unemployment rate does not hold.

To illustrate, let's look at the unemployment rate, which is computed by dividing the number of unemployed persons by the civilian labor force. For example, if 100,000 people are unemployed and the civilian labor force is 1 million, the unemployment rate is 10 percent. Let's say that at this 10 percent unemployment rate, Real GDP is $9,000 billion.

Now suppose Real GDP rises to $9,500 billion. If nothing else changes, we would expect the unemployment rate to drop. But suppose something else does change. Suppose that as the number of unemployed falls to 98,000, the civilian labor force does not stay constant at 1 million, but falls to 900,000 persons. When we divide the number of unemployed persons (98,000) by the civilian labor force (900,000), we get an unemployment rate of 10.9 percent. In other

---

3. Christina Romer, "The Nation in Depression," *Journal of Economic Perspectives* (spring 1993): 25.

Can Information Technology Cause People to Buy Bigger Homes?

For much of 1998 and 1999, the U.S. stock market was moving up, as measured by broad stock indexes like the Dow Jones Industrial Average and the Standard & Poor's 500. Business magazines were replete with stories wondering whether the bull market would ever run out of steam.

Some economists explained the rising stock market in terms of technology. They argued that technology, especially information technology, was getting cheaper, which helped businesses become more profitable. In fact, Alan Greenspan, chairman of the Board of Governors of the Federal Reserve System, made this argument in a speech before the 35th Annual Conference on Bank Structure and Competition.[4]

In his speech, Greenspan said that an unexpected leap in technology was responsible for the nation's "phenomenal" economic performance and extraordinary combination of strong growth, low unemployment, low inflation, high corporate profits—and soaring stock prices. The following is an excerpt from his speech:

I have hypothesized before this group on several occasions that the synergies that have developed, especially among the micro-processor, the laser, fiber-optics, and satellite technologies, have dramatically raised the potential rates of return, not only on new telecommunications investments, but more broadly on many types of equipment that embody or utilize the newer technologies.

The newest innovations, which we label information technologies, have begun to alter the manner in which we do business and create value, often in ways not readily foreseeable even five years ago.

Thus, development of information technology was considered by many to be the reason for the rising stock market.

How might the rising stock market affect other areas of the economy?

According to many economists, a rising stock market simply increases the wealth of many Americans, and a rise in wealth increases consumption. What were Americans consuming?

During much of the same time the stock market was rising, the housing market was also rising. Many economists thought this was not a coincidence. They believed that the new wealth generated in the stock market simply found its way into increased spending on houses—especially new and bigger homes with many more amenities.[5] In other words, we can trace a connection between information technology and the size and kind of homes being built and bought in the 1990s.

words, we witness a rising Real GDP (from $9,000 billion to $9,500 billion) associated with a rising unemployment rate (from 10 percent to 10.9 percent).

To repeat: the *ceteris paribus* condition makes all the difference. A higher Real GDP is associated with a lower unemployment rate, and a lower Real GDP is associated with a higher unemployment rate, *ceteris paribus*.

THINKING IN TERMS OF SHORT-RUN EQUILIBRIUM CHANGES IN THE ECONOMY

Earlier you learned that certain factors can lead to a change in aggregate demand. You also learned that certain factors can lead to a change in short-run aggregate supply. Then you learned that if either aggregate demand or short-run aggregate

---

4. This speech was given on May 6, 1999.

5. We should also mention that during this time, mortgage rates were relatively low, which also tends to stimulate the housing market.

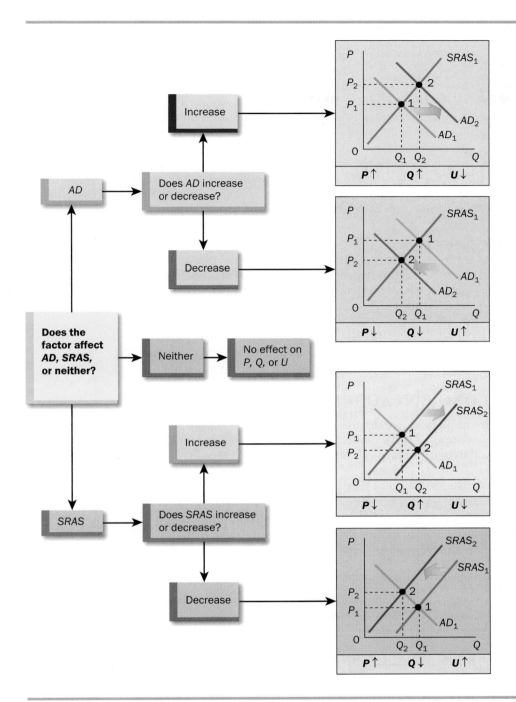

exhibit 11

How a Factor Affects the Price Level, Real GDP, and the Unemployment Rate in the Short Run
In the exhibit, P = price level, Q = Real GDP, and U = unemployment rate.

supply changes, the price level, Real GDP, and the unemployment rate will all change in the short run. Exhibit 11 puts all this information together in a flow chart.

Let's see how it works. With one eye on the exhibit, consider an adverse supply shock that hits the economy. Question: Does an adverse supply shock affect *AD, SRAS,* or neither? Answer: It affects *SRAS.*

Next question: Does it cause *SRAS* to increase or decrease? Answer: Decrease. We then see that as a result of the adverse supply shock, the price level (P) rises and Real GDP (Q) falls in the short run. And earlier you learned that when Real GDP falls, the unemployment rate (U) rises, *ceteris paribus.*

Exhibit 12 summarizes much of the discussion in this chapter up to this point.

THINKING LIKE AN ECONOMIST

In the flow chart in Exhibit 11, it is easy to see how one thing is related to another. For example, you can see how the change in Real GDP shown in the large box at the lower right of the exhibit is related to a change in a factor (represented in the middle far-left box). Lines in a flow chart connect factors that are linked in real life—thus visually establishing connections or causes and effects.

To a large degree, economists naturally think in terms of flow charts. Economics is about establishing a connection or link between an effect (such as a fall in Real GDP) and a correct cause (such as an adverse supply shock that shifts the SRAS *curve to the left). A flow chart is simply the graphical representation of the economic way of thinking.*

Self-Test

1. Identify what will happen to the price level and Real GDP (in the short run) as a result of each of the following:
   a. *SRAS* rises
   b. *SRAS* falls
   c. *AD* rises
   d. *AD* falls
   e. *AD* rises by more than *SRAS* rises
   f. *AD* falls by less than *SRAS* falls

2. Explain Exhibit 11 in your own words.

LONG-RUN AGGREGATE SUPPLY

In this section, we discuss long-run aggregate supply and draw a long-run aggregate supply (*LRAS*) curve. We also discuss long-run equilibrium and explain how it differs from short-run equilibrium.

GOING FROM THE SHORT RUN TO THE LONG RUN

Graphically, short-run equilibrium is at the intersection of the *AD* curve and the (upward-sloping) *SRAS* curve. As an earlier section explains, economists give dif-

exhibit 12

A Summary Exhibit of *AD* and *SRAS*

Economy in the Short Run

Aggregate Demand → **Real GDP Price Level** ← **Short-Run Aggregate Supply**

C
1. Wealth
2. Expectations about Future Prices and Income
3. Interest Rate (money supply is relevant here)
4. Income Taxes

I
1. Interest Rate (money supply is relevant here)
2. Expectations about Future Sales
3. Business Taxes

G

NX

EX
1. Foreign Real National Income
2. Exchange Rate

IM
1. Exchange Rate

Wage Rates

Prices of Nonlabor Inputs

Productivity

Supply Shocks

ferent reasons for an upward-sloping *SRAS* curve. Recall that those reasons have to do with:

1. Sticky wages
2. Sticky prices
3. Producers' misperceptions
4. Workers' misperceptions

It follows, then, that short-run equilibrium identifies the Real GDP the economy produces when any of these four conditions hold.

In time, though, wages and prices will become unstuck and misperceptions will turn into accurate perceptions. When this happens, the economy is said to be in the *long run*. In other words, in the long run, these four conditions do not hold.

An important macroeconomic question is: *Will the level of Real GDP the economy produces in the long run be the same as in the short run?* Most economists say that it will not be. They argue that in the long run, the economy produces the full-employment Real GDP or the **Natural Real GDP** (Q_N). The aggregate supply curve that identifies the output the economy produces in the long run is the **long-run aggregate supply (*LRAS*) curve.** It is portrayed as the vertical line in Exhibit 13.

It follows that **long-run equilibrium** identifies the level of Real GDP the economy produces when wages and prices have adjusted to their (final) equilibrium levels and there are no misperceptions on the part of either producers or workers. Graphically, this occurs at the intersection of the *AD* and *LRAS* curves. Furthermore, the level of Real GDP that the economy produces in long-run equilibrium is Natural Real GDP (Q_N).

Q: An earlier section describes the factors that can shift the *SRAS* curve—such as wage rates, productivity, and so on. Are there factors that can shift the *LRAS* curve?

A: Yes. In fact, some of the factors that shift the *LRAS* curve are the same factors that shift the *SRAS* curve. We discuss the factors that shift the *LRAS* curve in a later chapter when we discuss economic growth.

SHORT-RUN EQUILIBRIUM, LONG-RUN EQUILIBRIUM, AND DISEQUILIBRIUM

There are two equilibrium states in an economy—short-run equilibrium and long-run equilibrium. These two equilibrium states are graphically shown in Exhibit 14.

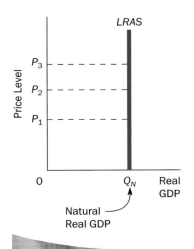

exhibit 13

Long-Run Aggregate Supply (*LRAS*) Curve
The *LRAS* curve is a vertical line at the level of Natural Real GDP. It represents the output the economy produces when all economy-wide adjustments have taken place and no economic agents have any (relevant) misperceptions.

Natural Real GDP
The Real GDP that is produced at the natural unemployment rate. The Real GDP that is produced when the economy is in long-run equilibrium.

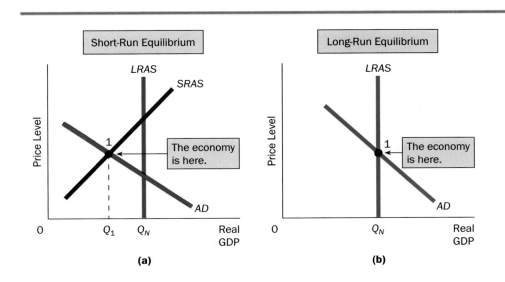

(a)

(b)

exhibit 14

Equilibrium States of the Economy
There are two equilibrium states in the economy: short-run equilibrium, shown in part (a), and long-run equilibrium, shown in part (b). During the time an economy moves from one equilibrium to another, it is said to be in disequilibrium.

In Exhibit 14a, the economy is at point 1, producing Q_1 amount of Real GDP. Notice that at point 1, the quantity supplied of Real GDP (in the short run) is equal to the quantity demanded of Real GDP and both are Q_1. The economy is in short-run equilibrium.

In Exhibit 14b, the economy is at point 1, producing Q_N. In other words, it is producing Natural Real GDP. The economy is in long-run equilibrium when it produces Q_N. When the economy is in neither short-run equilibrium nor long-run equilibrium, it is said to be in *disequilibrium*. Essentially, disequilibrium is the state of the economy as it moves from one short-run equilibrium to another or from short-run equilibrium to long-run equilibrium.

Q & A

Q: It appears that in both short-run and long-run equilibrium, the quantity supplied of Real GDP equals the quantity demanded. So what is the difference?

A: You are right that in both short-run and long-run equilibrium, the quantity supplied of Real GDP equals the quantity demanded. But it is what else they equal that matters. In long-run equilibrium, quantity supplied and demanded of Real GDP equal Natural Real GDP (see Exhibit 14b). But in short-run equilibrium, quantity supplied and demanded of Real GDP are either more than or less than Natural Real GDP. Let's illustrate with numbers. Suppose $Q_N =$ $9,000 billion. In long-run equilibrium, quantity supplied of Real GDP = quantity demanded of Real GDP = $9,000 billion. In short-run equilibrium, quantity supplied of Real GDP equals quantity demanded, but neither equals $9,000 billion. For example, it could be that quantity supplied of Real GDP = quantity demanded of Real GDP = $8,500 billion. Finally, in disequilibrium, quantity supplied of Real GDP and quantity demanded of Real GDP are not equal.

A FEW OF THE INTERESTING QUESTIONS MACROECONOMISTS ASK

Based on the aggregate demand–aggregate supply model, we can identify some of the questions macroeconomists try to answer. Much of the rest of this book will be concerned with these questions and answers, so you can consider this list a road map to future chapters.

1. **What can cause the economy to move from one short-run equilibrium position to another short-run equilibrium position?** For example, if the economy is in short-run equilibrium at point 1 in Exhibit 15a, what can cause it to move to point 2? (We have already started to answer this question in this chapter.)

2. **What happens to certain economic variables, such as the price level and Real GDP, as the economy moves from one short-run equilibrium to another short-run equilibrium?** In terms of Exhibit 15a, economists are asking what happens to the price level and Real GDP as the economy moves from, say, point 1 to point 2.

3. **If the economy is in short-run equilibrium, what path does it travel to long-run equilibrium?** For example, suppose the economy is in short-run equilibrium at point 1 in Exhibit 15b. In time, the economy may go from short-run equilibrium to long-run equilibrium. For a given *LRAS* curve, both points 2 and 3 may represent long-run equilibrium positions. Does the economy travel from point 1 to point 2 or from point 1 to point 3? Or is there some other path (not identified) that it travels?

4. **How long does it take the economy to move from short-run equilibrium to long-run equilibrium?** For example, suppose the economy is currently in short-run equilibrium at point 1 in Exhibit 15b and we know that it will travel from point 1 to point 2 to establish long-run equilibrium. How

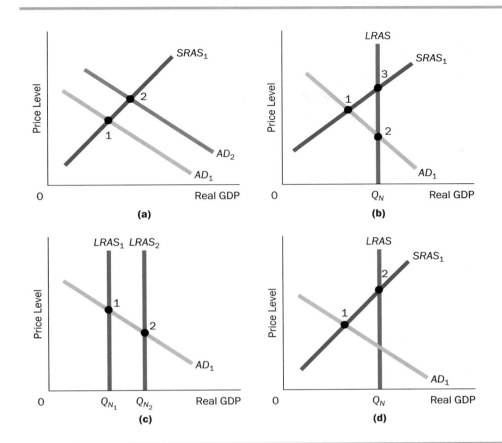

long will it take to move from point 1 to point 2? Will it take weeks, months, or years? Can the economy get stuck in short-run equilibrium?

5. **If the economy is in long-run equilibrium, what must happen to move it to another long-run equilibrium?** For example, suppose the economy is in long-run equilibrium at point 1 in Exhibit 15c. What has to happen to move the economy from point 1 to, say, point 2, another long-run equilibrium position?

6. **How long does it take to move from one long-run equilibrium position to another long-run equilibrium position?** For example, if the economy moves from long-run equilibrium at point 1 in Exhibit 15c to long-run equilibrium at point 2, how long does this take? Is it a matter of months or years?

7. **Are some of the states of an economy better than other states?** For example, is it better to be at point 1 or point 2 in Exhibit 15d?

8. **If some states of the economy are better than others, is there anything that government can do to move the economy from one state to another?** For example, suppose the economy is at point 1 in Exhibit 15d but the state of the economy would be better if it were at point 2. Is there anything government can do to move the economy from point 1 to point 2? If so, what can it do? Is there any chance that government actions might make matters worse?

Self-Test

1. What is the difference between short-run equilibrium and long-run equilibrium?

2. Diagrammatically represent an economy that is in neither short-run equilibrium nor long-run equilibrium.

Aggregate demand (AD) and short-run aggregate supply (SRAS) appear to determine Real GDP in the short run. Will AD *and* SRAS *also influence my job prospects after I graduate from college?*

Your job prospects will depend in part on your major, your grades, and your performance in job interviews. But your prospects will also depend on where the *AD* curve and the *SRAS* curve "intersect." That is, your job prospects will depend on whether *AD* and *SRAS* have been increasing, decreasing, or remaining constant.

To illustrate, suppose that some months before you graduate, interest rates rise and the dollar appreciates. An increase in interest rates tends to reduce durable goods spending and investment spending—so both consumption and investment decline. If the dollar appreciates, U.S. goods become more expensive for foreigners, so they buy less. Also, foreign goods become cheaper for Americans, so they buy more. The result is that exports fall and imports rise, or net exports decline.

If consumption, investment, and net exports fall, aggregate demand in the U.S. economy declines. In other words, the *AD* curve shifts to the left.

As a result of declining aggregate demand in the economy, there is a new short-run equilibrium. The new short-run equilibrium is at a lower Real GDP level. In other words, firms have cut back on the quantity of the goods and services they produce. Many of the firms that cut back may be the ones at which you hope to find a job after college. Your job prospects look slightly less rosy than they did before the changes in the economy.

A statement in the magazine *The Economist* provides further evidence of the connection between the state of the economy and your job prospects. In its November 1, 2001, edition, the magazine stated, "the downturn [in the economy] is plainly bad news for the [MBA] students, especially since banking and consulting—two of the industries which, in less interesting times, reliably hire hundreds of MBAs—have curtailed their recruiting."

Chapter Summary

Aggregate Demand

- Aggregate demand refers to the quantity demanded of all goods and services (Real GDP) at different price levels, *ceteris paribus.*
- The aggregate demand (*AD*) curve slopes downward, indicating an inverse relationship between the price level and the quantity demanded of Real GDP.
- The aggregate demand curve slopes downward because of the real balance, interest rate, and international trade effects.
- The real balance effect states that the inverse relationship between the price level and the quantity demanded of Real GDP is established through changes in the value of a person's monetary wealth or money holdings. Specifically, a fall in the price level causes purchasing power to rise, which increases a person's monetary wealth. As people become wealthier, they buy more goods. A rise in the price level causes purchasing power to fall, which reduces a person's monetary wealth. As people become less wealthy, they buy fewer goods.
- The interest rate effect states that the inverse relationship between the price level and the quantity

demanded of Real GDP is established through changes in household and business spending that is sensitive to changes in interest rates. If the price level rises, a person needs more money to buy a fixed bundle of goods. In an effort to acquire more money, the demand for credit rises, as does the interest rate. As the interest rate rises, businesses and households borrow less and buy fewer goods. Thus, the quantity demanded of Real GDP falls. If the price level falls, a person needs less money to buy a fixed bundle of goods. Part of the increase in a person's monetary wealth is saved, so the supply of credit rises, and the interest rate falls. As the interest rate falls, businesses and households borrow more and buy more goods. Thus, the quantity demanded of Real GDP rises.

- The international trade effect states that the inverse relationship between the price level and the quantity demanded of Real GDP is established through foreign sector spending. Specifically, as the price level in the United States rises, U.S. goods become relatively more expensive than foreign goods, and both Americans and foreigners buy fewer U.S. goods. The quantity demanded of (U.S.) Real GDP falls. As the price level in the United States falls, U.S. goods become relatively less expensive than foreign goods, and both Americans and foreigners buy more U.S. goods. The quantity demanded of (U.S.) Real GDP rises.

- At a given price level, a rise in consumption, investment, government purchases, or net exports will increase aggregate demand and shift the *AD* curve to the right. At a given price level, a fall in consumption, investment, government purchases, or net exports will decrease aggregate demand and shift the *AD* curve to the left.

Factors That Can Change *C, I,* and *NX* (*EX − IM*) and Therefore Can Change *AD*

- The following factors can change consumption: wealth, expectations about future prices and income, the interest rate, and income taxes. The following factors can change investment: the interest rate, expectations about future sales, and business taxes. The following factors can change net exports (exports − imports): foreign real national income and the exchange rate. A change in the money supply can affect one or more spending components (e.g., consumption) and therefore affect aggregate demand.

Short-Run Aggregate Supply

- Aggregate supply refers to the quantity supplied of all goods and services (Real GDP) at different price levels, *ceteris paribus.*
- The short-run aggregate supply (*SRAS*) curve is upward-sloping, indicating a direct relationship between the price level and the quantity supplied of Real GDP.
- A decrease in wage rates, a decrease in the price of nonlabor inputs, an increase in productivity, and beneficial supply shocks all shift the *SRAS* curve to the right. An increase in wage rates, an increase in the price of nonlabor inputs, a decrease in productivity, and adverse supply shocks all shift the *SRAS* curve to the left.

Short-Run Equilibrium

- Graphically, short-run equilibrium exists at the intersection of the *AD* and *SRAS* curves. A shift in either or both of these curves can change the price level and Real GDP. For example, an increase in aggregate demand increases the price level and Real GDP, *ceteris paribus.*

The Unemployment Rate in the Short Run

- A higher Real GDP level is associated with a lower unemployment rate, and a lower Real GDP level is associated with a higher unemployment rate, *ceteris paribus.*

Long-Run Aggregate Supply and Long-Run Equilibrium

- The long-run aggregate supply (*LRAS*) curve is vertical at the Natural Real GDP level.
- Graphically, long-run equilibrium exists at the intersection of the *AD* and *LRAS* curves. It is the condition that exists in the economy when all economy-wide adjustments have taken place and no economic agents hold any (relevant) misperceptions. In long-run equilibrium, quantity demanded of Real GDP = quantity supplied of Real GDP = Natural Real GDP.

Three States of an Economy

- An economy can be in short-run equilibrium, long-run equilibrium, or disequilibrium.

Key Terms and Concepts

Aggregate Demand
Aggregate Demand (*AD*) Curve
Real Balance Effect
Monetary Wealth
Purchasing Power
Interest Rate Effect
International Trade Effect

Wealth
Exchange Rate
Appreciation
Depreciation
Aggregate Supply
Short-Run Aggregate Supply (*SRAS*) Curve

Menu Costs
Short-Run Equilibrium
Natural Real GDP
Long-Run Aggregate Supply (*LRAS*) Curve
Long-Run Equilibrium

Economic facts, actions, and changes create ripples that move away from their point of origin. Eventually, these ripples can intersect your life and have an effect on you. Consider the following example.

The exchange rate is the price of one currency in terms of another currency. If the U.S. dollar depreciates and the Japanese yen appreciates, Japanese goods will become more expensive for Americans. If you are planning a trip to Japan this summer and,

on the day before you leave, the U.S. dollar depreciates, your trip will now be more expensive. Thus, there is a connection between the exchange rate and your overseas travel expenses—an economic connection to you.

Based on the material in this chapter, identify other ways in which economic facts, actions, and changes create ripples that eventually affect you.

Questions and Problems

1. Is aggregate demand a specific dollar amount? For example, would it be correct to say that aggregate demand is $1 trillion this year?
2. Explain each of the following: (a) real balance effect, (b) interest rate effect, and (c) international trade effect.
3. Graphically portray each of the following: (a) a change in the quantity demanded of Real GDP and (b) a change in aggregate demand.
4. The amount of Real GDP (real output) that households are willing and able to buy may change if there is a change in either (a) the price level, or (b) some nonprice factor, such as wealth, interest rates, and so on. Do you agree or disagree? Explain your answer.
5. Explain what happens to aggregate demand in each of the following cases:
   a. The interest rate rises.
   b. Wealth falls.
   c. The dollar depreciates relative to foreign currencies.
   d. Households expect lower prices in the future.
   e. Business taxes rise.
6. Will a direct increase in the price of U.S. goods relative to foreign goods lead to a change in the quantity demanded of Real GDP or to a change in aggregate demand? Will a change in the exchange rate that subsequently increases the price of U.S. goods relative to foreign goods lead to a change in the quantity demanded of Real GDP or to a change in aggregate demand? Explain your answers.
7. Explain how each of the following will affect short-run aggregate supply:
   a. An increase in wage rates
   b. A beneficial supply shock
   c. An increase in the productivity of labor
   d. A decrease in the price of a nonlabor resource (such as oil)

8. The text distinguishes between a change in the quantity demanded of Real GDP and a change in aggregate demand, but does not distinguish between a change in the quantity supplied of Real GDP and a change in short-run aggregate supply. What do you think the difference is between a change in the quantity supplied of Real GDP and a change in short-run aggregate supply? (Hint: Which of the two refers to a movement along a given *SRAS* curve and which refers to a shift in the *SRAS* curve?)
9. A change in the price level affects which of the following?
   a. The quantity demanded of Real GDP
   b. Aggregate demand
   c. Short-run aggregate supply
   d. The quantity supplied of Real GDP
10. In the short run, what is the impact on the price level, Real GDP, and the unemployment rate of each of the following:
   a. An increase in consumption brought about by a decrease in interest rates
   b. A decrease in exports brought about by an appreciation of the dollar
   c. A rise in wage rates
   d. A beneficial supply shock
   e. An adverse supply shock
   f. A decline in productivity
11. Explain why there is an inverse relationship between Real GDP and the unemployment rate, *ceteris paribus*.
12. Identify the details of each of the following explanations for an upward-sloping *SRAS* curve:
   a. Sticky-wage explanation
   b. Sticky-price explanation
   c. Worker-misperception explanation
13. What is the difference between short-run equilibrium and long-run equilibrium?

1. Suppose that at a price index of 154, the quantity demanded of (U.S.) Real GDP is $9,000 billion worth of goods. Do these data represent aggregate demand or a point on an aggregate demand curve? Explain your answer.

2. Diagrammatically represent the effect on the price level and Real GDP in the short run of each of the following:
   a. An increase in wealth
   b. An increase in wage rates
   c. An increase in labor productivity

3. Diagrammatically represent the following and identify the effect on Real GDP and the price level in the short run:
   a. An increase in SRAS that is greater than the increase in AD
   b. A decrease in AD that is greater than the increase in SRAS
   c. An increase in SRAS that is less than the increase in AD

4. In the following figure, which part is representative of each of the following:
   a. A decrease in wage rates
   b. An increase in the price level
   c. A beneficial supply shock
   d. An increase in the price of nonlabor inputs

5. In the following figure, which of the points is representative of each of the following:
   a. The lowest unemployment rate
   b. The highest unemployment rate
   c. A decrease in SRAS that is greater than an increase in AD

(a)

(b)

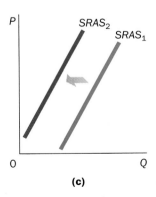

(c)

1. Go to *http://stats.bls.gov*. Click on "U.S. Economy at a Glance," and then select the graph icon next to "Unemployment."
   a. Using *AD-AS* analysis, what are two possible explanations for the change in the number of unemployed persons during the period 1990–1991?
   b. Using *AS-AD* analysis, what are two possible explanations for the change in the number of unemployed persons during the period 1995–1999?
2. Click "Back" and then click on the graph icon next to "Productivity."
   a. Using an *AD-AS* diagram, show how the change in productivity in the 1990s affected Real GDP and prices.
   b. Based on the diagram you drew in part (a), which of the two explanations you outlined in Activity 1 part (b) is more nearly accurate?
3. Go to *ftp://ftp.bls.gov/pub/special.requests/cpi/cpiai.txt* and determine the value for the annual CPI percentage change (December to December) for each year in the following table. Next, go to *http://www.bea.doc.gov/bea/dn1.htm* and click on "Percent change from preceding period" under the Time Series category. Determine the value for the change in Real GDP for each year in the following table. (We have already done this for 1933 and 1954.) Finally, for each year draw an *AD-AS* diagram that shows the shift(s) that is (are) most likely to have led to the changes in CPI and Real GDP.

Year	Change in CPI (percent)	Change in Real GDP (percent)
1933	A	−1.4
1954	B	−0.7
1974	C	G
1982	D	H
1996	E	I
latest year	F	J

Log on to the Arnold Xtra! Web site now (*http://arnoldxtra.swcollege.com*) for additional learning resources such as practice quizzes, help with graphing, video clips, and current event applications.

ch.8

THE SELF-REGULATING ECONOMY

For hundreds of years, scientists have tried to understand themselves and their surroundings. Biologists have observed and experimented to try to understand human and animal behavior. Ecologists have developed models to try to understand the relationships between plants and animals in forests and oceans. Astronomers have constructed increasingly more powerful telescopes to try to understand the phenomena in space. And economists have built and tested theories to try to understand the economy. This chapter and the next present two views about how the economy works.

Chapter Road Map

This chapter poses two questions: What are the possible
states of an economy? How does the economy work? To answer the
first question, we need to examine two types of short-run equilibria—a recessionary gap and an inflationary gap.

The second question essentially asks, If the economy is in short-run equilibrium, what happens next? Not all economists will give the same answer to this question. Some economists will argue that
the economy is self-regulating and that economic forces will smoothly move the economy from short-run equilibrium
into long-run equilibrium. Other economists will argue that the economy is inherently unstable and is not self-regulating.
These economists believe the economy may become stuck in short-run equilibrium and be unable to move itself smoothly
into long-run equilibrium.

Generally, those economists who believe the economy is self-regulating called themselves classical economists in
the past and today call themselves monetarists or new classical economists. This chapter focuses on these economists
and a self-regulating economy. Economists who call themselves Keynesians or New Keynesians usually fall into the camp
that believes the economy is inherently unstable. We begin to outline their theories in the next chapter.

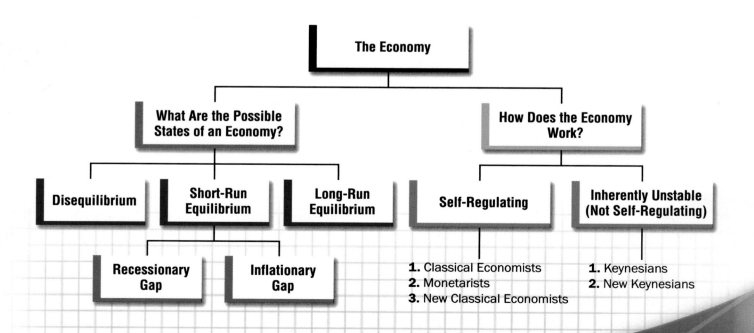

THE CLASSICAL VIEW

The term *classical economics* is often used to refer to an era in the history of economic thought that stretched from about 1750 to the late 1800s or early 1900s. Although classical economists lived and wrote many years ago, their ideas are often employed by some modern-day economists.

CLASSICAL ECONOMISTS AND SAY'S LAW

We know from our study of supply and demand that there can be temporary shortages and surpluses in markets. For example, there may be a surplus in the apple market. But can there be a general surplus (a general glut of goods and services) in the economy? The classical economists thought not. This is largely because they believed in Say's law. In its simplest version, **Say's law** says that supply creates its own demand.

Say's law is most easily understood in terms of a barter economy. Consider a person baking bread in a barter economy; he is a supplier of bread. According to Say, the baker works at his trade because he plans to demand other goods. As he is baking his bread, the baker is thinking of the goods and services he will obtain in exchange for it. Thus, his act of supplying bread is linked to his demand for other goods. Supply creates its own demand.

If the supplying of some goods is simultaneously the demanding of other goods, then Say's law implies that there cannot be either (1) a general overproduction of goods (where supply in the economy is greater than demand in the economy) or (2) a general underproduction of goods (where demand in the economy is greater than supply in the economy).

Now suppose the baker is baking bread in a money economy. Does Say's law hold? Over a period of time, the baker earns an income as a result of his supplying bread. But what does he do with his income? One thing he does is buy goods and services. However, his demand for goods and services does not necessarily match the income that he generates through his actions as a supplier of bread. The baker may spend less than his full income because he engages in saving. Noting this, we might think that Say's law does not hold in a money economy because the act of supplying goods and services, and thus earning income, need not create an equal amount of demand.

But the classical economists disagreed. They argued that even in a money economy, where individuals sometimes spend less than their full incomes, Say's law still holds. Their argument was partly based on the assumption of interest rate flexibility.

CLASSICAL ECONOMISTS AND INTEREST RATE FLEXIBILITY

For Say's law to hold in a money economy, funds saved must give rise to an equal amount of funds invested; that is, what leaves the spending stream through one door must enter through another door. If not, then some of the income earned from supplying goods may not be used to demand goods (goodbye Say's law). As a result, there will be an overproduction of goods.

The classical economists argued that saving is matched by an equal amount of investment because of interest rate flexibility in the credit market. We explain their argument using Exhibit 1, where *I* represents investment and *S* represents saving.

Notice that I_1 is downward sloping, indicating an inverse relationship between the amount of funds firms

Go to *http://www.frbsf.org/publications/education/greateconomists/*. Read the sections on Classical Economics, Adam Smith, David Ricardo, and Thomas Malthus. Does competition play a significant role in classical economics and in the theories of Smith, Ricardo, and Malthus? Do classical economists argue for or against government involvement in the economy?

Say's Law
Supply creates its own demand. Production creates demand sufficient to purchase all goods and services produced.

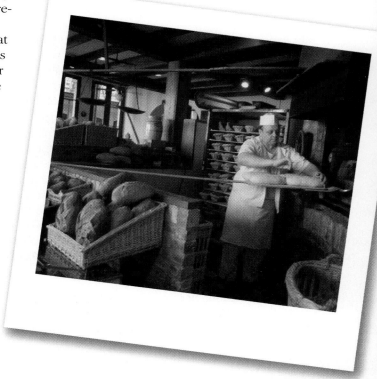

exhibit 1

The Classical View of the Credit Market

In classical theory, the interest rate is flexible and adjusts so that saving equals investment. Thus, if saving increases and the saving curve shifts rightward from S_1 to S_2 (arrow 1), the increase in saving eventually puts pressure on the interest rate and moves it downward from i_1 to i_2 (arrow 2). A new equilibrium is established at E_2 (arrow 3), where once again the amount households save equals the amount firms invest.

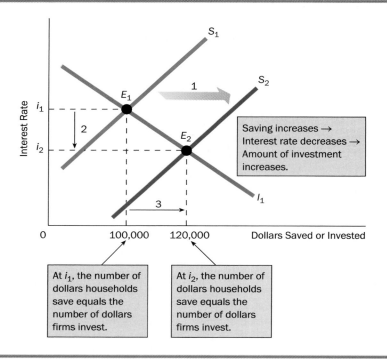

Saving increases → Interest rate decreases → Amount of investment increases.

At i_1, the number of dollars households save equals the number of dollars firms invest.

At i_2, the number of dollars households save equals the number of dollars firms invest.

invest and the interest rate (i). The reason for this is straightforward. The interest rate is the cost of borrowing funds. The higher the interest rate, the fewer funds firms borrow and invest; the lower the interest rate, the more funds firms borrow and invest.

Notice that S_1 is upward sloping, indicating a direct relationship between the amount of funds households save and the interest rate. The reason is that the higher the interest rate, the higher the reward for saving (or the higher the opportunity cost of consuming), and therefore, the fewer funds consumed and the more funds saved. Market-equilibrating forces move the credit market to interest rate i_1 and equilibrium point E_1. At E_1, the number of dollars households save ($100,000) equals the number of dollars firms invest ($100,000).

Suppose now that saving increases at each interest rate. We represent this by a rightward shift in our saving curve from S_1 to S_2. The classical economists believed that an increase in saving will put downward pressure on the interest rate, moving it to i_2, thereby increasing the number of dollars firms invest. Ultimately, the number of dollars households save ($120,000) will once again equal the number of dollars firms invest ($120,000). Interest rate flexibility ensures that saving equals investment. (What goes out one door comes in the other door.) In short, changes in the interest rate uphold Say's law in a money economy where there is saving.

Let's use a few numbers to show exactly what classical economists were saying. Suppose that at a given price level, total expenditures (TE) in a very tiny economy are $5,000. We know that total expenditures (total spending on domestic goods and services) equal the sum of consumption (C), investment (I), government purchases (G), and net exports ($EX - IM$). If $C = \$3,000$, $I = \$600$, $G = \$1,200$, and $EX - IM = \$200$,

$$TE = C + I + G + (EX - IM)$$
$$\$5,000 = \$3,000 + \$600 + \$1,200 + \$200$$

Furthermore, let's assume the $5,000 worth of goods and services that the four sectors of the economy want to purchase also happens to be the exact dollar amount of goods and services that suppliers want to sell.

Next, let's increase saving in the economy. Saving (S) is equal to the amount of a person's disposable income (Y_d) minus consumption (C). For example, if Harriet earns a disposable income of $40,000 a year and spends $38,000, she saves $2,000.

$$\text{Saving } (S) = \text{Disposable income } (Y_d) - \text{Consumption } (C)$$

For saving to increase, consumption must decrease. Let's say saving increases by $100; then, consumption must fall from $3,000 to $2,900. At first glance, this seems to imply that total expenditures will fall to $4,900. But classical economists disagreed. They said that investment will increase by $100, going from $600 to $700. Total expenditures will remain constant at $5,000 and will be equal to the dollar amount of goods and services suppliers want to sell.

$$TE = C + I + G + (EX - IM)$$
$$\$5,000 = \$2,900 + \$700 + \$1,200 + \$200$$

Exhibit 2 summarizes this discussion.

According to the classical view of the economy, then, Say's law holds both in a barter economy and in a money economy. In a money economy, according to classical economists, interest rates will adjust to equate saving and investment. Therefore, any fall in consumption (and consequent rise in saving) will be matched by an equal rise in investment. In essence, at a given price level, total expenditures will not decrease as a result of an increase in saving.

What does an increase in saving imply for aggregate demand (AD)? An earlier chapter explains that aggregate demand changes only if total spending in the economy changes at a given price level. Therefore, because there is no change in total spending as a result of an increase in saving, there is no change in aggregate demand.

CLASSICAL ECONOMISTS ON PRICES AND WAGES

Classical economists believed that most, if not all, markets are competitive. That is, supply and demand are operational in all markets. If, for example, there is a surplus of labor in the labor market, it will be temporary. Soon, the wage rate will decline and the quantity supplied of labor will equal the quantity demanded of labor. Similarly, if there is a shortage of labor in the labor market, the wage rate will rise and the quantity supplied will equal the quantity demanded.

exhibit 2

The Classical View of Say's Law in a Money Economy
According to classical economists, a decrease in consumption and subsequent increase in saving will be matched by an equal increase in investment. Thus, there is no change in total expenditures.

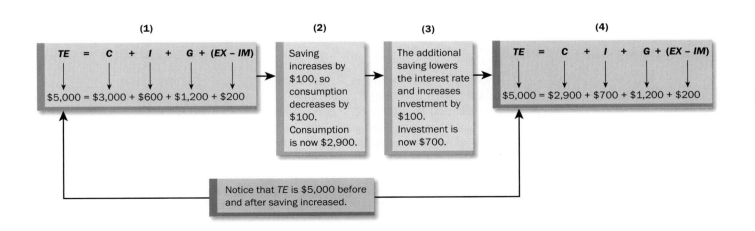

(1)	(2)	(3)	(4)
$TE = C + I + G + (EX - IM)$ $\$5,000 = \$3,000 + \$600 + \$1,200 + \$200$	Saving increases by $100, so consumption decreases by $100. Consumption is now $2,900.	The additional saving lowers the interest rate and increases investment by $100. Investment is now $700.	$TE = C + I + G + (EX - IM)$ $\$5,000 = \$2,900 + \$700 + \$1,200 + \$200$

Notice that TE is $5,000 before and after saving increased.

What holds for wages in the labor market, holds for prices in the goods and services market. Prices will adjust quickly to any surpluses or shortages and equilibrium will be quickly reestablished.

Q & A   **Q:** We have been examining the views of classical economists, who lived many years ago. Do some economists today hold these same views? For example, do some modern economists believe that wages and prices are flexible and that they quickly respond to changes in supply and demand?

A: Yes, there are economists today who ascribe to classical views. In particular, there are economists who believe that wages and prices are flexible and move up and down in response to market shortages and surpluses.

Self-Test *(Answers to Self-Test questions are in the Self-Test Appendix.)*

1. Explain Say's law in terms of a barter economy.
2. According to classical economists, if saving rises and consumption spending falls, will total spending in the economy decrease? Explain your answer.
3. What is the classical position on prices and wages?

THREE STATES OF THE ECONOMY

You will need the basic background information provided in this section before we discuss the views of economists who believe the economy is self-regulating. Specifically, we discuss three states of the economy, the correspondence between the labor market and the three states of the economy, and more in this section.

REAL GDP AND NATURAL REAL GDP: THREE POSSIBILITIES

In the last chapter, Natural Real GDP is defined as the Real GDP that is produced at the natural unemployment rate. It is the Real GDP that is produced when the economy is in long-run equilibrium.

Economists often refer to the three states of an economy that are possible when we consider the relationship between Real GDP and Natural Real GDP. The possibilities are an economy operating at a level of Real GDP (1) less than Natural Real GDP, (2) greater than Natural Real GDP, or (3) equal to Natural Real GDP.

Three possible states of an economy are:

- Real GDP is less than Natural Real GDP.
- Real GDP is greater than Natural Real GDP.
- Real GDP is equal to Natural Real GDP.

Let's now give a name to each of these three possible states of the economy and graphically portray each.

Real GDP Is Less Than Natural Real GDP (Recessionary Gap)

Exhibit 3a shows an *AD* curve, an *SRAS* curve, and the *LRAS* curve. It also shows that Natural Real GDP (Q_N) is produced in the long run.

Short-run equilibrium is at the intersection of the *AD* and *SRAS* curves, so in part (a) short-run equilibrium is at point 1. The Real GDP level that the economy is producing at point 1 is designated by Q_1.

Now compare Q_1 with Q_N. Obviously, Q_1 is less than Q_N. In other words, the economy is currently producing a level of Real GDP in the short run that is less than its Natural Real GDP level.

(a)

(b)

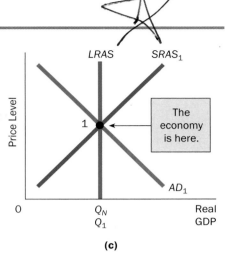

(c)

When the Real GDP the economy is producing is less than its Natural Real GDP, the economy is said to be in a **recessionary gap.**

Real GDP Is Greater Than Natural Real GDP (Inflationary Gap)

In Exhibit 3b, the *AD* and *SRAS* curves intersect at point 1, so short-run equilibrium is at point 1. The Real GDP level the economy is producing at point 1 is designated by Q_1.

Compare Q_1 with Q_N. Obviously, Q_1 is greater than Q_N. In other words, the economy is currently producing a level of Real GDP in the short run that is greater than its Natural Real GDP level or potential output.

When the Real GDP the economy is producing is greater than its Natural Real GDP, the economy is said to be in an **inflationary gap.**

Real GDP Is Equal to Natural Real GDP (Long-Run Equilibrium)

In Exhibit 3c, the *AD* and *SRAS* curves indicate that short-run equilibrium is at point 1. The Real GDP level the economy is producing at point 1 is designated by Q_1.

Again compare Q_1 and Q_N. This time Q_1 is equal to Q_N. In other words, the economy is currently producing a level of Real GDP that is equal to its Natural Real GDP or potential output.

When the Real GDP the economy is producing is equal to its Natural Real GDP, the economy is in *long-run equilibrium.*

THE LABOR MARKET AND THE THREE STATES OF THE ECONOMY

If the economy can be in three possible states, so can the labor market. We identify the three possible states of the labor market, and then tie each state to a possible state of the economy.

We know that the labor market consists of the demand for labor and the supply of labor. Like a goods market, the labor market can manifest (1) equilibrium, (2) a shortage, or (3) a surplus.

Three possible states of the labor market are:

- Equilibrium
- Shortage
- Surplus

exhibit 3

Real GDP and Natural Real GDP: Three Possibilities

In (a), the economy is currently in short-run equilibrium at a Real GDP level of Q_1. Q_N is Natural Real GDP or the potential output of the economy. Notice that $Q_1 < Q_N$. When this condition ($Q_1 < Q_N$) exists, the economy is said to be in a recessionary gap.

In (b), the economy is currently in short-run equilibrium at a Real GDP level of Q_1. Q_N is Natural Real GDP or the potential output of the economy. Notice that $Q_1 > Q_N$. When this condition ($Q_1 > Q_N$) exists, the economy is said to be in an inflationary gap.

In (c), the economy is currently operating at a Real GDP level of Q_1, which is equal to Q_N. In other words, the economy is producing its Natural Real GDP or potential output. When this condition ($Q_1 = Q_N$) exists, the economy is said to be in long-run equilibrium.

Recessionary Gap
The condition where the Real GDP the economy is producing is less than the Natural Real GDP and the unemployment rate is greater than the natural unemployment rate.

Inflationary Gap
The condition where the Real GDP the economy is producing is greater than the Natural Real GDP and the unemployment rate is less than the natural unemployment rate.

When equilibrium exists in the labor market, there are the same number of jobs available as the number of people who want to work. That is, the quantity demanded of labor is equal to the quantity supplied of labor.

When there is a shortage in the labor market, there are more jobs available than there are people who want to work. That is, the quantity demanded of labor is greater than the quantity supplied of labor.

When there is a surplus in the labor market, there are more people who want to work than there are jobs available; the quantity supplied of labor is greater than the quantity demanded of labor.

Recessionary Gap and the Labor Market

If the economy is in a recessionary gap, is the labor market in equilibrium, shortage, or surplus? To simplify, suppose the economy is in a recessionary gap producing a Real GDP level of $8,200 billion (worth of goods and services) when Natural Real GDP, or potential output, is $9,000 billion.

The unemployment rate that exists when the economy produces Natural Real GDP is, of course, the natural unemployment rate. Is the unemployment rate that exists when the economy is in a recessionary gap producing $8,200 billion worth of goods and services greater or less than the natural unemployment rate that exists when the economy is producing $9,000 billion worth of goods and services? The answer is that the unemployment rate is greater than the natural unemployment rate because fewer workers are needed to produce a Real GDP of $8,200 billion than are needed to produce a Real GDP of $9,000 billion. *Ceteris paribus,* the unemployment rate will be higher at a Real GDP level of $8,200 billion than it is at a level of $9,000 billion.

We conclude that when the economy is in a recessionary gap, the unemployment rate is *higher* than the natural unemployment rate. This implies there is a surplus in the labor market: quantity supplied of labor is greater than quantity demanded, or there are more people who want to work than there are jobs available.

If the economy is in a recessionary gap, the unemployment rate is higher than the natural unemployment rate and a surplus exists in the labor market.

Inflationary Gap and the Labor Market

Now suppose the economy is in an inflationary gap producing a Real GDP level of $9,500 billion (worth of goods and services) when Natural Real GDP, or potential output, is $9,000 billion.

Again, the unemployment rate that exists when the economy produces Natural Real GDP is the natural unemployment rate. Is the unemployment rate that exists when the economy is producing $9,500 billion worth of goods and services greater or less than the natural unemployment rate that exists when the economy is producing $9,000 billion worth of goods and services? The answer is that the unemployment rate is less than the natural unemployment rate because more workers are needed to produce a Real GDP of $9,500 billion than are needed to produce a Real GDP of $9,000 billion. *Ceteris paribus,* the unemployment rate will be lower at a Real GDP level of $9,500 billion than it is at a level of $9,000 billion.

We conclude that when the economy is in an inflationary gap, the unemployment rate is *lower* than the natural unemployment rate. This implies that there is a shortage in the labor market: quantity demanded of labor is greater than quantity supplied, or there are more jobs available than there are people who want to work.

If the economy is in an inflationary gap, the unemployment rate is less than the natural unemployment rate and a shortage exists in the labor market.

ECONOMICS IN...

March 1991–March 2001

On November 26, 2001, the *Associated Press* flashed a major headline: "Panel: U.S. Recession Began in March."

The "Panel" referenced in the headline was actually a committee—the National Bureau of Economic Research (NBER) Business Cycle Dating Committee. This committee determines the beginning of recessions. Essentially, it looks at various economic data and then determines whether or not the U.S. economy has slipped into a recession. The committee of six members—all economists—determined that the U.S. economy slipped into a recession in March 2001. This meant the economic expansion that started in March 1991 was now officially over. The expansion lasted 10 years or 120 months, the longest economic expansion in U.S. history.

One thing is particularly interesting about the NBER committee's dating of the recession as March 2001: It chose a quarter in which Real GDP was expanding, albeit by a tiny percentage. The usual definition of a recession is two consecutive quarters of decline in Real GDP. When the committee was asked why its definition of recession didn't go along with the widely accepted definition, it said:

> Most of the recessions identified by our procedures do consist of two or more quarters of declining Real GDP, but not all of them. But our procedure differs in a number of ways. First, we use monthly indicators to arrive at a monthly chronology. Second, we use indicators subject to much less frequent revision. Third, we consider the depth of the decline in economic activity. Recall that our definition includes the phrase, "a significant decline in activity."[1]

The phrase "a significant decline in activity" is part of NBER's definition of a recession. NBER states that "a recession is a significant decline in activity spread across the economy, lasting more than a few months, visible in industrial production, employment, real income, and wholesale-retail trade." Thus, the NBER considers four variables—industrial production, employment, real income, and wholesale-retail trade—in determining the beginning of a recession.

According to the NBER, employment peaked in March 2001 and then declined; industrial production peaked in September 2000 and then declined over the next 12 months; manufacturing and trade sales peaked around November 2000. In other words, three out of the four variables had peaked; only real income was yet to peak. About real income, the NBER committee said:

> The committee also determined that the continued growth of real personal income after March 2001 was consistent with the finding of that date as the peak in economic activity. Real income is not precisely a measure of activity—rather, it measures the command of households over resources. During the relevant period, continuing fast growth in productivity and sharp declines in the prices of imports, especially oil, raised purchasing power while employment was falling.[2]

Long-Run Equilibrium and the Labor Market

Finally, suppose the economy is in long-run equilibrium. In other words, it is producing a Real GDP level equal to Natural Real GDP. It follows that in this state, the unemployment rate (that exists in the economy) is the same as the natural unemployment rate. This implies that there is neither a shortage nor a surplus in the labor market; instead, equilibrium exists in the labor market.

If the economy is in long-run equilibrium, the unemployment rate equals the natural unemployment rate and equilibrium exists in the labor market.

The following table summarizes three possible states of the economy and the related states of the labor market.

---

1. See the NBER Web site at *http://cycles-www.nber.org/cycles/november2001/recessnov.html.*
2. Ibid.

State of the Economy	What Do We Call It?	Relationship between Unemployment Rate and Natural Unemployment Rate	State of the Labor Market
Real GDP < Natural Real GDP	Recessionary gap	Unemployment rate > Natural unemployment rate	Surplus exists
Real GDP > Natural Real GDP	Inflationary gap	Unemployment rate < Natural unemployment rate	Shortage exists
Real GDP = Natural Real GDP	Long-run equilibrium	Unemployment rate = Natural unemployment rate	Equilibrium exists

ONE NAGGING QUESTION: HOW CAN THE UNEMPLOYMENT RATE BE LESS THAN THE NATURAL UNEMPLOYMENT RATE?

Recall that when the economy is in an inflationary gap, the unemployment rate is less than the natural unemployment rate. For example, if the natural unemployment rate is 5 percent, the unemployment rate may be 4 percent.

You may have wondered how the economy can do better than the natural unemployment rate, which, after all, is equated with full employment or potential output. To explain, we need to use two production possibilities frontiers.

In Exhibit 4, the two production possibilities frontiers are the physical PPF (purple curve) and the institutional PPF (blue curve). The physical PPF illustrates different combinations of goods the economy can produce given the physical constraints of (1) finite resources and (2) the current state of technology.

The institutional PPF illustrates different combinations of goods the economy can produce given the physical constraints of (1) finite resources, (2) the current state of technology, and (3) any institutional constraints. Broadly defined, an institutional constraint is anything that prevents economic agents from producing the maximum Real GDP physically possible.

exhibit 4

The Physical and Institutional PPFs
A society has both a physical PPF and an institutional PPF. The physical PPF illustrates different combinations of goods the economy can produce given the physical constraints of (1) finite resources and (2) the current state of technology. The institutional PPF illustrates different combinations of goods the economy can produce given the physical constraints of (1) finite resources, (2) the current state of technology, and (3) any institutional constraints. The economy is at the natural unemployment rate if it is located on its institutional PPF, such as at points A, B, or C. An economy can never operate beyond its physical PPF, but it is possible for it to operate beyond its institutional PPF because institutional constraints are not always equally effective. If the economy does operate beyond its institutional PPF, such as at point D, then the unemployment rate in the economy is lower than the natural unemployment rate.

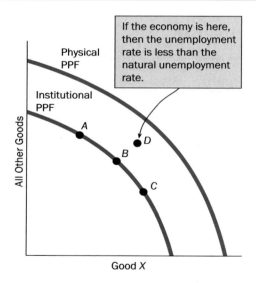

For example, the minimum wage law, which is an institutional constraint, specifies that workers must be paid a wage rate at least equal to the legislated minimum wage. One effect of this law is that unskilled persons whose value to employers falls below the legislated minimum wage will not be hired. Fewer workers means less output produced, *ceteris paribus*. (This is why the institutional PPF lies closer to the origin than the physical PPF.)

Within the confines of society's physical and institutional constraints, there is a natural unemployment rate. This state of affairs is represented by any point on the institutional PPF. In the exhibit, points *A, B,* and *C* are all such points.

An economy can never operate beyond its physical PPF, but it is possible for it to operate beyond its institutional PPF. For example, suppose inflation reduces the purchasing power of the minimum wage, thus reducing or eliminating the constraining properties of the minimum wage law on the unskilled labor market.[3] This would make one of society's institutional constraints ineffective, allowing the economy to temporarily move beyond the institutional constraint.

Logic dictates that if the economy is operating at the natural unemployment rate when it is located on its institutional PPF, then it must be operating at an unemployment rate lower than the natural rate when it is located beyond its institutional PPF (but below its physical PPF). Because society's institutional constraints are not always equally effective, it is possible for an economy to be operating at an unemployment rate below the natural rate.

Self-Test

1. What is a recessionary gap? an inflationary gap?

2. What is the state of the labor market when the economy is in a recessionary gap? in an inflationary gap?

3. If the economy is in an inflationary gap, locate its position in terms of the two PPFs discussed in this section.

THE SELF-REGULATING ECONOMY

Some economists believe that the economy is self-regulating. This means that if the economy is not at the natural unemployment rate (or full employment)—that is, it is not producing Natural Real GDP—then it can move itself to this position. The notion of a self-regulating economy is a very classical notion, but is also a view held by some modern-day economists. This section describes how a self-regulating economy works.

WHAT HAPPENS IF THE ECONOMY IS IN A RECESSIONARY GAP?

If the economy is in a recessionary gap, (1) it is producing a Real GDP level that is less than Natural Real GDP, (2) the unemployment rate is greater than the natural unemployment rate, and (3) a surplus exists in the labor market. Exhibit 5a illustrates this case for a Real GDP of $8,200 billion and a Natural Real GDP of $9,000 billion. What, if anything, happens in the economy?

According to economists who believe the economy is self-regulating, the surplus in the labor market begins to exert downward pressure on wages.[4] In other words, as old wage contracts expire, business firms will negotiate contracts that pay workers lower wage rates.

---

3. Inflation reduces the real (inflation-adjusted) minimum wage. If the minimum wage rate is $6 and the price level is 1.00, the real minimum wage is $6 ($6 divided by the price level, 1.00). If the price level rises to 2.00, then the real minimum wage rate falls to $3. The lower the real minimum wage, the greater the number of unskilled workers that employers will hire because the demand curve for unskilled workers is downward-sloping.

4. In this discussion of how the self-regulating economy eliminates a recessionary gap, we have emphasized wages (in the labor market) adjusting downward. Other resource prices besides wages may fall as well.

exhibit 5

The Self-Regulating Economy: Removing a Recessionary Gap
(a) The economy is at P_1 and Real GDP of $8,200 billion. Because Real GDP is less than Natural Real GDP ($9,000 billion), the economy is in a recessionary gap and the unemployment rate is higher than the natural unemployment rate. (b) Wage rates fall, and the short-run aggregate supply curve shifts from $SRAS_1$ to $SRAS_2$. As the price level falls, the real balance, interest rate, and international trade effects increase the quantity demanded of Real GDP. Ultimately, the economy moves into long-run equilibrium at point 2.

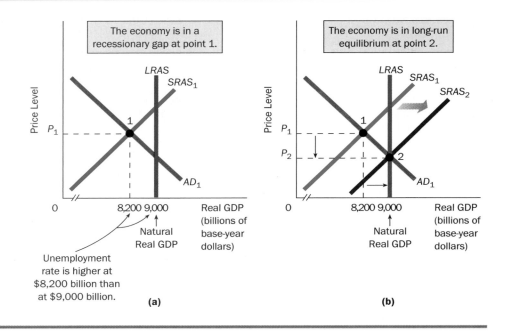

(a)

(b)

Recall from the last chapter that as wage rates fall, the *SRAS* curve begins to shift to the right, ultimately moving from $SRAS_1$ to $SRAS_2$ in Exhibit 5b. As a result of the increase in short-run aggregate supply, the price level falls. But as the price level falls, the quantity demanded of Real GDP rises due to the real balance, interest rate, and international trade effects (all of which are discussed in the last chapter). As the price level falls, the economy moves from one point on the *AD* curve to a point farther down the same curve. In Exhibit 5b, this is a move from point 1 to point 2.

As long as the economy's Real GDP is less than its Natural Real GDP, the price level will continue to fall. Ultimately, the economy moves to long-run equilibrium at point 2, corresponding to P_2, and a Natural Real GDP of $9,000 billion.

> Recessionary gap →
> Unemployment rate > Natural unemployment rate →
> Surplus in labor market → Wages fall → *SRAS* curve shifts to the right →
> Economy moves into long-run equilibrium

WHAT HAPPENS IF THE ECONOMY IS IN AN INFLATIONARY GAP?

If the economy is in an inflationary gap, (1) it is producing a Real GDP level that is greater than Natural Real GDP, (2) the unemployment rate is less than the natural unemployment rate, and (3) a shortage exists in the labor market. Exhibit 6a illustrates this case for a Real GDP of $9,500 billion and a Natural Real GDP of $9,000 billion.

Again, according to economists who believe the economy is self-regulating, the shortage in the labor market begins to exert upward pressure on wages. In other words, as old wage contracts expire, business firms will negotiate contracts that pay workers higher wage rates.

As wage rates rise, the *SRAS* curve begins to shift to the left, ultimately moving from $SRAS_1$ to $SRAS_2$ in Exhibit 6b. As a result of the decrease in short-run aggregate supply, the price level rises. But as the price level rises, the quantity demanded of Real GDP falls due to the real balance, interest rate, and international trade effects. As the price level rises, the economy moves from one point on the *AD* curve to a point farther up the same curve. In Exhibit 6b, this is a move from point 1 to point 2.

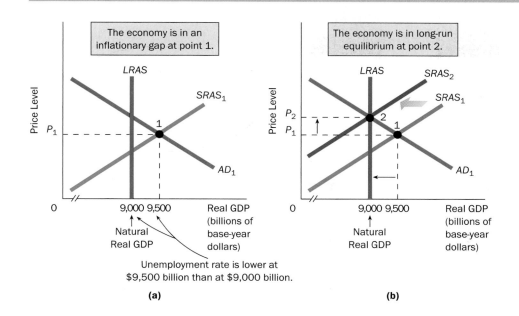

The economy is in an inflationary gap at point 1.

LRAS

Price Level

P_1

SRAS$_1$

1

AD$_1$

0   9,000 9,500   Real GDP (billions of base-year dollars)

↑   Natural Real GDP

Unemployment rate is lower at $9,500 billion than at $9,000 billion.

(a)

The economy is in long-run equilibrium at point 2.

LRAS   SRAS$_2$

Price Level

P_2 SRAS$_1$

P_1 2   1

AD$_1$

0   9,000 9,500   Real GDP (billions of base-year dollars)

↑   Natural Real GDP

(b)

exhibit 6

The Self-Regulating Economy: Removing an Inflationary Gap
(a) The economy is at P_1 and Real GDP of $9,500 billion. Because Real GDP is greater than Natural Real GDP ($9,000 billion), the economy is in an inflationary gap and the unemployment rate is lower than the natural unemployment rate. (b) Wage rates rise, and the short-run aggregate supply curve shifts from SRAS$_1$ to SRAS$_2$. As the price level rises, the real balance, interest rate, and international trade effects decrease the quantity demanded of Real GDP. Ultimately, the economy moves into long-run equilibrium at point 2.

As long as the economy's Real GDP is greater than its Natural Real GDP, the price level will continue to rise. Ultimately, the economy moves to long-run equilibrium at point 2, corresponding to P_2, and a Natural Real GDP of $9,000 billion.

Inflationary gap →
Unemployment rate < Natural unemployment rate →
Shortage in labor market → Wages rise → SRAS curve shifts to the left →
Economy moves into long-run equilibrium

THE SELF-REGULATING ECONOMY: A RECAP

We have shown that if the economy is in a recessionary gap, wage rates fall (along with other resource prices) and the SRAS curve shifts to the right. As this happens, the price level falls and the economy moves down the AD curve. The economy moves in the direction of long-run equilibrium, ultimately achieving the Natural Real GDP level.

If the economy is in an inflationary gap, wage rates rise (along with other resource prices) and the SRAS curve shifts to the left. As this happens, the price level rises and the economy moves up the AD curve. The economy moves in the direction of long-run equilibrium, ultimately achieving the Natural Real GDP level.

Flexible wage rates (and other resource prices) play a critical role in the self-regulating economy. For example, suppose wage rates are not flexible and do not fall in a recessionary gap. Then, the SRAS curve will not shift to the right. But if the SRAS curve does not shift to the right, the price level will not fall. And if the price level does not fall, the economy won't move down the AD curve toward long-run equilibrium. Similarly, if wage rates are not flexible and do not rise in an inflationary gap, then the economy won't move up the AD curve toward long-run equilibrium.

The economists who believe in a self-regulating economy—classical economists, monetarists, and new classical economists—believe that wage rates and other resource prices are *flexible* and move up and down in response to market conditions. Thus, these economists believe that *wage rates will fall* when there is a *surplus of labor.* They believe that *wage rates will rise* when there is a *shortage of labor.* You will see in the next chapter that the flexible wages and prices position taken by these economists has not gone unchallenged.

The following table summarizes how a self-regulating economy works for three possible states of the economy.

State of the Economy	What Happens If the Economy Is Self-Regulating?
Recessionary gap (Real GDP < Natural Real GDP)	Wages fall and *SRAS* curve shifts to the right until Real GDP = Natural Real GDP.
Inflationary gap (Real GDP > Natural Real GDP)	Wages rise and *SRAS* curve shifts to the left until Real GDP = Natural Real GDP.
Long-run equilibrium (Real GDP = Natural Real GDP)	No change in wages and no change in SRAS.

THINKING LIKE AN ECONOMIST   *Like other scientists, economists are often interested in knowing whether the phenomena they are studying have a natural resting place. For example, the natural resting place for a ball thrown high into the air is the ground. Gravity pulls the ball downward. Where is the natural resting place for a competitive market? It is where the quantity demanded of a good equals the quantity supplied of the good. Markets are "at rest" when they are in equilibrium.*

Macroeconomists want to know if the economy has a natural resting place. Some economists think it does. They think the natural resting place for the economy is where Natural Real GDP is being produced and the natural unemployment rate exists. Economists who believe that the economy can eliminate both recessionary and inflationary gaps smoothly and quickly by itself, and thus return to its natural state, use the analogy of a person's normal body temperature, which is 98.6 degrees.

When a person's body temperature rises above normal, he has a fever. In most cases, the body itself eliminates the fever in time; that is, the temperature returns to normal. When the person's body temperature is below normal, in most cases this is an aberration and his temperature will edge back up to normal in time. In short, a below-normal temperature and an above-normal temperature are temporary states. Just as the body has a natural resting place—at 98.6 degrees—so does the economy, some economists say. Thinking in terms of a "natural resting place," an "equilibrium," or a "benchmark" is part of some economists' way of thinking. However, not all economists agree on where the natural resting place of the economy is.

POLICY IMPLICATION OF BELIEVING THE ECONOMY IS SELF-REGULATING

Classical, new classical, and monetarist economists believe that the economy is self-regulating. For these economists, full employment is the norm: the economy always moves back to Natural Real GDP. Stated differently, if the economy becomes "ill"—in the form of a recessionary or an inflationary gap—it certainly is capable of healing itself through changes in wages and prices. This belief in how the economy works has led these economists to advocate a macroeconomic policy of **laissez-faire,** or noninterference. In the view of these economists, government does not have an economic management role to play.

CHANGES IN A SELF-REGULATING ECONOMY: SHORT RUN AND LONG RUN

Let's consider how a change in aggregate demand affects the economy in the short run and the long run if the economy is self-regulating. In Exhibit 7a, the economy is initially in long-run equilibrium at point 1. Suppose there is an increase in aggregate demand brought about by, say, an increase in government purchases (this possibility is discussed in the last chapter). The *AD* curve shifts

http://

Go to *http://www.cato.org*, and select "About Us." Read "Cato's Mission," and browse the Web page. How would you label Cato? How does Cato's mission statement relate to classical economics? What is the Friedman Prize?

Laissez-faire
A public policy of not interfering with market activities in the economy.

(a)

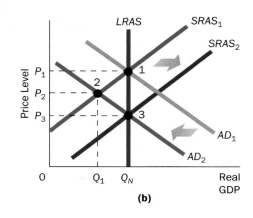

(b)

right from AD_1 to AD_2 and in the short run, the economy moves to point 2 with both Real GDP and the price level higher than each was at point 1.

Now at point 2, the economy is in an inflationary gap. If the economy is self-regulating, wages will soon rise and the *SRAS* curve will shift to the left—ultimately from $SRAS_1$ to $SRAS_2$. The economy will end up at point 3 in long-run equilibrium.

Now let's examine the changes in the short run and in the long run. As a result of an increase in aggregate demand, Real GDP rises and the price level rises in the short run. In addition, because Real GDP rises, the unemployment rate falls. In the long run, when the economy is at point 3, it is producing exactly the same level of Real GDP that it was producing originally (Q_N) but at a higher price level.

Conclusion: If the economy is self-regulating, an increase in aggregate demand can raise the price level and Real GDP in the short run but in the long run, the only effect of an increase in aggregate demand is a rise in the price level. In other words, in the long run all that we have to show for an increase in aggregate demand is higher prices.

Now let's consider what happens if aggregate demand falls. In Exhibit 7b, the economy is initially in long-run equilibrium at point 1. Suppose there is a decrease in aggregate demand. The *AD* curve shifts left from AD_1 to AD_2 and in the short run, the economy moves to point 2 with both Real GDP and the price level lower than each was at point 1.

Now at point 2, the economy is in a recessionary gap. If the economy is self-regulating, wages will soon fall and the *SRAS* curve will shift to the right—ultimately from $SRAS_1$ to $SRAS_2$. The economy will end up at point 3 in long-run equilibrium.

Now let's examine the changes in the short run and in the long run. As a result of a decrease in aggregate demand, Real GDP falls and the price level falls in the short run. In addition, because Real GDP falls, the unemployment rate rises. In the long run, when the economy is at point 3, it is producing exactly the same level of Real GDP that it was producing originally (Q_N) but at a lower price level.

Conclusion: If the economy is self-regulating, a decrease in aggregate demand can lower the price level and Real GDP in the short run but in the long run, the only effect of a decrease in aggregate demand is a lower price level.

Changes in a Self-Regulating Economy: Short Run and Long Run

In (a) the economy is initially at point 1 in long-run equilibrium. Aggregate demand rises and the *AD* curve shifts from AD_1 to AD_2. The economy is at point 2 in the short run, with a higher Real GDP and price level than at point 1. The economy is also in an inflationary gap at point 2. If the economy is self-regulating, wages will soon rise, the *SRAS* curve will shift left from $SRAS_1$ to $SRAS_2$, and the economy will be in long-run equilibrium at point 3. At point 3, the economy is producing the same Real GDP as it did at point 1. In other words, in the long run, an increase in aggregate demand only raises the price level. In (b) the economy is initially at point 1 in long-run equilibrium. Aggregate demand falls and the *AD* curve shifts from AD_1 to AD_2. The economy is at point 2 in the short run, with a lower Real GDP and price level than at point 1. The economy is also in a recessionary gap. If the economy is self-regulating, wages will soon fall, the *SRAS* curve will shift right from $SRAS_1$ to $SRAS_2$, and the economy will be in long-run equilibrium at point 3. At point 3, the economy is producing the same Real GDP as it did at point 1. In other words, in the long run, a decrease in aggregate demand only lowers the price level.

Change in *AD*	In the Short Run,	In the Long Run,
$AD\uparrow$	$P\uparrow, Q\uparrow$	$P\uparrow$, Q does not change
$AD\downarrow$	$P\downarrow, Q\downarrow$	$P\downarrow$, Q does not change

Technology   Popular Culture   Everyday Life   The World

The Natural Unemployment Rate, Technology, and Policy Errors

Recall that the natural unemployment rate is equal to the frictional unemployment rate plus the structural unemployment rate. Thus, anything that lowers either the frictional or the structural unemployment rate will also lower the natural unemployment rate. Let's consider how the frictional unemployment rate might be lowered.

Frictional unemployment occurs when changing market conditions cause qualified individuals with transferable skills to change jobs. A person's frictional unemployment lasts only as long as it takes him or her to find another job. The length of time it takes to find another job is a function of many things—one of which is the amount of information the individual has about jobs that she can perform.

Have advances in technology influenced the amount of information available to job seekers? For example, suppose telephones and newspapers did not exist. In this situation, the frictionally unemployed person would be likely to stay unemployed longer than if she could use telephones and newspapers to obtain information.

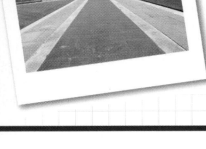

In recent years, technology has provided another way for a frictionally unemployed person to obtain information and find a job. She can post her résumé on the Internet and can use the Internet to easily look for jobs all across the country. By using the Internet, a frictionally unemployed person is likely to stay unemployed for a shorter time. As a result, the frictional unemployment rate will fall, as will the natural unemployment rate.

Now suppose technology lowers the natural unemployment rate in the way we have described, but this is as yet unknown to policymakers. Will errors in policy be made?

To illustrate, there is some evidence that the monetary authority in the United States—the Federal Reserve, or simply the Fed—sometimes uses the natural unemployment rate when making monetary policy. Specifically, it sometimes compares the actual unemployment rate to the natural unemployment rate in order to get an idea of the direction it should take in monetary policy.

Suppose the natural unemployment rate has fallen to 4.5 percent because of improvements in technology, but this is not yet known by the Fed. The Fed thinks the natural unemployment rate is 5 percent. Now assume the actual unemployment rate falls from 5.0 to 4.8 percent. The Fed believes the economy has gone below its natural unemployment rate (it is in an inflationary gap) and if it does nothing, the price level will soon rise. In order to offset the potential rise in prices down the road, the Fed decides to try to reduce aggregate demand by lowering the growth rate of the money supply.

Let's summarize the situation: The economy is still operating at an unemployment rate (4.8 percent) above the true natural unemployment rate (4.5 percent), but the Fed thinks it is operating at an unemployment rate (4.8 percent) below the natural unemployment rate (5.0 percent). Stated differently, while the economy is still in a recessionary gap, the Fed thinks it is in an inflationary gap.

By cutting back the rate of growth in the money supply, the Fed will lower aggregate demand and keep the unemployment rate above the natural unemployment rate. Thus, the economy will stay in a recessionary gap for longer than would have been the case if the Fed had not made the mistake that it did.

Q & A

Q: In Exhibit 7a, the economy starts at point 1 and then moves to point 2. At point 2, both the price level and Real GDP are higher than they were at point 1. In other words, if *AD* rises, both the price level and Real GDP rise in the short run.

Now if the economy is self-regulating, it will not remain at point 2. Instead it will move to point 3, where it is in long-run equilibrium. At point 3, the price level is higher than it was at point 2 but Real GDP is lower. Why, then, don't we say that Real GDP is lower in the long run than it is in the short run instead of saying that Real GDP does not change in the long run?

A: The long run is measured from one long-run equilibrium point to another long-run equilibrium point. In terms of Exhibit 7a, we are comparing point 1 and point 3. When we make this comparison, we notice two things: The price level is higher at point 3 than at point 1, and Real GDP is the same at both points.

Your question is not really about the long run, but is rather about the "journey" that the price level and Real GDP take in moving from one long-run equilibrium to another long-run equilibrium. The journey, as you point out, goes from point 1 to point 2 to point 3. You then note what happens to the price level and Real GDP on the journey. However, we do not equate what happens to, say, Real GDP in the long run with the journey Real GDP takes. While the journey proceeds from point 1 to 2 to 3, the long run is viewed as the movement from point 1 (one long-run equilibrium) to point 3 (another long-run equilibrium).

Self-Test

1. If the economy is self-regulating, what happens if it is in a recessionary gap?
2. If the economy is self-regulating, what happens if it is in an inflationary gap?
3. If the economy is self-regulating, how do changes in aggregate demand affect the economy in the long run?

A Reader Asks...
Why Don't All Economists Agree?

The chapter road map states that while some economists believe the economy is self-regulating, others believe it is inherently unstable. Why don't all economists agree on how the economy works?

One reason (but not the only reason) is because economists can't undertake controlled experiments. In a controlled experiment, it is possible to change one variable, leave all other variables unchanged, and then see what happens. Whatever happens must be the result of the one variable you changed.

To illustrate, suppose you want to know whether or not increasing your intake of vitamin C will reduce the number of colds you get in a year. In a controlled experiment, you would increase your intake of vitamin C and everything else in your life would stay the same—the amount of sleep you get each night, the amount of exercise you get, the people you are around, and so on. Then you would observe whether or not you got fewer colds. If you did get fewer colds, then you could be rea-

sonably sure that it was because of your higher intake of vitamin C.

Now let's see what happens in economics because economists cannot run controlled experiments. Suppose Real GDP falls in February 2003. Economist *A* argues that the decline in Real GDP was due to higher interest rates in July 2002 and not to higher taxes in August 2002. Economist *B* argues just the opposite: the decline in Real GDP was due to higher taxes in August 2002 and not to higher interest rates in July 2002.

Obviously, economist *A* has a theory that states that a change in interest rates affects Real GDP but a change in taxes does not. Economist *B* has a theory that states a change in taxes affects Real GDP but a change in interest rates does not. It would be nice to test each theory in a controlled environment: change taxes and nothing else, and see what happens; change interest rates and nothing else, and see what happens. You can see that if we could do this, some of the disagreements between economists *A* and *B* are likely to disappear.

Chapter Summary

Say's Law

- Say's law states that supply creates its own demand. All economists believe that Say's law holds in a barter economy. Here, there can be no general overproduction or underproduction of goods. Classical economists believed that Say's law also holds in a money

economy. In their view, even if consumption drops and saving rises, economic forces are at work producing an equal and offsetting increase in investment. According to classical economists, interest rates are flexible and equate the amount of saving and investment in an economy.

Classical Economists on Markets, Wages, and Prices

- Classical economists believed that most, if not all, markets are competitive and that wages and prices are flexible.

Three States of the Economy

- Natural Real GDP is the level of Real GDP that is produced when the economy is operating at the natural unemployment rate.
- The economy can be producing a Real GDP level that (1) is equal to Natural Real GDP, (2) is greater than Natural Real GDP, or (3) is less than Natural Real GDP. In other words, the economy can be in (1) long-run equilibrium, (2) an inflationary gap, or (3) a recessionary gap, respectively.
- In long-run equilibrium, the Real GDP that the economy is producing is equal to the Natural Real GDP. The unemployment rate that exists in the economy is equal to the natural unemployment rate, and the labor market is in equilibrium.
- In a recessionary gap, the Real GDP that the economy is producing is less than the Natural Real GDP. The unemployment rate that exists in the economy is greater than the natural unemployment rate, and a surplus exists in the labor market.
- In an inflationary gap, the Real GDP that the economy is producing is greater than the Natural Real GDP. The unemployment rate that exists in the economy is less than the natural unemployment rate, and a shortage exists in the labor market.

The Institutional and Physical Production Possibilities Frontiers

- The physical PPF illustrates different combinations of goods the economy can produce given the physical constraints of (1) finite resources and (2) the current state of technology. The institutional PPF illustrates different combinations of goods the economy can produce given the physical constraints of (1) finite resources, (2) the current state of technology, and (3) any institutional constraints.
- If an economy is operating on its institutional PPF, it is operating at the natural unemployment rate. If it is operating at a point beyond the institutional PPF but below the physical PPF, it is operating at an unemployment rate less than the natural unemployment rate.

The View That the Economy Is Self-Regulating

- Some economists (classical, new classical, monetarists) contend that the economy can eliminate both recessionary and inflationary gaps smoothly and quickly by itself.
- If the economy is self-regulating and in a recessionary gap, then: The unemployment rate in the economy is greater than the natural unemployment rate, and a surplus exists in the labor market. As old wage contracts expire, wage rates fall. As a result, the SRAS curve shifts to the right and the price level falls. As the price level falls, the quantity demanded of Real GDP rises. Ultimately, the economy will move into long-run equilibrium where it is producing Natural Real GDP.
- If the economy is self-regulating and in an inflationary gap, then: The unemployment rate in the economy is less than the natural unemployment rate, and a shortage exists in the labor market. As old wage contracts expire, wage rates rise. As a result, the SRAS curve shifts to the left and the price level rises. As the price level rises, the quantity demanded of Real GDP falls. Ultimately, the economy will move into long-run equilibrium where it is producing Natural Real GDP.

Key Terms and Concepts

Say's Law   Inflationary Gap   Laissez-faire
Recessionary Gap

Economic Connections to You

Economic facts, actions, and changes create ripples that move away from their point of origin. Eventually, these ripples can intersect your life and have an effect on you. Consider the following example.

If the economy is self-regulating and in an inflationary gap, wage rates will begin to rise. As a result of higher wage rates, the SRAS curve will shift to the left. Then, the price level will rise, Real GDP will drop, and the unemployment rate will increase. Some people will lose their jobs and have to live on their savings. If you are one of those people, you may have to move back in with your parents in order to reduce your living expenses. Thus, there is a connection between a self-regulating economy in an inflation- *ary gap and your employment and lifestyle—an economic connection to you.*

Based on the material in this chapter, identify other ways in which economic facts, actions, and changes create ripples that eventually affect you.

Questions and Problems

1. What is the classical economics position with respect to (a) wages, (b) prices, and (c) interest rates?
2. According to classical economists, does Say's law hold in a money economy? Explain your answer.
3. According to classical economists, does an increase in saving shift the *AD* curve to the left? Explain your answer.
4. What does it mean to say the economy is in a recessionary gap? in an inflationary gap? in long-run equilibrium?
5. Describe the relationship of the (actual) unemployment rate to the natural unemployment rate in each of the following economic states: (a) a recessionary gap, (b) an inflationary gap, and (c) long-run equilibrium.
6. Diagrammatically represent an economy in (a) an inflationary gap, (b) a recessionary gap, and (c) long-run equilibrium.
7. Explain how the economy can operate beyond its institutional PPF but not beyond its physical PPF.
8. According to economists who believe in a self-regulating economy, what happens—step by step—when the economy is in a recessionary gap? What happens when the economy is in an inflationary gap?

9. If wage rates are not flexible, can the economy be self-regulating? Explain your answer.
10. Explain the importance of the real balance, interest rate, and international trade effects to long-run (equilibrium) adjustment in the economy.
11. Suppose the economy is self-regulating, the price level is 132, the quantity demanded of Real GDP is $4,000 billion, the quantity supplied of Real GDP in the short run is $3,900, and the quantity supplied of Real GDP in the long run is $4,300 billion. Is the economy in short-run equilibrium? Will the price level in long-run equilibrium be greater than, less than, or equal to 132? Explain your answers.
12. Suppose the economy is self-regulating, the price level is 110, the quantity demanded of Real GDP is $4,000 billion, the quantity supplied of Real GDP in the short run is $4,900, and the quantity supplied of Real GDP in the long run is $4,100 billion. Is the economy in short-run equilibrium? Will the price level in long-run equilibrium be greater than, less than, or equal to 110? Explain your answers.

Working with Numbers and Graphs

1. In the following figure, which point is representative of:
   a. The economy on its *LRAS* curve
   b. The economy in a recessionary gap
   c. The economy in an inflationary gap

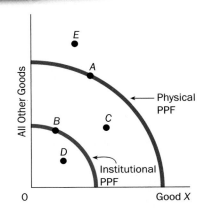

2. In the following figure, which of parts (a)–(c) is consistent with or representative of:
   a. The economy operating at the natural unemployment rate
   b. A surplus in the labor market
   c. A recessionary gap
   d. A cyclical unemployment rate of zero

(a)

(b)

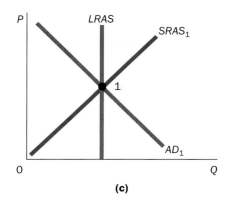

(c)

3. Diagrammatically represent the following:
   a. An economy in which *AD* increases as it is self-regulating out of a recessionary gap
   b. An economy in which *AD* decreases as it is self-regulating out of an inflationary gap
4. Economist Jones believes that there is always sufficient (aggregate) demand in the economy to buy all the goods and services supplied at full employment. Diagrammatically represent what the economy looks like for Jones.
5. Diagrammatically show what happens when the institutional constraints in the economy become less effective.

Internet Activities

1. Go to *http://w3.access.gpo.gov/eop/*. Enter "B-2" in the Search box and click "Submit." Find Table B-2 and click the "TXT" icon underneath it. The table is in two parts. The upper part shows GDP, consumption (*C*), and investment (*I*); the lower part shows net exports and government purchases (*G*). Write down GDP, *I, G,* and net exports for the years 1990, 1991, and 1992.
   a. Real GDP was lower in 1991 than in 1990, indicating that 1991 was a recession year. Was (nominal) GDP lower in 1991 than in 1990?
   b. Do you think the behavior of investment in 1991 was consistent with a recession? Explain your answer.
   c. Did government purchases in 1991 move in the same direction as Real GDP in 1991 (as compared to 1990) or in the opposite direction? What effect do you think government had on aggregate demand during the period 1990–1991?
   d. What effect do you think net exports had on aggregate demand during the period 1990–1991?
2. Go to *http://stats.bls.gov*. Under "At a Glance Tables," click on "REGIONS, STATES, and AREAS at a GLANCE." Click on the relevant state or metropolitan area to answer the following questions:
   a. What is the unemployment rate in California? in Connecticut? in Hawaii? Are the unemployment rates of these three states similar or dissimilar?
   b. What is the unemployment rate of Los Angeles–Long Beach (California) and of Orange County (California)? Are the unemployment rates similar or dissimilar? Since these two metropolitan areas adjoin each other, how might a significant difference in unemployment rates be explained?

Log on to the Arnold Xtra! Web site now (*http://arnoldxtra.swcollege.com*) for additional learning resources such as practice quizzes, help with graphing, video clips, and current event applications.

ch.9

ECONOMIC INSTABILITY: A CRITIQUE OF THE SELF-REGULATING ECONOMY

Every day, in every town and city in this country, people buy various goods and services: computers, cars, food, furniture. The act of buying is so much a part of our lives that we don't give it a second thought. Not so economists. They realize buying goods and services is an act of consumption and know that consumption spending can have a major impact on the economy. In this chapter, we introduce you to the ideas of a famous economist whose work focused on consumption, among other things. His name is John Maynard Keynes. His theories on a host of economic topics led to a revolution in economics.

Chapter Road Map

This chapter begins by outlining the differences between
the theories of John Maynard Keynes, the famous British economist,
and the theories of classical economists about Say's law, savings and investment, wages, and prices. As you will learn, Keynes's ideas about these subjects were very
different from the ideas of the classical economists.

We then begin to outline the details of the simple Keynesian model. The two critical parts of the model—
total expenditures and total production—are defined and discussed. We continue with an explanation of the equili-
brating process in the simple Keynesian model: How the economy goes from total expenditures either greater than or less
than total production to total expenditures equaling total production.

The underlying theme of this chapter is that the economy may not self-regulate; instead, the economy may, at times,
be inherently unstable. Stated differently, the economy may get stuck in a recessionary gap.

QUESTIONING THE CLASSICAL POSITION

The classical position on the economy consisted of four beliefs: (1) Say's law holds, so insufficient demand in the economy is unlikely. (2) Wages, prices, and interest rates are flexible. (3) The economy is self-regulating. (4) Laissez-faire is the right and sensible economic policy to implement. John Maynard Keynes challenged all four of these classical beliefs.

KEYNES'S CRITICISM OF SAY'S LAW IN A MONEY ECONOMY

Let's review the position expressed by classical economists on Say's law in a money economy. According to classical economists, if consumption spending fell because saving increased, then total spending would not fall because the added saving would simply bring about more investment spending. This would happen through changes in the interest rate. The added saving would put downward pressure on the interest rate, and at a lower interest rate, businesses would borrow and invest more. Through changes in the interest rate, the amount of saving would always equal the amount invested.

Keynes disagreed. He didn't think that added saving would necessarily stimulate an equal amount of added investment spending. Exhibit 1 illustrates Keynes's point of view. As in the last chapter, we let consumption = $3,000, investment = $600, government purchases = $1,200, and net exports = $200. Then saving increases by $100, which lowers consumption to $2,900. According to the classical economists, investment rose by $100 at the same time, going from $600 to $700. Keynes asked: What guarantee is there that an increase in saving will be equally matched by an increase in investment? What if saving rises by $100 (which means consumption goes down by $100), but investment rises by, say, only $40 (instead of $100)? In this situation, the equation $TE = C + I + G + (EX - IM)$ changes from

$$TE = \$3,000 + \$600 + \$1,200 + \$200$$
$$= \$5,000$$

to:

$$TE = \$2,900 + \$640 + \$1,200 + \$200$$
$$= \$4,940$$

Go to *http://www.frbsf.org/publications/ education/greateconomists*. Read the sections on John Maynard Keynes and the Keynesian School. When did Keynes develop his theory? According to the text, when did economists start looking for new theories? When did Keynes die? Do you think he had much chance to discuss and improve his theory after he published it?

exhibit 1

Keynes's View of Say's Law in a Money Economy
According to Keynes, a decrease in consumption and subsequent increase in saving may not be matched by an equal increase in investment. Thus, a decrease in total expenditures may occur.

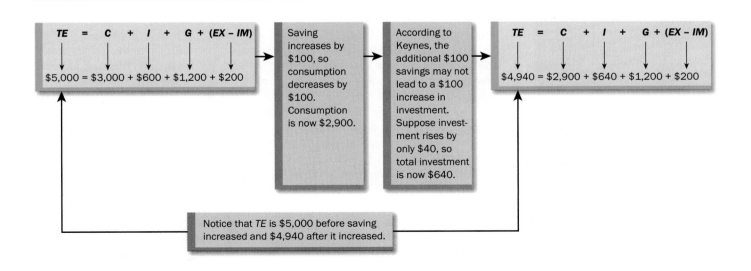

TE = C + I + G + (EX − IM)

$5,000 = $3,000 + $600 + $1,200 + $200

Saving increases by $100, so consumption decreases by $100. Consumption is now $2,900.

According to Keynes, the additional $100 savings may not lead to a $100 increase in investment. Suppose investment rises by only $40, so total investment is now $640.

TE = C + I + G + (EX − IM)

$4,940 = $2,900 + $640 + $1,200 + $200

Notice that *TE* is $5,000 before saving increased and $4,940 after it increased.

Thus, total expenditures decrease from $5,000 to $4,940. And if, at a given price level, total spending falls, so will aggregate demand. In other words, according to Keynes, it was possible for saving to increase and aggregate demand to fall.

Of course, a classical economist would retort that, as a result of a $100 increase in saving, interest rates would fall enough to guarantee that investment would increase by $100. But Keynes countered by saying that individuals save and invest for a host of reasons and that no single factor, such as the interest rate, links these activities.

Furthermore, Keynes believed that saving is more responsive to changes in income than to changes in the interest rate and that investment is more responsive to technological changes, business expectations, and innovations than to changes in the interest rate. In summary, whereas the classical economists believed that saving and investment depend on the interest rate, Keynes believed that both saving and investment depend on a number of factors that may be far more influential than the interest rate.

Consider the difference between Keynes and the classical economists on saving. As noted earlier, the classical economists held that saving is directly related to the interest rate: As the interest rate goes up, saving rises; as the interest rate goes down, saving falls, *ceteris paribus.*

Keynes thought this might not always be true. Suppose individuals are saving for a certain goal—say, a retirement fund of $100,000. They might save less per period at an interest rate of 12 percent than at an interest rate of 5 percent because a higher interest rate means that less saving is required per period to meet the goal within a set time. For example, if the interest rate is 5 percent, $50,000 in savings is needed to earn $2,500 in interest income per year. If the interest rate is 10 percent, only $25,000 in savings is needed to earn $2,500 in interest.

As to investment, Keynes believed that the interest rate is important in determining the level of investment, but he did not think it is as important as other variables, such as the expected rate of profit on investment. Keynes argued that if business expectations are pessimistic, then there is unlikely to be much investment, regardless of how low the interest rate is.

KEYNES ON WAGE RATES

In the last chapter, we state that if the unemployment rate in the economy is greater than the natural unemployment rate, a surplus exists in the labor market: the number of job seekers is high relative to the number of jobs available. Consequently, according to classical economists, wage rates will fall.

Keynes didn't believe the adjustment was so simple. Instead, he said, employees will naturally resist an employer's efforts to cut wages. Similarly, labor unions may resist wage cuts. In short, wage rates may be inflexible in a downward direction.

Suppose Keynes is correct and wage rates won't fall. Does this mean that if the economy is in a recessionary gap, it can't get itself out? The unequivocal answer is yes. If employee and labor union resistance prevent wage rates from falling, then the *SRAS* curve will not shift to the right. If the *SRAS* curve doesn't shift to the right, the price level won't come down. If the price level doesn't come down, buyers will not purchase more goods and services and remove the economy from a recessionary gap. In terms of Exhibit 2, the economy is stuck at point 1. It cannot get to point 2.

In summary, Keynes believed that the economy was inherently unstable—it may not automatically cure itself of a recessionary gap. It may not be self-regulating.

NEW KEYNESIANS AND WAGE RATES

Many economists criticized early versions of the Keynesian theory on the ground that it didn't offer a rigorous and complete explanation for inflexible wages. Some of the later versions—put forth by New Keynesian economists—made up

exhibit 2

The Economy Gets "Stuck" in a Recessionary Gap
If the economy is in a recessionary gap at point 1, Keynes held that wage rates may not fall. The economy may be stuck in the recessionary gap.

Keynesian View
Wages may be inflexible (in a downward direction), so if the economy is at point 1, it may be stuck there.

for this deficiency by focusing on, among other things, long-term contracts and efficiency reasons for firms paying higher-than-market wages.

For example, New Keynesians argue that long-term labor contracts are often advantageous for both employers and workers. Firms may perceive such benefits as (1) fewer labor negotiations (labor negotiations can be costly) and (2) a decreased likelihood of worker strikes (the firms avoid strikes during the time of the contract). Workers may perceive such benefits as (1) fewer strikes (which can be costly for them too) and (2) the sense of security long-term contracts provide.

Long-term contracts have costs as well as benefits for both firms and workers, but some economists believe that in many instances the benefits outweigh the costs and that firms and workers enter into the long-term contracts for mutually advantageous reasons. When they do, wage rates are "locked in" for the period of the contract and therefore cannot adjust downward. As a result, the economy may get stuck at point 1 in Exhibit 2 for a long time and experience high levels of unemployment for many years.

As another example, New Keynesian economists who work with **efficiency wage models** believe there are solid microeconomic reasons for inflexible wages. They argue that firms sometimes find it in their best interest to pay wage rates above market-clearing levels. According to efficiency wage models, labor productivity depends on the wage rate the firm pays its employees. Specifically, a cut in wages can cause labor productivity to decline, which, in turn, raises the firm's costs. (Basically, these models say that you are more productive when you are paid a higher wage than when you are paid a lower wage.) By paying a higher-than-market wage, firms provide an incentive to workers to be productive and do less shirking, among other things. If shirking declines, so do the monitoring (management) costs of the firm.

The economist Robert Solow has argued that "the most interesting and important line of work in current macroeconomic theory is the attempt to reconstruct plausible microeconomic underpinnings for a recognizably Keynesian macroeconomics."[1] Many Keynesian economists believe efficiency wage models can perform this task. They believe these models provide a solid microeconomic explanation for inflexible wages and thus are capable of explaining why continuing unemployment problems exist in some economies.

Efficiency Wage Models
These models hold that it is sometimes in the best interest of business firms to pay their employees higher-than-equilibrium wage rates.

---

1. Robert Solow, "Another Possible Source of Wage Stickiness," in *Efficiency Wage Models of the Labor Market*, ed. George Akerlof and Janet Yellen (Cambridge: Cambridge University Press, 1986), 41.

KEYNES ON PRICES

Again, think back to the process classical economists (among others) believe occurs when a recessionary gap exists. Wage rates fall, the *SRAS* curve shifts to the right, and the price level begins to decrease . . . Now stop right there! Notice that we said ". . . and the price level begins to decrease." This phrase tells us that classical economists believe that prices in the economy are flexible: they move up and down in response to market forces.

Keynes said that the internal structure of an economy is not always competitive enough to allow prices to fall. Recall from Chapter 3 how the forces of supply and demand operate when price is above equilibrium. In this case, a surplus is generated and price falls until the quantity supplied of the good equals the quantity demanded. Keynes suggested that anticompetitive or monopolistic elements in the economy would sometimes prevent price from falling.

Before continuing, use the following chart to quickly review some of the differences in the views of the classical economists and Keynes.

	Classical Economists	Keynes
Say's Law	Holds in a money economy. In other words, all output produced will be demanded.	May not hold in a money economy. In other words, more output may be produced than will be demanded.
Savings	Amount saved and interest rate are directly related. Savers save more at higher interest rates and save less at lower interest rates.	Savers may not save more at higher interest rates or save less at lower interest rates. If savers have a savings goal in mind, then a higher interest rate means savers can save less and still reach their goal.
Investment	Amount invested is inversely related to interest rate. Businesses invest more at lower interest rates and invest less at higher interest rates.	If expectations are pessimistic, a lower interest rate may not stimulate additional investment.
Wages	Flexible	May be inflexible downward
Prices	Flexible	May be inflexible downward

IS IT A QUESTION OF THE TIME IT TAKES FOR WAGES AND PRICES TO ADJUST?

Classical economists believed that both wages and prices are flexible and adjust downward in a recessionary gap. Keynes, however, suggested that wages and prices are not flexible (in a downward direction) and may not adjust downward in a recessionary gap.

Many economists today take a position somewhere between Keynes and the classical economists. For them, the question is not whether wages and prices are flexible downward, but *how long it takes for wages and prices to adjust downward.*

Consider Exhibit 3. Suppose the economy is currently in a recessionary gap at point 1. The relevant short-run aggregate supply curve is $SRAS_1$, where the wage rate is $10 per hour and the price level is P_1. Now classical economists said the wage rate and price level would fall, while Keynes said this may not happen.

Did Keynes mean that if the economy is in a recessionary gap, *the wage rate will never fall and the price level will never adjust downward?* Most economists think not. The question is *how long* the wage rate and price level will take to fall. Will they fall in just a few weeks? Will they fall in a few months? Or will they take five years to fall? The question is relevant because the answer determines how long an economy will be in a recessionary gap, and thus how long the economy takes to self-regulate.

A Question of How Long It Takes for Wage Rates and Prices to Fall
Suppose the economy is in a recessionary gap at point 1. Wage rates are $10 per hour, and the price level is P_1. The issue may not be whether wage rates and the price level fall, but how long they take to reach long-run levels. If they take a short time, then classical economists are right: the economy is self-regulating. If they take a long time—perhaps years—then Keynes is right: the economy is not self-regulating over any reasonable period of time.

Let's look at things this way: If it takes only a few weeks or months for wage rates to fall (say, to $8 an hour, thus shifting the short-run aggregate supply curve from $SRAS_1$ to $SRAS_2$) and for the price level to fall from P_1 to P_2, then for all practical matters the economy is almost instantaneously self-regulating. But if it takes years for this to happen, the economy can hardly be considered self-regulating over any reasonable amount of time.

The classical position is that the time required before wages and prices adjust downward is short enough to call the economy self-regulating. The Keynesian position is that the time is long enough to say that the economy is not self-regulating. Instead, the Keynesians believe that the economy is inherently unstable: it can exist in a recessionary gap for a long time.

KEYNESIANS AND THE GREAT DEPRESSION

Keynes's major work, *The General Theory of Employment, Income and Money,* was published in 1936. Just prior to its publication, the Great Depression had plagued many countries of the world. Looking around at the world during that time, one had to wonder if the classical view of the economy wasn't wrong. After all, unemployment was sky high in many countries and numerous economies had been contracting. Where was Say's law with its promise that there would not be general gluts? Where was the self-regulating economy healing itself of its depression illness? Where was full employment? And given the depressed state of the economy, could anyone any longer believe that laissez-faire was the right policy stance?

With the Great Depression as recent history, Keynes and the Keynesians thought that while their theory may not be right with respect to every detail, there certainly was enough evidence to say that the classical view of the economy was wrong.

Self-Test *(Answers to Self-Test questions are in the Self-Test Appendix.)*

1. What do Keynesians mean when they say the economy is inherently unstable?

2. "What matters is not whether the economy is self-regulating or not, but whether prices and wages are flexible and adjust quickly." Comment.

3. According to Keynes, why might aggregate demand be too low?

THE KEYNESIAN FRAMEWORK OF ANALYSIS

From previous chapters, you are familiar with the *AD-AS* framework of analysis. Keynesian ideas on the economy can be presented in this framework—as in Exhibit 2. These ideas can also be discussed in the *income-expenditure (I-E) framework,* sometimes referred to as the *Keynesian framework.*

In this section, we explain a simple Keynesian model, or *I-E* framework. In the next section, we look at some economic topics using this framework.

THE SIMPLE KEYNESIAN MODEL: THREE SIMPLIFYING ASSUMPTIONS

In the simple Keynesian model presented here, certain simplifying assumptions hold. First, the price level is assumed to be constant. This means that all factors—such as consumption, disposable income, investment, and so on—are real magnitudes. In other words, we talk about real consumption (consumption adjusted for prices), real investment, and so on, although we do not explicitly mention this each time.

Second, there is no foreign sector. In other words, the model is representative of a *closed economy,* not an *open economy.* It follows that total spending in the economy is the sum of consumption, investment, and government purchases.

Third, the monetary side of the economy is excluded.

TOTAL EXPENDITURES AND CONSUMPTION

Total expenditures is the sum of consumption, investment, and government purchases. Keynes was interested in the level of total expenditures in general, but he was particularly concerned about one component of total expenditures: consumption. Consumption (*C*) was of major concern because it is by far the largest slice of the total expenditures pie. For example, in any given year, consumption is approximately 68 percent of total expenditures.

We begin with a discussion of the consumption function, which specifies the relationship between disposable income and consumption in the Keynesian model. Before deriving a total expenditures curve, we explain some of the relationships between consumption, disposable income, and saving.

The Consumption Function

Keynes made three basic points about consumption and disposable income: (1) Consumption depends on disposable income. (2) Consumption and disposable income move in the same direction. (3) When disposable income changes, consumption changes by less. These three points make a specific statement about the relationship between consumption and disposable income. The statement specifying this relationship is called the **consumption function.** We can write the consumption function as:

$$C = C_0 + (MPC)(Y_d)$$

To understand the consumption function, you need to know what the variables represent. You know that *C* is consumption, and we use Y_d to specify disposable income. Let's look at *MPC* and C_0.

MPC stands for **marginal propensity to consume,** which is the ratio of the change in consumption to the change in disposable income:

Marginal propensity to consume = Change in consumption/Change in disposable income

$$MPC = \Delta C / \Delta Y_d$$

http://

Go to *http://w3.access.gpo.gov/eop/.* Enter "B-2" in the Search box, and click "Submit." Find Table B-2, and click on the "TXT" icon below it. Write the value of GDP for the earliest year and for the most recent year in the table. Next, scan down the page and identify the value of total exports for those two years. What percentage of GDP were exports in the earliest year? What percentage of GDP were exports in the most recent year? How realistic do you think the "closed economy" assumption was in the 1930s? Is it more or less realistic than today?

Consumption Function
The relationship between consumption and disposable income. In the consumption function used here, consumption is directly related to disposable income and is positive even at zero disposable income: $C = C_0 + (MPC)(Y_d)$.

Marginal Propensity to Consume (*MPC*)
The ratio of the change in consumption to the change in disposable income: $MPC = \Delta C / \Delta Y_d$.

The symbol Δ stands for "change in." Thus, the *MPC* is equal to the change in consumption divided by the change in disposable income. To illustrate, suppose consumption rises from $800 to $900 as disposable income rises from $1,000 to $1,200. If we divide the change in consumption, which is $100, by the change in disposable income, which is $200, we see that the *MPC* equals 0.50.

C_0 is **autonomous consumption.** Autonomous consumption does not change as disposable income changes; it changes due to factors other than disposable income. Think of consumption as being made up of two parts. One part, which is independent of disposable income, is called *autonomous consumption*. The second part, which depends on disposable income, is called *induced consumption*.

Now, let's look again at the consumption function:

Consumption = Autonomous consumption
+ (Marginal propensity to consume)(Disposable income)
$$C = C_0 + (MPC)(Y_d)$$

For example, suppose C_0 = $800, *MPC* = 0.80, and Y_d = $1,500. By substituting these numbers into the consumption function, we find that C = $800 + (0.80)($1,500) = $800 + $1,200 = $2,000. What will cause an increase in consumption?

Consumption, *C*, will increase if any of the variables, C_0, *MPC*, or Y_d, increases. Thus, *C* can be increased in three ways:

1. **Raise autonomous consumption.** Suppose in our example that autonomous consumption, C_0, goes from $800 to $1,000. This would raise consumption to $2,200: C = $1,000 + (0.80)($1,500) = $2,200.
2. **Raise disposable income.** Suppose disposable income, Y_d, goes from $1,500 to $1,800. This would raise consumption to $2,240: C = $800 + (0.80)($1,800) = $2,240. This increase in consumption from $2,000 to $2,240 is due to an increase of $240 in induced consumption. Specifically, the increased consumption was induced by an increase in disposable income.
3. **Raise the *MPC*.** Suppose the *MPC* rises to 0.90. This would raise consumption to $2,150: C = $800 + (0.90)($1,500) = $2,150.

In Exhibit 4, we set C_0 equal to $200 billion and the *MPC* equal to 0.80; thus, C = $200 billion + (0.8)($Y_d$). We then calculated different levels of consumption (column 3) for different levels of disposable income (column 1).

Saving and Consumption

In Exhibit 4, we also calculated the saving levels (column 5) at the different disposable income levels. How did we calculate this? We know that $C = C_0 + (MPC)(Y_d)$, and we also know that households can only consume or save. So it follows that saving, *S*, is the difference between disposable income and consumption:

Saving = Disposable Income − Consumption
= Disposable income − [Autonomous consumption
+ (Marginal propensity to consume)(Disposable income)]
$$S = Y_d - [C_0 + (MPC)(Y_d)].$$

The *MPC* and the *MPS*

In Exhibit 4, we set the *MPC* = 0.80. This means that for every $1 change in disposable income, there is an $0.80 change in consumption. For example, at a disposable income of $1,200 billion, consumption is $1,160 billion; but at a disposable income of $1,400 billion, consumption is $1,320 billion. This is a difference of $160 billion, or $0.80 additional consumption for every $1 of extra disposable income.

(1) Disposable Income Y_d	(2) Change in Disposable Income ΔY_d	(3) Consumption $C = C_0 + (MPC)(Y_d)$	(4) Change in Consumption $\Delta C = (MPC)(\Delta Y_d)$	(5) Saving $S = Y_d - [C_0 + (MPC)(Y_d)]$	(6) Change in Saving $\Delta S = \Delta Y_d - \Delta C$
$ 800	$___	$ 840	$___	−$40	$___
1,000	200	1,000	160	0	40
1,200	200	1,160	160	40	40
1,400	200	1,320	160	80	40
1,600	200	1,480	160	120	40
1,800	200	1,640	160	160	40

exhibit 4

Consumption and Saving at Different Levels of Disposable Income (in billions)
Our consumption function is $C = C_0 + (MPC)(Y_d)$, where C_0 has been set at $200 billion and $MPC = 0.80$. Saving is the difference between Y_d and C: $S = Y_d - [C_0 + (MPC)(Y_d)]$. All dollar amounts are in billions.

Marginal Propensity to Save (MPS)
The ratio of the change in saving to the change in disposable income: $MPS = \Delta S/\Delta Y_d$.

Average Propensity to Consume (APC)
Consumption divided by disposable income: $APC = C/Y_d$.

Average Propensity to Save (APS)
Saving divided by disposable income: $APC = S/Y_d$.

The **marginal propensity to save (MPS)** is the ratio of the change in saving to the change in disposable income:

Marginal propensity to save = Change in saving/Change in disposable income
$$MPS = \Delta S/\Delta Y_d$$

We know that disposable income can be used only for consumption or saving, that is, $C + S = Y_d$. So, any change to disposable income can only change consumption or saving. Thus, $\Delta Y_d = \Delta C + \Delta S$. It follows that:

$$MPC + MPS = \frac{\Delta C}{\Delta Y_d} + \frac{\Delta S}{\Delta Y_d} = \frac{\Delta C + \Delta S}{\Delta Y_d} = \frac{\Delta C + \Delta S}{\Delta C + \Delta S} = 1$$

Thus, the marginal propensity to consume (MPC) plus the marginal propensity to save (MPS) must equal 1.

Marginal propensity to consume + Marginal propensity to save = 1
$$MPC + MPS = 1$$

In Exhibit 4, we set the marginal propensity to consume at 0.80, so it follows that the marginal propensity to save is 0.20. Notice that for every $1 change in disposable income, saving changes by $0.20; or, for every $200 change in disposable income (column 2), there is a $40 change in saving (column 6).

The APC and APS
Another measure relating consumption and disposable income is the **average propensity to consume (APC).** It is the proportion of disposable income spent on consumption.

Average propensity to consume = Consumption/Disposable income
$$APC = C/Y_d$$

For example, in Exhibit 4 at an income level of $1,400, $APC = \$1,320/\$1,400 = 0.94$. At an income level of $1,800, $APC = \$1,640/\$1,800 = 0.91$.

A similar concept, the **average propensity to save (APS),** is the proportion of disposable income saved.

Average propensity to save = Saving/Disposable income
$$APS = S/Y_d$$

Once again, because saving and consumption are the only ways households can dispose of income, it follows that

$$\text{Average propensity to consume} + \text{Average propensity to save} = 1$$
$$APC + APS = 1$$

It is important to differentiate between "marginal" and "average" magnitudes. Although they may sound alike, the MPC and the APC, and the MPS and the APS, are not the same. The average magnitudes, APC and APS, refer to the *fractions* of disposable income that are consumed and saved, respectively. On an individual basis, if a person has a disposable income of \$1,000 and her consumption is \$600 and her saving is \$400, then her $APC = 0.60$ and her $APS = 0.40$.

The marginal magnitudes, MPC and MPS, refer to the *fractions of any change* in disposable income that are consumed and saved, respectively. On an individual basis, suppose that when a person's disposable income rises by \$100, her consumption rises by \$70 and her saving rises by \$30. Then her $MPC = 0.70$ and her $MPS = 0.30$.

Deriving a Total Expenditures (*TE*) Curve

Just as we derived AD and AS curves in the AD-AS framework, we want to derive a total expenditures (*TE*) curve in the Keynesian framework. Total expenditures is the sum of its parts—consumption, investment, and government purchases. To derive a *TE* curve, we must first derive a diagrammatic representation of consumption, investment, and government purchases, as shown in Exhibit 5 and explained below.

1. **Consumption.** As disposable income rises, so does consumption. This is shown arithmetically in columns (1) and (3) of Exhibit 4. Exhibit 4 also shows that if the MPC is less than 1, consumption rises by less than disposable income rises. Consumption also rises as Real GDP rises, but, again, by a smaller percentage. For example, if Real GDP rises by \$100, consumption may rise by \$80.

    In Exhibit 5a, we have drawn consumption as an upward-sloping curve. Notice that as Real GDP rises from Q_1 to Q_2, consumption rises from \$3,000 billion to \$3,600 billion.

2. **Investment.** We are going to simplify things in deriving *TE*. Look at the investment curve in Exhibit 5b. We assume investment is constant at \$700 billion, no matter whether Real GDP is Q_1 or Q_2.

3. **Government purchases.** We simplify the government spending curve, too. In Exhibit 5c, government purchases are constant at \$1,000 billion, regardless of the amount of Real GDP.

    In Exhibit 5d, we have derived a *TE* curve. We simply added the components of total expenditures at the two Real GDP levels, Q_1 and Q_2, plotted the relevant points, and then drew a line through the points. We see that at Q_1, total expenditures is \$4,700 billion; and at Q_2, it is \$5,300 billion. The *TE* curve is upward-sloping.

COMPARING TOTAL EXPENDITURES (*TE*) AND TOTAL PRODUCTION (*TP*)

Businesses produce the goods and services that are bought by the three sectors of the economy (household, business, and government). Sometimes, though, businesses produce too much or too little in comparison to what the three sectors buy. For example, suppose businesses produce \$9,000 billion worth of goods and services, but the three sectors of the economy buy only \$8,500 billion worth of goods and services. In this case, businesses have produced too much relative to what the three sectors of the economy buy.

Or, possibly, businesses produce \$9,000 billion worth of goods and services, but the three sectors of the economy buy \$9,500 billion worth of goods and services. In this case, businesses have produced too little relative to what the three sectors of the economy buy.

exhibit 5

The Derivation of the Total Expenditures (*TE*) Curve
At different levels of Real GDP, we sum consumption (a), investment (b), and government purchases (c) to derive the *TE* curve (d).

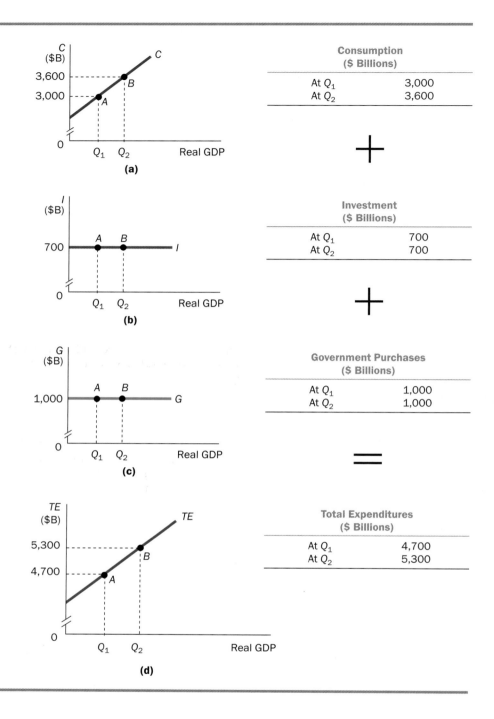

Consumption ($ Billions)	
At Q_1	3,000
At Q_2	3,600

+

Investment ($ Billions)	
At Q_1	700
At Q_2	700

+

Government Purchases ($ Billions)	
At Q_1	1,000
At Q_2	1,000

=

Total Expenditures ($ Billions)	
At Q_1	4,700
At Q_2	5,300

Finally, it is possible for businesses to produce $9,000 billion worth of goods and services, and for the three sectors of the economy to buy exactly $9,000 billion worth of goods and services. In this case, businesses have produced exactly the right amount of goods and services.

Thus, there are three possible states of the economy in the *I-E* framework. The total expenditures (*TE*) of the three sectors of the economy can be less than, greater than, or equal to the dollar value of total production (*TP*). In other words, each of the following states of the economy is possible:

$$TE < TP$$
$$TE > TP$$
$$TE = TP$$

According to many economists, if the economy is currently operating where $TE < TP$ or $TE > TP$ (both states are described as disequilibrium), it will eventually move to where $TE = TP$ (where the economy is in equilibrium). The next section explains how this happens.

MOVING FROM DISEQUILIBRIUM TO EQUILIBRIUM

Business firms hold an inventory of their goods to guard against unexpected changes in the demand for their product. For example, General Motors may hold an inventory of a certain type of car in case the demand for that car suddenly increases unexpectedly.

Although we know why business firms hold an inventory of their goods, we don't know *how much* inventory they will hold. For example, we don't know if General Motors will hold an inventory of 1,000 cars, 2,000 cars, or 10,000 cars. (Inventories are usually held in terms of, say, a 45- or 60-day supply, but we have simplified things here.) However, we do know that for General Motors, and all other business firms, there is some *optimum inventory*. This is "just the right amount" of inventory—not too much and not too little. With this in mind, consider two cases that illustrate how business inventory levels play an important role in the economy's adjustment from disequilibrium to equilibrium.

Case 1: $TE < TP$

Assume business firms hold an optimum inventory level of $300 billion worth of goods. Then firms produce $9,000 billion worth of goods and services, and the three sectors of the economy buy $8,800 billion worth of goods and services. Thus, producers produce more than individuals buy ($TE < TP$). The difference adds to inventories, and inventory levels rise unexpectedly to $500 billion, which is $200 billion more than the $300 billion firms see as optimal.

This unexpected rise in inventories signals to firms that they have *overproduced*. Consequently, they cut back on the quantity of goods they produce. The cutback in production causes Real GDP to fall, bringing Real GDP closer to the (lower) output level that the three sectors of the economy are willing and able to buy. Ultimately, TP will equal TE.

Case 2: $TE > TP$

Assume business firms hold their optimum inventory level, $300 billion worth of goods. Then firms produce $8,400 billion worth of goods, and members of the three sectors buy $8,600 billion worth of goods. But how can individuals buy more than firms produce? The answer is that firms make up the difference out of inventory. In our example, inventory levels fall from $300 billion to $100 billion because individuals purchase $200 billion more of goods than firms produced (to be sold). This example illustrates why firms maintain inventories in the first place: to be able to meet an unexpected increase in sales.

The unexpected fall in inventories signals to firms that they have *underproduced*. Consequently, they increase the quantity of goods they produce. The rise in production causes Real GDP to rise, in the process bringing Real GDP closer to the (higher) real output that the three sectors are willing and able to buy. Ultimately, TP will equal TE.

THE GRAPHICAL REPRESENTATION OF THE THREE STATES OF THE ECONOMY IN THE KEYNESIAN FRAMEWORK

The three states of the economy are represented in Exhibit 6. Notice that there is a TE curve, which we derived earlier, and a TP curve, which is simply a 45-degree line. (It is called a 45-degree line because it bisects the 90-degree angle at the origin.) It is important to notice that at any point on the TP curve, total production is equal to Real GDP (TP = Real GDP). This is because TP and Real GDP are different names for the same thing. Real GDP, remember, is simply the total market value of all final goods and services produced annually within a country's borders, adjusted for price changes.

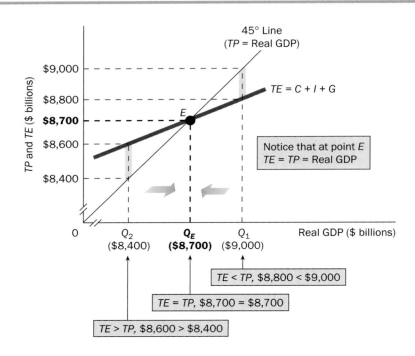

exhibit 6

The Three States of the Economy

At Q_E, $TE = TP$ and the economy is in equilibrium. At Q_1, $TE < TP$. This results in an unexpected increase in inventories, which signals firms that they have overproduced, which leads firms to cut back production. The cutback in production reduces Real GDP. The economy tends to move from Q_1 to Q_E. At Q_2, $TE > TP$. This results in an unexpected decrease in inventories, which signals firms that they have underproduced, which leads firms to raise production. The increased production raises Real GDP. The economy tends to move from Q_2 to Q_E.

Now let's look at three different Real GDP levels in the exhibit. We start with Q_1, where Real GDP = $9,000 billion. At this Real GDP level, what does TE equal? What does TP equal? We see that TE is $8,800 billion and TP is $9,000 billion. This illustrates Case 1, in which producers produce more than individuals buy ($TE < TP$). The difference adds to inventories. This unexpected rise in inventories signals to firms that they have overproduced. Consequently, they cut back on the quantity of goods they produce. The cutback in production causes Real GDP to fall, ultimately bringing Real GDP down to Q_E ($8,700 billion in the exhibit).

Now we look at Q_2, where Real GDP = $8,400 billion. At this Real GDP level, TE equals $8,600 billion and TP equals $8,400 billion. This illustrates Case 2, in which the three sectors of the economy buy more goods and services than business firms have produced ($TE > TP$). Business firms make up the difference between what they have produced and what the three sectors of the economy buy through inventories. Inventories fall below optimum levels. Consequently, businesses increase the quantity of goods they produce. The rise in production causes Real GDP to rise, ultimately moving Real GDP up to Q_E ($8,700 billion in the exhibit).

When the economy is producing Q_E, or $8,700 billion worth of goods and services, it is in equilibrium. At this Real GDP level, TP and TE are the same, $8,700 billion. The following table summarizes some key points about the state of the economy in the *I-E* framework.

State of the Economy	What Happens to Inventories?	What Do Firms Do?
$TE < TP$ Individuals are buying less output than firms produce.	Inventories rise above optimum levels.	Firms cut back production to reduce inventories to their optimum levels.
$TE > TP$ Individuals are buying more output than firms produce.	Inventories fall below optimum levels.	Firms increase production to raise inventories to their optimum levels.
$TE = TP$	Inventories are at their optimum levels.	Firms neither increase nor decrease production.

Economists often think in threes. For example, this chapter describes three possible states of the economy: (1) TE less than TP, (2) TE greater than TP, or (3) TE equal to TP. The last chapter also identifies three possible states of the economy: (1) Real GDP less than Natural Real GDP, (2) Real GDP greater than Natural Real GDP, or (3) Real GDP equal to Natural Real GDP. Chapter 3, which discusses supply and demand, describes three possible market conditions: (1) quantity demanded greater than quantity supplied, (2) quantity demanded less than quantity supplied, or (3) quantity demanded equal to quantity supplied. Economists often think in threes because economists often think in terms of equilibrium and disequilibrium—and usually there is one equilibrium position and two (categorically different) disequilibria positions.*

Self-Test

1. How is autonomous consumption different from consumption?

2. What happens in the economy if total production (*TP*) is greater than total expenditures (*TE*)?

ECONOMIC ANALYSIS IN THE KEYNESIAN FRAMEWORK

In this section, we use the Keynesian framework to examine some familiar macroeconomic concepts. We also expand our discussion of autonomous consumption to explore Keynes's theory about the relationship between autonomous spending and Real GDP.

CAN THE ECONOMY BE IN A RECESSIONARY GAP AND IN EQUILIBRIUM TOO?

In the last chapter, we primarily used the *AD-AS* framework to discuss the economy. In that framework, an economy could be in short-run equilibrium and in a recessionary gap too. Can the same situation exist in the Keynesian framework just outlined? Take another look at Exhibit 6. The economy is in equilibrium at point *E,* producing a Real GDP level of Q_E or $8,700 billion. Is there any guarantee that the Real GDP level of $8,700 is the Natural Real GDP level? Not at all. The economy could be in a situation like that shown in Exhibit 7. The economy is in equilibrium, producing Q_E, but the Natural Real GDP level is Q_N. Because the economy is producing at a Real GDP level that is less than Natural Real GDP, it is in a recessionary gap.

THINKING LIKE AN
ECONOMIST *An economist's view of the economy and his policy suggestions are often linked. For example, classical economists and their modern-day counterparts, who view the economy as inherently stable, believe in a policy of laissez-faire: Government should keep its hands off the economy. Keynesians, however, who view the economy as inherently unstable, suggest that government has an economic role to play (which we discuss in the next chapter). In short, policy suggestions are sometimes a consequence of how one views the internal or inherent workings of an economy.*

THE MULTIPLIER

Before we discuss the concept of the *multiplier,* we need to examine the difference between autonomous spending and induced spending. What is *autonomous spending?* It is any expenditure that is *not related* to a change in income or Real GDP. Autonomous consumption, which is defined earlier in this chapter, is one

exhibit 7

The Economy: In Equilibrium, and in a Recessionary Gap Too
Using the Keynesian framework, the economy is currently in equilibrium at point E, producing Q_E. Natural Real GDP, however, is greater than Q_E, so the economy is in a recessionary gap as well as being in equilibrium.

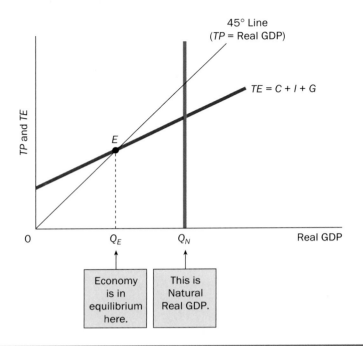

type of autonomous spending. Autonomous spending stands in contrast to an *induced spending* component, which is any expenditure that is *related* to a change in income or Real GDP.

To illustrate, we use an example from the business sector. Suppose investment is currently $600 billion at a Real GDP level of $8,000 billion. Now suppose Real GDP rises to $8,100 billion. As a result of the increase in Real GDP, business owners purchase more factories and other capital goods, and investment rises to $630 billion. This $30 billion increase in investment was induced by an increase in income or Real GDP. Thus, it is *induced spending* on the part of the business sector.

On the other hand, suppose investment is still $600 billion and Real GDP is still $8,000 billion. Now suppose many business owners become optimistic about the future of the economy. They believe that members of the household and government sectors will soon (perhaps in a matter of a few months) start buying more goods and services. In expectation of "better times," businesses buy more factories and other capital goods, and investment rises to $613 billion. In this case, investment rises even when Real GDP remains constant. Investment increased because business expectations about the future became more positive. This $13 billion increase in investment was *autonomous*: it changed *independently* of income or Real GDP. Thus, it is *autonomous spending* on the part of the business sector. We can also call it *autonomous investment,* just as we refer to autonomous spending by the household sector as autonomous consumption.

With this as background, look at Exhibit 8. Suppose the economy is in equilibrium at point E_1, where it is producing Q_1. Now suppose the business sector decides to increase its level of autonomous investment spending. It increases its spending from, say, I_1 to I_2. This increase causes the *TE* curve to shift upward from TE_1 to TE_2. According to our diagram, the new equilibrium in the economy will be at E_2 where the economy is producing Q_2.

Let's take a closer look at the *increase in autonomous investment spending* and the *increase in Real GDP*. The upward parallel shift in the *TE* curve represents the increase in autonomous investment spending; after all, it was the increase in auto-

exhibit 8

A Change in Autonomous Investment Spending Relative to a Change in Real GDP
An increase in autonomous investment spending shifts the *TE* curve from TE_1 to TE_2 and brings about an increase in Real GDP from Q_1 to Q_2. The increase in Real GDP is greater than the increase in autonomous investment—compare the length of arrow 2 with the length of arrow 1.

nomous investment spending that caused the *TE* curve to shift upward. This change in autonomous investment spending is identified by arrow 1.

The increase in Real GDP is represented by arrow 2. Notice that arrow 2 is longer than arrow 1, signifying that *the increase in Real GDP is greater than the increase in autonomous spending.* For example, it could be that for every \$1 increase in autonomous investment spending, Real GDP increases by \$2.50. Then, if autonomous investment spending increases by \$5 billion, Real GDP increases by \$12.5 billion.

Why does Real GDP increase by a greater amount than the increase in investment spending? This happens because the **multiplier** is at work. The multiplier is the number that is multiplied by the change in *any autonomous spending component* of total expenditures to give us the change in Real GDP.

To find the multiplier, we use this formula:

$$\text{Multiplier } (m) = \frac{1}{1 - MPC}$$

For example, if the marginal propensity to consume is 80 percent, then the multiplier is 5:

$$\text{Multiplier } (m) = \frac{1}{1 - 0.80}$$

$$= \frac{1}{0.20}$$

$$= 5$$

This means that if an autonomous spending component changes by \$1, Real GDP will change by \$5. Here is our formula:

$$\Delta \text{Real GDP} = m \times \Delta \text{Autonomous spending}$$

The Multiplier: One Step at a Time
It is easy to see the effect of the multiplier in Exhibit 8. Arrow 2, which represents the increase in Real GDP, is longer than arrow 1, which represents the change in autonomous investment.

Multiplier
The number that is multiplied by the change in autonomous spending to obtain the change in Real GDP: $m = 1/(1 - MPC)$.

But how exactly does a change in autonomous spending lead to a multiple change in Real GDP? We explain using Exhibit 9.

1. We start with a $60 million increase in autonomous investment spending (column 2).
2. This increase in autonomous investment spending generates income equal to itself: $60 million spent on goods by business is $60 million received as income by people who sell to business (column 3). (Remember from earlier in this chapter that prices are assumed to be constant, so this is a $60 million increase in real income. Our analysis is at the national level, so the increase is in real national income, which is a very close proxy for Real GDP. This is why column (3) is titled "Change in Real National Income or Real GDP.")
3. We assume that the *MPC* = 0.80. So, if real national income increases by $60 million, then consumption changes by 80 percent of $60 million, or $48 million.
4. The $48 million is spent, generating income equal to itself.
5. Again, if the *MPC* = 0.80, then consumption changes by 80 percent of $48 million, or $38.4 million.
6. And so on.

If we continue until the dollar amounts become tiny, we will find that a $60 million increase in autonomous investment spending leads to a $300 million increase in real national income or Real GDP. This is, of course, assuming the *MPC* = 0.80 (the multiplier is 5). Thus, the change in Real GDP ($300 million) is equal to *m* times the change in autonomous spending (5 × $60 million).

The Multiplier and Reality

We have discussed the multiplier in simple terms: A change in autonomous spending leads to a greater change in Real GDP.

We must note two points, however. First, the multiplier takes time to have an effect. In a textbook, it takes only seconds to go from an initial increase in autonomous spending to a multiple increase in Real GDP. In the real world, this process takes many months.

Second, for the multiplier to increase Real GDP (the way we have described), *idle resources must exist at each expenditure round.* Recall that one of our simplifying assumptions for the Keynesian framework is that prices are fixed or con-

---

exhibit 9

Autonomous Investment Spending and the Multiplier

A $60 million change in autonomous investment spending ultimately changes Real GDP or real national income by $300 million (*MPC* = 0.80). The process begins with an increase in autonomous investment spending, which leads to a change in income, a change in consumption, another change in income, another change in consumption, and so on.

(1) Expenditure Round	(2) Change in Autonomous Investment Spending ($ millions)	(3) Change in Real National Income or Real GDP ($ millions)	(4) MPC	(5) Change in Consumption ($ millions)
Round 1	$60.00	$ 60.00	0.80	$ 48.00
Round 2		48.00	0.80	38.40
Round 3		38.40	0.80	30.72
Round 4		30.72	0.80	24.57
.		.	.	.
.		.	.	.
.		.	.	.
All other rounds		122.88	0.80	98.88
TOTALS	$300.00			$240.00 (Approx.)

The Multiplier on Spring Break

During the week-long spring break, many college students put away their books, pack their shorts, swimsuits, and tanning oil, jump into their cars, and head for the beaches. As they are driving to Fort Lauderdale, Galveston, Myrtle Beach, Daytona Beach, San Diego, and other coastal cities, the multiplier is getting ready to go to work.

Look at it this way. When college students from around the country head for, say, Daytona Beach, they have dollars in their pockets. They will spend many of these dollars in Daytona Beach—on food and drink, motel rooms, dance clubs, and so on. As far as Daytona Beach is concerned, those dollars represent autonomous spending. More importantly, those dollars can raise the total income of Daytona Beach by some multiple of itself. College students buy pizzas, beer, and sodas. The people who sell these items find their incomes rising. They, in turn, spend some fraction of their increase in income, which generates additional income for still others, who spend some fraction of their increase in income, and so on and so on.

Let's take a hypothetical example. Suppose college students spend $7 million in Daytona Beach during spring break. If the *MPC* is, say, 0.60 in Daytona Beach, and all the added income generated is spent in Daytona Beach, then college students will increase income in Daytona Beach by $17.5 million.

$$\Delta \text{Daytona Beach income} = \frac{1}{1 - MPC} \times \frac{\Delta \text{Autonomous}}{\text{spending}}$$
$$= 2.5 \times \$7 \text{ million}$$
$$= \$17.5 \text{ million}$$

Do the people who live in Daytona Beach want college students to visit their city during spring break? Many of them do because it means extra dollars in their pockets. College students from out of town, together with the multiplier, often make for robust economic times!

stant. It follows that if we experience an increase in Real GDP (output is increasing) at each expenditure round, *idle resources must be available to be brought into production.* If this were not the case, then increased spending would simply result in higher prices without an increase in Real GDP. Thus, there would be an increase in GDP ($P \times Q$), but not in Real GDP (Q).

Q & A **Q:** Does the multiplier analysis work in reverse? That is, if autonomous investment spending declines by $60 million and the *MPC* equals 0.80, would Real GDP decrease by $300 million?

A: Yes.

WHAT DOES THE KEYNESIAN AGGREGATE SUPPLY CURVE LOOK LIKE?

Consider these two statements: (1) Idle resources must exist at each expenditure round for the multiplier to work as we have described. (2) Prices are constant. Let's put these two together and ask a question. If prices are constant and there are idle resources at each expenditure round, then what must the aggregate supply curve look like? Obviously, it must be horizontal. The easiest way to see this is to consider what would happen to the price level if the *AS* curve were upward-sloping or vertical. In these situations, any increase in total spending in the economy would shift the *AD* curve to the right and bring about a higher price level. The only way that an increase in total spending does not bring about a higher price level is if the aggregate supply curve is horizontal. We have shown this in Exhibit 10.

exhibit 10

The Keynesian *AS* Curve

In the simple Keynesian model we present in this chapter, the *AS* curve is horizontal. Changes in aggregate demand change only Real GDP and not the price level.

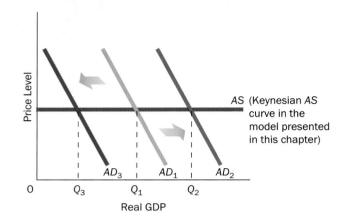

Notice in Exhibit 10 what happens in this simple Keynesian model when aggregate demand rises or falls. If aggregate demand rises from AD_1 to AD_2, Real GDP rises but there is no change in the price level. Alternatively, if aggregate demand falls from AD_1 to AD_3, Real GDP falls and still there is no change in the price level.

KEYNES ON THE PRIVATE SECTOR

Suppose the economy is in a recessionary gap: it is producing a level of Real GDP that is less than Natural Real GDP. Can the private sector (consisting of households and business firms in the simple Keynesian model) increase its autonomous spending, shift the *AD* curve to the right, and thus remove the economy from the recessionary gap?

Suppose, as shown in Exhibit 11, that the economy is currently at Q_1. Furthermore, suppose that Q_1 is less than Q_N. In terms of our previous terminology, the economy is in a recessionary gap. Our question is: Can private sector spending (consisting of both consumption and investment spending) rise enough to shift the *AD* curve from AD_1 to AD_2 and thus move the economy into producing Natural Real GDP, Q_N?

exhibit 11

Can the Private Sector Remove the Economy from a Recessionary Gap?

The economy is at point *A* producing Q_1. Q_1 is less than Q_N, so the economy is in a recessionary gap. The question is whether the private sector (consisting of consumption and investment spending) can remove the economy from the recessionary gap by increasing spending enough to shift the aggregate demand curve from AD_1 to AD_2. Keynes believed that sometimes it could not. No matter how low interest rates fell, investment spending would not rise because of pessimistic business expectations with respect to future sales.

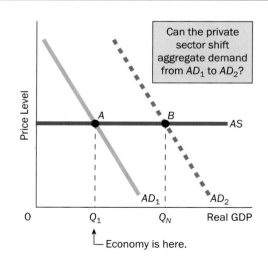

ECONOMICS IN...

Everyday Life   Popular Culture   Technology   The World

The Keynesian Explanation of the Great Depression

The years of the Great Depression were hard for many people. Jobs were extremely difficult to find and the unemployment rate was sky high. Many people did not have enough food to eat. Obviously, when the economy is "ill," many people suffer.

But what caused the economic downturn and the human hardship? Economist Christina Romer states that the Great Depression was caused by repeated declines in aggregate demand: "Between 1929 and 1933, a series of shocks caused aggregate demand to decline repeatedly in the United States. These declines in aggregate demand moved the economy down along an upward-sloping aggregate supply curve. The net result was both progressively worsening unemployment and deflation."[2]

This leads us to ask: What caused the repeated declines in aggregate demand? For Keynesians, it was a combination of repeated declines in investment and consumption spending.

To grasp the entire story, we need to look at conditions before the Great Depression. Keynesians point to the sharp increase in investment demand in the early 1920s. They argue that this increased demand arose for a number of reasons.

First, World War I had left much of Europe in ruins; Europeans therefore turned to the United States for many goods. Increased European demand for U.S. goods led to greater production in U.S. factories and to increased U.S. investment spending (on machinery and factories) to meet the higher demand.

Second, the end of the war unleashed American consumers' pent-up demand for goods. As a result, firms began to produce and invest more.

Third, after the war, people were optimistic about the future. They believed that the world was entering a period of peace and that advances in technology would lead to a higher standard of living. Some economists argue that this heightened positive outlook encouraged business firms to invest beyond the level that reality indicated.

In the mid-1920s, the productive capacity of many industries caught up with the increased European demand and unleashed American demand for goods. In some industries, firms had excess production capacity. As a result, investment spending began to fall, shifting the *AD* curve to the left.

Then the multiplier came into play, causing Real GDP to fall more than investment fell. In turn, the decline in Real GDP led to a fall in consumption (which shifted the *AD* curve leftward), suggesting even less need for productive capacity and therefore less investment spending (which shifted the *AD* curve leftward again). In other words, the economy began to fold in on itself: A decline in investment (and decline in *AD*) led to a decline in Real GDP, which led to a decline in consumption (and decline in *AD*), which led to another decline in investment (and another decline in *AD*), and so on.

Not all economists agree with this explanation of the Great Depression, which explicitly maintains that its cause or catalyst was a reduction in investment spending coming off an investment boom.

Given our discussion about the multiplier, it would seem that it could. But recall that our multiplier analysis depends on an autonomous spending component rising; in our example, it was a rise in autonomous investment spending. But whether autonomous investment spending will rise or not depends on what factors affect autonomous investment. Suppose autonomous investment is affected by both interest rates and business expectations of future sales. In other words, a change in interest rates or business expectations or *both* can cause a change in autonomous investment spending.

For example, suppose interest rates *fall,* and *nothing else changes*. In this case, we would expect that businesses would find it cheaper to borrow funds to

---

2. Christina Romer, "The Nation in Depression," *Journal of Economic Perspectives* (spring 1993): 25.

invest, so they would borrow and invest more. Or, suppose expectations become *pessimistic* and *nothing else changes*. In this case, we would expect that businesses would want to invest less.

But suppose both things happen at the same time: *interest rates fall and businesses become pessimistic about future sales.* One factor (lower interest rates) pushes autonomous investment spending up, but the other factor (business expectations about future sales) pushes autonomous investment spending down. What happens *on net?* Obviously, it depends on which factor is stronger. If the expectations factor outweighs the interest rate factor, then autonomous investment spending will decline; if the interest rate factor outweighs the expectations factor, then autonomous investment spending will rise; and if the two factors perfectly counter each other, there will be no change in autonomous investment spending.

Keynes believed that investment is not always responsive to lower interest rates. Specifically, he believed that business expectations with respect to future sales could be so negative that businesses wouldn't invest more *even if interest rates fell.* His conclusion was that the private sector may not be able to get the economy out of a recessionary gap. Well, then, if the private sector couldn't always remove the economy from a recessionary gap, what could? This question opened the door to a discussion of government's role in the economy, which we address in the next chapter.

Self-Test

1. Suppose that prices are not fixed and there are no idle resources. Can a rise in autonomous spending raise Real GDP by some multiple of the amount of the rise? Can a rise in autonomous spending raise GDP by some multiple of the amount of the rise? Explain your answer.

2. If the *MPS* equals 0.23, then what does the multiplier equal?

3. What is the relationship between a change in Real GDP (assuming a change in autonomous spending) and (the size of) the *MPC?*

A Reader Asks...
Do Firms Really Look at Their Inventories When Deciding What to Do?

In the simple Keynesian model, if spending is greater than output, inventories fall and firms increase production. Alternatively, if spending is less than output, inventories rise and firms cut back on production. Is this how things happen in the real world?

Many economists think so. In fact, many economists, especially those who make it their business to forecast the economy, often check the inventory-to-sales ratio to get some idea of where the economy is headed. The inventory-to-sales ratio is the ratio of inventories to monthly sales, or inventory value divided by monthly sales. To illustrate, suppose Jim has $24,000 in inventory and his sales for the month are $9,600. His inventory-to-sales ratio is $24,000/$9,600 = 2.5.

Economists usually look at the inventory-to-sales ratio over three consecutive months. If it has fallen in

each of the past three months, they reason that inventories have fallen relative to sales. In other words, sales are robust. They then predict that firms will have to increase output production in order to get their inventories back up to optimum levels.

If the inventory-to-sales ratio has risen in each of the past three months, economists reason that inventories have risen relative to sales. In other words, sales are weak. They then predict that firms will cut back on output production in order to get their inventories back down to optimum levels.

Finally, if there is either no change in the inventory-to-sales ratio over the past three months, or if a rising ratio in one month is matched by a falling ratio in another month, economists often predict no change in output production.

Keynes on Wage Rates and Prices

- Keynes believed that wage rates and prices may be inflexible downwards. He said that employees and labor unions would resist employer's wage cuts and that because of anticompetitive or monopolistic elements in the economy, prices would not fall.

Keynes on Say's Law

- Keynes did not agree that Say's law would necessarily hold in a money economy. He thought it was possible for consumption to fall (saving to increase) by more than investment increased. Consequently, a decrease in consumption (or increase in saving) could lower total expenditures and aggregate demand in the economy.

Consumption Function

- Keynes made three points about consumption and disposable income: (1) Consumption depends on disposable income. (2) Consumption and disposable income move in the same direction. (3) As disposable income changes, consumption changes by less. These three ideas are incorporated into the consumption function, $C = C_0 + (MPC)(Y_d)$, where C_0 is autonomous consumption, MPC is the marginal propensity to consume, and Y_d is disposable income.

Total Expenditures and Total Production

- If total expenditures (TE) equal total production (TP), the economy is in equilibrium. If $TE < TP$, the economy is in disequilibrium and inventories unexpectedly rise, signaling firms to cut back production. If $TE > TP$, the economy is in disequilibrium and inventories unexpectedly fall, signaling firms to increase production.

The Multiplier

- A change in autonomous spending will bring about a multiple change in Real GDP. This multiple change will be equal to $1/(1 - MPC)$ (the multiplier) times the change in autonomous spending.

A Keynesian Theme

- Keynes proposed that the economy could reach its equilibrium position with Real GDP below Natural Real GDP; that is, the economy can be in equilibrium and in a recessionary gap too. Furthermore, he argued that the economy may not be able to get out of a recessionary gap by itself.

Efficiency Wage Models
Consumption Function
Marginal Propensity to Consume
   (*MPC*)

Autonomous Consumption
Marginal Propensity to Save (*MPS*)
Average Propensity to Consume
   (*APC*)

Average Propensity to Save (*APS*)
Multiplier

Economic facts, actions, and changes create ripples that move away from their point of origin. Eventually, these ripples can intersect your life and have an effect on you. Consider the following example.

It may or may not be an economic fact that the economy is self-regulating. If it is a fact, then recessions will be temporary economic events. But if the economy is not self-regulating but inherently unstable, then it could get stuck in a recessionary gap. In a recessionary gap, price levels and the unemployment

rate are high in relation to their equilibrium values. If you are looking for a job when the economy is stuck in a recessionary gap, you could be looking for a very long time. Thus, there is a connection between whether or not an economy is self-regulating and the length of time it takes you to find a job—an economic connection to you.

Based on the material in this chapter, identify other ways in which economic facts, actions, and changes create ripples that affect you.

1. According to Keynes, why might the economy get stuck in a recessionary gap?
2. Give two reasons why wage rates may not fall.
3. According to New Keynesian economists, why might business firms pay wage rates above market-clearing levels?
4. According to Keynes, can an increase in saving shift the *AD* curve to the left? Explain your answer.
5. Explain how to derive a total expenditures (*TE*) curve.
6. Using the consumption function developed in this chapter, explain the ways in which consumption can increase.
7. Explain what happens in the economy if total production (*TP*) is greater than total expenditures (*TE*). Explain what happens if *TE* is greater than *TP*.
8. Will an increase in autonomous spending always increase Real GDP by some multiple of the spending increase? Why or why not?
9. Although we did not discuss an inflationary gap in this chapter, it can be diagrammatically represented within the Keynesian framework. Please do so.
10. Classical economists assumed that wage rates, prices, and interest rates were flexible and would adjust quickly. Consider an extreme case: Suppose classical economists believed wage rates, prices, and interest rates would adjust instantaneously. What would this imply the classical aggregate supply (*AS*) curve would look like? Explain your answer.

11. Suppose there is an increase in autonomous investment with no decline in any other component of total expenditures. Furthermore, suppose the multiplier is fully operable: there is a multiple increase in Real GDP equal to the change in investment times the multiplier. What does all this imply about the shape of the aggregate supply curve? Explain your answer.
12. According to Keynes, an increase in saving and decrease in consumption may lower total spending in the economy. But how could this happen if the increased saving lowers interest rates (as shown in the last chapter)? Wouldn't a decrease in interest rates increase investment spending, thus counteracting the decrease in consumption spending?
13. Can a person believe that wages are inflexible downward for, say, one year and also believe in a self-regulating economy? Explain your answer.
14. Given the Keynesian consumption function, how would a cut in income tax rates affect consumption? Explain your answer.
15. Economist Brown believes that a cut in income tax rates will stimulate consumption spending by something less than the *MPC* times the change in disposable (after-tax) income. Does it follow that he believes in the Keynesian consumption function identified in this chapter? Explain your answer.

1. Answer the following questions:
   a. Suppose the *MPC* = 0.80 and that it is the same at all Real GDP levels. Suppose autonomous consumption decreases by $500. How much does Real GDP change?
   b. Suppose the *MPS* = 0.10 and that it is the same at all Real GDP levels. Suppose autonomous investment increases by $100. How much does Real GDP change?
   c. Suppose the *MPC* = 0.70 and that it is the same at all Real GDP levels. Suppose autonomous consumption increases by $500 and autonomous investment decreases by $80. How much does Real GDP change?
2. In the simple Keynesian model, suppose the *MPC* = 0.75 and the *APC* = 0.90. If real national income is $4,000 billion, what does consumption equal?
3. If the *MPC* begins to decline, what will happen to the *APC*? Explain your answer with a numerical example.

4. Diagrammatically represent the following states of the economy in both the *I-E* and *AD-AS* frameworks.
   a. Recessionary gap
   b. Inflationary gap
5. Economist Smith believes that changes in aggregate demand affect only the price level, and economist Jones believes that changes in aggregate demand affect only Real GDP. What do the *AD* and *AS* curves look like for each economist?
6. Write an investment function (equation) that specifies two components: (a) autonomous investment spending and (b) induced investment spending.
7. The *TE* curve in Exhibit 5d is upward-sloping because the consumption function is upward-sloping. Explain.
8. Look at Exhibit 5d. What does the vertical distance between the origin and the point at which the *TE* curve cuts the vertical axis represent?

9. In the following figure, explain what happens if:
   a. The economy is at Q_1
   b. The economy is at Q_2

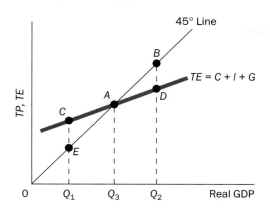

10. In the previous figure, if Natural Real GDP is Q_2, what state is the economy in at point A?

11. Explain the following using the figure below.

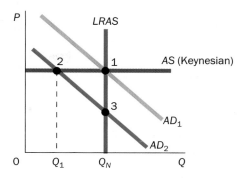

   a. According to Keynes, aggregate demand may be insufficient to bring about the full-employment output level (or Natural Real GDP).
   b. A decrease in consumption (due to increased saving) is not matched by an increase in investment spending.

Internet Activities

1. Go to *http://corp.bankofamerica.com/research*. Select "Global Economics and Financial Markets Weekly." Scroll to the pages for the United States and read the information on two economic indicators. Answer the following questions for each of the two indicators you chose.
   a. Which indicator did you pick? Is it a national or regional indicator? Is it a strictly macroeconomic indicator or might there be microeconomic implications to it?
   b. Did this indicator rise or fall? How much did it rise or fall? What time period does it cover (year, month, etc.)?
   c. What is the economic significance of the change in the indicator?
   d. How might unemployment and prices be affected by the change in the indicator?

   e. Draw the predicted effect of the change in the indicator in terms of aggregate demand and aggregate supply.
2. Now choose another country in the report, read the discussion, and then select an economic indicator for that country.
   a. What country and indicator did you choose and what happened to the indicator during the report period?
   b. What is the economic significance of the change in the indicator?
   c. How might unemployment and prices be affected by the change in the indicator?
   d. Draw the predicted effect of the change in the indicator in terms of aggregate demand and aggregate supply.

Log on to the Arnold Xtra! Web site now (*http://arnoldxtra.swcollege.com*) for additional learning resources such as practice quizzes, help with graphing, video clips, and current event applications.

ch.10
FISCAL POLICY

Suppose the economy is not self-regulating; suppose it can get stuck in a recessionary gap. What then? Some economists say that if the economy can't regulate itself (if it can't eliminate, say, a recessionary gap and move itself to its Natural Real GDP level), then government should. Enter fiscal policy, which refers to changes in government expenditures and/or taxes to achieve particular macroeconomic goals. The primary participants in formulating fiscal policy include the President and the U.S. Congress.

Chapter Road Map

Government uses fiscal policy in order to achieve particular macroeconomic goals, such as lowering the unemployment rate and raising Real GDP to eliminate a recessionary gap. In order to achieve these goals, fiscal policy must change either aggregate demand or aggregate supply. Fiscal policy designed to change aggregate demand is referred to as demand-side fiscal policy, *and fiscal policy designed to change aggregate supply is referred to as* supply-side fiscal policy. *In this chapter, we mainly discuss demand-side fiscal policy.*

Economists disagree on the effectiveness of demand-side fiscal policy. Some argue that demand-side fiscal policy works in intended ways. Others argue that it does not always work in ways that were intended. Still others argue that it does not work at all.

When fiscal policy either does not work at all or works in a way that is unintended, it is natural to ask why. Usually, the answer has to do with (1) crowding out, (2) lags, or (3) incomplete information, all of which we discuss in this chapter.

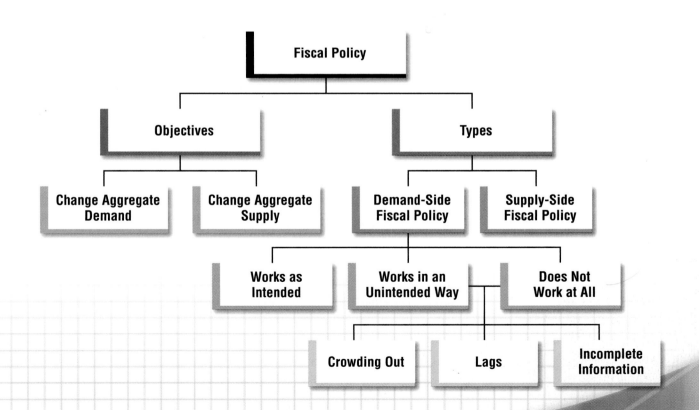

FISCAL POLICY

Some economists, such as the Keynesians and New Keynesians, believe the economy is inherently unstable and argue that the government should play a role in managing the economy. One of the major ways government can influence the economy is through its *fiscal policy.*

Fiscal policy refers to changes in government expenditures and/or taxes to achieve particular economic goals, such as low unemployment, price stability, and economic growth. Because fiscal policy deals with both government expenditures and taxes, it can affect the federal budget.

THE FEDERAL BUDGET

The federal budget is composed of two, not necessarily equal, parts: government expenditures and tax revenues. If expenditures are greater than tax revenues, a **budget deficit** exists. If tax revenues are greater than expenditures, a **budget surplus** exists. If expenditures equal tax revenues, a **balanced budget** exists.

SOME RELEVANT FISCAL POLICY TERMS

Notice in our definition of fiscal policy that we use the term *government expenditures* instead of *government purchases,* the term you are familiar with from earlier chapters. Government expenditures—which is sometimes simply called *government spending*—is not the same as *government purchases.* Government expenditures is the sum of government purchases and (government) transfer payments.[1]

Expansionary fiscal policy refers to increases in government expenditures and/or decreases in taxes to achieve macroeconomic goals. **Contractionary fiscal policy** refers to decreases in government expenditures and/or increases in taxes to achieve these goals.

> Expansionary fiscal policy: Government expenditures up and/or taxes down
> Contractionary fiscal policy: Government expenditures down and/or taxes up

When changes in government expenditures and taxes are brought about deliberately through government actions, fiscal policy is said to be *discretionary.* For example, if Congress decides to increase government spending by, say, $10 billion in an attempt to lower the unemployment rate, this is an act of **discretionary fiscal policy.** In contrast, a change in either government expenditures or taxes that occurs automatically in response to economic events is referred to as **automatic fiscal policy.** To illustrate, suppose Real GDP in the economy turns down, causing more people to become unemployed. As a result, more people automatically receive unemployment benefits. These added unemployment benefits automatically boost government spending.

TWO IMPORTANT NOTES

In your study of this chapter, keep in mind the following two important points:

1. In our discussion of fiscal policy in this chapter, we deal only with *discretionary fiscal policy.* In other words, we will consider deliberate actions on the part of policymakers to affect the economy through changes in government spending and/or taxes.
2. We assume that any change in government spending is due to a change in government purchases and not to a change in transfer payments. Stated differently, we assume that transfer payments are constant so that changes in government spending are a reflection of changes in government purchases only.

---

1. Remember from an earlier chapter that government purchases refer to the purchases of goods and services by government and all levels. Transfer payments are payments to persons that are not made in return for goods and services currently supplied. For example, Social Security payments are transfer payments.

Sidebar Definitions

Fiscal Policy
Changes in government expenditures and/or taxes to achieve particular economic goals, such as low unemployment, stable prices, and economic growth.

Budget Deficit
Government expenditures greater than tax revenues.

Budget Surplus
Tax revenues greater than government expenditures.

Balanced Budget
Government expenditures equal to tax revenues.

Expansionary Fiscal Policy
Increases in government expenditures and/or decreases in taxes to achieve particular economic goals.

Contractionary Fiscal Policy
Decreases in government expenditures and/or increases in taxes to achieve particular economic goals.

Discretionary Fiscal Policy
Deliberate changes of government expenditures and/or taxes to achieve particular economic goals.

Automatic Fiscal Policy
Changes in government expenditures and/or taxes that occur automatically without (additional) congressional action.

Everyday Life   Popular Culture   Technology   The World

JFK and the 1964 Tax Cut

In 1962, John F. Kennedy was president of the United States and Walter Heller was one of Kennedy's economic advisers. Heller told the president that the economy needed a tax cut (a form of expansionary fiscal policy) to keep it from sputtering. In December, in a speech before the Economic Club of New York, President Kennedy said, "An economy hampered by restrictive tax rates will never produce enough revenue to balance our budget just as it will never produce enough jobs or enough profits."

Then in January 1963, he said, "It has become increasingly clear that the largest single barrier to full employment . . . and to a higher rate of economic growth is the unrealistically heavy drag of federal income taxes on private purchasing power, initiative and incentive."

Kennedy proposed expansionary fiscal policy—in the form of a tax cut—to raise economic growth and lower the unemployment rate. He proposed lowering the top personal income tax rate, the bottom personal income tax rate, the corporate income tax, and the capital gains tax. He was assassinated in Dallas before Congress passed his tax program, but Congress did pass it. What was the result?

When the tax bill passed in 1964, the unemployment rate was 5.2 percent; in 1965, it was down to 4.5 percent; in 1966, it was down further, to 3.8 percent. The tax cut is widely credited with bringing the unemployment rate down.

As for economic growth, when the tax cut was passed in 1964, it was 5.8 percent; one year later, in 1965, the growth rate was up to 6.4 percent; and in 1966, the growth rate was even higher, at 6.6 percent. Again, the tax cut received much of the credit for stimulating economic growth.

DEMAND-SIDE FISCAL POLICY

Fiscal policy can affect the demand-side of the economy—that is, it can affect aggregate demand. This section focuses on how government spending and taxes can affect aggregate demand.

HOW DO CHANGES IN *G* AND *T* AFFECT AGGREGATE DEMAND?

Before discussing demand-side fiscal policy, we need to know how changes in government purchases (G) and taxes (T) affect aggregate demand. Recall from an earlier chapter that a change in consumption, investment, government purchases, or net exports can change aggregate demand and therefore shift the AD curve. For example, an increase in government purchases (G) increases aggregate demand and shifts the AD curve to the right. A decrease in G decreases aggregate demand and shifts the AD curve to the left.[2]

A change in taxes (T) can affect consumption or investment or both and therefore can affect aggregate demand. For example, a decrease in income taxes increases disposable (after-tax) income, which permits individuals to increase their consumption. As consumption rises, the AD curve shifts to the right. An increase in taxes decreases disposable income, lowers consumption, and shifts the AD curve to the left.

FISCAL POLICY: A KEYNESIAN PERSPECTIVE

In Exhibit 1a, the economy is initially in a recessionary gap at point 1. Aggregate demand is too low to move the economy to equilibrium at the Natural Real GDP level. The Keynesian prescription is to enact expansionary fiscal policy measures

http://

Go to *http://www.ism.ws*. Under the "ISM REPORT ON BUSINESS" menu, select "Overview of the PMI" and read the page. What is the PMI? How does the PMI indicate expansions and contractions of the economy? Now, select "PMI History." Is the U.S. economy currently in a contraction or an expansion? From a Keynesian perspective, what fiscal policy measures would be appropriate based on this information?

---

2. Later in this chapter, when we discuss crowding out, we question the effect of an increase in government purchases on aggregate demand.

| (a) | (b) |
| Expansionary Fiscal Policy for a Recessionary Gap | Contractionary Fiscal Policy for an Inflationary Gap |

exhibit 1

Fiscal Policy in Keynesian Theory: Ridding the Economy of Recessionary and Inflationary Gaps
(a) In Keynesian theory, expansionary fiscal policy eliminates a recessionary gap. Increased government purchases, decreased taxes, or both lead to a rightward shift in the aggregate demand curve from AD_1 to AD_2, restoring the economy to the natural level of Real GDP, Q_N. (b) Contractionary fiscal policy is used to eliminate an inflationary gap. Decreased government purchases, increased taxes, or both lead to a leftward shift in the aggregate demand curve from AD_1 to AD_2, restoring the economy to the natural level of Real GDP, Q_N.

Crowding Out
The decrease in private expenditures that occurs as a consequence of increased government spending or the financing needs of a budget deficit.

(an increase in government purchases or a decrease in taxes), to shift the aggregate demand curve rightward from AD_1 to AD_2 and move the economy to the Natural Real GDP level at point 2.

At this point someone might ask, Why not simply wait for the short-run aggregate supply curve to shift rightward and intersect the aggregate demand curve at point 2′? The Keynesians usually respond that (1) the economy is stuck at point 1 and won't move naturally to point 2′—perhaps the economy is stuck because wage rates won't fall; or (2) the short-run aggregate supply curve takes too long to shift rightward, and in the interim, we must deal with the high cost of unemployment and a lower level of Real GDP.

In Exhibit 1b, the economy is initially in an inflationary gap at point 1. In this situation, Keynesians are likely to propose a contractionary fiscal measure (a decrease in government purchases or an increase in taxes) to shift the aggregate demand curve leftward from AD_1 to AD_2 and move the economy to point 2.

In Exhibit 1, fiscal policy has worked as intended. In (a), the economy was in a recessionary gap and expansionary fiscal policy eliminated the recessionary gap. In (b), the economy was in an inflationary gap and contractionary fiscal policy eliminated the inflationary gap. In (a) and (b), fiscal policy is at its best: working as intended.

CROWDING OUT: QUESTIONING THE EFFECTIVENESS OF FISCAL POLICY

Not all economists believe that fiscal policy works the way we have described. Some economists bring up the subject of *crowding out*. **Crowding out** refers to a decrease in private expenditures (consumption, investment, and so on) that occurs as a consequence of increased government spending or the financing needs of a budget deficit.

Two examples of crowding out are:

1. The government spends more on public libraries, and individuals buy fewer books at bookstores.[3]
2. The government spends more on social programs and defense without increasing taxes; as a result, the size of the budget deficit increases. Consequently, the government must borrow more funds to finance the larger deficit. This

---

3. We are not saying that if the government spends more on public libraries, individuals will necessarily buy fewer books at bookstores; rather, if they do, this would be an example of crowding out. The same holds for example 2.

increase in borrowing causes the demand for credit (or demand for loanable funds) to rise, which, in turn, causes the interest rate to rise. As a result, investment drops.

Analysis of the First Example

Let's consider our first example in which the government spends more on public libraries. To be specific, let's say that the government spends $2 billion more on public libraries. Suppose that after the government has spent $2 billion more on public libraries, consumers choose to spend not one dollar less on books at bookstores. Obviously, then, there is no crowding out, or *zero crowding out*.

Now, suppose that after the government has spent $2 billion more on public libraries, consumers choose to spend $2 billion less on books at bookstores. Obviously, crowding out exists and the degree of crowding out is dollar for dollar. When one dollar of government spending offsets one dollar of private spending, **complete crowding out** is said to exist.

Finally, suppose that after the government has spent $2 billion more on public libraries, consumers end up spending $1.2 billion less on books at bookstores. Again, there is crowding out, but it is not dollar-for-dollar crowding out; it is not complete crowding out. In this case, incomplete crowding out exists. **Incomplete crowding out** occurs when the decrease in one or more components of private spending only partially offsets the increase in government spending.

The following table summarizes the different types of crowding out outlined in our discussion of the first example.

Type of Crowding Out	Example
Zero crowding out (sometimes called "no crowding out")	Government spends $2 billion more, and private sector spending stays constant.
Complete crowding out	Government spends $2 billion more, and private sector spends $2 billion less.
Incomplete crowding out	Government spends $2 billion more, and private sector spends $1.2 billion less.

If *complete* or *incomplete crowding out* occurs, it follows that expansionary fiscal policy will have less impact on aggregate demand and Real GDP than Keynesian theory predicts. Let's look at the graphical representation of crowding out.

Exhibit 2 illustrates the consequences of complete and incomplete crowding out. For comparison, the exhibit also includes the case in Keynesian theory where there is zero crowding out.

Complete Crowding Out
A decrease in one or more components of private spending completely offsets the increase in government spending.

Incomplete Crowding Out
The decrease in one or more components of private spending only partially offsets the increase in government spending.

exhibit 2

Zero (No), Incomplete, and Complete Crowding Out
The effects of zero, incomplete, and complete crowding out in the AD-AS framework. Starting at point 1, expansionary fiscal policy shifts the aggregate demand curve to AD_2 and moves the economy to point 2 and Q_N. The Keynesian theory that predicts this outcome assumes zero, or no, crowding out; an increase in, say, government spending does not reduce private expenditures. With incomplete crowding out, an increase in government spending causes private expenditures to decrease by less than the increase in government spending. The net result is a shift in the aggregate demand curve to AD_2'. The economy moves to point 2' and Q_2'. With complete crowding out, an increase in government spending is completely offset by a decrease in private expenditures, and the net result is that aggregate demand does not increase at all. The economy remains at point 1 and Q_1.

ECONOMICS IN...

Popular Culture   Technology   Everyday Life   The World

Harry Potter

The blockbuster movie *Harry Potter and the Sorcerer's Stone* was released on Friday, November 16, 2001. In that first weekend, it earned a whopping $90 million.

As movie releases go, $90 million is an extraordinarily large dollar amount. Some people said this dollar amount indicated that the public was spending more money on going to the movies.

But is this necessarily true? Certainly it doesn't have to be. There may be such a thing as "movie crowding out."

To illustrate, we assume the movie-going public spends $70 million each weekend on ten movies. Let's say this dollar amount is evenly distributed across all ten movies so that each movie earns $7 million. A blockbuster movie may simply have a larger share of the $70 million pie. The blockbuster may earn, say, $20 million and the nine remaining movies evenly divide the remaining $50 million. In other words, spending on the blockbuster comes at the expense of other movies on a dollar-for-dollar basis. Blockbuster spending crowds out non-

blockbuster spending much the same way that government spending can crowd out household spending.

Movie crowding out could also work another way. It could be that because of the blockbuster, total spending on movies rises when the blockbuster is released. In other words, the movie-going public increases the amount it spends on movies in the first few weekends after a blockbuster is released. Thus, spending may rise to, say, $100 million each weekend for three consecutive weekends after the release of a blockbuster. But, then, the "blockbuster effect" fades away and spending on movies falls below the usual $70 million per weekend. It may fall to, say, $50 million per weekend for a few weekends. Blockbuster spending has still "crowded out" nonblockbuster spending, although it doesn't do it so quickly as in the first case.

There is also a related issue. It could be that a blockbuster doesn't crowd out other movie spending, but does crowd out non-movie spending. To illustrate, suppose because of a blockbuster, spending on movies actually does rise (over a year). The new average goes from $70 million each weekend to, say, $80 million. But because people are spending more on movies, they spend less on other things. In other words, "movie spending" crowds out "non-movie spending." People end up spending less on books, restaurant meals, clothes, and so on. One sector of the economy (the movie sector) expands as another contracts.

As we discuss Exhibit 2, keep in mind the three possibilities concerning crowding out:

- Zero crowding out (no crowding out)
- Incomplete crowding out
- Complete crowding out

In Exhibit 2, the economy is initially at point 1, with Real GDP at Q_1. In Keynesian theory, expansionary fiscal policy shifts the aggregate demand curve to AD_2 and moves the economy to point 2. Among other things, this implicitly assumes there is zero crowding out (or no crowding out). Notice that Real GDP has increased from Q_1 to Q_N. It follows that the unemployment rate will fall from its level at Q_1 to a lower level at Q_N. Summary: If there is no crowding out, expansionary fiscal policy increases Real GDP and lowers the unemployment rate.

With incomplete crowding out, the aggregate demand curve only shifts (on net) to AD_2' because the initial stimulus in aggregate demand due to increased government spending is *partially offset* by a fall in private expenditures. The economy moves to point 2'. Notice that Real GDP has increased from Q_1 to Q_2'. It follows that the unemployment rate will fall from what it was at Q_1 to what it

A Closer Look

```
Government spending increases. → Did the increased government spending cause private spending to fall?
    → Yes → Did private spending fall less than or equal to the amount government spending increased?
        → Less than → There is incomplete crowding out. → AD increases, but not as much as for zero crowding out. Real GDP increases, but not as much as for zero crowding out. The unemployment rate drops, but not as much as for zero crowding out.
        → Equal to → There is complete crowding out. → AD does not change at all. Real GDP and the unemployment rate do not change at all.
    → No → There is zero crowding out and AD increases. Real GDP increases and the unemployment rate decreases.
```

exhibit 3

Expansionary Fiscal Policy (Government Spending Increases), Crowding Out, and Changes in Real GDP and the Unemployment Rate

is at Q_2'. But also notice that the changes in both Real GDP and the unemployment rate are smaller with incomplete crowding out than they are with zero crowding out. Summary: If there is incomplete crowding out, expansionary fiscal policy increases Real GDP and lowers the unemployment rate, but not as much as if there is zero crowding out.

In the case of complete crowding out, the initial stimulus in aggregate demand due to increased government spending is *completely offset* by a fall in private expenditures and the aggregate demand curve does not move (on net) at all. Notice that Real GDP does not change, and neither does the unemployment rate. Summary: If there is complete crowding out, expansionary fiscal policy has no effect on the economy. The economy remains at point 1.

See Exhibit 3 for a summary flow chart of the different types of crowding out.

Analysis of the Second Example

Let's look at our second example of crowding out. Assume the federal budget is currently in deficit. Government increases its spending without raising taxes, so the deficit becomes larger. As a consequence of the larger deficit, the government needs to borrow more funds. Therefore, the demand for credit (or demand for loanable funds) increases. In turn, this raises the interest rate and causes investment spending to decline. Thus, there is crowding out.

At this point, some economists suggest part of the story may have been left out. They ask, Will there be less crowding out if the *higher* interest rate attracts loanable funds from abroad? Many economists argue that foreigners in search of the highest rates of return (actually, the highest after-tax real returns) will help finance the deficit by lending funds to the federal government through their purchases of U.S. Treasury securities. This action increases the supply of credit (or the supply of loanable funds) and keeps the interest rate from rising, or from rising as much.

How does the inflow of foreign funds affect crowding out? At first glance, the foreign funds might appear to moderate the crowding-out effect because they dampen the increase in the interest rate and thus the fall in investment.

But a closer look is required. Before foreigners buy U.S. Treasury securities, they must exchange their domestic currency for U.S. dollars. This action increases the demand, and price, of U.S. dollars in the foreign exchange market. In short, the dollar will appreciate in value relative to other currencies.

In turn, this will make foreign goods cheaper for Americans and American goods more expensive for foreigners. Economists predict that Americans will import more and export less. We conclude that some of the crowding out of private expenditures will come in the form of a decrease in net exports.

Q & A

Q: Does it follow that an increase in the size of a federal budget deficit can affect U.S. international trade?

A: Yes. To explain more fully, the United States is said to have a **trade deficit** if the value of its exports is less than the value of its imports. Let's suppose that the United States currently has a budget deficit of $30 billion and a trade deficit of $100 billion. If the government increases spending but does not raise taxes, the budget deficit gets bigger.

Consequently, the U.S. Treasury demands more funds in the credit market and the interest rate rises. Then, as we said, the higher interest rate causes foreign lenders to purchase interest-paying U.S. Treasury securities. To buy the securities, foreigners increase their demand for U.S. dollars; thus, the dollar appreciates in value relative to foreign currencies.

This makes foreign goods cheaper for Americans and American goods more expensive for foreigners. Americans import more and export less, thus widening the trade deficit beyond the original $100 billion. In this way, a bigger budget deficit can lead to a bigger trade deficit.

Q & A

Q: It appears that increased government spending can crowd out investment, consumption, and net exports. In other words, if government spending increases by, say, $100 billion, investment may go down by $30 billion, consumption may fall by $60 billion, and net exports may decrease by $10 billion. The sum of the spending in the private sector (by the household, business, and foreign sectors) goes down as a result of government spending going up. Is this an accurate description of what can happen?

A: Yes, it is. An increase in government spending can lead to declines in consumption, investment, and net exports. The real question, though, is *how much* they decline. In other words, is there complete crowding out or incomplete crowding out? And if it is the latter, how much is it? Is it a decline of 10 cents in private spending for every additional $1 spent by government, or is it a decline of 90 cents in private spending for every additional $1 spent by government?

THINKING LIKE AN ECONOMIST

Economic changes, like a stone thrown into a lake, often have a ripple effect. We have just seen how an increase in government spending can affect (1) a budget deficit, (2) interest rates, (3) the value of the dollar relative to other currencies, (4) the purchases of both foreigners and Americans, and (5) the U.S. trade deficit. These are quite a few ripples, and there are plenty more that we have not discussed. The economic way of thinking takes the ripple effect into account: A change over here brings about a change way over there.

The laws of economics do not take notice of a nation's borders. Economic effects do not ripple outward until they reach a national frontier and then stop; instead, they may be worldwide in scope. This is where the political and economic ways of thinking differ. Political thinking views the world as composed of hundreds of sovereign nations; economic thinking views the world as essentially one country.

Trade Deficit
The situation where the value of exports is less than the value of imports.

The New Classical View of Fiscal Policy

Our examples and analysis of crowding out consider both direct substitution and indirect effects. In the first example, crowding out is a result of individuals thinking along this line: "Government has increased its spending on books for public libraries, so I'll decrease my private spending on books because I can get them from the library."

In the second example, business owners and managers are thinking this way: "The interest rate has gone up (as a result of increased financing needs related to the deficit), so we'll reduce investment." Here, then, are two ways of understanding individuals' motives behind the crowding-out phenomenon.

The new classical school of economics proposes another way of looking at what people may do. These economists believe that individuals respond to expansionary fiscal policy, a larger deficit, and greater deficit-financing requirements by thinking the following: "A larger deficit implies more debt this year and higher future taxes. I'll simply save more in the present so I can pay the higher future taxes required to pay interest and to repay principal on the new debt. But, of course, if I'm going to save more, I have to consume less."

Thus, new classical economists offer a few predictions:

1. **Current consumption will fall as a result of expansionary fiscal policy.** How so? Again, an increase in government spending that increases the deficit and the amount of debt financing will cause individuals to save more (consume less) to prepare for higher future taxes.

2. **Deficits do not necessarily bring higher interest rates.** The reason is simple: A deficit simply means less tax to pay today and more tax to pay in the future. Knowing this, individuals save more to pay their higher future taxes. The increased saving increases the supply of credit (or supply of loanable funds) and offsets the increased demand for credit that is a consequence of the need to finance the deficit.

These two new classical predictions are illustrated in Exhibit 4. In part (a), the economy is initially at point 1. If individuals do not anticipate higher future

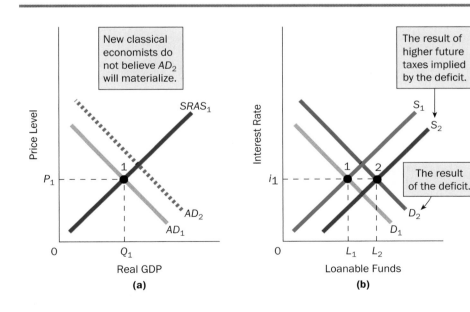

(a)

(b)

exhibit 4

The New Classical View of Expansionary Fiscal Policy
New classical economists argue that individuals will link expansionary fiscal policy to higher future taxes and decrease their current consumption and increase their saving as a result. (a) The decreased consumption prevents the aggregate demand curve from shifting rightward from AD_1 to AD_2. (b) The increased saving causes the supply of credit (or supply of loanable funds) to shift rightward from S_1 to S_2, thus offsetting the increased demand for credit (or demand for loanable funds) and maintaining the existing level of interest rates. The new classical position on both (anticipated) expansionary and contractionary fiscal policy is that neither affects Real GDP, unemployment, the price level, or interest rates.

taxes as a result of expansionary fiscal policy, the aggregate demand curve will shift rightward from AD_1 to AD_2.

However, new classical economists believe that individuals will anticipate higher future taxes and will therefore reduce their consumption (and increase their saving) to pay those taxes. In this case, the aggregate demand curve does not shift at all. What is the conclusion? Given the condition of anticipated higher future taxes, expansionary fiscal policy leaves Real GDP, unemployment, and the price level unchanged. Expansionary fiscal policy is not stimulative—it is not effective at increasing Real GDP and lowering the unemployment rate.

In part (b), the credit market is initially in equilibrium at point 1 and the interest rate is i_1. The result of the government implementing an expansionary fiscal policy measure is a deficit. The deficit requires financing, so the demand for credit (or demand for loanable funds) shifts rightward from D_1 to D_2. At the same time, individuals perceive the deficit in terms of higher future taxes and increase their saving by enough to offset those taxes. This action shifts the supply of credit (or supply of loanable funds) from S_1 to S_2. What is the conclusion? The interest rate does not change.

The new classical position on expansionary fiscal policy may be summarized as follows: As long as expansionary fiscal policy is translated into higher future taxes (which new classical economists think is likely), there will be no change in Real GDP, unemployment, the price level, or interest rates. The analysis also holds for contractionary fiscal policy.

Q & A

Q: It seems unlikely that people will save enough to offset their higher future taxes completely because many people won't live long enough to pay the higher taxes. Won't some simply say: "I'd rather have a government deficit and lower taxes now because when the higher taxes roll around, I won't be here. Future taxpayers will have to pay for the increased government spending that I enjoyed."

In other words, if people assume they won't be paying the future taxes, they will have no reason to save more. Have the new classical economists thought of this?

A: They have. One new classical economist, Robert Barro, points out that individuals leave bequests to their children, implying that they care about their children's welfare and, indirectly, about the tax burden their children will one day face. He argues that today's taxpayers will react to an increased budget deficit by increasing their saving in order to leave more to their children, who will pay the higher future taxes.

LAGS AND FISCAL POLICY

Suppose we proved, beyond a shadow of a doubt, that there is no, or zero, crowding out. Would it then hold that fiscal policy should be used to solve the problems of inflationary and recessionary gaps? Many economists would answer "not necessarily." The reason is that *lags* exist. There are five types of lags:

1. **The data lag.** Policymakers are not aware of changes in the economy as soon as they happen. For example, if the economy turns down in January, the decline may not be apparent for two to three months.
2. **The wait-and-see lag.** After policymakers are aware of a downturn in economic activity, they rarely enact counteractive measures immediately. Instead, they usually adopt a more cautious, wait-and-see attitude. They want to be sure that the observed events are not just a short-run phenomenon.
3. **The legislative lag.** After policymakers decide that some type of fiscal policy measure is required, Congress or the president will have to propose the measure, build political support for it, and get it passed. This can take many months.
4. **The transmission lag.** After enacted, a fiscal policy measure takes time to be put into effect. For example, a discretionary expansionary fiscal policy measure mandating increased spending for public works projects will require

construction companies to submit bids for the work, prepare designs, negotiate contracts, and so on.

5. **The effectiveness lag.** After a policy measure is actually implemented, it takes
   time to affect the economy. If government spending is increased on Monday,
   the aggregate demand curve does not shift rightward on Tuesday.

Taking these five lags together, some economists argue that discretionary fiscal policy is not likely to have the impact on the economy that policymakers
hope. By the time the full impact of the policy is felt, the economic problem it
was designed to solve (1) may no longer exist, (2) may not exist to the degree it
once did, or (3) may have changed altogether. Exhibit 5 illustrates the effect of
lags. Suppose the economy is currently in a recessionary gap at point 1. The
recession is under way before government officials recognize it. After it is recog-
nized, however, Congress and the President consider enacting expansionary fiscal
policy in the hope of shifting the AD curve from AD_1 to AD_2 so it will intersect the
$SRAS$ curve at point 1', at Natural Real GDP.

But in the interim, unknown to everybody, the economy is "healing" or regulating itself: The $SRAS$ curve is shifting to the right. Government officials don't see
this change because it takes time to collect and analyze data about the economy.

Thinking that the economy is not healing itself or not healing itself quickly
enough, the government enacts expansionary fiscal policy. In time, the AD curve
shifts rightward. But by the time the increased demand is felt in the goods and
services market, the AD curve intersects the $SRAS$ curve at point 2. In short, the
government has moved the economy from point 1 to point 2, and not, as it had
hoped, from point 1 to point 1'. The government has moved the economy into an
inflationary gap. Instead of stabilizing and moderating the ups and downs in economic activity (the business cycle), the government has intensified the fluctuations.

CROWDING OUT, LAGS, AND THE EFFECTIVENESS OF FISCAL POLICY

Those economists who believe there is zero crowding out and that lags are insignif-
icant conclude that fiscal policy is effective at moving the economy out of a recessionary gap. Those economists who believe crowding out is complete and/or that
lags are significant conclude that fiscal policy is ineffective at moving the economy

http://

Go to *http://www.whitehouse.gov/
OMB/budget*. When was the most
recent budget submitted by the President to Congress? When does it take
effect? How long does this make the
legislative lag under normal circumstances? If a recession starts during
the summer and the President waits
until the next regular budget submission
to propose policy to deal with it, how
long would it be until his proposals are
submitted? How long until they would
go into effect?

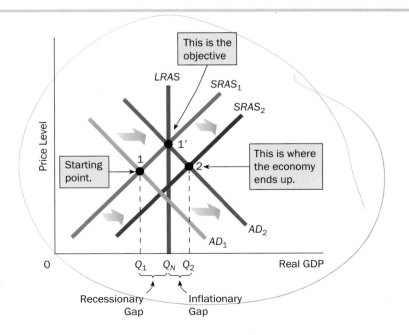

exhibit 5

**Fiscal Policy May Destabilize
the Economy**
In this scenario, the *SRAS* curve is
shifting rightward (healing the economy of its recessionary gap), but this
information is unknown to policymakers.
Policymakers implement expansionary
fiscal policy, and the *AD* curve ends
up intersecting *SRAS*$_2$ at point 2
instead of intersecting *SRAS*$_1$ at point
1'. Policymakers thereby move the
economy into an inflationary gap, thus
destabilizing the economy.

out of a recessionary gap. Keynesians usually view fiscal policy as effective, and monetarists and new classical economists usually view it as ineffective.

INCOMPLETE INFORMATION

The last chapter introduces a simple Keynesian model in which prices are constant and the *AS* curve is horizontal. Let's return to that model to discuss a few last important things about demand-side fiscal policy.

Suppose, as shown in Exhibit 6, the economy is producing Q_1. Since Q_1 is less than Q_N, the economy is in a recessionary gap. An economist advocates the use of expansionary fiscal policy in order to raise aggregate demand so that the *AD* curve shifts right from AD_1 to AD_2.

Now let's assume there are no lags and zero (no) crowding out. It would seem that under these conditions, expansionary fiscal policy—either increasing government spending or cutting taxes—will work at removing the economy from a recessionary gap. We consider both types of expansionary fiscal policy.

Increasing Government Spending

What information does government need to know in order to use the expansionary fiscal policy of increasing government spending effectively? To find out, let's go back to an equation from the last chapter:

$$\Delta \text{Real GDP} = m \times \Delta \text{Autonomous spending}$$

where *m* stands for the multiplier.

Rearranging terms,

$$\Delta \text{Autonomous spending} = \frac{\Delta \text{Real GDP}}{m}$$

exhibit 6

Will Fiscal Policy Be Effective?
The exhibit shows the economy in terms of the Keynesian model introduced in the last chapter. Prices are constant and the *AS* curve is horizontal. The economy is at Q_1 in a recessionary gap. Will expansionary fiscal policy be effective at removing the economy from the recessionary gap and moving it to producing its Natural Real GDP, Q_N? Suppose there are no lags and zero (no) crowding out. It would seem that under these conditions, fiscal policy has a chance at being effective. But still there are problems. Government will have to know the dollar difference between Q_1 and Q_N and it will have to know the *MPC*. With this kind of information, expansionary fiscal policy will be effective; without it, expansionary fiscal policy may not have the intended effect.

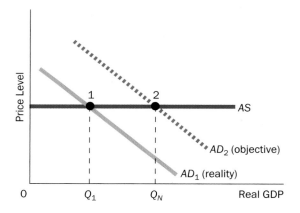

$$\Delta \text{Real GDP} = m \times \Delta \text{Autonomous government spending}$$

$$\Delta \text{Autonomous government spending} = \frac{\Delta \text{Real GDP}}{m}$$

$$\Delta \text{Real GDP} = -(MPC)(m) \times \Delta T$$

$$\Delta T = -\frac{\Delta \text{Real GDP}}{(MPC)(m)}$$

Thus, in order to know *how much* to increase spending, government has to know (1) how much Real GDP should increase and (2) the value of the multiplier.

How much Real GDP should change is the dollar difference between Q_N and Q_1. While the government may know what Q_1 is, economists sometimes differ as to what Q_N equals. This is because they sometimes differ as to what the natural unemployment rate is. Is it 4.0 percent, 4.5 percent, or 5.0 percent?

Now, let's consider the multiplier. From the last chapter, we know that, given the conditions we specified (prices constant, no foreign sector, and so on), the multiplier is equal to $1/(1-MPC)$. It is obvious that in order to know the multiplier, government must know the *MPC*. Is it 0.60, 0.70, 0.80, or some other value? The actual value matters because if government estimates the *MPC* too low, then the multiplier will be less than it should be. Then, government will raise spending too much and instead of hitting its Q_N target, it will go past it (from a recessionary gap to an inflationary gap).

We conclude: If government knows the difference between Q_1 and Q_N (so that it knows how much to change Real GDP) and it knows the *MPC*, then it can use fiscal policy to get the economy out of a recessionary gap and producing Natural Real GDP. To illustrate, suppose the difference between Q_1 and Q_N is $1,400 billion and the *MPC* is 0.80. This means the multiplier is 5. Then government can simply solve the previous equation:

$$\Delta\text{Autonomous government spending} = \frac{\$1,400 \text{ billion}}{5} = \$280 \text{ billion}$$

In other words, if the government simply raises its purchases by $280 billion, the recessionary gap will soon vanish and the economy will be producing Q_N or Natural Real GDP. But, again, look at the information that the government has to know. If it doesn't know the actual *MPC* and it doesn't know the actual difference between Q_1 and Q_N—in other words, if the government has *incomplete information*—then fiscal policy isn't likely to work as intended.

Tax Cuts Instead: Are Things Any Different?

Are things any different if the government wants to use tax cuts as its expansionary fiscal policy measure instead of raising its spending? The information needs of the government are the same; the only difference is the equation the government uses to determine how much it should cut taxes. The equation is:

$$\Delta\text{Real GDP} = -(MPC)(m) \times \Delta T$$

Rearranging terms,

$$\Delta T = -\frac{\Delta\text{Real GDP}}{(MPC)(m)}$$

Let's use the same numbers as before to see by how much government should cut taxes.

$$\Delta T = -\frac{\$1,400 \text{ billion}}{(0.80)(5)}$$
$$= -\frac{\$1,400 \text{ billion}}{4}$$
$$= -\$350 \text{ billion}$$

The change in taxes is a negative number because taxes are to be reduced.

Notice that to get Real GDP to rise by $1,400 billion (under the conditions specified) government has to cut taxes $350 billion or raise government purchases by $280 billion. Why does it have to cut taxes by a greater amount than it has to

ECONOMICS IN...

The Politics of Fiscal Policy

Suppose the economy is in a recessionary gap and the president and Congress agree to enact some form of expansionary fiscal policy. Will they do so simply and easily? Not usually. Agreeing to enact expansionary fiscal policy is usually easy. However, agreeing to the *specifics* of the expansionary fiscal policy is usually hard. Why? Because of politics. Let's look at some of the ways politics can make agreement difficult when trying to determine the specifics of expansionary fiscal policy.

First, will the expansionary fiscal policy take the form of only tax cuts, only government spending increases, or some combination of a tax cut and a spending increase? In late 2001, Congress and President Bush were debating an expansionary fiscal policy package ("fiscal stimulus"). President Bush initially stressed tax cuts; much of Congress initially stressed increases in government spending.

Second, suppose that after some debate, Congress and the President eventually agree to some combination of tax cuts and spending increases. Still they could differ as to which taxes are to be cut and by how much. This difference in opinion might exist between the president and Congress or between various members of Congress. For example, if we again return to late 2001, some members of Congress were calling for general, across-the-board tax cuts while other members of Congress were calling for targeted tax cuts—that is, tax cuts targeted toward certain types of companies in certain industries or toward certain income groups.

Congress and the president could also disagree about where the money should be spent. Just because there is agreement to raise government spending by, say, $100 billion, it doesn't follow that there will be easy agreement on how to spend the $100 billion. Should more money be spent on health care or on education? Should more money be spent on national defense or on the country's infrastructure?

---

increase purchases in order to get the same result? Here's what some economists say: When government purchases increase, 100 percent of every extra dollar goes to increase total spending in the economy. But when taxes are decreased, households experience an increase in disposable income. They end up spending part of the tax cut and saving the rest. The amount saved depends on the marginal propensity to save. For example, if the marginal propensity to save is 0.20 (and the $MPC = 0.80$), then 20 percent of each tax dollar reduction is saved and the remainder is consumed, which in turn increases aggregate demand. What do we conclude? A dollar spent by government is a dollar spent; a dollar tax cut is a dollar partly saved and partly spent. So, in order get the same change in Real GDP, government has to cut taxes more than it has to raise its purchases.

Self-Test *(Answers to Self-Test questions are in the Self-Test Appendix).*

1. How does crowding out question the effectiveness of expansionary demand-side fiscal policy?

2. Do budget deficits raise interest rates?

3. How can an increase in the size of the federal budget deficit affect the trade deficit?

SUPPLY-SIDE FISCAL POLICY

Fiscal policy effects may be felt on the supply side as well as on the demand side of the economy. For example, a reduction in tax rates may alter an individual's incentive to work and produce, thus altering aggregate supply.

MARGINAL TAX RATES AND AGGREGATE SUPPLY

When fiscal policy measures affect tax rates, they may affect both aggregate supply and aggregate demand. Consider a reduction in an individual's marginal tax rate. The **marginal (income) tax rate** is equal to the change in a person's tax payment divided by the change in the person's taxable income.

$$\text{Marginal tax rate} = \Delta\text{Tax payment}/\Delta\text{Taxable income}$$

For example, if Serena's taxable income increases by $1 and her tax payment increases by $0.28, her marginal tax rate is 28 percent; if her taxable income increases by $1 and her tax payment increases by $0.36, then her marginal tax rate is 36 percent.

All other things held constant, lower marginal tax rates increase the incentive to engage in productive activities (work) relative to leisure and tax-avoidance activities. As resources shift from leisure to work, short-run aggregate supply increases. If the lower marginal tax rates are permanent and not simply a one-shot affair, most economists predict that not only will the short-run aggregate supply curve shift rightward but the long-run aggregate supply curve will shift rightward too. Exhibit 7 illustrates the predicted effect of a permanent marginal tax rate cut on aggregate supply.

Marginal (Income) Tax Rate
The change in a person's tax payment divided by the change in the person's taxable income: ΔTax payment/ΔTaxable income.

Q & A

Q: Why will individuals want to work more and have less leisure time if marginal tax rates are reduced? Won't they want to do the opposite? After all, lower marginal tax rates will leave individuals with higher disposable incomes, and therefore they will have less need to work.

A: What we actually have here are two forces pulling in opposite directions. Given a cut in marginal tax rates, two things will happen: (1) Individuals will have more disposable income. (2) The amount of money they can earn (and keep) by working increases. As a result of effect 2, individuals will choose to work more. (Would you want to work more or fewer hours if you could keep 90 cents out of every dollar earned as opposed to, say, 50 cents?) As a result of effect 1, individuals will choose to work less. Whether an individual works more or less on net depends on whether effect 1 or effect 2 is stronger. If effect 2 is stronger than effect 1, the individual (on net) will work more; if effect 1 is stronger than effect 2, the individual (on net) will work less. In the analysis of marginal tax rates and aggregate supply, we implicitly assume that in the aggregate, a marginal tax rate cut (on net) increases work activity.[4]

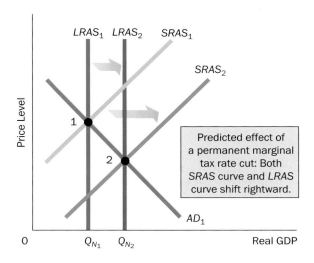

exhibit 7

The Predicted Effect of a Permanent Marginal Tax Rate Cut on Aggregate Supply
A cut in marginal tax rates increases the attractiveness of productive activity relative to leisure and tax-avoidance activities and shifts resources from the latter to the former, thus shifting rightward both the short-run and the long-run aggregate supply curves.

---

4. Students of microeconomics will recognize "effect 1" as the income effect and "effect 2" as the substitution effect.

THE LAFFER CURVE: TAX RATES AND TAX REVENUES

High tax rates are followed by attempts of ingenious men to beat them as surely as snow is followed by little boys on sleds.

—Arthur Okun, economist, 1928–1980

If (marginal) income tax rates are reduced, will income tax revenues increase or decrease? Most people think the answer is obvious—lower tax rates mean lower tax revenues. The economist Arthur Laffer explained why this may not be the case.

As the story is told, Laffer, while dining with a journalist at a restaurant in Washington, D.C., drew the curve in Exhibit 8 on a napkin. The curve came to be known as the **Laffer curve.** Laffer's objective was to explain the different possible relationships between tax rates and tax revenues.

In the exhibit, tax revenues are on the vertical axis and tax rates are on the horizontal axis. Laffer made three major points using the curve:

1. There are two (marginal) tax rates at which zero tax revenues will be collected— 0 percent and 100 percent. Obviously, no tax revenues will be raised if the tax rate is zero; and if the tax rate is 100 percent, no one will work and earn income because the entire amount would be taxed away.
2. An increase in tax rates could cause tax revenues to increase. For example, an increase in tax rates from X percent to Y percent (see the exhibit) will increase tax revenues from T_X to T_Y.
3. A decrease in tax rates could cause tax revenues to increase. For example, a decrease in tax rates from Z percent to Y percent will increase tax revenues from T_Z to T_Y (see the exhibit). This was the point that brought public attention to the Laffer curve.

How can an *increase* in tax rates and a *decrease* in tax rates at different times both increase tax revenues? This can happen because of the interrelationship of tax rates, the **tax base,** and tax revenues.

Tax revenues equal the tax base times the (average) tax rate:[5]

$$\text{Tax revenues} = \text{Tax base} \times \text{(average) Tax rate}$$

exhibit 8

The Laffer Curve
When the tax rate is either 0 or 100 percent, tax revenues are zero. Starting from a zero tax rate, increases in tax rates first increase (region A to B) and then decrease (region B to C) tax revenues. Starting from a 100 percent tax rate, decreases in tax rates first increase tax revenues (region C to B) and then decrease tax revenues (region B to A). This suggests there is some tax rate that maximizes tax revenues.

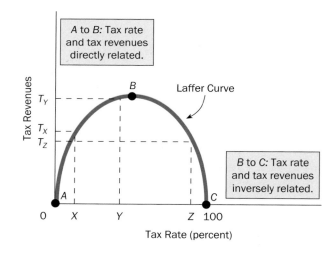

A to B: Tax rate and tax revenues directly related.

Laffer Curve

B to C: Tax rate and tax revenues inversely related.

Tax Revenues : T_Y, T_X, T_Z

Tax Rate (percent): 0, X, Y, Z, 100

5. First, the average tax rate is equal to an individual's tax payment divided by his or her taxable income (tax payment/taxable income). Second, a lower average tax rate requires a lower marginal tax rate. This follows from the average-marginal rule, which states that if the marginal magnitude is below the average magnitude, then the average is pulled down; if the marginal is above the average, the average is pulled up. Simply put, if an individual pays less tax on an additional taxable dollar (which is evidence of a marginal tax rate reduction), then his or her average tax naturally falls.

Popular Culture Technology Everyday Life The World

Does Mick Jagger Care about Taxes?

In 1987, Arthur Laffer was asked how he defined supply-side economics. He answered:

Supply-side economics is the economics of incentives. Very simply, people like doing things they find attractive, and they are repelled by things they find unattractive. The basic notion here is that the government can, through its policies, affect the attractiveness of activities. For example, when you tax an activity, you make it less attractive and people do less of it . . .[6]

With Laffer's words as background, let's see how taxes affected the behavior of the Rolling Stones.

In 1977, the government of the United Kingdom passed into law the Foreign Earnings Deduction.[7] As a result, British citizens living and working in foreign countries did not have to pay British income taxes as long as they didn't spend more than 62 days in the U.K.

In 1998, the Rolling Stones, one of the most famous rock bands in history, were on a world tour. They were scheduled to play four dates in the United Kingdom. Ordinarily, they wouldn't have had to pay British taxes on their world tour

earnings because of the Foreign Earnings Deduction. However, the deduction had been repealed in 1998 because it had increasingly come to be seen as a "giveaway" to the rich. As a result of the elimination of the deduction, the Rolling Stones would have to pay $20 million in British taxes if they played their four U.K. dates. If they were forced to pay these taxes, the entire world tour would have taken a loss.

Mick Jagger, lead singer for the Stones, said that the band would play the four U.K. dates for charity if they could have the tax deduction. His request was denied. As a result, the four dates were canceled.

Do taxes act as disincentives that affect behavior? Well, they certainly affected the behavior of the Rolling Stones.

For example, a tax rate of 20 percent multiplied by a tax base of $100 billion generates $20 billion of tax revenues.

Now, obviously, tax revenues are a function of two variables: (1) the tax rate and (2) the tax base. Whether tax revenues increase or decrease as the average tax rate is lowered depends on whether the tax base expands by a greater or lesser percentage than the percentage reduction in the tax rate. Exhibit 9 illustrates the point.

We start with a tax rate of 20 percent, a tax base of $100 billion, and tax revenues of $20 billion. We assume that as the tax rate is reduced, the tax base expands: The rationale is that individuals work more, invest more, enter into more trades, and shelter less income from taxes at lower tax rates.

However, the real question is: *How much* does the tax base expand following the tax rate reduction? Suppose the tax rate in Exhibit 9 is reduced to 15 percent. In Case 1, this increases the tax base to $120 billion: A 25 percent decrease in the tax rate (from 20 to 15 percent) causes a 20 percent increase in the tax base (from $100 billion to $120 billion). Tax revenues drop to $18 billion. In Case 2, the tax base expands by 50 percent to $150 billion. Because the tax base increases by a greater percentage than the percentage decrease in the tax rate, tax revenues increase (to $22.5 billion).

---

6. Roger A. Arnold, *Economics* (St. Paul, Minnesota: West Publishing Company, 1989), 384.

7. This feature is adapted from "The Jagger Curve," an editorial in the *Wall Street Journal,* 9 June 1998.

	(1) Tax Rate	(2) Tax Base	(3) Tax Revenues (1) × (2)	Summary	
Start with:	20%	$100	$20	—	
Case 1:	15	120	18	↓Tax rate	↓Tax revenues
Case 2:	15	150	22.5	↓Tax rate	↑Tax revenues

exhibit 9

Tax Rates, the Tax Base, and Tax Revenues

Tax revenues equal the tax base times the (average) tax rate. If the percentage reduction in the tax rate is greater than the percentage increase in the tax base, tax revenues decrease (Case 1). If the percentage reduction in the tax rate is less than the percentage increase in the tax base, tax revenues increase (Case 2). All numbers are in billions of dollars.

Of course, either case is possible. In the Laffer curve, tax revenues increase if a tax rate reduction is made in the downward-sloping portion of the curve (between points *B* and *C* in Exhibit 8); tax revenues decrease following a tax rate reduction in the upward-sloping portion of the curve (between points *A* and *B*).

Q: Suppose a country's income tax rate is 40 percent. Would it follow that a reduction in the tax rate to 35 percent would increase tax revenues?

A: It would depend on whether the 40 percent tax rate was in the downward-sloping portion of the Laffer curve (between points *B* and *C* in Exhibit 8) or in the upward-sloping portion (between points *A* and *B*). If the former, then tax revenues would increase; if the latter, then tax revenues would decrease. This is largely an empirical issue. We say "largely" because most economists believe it is obvious that a tax rate reduction from an extreme 100 percent to some lower rate will increase tax revenues.

THINKING LIKE AN ECONOMIST

Contrast the way economist Laffer thinks about a tax cut with the way the layperson thinks about it. As we said earlier, the layperson probably believes that a reduction in tax rates will reduce tax revenues. The layperson focuses on the "arithmetic" of the situation. Laffer, however, focuses on the economic incentives. He asks: What does a lower tax rate imply in terms of a person's incentive to engage in productive activity? How does a lower tax rate affect one's tradeoff between work and leisure? The layperson likely sees only the "arithmetic" effect of a tax cut; the economist sees the incentive effect.

MACROECONOMICS INTERMISSION

Before going to the next chapter, let's take some time out to put your study of macroeconomics in perspective.

A key question in macroeconomics is, *How does the economy work?* In answering this question, some economists—notably classical economists, monetarists, and new classical economists—say that the economy is self-regulating. In other words, they believe the economy can remove itself from either a recessionary gap or an inflationary gap. The reason the economy can remove itself from both recessionary and inflationary gaps is because wages (and other resource prices) are sufficiently flexible. Other economists—notably Keynesians—believe the economy may be inherently unstable (not self-regulating). It may, at times, get stuck in a recessionary gap because wages are inflexible downwards.

Now if the economy is inherently unstable—if it can and does get stuck in a recessionary gap—it is natural to propose a policy solution to this economic problem. As you learned in this chapter, some economists—notably Keynesians—propose demand-side fiscal policy as the solution to this economic problem. However, other economists say, "But fiscal policy may not work, or if it does work, it may not work as intended." These economists then outline and discuss what they see as the problems with the policies proposed to solve the economic problem. See Exhibit 10.

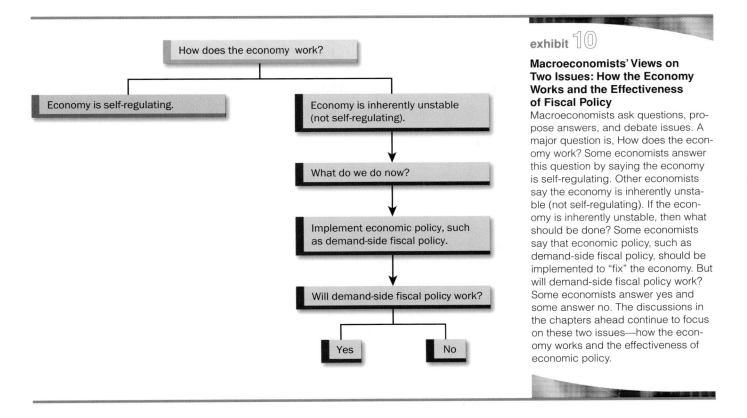

exhibit 10

Macroeconomists' Views on Two Issues: How the Economy Works and the Effectiveness of Fiscal Policy

Macroeconomists ask questions, propose answers, and debate issues. A major question is, How does the economy work? Some economists answer this question by saying the economy is self-regulating. Other economists say the economy is inherently unstable (not self-regulating). If the economy is inherently unstable, then what should be done? Some economists say that economic policy, such as demand-side fiscal policy, should be implemented to "fix" the economy. But will demand-side fiscal policy work? Some economists answer yes and some answer no. The discussions in the chapters ahead continue to focus on these two issues—how the economy works and the effectiveness of economic policy.

Future chapters proceed much the same way. You will read more about what economists say about how the economy works. You will also read more about the policies designed to "fix" the economy and about what is right or wrong with those policies.

Self-Test

1. Give an arithmetical example to illustrate the difference between the marginal and average tax rates.

2. If income tax rates rise, will income tax revenues rise too?

A Reader Asks...

Are Americans Overtaxed?

On a television news program I was watching the other day, a person said that Americans are overtaxed. He went on to back this up by saying that Americans work from January 1 to around the second week of May just to pay their taxes. If this is true, then perhaps Americans are overtaxed. What do the economists say, though? Do they say Americans are overtaxed?

Most economists do not usually comment on whether Americans are overtaxed, undertaxed, or taxed just the right amount. Instead, they mainly report on what taxes people pay, how much taxes people pay, and so on.

For example, what you heard on your television news program about how many days Americans work each year to pay their taxes is essentially correct. In 2002, the "average American taxpayer" worked from January 1 to April 27 to pay all her taxes (federal, state, and local). That is a total of 117 days out of a 365-day year. Is that too much? Some people, speaking for themselves, would say yes. After all, they might say, working one-third of the year just to pay your taxes is too much.

But consider a different measure of the tax burden: the ratio of tax revenues to GDP. This tax ratio for the United States was about 29 percent in 1998. The same ratio was 51 percent for Sweden, 43 percent for Austria, and 44 percent for France. In fact, of 29 countries studied, the United States had a lower tax-revenue-to-GDP ratio than 24 countries. The same people who said Americans were overtaxed might change their minds when they learn that the United States has a relatively lower tax burden than many other countries have.

Another issue to consider is how the tax burden is distributed among American workers. For example, in 1999, the top 1 percent of income earners in the United States paid 36.2 percent of all federal income taxes while the bottom 50 percent of all income earners paid 4.0 percent of all federal income taxes. Were the top 1 percent of income earners overtaxed and the bottom 50 percent undertaxed?

Finally, there is the issue of who benefits from the taxes. For example, suppose Smith pays $400 in taxes and Jones pays $200 in taxes. Is Smith overtaxed relative to Jones? Maybe not. Smith could receive $500 worth of benefits for the $400 he pays in taxes, whereas Jones could receive $100 worth of benefits for the $200 he pays in taxes. Even though Smith pays twice the taxes that Jones pays, Smith may consider himself much better off than Jones. And Jones may agree.

Chapter Summary

Fiscal Policy: General Remarks

- Fiscal policy refers to changes in government expenditures and/or taxes to achieve particular economic goals. Expansionary fiscal policy refers to increases in government expenditures and/or decreases in taxes. Contractionary fiscal policy refers to decreases in government expenditures and/or increases in taxes.

Demand-Side Fiscal Policy: A Keynesian Perspective

- In Keynesian theory, demand-side fiscal policy can be used to rid the economy of a recessionary gap or an inflationary gap. A recessionary gap calls for expansionary fiscal policy and an inflationary gap calls for contractionary fiscal policy. Ideally, fiscal policy changes aggregate demand by enough to rid the economy of either a recessionary gap or an inflationary gap.

Crowding Out

- Crowding out refers to the decrease in private expenditures that occurs as a consequence of increased government spending and/or the greater financing needs of a budget deficit. The crowding-out effect suggests that expansionary fiscal policy does not work to the degree that Keynesian theory predicts.
- Complete (incomplete) crowding out occurs when the decrease in one or more components of private spending completely (partially) offsets the increase in government spending.
- New classical economists argue that crowding out occurs when individuals decrease consumption spending in order to increase saving to pay the higher future taxes brought on by debt financing of the deficit.

Reasons Why Demand-Side Fiscal Policy May Be Ineffective

- Demand-side fiscal policy may be ineffective at achieving certain macroeconomic goals because of (1) crowding out, (2) lags, or (3) government's lack of information as to the value of the marginal propensity to consume and the difference between Natural Real GDP and the Real GDP produced in a recessionary gap.

Supply-Side Fiscal Policy

- When fiscal policy measures affect tax rates, they may affect both aggregate supply and aggregate demand. It is generally accepted that a marginal tax rate reduction increases the attractiveness of work relative to leisure and tax-avoidance activities and thus leads to an increase in aggregate supply.
- Tax revenues equal the tax base multiplied by the (average) tax rate. Whether tax revenues decrease or increase as a result of a tax rate reduction depends on whether the percentage increase in the tax base is greater or less than the percentage reduction in the tax rate. If the percentage increase in the tax base is greater than the percentage reduction in the tax rate, then tax revenues will increase. If the percentage increase in the tax base is less than the percentage reduction in the tax rate, then tax revenues will decrease.

Fiscal Policy
Budget Deficit
Budget Surplus
Balanced Budget
Expansionary Fiscal Policy

Contractionary Fiscal Policy
Discretionary Fiscal Policy
Automatic Fiscal Policy
Crowding Out
Complete Crowding Out

Incomplete Crowding Out
Trade Deficit
Marginal (Income) Tax Rate
Laffer Curve
Tax Base

Economic Connections to You

Economic facts, actions, and changes create ripples that move away from their point of origin. Eventually, these ripples can intersect your life and have an effect on you. Consider the following example.

> *Unbeknownst to members of Congress, the economy is on the downward-sloping portion of the Laffer curve at the time they pass legislation to raise income tax rates. As a result, higher tax rates lower tax revenues. The budget deficit widens and the U.S. Treasury increases its demand for credit. There is a slight increase in the supply of credit, but still the demand*

for credit rises by more than the supply of credit. Consequently, the interest rate rises. You must pay more for a car because the higher interest rate increases the cost of your car loan. Thus, there is a connection between tax legislation, the Laffer curve, and the cost of your car loan—an economic connection to you.

Based on the material in this chapter, identify other ways in which economic facts, actions, and changes create ripples that eventually affect you.

Questions and Problems

1. Explain three ways crowding out may occur.
2. Why is crowding out an important issue in the debate over the use of fiscal policy?
3. Some economists argue for the use of fiscal policy to solve economic problems; some argue against its use. What are some of the arguments on both sides?
4. The debate over using government spending and taxing powers to stabilize the economy involves more than technical economic issues. Do you agree or disagree? Explain your answer.
5. The Laffer curve, which shows (among other things) that a tax rate reduction can increase tax revenues, became very popular and was widely cited a couple of years before, during, and for a few years after the presidential election of 1980. Why do you think this happened?
6. Is crowding out equally likely under all economic conditions? Explain your answer.
7. Tax cuts will likely affect aggregate demand and aggregate supply. Does it matter which is affected more? Explain in terms of the *AD-AS* framework.

8. Explain how a growing federal budget deficit may lead to a growing trade deficit.
9. The discussion of the multiplier in the last chapter shows how a change in autonomous spending increases Real GDP by a multiple of itself. For example, if the multiplier is 4 and the change in autonomous spending is $100, then Real GDP changes by $400. What does complete crowding out imply about the value of the multiplier? Explain your answer.
10. Explain how expansionary fiscal policy can, under certain conditions, destabilize the economy.
11. The economy is in a recessionary gap and both Smith and Jones advocate expansionary fiscal policy. Does it follow that both Smith and Jones favor "big government"?
12. Will tax cuts that are perceived to be temporary affect the *SRAS* and *LRAS* curves differently than tax cuts that are perceived to be permanent? Explain your answer.

1. Graphically show how fiscal policy works in the ideal case.
2. Illustrate zero crowding out using the income-expenditure diagram introduced in the last chapter.
3. In the Keynesian model with constant prices and a horizontal *AS* curve, the *MPC* = 0.75, current Real GDP = $4,300 billion, and Q_N = $5,400 billion. Identify (a) the amount government will have to raise its purchases and (b) the amount it will have to cut taxes in order to move the economy to producing Q_N.
4. A $1 rise in government purchases increases Real GDP by $5. What is the *MPC?* The *MPS?* the multiplier?

5. A $1 cut in taxes increases Real GDP by $4. What is the *MPC?* the *MPS?* the multiplier?
6. Graphically illustrate how government can use supply-side fiscal policy to get an economy out of a recessionary gap.
7. Graphically illustrate the following:
   a. Fiscal policy destabilizes the economy
   b. Fiscal policy eliminates an inflationary gap
   c. Fiscal policy only partly eliminates a recessionary gap

Go to *http://w3.access.gpo.gov/usbudget/*. Click on the most recent budget (e.g., FY2003 Budget), then on "Analytical Perspectives," and finally on "Economic and Accounting Analyses." Read the section on economic Assumptions.

1. How does the Office of Management and Budget (OMB) describe the current economic condition of the United States and how does it justify what it states?
2. Does the OMB view the management of inflation as a fiscal responsibility of the President, a monetary responsibility of the Federal Reserve, or both? Explain your answer.

3. Of all the economic policy tools available, to which does the OMB give the greatest weight? Is this a fiscal policy tool?
4. Is there a prediction about unemployment in the future? What is it?
5. Is there a prediction about inflation in the future? What is it?
6. What is the dollar amount of the projected budget deficit or surplus? Would Keynesians consider this indicative of expansionary or contractionary fiscal policy? What would new classical economists or supply-side economists have to say about it?

Log on to the Arnold Xtra! Web site now (*http://arnoldxtra.swcollege.com*) for additional learning resources such as practice quizzes, help with graphing, video clips, and current event applications.

MORE ON GOVERNMENT SPENDING AND TAXES: BEYOND FISCAL POLICY

The nightly news on television doesn't usually have stories about aggregate demand, aggregate supply, fiscal policy, crowding out, and so on. But this doesn't mean it doesn't report economic news. Economics is a hot topic of discussion on a regular basis on the nightly news shows. Usually, the economic news has something to do with taxes, government spending, the state of the budget, Social Security, or Medicare. This chapter discusses some of these more popular and widely publicized economic stories.

The last chapter discusses government spending and taxes in the context of fiscal policy. In that chapter, the objective of changing government spending and taxes was to change aggregate demand or aggregate supply in order to achieve some particular macroeconomic goal.

This chapter discusses government spending and taxes *outside* the context of fiscal policy. *In short, government can increase or decrease its spending, and it can raise or lower taxes, without having a fiscal policy objective in mind. All government spending designed for non-fiscal policy purposes (and fiscal policy purposes too) will benefit someone. For our purposes, spending will benefit either (1) the general public or (2) a special interest group. With respect to the general public, we discuss the issue of nonexcludable public goods.*

A discussion of federal government spending and tax revenues leads to an examination of how the government balances its income and expenditures. So, we also spend some time in this chapter discussing the various states of the federal budget, in particular budget surpluses and deficits, and the public debt.

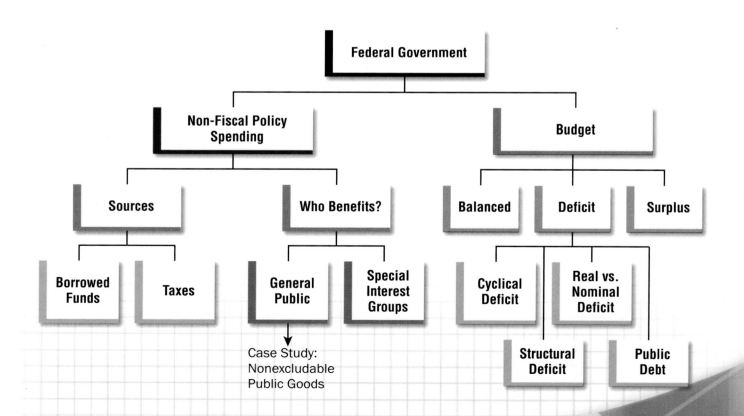

MAJOR FEDERAL GOVERNMENT SPENDING PROGRAMS AND TAX SOURCES

In this section, we discuss how the federal government spends money, the sources of its spending, and the major sources of tax revenues.

MAJOR SPENDING PROGRAMS

Public finance economists often talk about the various functions of government, which include: (1) economic stabilization, (2) protection, (3) allocation, and (4) distribution. In other words, the government can spend money with the purpose in mind of stabilizing the economy as discussed in the last chapter. It can spend money to protect personal property and the rights of individuals, such as spending money for courts, police, and so on. Government spending can also be used to allocate or shift resources. For example, if the government spends more on health care, the number of resources that flow into the health care industry may increase. Finally, the government can change the distribution of income by increasing spending on a specific segment of the population, such as farmers or poor people.

In 2000, the federal government spent about $1.8 trillion. This was 18.2 percent of the country's GDP. How did the federal government spend this $1.8 trillion? About 87 percent of the money went for national defense, income security, health, Medicare, Social Security, and net interest on the public debt. The remaining percentage of the money went for such things as transportation, the administration of justice, agriculture, education, international affairs, and so on.

WHERE DOES THE FEDERAL GOVERNMENT GET THE MONEY IT SPENDS?

Before the federal government can spend a dollar, it must get a dollar. The federal government can get a dollar in two ways. First, it can borrow the dollar in the loanable funds market. (We discussed this market in the previous chapter).

Second, the federal government can tax someone or something. In 2000, the federal government took in $2.025 trillion in tax revenues. Most of this came from three taxes—the personal income tax, the corporation income tax, and the Social Security tax. Specifically, 49 percent came from the personal income tax, 10.2 percent came from the corporate income tax, and 32.2 percent came from the Social Security tax. Other taxes accounted for 8.6 percent of total tax revenues. See Exhibit 1.

Q & A   **Q:** The government can get a dollar by borrowing it from someone or by taxing it away from someone. Can the federal government also get a dollar by printing it?

A: Before we can answer this question completely, you need to understand the monetary system of the United States. We begin to discuss this in the next chapter. In short, you will soon learn about money, banking, the Federal Reserve System, and more. For now, keep in mind that we are discussing how the federal government gets the money that Congress and the president of the United States have agreed to spend in the face of a constant money supply.

THE FEDERAL PERSONAL INCOME TAX

The following paragraphs examine some aspects of the federal personal income tax, the largest portion of the government's tax revenues.

Who Pays Most of the Federal Personal Income Tax?[1]

Economists often look at the tax situation for different income groups. For example, in 1999, the top 1 percent of income earners in the United States earned 19.5 percent of the total income earned that year and paid 36.2 percent of the total

Go to *http://www.irs.gov*. In the box titled "Search Forms and Publications for," key "How is my tax figured?" and then click "Go." Select "2000 Publication 4," and read page #2 of the publication. How many income tax rates do we have in the United States? What is your marginal tax rate? Is the U.S. income tax a progressive, regressive, or proportional tax?

exhibit 1

Major Federal Taxes

For each dollar the federal government raised from taxes in 2000, 49 percent came from the personal income tax, 10.2 percent came from the corporate income tax, 32.2 percent came from the Social Security tax, and 8.6 percent came from other federal taxes.

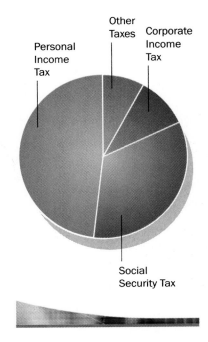

Other Taxes

Corporate Income Tax

Personal Income Tax

Social Security Tax

---

1. The source of the income and tax data in this section is the Tax Foundation.

Two Plumbers on New Year's Eve and Progressive Taxation

Many people believe that if two people do the same job, they should be paid the same dollar amount. This notion of *equal pay for equal work* often arises in discussions about the jobs performed by men and women. In other words, if a man and a woman do the same job, many people say that they should be paid the same dollar amount.

Sometimes the notion of equal pay for equal work is extended to *equal after-tax pay for equal work*. In other words, if two people do the same job, then they should earn the same after-tax income. However, a progressive income tax structure sometimes makes this impossible.

To illustrate, suppose under a progressive income tax structure, a person who earns between $50,000 and $60,000 pays income tax at a tax rate of 10 percent. For every dollar earned over $60,000 but under $70,000, a person pays at a tax rate of 15 percent.

Now, let's consider two plumbers, Smith and Jones. By December 30, Jones has earned $58,000 for the year and Smith has earned $60,000. Each is asked to do the same kind of plumbing job on December 31, New Year's Eve. Each plumber charges $1,000 for the job. Thus, Jones and Smith receive equal pay for equal work.

Let's look at the after-tax income that each receives for the job. On the additional $1,000 that Jones earns, she pays at a tax rate of 10 percent. So, she pays $100 in taxes and gets to keep $900 in after-tax income. Smith, on the other hand, now has an income of $61,000 and thus falls into a higher marginal tax bracket. He pays at a tax rate of 15 percent on the additional $1,000. So, Smith pays $150 in taxes and has $850 in after-tax income. Smith does the same job as Jones but Smith earns only $850 in after-tax pay while Jones earns $900 in after-tax pay.

Our conclusion: The progressive income tax structure can turn *equal pay for equal work* into *unequal after-tax pay for equal work*. Stated differently, a person can be in favor of progressive income taxes or equal after-tax pay for equal work, but not both. Sometimes it is a matter of one or the other.

---

federal income taxes. The following data show the income and taxes for additional income groups.

Income Group	Group's Share of Total Income	Group's Share of Federal Income Taxes
Top 1%	19.5%	36.2%
Top 5%	34.0	55.5
Top 10%	44.9	66.5
Top 25%	66.5	83.5
Top 50%	86.7	96.0
Bottom 50%	13.3	4.0

Progressive Income Tax
An income tax system in which one's tax rate rises as one's taxable income rises (up to some point).

Proportional Income Tax
An income tax system in which one's tax rate is the same no matter what one's taxable income is.

Regressive Income Tax
An income tax system in which one's tax rate declines as one's taxable income rises.

The Income Tax Structure

An income tax structure can be progressive, proportional, or regressive. Under a **progressive income tax,** the tax rate increases as a person's taxable income level rises. To illustrate, suppose Davidson pays taxes at the rate of 15 percent on a taxable income of $20,000. When his (taxable) income rises to, say, $30,000, he pays at a rate of 28 percent. And when his income rises to, say, $55,000, he pays at a rate of 31 percent. A progressive income tax is usually capped at some tax rate. Currently, the U.S. income tax structure is progressive.

Under a **proportional income tax,** the same tax rate is used for all income levels. A proportional income tax is sometimes referred to as a *flat tax.* For example, if Kuan's taxable income is $10,000, she pays taxes at a rate of 10 percent; if her taxable income rises to $100,000, she still pays at a rate of 10 percent.

Under a **regressive income tax,** the tax rate decreases as a person's taxable income level rises. For example, Lowenstein's tax rate is 10 percent when her taxable income is $10,000 and 8 percent when her taxable income rises to $20,000.

See Exhibit 2 for a review of the three income tax structures.

exhibit 2

Three Income Tax Structures
The three income tax structures outlined are the progressive, proportional, and regressive.

FDR's Taxes

In 1938, Franklin D. Roosevelt, U.S. president at the time, found it too difficult to compute the income taxes he owed. So he sent a check for part of what he thought he owed in taxes, along with the following letter, to the commissioner of the Internal Revenue Service:

My dear Commissioner Helvering:

I am enclosing my income tax return for the calendar year 1937, together with my check for $15,000. [Roosevelt's income that year was $93,601.]

I am wholly unable to figure out the amount of the tax for the following reasons:

The first twenty days of January 1937 were a part of my first term of office and to these twenty days the income tax rates as of March 4, 1933 apply. To the other 345 days of the year 1937, the income tax rates as they existed on January 30, 1937 apply.

As this is a problem in higher mathematics, may I ask that the Bureau let me know the amount of the balance due? The payment of $15,000 doubtless represents a good deal more than half what the eventual tax will prove to be.[2]

2. The original letter is in the Franklin D. Roosevelt Library.

ECONOMICS IN...

The World • Popular Culture • Technology • Everyday Life

Taxes, Smuggling, and Gangs with Machetes[3]

The high duties which have been imposed upon the importation of many different sorts of foreign goods, in order to discourage their consumption, have served only to encourage smuggling.

—Adam Smith

In recent years, many countries have increased the taxes on cigarettes and alcohol. These taxes—often called *sin taxes*—are justified on the basis of health and revenue reasons. Taxes make the price of cigarettes and alcohol higher, which leads to a reduction in cigarette and alcohol consumption, which is presumed to be good for one's health. Also, the sin taxes raise much-needed revenues for the countries that impose them, allowing countries to spend more on such things as education and infrastructure.

If neighboring countries have very different sin tax rates, an unintended effect can occur. For example, in recent years, the British taxes on cigarettes and alcohol have been much higher than the taxes imposed by many of its neighboring countries (such as France and Belgium). The tax discrepancy creates a price discrepancy, which if substantial, makes it profitable to smuggle cigarettes and alcohol into the country imposing the higher taxes.

This is currently happening in Great Britain. Because of the tax differences, a box of 200 Silk Cut cigarettes sells for $32 in Belgium and $61 in Great Britain; the price of wine and beer in France is about two-thirds of the British price. With these kinds of profit opportunities available, people buy cigarettes and alcohol in Belgium and France and then smuggle them into Britain. Presently, two-thirds of the British market in hand-rolling tobacco is illegal imports. It is reported that 1 million people in Britain buy illegally smuggled cigarettes each week.

The huge profits that can be earned by smuggling have attracted organized crime and numerous gangs. Gangs have used knives, baseball bats, guns, and machetes in attempts to steal illegal cigarettes and alcohol from each other. As of this writing, Great Britain is thinking of lowering its sin tax rates to stop some of the smuggling and crime.

Self-Test *(Answers to Self-Test questions are in the Self-Test Appendix.)*

1. Explain the differences among progressive, proportional, and regressive income tax structures.

2. What percentage of all income taxes was paid by the top 5 percent of income earners in 1999? What percentage of total income did this income group receive in 1999?

3. What three federal taxes account for the bulk of federal tax revenues?

GOVERNMENT SPENDING: WHO BENEFITS?

All government spending benefits someone. When government spends for reasons other than to meet fiscal policy objectives, two possible beneficiaries are the general public and special interest groups. In this section, we first discuss government spending on public goods, that is, spending that benefits the general public. We then look at spending that benefits special interest groups.

GOVERNMENT SPENDING ON NONEXCLUDABLE PUBLIC GOODS

Before examining the specific issue of nonexcludable public goods, we define and discuss how economists look at various types of goods.

---

3. This feature is based on "Smuggling: The Belgian Job," in *The Economist*, 8 May 1999.

Types of Goods

Economists talk about two kinds of goods—private goods and public goods. A *private good* is a good the consumption of which by one person reduces the consumption for another person. For example, a sweater, an apple, and a computer are all private goods. If one person is wearing a sweater, another person cannot wear (consume) the same sweater. If one person takes a bite of an apple, there is that much less apple for someone else to consume. If someone is using a computer, someone else can't use the same computer. A private good is said to be **rivalrous in consumption.**

A **public good,** in contrast, is a good the consumption of which by one person does not reduce the consumption by another person. For example, a movie in a movie theater is a public good. If there are 200 seats in the theater, then 200 people can see the movie at the same time and no one person's viewing of the movie detracts from another person's viewing of the movie. An economics lecture is also a public good. If there are 30 seats in the classroom, then 30 people can consume the economics lecture at the same time and one person's consumption does not detract from any other person's consumption. The chief characteristic of a public good is that it is **nonrivalrous in consumption**—which means that its consumption by one person does not reduce its consumption by others.

While all public goods are nonrivalrous in consumption, they are not all the same. Some public goods are excludable and some are nonexcludable.

Two Types of Public Goods
- Excludable Public Good
- Nonexcludable Public Good

A public good is **excludable** if it is possible, or not prohibitively costly, to exclude someone from obtaining the benefits of the good after it has been produced. For example, a movie in a movie theater is excludable, in that persons who do not pay to see the movie can be excluded from seeing it. The same holds for an economics lecture. If someone does not pay the tuition to obtain the lecture, he or she can be excluded from consuming it. We summarize by noting that both movies in movie theaters and economics lectures in classrooms are *excludable public goods.*

A public good is **nonexcludable** if it is impossible, or prohibitively costly, to exclude someone from obtaining the benefits of the good after it has been produced. Consider national defense. First, national defense is a public good in that it is nonrivalrous in consumption. For example, if the U.S. national defense system is protecting people in New Jersey from incoming missiles, then it is automatically protecting people in New York as well. And just as important, protecting people in New Jersey does not reduce the degree of protection for the people in New York. Second, once national defense has been produced, it is impossible (or prohibitively costly) to exclude someone from consuming its services. In other words, national defense is a *nonexcludable public good.* The same holds for flood control or large-scale pest control. After the dam has been built or the pest spray has been sprayed, it is impossible to exclude persons from benefiting from it.

Does the Market Fail to Provide Some Goods?

When a good is excludable (whether it is a private good or a public good), individuals can obtain the benefits of the good only if they pay for it. For example, no one can consume an apple (a private good) or a movie in a movie theater (a public good) without first paying for the good. This is not the case with a nonexcludable public good, though. Individuals can obtain the benefits of a nonexcludable public good without paying for it. Persons who do so are referred to as **free riders.** Because of the so-called *free rider problem,* most economists hold that the market will fail to produce nonexcludable public goods, or at least fail to produce them at a desired level.

Rivalrous in Consumption
A good is rivalrous in consumption if its consumption by one person reduces its consumption by others.

Public Good
A good the consumption of which by one person does not reduce the consumption by another person—that is, a public good is characterized by nonrivalry in consumption. There are both excludable and nonexcludable public goods. An excludable public good is a good that while nonrivalrous in consumption can be denied to a person who does not pay for it. A nonexcludable public good is a good that is nonrivalrous in consumption and that cannot be denied to a person who does not pay for it.

Nonrivalrous in Consumption
A good is nonrivalrous in consumption if its consumption by one person does not reduce its consumption by others.

Excludability
A good is excludable if it is possible, or not prohibitively costly, to exclude someone from receiving the benefits of the good after it has been produced.

Nonexcludability
A good is nonexcludable if it is impossible, or prohibitively costly, to exclude someone from receiving the benefits of the good after it has been produced.

Free Rider
Anyone who receives the benefits of a good without paying for it.

To illustrate, consider someone contemplating the production of nonexcludable public good X, which because it is a public good, is also nonrivalrous in consumption. After good X has been produced and provided to one person, there is no incentive for others to pay for it (even if they demand it) because they can receive all of its benefits without paying. No one is likely to supply a good that people can consume without paying for it. The market, it is argued, will not produce nonexcludable public goods. The door then is opened to government involvement in the production of nonexcludable public goods. It is often stated that if the market will not produce nonexcludable public goods, although they are demanded, then the government must.

The free rider argument is the basis for accepting government provision of nonexcludable public goods. In other words, if a nonexcludable public good is demanded, but the market won't supply it, then who or what will? The answer: government. Today, the federal government provides such things as national defense and it largely pays for national defense spending with taxes.

 Q: Are all the goods that the government provides nonexcludable public goods?

A: No. We need to make a distinction between a *nonexcludable public good* and a *government-provided good*. A nonexcludable good is a good that is nonrivalrous in consumption and nonexcludable. A government-provided good is self-defined: it a good that government provides.

In some instances, a government-provided good is a nonexcludable public good, such as when the government furnishes national defense. But it need not be. The government furnishes mail delivery and education, two goods that are also provided privately and are excludable and thus not subject to free riding.

GOVERNMENT SPENDING AND SPECIAL INTEREST GROUPS

So far we know that government sometimes spends and taxes (1) in order to meet fiscal policy objectives and (2) to provide public goods. Of course, this isn't the only kind of spending (and taxing) that government is involved in. In this section we discuss government spending that has the effect of benefiting a *special interest group* at the expense of the general taxpayer.

An Example

Scottie Pippen plays basketball for the Portland Trailblazers. In 2001, he earned a salary of about $18.1 million. Pippen supplemented his income with a payment of $131,575 that he received in farm subsidies over a period of five years. Specifically, the federal government paid Pippen $131,575 for not planting crops on land he had purchased in Arkansas.

Ted Turner, of Turner Broadcasting, has a net worth of $6.2 billion. Turner regularly applies for and receives farm subsidies to grow wheat, oats, and barley on his ranches. During the period 1996–2001, he received about $176,000 in subsidies.

Why did government pay both Pippen and Turner? Did it pay the money because it wanted to raise aggregate demand in the economy? In other words, did government try to meet a fiscal policy objective by paying Pippen and Turner? Probably not. Did it pay the money because it wanted to provide a nonexcludable public good? Well, if it did, it is difficult to see what the nonexcludable public good is.

Payments to Special Interest Groups

Most economists would argue that the payments to Pippen and Turner had nothing to do with fiscal policy or nonexcludable public goods. Instead, these payments are an example of a special interest group benefiting from government spending. A **special interest group** is a subset of the general population that

Special Interest Group
A subset of the general population that holds (usually) intense preferences for or against a particular government service, activity, or policy. Often special interest groups gain from public policies that may not be in accord with the interests of the general public.

ECONOMICS IN...

Everyday Life   **Popular Culture**   **Technology**   **The World**

Special Interests Dressed in Fiscal-Policy and Public-Goods Clothing

The federal government spends a dollar. Is that a dollar spent to meet a fiscal policy objective, to buy a nonexcludable public good, or to satisfy a special interest group at the expense of the general taxpayer?

Without more information, it is hard to know the answer to this question. And because it is hard to know the answer without more information, special interest groups can sometimes disguise their requests for money. Consider the following two things that occurred soon after the terrorist attacks of September 11, 2001:

1. There was more government spending on both homeland and national security. If homeland and national security is a nonexcludable good, then we can say there was a call for more of this particular nonexcludable public good.
2. Economists, government officials, and the "man and woman in the street," began to talk about the strong possibility that the United States was in the middle of a recession. In Washington, D.C., talk turned to the need for "fiscal stimulus"—in other words, expansionary fiscal policy (spend more, tax less).

Some people argued that the call for more homeland and national security (more of a particular nonexcludable public good), along with a call for fiscal stimulus, gave special interest groups an opportunity to disguise their pleas as public interest talk. Special interest group *A* doesn't want more money or a tax cut because it wants to make itself better off.

It needs both because it serves the national interest (public goods argument) or because it will stimulate the economy (fiscal policy argument).

Let's look at some examples. Start with the Farm Security Act—notice its middle name "Security." Congressman Terry Everett argued for the peanut subsidies in the act because, as he said, it "strengthens America's national security." The *Wall Street Journal* said of Mr. Everett, "The man who chairs a key agriculture subcommittee is himself the proud owner of a federal quota that stands to make him about $30,000 in subsidies over five years if the bill [the Farm Security Act] passes."[4]

In a similar vein, Senator Tom Daschle argued that "poultry waste and waste of all agricultural products is something that continues to *threaten* our country."

On the issue of fiscal stimulus, Senator Frank Murkowski argued that one of the best ways to stimulate the economy is for the government to pay for a pipeline to be built from Alaska to Chicago. Senator Murkowski represents the state of Alaska.

holds (usually) intense preferences for or against a particular government service, activity, or policy. Both Pippen and Turner are members of a special interest group—they are farmers.

The dollars that the government pays to Pippen, Turner, other farmers, and the other members of various special interest groups have to be obtained from someone. As is true for all government spending, these dollars can be obtained from lenders or from taxpayers. For now, let's assume they are obtained from taxpayers. Why do taxpayers accept this kind of spending? Why do our elected representatives permit it? After all, taxpayers outnumber the members of any particular special interest group by a large amount. Why don't our elected representatives simply "count votes" and decide accordingly?

Before we answer these questions, let's consider the following. Suppose special interest group A, composed of 5,000 individuals, favors a policy that will result in the redistribution of $50 million from 100 million general taxpayers to

4. *Wall Street Journal*, 3 October 2001, p. A22.

the group. The dollar benefit for each member of the special interest group is $10,000. Given this substantial dollar amount, it is likely that the members of the special interest group (1) will have proposed the legislation in the first place and (2) will lobby the elected representatives who will decide the issue.

But will the elected representatives also hear from the general voter (general taxpayer)? The general voter-taxpayer will probably be less informed about the legislation than the members of the special interest group, and even if he or she were informed, each person would have to calculate the benefits and costs of lobbying against the proposed legislation. If the legislation passes, the average taxpayer will pay approximately 50 cents. The benefits of lobbying against the legislation are probably not greater than 50 cents. Therefore, we can reasonably conclude that even if the general taxpayer were informed about the legislation, he or she would not be likely to argue against it. The benefits just wouldn't be worth the time and effort. In other words, it is likely that the special interest group will have a good chance of getting what it wants.

Self-Test

1. Why won't the market produce nonexcludable public goods?

2. Identify each of the following goods as a nonexcludable public good, an excludable public good, or a private good: (a) personal computer, (b) Broadway play, (c) tree in a person's yard, (d) telephone in service, (e) sunshine.

3. Give an example, other than a movie in a movie theater or a play in a theater, of a good that is nonrivalrous and excludable.

4. Consider two groups, *A,* and *B.* If one group is trying to redistribute income away from the other group to itself (by passing some type of special interest legislation), will it have a better chance of accomplishing this objective if each group has the same number of members or a different number of members? Explain your answer.

DEFICITS, SURPLUSES, AND THE PUBLIC DEBT

As we state in the previous chapter, the federal budget is composed of two, not necessarily equal, parts: government expenditures and tax revenues. If expenditures are greater than tax revenues, a *budget deficit* exists. If tax revenues are greater than expenditures, a *budget surplus* exists. If expenditures equal tax revenues, a *balanced budget* exists.

The federal government ran a budget deficit in every year of the period 1970–1997. The federal government ran a budget surplus in every year of the period 1998–2000. As of this writing, the Congressional Budget Office projects budget deficits (in the unified budget) for the period 2002–2005.[5]

BUDGET DEFICITS

Budget deficits are a part of our recent history. In 1996, the budget deficit was $108 billion. Does it follow that in 1996 the government was implementing expansionary fiscal policy by increasing government spending and/or lowering taxes? Not necessarily. A budget deficit can result from a downturn in economic activity unrelated to any spending and taxing decisions made by government. In our analysis of budget deficits, we look at different types of deficits, the size of the deficit, and how the deficit is measured.

---

5. The unified budget takes into account both on-budget items (such as national defense) and off-budget items (such as Social Security).

Structural and Cyclical Deficits

Suppose the budget is currently balanced and then Real GDP in the economy drops. As Real GDP drops, the tax base of the economy falls, and if tax rates are held constant, tax revenues will fall. Also, as a result of the decline in Real GDP, transfer payments (such as unemployment compensation) will rise. Thus, government expenditures will rise and tax revenues will fall. As a result, a balanced budget turns into a budget deficit. This budget deficit resulted from the downturn in economic activity, and not from any current spending and taxing decisions of the government.

Economists use the term **cyclical deficit** to refer to that part of the budget deficit that is a result of a downturn in economic activity. The remainder of the deficit—or that part of the deficit that would exist if the economy were operating at full employment—is called the **structural deficit.** In other words,

$$\text{Total budget deficit} = \text{Structural deficit} + \text{Cyclical deficit}$$

To illustrate, suppose the economy is in a recessionary gap, government expenditures are currently $1,500 billion, and tax revenues are $1,300 billion. Thus, the (total) budget deficit is $200 billion. Economists estimate what government expenditures and tax revenues would be if the economy were operating at full employment. Assume they estimate government expenditures would be only $1,400 billion and tax revenues would be $1,350 billion. This means that the structural deficit—the deficit that would exist at full employment—is $50 billion. The cyclical deficit—the part of the budget deficit that is a result of economic downturn—is $150 billion. It is the difference between the total budget deficit ($200 billion) and the structural deficit ($50 billion).

Total Budget Deficit	Structural Deficit (Deficit that would exist if the economy were at full employment.)	Cyclical Deficit (Total budget deficit − structural deficit)
$200 billion	$50 billion	$150 billion

Why is it important to separate the structural and cyclical deficits from the (total) budget deficit? The answer is that only by focusing on the structural deficit do we get a correct reading of fiscal policy. With a structural deficit of $50 billion, clearly fiscal policy is expansionary, but not as expansionary as a simple reading of the total budget deficit ($200 billion) indicates.

The Size of the Deficit and How It Is Measured

When the federal government runs deficits, two, not unrelated, issues are discussed: (1) the size of the deficit and (2) how the deficit is measured. Social Security is often discussed with respect to the first issue. Consider that federal government spending includes Social Security benefits paid to people and that federal tax revenues include Social Security (payroll) taxes. Currently, the revenues from Social Security taxes are greater than the benefits paid, which means that the Social Security system has a surplus. The Social Security surplus makes any budget deficit smaller than it would be if Social Security payments and revenues were not a part of government expenditures and tax revenues. In 1998, there would not have been a budget surplus if an adjustment had been made for the Social Security surplus. Instead, there would have been a budget deficit.

On a related issue, economist Robert Eisner has argued that the budget deficit that matters is the *real budget deficit,* not the *nominal budget deficit.* Eisner says that to obtain the real deficit, the public debt (the amount the government owes) should be adjusted each year for inflation and then subtracted from the actual or nominal deficit.

http://

Go to *http://www.odci.gov.* Under "Library and Reference," select "The World Factbook," and then "Country Listing." Using the links and the "Back" button, identify the size of the budget deficits or surpluses for Brazil, Japan, and Russia. Of the countries with budget deficits, are any of the deficits viewed as a serious economic problem?

$$\text{Real budget deficit} = \text{Nominal budget deficit} - (\text{Public debt} \times \text{Inflation rate})$$

To illustrate, suppose the public debt one year is $4,000 billion and the (nominal) budget deficit that year is $250 billion. Now suppose the price level rises by 5 percent during the year. This means the real value of the original $4,000 billion debt declines by 5 percent, or $200 billion ($4,000 billion × 0.05 = $200 billion). The real budget deficit for the year is then only $50 billion.

$$\text{Real budget deficit} = \$250 \text{ billion} - (\$4{,}000 \text{ billion} \times 0.05) = \$50 \text{ billion}$$

What then is the *real public debt* if the real budget deficit is simply $50 billion instead of $250 billion? It is $50 billion higher than it was before the deficit was run. In other words, if the public debt was originally $4,000 billion, it is now $4,050 billion.

The essence of what Eisner is saying is that while spending more than tax revenues adds to the value of the debt, inflation reduces the value of the debt. We want to see how things turn out on net.

Consider a simple example. Suppose a person borrows $100 and promises to pay it back in a year. During the year, the price level rises 10 percent, so she pays back the loan with dollars that have 10 percent less purchasing power than the dollars she borrowed. For the lender, it is as if he received 10 percent fewer dollars than he thought he would receive at the time the loan was made. Simply put, increases in the price level redistribute buying power from creditors to debtors. With regard to the public debt, the federal government is a debtor.

THE PUBLIC DEBT

A budget deficit occurs when federal government expenditures are greater than taxes for a single year. The **public debt,** which is sometimes called the federal or national debt, is the total amount the federal government owes its creditors. The public debt was $6.2 trillion on September 6, 2002. You can find the public debt as of today if you go to the Bureau of the Public Debt Web site at *http://www .publicdebt.treas.gov/opd/opd.htm*.

About 41 percent of the public debt was held by agencies of the U.S. government—which means that one entity in the government owed it to another. The remainder of the debt (59 percent) was held by the public. Economists distinguish between these amounts by referring to the entire debt as the *public debt,* or *gross public debt,* and the part of the debt held exclusively by the public as the *net public debt.*

 Q: In what year was the public debt the lowest?

A: 1835. On January 1, 1835, it was $33,733.05.

Who bears the burden of the debt? Or, to put it differently, who bears the burden of public spending financed by borrowing from the public? There are two main schools of thought: One argues that the current generation bears the burden of the debt. The other maintains that the future generation bears the burden of the debt.

The Current Generation Bears the Burden of the Debt

According to one view, public borrowing imposes a burden only on the current generation. To illustrate, suppose government increases its spending on national defense. To finance the spending it borrows the funds from the public by issuing bonds. Because more resources are devoted to building planes, ships, and tanks, fewer resources are available to produce television sets, radios, and cars. Some economists argue that the current generation must give up private goods (television sets and the like) to pay for the increased national defense, so the current generation bears the burden of the debt.

Public Debt
The total amount the federal government owes its creditors.

Go to *http://w3.access.gpo.gov/eop*. Enter "B-89" into the box, and click "Submit." From the list, find "Table B-89, Estimated Ownership . . ." and click on the "TXT" icon beneath it. What percent of the federal debt was owned by foreigners in the earliest year in the table? In the most recent year in the table? Has there been a significant change in ownership between these two years?

But what happens when the bonds issued in the current year come due, say, 30 years from now? Don't future taxpayers have to pay them off? The economist Abba Lerner answered yes, but added that as long as the debt is domestically held (only Americans hold the debt), American *taxpayers* will be making payments to American *bondholders*. And if we lump both taxpayers and bondholders together and realize that together they make up the future generation, then we can say that the future generation doesn't bear the burden of the debt. There is simply a transfer of funds from one part of the future generation, taxpayers, to another part of the future generation, bondholders. This is the *we-owe-it-to-ourselves* argument. According to this view, the future generation, as a whole, sacrifices nothing for the increased government expenditures in an earlier period.

There is one proviso, however, and it is that the entire public debt is held by Americans, which is not the case. To the degree that the public debt is held by foreigners, the future American generation (specifically, future American taxpayers) does not completely escape the burden of the debt.

One other point should be kept in mind. The current-generation-bears-the-burden-of-the-debt argument does not account for the possibility of current budget deficits (and current additions to the debt) reducing the amount of capital investment by the current generation. In other words, it doesn't take into account crowding out.

To illustrate, suppose the economy is at or near full employment and the federal government increases the size of the budget deficit by spending more on current operations (instead of on capital investment projects). To finance the larger budget deficit, the government must borrow more funds in the credit market, which, in turn, drives up the interest rate. The higher interest rate will cause some businesses to cut back on their investment plans. Thus, per capita Real GDP for future generations may be lower than it would have been because there was less capital investment in the current period.

The Future Generation Bears the Burden of the Debt

Economist James Buchanan has argued that although resources are drawn from the private sector when debt-financed public expenditures are made, the people who give up these resources do not pay for, or bear the burden of, the public expenditures secured. To illustrate, suppose again that the government issues debt to pay for more national defense. Some people buy the government bonds—these are current bondholders. As a result of this voluntary exchange, resources shift from the private to the public sector. Society ends up with more planes, ships, and tanks and fewer television sets and the like. So far, the debt situation is the same as described earlier.

Have the bondholders paid for the weapons systems? Buchanan would say no. What the bondholders have done, he argues, is entered into a voluntary trade. They have voluntarily decided to consume a little less today (by buying bonds they have less income to devote to consumption) and to consume a little more when their bonds are paid off (because they will receive the principal plus interest, they can consume more over their lifetimes than if they had not purchased the bonds). By sacrificing current private consumption, bondholders have paid for more future private consumption; they have not paid for more weapons systems. Buchanan argues that the persons who pay for the weapons systems are the future taxpayers, who must retire the debt when it comes due.

In summary, Buchanan's argument works like this: The government in year 1 says, "Who among you wants to buy our government bonds?" Some people voluntarily raise their hands. What they are buying and "paying for" is the opportunity to increase their private consumption in the future above what it would have been had they not purchased the bonds. When the future comes, say, in year 30 and the bonds have to be paid off, the government doesn't say, "Who among you wants to pay your taxes so that the debt can be paid off?" Instead, it

Go to *http://w3.access.gpo.gov/ usbudget/*. Under the most recent Fiscal Year Budget, select "Searching and Viewing Documents On-line." Key "function" in the "Search Terms Box," and click "SUBMIT." Finally, select the "TXT" icon under "Outlays by Function and Subfunction." Look over the complete list of government functions. Identify those government functions that you believe fall under the category of non-excludable public goods.

simply takes the funds from taxpayers. These taxpayers are not paying for the opportunity of greater future private consumption, as were the bondholders in year 1; they are paying for debt-financed expenditures in year 1.

How does Buchanan answer the argument that because the taxpayers in year 30 pay the bondholders in year 30, and what the taxpayers lose, the bondholders gain, wouldn't the burden of the debt for the next generation on net be zero? Buchanan says that this argument is misleading. The bondholders in year 30 don't really gain anything; all they do is trade one asset (bonds) for another asset (money) of equal value. This generation of bondholders gains no more from this transaction than if it had exchanged a $20 bill for four $5 bills. The taxpayers in year 30 do lose something, however—taxes. In conclusion, bondholders do not gain anything, and taxpayers lose something, so on net the next generation loses.

Self-Test

1. How is the cyclical deficit computed?
2. Suppose the nominal deficit is $100 billion, the inflation rate is 1 percent, and the public debt is $4,000 billion. What is the real budget deficit?
3. Explain the argument that states the current generation bears the burden of the public debt.
4. What is the unified budget?

SOCIAL SECURITY

The critics of the Social Security system often point out that it is a *pay-as-you-go* system. In other words, workers today pay workers who have retired, and in turn will be paid by the workers of tomorrow. That may be all right, say the critics, as long as the number of workers paying for retirees does not drop dramatically. But it has dropped over the years. In 1940, there were more than 40 workers for every retiree. By 1960, there were 5 workers for every retiree. In 2002, there were 3.4 workers for every retiree. By 2050, actuaries estimate that there will be only 2 workers for every retiree.

A presidential commission on Social Security reported in December 2001 that beginning in 2016, the Social Security program would begin running deficits: annual payments would be greater than annual tax revenue. The commission estimated that if the deficits in, say, 2020 were faced today, a two-earner couple with $50,000 income would have to pay $860 more in annual taxes. The deficit in 2030 is estimated to be even larger than the one in 2020; the same couple would be faced with $2,100 more in annual taxes.

Of course, taxes don't have to rise if benefits fall. Without a rise in taxes, a wage earner retiring at age 65 in 2020 would receive $2,227 less in annual benefits; retiring at age 65 in 2030 would mean $4,605 less in annual benefits.

Some people argue that cutting Social Security payments (in the future) is not necessary if other cuts are made instead. However, if payments were held constant, then the required cuts in 2020 would equal the combined size of Head Start, and the Departments of Education, Interior, Commerce, and the Environmental Protection Agency. In 2025, NASA and the Department of Veterans Affairs would need to be added to this list.

Finally, nothing needs to be cut, of course, if government simply borrows the funds to keep payments constant. But this would necessitate a lot of borrowing. The total government borrowing required to finance Social Security's deficit would equal $7 trillion by 2040, $14 trillion by 2050, and $47 trillion by 2075 (all in 2001 dollars).

The presidential commission recommended moving the Social Security system from a pay-as-you-go system to a save-and-invest system. This recommendation was based partly on the return on Social Security contributions, which was seen as meager. For example, Social Security actuaries estimate that for a single male worker born in 2000 with average earnings, the real annual return on his scheduled Social Security contributions will be only 0.86 percent. For workers who earn the maximum amount taxed ($80,400 in 2001), the real annual return was a *minus* 0.72 percent.

The presidential commission recommended three alternative models for Social Security reform. A common feature of all the plans was a voluntary personal retirement account that would not only permit workers more control over their retirement benefits but also produce a higher return for them. As of this writing, Congress has not decided whether or not any of the commission's suggestions will be acted upon.

A Reader Asks...
Will Social Security Be There for Me?

I'm a college student today. If I go to work tomorrow, I'll probably retire in 2040—just at the time of the big Social Security shortfalls. Do most economists think Social Security will be there for me? What do they say I should do to plan for my retirement?

Most economists would say that whether or not Social Security will be there for you depends on many things. It depends on whether Social Security reforms are enacted in the near future, the nature of those reforms, the health of the economy during the next decades, how long people work and live, and so on.

What do economists say you should do to plan for your retirement? Here, much depends on your income, circumstances, and so on. Generally, though, most economists would probably agree that you should save in one way or another. In other words, you might want to save by buying Treasury securities, corporation bonds, or stock. Which is the best type of investment? Let's look at some numbers.

Between 1926 and 1997, the average annual return was 3.8 percent on U.S. Treasury bills, 5.3 percent on intermediate-term government bonds, and 5.7 percent on long-term government bonds. In contrast, the return was 11 percent in the stock market (as measured by the Standard & Poor's 500). To put things differently, if you had invested $1 in the stocks that make up the Standard & Poor's 500 in 1926, your $1 would be worth $1,828 in 1997. But $1 invested in long-term bonds would have been worth $55.38.

Generally, the stock market (over the past) has shown to be a good investment if you do not need the money for a long time. There is, of course, no guarantee that putting, say, $1,000 in the stock market this year will give you a positive return next year.

Also, keep in mind the computations made by the editors of *The Economist* magazine at the end of 1999. First, they found the highest-returning investment in each year of the twentieth century—starting in 1900 and ending in 1999. They then computed the amount of money a person would have earned at the end of 1999 if she had (1) invested $1 in the highest returning investment in 1900, (2) taken the return from that investment and invested it in the highest-returning investment in 1901, and (3) continued in this way throughout the century. In other words, what are the returns if a person has perfect foresight? The answer is $1.3 quadrillion (after taxes)—or 15,000 times more money than Bill Gates has.

The editors of *The Economist* know that the typical investor does not, of course, have perfect foresight. According to them, the typical investor is one who follows fashion and buys the stocks that are popular. The typical investor buys what people are currently talking about. The problem is that by the time people start talking about an investment, it has usually already reached its maximum gains. (It is the high gains that get people talking.)

So, what would a person, starting with $1 in 1900, have earned by 1999 if she had missed the highest-earning investment of each year by one year? In other words, if gold is the highest-returning investment in 1982, buy it in 1983. The answer is $290.

According to the editors of *The Economist*, there are two lessons to be learned. First, the best investments are often the ones that you don't hear about until it is too late. Second, ignoring the first lesson and thinking that a popular investment is a good investment is often the way to low returns.

Government Spending

- In 2000, the federal government spent about $1.8 trillion. This was 18.2 percent of the country's GDP. About 87 percent of the money went for national defense, income security, health, Medicare, Social Security, and net interest on the public debt.

Taxes

- In 2000, the federal government took in $2.025 trillion in tax revenues. Most of this came from three taxes—the personal income tax, the corporation income tax, and the Social Security tax.
- With a proportional income tax, everyone pays taxes at the same rate, whatever their income level. With a progressive income tax, a person pays taxes at a higher rate (up to some top rate) as his or her income level rises. With a regressive income tax, a person pays taxes at a lower rate as his or her income level rises.
- The federal income tax is a progressive income tax.

Public Goods

- A public good is a good characterized by nonrivalry in consumption. A public good can be excludable or nonexcludable. Excludable public goods are goods that while nonrivalrous in consumption can be denied to people if they do not pay for them. Nonexcludable public goods are goods that are nonrivalrous in consumption and cannot be denied to people who do not pay for them. The market will not provide nonexcludable public goods because of the free rider problem—that is, a supplier of a good would not be able to extract payment for the good because its benefits can be received without making payment.

Special Interest Groups

- Special interest groups are usually well-informed about their issues. Individuals have a greater incentive to become informed about issues the more directly and intensely the issue affects them.
- Legislation that concentrates the benefits on a few and disperses the costs over many is likely to pass because the beneficiaries will have an incentive to lobby for it, whereas those who pay the bill will not lobby against it because each of them pays such a small part of the bill.

Deficits, Surpluses, and the Public Debt

- If government expenditures are greater than tax revenues, there is a budget deficit; if government expenditures are less than tax revenues, there is a budget surplus. For the most part, our recent budgetary history is one of budget deficits. In 1998, the federal government ran its first budget surplus in almost three decades. Budget deficits are predicted for the near future.
- A cyclical deficit refers to the part of the budget deficit that is a result of a downturn in economic activity.
- A structural deficit refers to the part of the deficit that would exist if the economy were operating at full employment.
- Total budget deficit = Structural deficit + Cyclical deficit.
- The public debt is the total amount the federal government owes its creditors.
- Because some of the public debt is held by agencies of the U.S. government and some is held by the public, economists refer to the entire debt as the *public debt* or *gross public debt* and to that part of the entire debt that is held by the public as the *net public debt*.
- There is a continuing debate in economics about who bears the burden of the public debt. Economists who hold that the burden of the debt falls on the current generation argue that resources are used up only in the periods when spending programs take place. Thus, if government debt finances an expenditure on, say, weapons, the resources that go into producing the weapons must be given up by some persons during that current period, not later.
- Economists who hold that the burden of the debt falls on future generations argue that when an expenditure is financed by government debt, the government issues debt that is purchased by bondholders. These bondholders voluntarily trade one asset (money) for another (bonds). What they purchase is greater future consumption, not government expenditure. The people who pay for the government expenditure are those who pay higher taxes to retire the previously issued debt.

Social Security

- In 1940, there were more than 40 workers for every retiree. By 1960, there were 5 workers for every retiree. In 2002, there were 3.4 workers for every retiree. By 2050, actuaries estimate that there will be only 2 workers for every retiree.
- A presidential commission on Social Security reported in December 2001 that beginning in 2016, the Social Security program would begin running deficits.

Progressive Income Tax
Proportional Income Tax
Regressive Income Tax
Rivalrous in Consumption
Public Good

Nonrivalrous in Consumption
Excludability
Nonexcludability
Free Rider
Special Interest Group

Cyclical Deficit
Structural Deficit
Public Debt

Economic Connections to You

Economic facts, actions, and changes create ripples that move away from their point of origin. Eventually, these ripples can intersect your life and have an effect on you. Consider the following example.

The economy expands and tax revenues rise. As a result, the deficit disappears. Because there is no longer a deficit, the U.S. Treasury reduces its borrowing in the credit market, and the interest rate

drops. You end up paying a lower interest rate for a car loan. Thus, there is a connection between the state of the economy and what you pay for a car— an economic connection to you.

Based on the material in this chapter, identify other ways in which economic facts, actions, and changes create ripples that eventually affect you.

Questions and Problems

1. Is it true that under a proportional income tax structure a person who earns a higher income will pay more in taxes than a person who earns a lower income? Explain your answer.

2. A progressive income tax always raises more revenue than a proportional income tax. Do you agree or disagree? Explain your answer.

3. Why does the market fail to provide nonexcludable public goods?

4. Will the market fail to provide excludable public goods? Explain your answer.

5. Your objective is to pass as much spending-and-tax legislation as possible. Does the spending-and-tax legislation have a better chance of passing if it (1) concentrates the benefits on few and disperses the costs over many or (2) concentrates the costs on few and disperses the benefits over many? Explain your answer.

6. Why is it important to separate a structural deficit from a cyclical deficit?

7. "The public debt is a fraction (something less than 100 percent) of the GDP. The Jensens' private debt is

equal to their family income. It follows that the public debt is less of a problem than the Jensens' private debt. No one seems very concerned about the Jensens' private debt, so there is less reason to get upset about the public debt. All this discussion about the seriousness of the public debt is simply empty talk." Discuss.

8. The last chapter discusses how an increase in the size of the budget deficit might affect interest rates, the demand for loanable funds, and ultimately the value of U.S. exports and foreign imports. How might a decrease in the size of the budget deficit or a movement from deficit to surplus affect interest rates, the demand for loanable funds, and ultimately the value of U.S. exports and foreign imports?

9. According to the "current generation bears the burden of the debt" argument, *why* (or *in what way*) does the current generation bear the burden of the debt?

10. Explain the "future generation bears the burden of the debt" argument.

Working with Numbers and Graphs

Use the following table to answer questions 1–4.

Taxable Income	Taxes
$1,000–$5,000	10% of taxable income
$5,001–$10,000	$500 + 12% of everything over $5,000
$10,001–$15,000	$1,100 + 15% of everything over $10,000

1. If a person's income is $6,000, how much does he pay in taxes?
2. If a person's income is $14,000, how much does he pay in taxes?
3. What is the marginal tax rate on the 10,001st dollar? What is the marginal tax rate on the 10,000th dollar?
4. What is the average tax rate of someone with a taxable income of $13,766?
5. There are three income earners in society and all three must pay income taxes. The taxable income of Smith is $40,000, the taxable income of Jones is $100,000, and the taxable income of Brown is $200,000.
   a. How much tax revenue is raised under a proportional income tax where the tax rate is 10 percent? 15 percent?
   b. Would a progressive tax with a rate of 5 percent on an income of $0–$40,000, a rate of 8 percent on everything over $40,000 and under $100,000, and a rate of 15 percent of everything over $100,000 raise more or less tax revenue than a proportional tax rate of 10 percent? Explain your answer.
6. Suppose the supply curve of labor (in the aggregate) is upward-sloping and that the entire Social Security tax is placed on the employee.
   a. Does it follow that the employee will end up being paid a higher wage rate after the Social Security tax is imposed than before? Explain your answer.
   b. Will the wage rate increase by a dollar amount equal to the Social Security tax (on an hourly basis), or will the wage rate increase by a dollar amount less than the Social Security tax? Explain your answer in words and with a graph.

Internet Activities

1. Go to *http://w3.access.gpo.gov/usbudget/*. Under the latest FY Budget, i.e. "FY 2003 Budget," select "Searching and Viewing Document On-line." Click "Historical Tables" and enter "Public Debt" in the Search Terms box. Next, click "Submit" and then locate Table 7.1. Click the "TXT" icon below it.
   a. Fill in the blanks in the following table.

Year	Federal Gross Debt as a Percentage of GDP	Federal Gross Debt (held by federal government) as a Percentage of GDP
1946	A	F
1970	B	G
1980	C	H
1990	D	I
2000	E	J

   b. In which year is the federal debt as a percentage of GDP the highest? Is it possible for the gross federal debt to rise as the federal gross debt as a percentage of GDP falls? Explain your answer.
   c. What percentage of the federal debt is held by the Federal Reserve System?
2. Return to the main page. Under "FY 2001 Federal Budget Publications and the 2000 Economic Report of the President," click "A Citizen's Guide to the Federal Budget. Then select "Section 2."
   a. What percentage of federal revenues are raised by the personal income tax?
   b. Give an example of a federal excise tax and what it is used for.
   c. At one time the federal government primarily relied on custom duties for its revenue. How important are custom duties today?
   d. How do taxes in the United States compare with taxes in other developed countries?

Log on to the Arnold Xtra! Web site now (*http://arnoldxtra.swcollege.com*) for additional learning resources such as practice quizzes, help with graphing, video clips, and current event applications.

ch.12

MONEY AND BANKING

Banks are more important for what you don't see than for what you do see. When you enter a bank, you may see a customer depositing a paycheck, a loan officer talking to a prospective borrower, or a teller handing $200 to a customer who needs some cash for the next few days. All very ordinary. But what isn't so ordinary is what most of us don't see. What we don't see is banks creating money. No, there are no printing presses in back rooms. But, still, money is being created, as this chapter explains.

Chapter Road Map

Everybody knows about money—or do they? What is money? How did it come to be? What does it do? What benefits does it provide? After answering these questions, we discuss two common definitions of the money supply. Then, we examine the money creation and destruction process, which leads to a discussion of banks and money. Suppose the money supply rises from $1,500 billion to $1,600 billion. How does this happen? Or suppose the money supply falls from $1,500 billion to $1,400 billion. How does this happen?

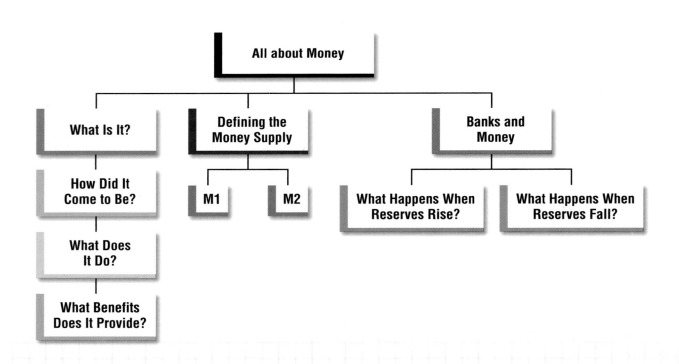

MONEY: WHAT IS IT AND HOW DID IT COME TO BE?

The story of money starts with a definition and a history lesson. This section discusses what money is and isn't (the definition) and how money came to be (the history lesson).

MONEY: A DEFINITION

To the layperson, the words *income, credit,* and *wealth* are synonyms for *money.* In each of the next three sentences, the word *money* is used incorrectly; the word in parentheses is the word an economist would use.

1. "How much money (income) did you earn last year?"
2. "Most of her money (wealth) is tied up in real estate."
3. "It sure is difficult to get much money (credit) in today's tight mortgage market."

In economics, the words *money, income, credit,* and *wealth* are not synonyms. The most general definition of **money** is any good that is widely accepted for purposes of exchange (payment for goods and services) and in the repayment of debts.

Money
Any good that is widely accepted for purposes of exchange and in the repayment of debts.

THREE FUNCTIONS OF MONEY

Money has three major functions. It functions as a medium of exchange, a unit of account, and a store of value.

Money as a Medium of Exchange

If money did not exist, goods would have to be exchanged by **barter.** Suppose you wanted a shirt. You would have to trade some good in your possession, say, a jackknife, for the shirt. But first, you would have to locate a person who has a shirt and wants to trade it for a knife. In a money economy, this step is not necessary. You can simply (1) exchange money for a shirt or (2) exchange the knife for money and then the money for the shirt. The buyer of the knife and the seller of the shirt do not have to be the same person. Money is the medium through which exchange occurs; hence, it is a **medium of exchange.** As such, money reduces the *transaction costs* of making exchanges. Exchange is easier and less time-consuming in a money economy than in a barter economy.

Barter
Exchanging goods and services for other goods and services without the use of money.

Medium of Exchange
Anything that is generally acceptable in exchange for goods and services. A function of money.

Money as a Unit of Account

A **unit of account** is a common measure in which values are expressed. Consider a barter economy. The value of every good is expressed in terms of all other goods, and there is no common unit of measure. For example, one horse might equal 100 bushels of wheat, or 200 bushels of apples, or 20 pairs of shoes, or 10 suits, or 55 loaves of bread, and so on. In a money economy, a person doesn't have to know the price of an apple in terms of oranges, pizzas, chickens, or potato chips, as would be the case in a barter economy. He or she only needs to know the price in terms of money. And because all goods are denominated in money, determining relative prices is easy and quick. For example, if 1 apple is $1 and 1 orange is 50 cents, then 1 apple = 2 oranges.

Unit of Account
A common measure in which relative values are expressed. A function of money.

Money as a Store of Value

The **store of value** function refers to a good's ability to maintain its value over time. This is the least exclusive function of money because other goods—for example, paintings, houses, and stamps—can do this too. At times, money has not maintained its value well, such as during high inflationary periods. For the most part, though, money has served as a satisfactory store of value. This allows us to accept payment in money for our productive efforts and to keep that money until we decide how we want to spend it.

Store of Value
The ability of an item to hold value over time. A function of money.

FROM A BARTER TO A MONEY ECONOMY: THE ORIGINS OF MONEY

The thing that differentiates man and animals is money.

—Gertrude Stein

At one time, there was trade but no money. Instead, people bartered. They would trade an apple for two eggs, a banana for a peach.

Today we live in a money economy. How did we move from a barter to a money economy? Did some king or queen issue the edict "Let there be money"? Not likely. Money evolved in a much more natural, market-oriented manner.

Making exchanges takes longer (on average) in a barter economy than in a money economy. That's because the *transaction costs* of making exchanges are higher in a barter economy than they are in a money economy. Stated differently, the time and effort one has to incur to consummate an exchange is greater in a barter economy than in a money economy. To illustrate, suppose Smith, living in a barter economy, wants to trade apples for oranges. He locates Jones, who has oranges. Smith offers to trade apples for oranges, but Jones tells Smith that she does not like apples and would rather have peaches.

In this situation, Smith must either (1) find someone who has oranges and wants to trade oranges for apples or (2) find someone who has peaches and wants to trade peaches for apples, after which he must return to Jones and trade peaches for oranges.

Suppose Smith continues to search and finds Brown, who has oranges and wants to trade oranges for (Smith's) apples. In economics terminology, Smith and Brown are said to have a **double coincidence of wants.** Two people have a double coincidence of wants if what the first person wants is what the second person has and what the second person wants is what the first person has. A double coincidence of wants is a necessary condition for trade to take place.

Double Coincidence of Wants
In a barter economy, a requirement that must be met before a trade can be made. It specifies that a trader must find another trader who is willing to trade what the first trader wants and at the same time wants what the first trader has.

In a barter economy, some goods are more readily accepted in exchange than other goods are. This may originally be the result of chance, but when traders notice the difference in marketability, their behavior tends to reinforce the effect. Suppose there are 10 goods, *A–J,* and that good *G* is the most marketable of the 10. On average, good *G* is accepted 5 out of every 10 times it is offered in an exchange, while the remaining goods are accepted, on average, only 2 out of every 10 times. Given this difference, some individuals accept good *G* simply because of its relatively greater acceptability, even though they have no plans to consume it. They accept good *G* because they know that it can easily be traded for most other goods at a later time (unlike the item originally in their possession).

The effect snowballs. The more people accept good *G* for its relatively greater acceptability, the greater its relative acceptability becomes, which in turn causes more people to agree to accept it. This is how money evolved. When good *G*'s acceptance evolves to the point where good *G* is widely accepted for purposes of exchange, good *G* is money. Historically, goods that have evolved into money include gold, silver, copper, cattle, salt, cocoa beans, and shells.

Q & A

Q: Isn't money an invention of government? After all, didn't the kings and emperors of long ago stamp their likenesses on money?

A: Kings and emperors may have stamped their likenesses on a certain form of money—coins—but no government invented money. Money predates government. Money largely evolved out of the self-interested actions of individuals who were trying to reduce the time and effort it took to make trades in a barter economy.

MONEY IN A PRISONER OF WAR CAMP

During World War II, an American, R. A. Radford, was captured and imprisoned in a POW camp. While in the camp, he made some observations about economic happenings, which he later described in the journal *Economica.* He noted

English and Money

In a world of barter, some goods are more widely accepted than other goods.

In a world of languages, some languages may be more widely used than other languages. Today, the most widely used language appears to be English.

English is spoken not only by native English speakers but by many other people around the world. English is the language of computers and the Internet. You can see English on posters everywhere in the world. You can hear English in pop songs sung in Tokyo. English is the working language of the Asian trade group ASEAN (Association of South East Asian Nations). It is the language of 98 percent of German research physicists and 83 percent of German research chemists. It is the official language of the European Central Bank, even though the bank is in Frankfurt, Germany. It is found in official documents in Phnom Penh, Cambodia. Singers all over the world sing in English. Alcatel, a French telecommunications company, uses English as its internal language. By 2050, half the world's population is expected to be proficient in English.

In a barter economy, if more people accept a particular good in exchange, then more people will want to accept that good. Might the same be true with a language? In other words, if more people speak English, then more non-English-speaking people will want to learn English. Just as money lowers the transaction costs of making exchanges, English might lower the transaction costs of communicating.

Is the world evolving toward one universal language and is that language English?

---

that the Red Cross would periodically distribute packages to the prisoners that contained such goods as cigarettes, toiletries, chocolate, cheese, jam, margarine, and tinned beef. Not all the prisoners had the same preferences for the goods. For example, some liked chocolate more than others; some smoked cigarettes, others did not. Because of their different preferences, the prisoners began to trade, say, a chocolate bar for some cheese, and a barter system emerged. After a short while, money appeared in the camp, but it was not U.S. dollars or any other government currency. The good that emerged as money—the good that was widely accepted for purposes of exchange—was cigarettes. As Radford noted, "The cigarette became the standard of value. In the permanent camp people started by wandering through the bungalows calling their offers—'cheese for seven [cigarettes] . . .'"

MONEY, LEISURE, AND OUTPUT

Exchanges take less time in a money economy than in a barter economy because a double coincidence of wants is irrelevant. Everyone is willing to trade what he or she has for money. It follows that the movement from a barter to a money economy releases some time that people can use in different ways.

To illustrate, suppose it takes 10 hours a week in a barter economy to make trades, but it takes only 1 hour in a money economy. In a money economy, then, there are 9 hours a week that don't have to be spent making exchanges. How will people use these 9 hours? Some people will use them to work, some people will use them for leisure, and some people will divide the 9 hours between work and leisure. Thus, there is likely to be both more output (because of the increased production) and more leisure in a money economy than in a barter economy. In other words, a money economy is likely to be richer in both goods and leisure than is a barter economy.

A person's standard of living is, to a degree, dependent on the number and quality of goods he consumes and the amount of leisure he consumes. We would expect the average person's standard of living to be higher in a money economy than in a barter economy.

Would Chris Rock Be Funny in a Barter Economy?

Suppose Chris Rock lived in a barter economy. Would he be funny?

Before we answer that question, let's look at what Chris Rock does on an average day, living in a money economy. He wakes up in the morning, eats breakfast, and then drives to a movie or television studio. Many of the next few hours are spent before the camera. In most of his TV shows, his objective is to be funny—to say funny things, to make funny faces. For this work, Chris Rock gets paid. Moreover, he gets paid with money. He then uses the money to buy food, clothes, cars, houses, and so on.

Now let's place Chris Rock in a barter economy and look at his average day. He wakes up in the morning and goes out to see if he can trade a few jokes or a few funny faces for some food. He meets a man who bakes bread. Chris asks the man if he will trade some of his bread for a few laughs. The man tells Chris that he is not interested in making that trade. In economic terms, Chris and the man do not have a double coincidence of wants: although the man has what Chris wants (bread), Chris doesn't have what the man wants.

Chris spends the rest of the day looking for people who have food and are willing to trade it for a few laughs. At the end of the day, he finally finds a person who wants to trade some food for a few laughs.

After a few days, Chris would realize that having only one thing to trade in a barter economy— jokes and funny faces—

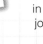

is somewhat problematic. He would decide to produce some of his own food so he wouldn't have to trade for so many things. In economic terms, if trading is difficult, reduce the number of trades you have to make by producing much of what you want to consume.

After making this decision, Chris's average day would change. He would spend most of his time planting seed to grow corn and apples, baking bread, and raising cows. He would have little time to think up jokes or to hone his comedic routine.

Why is Chris Rock's life so different in a money economy from what it would be in a barter economy? In a money economy, he specializes in producing only one thing—funny jokes and faces. In a barter economy, he would produce many things—corn, apples, meat and milk from cows, and a few laughs. Thus in a money economy, Chris specializes, and in a barter economy, he would not.

In fact, few people would specialize in a barter economy to the degree they do in a money economy. They wouldn't specialize for the same reason Chris Rock wouldn't specialize— it's just too risky. When you produce only one thing, it is extremely unlikely that you are going to obtain your preferred bundle of goods through (barter) trade. After all, what is the probability that everyone whose goods you want will want the one thing that you produce? In other words, you're not likely to have a double coincidence of wants with everyone whose goods you want.

But in a money economy, everyone is willing to trade what they have for money. There is no double-coincidence-of-wants problem, and so people specialize in one good or service. There's not so much risk to specializing as there would be in a barter economy. So people produce one thing (jokes, attorney services, corn, and so on), sell it for money, and then use the money to make their preferred purchases.

WHAT GIVES MONEY ITS VALUE?

In the days when the dollar was backed by gold, people would say that gold gave paper money its value. Very few ever asked, What gives gold its value?

It is a myth that paper money has to be backed by some commodity (such as gold) before it can have value. Today our money is not backed by gold. Our money has value because of its *general acceptability*. You accept a dollar bill in payment for your goods and services because you know others will accept the dollar bill in payment for their goods and services.

This system may sound odd, but suppose our money was not generally accepted. Suppose one day the grocery store clerk would not accept the paper dollars you offered as payment for the groceries you wanted to buy. Also, the plumber and the gas station attendant would not accept your paper dollars for fixing your kitchen drain and for servicing your car. If this were to happen, would you be as likely to accept paper dollars in exchange for what you sell? We think not. You accept paper dollars because you know that other people will accept paper dollars later when you try to spend them. Money has value to people because it is widely accepted in exchange for other goods that are valuable.

DEFINING THE MONEY SUPPLY

Money is any good that is widely accepted for purposes of exchange. We now ask, Is a ten-dollar bill money? Is a dime money? Is a checking account or a savings account money? What does money include? In other words, what is included in the money supply? Two of the more frequently used definitions of the money supply are M1 and M2.

M1

M1 is sometimes referred to as the *narrow definition of the money supply* or as *transactions money*. It is money that can be directly used for everyday transactions—to buy gas for the car, groceries to eat, and clothes to wear. **M1** consists of currency held outside banks (by members of the public for use in everyday transactions), checkable deposits, and traveler's checks.

$$M1 = \text{Currency held outside banks} + \text{Checkable deposits} + \text{Traveler's checks}$$

How are the components of M1 defined? **Currency** includes coins minted by the U.S. Treasury and paper money. About 99 percent of the paper money in circulation is **Federal Reserve notes** issued by the Federal Reserve District Banks. **Checkable deposits** are deposits on which checks can be written. There are different types of checkable deposits, including demand deposits, which are checking accounts that pay no interest, and NOW (negotiated order of withdrawal) and ATS (automatic transfer from savings) accounts, which do pay interest on their balances.

In June 2002, checkable deposits equaled $569 billion, currency held outside banks equaled $611 billion, and traveler's checks were $8 billion. M1, the sum of these figures, was $1,188 billion (see Exhibit 1).

THINKING LIKE AN ECONOMIST
When a layperson hears the word money, she usually thinks of currency—paper money (dollar bills) and coins. For example, if you are walking along a dark street at night and a thief stops you and says, "Your money or your life," you can be sure he wants your currency. To an economist, though, money is more than simply currency. One definition of money (the M1 definition) is that it is currency, checkable deposits, and traveler's checks. (Still, if stopped by a thief, an economist would be unlikely to hand over his currency and then write a check too.)

M2

M2 is sometimes referred to as the (most common) *broad definition of the money supply*.[1] **M2** is made up of M1 plus savings deposits (including money market deposit accounts, MMDAs), small-denomination time deposits, and money market mutual funds (noninstitutional). In June 2002, M2 was $5,571 billion. See Exhibit 2.

---

1. There are other definitions (or measures) of the money supply besides M1 and M2. For example, other definitions or measures include M3 and MZM. This book discusses the details of only M1 and M2.

http://

Go to *http://www.frbsf.org/currency/ independence/show.html*. This site shows the bills that have existed throughout U.S. history. Look at the continental currency, one-third dollar. What backed this currency of 1776? How would victories and defeats in the American Revolution affect the value of this bill? Are the other bills on the page backed by something other than a promise?

M1
Includes currency held outside banks + checkable deposits + traveler's checks.

Currency
Coins and paper money.

Federal Reserve Notes
Paper money issued by the Fed.

exhibit 1

The Components of M1
M1 includes currency held outside banks, checkable deposits, and traveler's checks. Data are for June 2002.

Source: Board of Governors of the Federal Reserve System

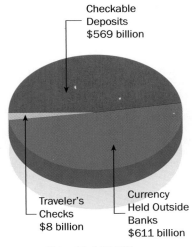

Checkable Deposits $569 billion

Traveler's Checks $8 billion

Currency Held Outside Banks $611 billion

M1 = $1,188 billion

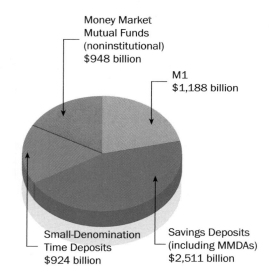

The Components of M2

M2 includes M1, savings deposits (including money market deposit accounts), small-denomination time deposits, and money market mutual funds (noninstitutional). Data are for June 2002.

Source: Board of Governors of the Federal Reserve System

Money Market Mutual Funds (noninstitutional) $948 billion

M1 $1,188 billion

Small-Denomination Time Deposits $924 billion

Savings Deposits (including MMDAs) $2,511 billion

Checkable Deposits
Deposits on which checks can be written.

M2
Includes M1 + savings deposits (including money market deposit accounts) + small-denomination time deposits + money market mutual funds (noninstitutional).

Savings Deposit
An interest-earning account at a commercial bank or thrift institution. Normally, checks cannot be written on savings deposits and the funds in a savings deposit can be withdrawn (at any time) without a penalty payment.

Money Market Deposit Account
An interest-earning account at a bank or thrift institution. Usually a minimum balance is required for an MMDA. Most MMDAs offer limited check-writing privileges.

Time Deposit
An interest-earning deposit with a specified maturity date. Time deposits are subject to penalties for early withdrawal. Small-denomination time deposits are deposits of less than $100,000.

Money Market Mutual Fund
An interest-earning account at a mutual fund company. Usually a minimum balance is required for an MMMF account. Most MMMF accounts offer limited check-writing privileges. Only noninstitutional MMMFs are part of M2.

M2 = M1
+ Savings deposits (including money market deposit accounts)
+ Small-denomination time deposits
+ Money market mutual funds (noninstitutional)

Let's look at some of the components of M2. A **savings deposit,** sometimes called a *regular savings deposit,* is an interest-earning account at a commercial bank or thrift institution. (Thrift institutions include savings and loan associations, mutual savings banks, and credit unions). Normally, checks cannot be written on savings deposits and the funds in savings deposits can be withdrawn (at any time) without a penalty payment.

A **money market deposit account** (MMDA) is an interest-earning account at a bank or thrift institution. Usually, a minimum balance is required for an MMDA. Most MMDAs offer limited check-writing privileges. For example, the owner of an MMDA might be able to write only a certain number of checks each month, and/or each check may have to be above a certain dollar amount (say, $500).

A **time deposit** is an interest-earning deposit with a *specified maturity date.* Time deposits are subject to penalties for early withdrawal. Small-denomination time deposits are deposits of less than $100,000.

A **money market mutual fund** (MMMF) is an interest-earning account at a *mutual fund company.* MMMFs held by large institutions are referred to as institutional MMMFs. MMMFs held by all others (for example, the MMMF held by an individual) are referred to as noninstitutional MMMFs. *Only noninstitutional MMMFs are part of M2.* Usually, a minimum balance is required for an MMMF account. Most MMMF accounts offer limited check-writing privileges.

WHERE DO CREDIT CARDS FIT IN?

Credit cards are commonly referred to as money—plastic money. But they are not money. A credit card is an instrument or document that makes it easier for the holder to obtain a loan. When Tina Ridges hands the department store clerk her MasterCard or Visa, she is, in effect, spending someone else's money (that already existed). The department store submits the claim to the bank, the bank pays the department store, and then the bank bills the holder of its credit card. By using her credit card, Tina has spent someone else's money, and she ultimately must repay her credit card debt with money. These transactions shift

ECONOMICS IN...

Is Money the Best Gift?

Consider what happens when one person gives another person a gift. First, the gift giver has to decide about how much money to spend on the gift. Is it an amount between $10 and $20 or between $50 and $80? After the dollar range has been decided, the gift giver has to decide what to buy. Will it be a book, a shirt, a gift certificate to a restaurant, or what? Deciding on what to buy requires the gift giver to guess the preferences of the gift recipient. This is no easy task, even if the gift giver knows the gift recipient fairly well. Often, guessing preferences is done poorly, which means that each year hundreds of thousands of people end up with gifts they would prefer not to have received. Every year, shirts go unworn, books go unread, and closets fill up with unwanted items.

At the end of a holiday season in 1993, Joel Waldfogel, then an economist at Yale University, asked a group of students two questions. First, he asked them what dollar value they would estimate was paid by the gift givers for all the holiday gifts they (the students) received. Second, he asked the students how much *they* would have paid to get the gifts they received. What Waldfogel learned was that, on average, gift recipients were willing to pay less for the gifts they received than gift givers paid for the gifts. For example, a gift recipient might be willing to pay $25 for a book that a gift giver bought for $30. The most conservative estimate put the average gift recipient's valuation at 90 percent of the buying price. This means that if the gift giver had given the cash value of the purchase instead of the gift itself, the recipient could then buy what was really wanted and been better off at no additional cost. In other words, some economists have concluded that when you don't know the preferences of the gift recipient very well, it just may be better to give money.

---

around the existing quantity of money between various individuals and firms but do not change the total.

Self-Test *(Answers to Self-Test questions are in the Self-Test Appendix.)*

1. Why (not how) did money evolve out of a barter economy?
2. If individuals remove funds from their checkable deposits and transfer them to their money market accounts, will M1 fall and M2 rise? Explain your answer.
3. How does money reduce the transaction costs of making trades?

HOW BANKING DEVELOPED

Just as money evolved, so did banking. This section discusses the origins of banking. The discussion will shed some light on and aid in understanding modern banking.

THE EARLY BANKERS

Our money today is easy to carry and transport. But money was not always so portable. For example, when money was principally gold coins, carrying it about was neither easy nor safe. First, gold is heavy. Second, a person transporting thousands of gold coins can easily draw the attention of thieves. But storing gold at home can also be risky. Most individuals turned to their local goldsmith for help because he was already equipped with safe storage facilities. Goldsmiths were the first bankers. They took in other people's gold and stored it for them. To acknowledge that they held deposited gold, goldsmiths issued receipts called *warehouse receipts* to their customers.

After people's confidence in the receipts was established, they used the receipts to make payments instead of using the gold itself. (Gold was not only

http://

Go to *http://www.frbsf.org/currency/civilwar/show.html*. Why aren't living persons portrayed on U.S. money? What do you think explains the reason postage stamps were used as a substitute for coins during the Civil War? What is a greenback?

http://

Go to *http://www.jpmchase.com*. Under the "About the firm" menu, select "History" and then "JPMorgan." When was J. P. Morgan founded? Who were the customers of J. P. Morgan? What effect did the Glass-Steagall Act have on J. P. Morgan? Do you think large companies use banks the same way today as they did 100 years ago?

Economics on the Yellow Brick Road

I'll get you, my pretty.
—Wicked Witch of the West in *The Wizard of Oz*

In 1893, the United States fell into economic depression: the stock market crashed, banks failed, workers were laid off, and many farmers lost their farms. Some people blamed the depression on the gold standard. They proposed that instead of only gold backing U.S. currency, there should be a bimetallic monetary standard where both gold and silver backed the currency. This would lead to an increase in the money supply. Many people thought that with more money in circulation, the economic hard times would soon be a thing of the past.

One of the champions of silver was William Jennings Bryan, who was the Democratic candidate for the U.S. presidency in 1896. Bryan had established himself as a friend to the many Americans who had been hurt by the economic depression—especially farmers and industrial workers. Bryan's views were shared by L. Frank Baum, the author of *The Wonderful Wizard of Oz*, the book that was the basis for the 1939 movie *The Wizard of Oz*.

Baum blamed the gold standard for the hardships faced by farmers and workers during the depression. Baum saw farmers and industrial workers as the "common man," and he saw William Jennings Bryan as the best possible hope for the common man in this country.

Numerous persons believe that Baum's most famous work, *The Wonderful Wizard of Oz*, is an allegory for the presidential election of 1896.[2] Some say that Dorothy, in the book and the movie, represents Bryan. Both Dorothy and Bryan were young (Bryan was a 36-year-old presidential candidate). Like the cyclone in the movie that transported Dorothy to the Land of Oz, the delegates at the 1896 Democratic convention lifted Bryan into a new political world, the world of presidential politics.

As Dorothy begins her travels to the Emerald City (Washington, D.C.) with Toto (who represents the Democratic Party) to meet the Wizard of Oz, she travels down a yellow brick road (the gold standard). On her way, she meets the scarecrow (who represents the farmer), the tin man (who represents the industrial worker), and the cowardly lion, who some believe represents the Populist Party of the time. (The Populist Party was sometimes represented as a lion in cartoons of the time. It was a "cowardly" lion because, some say, it did not have the courage to fight an independent campaign for the presidency in 1896.) The message is clear: Bryan, with the help of the Democratic and Populist parties and the votes of the farmers and the industrial workers, will travel to Washington.

But then, when Dorothy and the others reach the Emerald City, they are denied their wishes, just as Bryan is denied the presidency. He loses the election to William McKinley.

But all is not over. There is still the battle with the Wicked Witch of the West, who wears a golden cap (gold standard). When the Wicked Witch sees Dorothy's silver shoes—they were changed to ruby shoes in the movie—she desperately wants them for their magical quality. But that is not to be. Dorothy kills the Wicked Witch of the West; she then clicks her silver shoes together and they take her back home, where all is right with the world.

inconvenient for customers to carry, it was also inconvenient for merchants to accept.) In short, the paper warehouse receipts circulated as money. For instance, if Franklin wanted to buy something from Mason that was priced at 10 gold pieces, he could simply give his warehouse receipt to Mason instead of going to the goldsmith, obtaining the gold, and then delivering it to Mason. For both Franklin and Mason, using the receipts was easier than dealing with the actual gold.

At this stage of banking, warehouse receipts were fully backed by gold; they simply represented gold in storage. Goldsmiths later began to recognize that on an average day few people came to redeem their receipts for gold. Many individuals were simply trading the receipts for goods and seldom requested the

---

2. The interpretation here is based on "William Jennings Bryan on the Yellow Brick Road" by John Geer and Thomas Rochon (*Journal of American Culture*, Winter 1993) and "The Wizard of Oz: Parable on Populism" by Henry Littlefield (*American Quarterly*, 1964).

gold that the receipts represented. In short, the receipts had become money, widely accepted for purposes of exchange.

Sensing opportunity, some goldsmiths began to lend some of the stored gold, realizing that they could earn interest on the loans without defaulting on their pledge to redeem the warehouse receipts when presented. In most cases, the borrowers of the gold also preferred warehouse receipts to the actual gold. Thus, the amount of gold represented by the warehouse receipts was greater than the actual amount of gold on deposit. The consequence of this lending activity was an increase in the money supply—measured in terms of gold and the paper warehouse receipts issued by the goldsmith-bankers.

This was the beginning of **fractional reserve banking.** Under a fractional reserve system, banks create money by holding on reserve only a fraction of the money deposited with them and lending the remainder. Our modern-day banking system operates under a fractional reserve banking arrangement.

Fractional Reserve Banking
A banking arrangement that allows banks to hold reserves equal to only a fraction of their deposit liabilities.

THE FEDERAL RESERVE SYSTEM

The next chapter discusses the structure of **the Fed** (the popular name for the **Federal Reserve System**) and the tools it uses to change the money supply. For now, we need only note that the Federal Reserve System is the central bank; essentially, it is a bank's bank. Its chief function is to control the nation's money supply.

Federal Reserve System (the Fed)
The central bank of the United States.

THE MONEY CREATION PROCESS

This section describes the important money supply process, specifically, how the banking system, working under a fractional reserve requirement, creates money.

THE BANK'S RESERVES AND MORE

Many banks have an account with the Fed, in much the same way that an individual has a checking account with a commercial bank. Economists refer to this account with the Fed as either a reserve account or bank deposits at the Fed. Banks also have currency or cash in their vaults—simply called vault cash—on the bank premises. The sum of (1) bank deposits at the Fed and (2) the bank's vault cash is (total bank) **reserves.**

Reserves = Bank deposits at the Fed + Vault cash

Reserves
The sum of bank deposits at the Fed and vault cash.

For example, if a bank currently has $4 million in deposits at the Fed and $1 million in vault cash, it has $5 million in reserves.

The Required Reserve Ratio and Required Reserves

The Fed mandates that member commercial banks must hold a certain fraction of their checkable deposits in reserve form. What does "reserve form" mean here? It means in the form of "bank deposits at the Fed" and/or "vault cash" because the sum of these two equals reserves.

The fraction of checkable deposits that banks must hold in reserve form is called the **required reserve ratio (r).** The actual dollar amount of deposits held in reserve form is called **required reserves.** In other words, to find the required reserves for a given bank, multiply the required reserve ratio by checkable deposits (in the bank):

Required reserves = r × Checkable deposits

Required Reserve Ratio (r)
A percentage of each dollar deposited that must be held on reserve (at the Fed or in the bank's vault).

Required Reserves
The minimum amount of reserves a bank must hold against its checkable deposits as mandated by the Fed.

For example, assume that customers have deposited $40 million in a neighborhood bank and that the Fed has set the required reserve ratio at 10 percent. It follows that required reserves for the bank equal $4 million (0.10 × $40 million = $4 million).

Excess Reserves

Excess Reserves
Any reserves held beyond the required amount. The difference between (total) reserves and required reserves.

The difference between a bank's (total) reserves and its required reserves is its **excess reserves:**

$$\text{Excess reserves} = \text{Reserves} - \text{Required reserves}$$

For example, if the bank's (total) reserves are $5 million and its required reserves are $4 million, then it holds excess reserves of $1 million.

The important point to remember about excess reserves is that banks use them to make loans. In fact, banks have a monetary incentive to use their excess reserves to make loans: If the bank uses the $1 million excess reserves to make loans, it earns interest income. If it does not make any loans, it does not earn interest income.

THE BANKING SYSTEM AND THE MONEY EXPANSION PROCESS

The banks in the banking system are prohibited from printing their own currency. Nevertheless, the banking system can create money by increasing checkable deposits. (Remember, checkable deposits are a component of the money supply.)

The process starts with the Fed. For now, suppose the Fed prints $1,000 in new paper money and gives it to Bill. Bill takes the newly created $1,000 and deposits it in bank *A*. We can see this transaction in the following T-account. A **T-account** is a simplified balance sheet that records the *changes* in the bank's assets and liabilities.

T-Account
A simplified balance sheet that shows the changes in a bank's assets and liabilities.

BANK *A*			
Assets		**Liabilities**	
Reserves	+$1,000	Checkable deposits (Bill)	+$1,000

Because the deposit initially is added to vault cash, *the bank's reserves have increased by $1,000.* The bank's liabilities also have increased by $1,000 because it owes Bill the $1,000 he deposited in the bank.

Next, the banker divides the $1,000 reserves into two categories: required reserves and excess reserves. The amount of required reserves depends on the required reserve ratio specified by the Fed. We'll set the required reserve ratio at 10 percent. This means the bank holds $100 in required reserves against the deposit and holds $900 in excess reserves. The previous T-account can be modified to show this:

BANK *A*			
Assets		**Liabilities**	
Required reserves	+$100	Checkable deposits (Bill)	+$1,000
Excess reserves	+$900		

On the left side of the T-account, the total is $1,000, and on the right side, the total is also $1,000. By dividing total reserves into required reserves and excess reserves, we can see how many dollars the bank is holding above the Fed requirements. These excess reserves can be used to make new loans.

Suppose bank *A* makes a loan of $900 to Jenny. The left (assets) side of the bank's T-account looks like this:

BANK *A*			
Assets		**Liabilities**	
Required reserves	+$100	See the next T-account.	
Excess reserves	+$900		
Loans	+$900		

Now when bank *A* gives Jenny a $900 loan, it doesn't give her $900 cash. Instead, it opens a checking account for Jenny at the bank, and the balance in the account is $900. This is how things are shown in the T-account:

BANK *A*		
Assets	**Liabilities**	
See the previous T-account.	Checkable deposits (Bill)	+$1,000
	Checkable deposits (Jenny)	+$900

Before we continue, *notice that the money supply has increased.* When Jenny borrowed $900 and the bank put that amount in her checking account, *no one else in the economy had any less money and Jenny had more than before.* Consequently, the money supply has increased. (Think of M1 as equal to currency + checkable deposits + traveler's checks. Through the lending activity of the bank, checkable deposits have increased by $900 and there has been no change in the amount of currency or traveler's checks. It follows that M1 has increased.) In other words, the money supply is $900 more than it was previously.

Now suppose that Jenny spends the $900 on a new CD player. She writes a $900 check to the CD retailer, who deposits the full amount of the check in bank *B*. First, what happens to bank *A*? It uses its excess reserves to honor Jenny's check when it is presented by bank *B* and simultaneously reduces her checking account balance from $900 to zero. Bank *A*'s situation is shown here:

BANK *A*			
Assets		**Liabilities**	
Required reserves	+$100	Checkable deposits (Bill)	+$1,000
Excess reserves	$0		
Loans	+$900	Checkable deposits (Jenny)	$0

The situation for bank *B* is different. Because of the CD retailer's deposit, bank *B* now has $900 that it didn't have previously. This increases bank *B*'s reserves and liabilities by $900:

BANK *B*			
Assets		**Liabilities**	
Reserves	+$900	Checkable deposits (CD Retailer)	+$900

Note that the CD purchase has not changed the overall money supply. Dollars have simply moved from Jenny's checking account to the CD retailer's checking account.

The process continues in much the same way for bank *B* as it did earlier for bank *A*. Only a fraction (10 percent) of the CD retailer's $900 has to be kept on reserve (required reserves on $900 = $90). The remainder ($810) constitutes excess reserves that can be lent to still another borrower. That loan will create $810 in new checkable deposits and thus expand the money supply by that amount. The process continues with banks *C, D, E,* and so on until the dollar figures become so small that the process comes to a halt. Exhibit 3 summarizes what happens as the $1,000 originally created by the Fed works its way through the banking system.

Looking back over the entire process, this is what has happened:

- The Fed created $1,000 worth of new money and gave it to Bill, who then deposited it in bank *A.*
- The reserves of bank *A* increased. The reserves of no other bank decreased.

exhibit 3

The Banking System Creates Checkable Deposits (Money)
In this exhibit, the required reserve ratio is 10 percent. We have assumed that there is no cash leakage and that excess reserves are fully lent out; that is, banks hold zero excess reserves.

(1) Bank	(2) New Deposits (new reserves)	(3) New Required Reserves	(4) Checkable Deposits Created by Extending New Loans (equal to new excess reserves)
A	$1,000.00	$100.00	$900.00
B	900.00	90.00	810.00
C	810.00	81.00	729.00
D	729.00	72.90	656.10
E	656.10	65.61	590.49
• • •	• • •	• • •	• • •
TOTALS (rounded)	$10,000	$1,000	$9,000

- The banking system, with the newly created $1,000 in hand, made loans and, in the process, created checkable deposits for the people who received the loans.
- Remember, checkable deposits are part of the money supply. So, in effect, by extending loans and, in the process, creating checkable deposits, the banking system has increased the money supply.

The $1,000 in new funds deposited in bank A was the basis of several thousand dollars' worth of new bank loans and new checkable deposits. In this instance, the $1,000 initially injected into the economy ultimately caused bankers to create $9,000 in new checkable deposits. When this amount is added to the newly created $1,000 the Fed gave to Bill, the money supply has expanded by $10,000. A formula that shows this result is

$$\text{Maximum change in checkable deposits} = (1/r) \times \Delta R$$

where $r =$ the required reserve ratio and $\Delta R =$ the change in reserves resulting from the original injection of funds.[3] In the equation, the reciprocal of the required reserve ratio $(1/r)$ is known as the **simple deposit multiplier.** The arithmetic for this example is

Simple Deposit Multiplier
The reciprocal of the required reserve ratio, $1/r$.

$$\begin{aligned} \text{Maximum change in checkable deposits} &= (1/0.10) \times \$1,000 \\ &= 10 \times \$1,000 \\ &= \$10,000 \end{aligned}$$

---

3. Because only checkable deposits, and no other components of the money supply, change in this example, we could write "Maximum change in checkable deposits = $(1/r) \times \Delta R$" as "Maximum $\Delta M = (1/r) \times \Delta R$" where $\Delta M =$ the change in the money supply. In this chapter, the only component of the money supply that we allow to change is checkable deposits. For this reason, we can talk about changes in checkable deposits and the money supply as if they are the same—which they are, given our specification.

WHY MAXIMUM? ANSWER: NO CASH LEAKAGES AND ZERO EXCESS RESERVES

We made two important assumptions in our discussion of the money expansion process.

First, we assumed that all monies were deposited in bank checking accounts. For example, when Jenny wrote a check to the CD retailer, the retailer endorsed the check and deposited the full amount in bank *B*. In reality, the retailer might have deposited less than the full amount and kept a few dollars in cash. This is referred to as a **cash leakage.** If there had been a cash leakage of $300, then bank *B* would have received only $600, not $900. This would change the second number in column 2 in Exhibit 3 to $600 and the second number in column 4 to $540. Therefore, the total in column 2 of Exhibit 3 would be much smaller. A cash leakage that reduces the flow of dollars into banks means that banks have fewer dollars to lend. Fewer loans mean banks put less into borrowers' accounts, so less money is created than when cash leakages = 0.

Second, we assumed that every bank lent all its excess reserves, leaving every bank with zero excess reserves. After Bill's $1,000 deposit, for example, bank *A* had excess reserves of $900 and made a new loan for the full amount. Banks generally want to lend all of their excess reserves to earn additional interest income, but there is no law, natural or legislated, that says every bank has to lend every penny of excess reserves. If banks do not lend all their excess reserves, then checkable deposits and the money supply will increase by less than in the original situation (where banks did lend all their excess reserves).

If we had not made our two assumptions, the change in checkable deposits would have been much smaller. Because we assumed no cash leakages and zero excess reserves, the change in checkable deposits is the *maximum* possible change.

Cash Leakage
Occurs when funds are held as currency instead of being deposited into a checking account.

WHO CREATED WHAT?

The money expansion process described had two major players: (1) the Fed, which created the new $1,000, and (2) the banking system. Together they created or expanded the money supply by $10,000. The Fed directly created $1,000 and thus made it possible for banks to create $9,000 in new checkable deposits as a by-product of extending new loans.

An easy formula for finding the maximum change in checkable deposits brought about by the banking system (and *only* the banking system) is

$$\text{Maximum change in checkable deposits (brought about by the banking system)} = (1/r) \times \Delta ER$$

where r = the required reserve ratio and ΔER = the change in excess reserves of the first bank to receive the new injection of funds. The arithmetic here is

$$\text{Maximum change in checkable deposits (brought about by the banking system)} = (1/0.10) \times \$900$$
$$= 10 \times \$900$$
$$= \$9,000$$

Q & A

Q: What would have happened if Bill had decided to keep the original $1,000 in his pocket rather than depositing it in bank *A*?

A: If Bill had kept the money rather than depositing it, the money expansion process in Exhibit 3 would not have taken place. For the money expansion process to proceed as described, dollars must be deposited in checking accounts and banks must extend loans. This process began when Bill placed the $1,000 in his checking account.

IT WORKS IN REVERSE: THE "MONEY DESTRUCTION" PROCESS

In the preceding example, the Fed created $1,000 of new money and gave it to Bill, who then deposited it in bank *A*. This simple act created a multiple increase in checkable deposits and the money supply. The process also works in reverse. Suppose Bill withdraws the $1,000 and gives it back to the Fed. The Fed then destroys the $1,000. As a result, bank reserves decline. The multiple deposit contraction process is symmetrical to the multiple deposit expansion process.

Again, we set the required reserve ratio at 10 percent. The situation for bank *A* looks like this:

BANK *A*			
Assets		**Liabilities**	
Reserves	−$1,000	Checkable deposits (Bill)	−$1,000

Losing $1,000 in reserves places bank *A* in a *reserve deficiency position*. Specifically, it is $900 short. Remember, bank *A* held $100 reserves against the initial $1,000 deposit, so it loses $900 in reserves that backed other deposits ($1,000 − $100 = $900). If this is not immediately obvious, consider the following example.

Suppose the checkable deposits in a bank total $10,000 and the required reserve ratio is 10 percent. This means the bank must hold $1,000 in reserve form. Now let's suppose this is exactly what the bank holds in reserves, $1,000. (We'll assume that the $1,000 is being held as vault cash.) Is the bank reserve deficient at this point? No, it is holding exactly the right amount of reserves given its checkable deposits. Not one penny more, not one penny less.

Now one day a customer of the bank asks to withdraw $1,000. The bank teller goes to the vault, collects $1,000, and hands it to the customer. Two things have happened: (1) reserves of the bank have fallen by $1,000 and (2) checkable deposits in the bank have fallen by the same amount. In other words, checkable deposits go from $10,000 to $9,000.

Does the bank currently have reserves? The answer is no. The bank's reserves of $1,000 were given to the customer, so the bank has $0 in reserves. If the required reserve ratio is 10 percent, how much does the bank need in reserves given that checkable deposits are now $9,000? The answer is $900. In other words, the bank is $900 reserve deficient.

When a bank is reserve deficient, it must take immediate action to correct this situation. What can it do? One thing it can do is to reduce its outstanding loans. Funds from loan repayments can be applied to the reserve deficiency rather than being used to extend new loans. As borrowers repay $900 worth of loans, they reduce their checking account balances by that amount, causing the money supply to decline by $900.

Let's assume that the $900 loan repayment to bank *A* is written on a check issued by bank *B*. After the check has cleared, reserves and customer deposits at bank *B* fall by $900. This situation is reflected in bank *B*'s T-account:

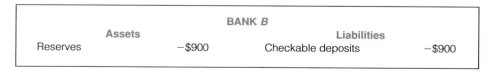

BANK *B*			
Assets		**Liabilities**	
Reserves	−$900	Checkable deposits	−$900

Bank *B* now faces a situation similar to bank *A*'s earlier situation. Losing $900 in reserves places bank *B* in reserve deficiency. It is $810 short. Remember, bank *B* held $90 in reserve form against the $900 deposit, so it loses $810 that backed other deposits ($900 − $90 = $810). Bank *B* seeks to recoup $810 by reducing its outstanding loans by an equal amount. If a customer is asked to pay off an $810 loan and does so by writing a check on his account at bank *C*, that bank's reserves and deposits both decline by $810. As a result, bank C is now in reserve deficiency; it is $729 short. Remember, bank C held $81 in reserve form against the $810 deposit, so it is short $729 that backed other deposits ($810 − $81 = $729).

As you can see, the figures are the same ones given in Exhibit 3, with the exception that each change is negative rather than positive. When Bill withdrew $1,000 from his account and returned it to the Fed (which then destroyed the $1,000), the money supply declined by $10,000.

Exhibit 4 shows the money supply expansion and contraction process in brief.

Q & A

Q: Suppose a bank gives Jim a $900 loan on Monday. On Tuesday, the bank learns that it is $900 reserve deficient. On Wednesday, Jim repays the $900 loan and the bank applies the $900 to its reserve deficiency position instead of creating a new loan with it. According to the text, if the bank applies the $900 to its reserve deficiency position instead of creating a new loan with it, the money supply falls. Why isn't the money supply the same as it was on Monday? Why did it fall?

A: The money supply rises and then falls. To see this clearly, let's say the money supply on Monday is $1,000. Now after the bank gives the $900 loan to Jim, the money supply *rises* to $1,900. That's because loans are made in the form of checkable deposits and checkable deposits are part of the money supply. Remember: M1 = currency held outside banks + checkable deposits + traveler's checks.

Now let's change your scenario. Suppose the bank is *not* reserve deficient and Jim repays the $900 loan (on Wednesday). What would the bank do with that $900? It would lend it to someone else. In other words, it would take in the $900 loan repayment from Jim and turn around and lend the $900 to, say, Nancy. Doing this would keep the money supply constant at $1,900. But when the bank is reserve deficient, it chooses another path. Instead of extending a $900 loan to Nancy—instead of creating a checkable deposit for Nancy with a balance of $900 in it—the bank applies the $900 to its reserve deficiency position. In other words, the bank puts the $900 in, say, its vault (where it is part of vault cash and thus part of reserves). Now what is the money supply? It is $1,000, not $1,900. Thus, the money supply *falls*.

WE CHANGE OUR EXAMPLE

Let's change our example somewhat. This time the Fed does not create new money. Instead, let's consider Jack, who currently has $1,000 in cash in a shoebox in his bedroom. He decides that he doesn't want to keep this much cash around the house, so he takes it to bank A and opens a checking account. So far, this act does not change the money supply. Initially, the $1,000 in the shoebox was currency outside a bank and thus was part of the money supply. When Jack took the $1,000 from his shoebox and placed it in a bank, there was $1,000 less

exhibit 4

The Money Supply Expansion and Contraction Processes
The money supply expands if reserves enter the banking system; the money supply contracts if reserves exit the banking system. In expansion, reserves rise; thus, excess reserves rise, more loans are made, and checkable deposits rise. Because checkable deposits are part of the money supply, the money supply rises. In contraction, reserves fall; thus, excess reserves fall, fewer loans are made, and checkable deposits fall. Because checkable deposits are part of the money supply, the money supply falls.

Money Supply Expansion

Reserves in banking system → Excess reserves → Loans → Checkable deposits → Money supply

Money Supply Contraction

Reserves in banking system → Excess reserves → Loans → Checkable deposits → Money supply currency outside a bank and $1,000 more checkable deposits. So far, this act has changed the *composition* of the money supply, but not its *size*.

The $1,000 could not create a multiple of itself when it was in a shoebox in Jack's bedroom. When the $1,000 is placed in a checking account, however, the banking system has $1,000 more reserves than before and thus has excess reserves that can be used to extend new loans and create new checkable deposits. This means the money supply can expand in much the same way as earlier. At maximum, the banking system can create $9,000 worth of new loans and checkable deposits. (We have assumed again that $r = 0.10$.) The primary difference between the two examples is their *starting point*. The first example started with the Fed creating new money. The second example began with Jack removing $1,000 from a shoebox and depositing it in a bank. Despite this difference, in both examples, the banking system created the identical maximum amount of new checkable deposits.

Self-Test

1. If a bank's deposits equal $579 million and the required reserve ratio is 9.5 percent, what dollar amount must the bank hold in reserve form?

2. If the Fed creates $600 million in new reserves, what is the maximum change in checkable deposits that can occur if the required reserve ratio is 10 percent?

3. Bank *A* has $1.2 million in reserves and $10 million in deposits. The required reserve ratio is 10 percent. If bank *A* loses $200,000 in reserves, by what dollar amount is it reserve deficient?

A Reader Asks...

Do People Desire to Economize on Time?

It takes less time to make exchanges in a money economy than in a barter economy. In other words, by moving from a barter economy to a money economy, individuals economize on time. Are there other examples in economics of individuals economizing on time?

Some economists have argued that one of the hallmarks of a money economy is the gradual reduction of "dead" time spent to consume a good or service. Examples abound. Today, the use of bar codes and scanners permits consumers to get through supermarket and department store lines faster. Touchtone telephones allow people to refill prescriptions without going to the pharmacy. With the Internet, we can make price comparisons without traveling from store to store and can order a wide variety of goods and services.[4]

Some economists go on to argue that brand names also help individuals economize on time. Instead of spending time making price and quality comparisons on everything we purchase, we sometimes rely on brand names to provide a certain level of service or quality. We can read a few pages of every book in a bookstore to see if a book looks "good enough to buy," or we can save time by just buying a book written by an author who has already satisfied our reading propensities. When traveling to a new city, we can spend time learning about the different local hotels, or we can save time by checking into a Marriott or Holiday Inn.

---

4. Many of the examples in this feature come from "Time: Economics' Neglected Stepchild," by Gene Epstein, *Barron's*, 31 December 2001.

What Money Is

- Money is any good that is widely accepted for purposes of exchange and in the repayment of debts.
- Money serves as a medium of exchange, a unit of account, and a store of value.
- Money evolved out of a barter economy as traders attempted to make exchange easier. A few goods that have been used as money include gold, silver, copper, cattle, rocks, and shells.
- Our money today has value because of its general acceptability.

The Money Supply

- M1 includes currency held outside banks, checkable deposits, and traveler's checks. M2 includes M1, savings deposits (including money market deposit accounts), small-denomination time deposits, and money market mutual funds (noninstitutional).
- Credit cards are not money. When a credit card is used to make a purchase, a liability is incurred. This is not the case when money is used to make a purchase.

The Money Creation Process

- Banks in the United States operate under a fractional reserve system in which they must maintain only a fraction of their deposits in the form of reserves (that is, in the form of deposits at the Fed and vault cash). Excess reserves are typically used to extend loans to customers. When banks make these loans, they credit borrowers' checking accounts and thereby increase the money supply. When banks reduce the volume of loans outstanding, they reduce checkable deposits and reduce the money supply.
- A change in the composition of the money supply can change the size of the money supply. For example, suppose M1 = $1,000 billion, where the breakdown is $300 billion currency outside banks and $700 billion in checkable deposits. Now suppose the $300 billion in currency is put in a checking account in a bank. Initially, this changes the composition of the money supply but not its size. M1 is still $1,000 billion but now includes $0 in currency and $1,000 billion in checkable deposits. Later, when the banks have had time to create new loans (checkable deposits) with the new reserves provided by the $300 billion deposit, the money supply expands.

Money	Federal Reserve Notes	Federal Reserve System (the Fed)
Barter	Checkable Deposits	Reserves
Medium of Exchange	M2	Required Reserve Ratio (r)
Unit of Account	Savings Deposit	Required Reserves
Store of Value	Money Market Deposit Account	Excess Reserves
Double Coincidence of Wants	Time Deposit	T-Account
M1	Money Market Mutual Fund	Simple Deposit Multiplier
Currency	Fractional Reserve Banking	Cash Leakage

Economic facts, actions, and changes create ripples that move away from their point of origin. Eventually, these ripples can intersect your life and have an effect on you. Consider the following example.

The economic change from a barter economy to a money economy was a slow process that took many years. People in a barter economy were not trying to create the institution of money; they were simply trying to make trading easier. In pursuit of their own gain, individuals began to accept that good (among many goods) that had relatively greater acceptability. In time, that good became money. In a money economy, people don't have to deal with the inefficiencies of a barter economy. You can go to a store and pay money for the shoes you want instead of trying to find a shoemaker who is willing to trade a pair of shoes for a good you've produced. Thus, there is a connection between the change from a barter to a money economy and the conveniences in your life you take for granted—an economic connection to you.

Based on the material in this chapter, identify other ways in which economic facts, actions, and changes create ripples that eventually affect you.

Questions and Problems

1. Does inflation, which is an increase in the price level, affect the three functions of money? If so, how?

2. Some economists have proposed that the Fed move to a 100 percent required reserve ratio. This would make the simple deposit multiplier 1 ($1/r = 1/1.00 = 1$). Do you think banks would argue for or against the move? Explain your answer.

3. Money makes trade easier. Would having a money supply twice as large as it is currently make trade twice as easy? Would having a money supply half its current size make trade half as easy?

4. Explain why gold backing is not necessary to give paper money value.

5. "Money is a means of lowering the transaction costs of making exchanges." Do you agree or disagree? Explain your answer.

6. If you were on an island with 10 other people and there was no money, do you think money would emerge on the scene? Why or why not?

7. Can M1 fall as M2 rises? Can M1 rise without M2 rising too? Explain your answers.

8. Why isn't a credit card money?

9. If Smith, who has a checking account at bank *A*, withdraws his money and deposits all of it into bank *B*, do reserves in the banking system change? Explain your answer.

10. If Jones, who has a checking account at bank *A*, withdraws his money, deposits half of it into bank *B*, and keeps the other half in currency, do reserves in the banking system change?

11. Give an example that illustrates a change in the composition of the money supply.

12. Describe the money supply expansion process.

13. Describe the money supply contraction process.

14. Does a cash leakage affect the change in checkable deposits and the money supply expansion process? Explain your answer.

Working with Numbers and Graphs

1. Suppose that $10,000 in new dollar bills (never seen before) falls magically from the sky into the hands of Joanna Ferris. What are the minimum increase and the maximum increase in the money supply that may result? Assume the required reserve ratio is 10 percent.

2. Suppose Joanna Ferris receives $10,000 from her friend Ethel and deposits the money in a checking account. Ethel gave Joanna the money by writing a check on her checking account. Would the maximum increase in the money supply still be what you found it to be in question 1 where Joanna received the money from the sky? Explain your answer.

3. Suppose that instead of Joanna getting $10,000 from the sky or through a check from a friend, she gets the money from her mother who had buried it in a can in her backyard. In this case, would the maximum increase in the money supply be what you found it to be in question 1? Explain your answer.

4. Suppose $r = 10$ percent and the Fed creates $20,000 in new money that is deposited in someone's check-

ing account in a bank. What is the maximum change in the money supply as a result?

5. Suppose $r = 10$ percent and John walks into his bank, withdraws $2,000 in cash, and burns the money. What is the maximum change in the money supply as a result?

6. The Fed creates $100,000 in new money that is deposited in someone's checking account in a bank. What is the maximum change in the money supply if the required reserve ratio is 5 percent? 10 percent? 20 percent?

7. Use the table below to answer the questions that follow.

Bank	New Deposits (new reserves)	New Required Reserves	Checkable Deposits Created by Extending New Loans (equal to new excess reserves)
A	(1)	$500	$1,400
B	(2)	$342	(3)

a. What dollar amount goes in blank (1)?

b. What does the required reserve ratio equal?

c. What does the cash leakage between bank *A* and bank *B* equal?

d. What dollar amount goes in blank (2)?

e. What dollar amount goes in blank (3)?

Internet Activities

1. Go to *http://research.stlouisfed.org/index.html*. Click on "Economic Data—FRED II" and then on "Monetary Aggregates."

a. Click on "M1 Money Stock and Components." First, look at the bottom of the page to see what the various abbreviations mean (for example, SA = seasonally adjusted). What is the most recent figure for M1 (seasonally adjusted and monthly)? What is the most recent figure for currency (seasonally adjusted and monthly)? What is the most recent figure for total checkable deposits (seasonally adjusted and monthly)?

b. Click the "Back" button, and then click on "M2 Money Stock and Components." What is the most recent figure for M2 (seasonally adjusted and monthly)? What is the most recent figure for total savings deposits (seasonally adjusted and monthly)?

2. Go to *http://www.census.gov/main/www/popclock.html*, and find the current population of the United States. Next, divide the most recent currency figure (from Activity 1a) by the population to find the currency per person. Is this about the amount of currency that you carry?

Log on to the Arnold Xtra! Web site now (*http://arnoldxtra.swcollege.com*) for additional learning resources such as practice quizzes, help with graphing, video clips, and current event applications.

ch.13

THE FEDERAL RESERVE SYSTEM

Tourists in Washington, D.C., usually visit the White House, the Capitol building, and the Supreme Court building. In these buildings, major decisions are made that affect peoples' lives.

There is another building in Washington, D.C., where major decisions are made that affect peoples' lives. But tourists rarely visit it. It is the Federal Reserve building. In this building, the Board of Governors of the Federal Reserve System and the members of the Federal Open Market Committee determine U.S. monetary policy. We provide you with many of the details of the Federal Reserve System in this chapter.

Chapter Road Map

Your goal in this chapter is an understanding of how the Fed changes the money supply. As shown below, the Fed principally uses three tools to change the money supply: (1) open market operations, (2) the required reserve ratio, and (3) the discount rate. Before discussing these three tools, we explain the structure and functions of the Fed.

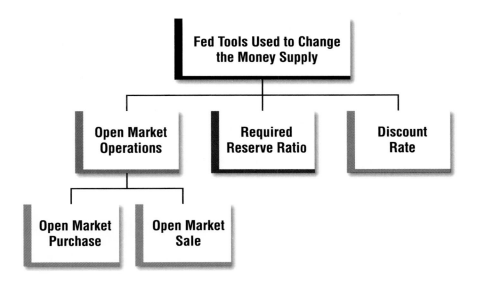

THE FEDERAL RESERVE SYSTEM

The Federal Reserve System is the central bank of the United States. Other nations also have central banks, such as the Bank of Sweden, the Bank of England, the Banque de France, the Bank of Japan, the Deutsche Bundesbank, and so on.

THE STRUCTURE OF THE FED

The Federal Reserve System came into existence with the Federal Reserve Act of 1913 and began operations in November 1914. The act divided the country into Federal Reserve Districts. As Exhibit 1 shows, there are 12 districts; each has a Federal Reserve Bank with its own president.

Within the Fed, a seven-member **Board of Governors** coordinates and controls the activities of the Federal Reserve System. The Board members serve 14-year terms and are appointed by the President with Senate approval. To limit political influence on Fed policy, the terms of the governors are staggered—with one new appointment every other year—so a President cannot "pack" the Board. The President also designates one member as chairman of the Board for a four-year term.

The major policymaking group within the Fed is the **Federal Open Market Committee (FOMC)**. Authority to conduct **open market operations**—or the buying and selling of government securities—rests with the FOMC (more on open market operations later). The FOMC has 12 members, including the 7-member Board of Governors and 5 Federal Reserve District Bank presidents. The president of the Federal Reserve Bank of New York holds a permanent seat on the FOMC because a large amount of financial activity takes place in New York City and because the New York Fed is responsible for executing open market operations. The other four positions are rotated among the Federal Reserve District Bank presidents.

The most important responsibility of the Fed is to control the nation's money supply. In meeting its responsibility, the Fed is theoretically independent of politics, Congress, and the President of the United States. The Fed is not obligated to seek the advice of Congress or the President on monetary matters; it must

Board of Governors
The governing body of the Federal Reserve System.

Federal Open Market Committee (FOMC)
The 12-member policymaking group within the Fed. This committee has the authority to conduct open market operations.

Open Market Operations
The buying and selling of government securities by the Fed.

exhibit 1

Federal Reserve Districts and Federal Reserve Bank Locations
The boundaries of the Federal Reserve Districts, the cities in which a Federal Reserve Bank is located, and the location of the Board of Governors (Washington, D.C.) are all noted on the map.

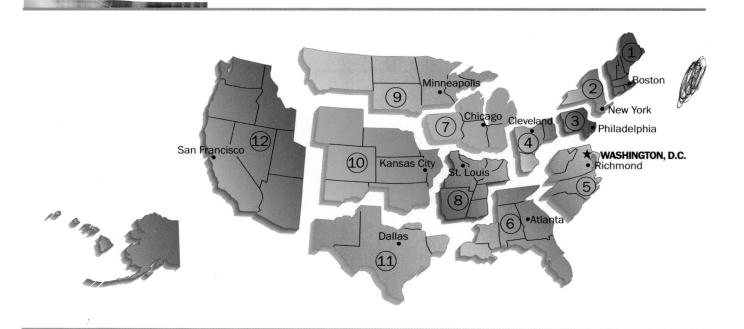

only inform both of its plans. Many economists argue, however, that although the Fed is theoretically independent, its behavior has not always reflected that independence. In general, it may be more accurate to say that the Fed is independent of day-to-day politics but probably is subject to political influence (to what degree is a point of debate) over longer periods when general economic policy is set.

FUNCTIONS OF THE FEDERAL RESERVE SYSTEM

The Fed has eight major responsibilities or functions. The first has already been mentioned.

1. **Control the money supply.** A full explanation of how the Fed does this comes later in this chapter.
2. **Supply the economy with paper money (Federal Reserve notes).** The Federal Reserve Banks have Federal Reserve notes on hand to meet the demands of the banks and the public. During the Christmas season, for example, more people withdraw larger-than-usual amounts of $1, $5, $20, $50, and $100 notes from banks. Banks need to replenish their vault cash, so they turn to their Federal Reserve Banks. The Federal Reserve Banks meet this cash need by issuing more paper money (they act as passive suppliers of paper money). The money is actually printed at the Bureau of Engraving and Printing in Washington, D.C., but it is issued to commercial banks by the 12 Federal Reserve Banks.
3. **Provide check-clearing services.** When someone in, say, San Diego writes a check to a person in, say, Los Angeles, what happens to the check? The process by which funds change hands when checks are written is called the *check-clearing process.* The following process is summarized in Exhibit 2.
   a. Harry Saito writes a $1,000 check on his San Diego bank and sends it to Ursula Pevins in Los Angeles.
   b. Ursula takes the check to her local bank, endorses it, and deposits it in her checking account. The balance in her account rises by $1,000.
   c. Ursula's Los Angeles bank sends the check to its Federal Reserve District Bank, which is located in San Francisco. The Federal Reserve Bank of San Francisco increases the reserve account of the Los Angeles bank by $1,000 and decreases the reserve account of the San Diego bank by $1,000.
   d. The Federal Reserve Bank of San Francisco sends the check to Harry's bank in San Diego, which then reduces the balance in Harry's checking account by $1,000. Harry's bank in San Diego either keeps the check on record or sends it to Harry with his monthly bank statement.

Go to *http://www.federalreserve.gov/,* click "About the Fed," and then "Structure of the Federal Reserve System." In making appointments to the Board of Governors, what does the law direct the President of the United States to do?

exhibit 2

The Check-Clearing Process

(a)	(b)	(c)	(d)
Harry and Ursula	**Ursula and her Los Angeles Bank**	**The Los Angeles Bank and the Federal Reserve Bank of San Francisco**	**The Federal Reserve Bank of San Francisco and the San Diego Bank**
Harry Saito writes a $1,000 check on his San Diego bank and sends it to Ursula Pevins in Los Angeles.	Ursula endorses the check and deposits it in her local (Los Angeles) bank. The balance in her account rises by $1,000.	Ursula's local (Los Angeles) bank sends the check to the Federal Reserve Bank of San Francisco, which increases the reserve account of the Los Angeles bank by $1,000 and decreases the reserve account of the San Diego bank by $1,000.	The Federal Reserve Bank of San Francisco sends the check to Harry's bank in San Diego, which then reduces the balance in Harry's account by $1,000.

http://

Go to *http://www.fdic.gov/regulations/laws/important/*, and read the page. What does the FDIC do? Was the FDIC created before or after the establishment of the Federal Reserve System? Besides the Fed and the FDIC, what government agencies regulate the activities of banks?

U.S. Treasury Securities
Bonds and bondlike securities issued by the U.S. Treasury when it borrows.

4. **Hold depository institutions' reserves.** As noted in the last chapter, banks are required to keep reserves against customer deposits either in their vaults or in reserve accounts at the Fed. These accounts are maintained by the 12 Federal Reserve Banks for member banks in their respective districts.

5. **Supervise member banks.** Without warning, the Fed can examine the books of member commercial banks to see the nature of the loans the banks have made, monitor compliance with bank regulations, check the accuracy of bank records, and so on. If the Fed finds that a bank has not been maintaining established banking standards, it can pressure it to do so.

6. **Serve as the government's banker.** The federal government collects and spends large sums of money. As a result, it needs a checking account for many of the same reasons an individual does. Its primary checking account is with the Fed. The Fed is the government's banker.

7. **Serve as the lender of last resort.** A traditional function of a central bank is to serve as the lender of last resort for banks suffering cash management, or liquidity, problems.

8. **Serve as a fiscal agent for the Treasury.** The U.S. Treasury often issues (auctions) Treasury bills, notes, and bonds. These **U.S. Treasury securities** are sold to raise funds to pay the government's bills. The Federal Reserve District Banks receive the bids for these securities and process them in time for weekly auctions.

   Q: What is the difference between the Treasury and the Fed?

A: The U.S. Treasury is a budgetary agency; the Fed is a monetary agency. When the federal government spends funds, the Treasury collects the taxes and borrows the funds needed to pay suppliers and others. In short, the Treasury has an obligation to manage the financial affairs of the federal government. Except for coins, the Treasury does not issue money. It cannot create money "out of thin air" as the Fed can. The Fed is principally concerned with the availability of money and credit for the entire economy. It does not issue Treasury securities. It does not have an obligation to meet the financial needs of the federal government. Its responsibility is to provide a stable monetary framework for the economy.

Self-Test *(Answers to Self-Test questions are in the Self-Test Appendix.)*

1. The president of which Federal Reserve District Bank holds a permanent seat on the Federal Open Market Committee (FOMC)?

2. What is the most important responsibility of the Fed?

3. What does it mean to say the Fed acts as "lender of last resort."

FED TOOLS FOR CONTROLLING THE MONEY SUPPLY

The money supply is, say, $1,000 billion one month and $1,100 billion the next month. How did this happen? Fact is, the Fed can change the money supply; it can cause the money supply to rise and to fall. The Fed has three tools at its disposal that it can use to change (or control) the money supply: (1) open market operations, (2) the required reserve ratio, and (3) the discount rate. This section explains how the Fed uses these tools to control the money supply.

OPEN MARKET OPERATIONS

When the Fed either buys or sells U.S. government securities in the financial markets, it is said to be engaged in *open market operations.*[1] Specifically, when

---

1. Actually, what the Fed buys and sells when it conducts open market operations are U.S. Treasury bills, notes, and bonds and government agency bonds. Government securities is a broad term that includes all of these financial instruments.

ECONOMICS IN...

Federal Reserve District Banks and the U.S. Attorney General

Slightly before the passage of the Federal Reserve Act in 1913, there was disagreement about how many districts and banks there should be. Many people thought there should be as few banks as possible—6 to 8—because concentrating activities in only a few cities would enhance efficiency and ease of operation. The Secretary of State at the time, William Jennings Bryan, wanted 50 district banks. He called for a "branch at every major crossroad." It was to be neither 6 nor 50; instead, there was a compromise. Section 2 of the Federal Reserve Act states that "not less than eight nor more than twelve cities" would be designated as Federal Reserve cities.

After the number of cities was determined to be 8 to 12, a commission was set up to identify both the boundaries of the Federal Reserve Districts and the locations of the district banks. The commission was composed of the Comptroller of the Currency, the Secretary of the Treasury, and the Secretary of Agriculture. They had to choose from among the 37 cities that had applied to be a location of a district bank. The commission settled on a 12-bank, 12-city plan. It decided the boundaries of the districts on the basis of trade. In other words, the commission decided the boundaries should include those cities or towns that traded most with each other. If the residents of cities X and Y traded a lot with each other but the residents of city Z did not trade much with the residents of cities X and Y, then cities X and Y should be included in the same district but Z should not. Instead, city Z should be part of the district that included cities with which it traded.

Some commercial banks protested both the number of district banks and the boundaries decided upon by the com-

mittee. These banks filed petitions for review of the plan with the Federal Reserve Board, thought to be the only group that could alter the plan.[2]

The petitions for review are said to have rekindled the debate about the actual number of district cities. Three members of the Federal Reserve Board wanted to reduce the number of district banks because they thought that half the banks were stronger than the other half and they wanted all banks to be of equal strength. Three other members of the Board wanted to stay with the original plan of 12 district banks. This left one member of the Board to break the tie. When it looked like that person's vote was going to be cast for a reduction in the number of district banks, one of the supporters of the original 12-bank plan went to the attorney general of the United States. He asked the attorney general for an opinion that stated the Board did not have the authority to alter the original plan. The attorney general gave that opinion. The Board, afraid of attracting any negative publicity by disagreeing and challenging the opinion, accepted it.

it buys securities, it is engaged in an **open market purchase;** when it sells securities, it is engaged in an **open market sale.** The following paragraphs explain how an open market purchase or sale affects the money supply.

Open Market Purchases

When the Fed buys securities, someone has to sell securities. Suppose bank *ABC* in Denver is the seller. In other words, suppose the Fed buys $5 million worth of government securities from bank *ABC*. When this happens, the securities leave the possession of bank *ABC* and go to the Fed.

Bank ABC, of course, wants something in return for the securities—it wants $5 million. The Fed pays for the government securities by increasing the balance in bank *ABC*'s reserve account. In other words, if before bank *ABC* sold the

Open Market Purchase
The buying of government securities by the Fed.

Open Market Sale
The selling of government securities by the Fed.

---

2. Before there was the Board of Governors of the Federal Reserve System, there was the Federal Reserve Board. The Banking Act of 1935, approved on August 23, 1935, changed the name of the Federal Reserve Board to the Board of Governors of the Federal Reserve System.

securities to the Fed, it had $0 on deposit with the Fed, then after it sells the securities to the Fed, it has $5 million on deposit with the Fed.

Now at this point someone will ask, Where did the Fed get the $5 million to put into bank *ABC*'s reserve account? The answer, as odd as it seems, is: *Out of thin air*. This simply means that the Fed has the legal authority to create money. In other words, what the Fed is effectively doing is deleting the "$0" balance in bank *ABC*'s account and, with a few keystrokes, replacing it with the number five and six zeroes—$5,000,000.

As in the last chapter, we use T-accounts to show the changes to the accounts affected by the transaction. After the open market purchase, the Fed's T-account looks like this:

THE FED	
Assets	**Liabilities**
Government securities +$5 million	Reserves on deposit in bank *ABC*'s – account +$5 million

In other words, the Fed now has assets of $5 million more in government securities, and it is holding (as liabilities) $5 million more for bank *ABC*.

After the open market purchase, bank *ABC*'s T-account looks like this:

BANK *ABC*	
Assets	**Liabilities**
Government securities −$5 million	No change
Reserves on deposit at the Fed +$5 million	

Bank *ABC* has $5 million less in securities and $5 million more in reserves.

Recall that as the reserves of one bank increase with no offsetting decline in reserves for other banks, the money supply expands through a process of increased loans and checkable deposits. In summary, an open market purchase by the Fed ultimately increases the money supply.

Q & A   Q: Is the transaction called an open market *purchase* because this is what the Fed is doing?

A: Yes. In our example, the Fed purchased government securities and bank *ABC* sold government securities. This might lead one to wonder why we don't call this operation an open market sale instead of an open market purchase; after all, something is being sold. True, but the Fed is not selling; the Fed is purchasing (or buying). It is what the Fed does that matters here.

Q & A   Q: If the Fed purchases a government security from a bank, where did the bank get the security in the first place?

A: Banks often purchase government securities from the U.S. Treasury. To illustrate, suppose the federal government wants to spend $1.6 trillion and tax revenues are $1.4 trillion. This budget deficit of $200 billion must be financed. The federal government has to raise the $200 billion in some way. It is the U.S. Treasury's task to raise the $200 billion by offering (for sale) Treasury securities—which include Treasury bills, notes, and bonds. These Treasury securities are promises by the U.S. government to pay the holder of the securities at some future date. For example, if Taylor buys a Treasury security and its face value is $10,000, then the U.S. Treasury is making a promise to Taylor that it will redeem the security at maturity for $10,000.

Suppose a bank purchased some Treasury securities a few months ago. Now the Fed offers to buy those Treasury securities from the bank. The bank agrees. This transaction is an open market purchase of government (Treasury) securities.

Open Market Sales

Sometimes the Fed sells government securities to banks and others. Suppose the Fed sells $5 million worth of government securities to bank *XYZ* in Atlanta. The Fed surrenders the securities to bank *XYZ* and is paid with $5 million previously deposited in bank *XYZ*'s account at the Fed. In other words, the Fed simply reduces the balance in bank *XYZ*'s account by $5 million.

After the open market sale, the Fed's T-account looks like this:

THE FED	
Assets	**Liabilities**
Government securities −$5 million	Reserves on deposit in bank *XYZ*'s account −$5 million

Bank *XYZ*'s T-account looks like this:

BANK *XYZ*	
Assets	**Liabilities**
Government securities +$5 million	No change
Reserves on deposit at the Fed −$5 million	

Now that bank *XYZ*'s reserves have declined by $5 million, it is reserve deficient. As bank *XYZ* and other banks adjust to the lower level of reserves, they reduce their total loans outstanding, which reduces the total volume of checkable deposits and money in the economy.

Exhibit 3 summarizes how open market operations affect the money supply.

Q: What happened to the $5 million the Fed got from bank *XYZ*'s account?

A: It is as if it disappears from the face of the earth. This is simply the other side of the "Fed can create money out of thin air" coin. The Fed can destroy money too.

THE REQUIRED RESERVE RATIO

The Fed can influence the money supply by changing the required reserve ratio. Recall from the last chapter that we can find the maximum change in checkable deposits (for a given change in reserves) by using the following formula:

$$\text{Maximum change in checkable deposits} = (1/r) \times \Delta R$$

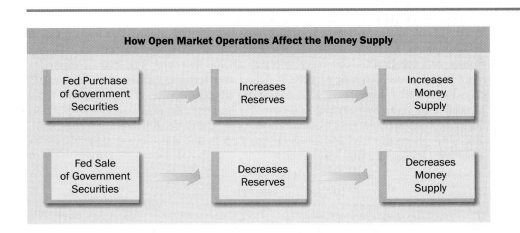

How Open Market Operations Affect the Money Supply

Fed Purchase of Government Securities → Increases Reserves → Increases Money Supply

Fed Sale of Government Securities → Decreases Reserves → Decreases Money Supply

exhibit 3

Open Market Operations
An open market purchase increases reserves, which leads to an increase in the money supply. An open market sale decreases reserves, which leads to a decrease in the money supply. (Note: We have assumed here that the Fed purchases government securities from and sells government securities to commercial banks.)

For example, if reserves increase by $1,000, and the required reserve ratio is 10 percent, then the maximum change in checkable deposits is $10,000:

$$\text{Maximum change in checkable deposits} = (1/0.10) \times \$1,000$$
$$= 10 \times \$1,000$$
$$= \$10,000$$

Now suppose Fed officials increase the required reserve ratio from 10 percent to 20 percent. How will this change the amount of checkable deposits? As you can see, the amount of checkable deposits will decline:

$$\text{Maximum change in checkable deposits} = (1/0.20) \times \$1,000$$
$$= 5 \times \$1,000$$
$$= \$5,000$$

If, instead, the Fed lowers the required reserve ratio to 5 percent, the maximum change in checkable deposits will increase:

$$\text{Maximum change in checkable deposits} = (1/0.05) \times \$1,000$$
$$= 20 \times \$1,000$$
$$= \$20,000$$

We conclude that an increase in the required reserve ratio leads to a decrease in the money supply, and a decrease in the required reserve ratio leads to an increase in the money supply. In other words, there is an inverse relationship between the required reserve ratio and the money supply. As r goes up, the money supply goes down; as r goes down, the money supply goes up.

THE DISCOUNT RATE

In addition to providing loans to customers, banks themselves borrow funds when they need them. Consider bank *ABC* that currently has zero excess reserves. Then either of the following two events occurs:

- **Case 1:** Mike Worls applies for a loan to buy new equipment for his horse ranch. The bank loan officer believes he is a good credit risk and that the bank could profit by granting him the loan. But the bank has no funds to lend.
- **Case 2:** Lisa Lysne closes her checking account. As a result, the bank loses reserves and now is reserve deficient.

In Case 1, the bank wants funds so that it can make a loan to Mike Worls and increase its profits. In Case 2, the bank needs funds to meet its **reserve requirement.** In either case, there are two major places the bank can go to acquire a loan: (1) the **federal funds market,** which basically means the bank goes to another bank for a loan, or (2) the Fed (the bank's Federal Reserve District Bank). At both places, the bank will pay an interest rate. The rate it pays for a loan in the federal funds market is called the **federal funds rate.** The rate it pays for the loan from the Fed is called the **discount rate.** Bank *ABC* will try to minimize its costs by borrowing where the interest rate is lower, *ceteris paribus.* Suppose the discount rate is much lower than the federal funds rate; then bank *ABC* will go to the Fed for funds. If the Fed grants the bank a loan, the Fed's T-account looks like this:

THE FED	
Assets	**Liabilities**
Loan to bank *ABC* +$1 million	Reserves on deposit in bank *ABC*'s account +$1 million

Reserve Requirement
The rule that specifies the amount of reserves a bank must hold to back up deposits.

Federal Funds Market
A market where banks lend reserves to one another, usually for short periods.

Federal Funds Rate
The interest rate in the federal funds market; the interest rate banks charge one another to borrow reserves.

Discount Rate
The interest rate the Fed charges depository institutions that borrow reserves from it.

Bank *ABC*'s T-account reflects the same transaction from its perspective:

BANK *ABC*	
Assets	**Liabilities**
Reserves on deposit at the Fed +$1 million	Loan from the Fed +$1 million

Notice that when bank *ABC* borrows from the Fed, its reserves increase while the reserves of no other bank decrease. The result is increased reserves for the banking system as a whole, so the money supply increases. In summary: When a bank borrows at the Fed's discount window, the money supply increases.

Q & A

Q: Do banks borrow from other banks when the discount rate is greater than the federal funds rate and borrow from the Fed when the discount rate is less than the federal funds rate?

A: Not necessarily. Banks do not like to borrow from the Fed for a number of reasons, which we discuss shortly. If the federal funds rate and the discount rate are equal (say, both are 7 percent), most banks prefer to borrow funds from other banks rather than borrowing from the Fed. But, of course, as the discount rate falls relative to the federal funds rate (say, the discount rate falls to 5 percent, and the federal funds rate stays at 7 percent), this preference on the part of the banks becomes more expensive to satisfy—and the banks will be less likely to satisfy it. So, the answer is: As the discount rate falls relative to the federal funds rate, banks are more likely to borrow from the Fed. As the discount rate rises relative to the federal funds rate, banks are more likely to borrow from other banks. In effect, it is the spread (or difference) between the two rates that often matters.

THE SPREAD BETWEEN THE DISCOUNT RATE AND THE FEDERAL FUNDS RATE

The discount rate may be lower than the federal funds rate, and a bank may still go to the federal funds market for a loan. Here are the reasons why:

1. The bank may know that the Fed is hesitant to extend loans to banks that want to take advantage of profit-making opportunities, such as the loan to Mike Worls (Case 1).
2. The bank doesn't want to deal with the Fed bureaucracy that regulates it, particularly if Fed officials interpret a request for a loan as mismanagement.
3. The bank realizes that acquiring a loan from the Fed is a privilege and not a right, and the bank doesn't want to abuse this privilege. The bank doesn't know when it may need the borrowing privilege the Fed has extended more than it currently needs to borrow.

Banks basically look at the spread (the difference) between the federal funds rate and the discount rate in deciding where to borrow funds. If the discount rate is only slightly lower than the federal funds rate, most banks will pay the extra charge and borrow from other commercial banks. If the discount rate is significantly lower than the federal funds rate, most banks will borrow from the Fed.

It follows that an increase in the discount rate relative to the federal funds rate reduces bank borrowings from the Fed. As banks borrow less from the Fed and pay back Fed loans previously taken out, reserves fall and, ultimately, the money supply declines.

A decrease in the discount rate relative to the federal funds rate increases bank borrowings from the Fed. As banks borrow more from the Fed, reserves rise and, ultimately, the money supply increases.

WHICH TOOL DOES THE FED PREFER TO USE?

The Fed can use open market operations, the required reserve ratio, or the discount rate to influence the money supply. Does the Fed use one monetary tool more than the others when it wants to change the money supply?

The Fed today uses open market operations much more than it uses the other two tools. It believes that open market operations have certain advantages over the other two tools. These advantages include the following:

1. **Open market operations are flexible.** The Fed can buy or sell small, medium, or large amounts of government securities and can control the size of the transaction.

2. **Open market operations can easily be reversed.** If the Fed purchased $50 million worth of government securities yesterday but now realizes that $40 million would have been a more appropriate figure, it can sell $10 million worth of securities today to correct the situation.

3. **Open market operations can be implemented quickly.** If the Fed decides it wants to change the money supply, it places an order with a government securities dealer and the trade is executed immediately.

A summary of the effects of the Fed's different monetary tools is shown in Exhibit 4.

Q & A

Q: Sometimes we hear on the news that the Fed is thinking about changing the federal funds rate. But the Fed doesn't have control over the federal funds rate, does it? Doesn't it only have control over the discount rate?

A: The Fed can change the discount rate *directly* and the federal funds rate *indirectly.* The federal funds rate is a market interest rate determined by the supply of and demand for reserves. The Fed can change the supply of reserves through its open market operations. In other words, the Fed could, say, conduct an open market purchase and increase the supply of reserves in the banking system. In turn, this would impact the federal funds rate.

Self-Test

1. How does the money supply change as a result of (a) an increase in the discount rate, (b) an open market purchase, (c) an increase in the required reserve ratio?

2. What is the difference between the federal funds rate and the discount rate?

3. If bank *A* borrows $10 million from bank *B*, what happens to the reserves in bank *A*? in the banking system?

4. If bank *A* borrows $10 million from the Fed, what happens to the reserves in bank *A*? in the banking system?

exhibit 4

Fed Monetary Tools and Their Effects on the Money Supply

The following Fed actions increase the money supply: purchasing government securities on the open market, lowering the required reserve ratio, and lowering the discount rate relative to the federal funds rate. The following Fed actions decrease the money supply: selling government securities on the open market, raising the required reserve ratio, and raising the discount rate relative to the federal funds rate.

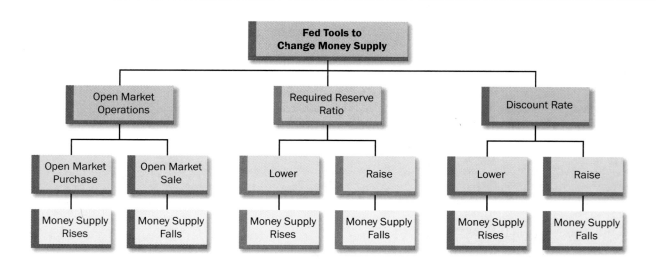

A Reader Asks...

How Do I Get a Job at the Fed?

I'm a junior in college, majoring in economics. Are there any career opportunities at the Fed that I might apply for while I'm still a student?

The Fed operates both summer internships and a Cooperative Education Program for college students. The Fed's summer internship program is "designed to provide valuable work experience for undergraduate and graduate students considering careers in economics, finance, and computer science." The following three divisions at the Federal Reserve Board in Washington, D.C., regularly offer internships:

- Banking Supervision and Regulation
- Information Technology
- Research and Statistics

Summer internships are usually available to college sophomores, juniors, and seniors. Internships are usually unpaid and run from June 1 to September 1.

As an economics major, you may be interested in applying for an internship in the Division of Research and Statistics. This division collects economic and financial information and develops economic analyses that are used by the Board of Governors, the Federal Open Market Committee, and other Fed officials in formulating monetary and regulatory policies.

The Fed's Cooperative Education Program provides paid and unpaid professional work experience to undergraduate and graduate students in economics, finance and accounting, information systems, and law. Here are the assignments in three of these areas:

- Economics: Students have the opportunity to apply their quantitative skills on projects in financial and nonfinancial areas, bank structure and competition, international trade, and foreign and exchange markets.
- Finance and Accounting: Students analyze the financial condition of domestic and foreign banking organizations and process applications filed by these financial institutions.

- Information Systems: Student assignments include creating public and intranet Web pages and assisting application developers in program maintenance, design, and coding.

Generally, employment in the Cooperative Education Program is for a summer or a year, although other assignment lengths are considered. Candidates are selected on the basis of scholastic achievement, recommendations, and completed course work in relevant areas of study.

To obtain more information about the summer internships and the Cooperative Education Program, go to the Federal Reserve Web site at http://www.federalreserve .gov/, and click on "Career Opportunities." You can also call the Fed's 24-hour job vacancy line at 1-800-448-4894.

The Federal Reserve Board

Career Opportunities
at the Federal Reserve Board

To meet its goals, the Board needs a highly educated and diverse staff. The Board recruits professionals in economics, finance, law, computer science, and other fields. It has full-time positions, generally two years in duration, for research assistants and offers summer internships and cooperative education opportunities. For information on various positions and on how to apply, see the following table. You may also call the Board's 24-hour job vacancy line (1-800-448-4894) or the TDD line (202-872-4894).

Chapter Summary

The Federal Reserve System

- There are 12 Federal Reserve Districts. The Board of Governors controls and coordinates the activities of the Federal Reserve System. The Board is made up of 7 members, each appointed to a 14-year term. The major policymaking group within the Fed is the Fed-

eral Open Market Committee (FOMC). It is a 12-member group, made up of the 7 members of the Board of Governors and 5 Federal Reserve District Bank presidents.

- The major responsibilities of the Fed are to (1) control the money supply, (2) supply the economy with paper money (Federal Reserve notes), (3) provide check-clearing services, (4) hold depository institutions' reserves, (5) supervise member banks, (6) serve as the government's banker, (7) serve as the lender of last resort, and (8) serve as a fiscal agent for the Treasury.

Controlling the Money Supply

- The following Fed actions increase the money supply: lowering the required reserve ratio, purchasing government securities on the open market, and lowering the discount rate relative to the federal funds rate. The following Fed actions decrease the money supply: raising the required reserve ratio, selling government securities on the open market, and raising the discount rate relative to the federal funds rate.

Open Market Operations

- An open market purchase by the Fed increases the money supply. An open market sale by the Fed decreases the money supply.

The Required Reserve Ratio

- An increase in the required reserve ratio leads to a decrease in the money supply. A decrease in the required reserve ratio leads to an increase in the money supply.

The Discount Rate

- An increase in the discount rate relative to the federal funds rate leads to a decrease in the money supply.
- A decrease in the discount rate relative to the federal funds rate leads to an increase in the money supply.

Key Terms and Concepts

Board of Governors
Federal Open Market Committee (FOMC)
Open Market Operations

U.S. Treasury Securities
Open Market Purchase
Open Market Sale
Reserve Requirement

Federal Funds Market
Federal Funds Rate
Discount Rate

Economic Connections to You

Economic facts, actions, and changes create ripples that move away from their point of origin. Eventually, these ripples can intersect your life and have an effect on you. Consider the following example.

On Tuesday, the chairman of the Board of Governors of the Federal Reserve System appears before a congressional committee and reports that labor markets are tight and that the inflation rate is edging higher than had been expected. The stock market interprets this to mean that the Fed will soon restrain growth in the money supply, which will raise short-

term interest rates. Higher interest rates will dampen business investment and, some think, hurt the long-term profit prospects of firms. Stock prices begin to fall. The 100 shares of stock you bought yesterday is worth less than when you purchased it. Thus, there is a connection between the actions of the chairman of the Board of Governors of the Fed and the value of your stock—an economic connection to you.

Based on the material in this chapter, identify other ways in which economic facts, actions, and changes create ripples that eventually affect you.

Questions and Problems

1. Identify the major responsibilities of the Federal Reserve System.
2. What is the difference between the Fed and the U.S. Treasury?
3. Explain how an open market purchase increases the money supply.

4. Explain how an open market sale decreases the money supply.
5. Suppose the Fed raises the required reserve ratio, a move that is normally thought to reduce the money supply. However, banks find themselves with a reserve deficiency after the required reserve ratio is

increased and are likely to react by requesting a loan from the Fed. Does this action prevent the money supply from contracting as predicted?

6. Suppose bank *A* borrows reserves from bank *B*. Now that bank *A* has more reserves than previously, will the money supply increase?

7. Explain how a decrease in the required reserve ratio increases the money supply.

8. Suppose you read in the newspaper that all last week the Fed conducted open market purchases and that on Tuesday of last week it lowered the discount rate. What would you say the Fed was trying to do?

9. Some people have referred to the Fed as a "legal counterfeiter." Do you think this terminology misrepresents the Fed's role? Explain your answer.

10. Explain how a check is cleared through the Federal Reserve System.

11. The Fed can change the discount rate directly and the federal funds rate indirectly. Explain.

12. If the federal funds rate equals the discount rate, from whom will banks borrow—other banks or the Fed? Explain your answer.

Working with Numbers and Graphs

1. If reserves increase by $2 million and the required reserve ratio is 8 percent, then what is the maximum change in checkable deposits?

2. If reserves increase by $2 million and the required reserves ratio is 10 percent, then what is the maximum change in checkable deposits?

3. If the federal funds rate is 6 percent and the discount rate is 5.1 percent, to whom will a bank be more likely to go for a loan—another bank or the Fed? Explain your answer.

4. Complete the following table:

Federal Reserve Action	Effect on the Money Supply (up or down?)
Lower the discount rate	A
Conduct open market purchase	B
Lower required reserve ratio	C
Raise the discount rate	D
Conduct open market sale	E
Raise the required reserve ratio	F

Internet Activities

1. Go to *http://www.federalreserve.gov/Regulations/default.htm*. Using this page, the regulations link on the page, and the "Back" button, identify each of the following statements as either true or false.
   a. The Fed controls the amount of credit that can be borrowed for purposes of buying stocks.
   b. The Fed insures deposits in commercial banks.
   c. The Fed controls the manner in which loan and lease terms are disclosed to borrowers.
   d. The Fed permits the payment of interest on demand deposits.
   e. The Fed lacks regulatory authority over electronic funds transfers.
   f. The Fed controls only the domestic operations of U.S. banks.
   g. Foreign banks operating in the United States remain under the control of their central banks.
   h. The FBI, not the Fed, is responsible for bank security against robbery.
   i. The Federal Trade Commission, not the Fed, controls unfair and deceptive business practices of banks.

2. Go to *http://www.bep.treas.gov/document.cfm/18/106*. Read the Fun Facts page and answer the following questions.
   a. What is the "average life" of a $1 Federal Reserve note?
   b. Who is the only woman whose portrait has appeared on a U.S. currency note?

Log on to the Arnold Xtra! Web site now (*http://arnoldxtra.swcollege.com*) for additional learning resources such as practice quizzes, help with graphing, video clips, and current event applications.

ch.14
MONEY AND THE ECONOMY

How do increases in prices affect people's lives? A couple moving to a new apartment may have to pay more in rent. A person may want to buy a house but not have enough money for the down payment or enough income for the mortgage payment. A college student may have to drop out of school for a year because tuition has increased.

What happens in the economy when the price level rises, rather than just the prices of some goods? What causes the price level to rise? Economists have developed theories to try to answer these questions.

Chapter Road Map

This chapter deals with one important question:

Can a change in the money supply change Real GDP and the price level? In search of the answer, we begin by outlining the details of an important equation in economics—the equation of exchange. The equation of exchange leads to the simple quantity theory of money, which speaks directly to the relationship between changes in the money supply and changes in the price level.

Next, we present the views of economists who call themselves monetarists. Specifically, we address how monetarists look at both the demand side and supply side of the economy.

We then examine the topic of inflation and discuss two types of inflation—one-shot inflation and continued inflation. Finally, we discuss the relationship between changes in the money supply and interest rates.

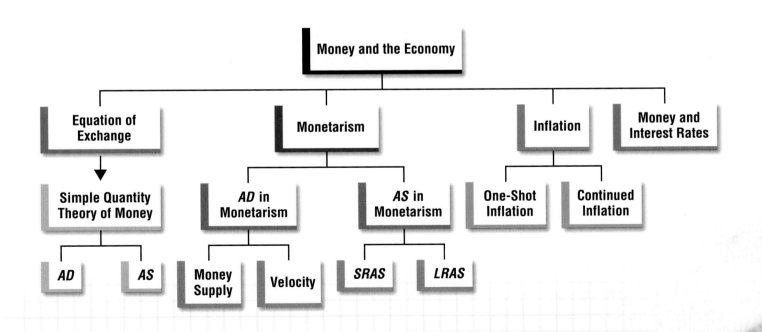

MONEY AND THE PRICE LEVEL

Do changes in the money supply affect the price level in the economy? Classical economists believed so. Their position was based on the equation of exchange and the simple quantity theory of money.

THE EQUATION OF EXCHANGE

The equation of exchange is an identity that states that the money supply (M) multiplied by velocity (V) must be equal to the price level (P) times Real GDP (Q).

$$MV = PQ$$

What is **velocity**? It is the average number of times a dollar is spent to buy final goods and services in a year. For example, assume an economy has only five one-dollar bills. In January, the first of the one-dollar bills moves from Smith's hands to Jones's hands to buy good X. Then in June it goes from Jones's hands to Brown's hands to buy good Y. And in December it goes from Brown's hands to Peterson's hands to buy good Z. Over the course of the year, this dollar bill has changed hands 3 times.

The other dollar bills also change hands during the year. The second dollar bill changes hands 5 times; the third, 6 times; the fourth, 2 times; the fifth, 7 times. Given this information, we calculate the number of times a dollar changes hands on average in making a purchase. In this case, the number is 4.6. This number (4.6) is velocity.

In a large economy such as ours, it is impossible to figure out how many times each dollar changes hands; therefore, it is impossible to calculate velocity as in our example. Instead, a different method is used.

First, we calculate GDP; next, we calculate the average money supply; finally, we divide GDP by the average money supply to obtain velocity. For example, if $4,800 billion worth of transactions occur in a year and the average money supply during the year is $800 billion, a dollar must have been used on average 6 times during the year to purchase goods and services. In symbols, we have

$$V \equiv GDP/M$$

(The sign $\equiv$ means "must be equal to"; this is an identity.) GDP is equal to $P \times Q$, so the identity can be written

$$V \equiv (P \times Q)/M$$

Multiplying both sides by M, we get

$$MV \equiv PQ$$

which is the **equation of exchange** shown at the beginning of this section.

The equation of exchange can be interpreted in different ways:

1. The money supply multiplied by velocity must equal the price level times Real GDP: $M \times V \equiv P \times Q$.
2. The money supply multiplied by velocity must equal GDP: $M \times V \equiv GDP$ (because $P \times Q \equiv GDP$).
3. Total spending or expenditures (measured by MV) must equal the total sales revenues of business firms (measured by PQ): $MV \equiv PQ$.

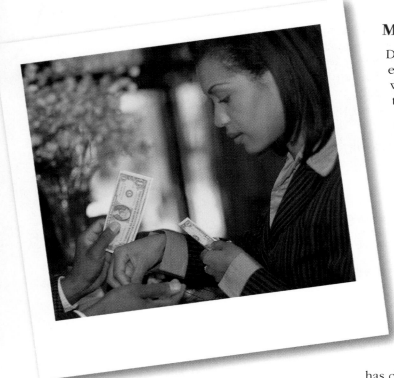

http://

Go to *http://research.stlouisfed.org/ publications/mt/* and click on "Velocity." How is M2 velocity calculated? Is there any trend? What is the most recent M2 velocity value?

Velocity
The average number of times a dollar is spent to buy final goods and services in a year.

Equation of Exchange
An identity stating that the money supply times velocity must be equal to the price level times Real GDP.

The third way of interpreting the equation of exchange is perhaps the most intuitively simple to understand. It simply says that the total expenditures (of buyers) must equal the total sales (of sellers). Consider a simple economy where there is only one buyer and one seller. If the buyer buys a book for $20, then the seller receives $20. Stated differently, the money supply in the example, or $20, times velocity, 1, is equal to the price of the book, $20, times the quantity of the book.

Q & A

Q: Can a given money supply support spending greater than itself? For example, can every $1 of the money supply support $3 worth of spending?

A: Yes. We can see this from the equation of exchange. Specifically, a given money supply will support a greater level of spending if velocity is greater than one. To illustrate, suppose the money supply is only $1 and it changes hands only once during the year. It follows that the $1 supports only $1 worth of spending. Now suppose that the $1 changes hands three times during the year. The first time Jack uses the dollar to buy something (priced at $1) from Sally. The second time Sally uses the dollar to buy something from Nancy. The third time Nancy uses the dollar to buy something from David. Velocity is 3 in this case and therefore $1 (money supply) has supported $3 worth of spending.

FROM THE EQUATION OF EXCHANGE TO THE SIMPLE QUANTITY THEORY OF MONEY

The equation of exchange is an identity, not an economic theory. To turn it into a theory, we make some assumptions about the variables in the equation. Many eighteenth-century classical economists, as well as the American economist Irving Fisher (1867–1947) and the English economist Alfred Marshall (1842–1924), assumed (1) changes in velocity are so small that for all practical purposes velocity can be assumed to be constant (especially over short periods of time) and (2) Real GDP, or Q, is fixed in the short run. Hence, they turned the equation of exchange, which is simply true by definition, into a theory by assuming that both V and Q are fixed, or constant. With these two assumptions, we have the **simple quantity theory of money:** If V and Q are constant, we would predict that changes in M will bring about *strictly proportional* changes in P. In other words, the simple quantity theory of money predicts that changes in the money supply will bring about strictly proportional changes in the price level.

Exhibit 1 shows the assumptions and predictions of the simple quantity theory. On the left side of the exhibit, the key assumptions of the simple quantity theory are noted: V and Q are constant. Also, $M \times V = P \times Q$ is noted. We use the equal sign (=) instead of the identity sign (≡) because we are speaking about the simple quantity theory and not the equation of exchange. (The = sign here

Simple Quantity Theory of Money The theory that assumes that velocity (V) and Real GDP (Q) are constant and predicts that changes in the money supply (M) lead to strictly proportional changes in the price level (P).

Assumptions of Simple Quantity Theory						Predictions of Simple Quantity Theory	
M	$\times$ $\bar{V}$	$=$	P	$\times$ $\bar{Q}$		% Change in M	% Change in P
$ 500	4		$2	1,000			
1,000	4		4	1,000		+ 100%	+ 100%
1,500	4		6	1,000		+ 50	+ 50
1,200	4		4.80	1,000		− 20	− 20

exhibit 1

Assumptions and Predictions of the Simple Quantity Theory of Money

The simple quantity theory of money assumes that both V and Q are constant. (A bar over each indicates this in the exhibit.) The prediction is that changes in M lead to strictly proportional changes in P. (Note: For purposes of this example, think of Q as "so many units of goods" and of P as the "average price paid per unit of these goods.")

Money and Inflation

The simple quantity theory of money predicts that the larger the percentage increase in the money supply, the larger the percentage increase in the price level. There is some evidence that confirms this theory.

Exhibit 2a shows the average annual growth rate in the money supply and the average annual inflation rate for the period 1980–1990 in Switzerland, Italy, Germany, the United States, Israel, Peru, and Argentina. It is easy to see that the countries with the higher money supply growth rates are also the countries with the higher inflation rates.

Exhibit 2b shows the average annual growth rate in the money supply and the average annual inflation rate for the period 1986–1996 for several Latin American countries. Again, the relationship predicted by the simple quantity theory of

exhibit 2

Money and Inflation
Parts (a) and (b) show that the higher the average annual money supply growth rate in a country, the higher the average annual inflation rate in the country. Part (c) shows annual money supply growth rates and inflation rates in four countries. Usually, countries with higher money supply growth rates have higher inflation rates.

Source: Financial International Statistics Yearbook and Handbook of International Economic Statistics, 1993 and 1996.

(a)

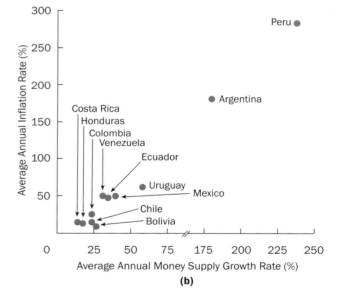

(b)

	Brazil			India			Mexico			South Korea	
Year	Money Supply Growth Rate (%)	Inflation Rate (%)	Year	Money Supply Growth Rate (%)	Inflation Rate (%)	Year	Money Supply Growth Rate (%)	Inflation Rate (%)	Year	Money Supply Growth Rate (%)	Inflation Rate (%)
1990	2,350.8	1,795.0	1990	14.3	9.0	1990	62.6	26.7	1990	21.2	8.6
1991	325.6	478.5	1991	22.5	13.9	1991	119.8	22.7	1991	18.6	9.7
1992	881.6	1,158.0	1992	12.3	11.7	1992	17.0	15.5	1992	18.4	6.2
1993	2,082.1	2,708.6	1993	16.9	6.4	1993	15.8	9.8	1993	17.4	5.8

(c)

money holds: the higher the money supply growth rate, the higher the growth rate in prices.

In Exhibit 2c, we look at annual changes (not average annual changes) in both the money supply and prices for four countries: Brazil, India, Mexico, and South Korea. Notice, for example, that the growth rate in the money supply in 1993 in Brazil was 2,082.1 percent. The percentage increase in prices (the inflation rate) in that year in Brazil was 2,708.6 percent. In contrast, the growth rate in the money supply in 1993 in Mexico was 15.8 percent, and the percentage increase in prices was 9.8 percent.

If we were to average the data in Exhibit 2c and compare the average annual growth rates in the money supply to the average annual increase in prices, we'd find that during the period 1990–1993, the money supply in Brazil grew by an average annual rate of 1,410 percent and prices increased by an average annual rate of 1,535 percent. In India, the money supply grew by an average annual rate of 16.5 percent and prices increased by an average annual rate of 10.25 percent. In Mexico, the respective figures were 53.8 percent (money supply) and 18.67 percent (prices). Finally, in South Korea the respective figures were 18.9 percent (money supply) and 7.57 percent (prices). Again the relationship between money and prices predicted by the simple quantity theory of money holds: the higher the growth rate of the money supply, the higher the growth rate in prices.

represents "is predicted to be equal"; that is, given our assumptions, $M \times V$, or MV, is predicted to be equal to $P \times Q$, or PQ.)

Starting with the first row, the money supply is $500, velocity is 4, Real GDP (Q) is 1,000 units, and the price level, or price index, is $2.[1] Therefore GDP equals $2,000. In the second row, the money supply increases by 100 percent, from $500 to $1,000, and both V and Q are constant, at 4 and 1,000, respectively. The price level moves from $2 to $4. On the right side of the exhibit, we see that a 100 percent increase in M predicts a 100 percent increase in P. Changes in P are predicted to be strictly proportional to changes in M.

In the third row, M increases by 50 percent, and P is predicted to increase by 50 percent. In the fourth row, M decreases by 20 percent, and P is predicted to decrease by 20 percent.

In summary, the simple quantity theory assumes that both V and Q are constant in the short run, and therefore predicts that changes in M lead to strictly proportional changes in P.

Q & A   Q: Does the simple quantity theory of money predict well? Does it make predictions that are consistently substantiated by the facts?

A: The simple quantity theory of money says that changes in the money supply bring about strictly proportional changes in prices. We do not always observe this strict proportionality. But we do observe that countries with higher money supply growth rates tend to have higher price level growth rates than countries with lower money supply growth rates. And this definitely is a theme of the simple quantity theory of money. As Exhibit 1 makes clear, the simple quantity theory of money predicts that larger percentage increases in the money supply will bring about greater percentage increases in the price level.

THE SIMPLE QUANTITY THEORY OF MONEY IN AN *AD-AS* FRAMEWORK

You are familiar with the *AD-AS* framework from earlier chapters. In this section, we analyze the simple quantity theory of money in this framework.

The *AD* Curve of the Simple Quantity Theory of Money

The simple quantity theory of money builds on the equation of exchange, $MV \equiv PQ$. As we stated earlier, one way of interpreting the equation of exchange is that the total expenditures of buyers must equal the total sales of sellers. Thus, we are saying that MV is the total expenditures of buyers and PQ is the total sales of sellers. For now, we concentrate on MV as the total expenditures of buyers:

$$MV = \text{Total expenditures}$$

---

1. You are used to seeing Real GDP expressed as a dollar figure and a price index as a number without a dollar sign in front of it. We have switched things for purposes of this example, as it is easier to think of Q as "so many units of goods" and P as "the average price paid per unit of these goods."

In an earlier chapter, total expenditures (TE) is defined as the sum of the expenditures made by the four sectors of the economy. In other words,

$$TE = C + I + G + (EX - IM)$$

Because $MV = TE$,

$$MV = C + I + G + (EX - IM)$$

Now recall that at a given price level, anything that changes C, I, G, EX, or IM changes aggregate demand and thus shifts the aggregate demand (AD) curve. But MV equals $C + I + G + (EX - IM)$, so it follows that *a change in the money supply (M) or a change in velocity (V) will change aggregate demand and therefore lead to a shift in the AD curve.* Another way to say this is that aggregate demand depends on *both* the money supply and velocity.

Specifically, an increase in the money supply will increase aggregate demand and shift the AD curve to the right. A decrease in the money supply will decrease aggregate demand and shift the AD curve to the left. An increase in velocity will increase aggregate demand and shift the AD curve to the right. A decrease in velocity will decrease aggregate demand and shift the AD curve to the left. But, *in the simple quantity theory of money, velocity is assumed to be constant.* Thus, we are left with only changes in the money supply being able to shift the AD curve.

The AD curve is shown in Exhibit 3a. The $(M, \bar{V})$ in parentheses next to the curve is a reminder of what factors can shift the AD curve. The bar over V (for velocity) indicates that velocity is assumed to be constant.

The *AS* Curve in the Simple Quantity Theory of Money

In the simple quantity theory of money, the level of Real GDP is assumed to be constant in the short run. Exhibit 3b shows Real GDP fixed at Q_1. The AS curve is vertical at this level of Real GDP.

AD and *AS* in the Simple Quantity Theory of Money

Exhibit 3c shows both the AD and AS curves in the simple quantity theory of money. Suppose that AD_1 is initially operational. In the exhibit, AD_1 is based on a money supply of \$800 billion and a velocity of 2. The price level is P_1.

exhibit 3

The Simple Quantity Theory of Money in the *AD-AS* Framework
(a) In the simple quantity theory of money, the *AD* curve is downward sloping. Velocity is assumed to be constant, so changes in the money supply will change aggregate demand. (b) In the simple quantity theory of money, Real GDP is fixed in the short run. Thus, the *AS* curve is vertical. (c) In the simple quantity theory of money, an increase in the money supply will shift the *AD* curve rightward and increase the price level. A decrease in the money supply will shift the *AD* curve leftward and decrease the price level.

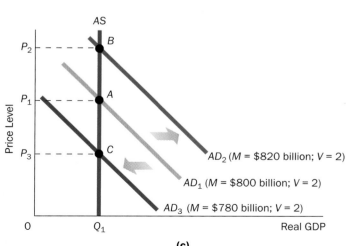

ECONOMICS IN...

The California Gold Rush, or an Apple for $72

Soon there was too much money in California and too little of everything else.
—J. S. Holiday, author of "The World Rushed In"

The only peacetime rise [in prices] comparable in total magnitude [to the 40 to 50 percent in prices from 1897 to 1914] followed the California gold discoveries in the early 1850s...
—Milton Friedman and Anna Schwartz, *A Monetary History of the United States, 1867–1960*

John Sutter was a Swiss immigrant who arrived in California in 1839. James Marshall, a carpenter, was building a sawmill for Sutter. On the chilly morning of January 24, 1848, Marshall was busy at work when something glistening caught his eye. He reached down and picked up the object. Marshall said to the workers he had hired, "Boys, by God I believe I have found a gold mine." Marshall later wrote, "I reached my hand down and picked it up; it made my heart thump, for I was certain it was gold. The piece was about half the size and shape of a pea. Then I saw another."

In time, Marshall and his workers came across more gold and before long people from all across the United States, and many other countries, headed to California. The California gold rush had begun.

The California gold rush, which resulted in an increase in the amount of money in circulation, provides an illustration of how a fairly dramatic increase in the money supply can affect prices. As more gold was mined and the supply of money increased, prices began to rise. There was a general rise in prices across the country, but the earliest and most dramatic increases in prices occurred in and near the areas in which gold was discovered. Near the gold mines, the prices of food and clothing sharply increased. For example, at the time, a loaf of bread sold for 4 cents in New York (equivalent to 72 cents today). Near the mines, the price was 75 cents (the equivalent of $13.50 today). Eggs sold for about $2 each (the equivalent of $36 today), apples for $4 (the equivalent of $72 today), a butcher's knife for $30 (the equivalent of $540 today), and boots went for $100 a pair (the equivalent of $1,800 today).

In San Francisco, land prices rose dramatically because of the city's relative closeness to the mines. Real estate that cost $16 (the equivalent of $288 today) before gold was discovered jumped to $45,000 (the equivalent of $810,000 today) in 18 months.

The sharp rise in prices that followed the California gold discoveries followed other gold discoveries too. For example, the gold stock of the world is estimated to have doubled from 1890 to 1914, due both to discoveries (in South Africa, Alaska, and Colorado) and to improved methods of mining and refining gold. During this period world prices increased too.

Now suppose we increase the money supply to $820 billion. Velocity remains constant at 2. According to the simple quantity theory of money, the price level will increase. We see that it does. The increase in the money supply shifts the AD curve from AD_1 to AD_2 and pushes up the price level from P_1 to P_2.

Suppose that instead of increasing the money supply, we decrease it to $780 billion. Again, velocity remains constant at 2. According to the simple quantity theory of money, the price level will decrease. We see that it does. The decrease in the money supply shifts the AD curve from AD_1 to AD_3 and pushes down the price level from P_1 to P_3.

DROPPING THE ASSUMPTIONS THAT V AND Q ARE CONSTANT

If we drop the assumptions that velocity (V) and Real GDP (Q) are constant, we have a more general theory of the factors that cause changes in the price level. Stated differently, changes in the price level depend on three variables: the money supply, velocity, and Real GDP. To see this, let's again start with the equation of exchange.

$$M \times V \equiv P \times Q \qquad (1)$$

If the equation of exchange holds, then it follows that:

$$P = \frac{M \times V}{Q} \qquad (2)$$

By looking at equation 2, we can see that the money supply, velocity, and Real GDP determine the price level. In other words, the price level depends on the money supply, velocity, and Real GDP.

What kinds of changes in *M, V,* and *Q* will bring about inflation (an increase in the price level)? Obviously, *ceteris paribus,* an increase in *M* or *V* or a decrease in *Q* will cause the price level to rise. For example, if velocity rises, *ceteris paribus,* the price level will rise. In other words, an increase in velocity is inflationary, *ceteris paribus.*

Inflationary Tendencies: $M\uparrow, V\uparrow, Q\downarrow$

What will bring about deflation (a decrease in the price level)? Obviously, *ceteris paribus,* a decrease in *M* or *V* or an increase in *Q* will cause the price level to fall. For example, if the money supply declines, *ceteris paribus,* the price level will drop. In other words, a decrease in the money supply is deflationary, *ceteris paribus.*

Deflationary Tendencies: $M\downarrow, V\downarrow, Q\uparrow$

Self-Test *(Answers to Self-Test questions are in the Self-Test Appendix.)*

1. If *M* times *V* increases, why does *P* times *Q* have to rise?
2. What is the difference between the equation of exchange and the simple quantity theory of money?
3. Predict what will happen to the *AD* curve as a result of each of the following:
   a. The money supply rises.
   b. Velocity falls.
   c. The money supply rises by a greater percentage than velocity falls.
   d. The money supply falls.

MONETARISM

Economists who call themselves monetarists have not been content to rely on the simple quantity theory of money. They do not hold that velocity is constant, nor do they hold that output is constant. Monetarist views on the money supply, velocity, aggregate demand, and aggregate supply are discussed in this section.

MONETARIST VIEWS

We begin with a brief explanation of the four positions held by monetarists. Then, we will discuss how, based on these positions, monetarists view the economy.

Velocity Changes in a Predictable Way

In the simple quantity theory of money, velocity is assumed to be constant. It follows from this that any changes in aggregate demand are brought about by changes in the money supply only.

Monetarists do not assume velocity is constant. Instead, they assume that velocity can and does change. It is important to note, however, that monetarists believe velocity changes in a predictable way. In other words, it does not change randomly, but rather it changes in a way that can be understood and predicted. Monetarists hold that velocity is a function of certain variables—the interest rate, the expected inflation rate, the frequency with which employees receive paychecks, and more—and that changes in it can be predicted.

Aggregate Demand Depends on the Money Supply and on Velocity

Earlier we showed that total expenditures in the economy (TE) equal MV. To better understand the economy, some economists—such as Keynesians—focus on the spending components of TE—such as C, I, G, EX, and IM. Other economists—such as monetarists—focus on the money supply (M) and velocity (V). For example, while Keynesians often argue that changes in C, I, G, EX, or IM can change aggregate demand, monetarists often argue that M and V can change aggregate demand.

The SRAS Curve Is Upward-Sloping

In the simple quantity theory of money, the level of Real GDP (Q) is assumed to be constant in the short run. So, the aggregate supply curve is vertical, as shown in Exhibit 3. According to monetarists, Real GDP may change in the short run. It follows that monetarists believe that the $SRAS$ curve is upward sloping.

The Economy Is Self-Regulating (Prices and Wages Are Flexible)

Monetarists believe that prices and wages are flexible. It follows that monetarists believe the economy is self-regulating—it can move itself out of a recessionary or an inflationary gap and into long-run equilibrium producing Natural Real GDP.

MONETARISM AND AD-AS

As we mentioned, monetarists tend to stress velocity and the money supply when discussing how the economy works. We describe the monetarist view using our *AD-AS* framework. Exhibit 4 helps to explain some of the highlights of monetarism. Each of the four parts (a)–(d) is considered separately.

Part (a)

In (a), the economy is originally in long-run equilibrium producing Natural Real GDP (Q_N) at price level P_1. Monetarists believe that changes in the money supply will change aggregate demand. For example, suppose the money supply rises from \$800 billion to \$820 billion. If velocity is constant, the AD curve shifts to the right, from AD_1 to AD_2 in the exhibit. As a result, Real GDP rises to Q_1 and the price level rises to P_2. And, of course, if Real GDP rises, the unemployment rate falls, *ceteris paribus*.

According to monetarists, the economy is an inflationary gap at Q_1. Monetarists believe in a self-regulating economy. Thus, because the unemployment rate is less than the natural unemployment rate in an inflationary gap, soon wages will be bid up. This will cause the $SRAS$ curve to shift leftward, from $SRAS_1$ to $SRAS_2$. The economy will return to long-run equilibrium, producing the same level of Real GDP it did originally (Q_N), but at a higher price level.

We can separate what monetarists predict will happen to the economy in the short run due to an increase in the money supply from what they predict will happen in the long run. In the short run, Real GDP will rise and the unemployment rate will fall. In the long run, Real GDP will return to its natural level, as will the unemployment rate, and the price level will be higher.

Part (b)

In (b), the economy is originally in long-run equilibrium producing Natural Real GDP (Q_N) at price level P_1. A decrease in the money supply, holding velocity constant, will shift the AD curve to the left, from AD_1 to AD_2. This will reduce Real

(a)

(b)

(c)

(d)

exhibit 4

Monetarism in an *AD-AS* Framework

According to monetarists, changes in the money supply and velocity can change aggregate demand. In (a), an increase in the money supply shifts the *AD* curve to the right and raises Real GDP and the price level. Monetarists believe the economy is self-regulating; in time it moves back to its Natural Real GDP level at a higher price level. The same self-regulating properties are present in (b)–(d).

GDP to Q_1 and reduce the price level to P_2. Because Real GDP has fallen, the unemployment rate will rise.

According to monetarists, the economy in (b) is in a recessionary gap. Can the economy get itself out of a recessionary gap? Monetarists think so; they believe the economy is self-regulating. In time, wages will fall, the *SRAS* curve will shift to the right, and the economy will be back in long-run equilibrium producing Q_N—albeit at a lower price level.

Again, we separate the short-run and long-run effects of a decrease in the money supply, according to monetarists. In the short run, Real GDP will fall and the unemployment rate will rise. In the long run, Real GDP will return to its natural level, as will the unemployment rate, and the price level will be lower.

Part (c)

Again, we start with the economy in long-run equilibrium. Now, instead of changing the money supply, we change velocity. An increase in velocity causes the *AD* curve to shift to the right, from AD_1 to AD_2. As a result, Real GDP rises, as does the price level. The unemployment rate falls as Real GDP rises.

According to monetarists, the economy is in an inflationary gap. In time, it will move back to long-run equilibrium. So, in the short run, an increase in velocity raises Real GDP and lowers the unemployment rate. In the long run, Real GDP returns to its natural level, as does the unemployment rate, and the price level is higher.

Part (d)

We start with the economy in long-run equilibrium. A decrease in velocity causes the AD curve to shift to the left from AD_1 to AD_2. As a result, Real GDP falls, as does the price level. The unemployment rate rises as Real GDP falls.

According to monetarists, the economy is in a recessionary gap. In time, it will move back to long-run equilibrium. So, in the short run, a decrease in velocity lowers Real GDP and increases the unemployment rate. In the long run, Real GDP returns to its natural level, as does the unemployment rate, and the price level is lower.

THE MONETARIST VIEW OF THE ECONOMY

Based on our diagrammatic exposition of monetarism so far, we know the following about monetarists:

1. Monetarists believe the economy is self-regulating.
2. Monetarists believe changes in velocity and the money supply can change aggregate demand.
3. Monetarists believe changes in velocity and the money supply will change the price level and Real GDP in the short run, but only the price level in the long run.

We need to make one other important point with respect to monetarists. But first, consider this question: Can a change in velocity offset a change in the money supply? To illustrate, suppose velocity falls and the money supply rises. By itself, a decrease in velocity will shift the AD curve to the left. And by itself, an increase in the money supply will shift the AD curve to the right. Can the decline in velocity shift the AD curve to the left by the same amount as the increase in the money supply shifts the AD curve to the right? This is, of course, possible. If it happens, then a change in the money supply would have no effect on Real GDP and the price level (in the short run) and on the price level (in the long run). In other words, we would have to conclude that changes in monetary policy may be ineffective at changing Real GDP and the price level.

Does this condition—a change in velocity completely offsetting a change in the money supply—occur often? Monetarists generally think not because they believe: (1) Velocity does not change very much from one period to the next, that is, it is relatively stable. (2) As mentioned earlier, changes in velocity are predictable. In other words, monetarists believe velocity is relatively stable and predictable.

So, in the monetarist view of the economy, changes in velocity are not likely to offset changes in the money supply. This means that changes in the money supply will largely determine changes in aggregate demand and, therefore, changes in Real GDP and the price level. For all practical purposes, an increase in the money supply will raise aggregate demand, increase both Real GDP and the price level in the short run, and increase the price level in the long run. A decrease in the money supply will lower aggregate demand, decrease both Real GDP and the price level in the short run, and decrease the price level in the long run.

Self-Test

1. What do monetarists predict will happen in the short run and in the long run as a result of each of the following (in each case, assume the economy is currently in long-run equilibrium)?
   a. Velocity rises.

b. Velocity falls.
c. The money supply rises.
d. The money supply falls.

2. Can a change in velocity offset a change in the money supply (on aggregate demand)? Explain your answer.

INFLATION

In everyday usage, the word *inflation* refers to any increase in the price level. Economists, though, like to differentiate between two types of increases in the price level: a one-shot increase and a continued increase. These two types of inflation are discussed in this section.

ONE-SHOT INFLATION

One-Shot Inflation
A one-time increase in the price level. An increase in the price level that does not continue.

One-shot inflation is exactly what it sounds like: it is a one-shot, or one-time, increase in the price level. Suppose the CPI for years 1–5 is as follows:

Year	CPI
1	100
2	110
3	110
4	110
5	110

Notice that the price level is higher in year 2 than in year 1 but that after year 2, it does not change. In other words, it takes a "one-shot" jump in year 2 and then stabilizes. This is an example of one-shot inflation.

 Q: Suppose there is an increase in a particular price, say, the price of television sets, but not in the price level. Is this inflation?

A: No, it isn't. A rise in the price of one good may be offset by a decline in the price of another good, leaving the price level unchanged. A rise in a single price is not inflation. A rise in the price level is inflation.

One-shot inflation can originate on either the demand side or the supply side of the economy.

One-Shot Inflation: Demand-Side Induced

In Exhibit 5a, the economy is initially in long-run equilibrium at point 1. Suppose the aggregate demand curve shifts rightward from AD_1 to AD_2. As this happens, the economy moves to point 2, where the price level is P_2. At point 2 in Exhibit 5b, the Real GDP the economy is producing (Q_2) is greater than Natural Real GDP. This means that the unemployment rate that exists in the economy is lower than the natural unemployment rate. Consequently, as old wage contracts expire, workers are paid higher wage rates because unemployment is relatively low. As wage rates rise, the *SRAS* curve shifts leftward from $SRAS_1$ to $SRAS_2$. The long-run equilibrium position is at point 3. The price level and Real GDP at each of the three points are as follows:

Point	Price Level	Real GDP
1 (start)	P_1	$Q_1 = Q_N$
2	P_2	Q_2
3 (end)	P_3	$Q_1 = Q_N$

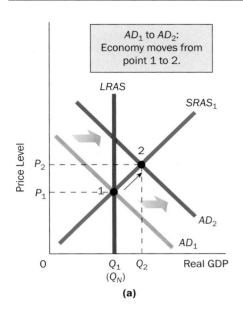

AD₁ to AD₂:
Economy moves from
point 1 to 2.

(a)

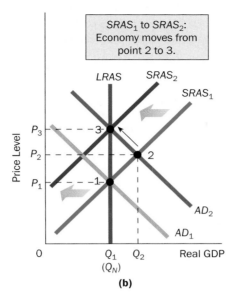

SRAS₁ to SRAS₂:
Economy moves from
point 2 to 3.

(b)

exhibit 5

**One-Shot Inflation: Demand-
Side Induced**
(a) The aggregate demand curve
shifts rightward from AD_1 to AD_2. As
a result, the price level increases from
P_1 to P_2; the economy moves from
point 1 to point 2. (b) Because the
Real GDP the economy produces (Q_2)
is greater than Natural Real GDP, the
unemployment rate that exists is less
than the natural unemployment rate.
Wage rates rise, and the short-run
aggregate supply curve shifts leftward
from $SRAS_1$ to $SRAS_2$. Long-run equilibrium is at point 3.

Notice that at point 3 the economy is at a higher price level than at point 1, but
at the same Real GDP level.

Q & A   **Q:** In the example, the price level goes from P_1 to P_2 to P_3. Why is this
one-shot inflation when the price level continues to increase?

A: In the example, the price level rises (from P_1 to P_2 to P_3) and then stabilizes at P_3. Because
the price level stabilizes, we cannot characterize it as continually rising. So the change in the
price level is representative of one-shot inflation.

One-Shot Inflation: Supply-Side Induced

In Exhibit 6a, the economy is initially in long-run equilibrium at point 1. Suppose
the short-run aggregate supply curve shifts leftward from $SRAS_1$ to $SRAS_2$, say,
because oil prices increase. As this happens, the economy moves to point 2
where the price level is P_2.

At point 2 in Exhibit 6b, the Real GDP the economy is producing (Q_2) is less
than Natural Real GDP. This means that the unemployment rate that exists in the
economy is greater than the natural unemployment rate. Consequently, as old
wage contracts expire, workers are paid lower wage rates because unemployment is relatively high. As wage rates fall, the short-run aggregate supply curve
shifts rightward from $SRAS_2$ to $SRAS_1$. The long-run equilibrium position is at
point 1 again. (If wage rates are somewhat inflexible, it may take a long time to
move from point 2 back to point 1.) The price level and Real GDP at each of the
three points are as follows:

Point	Price Level	Real GDP
1 (start)	P_1	$Q_1 = Q_N$
2	P_2	Q_2
1 (end)	P_1	$Q_1 = Q_N$

exhibit 6

One-Shot Inflation: Supply-Side Induced

(a) The short-run aggregate supply curve shifts leftward from $SRAS_1$ to $SRAS_2$. As a result, the price level increases from P_1 to P_2; the economy moves from point 1 to point 2. (b) Because the Real GDP the economy produces (Q_2) is less than Natural Real GDP, the unemployment rate that exists is greater than the natural unemployment rate. Some economists argue that when this happens, wage rates will fall and the short-run aggregate supply curve will shift rightward from $SRAS_2$ (back to $SRAS_1$). Long-run equilibrium is at point 1.

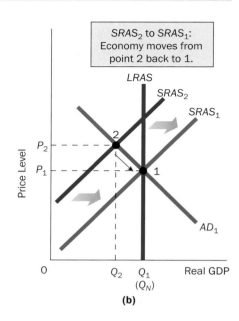

(a)

(b)

Q: In this example of SRAS declining, was there one-shot inflation?

A: Yes; the price level initially increased from P_1 to P_2.

Confusing Demand-Induced and Supply-Induced One-Shot Inflation

Demand-induced and supply-induced one-shot inflation are easy to confuse.[2] To illustrate, suppose the Federal Reserve System increases the money supply. Because there is more money in the economy, there can be greater total spending at any given price level. Consequently, the *AD* curve shifts rightward.

Next, prices begin to rise. Soon after, wage rates begin to rise. Many employers, perhaps unaware that the money supply has increased, certainly are aware that they are paying their employees higher wages. Thus, it is possible that the employers will think the higher price level is due to higher wage rates and not to the increased money supply that preceded the higher wage rates. But they would be wrong. What may look like a supply-induced rise in the price level is really a demand-induced rise in the price level.

We can tell this same story in terms of the diagrams in Exhibit 5. In (a), the *AD* curve shifts rightward because, as we said, the money supply increases. Employers, however, are unaware of what has happened in part (a). What they see is part (b). They end up paying higher wage rates to their employees, and the *SRAS* curve shifts leftward. Unaware that the *AD* curve shifted rightward in (a), but aware that the *SRAS* curve shifted leftward in (b), the employers mistakenly conclude that the rise in the price level originated with a supply-side factor (higher wage rates) and not with a demand-side factor (an increase in the money supply).

THINKING LIKE AN ECONOMIST

People tend to believe that what they see with their own eyes or experience in their daily lives causes the effects they notice. Witness, in our last example, employers' mistaken belief that the stimulus for the rise in the price level was a rise in wage rates (which they had experienced firsthand) and not an increase in the money supply

---

2. Sometimes the terms *demand-side inflation* and *supply-side inflation* are used.

(which they probably did not know had occurred). But the economist knows that the cause of a phenomenon may be far removed from our personal orbit. This awareness is part of the economic way of thinking.

CONTINUED INFLATION

Suppose the CPI for years 1–5 is as follows:

Year	CPI
1	100
2	110
3	120
4	130
5	150

Notice that the CPI goes from 100 to 110, then from 110 to 120, and so on. Each year the CPI is higher than it was in the year before. There is a continued increase in the price level. This is an example of **continued inflation.**

Continued Inflation
A continued increase in the price level.

From One-Shot Inflation to Continued Inflation

What can turn one-shot inflation into continued inflation? The answer is continued increases in aggregate demand. The process is illustrated in Exhibit 7.

Beginning at point 1 in Exhibit 7a, the aggregate demand curve shifts rightward from AD_1 to AD_2. The economy moves from point 1 to point 2. We know from the previous discussion that this is not the end of the story. At point 2, the unemployment rate that exists in the economy is less than the natural unemployment rate. As a result, wage rates rise and cause the short-run aggregate supply curve to shift leftward from $SRAS_1$ to $SRAS_2$. The economy moves from point 2 to point 3. At point 3, the economy is in long-run equilibrium.

Suppose that at point 3, the economy experiences another rightward shift in the aggregate demand curve (to AD_3). The process repeats itself, and the economy moves from point 3 to point 4 to point 5. Still another rightward shift in the aggregate demand curve moves the economy from point 5 to point 6 to point 7. We

(a)

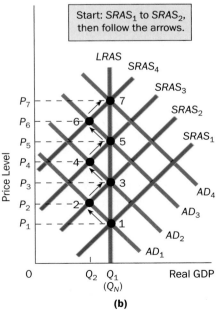

(b)

exhibit 7

Changing One-Shot Inflation into Continued Inflation
(a) The aggregate demand curve shifts rightward from AD_1 to AD_2. The economy initially moves from point 1 to point 2 and finally to point 3. Continued increases in the price level are brought about through continued increases in aggregate demand.
(b) The short-run aggregate supply curve shifts leftward from $SRAS_1$ to $SRAS_2$. The economy initially moves from point 1 to point 2. The economy will return to point 1 unless there is an increase in aggregate demand. We see here, as in (a), that continued increases in the price level are brought about through continued increases in aggregate demand.

have stopped at point 7, but we could have continued. Notice that the result of this process is a continually rising price level—from P_1 to P_7 and beyond. We conclude that continued increases in aggregate demand cause continued inflation.

Now let's look at continued inflation from the supply side of the economy. Beginning at point 1 in Exhibit 7b, the short-run aggregate supply curve shifts leftward from $SRAS_1$ to $SRAS_2$. The economy moves from point 1 to point 2. At point 2, the unemployment rate that exists in the economy is greater than the natural unemployment rate. According to some economists, there is a natural tendency for wage rates to fall and the $SRAS$ curve to shift rightward, moving the economy back to point 1.

This natural tendency of the economy to return to point 1 will be offset, however, if the aggregate demand curve shifts rightward. Then, instead of moving from point 2 back to point 1, the economy moves from point 2 to point 3. At point 3, the economy is in long-run equilibrium, and a higher price level exists than existed at point 2.

Suppose the economy experiences another leftward shift in the aggregate supply curve (to $SRAS_3$). The economy moves from point 3 to point 4 and would naturally return to point 3 unless the aggregate demand curve shifts rightward. If the latter occurs, the economy moves to point 5. The same process moves the economy from point 5 to 6 to 7, where we have decided to stop. Notice that this process results in a continually rising price level—from P_1 to P_7 and beyond. Again, we conclude that continued increases in aggregate demand cause continued inflation.

Q & A

Q: Can't continued declines in short-run aggregate supply (*SRAS*) also propel the price level continually higher? For example, suppose a labor union continually bargains for and receives higher wage rates for its members. Each time the union receives higher wage rates, the *SRAS* curve shifts leftward. And each time the *SRAS* curve shifts leftward, wouldn't the economy experience a higher price level?

A: Theoretically, continued declines in *SRAS* can lead to continued rises in the price level, *ceteris paribus*. It is possible, but not likely, for *SRAS* to continually decline. For it to do so, workers would have to continually increase their wage demands as unemployment rises above its natural level. This is not consistent with the supply-and-demand model outlined in Chapter 3 that shows that a surplus leads to downward pressure on price (wages).

http://

Go to *http://w3.access.gpo.gov/eop/*, and key "Major Industrial Countries" in the Search box (include the quotes). Click on "Submit." Find the table that includes consumer prices, and select the "TXT" icon below it. Find the consumer prices (index) table on the page. Find the index values for the United States, Japan, and Germany. Next, compute the inflation rate for each country for the years 1974, 1975, and 1979. (You may want to refer to an earlier chapter to see how to calculate the inflation rate.) There was a major oil price shock in the world in 1973. Does it look like the oil price shock affected the prices in each of the three countries the same way?

What Causes Continued Increases in Aggregate Demand?

So far, we know that continued increases in aggregate demand cause continued inflation. *But what causes continued increases in aggregate demand?*

To answer this question, recall that at a given price level, anything that increases total expenditures increases aggregate demand and shifts the *AD* curve to the right. With this in mind, consider an increase in the money supply. If there is more money in the economy, there can be greater total expenditures at a given price level. Consequently, aggregate demand increases and the *AD* curve shifts rightward.

Economists are widely agreed that the only factor that can change continually in such a way as to bring about continued increases in aggregate demand is the money supply. Specifically, continued increases in the money supply lead to continued increases in aggregate demand, which generate continued inflation.

Continued increases in the money supply $\rightarrow$ Continued increases in aggregate demand $\rightarrow$ Continued inflation

It is important to realize that the money supply is the *only* factor that can continually increase without causing a reduction in one of the four components of total expenditures—that is, consumption, investment, government purchases, or net exports.

Everyday Life   Popular Culture   Technology   The World

Grade Inflation: It's All Relative

Inflation can sometimes be deceptive. To illustrate, suppose Jones produces and sells motorcycles. The average price for one of his motorcycles is $10,000. Unbeknownst to Jones, the Fed increases the money supply. Months pass, and then one day, Jones notices that the demand for his motorcycles has increased. Jones raises the prices of his motorcycles and earns a higher dollar income.

Jones is excited about earning more income. But soon he realizes that the prices of many of the things he buys have increased too. Food, clothing, and housing prices have all gone up. Jones is earning a higher dollar income, but he is also paying higher prices. In relative terms, Jones's financial position may be the same as it was before the price of motorcycles increased.

Now let's consider grade inflation. Beginning in the 1960s, the average GPA at most colleges and universities across the country began to rise. Whereas professors once gave out the full range of grades—A, B, C, D, and F—today many professors give only A's and B's and a few C's. It's been said that the "Gentleman's C," once a mainstay on many college campuses, has been replaced by the "Gentleperson's B."

Grade inflation can deceive you, just as general price inflation deceived Jones. To illustrate, suppose you get higher grades (without studying more or working harder). Your average grade goes from, say, a C+ to a B, and you believe you have an advantage over other college and university students. You reason that with higher grades, you will have a better chance of getting a good job or of getting into graduate school.

But this is true only if your grades go up and no one else's do. In other words, your relative position must improve. But grade inflation at thousands of colleges and universities across the country prevents this from happening. You get higher grades, but so does everyone else. Your GPA increases from, say, a 2.90 to a 3.60, but other students' GPA's also increase.

So, do higher grades for you necessarily mean it will be easier for you to compete with others for a job or for admission to graduate school? No, not as long as other students are getting higher grades too. In essence, grade inflation, like general price inflation, is deceptive. When there is price inflation, you may initially think your financial position has improved because you are earning more for what you sell. But then you realize that you have to pay more for the things you buy. When there is grade inflation, you may initially think you have an advantage over other students because you are receiving higher grades. But then you learn that everyone else is receiving higher grades too. Your relative position may be the same as it was before grade inflation boosted your grades.

We mention this because someone might ask, Can't government purchases continually increase and so cause continued inflation? There are two reasons why this is unlikely to occur. First, there are both real and political limits beyond which government purchases cannot go. The real upper limit is 100 percent of GDP. We do not know what the political upper limit is, but it is likely to be less than 100 percent of GDP. In either case, once the limit is reached, government purchases can no longer increase.

Second, some economists argue that government purchases that are not financed with new money may crowd out one of the other expenditure components (see the discussion of crowding out in an earlier chapter). Thus, increases in government purchases are not guaranteed to raise total expenditures because if government purchases rise, consumption, say, may fall to the degree that government purchases have increased. For example, for every additional dollar government spends on public education, households may spend one less dollar on private education.

The emphasis on the money supply as the only factor that can continue to increase and thus cause continued inflation has led most economists to agree with Nobel Laureate Milton Friedman that "inflation is always and everywhere a monetary phenomenon." (The inflation that Friedman is referring to is continued inflation.)

Q & A

Q: Suppose the following scenario occurs: (1) The federal government runs continual budget deficits, that is, government expenditures are greater than tax revenues year after year. (2) The U.S. Treasury finances the budget deficits by selling Treasury securities to the public. (3) In response to step 2, the Fed conducts open market operations and purchases a large percentage of the Treasury securities. As long as steps 1 through 3 are repeated continually, would continued inflation result?

A: This question is based on a condition, and the answer is, "Yes, given the condition specified, and holding all other things constant." If there are continued deficits and if the Fed continues to conduct open market purchases in response to Treasury financing of the deficits, continued increases in aggregate demand and continued inflation will occur. Notice, though, that the money supply is continuing to increase; thus, inflation has a monetary origin.

Self-Test

1. The prices of houses, cars, and television sets have increased. Has there been inflation?

2. Is continued inflation likely to be supply-induced? Explain your answer.

3. What type of inflation is Milton Friedman referring to when he says, "Inflation is always and everywhere a monetary phenomenon"?

MONEY AND INTEREST RATES

Before we discuss how a change in the money supply affects interest rates, we review some of the ways changes in the money supply affect different economic variables.

WHAT ECONOMIC VARIABLES ARE AFFECTED BY A CHANGE IN THE MONEY SUPPLY?

Throughout this text, we have talked about money and have shown how changes in the money supply affect different economic variables. Let's review some of these effects.

http://

Go to *http://stlouisfed.org/publications/pleng/welcome.html*. Discover who makes up the Federal Reserve and what exactly they do by selecting the "next" icon after reading the welcoming Web page. Take the "Quiz" under the "What It All Means" menu, and get your "Certificate of Merit."

1. **Money and the supply of loans.** The last chapter discusses the actions of the Fed that change the money supply. For example, when the Fed undertakes an open market purchase, the money supply increases and reserves in the banking system increase. With greater reserves, banks can extend more loans. In other words, as a result of the Fed conducting an open market purchase, the supply of loans rises. Similarly, when the Fed conducts an open market sale, the supply of loans decreases.

2. **Money and Real GDP.** This chapter shows how a change in the money supply can change aggregate demand and, therefore, change the price level and Real GDP in the short run. For example, look back at Exhibit 4a. The economy starts at point 1, producing Q_N. An increase in the money supply shifts the AD curve rightward from AD_1 to AD_2. In the short run, the economy moves to point 2, and produces a higher level of Real GDP (Q_1). Similarly, in the short run, a decrease in the money supply produces a lower level of Real GDP. (See Exhibit 4b.)

3. **Money and the price level.** This chapter also shows how a change in the money supply can change the price level. Again, look back at Exhibit 4a. Initially, at point 1, the price level is P_1. An increase in the money supply shifts the AD curve rightward from AD_1 to AD_2. In the short run, the price level in the economy moves from P_1 to P_2. In the long run, the economy is at point 3, and the price level is P_3. Exhibit 4b shows how a decrease in the money supply affects the price level.

Thus, we know that changes in the money supply affect (1) the supply of loans, (2) Real GDP, and (3) the price level. Is there anything else the money supply can affect? Many economists say that because the money supply affects the price level, it also affects the *expected inflation rate*.

The expected inflation rate is the inflation rate that you expect. For example, your expected inflation rate—the inflation rate you expect will be realized over the next year—may be 5 percent, 6 percent, or a different rate. Changes in the money supply affect the expected inflation rate—either directly or indirectly. We know from working with the equation of exchange that the greater the increase in the money supply, the greater the rise in the price level. And, we would expect that the greater the rise in the price level, the higher the expected inflation rate, *ceteris paribus*. For example, we would predict that a money supply growth rate of, say, 10 percent a year generates a greater actual inflation rate, and a larger expected inflation rate, than a money supply growth rate of 2 percent a year.

To summarize: Changes in the money supply (or changes in the rate of growth of the money supply) can affect (1) the supply of loans, (2) Real GDP, (3) the price level, and (4) the expected inflation rate.

THE MONEY SUPPLY, THE LOANABLE FUNDS MARKET, AND INTEREST RATES

The loanable funds or credit market is shown in Exhibit 8a. The demand for loanable funds is downward-sloping, indicating that borrowers will borrow more funds as the interest rate declines. The supply of loanable funds is upward-sloping, indicating that lenders will lend more funds as the interest rate rises. The equilibrium interest rate, i_1 percent in the exhibit, is determined through the forces of supply and demand. If there is a surplus of loanable funds, the interest rate falls; if there is a shortage of loanable funds, the interest rate rises.

Anything that affects either the supply of loanable funds or the demand for loanable funds will obviously affect the interest rate. All four of the factors that are affected by changes in the money supply—the supply of loans, Real GDP, the price level, and the expected inflation rate—affect either the supply of or demand for loanable funds.

The Supply of Loans

A Fed open market purchase increases reserves in the banking system and therefore increases the supply of loanable funds. As a result, the interest rate declines. See Exhibit 8b. This change in the interest rate due to a change in the supply of loanable funds is called the **liquidity effect.**

Liquidity Effect
The change in the interest rate due to a change in the supply of loanable funds.

Real GDP

A change in Real GDP affects the supply of and demand for loanable funds. To understand this, you need to realize that there is (1) a link between supplying bonds and demanding loanable funds and (2) a link between demanding bonds and supplying loanable funds. In other words,

> To *supply bonds* is to *demand loanable funds*.
> To *demand bonds* is to *supply loanable funds*.

To explain, let's suppose that corporations are the only economic actors that supply (sell) bonds and that people (like you) are the only economic actors that demand (buy) bonds. Now when a corporation supplies a bond it is effectively seeking to borrow funds from you. It is saying, "If you will buy this bond from the corporation for, say, $10,000, the corporation promises to repay you $11,000 at some specified date in the future."

In other words, when the corporation supplies bonds for sale, it (the corporation) demands loanable funds (from you) and you, if you buy or demand the bonds, supply loanable funds to the corporation.

The Interest Rate and the Loanable Funds Market

The loanable funds market is shown in part (a). The demand for loanable funds is downward-sloping; the supply of loanable funds is upward-sloping. Part (b) shows the liquidity effect, part (c) shows the income effect, part (d) shows the price-level effect, and part (e) shows the expectations effect.

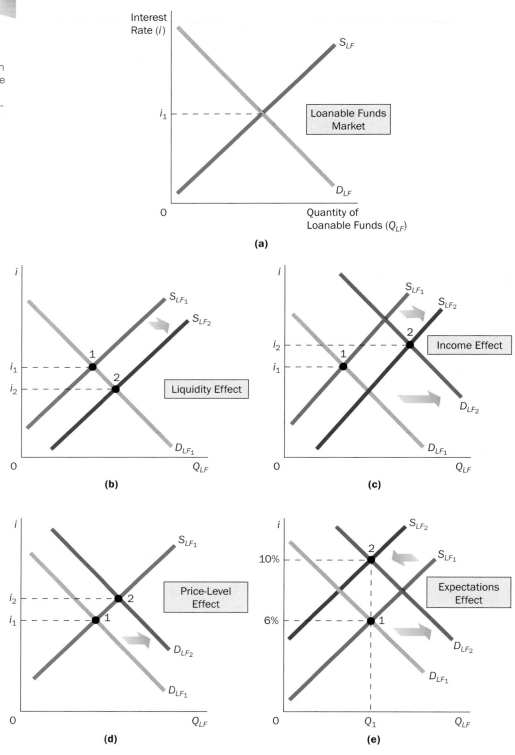

(a)

(b)

(c)

(d)

(e)

Think of a simpler transaction to understand how it is possible that when you supply one thing you demand something else. When you *supply* the desk for sale that you produced, aren't you effectively *demanding* money? And isn't the person who buys or *demands* the desk from you effectively *supplying* money to you?

With this as background, let's now ask two questions. First, how does Real GDP affect the supply of loanable funds? When Real GDP rises, peoples' wealth is greater (Real GDP consists of goods and goods are one component of wealth). When people became wealthier, they often demand more bonds (in much the same way that they may demand more houses, cars, and jewelry). But as we have just learned, to demand more bonds is to supply more loanable funds. So, when Real GDP rises, people (demand more bonds and thereby) supply more loanable funds.

Second, how does Real GDP affect the demand for loanable funds? When Real GDP rises, profitable business opportunities usually abound. Businesses decide to issue or supply more bonds to take advantage of these profitable opportunities. But, again, we know that to supply more bonds is to demand more loanable funds. So, when Real GDP rises, corporations (issue or supply more bonds and thereby) demand more loanable funds.

In summary, then, when Real GDP increases, both the supply of and demand for loanable funds increase. What is the overall effect on the interest rate? Usually, the demand for loanable funds increases by more than the supply of loanable funds, so that the interest rate rises. The change in the interest rate due to a change in Real GDP is called the **income effect.** See Exhibit 8c.

The Price Level

An earlier chapter discusses the reasons the *AD* curve slopes downward. A downward-sloping *AD* curve is explained by (1) the real balance effect, (2) the interest rate effect, and (3) the international trade effect. With respect to the interest rate effect, we said: When the price level rises, the purchasing power of money falls, and people may increase their demand for credit or loanable funds in order to borrow the funds necessary to buy a fixed bundle of goods. This change in the interest rate due to a change in the price level is called the **price-level effect.** See Exhibit 8d.

The Expected Inflation Rate

A change in the expected inflation rate affects both the supply of and demand for loanable funds. To see how, let's suppose the expected inflation rate is currently zero. Let's also assume that when the expected inflation rate is zero, the equilibrium interest rate is 6 percent, as in Exhibit 8e. Now suppose the expected inflation rate rises from 0 percent to 4 percent. What will this rise in the expected inflation rate do to the demand for and supply of loanable funds? Borrowers (demanders of loanable funds) will be willing to pay 4 percent more interest for their loans because they expect to be paying back the loans with dollars that have 4 percent less buying power than the dollars they are being lent. (Another way to look at this: If they wait to buy goods, the prices of the goods they want will have risen by 4 percent. To beat the price rise, they are willing to pay up to 4 percent more to borrow and purchase the goods now.) In effect, the demand for loanable funds curve shifts rightward, so that at Q_1 borrowers are willing to pay a 4 percent higher interest rate. See Exhibit 8e.

On the other side of the loanable funds market, the lenders (the suppliers of loanable funds) require a 4 percent higher interest rate to compensate them for the 4 percent less valuable dollars in which the loan will be repaid. In effect, the supply of loanable funds curve shifts leftward, so that at Q_1 lenders will receive an interest rate of 10 percent. See Exhibit 8e.

Thus, an expected inflation rate of 4 percent increases the demand for loanable funds and decreases the supply of loanable funds, so that the interest rate is 4 percent higher than it was when there was a zero expected inflation rate. A change in the interest rate due to a change in the expected inflation rate is referred to as the **expectations effect** (or *Fisher effect,* after economist Irving Fisher).

Exhibit 9 summarizes how a change in the money supply directly and indirectly affects the interest rate.

Income Effect
The change in the interest rate due to a change in Real GDP.

Price-Level Effect
The change in the interest rate due to a change in the price level.

Expectations Effect
The change in the interest rate due to a change in the expected inflation rate.

exhibit 9

How the Fed Affects the Interest Rate

This exhibit summarizes the way the Fed (through changes in the money supply) affects the interest rate. For example, an open market operation (OMO) directly affects the supply of loanable funds and affects the interest rate. An OMO also affects Real GDP, the price level, and the expected inflation rate, and therefore indirectly affects either the supply of or demand for loanable funds, which in turn affects the interest rate.

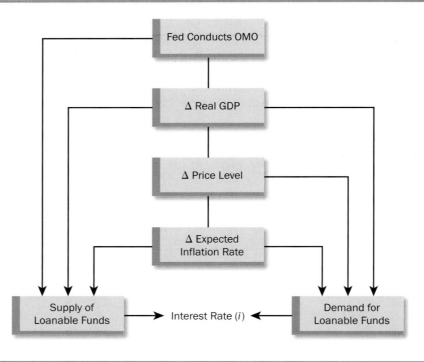

Q: The price-level effect sounds the same as the expectations effect. After all, both have something to do with the price level. What is the difference?

A: To illustrate the difference, consider a one-shot change in the money supply that ultimately moves the price level from a price index of 120 to a price index of 135. The price-level effect refers to the change in the interest rate that is related to the fact that the actual price level is rising. Think of the demand for loanable funds creeping up steadily as the price index rises from 120 to 121 to 122 to 123 and so on to 135. Once the price index has hit 135, there is no further reason for the demand for loanable funds to rise. After all, the price level isn't rising anymore. Now as the price level is rising, peoples' expected inflation rate is rising. In other words, they may see (in their mind's eye) where the price level is headed (from 120 to 135) and adjust accordingly. Once the price level hits 135 (and given that we are talking about a one-shot change in the money supply), the expected inflation rate falls to zero. In other words, any change in the interest rate due to a rise in the expected inflation rate is now over and therefore no longer has an effect on the interest rate. But certainly the price level still has an effect on the interest rate because the price level is higher. In the end, the effect on the interest rate due to a rise in the price level remains and the effect on the interest rate due to a rise in the expected inflation rate disappears.

SO, WHAT HAPPENS TO THE INTEREST RATE AS THE MONEY SUPPLY CHANGES?

Suppose the Fed decides to raise the rate of growth of the money supply, say, from 3 percent to 5 percent a year. What effect will this have on the interest rate? Some people will quickly say, "It will lower the interest rate." They may be thinking that the only effect on the interest rate is the liquidity effect. In other words, as the Fed increases the rate of growth of the money supply, more reserves enter the banking system, more loans are extended, and the interest rate falls.

That would be the right answer if the only thing that an increase in the money supply growth rate did was to affect the supply of loanable funds. But as we have discussed, this isn't the only thing that happens. Real GDP changes, the price level changes, and the expected inflation rate changes, and changes in these factors affect the loanable funds market just as the Fed action did. Figuring out what happens to the interest rate is a matter of trying to figure out when each effect (liquidity, income, price-level, and expectations) occurs and how strong each effect is.

To illustrate, suppose everyone expects the Fed to continue to increase the money supply at a growth rate of 2 percent a year. Then, on January 1, the Fed announces that it will increase the rate of growth in the money supply to 4 percent and will begin open market purchases to effect this outcome immediately. It's possible that one second after the announcement, people's expected inflation rate rises. In other words, the expectations effect begins immediately and affects interest rates accordingly. On January 2, the interest rate is higher than it was one day earlier. At this point, someone could say, "See, an increase in the rate of growth in the money supply raises the interest rate." The problem with saying this, though, is that not all the effects (liquidity, income, and so on) have occurred yet. In time, the liquidity effect puts downward pressure on the interest rate. Suppose this begins to happen on January 15, and the interest rate begins to fall from what it was on January 2. Then, someone on January 15 could say, "It is obvious that an increase in the rate of growth of the money supply lowers interest rates."

Our point is: A change in the money supply affects the economy in many ways—changing the supply of loanable funds directly, changing Real GDP and therefore changing the demand for and supply of loanable funds, changing the expected inflation rate, and so on. The timing and magnitude of these effects determine changes in the interest rate.

THE NOMINAL AND REAL INTEREST RATES

If you were to call a bank and ask what it charges for a given type of loan, the bank would quote some interest rate. The interest rate that it quotes is the interest rate we have been discussing. It is the interest rate that comes about through the interaction of the demand for and supply of loanable funds. Sometimes this interest rate is called the **nominal interest rate** or market interest rate.

The nominal interest rate may not be the true cost of borrowing because part of the nominal interest rate is a reflection of the expected inflation rate. To illustrate, let's suppose the nominal interest rate is 9 percent and the expected inflation rate is 2 percent. If you take out a loan for $10,000 at 9 percent, you will have to pay back the loan amount ($10,000) plus $900 in interest at the end of the year. In other words, for a $10,000 loan, you will have to repay $10,900.

Now let's suppose that the expected inflation rate turns out to be the actual inflation rate. In other words, people expected the inflation rate to be 2 percent and it turns out to be 2 percent. In this case, the dollars you pay back will be worth less than the dollars you borrowed—by 2 percent. In other words, you borrowed dollars that were worth 2 percent more in purchasing power than the dollars you repaid.

This fact should be taken into account in determining your real cost of borrowing. Was the real cost of borrowing 9 percent or 7 percent? Economists would say it was 7 percent. The real cost of borrowing is sometimes called the **real interest rate.** It is equal to the nominal interest rate minus the expected inflation rate.[3]

Nominal Interest Rate
The interest rate actually charged (or paid) in the market; the market interest rate. The nominal interest rate = Real interest rate + Expected inflation rate.

Real Interest Rate
The nominal interest rate minus the expected inflation rate. When the expected inflation rate is zero, the real interest rate equals the nominal interest rate.

Real interest rate = Nominal interest rate − Expected inflation rate

Based on this equation, it follows that the nominal interest rate is equal to the real interest rate plus the expected inflation rate.

Nominal interest rate = Real interest rate + Expected inflation rate

---

3. A broader definition is "Real interest rate = Nominal interest rate − Expected rate of change in the price level." This definition is useful because we will not always be dealing with an expected inflation rate; we could be dealing with an expected deflation rate.

Q: Suppose the *actual inflation rate* turns out to be different from the *expected inflation rate*. For example, suppose the expected inflation rate is 2 percent, but the actual inflation rate turns out to be 1 percent. Does it still follow that the real interest rate is equal to the nominal interest rate minus the expected inflation rate?

A: When the expected inflation rate is different from the actual inflation rate, we must differentiate between the *ex ante real interest rate* and the *ex post real interest rate*. Ex ante means "before" and ex post means "after." Here *ex ante* refers to before the actual inflation rate has been realized, and *ex post* refers to after the actual inflation rate has been realized.

Ex ante real interest rate = Nominal interest rate − Expected inflation rate
Ex post real interest rate = Nominal interest rate − Actual inflation rate

To illustrate the difference, suppose the nominal interest rate is 8 percent and the expected inflation rate is 3 percent. If follows that the ex ante real interest rate is 5 percent. Now suppose the actual inflation rate turns out to be lower than expected; it turns out to be 2 percent. It follows that the ex post real interest rate is 6 percent.

Self-Test

1. If the expected inflation rate is 4 percent and the nominal interest rate is 7 percent, what is real interest rate?

2. Is it possible for the nominal interest rate to immediately rise following an increase in the money supply? Explain your answer.

3. "The Fed only affects the interest rate via the liquidity effect." Do you agree or disagree? Explain your answer.

A Reader Asks...

How Do We Know What the Expected Inflation Rate Equals?

Is there some way to figure out what the expected inflation rate equals at any given time?

One way to find out what the expected inflation rate equals is to look at the spread—the difference—between the yield on conventional bonds and the yield on indexed bonds with the same maturity. For example, we can look at the spread between the yield on a 10-year Treasury bond (Treasury bond that matures in 10 years) and the yield on an inflation-indexed Treasury bond (inflation-indexed Treasury bond that matures in 10 years).

Before we do this, let's look at the difference between a conventional bond and an inflation-indexed bond. An inflation-indexed bond guarantees the purchaser a certain real rate of return, but a conventional, or non-indexed, bond does not. For example, suppose you purchase an inflation-indexed, 10-year, $1,000 security that pays 4 percent interest. If there is no inflation, the annual interest payment is $40. But, if the inflation rate is 3 percent, the bond issuer "marks up" the value of your security by 3 percent—from $1,000 to $1,030. Furthermore, your annual interest payment is 4 percent of this new higher amount—that is, it is 4 percent of $1,030, or $41.20.

Investors are willing to accept a lower yield on inflation-indexed bonds because they are receiving something with them that they are not receiving on conventional bonds—protection against inflation. So while a conventional bond may yield, say, 6 percent, an inflation-indexed bond may yield 4 percent.

What does the difference, or spread, signify? It is a measure of the inflation rate that investors expect will exist over the life of the bond.

To illustrate with some real numbers, we went to bloomberg.com and checked the yield on securities. An inflation-indexed 10-year Treasury bond had a yield of 3.29 percent. A conventional 10-year Treasury bond had a yield of 5.51. The difference, or spread, was 2.22 percent. This means that on this day, investors (or "the market") expected that the inflation rate was going to be 2.22 percent.

So, by checking the spread between yields on conventional and inflation-indexed bonds of the same maturity, you can see what the market expects the inflation rate will be. As the spread widens, the market expects a higher inflation rate; as the spread narrows, the market expects a lower inflation rate.

Once again, here is the process to follow:

1. Go to *http://www.bloomberg.com*.
2. Click on "U.S. Treasuries."
3. Write down the yield on conventional 10-year Treasury bonds.
4. Write down the yield on inflation-indexed 10-year Treasury bonds.
5. Find the spread between the yields. The spread is the market's expected inflation rate.
6. By doing this daily, you can see if the market's perception of inflation is changing. For example, if the spread is widening, the market believes inflation will be increasing. If the spread is narrowing, the market believes inflation will be decreasing.

Chapter Summary

$MV \equiv PQ$

- The equation of exchange is an identity: $MV \equiv PQ$. The equation of exchange can be interpreted in different ways: (1) The money supply multiplied by velocity must equal the price level times Real GDP: $M \times V \equiv P \times Q$. (2) The money supply multiplied by velocity must equal GDP: $M \times V \equiv GDP$. (3) Total expenditures (measured by MV) must equal the total sales revenues of business firms (measured by PQ): $MV \equiv PQ$.

- The equation of exchange is not a theory of the macroeconomy. However, the equation of exchange can be turned into a theory by making assumptions about some of the variables in the equation. For example, if we assume that both V and Q are constant, then we have the simple quantity theory of money, which predicts that changes in the money supply cause strictly proportional changes in the price level.

- A change in the money supply or a change in velocity will change aggregate demand and therefore lead to a shift in the AD curve. Specifically, either an increase in the money supply or an increase in velocity will increase aggregate demand and therefore shift the AD curve to the right. A decrease in the money supply or a decrease in velocity will decrease aggregate demand and therefore shift the AD curve to the left.

- In the simple quantity theory of money, Real GDP is assumed to be constant in the short run. This means the AS curve is vertical. Also, velocity is assumed to be constant. This means the only thing that can change aggregate demand is a change in the money supply. In the face of a vertical AS curve, any change in the money supply shifts the AD curve and changes only the price level, not Real GDP.

Monetarism

- According to monetarists, if the economy is initially in long-run equilibrium, (1) an increase in the money supply will raise the price level and Real GDP in the short run, and will raise only the price level in the long run; (2) a decrease in the money supply will lower the price level and Real GDP in the short run, and will lower only the price level in the long run; (3) an increase in velocity will raise the price level and Real GDP in the short run, and will raise only the price level in the long run; (4) a decrease in velocity will lower the price level and Real GDP in the short run, and will lower only the price level in the long run.

One-Shot Inflation and Continued Inflation

- One-shot inflation can result from an increase in aggregate demand or a decrease in short-run aggregate supply.
- For one-shot inflation to change to continued inflation, it is necessary and sufficient to have a continued increase in aggregate demand. Continued increases in the money supply cause continued increases in aggregate demand and continued inflation.

The Money Supply and Interest Rates

- Changes in the money supply can affect the interest rate via the liquidity, income, price level, and expectations effects.
- The change in the interest rate due to a change in the supply of loanable funds is called the liquidity effect. The change in the interest rate due to a change in Real GDP is called the income effect. The change in the interest rate due to a change in the price level is called the price-level effect. The change in the interest rate due to a change in the expected inflation rate is called the expectations effect (or Fisher effect).

Nominal and Real Interest Rates

- The Real interest rate = Nominal interest rate − Expected inflation rate.
- The Nominal interest rate = Real interest rate + Expected inflation rate.

Velocity

Equation of Exchange

Simple Quantity Theory of Money

One-Shot Inflation

Continued Inflation

Liquidity Effect

Income Effect

Price-Level Effect

Expectations Effect

Nominal Interest Rate

Real Interest Rate

Economic Connections to You

Economic facts, actions, and changes create ripples that move away from their point of origin. Eventually, these ripples can intersect your life and have an effect on you. Consider the following example.

The Fed sharply and unexpectedly increased the money supply last year. Also, last year a contractor won a bid to construct a new elementary school beginning this year. Prices started to rise this year and the contractor has had to pay more for many of the materials he needs to build the school. There is

no doubt he will earn less profit unless he can cut his costs. He decides to fire a few part-time workers, one of whom is you. Thus, there is a connection between a sharp and unexpected increase in the money supply and your part-time job—an economic connection to you.

Based on the material in this chapter, identify other ways in which economic facts, actions, and changes create ripples that eventually affect you.

Questions and Problems

1. What are the assumptions and predictions of the simple quantity theory of money? Does the simple quantity theory of money predict well?

2. In the simple quantity theory of money, the *AS* curve is vertical. Explain why.

3. In the simple quantity theory of money, what will lead to an increase in aggregate demand? In monetarism, what will lead to an increase in aggregate demand?

4. In monetarism, how will each of the following affect the price level in the short run?
   a. An increase in velocity
   b. A decrease in velocity
   c. An increase in the money supply
   d. A decrease in the money supply

5. Suppose the objective of the Fed is to increase Real GDP. To this end, it increases the money supply. Is there anything that can offset the increase in the money supply so that Real GDP does not rise? Explain your answer.

6. "A loaf of bread, a computer, and automobile tires have gone up in price; therefore, we are experiencing inflation." Do you agree or disagree with this statement? Explain your answer.

7. What is the difference in the long run between a one-shot increase in aggregate demand and a one-shot decrease in short-run aggregate supply?

8. "One-shot inflation may be a demand-side (of the economy) or a supply-side phenomenon, but continued inflation is likely to be a demand-side phenomenon." Do you agree or disagree with this statement? Explain your answer.

9. Explain how demand-induced one-shot inflation may appear as supply-induced one-shot inflation.

10. In recent years, economists have argued about what the true value of the real interest rate is at any one time and over time. Given that the Nominal interest rate = Real interest rate + Expected inflation rate, it follows that the Real interest rate = Nominal interest rate − Expected inflation rate. Why do you think there is so much disagreement over the true value of the real interest rate?

11. To a potential borrower, which would be more important—the nominal interest rate or the (ex ante) real interest rate? Explain your answer.

12. The money supply rises on Tuesday and by Thursday the interest rate has risen. Is this more likely to be the result of the income effect or the expectations effect? Explain your answer.

13. Suppose the money supply increased 30 days ago. Whether the nominal interest rate is higher, lower, or the same today as it was 30 days ago depends upon what? Explain your answer.

1. How will things change in the *AD-AS* framework if a change in the money supply is completely offset by a change in velocity?
2. Graphically show each of the following:
   a. Continued inflation due to supply-side factors
   b. One-shot demand-induced inflation
   c. One-shot supply-induced inflation
3. Use the figure at the right to answer the following questions.
   a. The economy is at point *A* when there is a one-shot demand-induced inflation. Assuming no other changes in the economy, at what point will the economy settle (assuming the economy is self-regulating)?
   b. The economy is at point *A* when it is faced with two adverse supply-side shocks. The Fed tries to counter these shocks by increasing aggregate demand. What path will the economy follow?

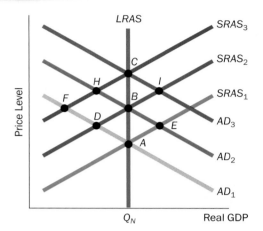

1. Go to *http://www.federalreserve.gov/releases/H41/Current/* and find the section titled "Consolidated Statement of Condition of All Federal Reserve Banks."
   a. What is the dollar value of gold certificates held by the Fed?
   b. What is the dollar value of all U.S. government securities "bought outright" by the Fed?
   c. What is the dollar value of Federal Reserve notes in the Fed's balance sheet?
   d. Are deposits in banks and other institutions, such as checking and savings accounts, represented in the Fed's balance sheet?
2. Go to *http://www.bls.gov/data/top20.htm*, and click on "CPI-All Urban Consumers (Current Series)." Next, click on the box "U.S. All Items 1982-84 = 100" (or most recent), and then click "Retrieve data." Now, reformat the series by selecting "REFORMAT" and specify year range from 1913 to the most recent year available.
   a. Find the most recent January price index. A market basket of goods that cost $9.80 in January 1913 would cost how much today?

   b. What was the last year in which prices declined from January to January? When was the last time this happened for two consecutive years?
   c. Was there inflation in the 1930s? If so, when? Was there deflation in the 1930s? If so, when?
   d. What was the price index in 1970? Double that index number and compare it with the actual index number for 1980. How do they compare? Would someone growing up in the 1970s think that inflation was a permanent part of the economic landscape? Explain.
   e. In what year were prices first twice what they were in 1913? How many years are there between the year you identified and 1913? In what year were prices first triple what they were in 1970? How many years are there between the year you identified and 1970? What do you conclude?

Log on to the Arnold Xtra! Web site now (*http://arnoldxtra.swcollege.com*) for additional learning resources such as practice quizzes, help with graphing, video clips, and current event applications.

ch.15

MONETARY POLICY

Economists have different theories about how the economy works. Monetarists have theories, new classical economists have theories, New Keynesians have theories, and others have theories. Sometimes economists disagree and sometimes they agree. Economists agree that the goals of monetary policy are to stabilize the price level, achieve low unemployment, and promote economic growth, among other things. Also, economists generally agree that monetary policy affects the economy. However, they disagree about the degree to which, and under what conditions, it does this. This chapter describes both the disagreements and the agreements economists have about **monetary policy.**

Chapter Road Map

In this chapter we discuss three issues that relate

to money. First, we examine the money market—focusing on

both the demand for and supply of money—in order to see how interest

rates are determined. An understanding of the money market is necessary for our

discussion of transmission mechanisms. Essentially, we discuss two transmission mechanisms:

the Keynesian and the monetarist.

   Next, we examine how monetary policy may be used to eliminate both inflationary and recessionary

gaps. Then we discuss the activist-nonactivist debate with respect to monetary policy.

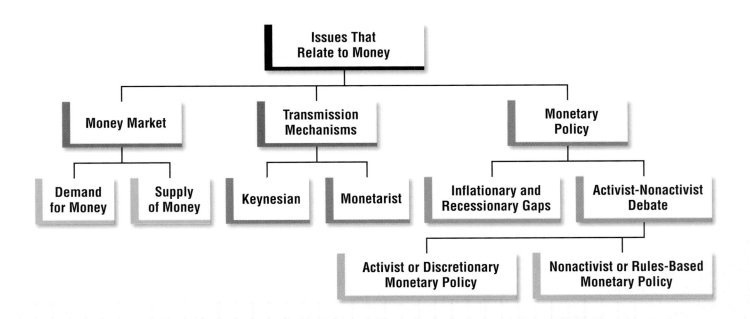

THE MONEY MARKET

Like all markets, the money market has two sides: a demand side and a supply side.[1] Both are discussed in this section.

THE DEMAND FOR MONEY

An illustration of the demand for a good has the price of the good on the vertical axis and the quantity of the good on the horizontal axis. An illustration of the **demand for money (balances)** has the price of holding money balances on the vertical axis and the quantity of money on the horizontal axis. But what is the price of holding money balances?

The price of holding money balances—specifically, the opportunity cost of holding money—is the interest rate. Money is one of many forms in which individuals may hold their wealth. By holding money, individuals forfeit the opportunity to hold that amount of their wealth in other forms. For example, the person who holds $1,000 in cash gives up the opportunity to purchase a $1,000 asset that yields interest (for example, a bond). Thus, the interest rate is the opportunity cost of holding money. One pays the price of forfeited interest by holding money.

Exhibit 1a illustrates the demand for money (balances). As the interest rate increases, the opportunity cost of holding money increases, and individuals choose to hold less money. As the interest rate decreases, the opportunity cost of holding money decreases, and individuals choose to hold more money.

THE SUPPLY OF MONEY

Exhibit 1b shows the supply of money as a vertical line at the quantity of money, which is largely determined by the Fed. The money supply is not exclusively determined by the Fed because both banks and the public are important players in the money supply process, as discussed in earlier chapters. For example, when banks do not lend their entire excess reserves, the money supply is not as large as it is when they do.

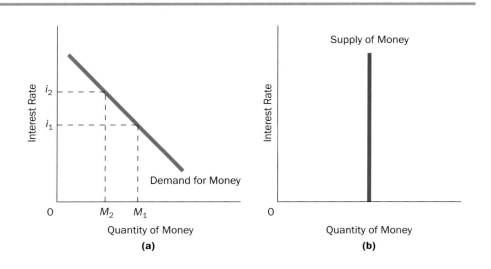

exhibit 1

The Demand for and Supply of Money
(a) The demand curve for money is downward-sloping. (b) The supply curve of money is a vertical line at the quantity of money, which is largely, but not exclusively, determined by the Fed.

---

1. In everyday language, the term *money market* is often used to refer to the market for short-term securities, where there is a demand for and supply of short-term securities. This is not the money market discussed here. In this money market, there is a demand for and supply of money.

EQUILIBRIUM IN THE MONEY MARKET

Equilibrium in the money market exists when the quantity demanded of money equals the quantity supplied. In Exhibit 2, equilibrium exists at the interest rate i_1. At a higher interest rate, i_2, the quantity supplied of money is greater than the quantity demanded, and there is an excess supply of money ("too much" money). At a lower interest rate, i_3, the quantity demanded of money is greater than the quantity supplied, and there is an excess demand for money ("too little" money). Only at i_1 are the quantity demanded and the quantity supplied of money equal. Here there are no shortages or surpluses of money, no excess demands or excess supplies. Individuals are holding the amount of money they want to hold.

Q&A

Q: At i_2 in Exhibit 2, there is an excess supply of money; there is "too much" money. How can an individual ever have "too much" money? Isn't money one of those things that you can never have enough of?

A: A person can have "too much" money relative to other things. For example, suppose you have $100,000 and nothing else—no food, no car, no television set. In this case, you might think that you have "too much" money and too few other things. In other words, you might be willing to trade some of your money for, say, some food, a car, and a TV set.

TRANSMISSION MECHANISMS

Consider two markets: (1) the money market and (2) the goods and services market. Economists have different ideas about the impact that changes in the money market have on the goods and services market and whether that impact is direct or indirect. The routes or channels that ripple effects created in the money market travel to affect the goods and services market are known as the **transmission mechanism.** We discuss two major transmission mechanisms: the Keynesian and the monetarist.

THE KEYNESIAN TRANSMISSION MECHANISM: INDIRECT

The Keynesian link between the money market and the goods and services market is an indirect one. Refer to Exhibit 3, as the Keynesian transmission mechanism is described market by market in the following paragraphs.

1. **The money market.** Suppose the money market is in equilibrium at interest rate i_1 in part (a). Then, the Fed increases the reserves of the banking system through an open market purchase. This results in an increase in the money

Go to *http://stats.bls.gov/*. Select "Consumer Price Index" under the "Inflation & Consumer Spending" menu. Click "Tables Created by BLS," and then "Annual Percent Changes From 1913 to Present." Find the inflation rate (DEC-DEC) for 1933, 1960, 1981, and 1999. Now go to *http://research.stlouisfed.org/fred/data/irates/prime*, and find the nominal interest rate for each of these years (use the lower value if a range is specified). Calculate the (ex post) real interest rate for each year. In which year was the real interest rate the highest? the lowest? Was the average real interest rate in the recession years of 1933 and 1981 higher or lower than the average real interest rate in the prosperous years of 1960 and 1999? In which year was the nominal interest rate the highest?

Transmission Mechanism
The routes or channels that ripple effects created in the money market travel to affect the goods and services market (represented by the aggregate demand and aggregate supply curves in the *AD-AS* framework).

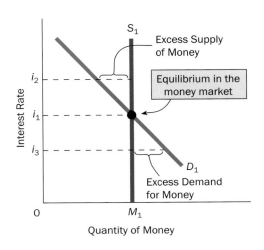

exhibit 2

Equilibrium in the Money Market
At an interest rate of i_1, the money market is in equilibrium: There is neither an excess supply of money nor an excess demand for money.

(a)
Money Market

(b)
Investment Goods Market

(c)
**Goods and Services Market
(AD–AS framework)**

exhibit 3

The Keynesian Transmission Mechanism

The exhibit shows how the Keynesian transmission mechanism operates given an increase in the money supply. (a) An increase in the money supply brings on a lower interest rate. (b) As a result, investment increases. (c) As investment increases, total expenditures rise and the aggregate demand curve shifts rightward. Real GDP rises from Q_1 to Q_2.

supply. The money supply curve shifts rightward from S_1 to S_2. The process increases the reserves of the banking system and therefore results in more loans being made. A greater supply of loans (or credit) puts downward pressure on the interest rate, as reflected in the movement from i_1 to i_2.

2. **The investment goods market.** A fall in the interest rate stimulates investment. In the investment goods market in part (b), investment rises from I_1 to I_2.

3. **The goods and services market (*AD-AS* framework).** Recall from an earlier chapter that our Keynesian model has a horizontal aggregate supply curve in the goods and services market. The decline in the interest rate has brought about an increase in investment, as shown in part (b). Rising investment increases total spending in the economy and shifts the *AD* curve to the right in part (c). As a result, Real GDP rises from Q_1 to Q_2, and the price level does not change. Due to the increase in Real GDP, the unemployment rate (*U*) drops.

In summary, when the money supply increases, the Keynesian transmission mechanism works as follows: An increase in the money supply lowers the interest rate, which causes investment to rise and the *AD* curve to shift rightward. As a result, Real GDP increases and the unemployment rate drops. The process works in reverse for a decrease in the money supply.

$$\text{Money supply}\uparrow \rightarrow i\downarrow \rightarrow I\uparrow \rightarrow AD\uparrow \rightarrow Q\uparrow, \bar{P}, U\downarrow$$
$$\text{Money supply}\downarrow \rightarrow i\uparrow \rightarrow I\downarrow \rightarrow AD\downarrow \rightarrow Q\downarrow, \bar{P}, U\uparrow$$

THE KEYNESIAN MECHANISM MAY GET BLOCKED

The Keynesian transmission mechanism is indirect. Changes in the money market *do not* directly affect the goods and services market (and thus Real GDP) because the investment goods market stands between the two markets. It is possible (although not likely) that the link between the money market and the goods and services market could be broken in the investment goods market. We explain.

Interest-Insensitive Investment

Some Keynesian economists believe that investment is not always responsive to interest rates. For example, when business firms are pessimistic about future economic activity, a decrease in interest rates will do little, if anything, to increase investment. When investment is completely insensitive to changes in interest rates, the investment demand curve is vertical, as in Exhibit 4a.

Consider what happens to the Keynesian transmission mechanism described in Exhibit 3. If the investment demand curve is vertical (instead of downward-sloping), a fall in interest rates will not increase investment; and if investment does not increase, neither will aggregate demand or Real GDP. In addition, unemployment won't fall. Thus, the Keynesian transmission mechanism would be short-circuited in the investment goods market, and the link between the money market in part (a) of Exhibit 3 and the goods and services market in part (c) would be broken.

> Money supply↑ → i↓
> Investment insensitive to changes in $i → \overline{I} → \overline{AD} → \overline{Q}, \overline{P}, \overline{U}$

The Liquidity Trap

Keynesians have sometimes argued that the demand curve for money could become horizontal at some low interest rate. Before we discuss why this might occur, let's look at the consequences. Notice that in Exhibit 4b, the demand curve for money becomes horizontal at i_1. This horizontal section of the demand curve for money is referred to as the **liquidity trap.**

What happens if the money supply is increased (for example, from S_1 to S_2) when the money market is in the liquidity trap? The money market moves from point 1 to point 2, and individuals are willing to hold all the additional money supply at the given interest rate. What happens to the Keynesian transmission mechanism illustrated in Exhibit 3? Obviously, if an increase in the money supply does not lower the interest rate, then there will be no change in investment, aggregate demand, or Real GDP. The liquidity trap can break the link between the money market and the goods and services market.

Liquidity Trap
The horizontal portion of the demand curve for money.

$\frac{1}{0.75}$

> Money supply↑
> Liquidity trap → $\overline{i} → \overline{I} → \overline{AD} → \overline{Q}, \overline{P}, \overline{U}$

(a)
Interest–Insensitive Investment

(b)
Liquidity Trap

exhibit 4

Breaking the Link between the Money Market and the Goods and Services Market: Interest-Insensitive Investment and the Liquidity Trap
The Keynesian transmission mechanism allows the link between the money market and the goods and services market to be broken in two places. (a) If investment is totally interest insensitive, a change in the interest rate will not change investment; therefore, aggregate demand, Real GDP, and unemployment will not change. (b) If the money market is in the liquidity trap, an increase in the money supply will not lower the interest rate. It follows that there will be no change in investment, aggregate demand, Real GDP, and unemployment.

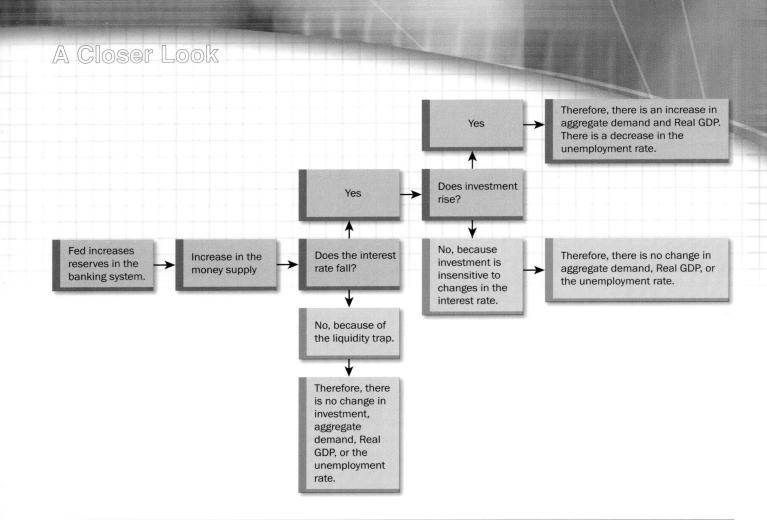

exhibit 5

The Keynesian View of Monetary Policy
According to the Keynesian transmission mechanism, if the Fed increases reserves in the banking system and therefore raises the money supply, the interest rate will drop, stimulating investment and aggregate demand. Consequently, Real GDP will rise, and the unemployment rate will drop. However, things may not work out this way if there is a liquidity trap or if investment is insensitive to changes in the interest rate.

Because the Keynesian transmission mechanism is indirect, both *interest-insensitive investment demand* and the *liquidity trap* may occur. Therefore, Keynesians conclude, there may be times when monetary policy will be unable to increase Real GDP and decrease unemployment. Viewing the money supply as a string, some economists have argued that "you can't push on a string." In other words, you can't always force Real GDP up by increasing (pushing up) the money supply.

See Exhibit 5 for a review of the Keynesian transmission mechanism and how it may get blocked.

Q & A

Q: The liquidity trap, or the horizontal section of the demand curve for money, seems to come out of the clear blue sky. Why might the demand curve for money become horizontal at some low interest rate?

A: To understand an explanation of the liquidity trap, one must first understand the relationship between bond prices and interest rates, which is the topic of the next section.

BOND PRICES AND INTEREST RATES

Consider Jessica Howard, who buys good *X* for $100 today and sells it one year later for $110. What is her actual rate of return? It is 10 percent because the difference between the selling price and buying price ($10) divided by the buying price ($100) is 10 percent.

Now suppose good X is a bond. Jessica buys the bond for $100 and sells it one year later for $110. This time we phrase our question another way: What is her actual interest rate return, or what interest rate did Jessica earn? The answer is the same: 10 percent.

Staying with the example, suppose Jessica buys the bond for $90 instead of $100, but still sells it for $110. What is her interest rate return? It is 22 percent ($20/$90 is 22 percent). Our point is simple: *As the price of a bond decreases, the actual interest rate return, or simply the interest rate, increases.*

Let's look at a slightly more complicated example that illustrates the inverse relationship between bond prices and interest rates in another way. Suppose last year Rob Lewis bought a bond for $1,000 that promises to pay him $100 a year. The annual interest rate return is 10 percent ($100/$1,000 = 10%). Suppose, however, that market or nominal interest rates are higher now than they were last year when Rob bought his bond. Now bond suppliers have to promise to pay $120 a year to someone who buys a $1,000 bond.

What will this do to the price Rob can get in the market for his $1,000 bond bought last year, assuming he wants to sell it? Will anyone pay Rob $1,000 for an (old) bond that pays $100 a year when a new $1,000 bond that pays $120 a year can be purchased? The answer is a definite no. This means that Rob will have to lower the price of his bond below $1,000. How far below $1,000 will he have to lower it? The price will have to be far enough below $1,000 so that the interest rate return on his old bond will be competitive with (equal to) the interest rate return on new bonds.

Rob's bond will sell for $833. At a price of $833, a buyer of his bond will receive $100 a year and an interest rate of 12 percent, which is the same interest rate he or she would receive by buying a new bond for $1,000 and receiving $120 a year. Thus, $100 is the same percentage of $833 as $120 is of $1,000—12 percent. We conclude that *the market interest rate is inversely related to the price of old or existing bonds.*

Keeping this in mind, consider the liquidity trap again. The reason an increase in the money supply does not result in an excess supply of money at a low interest rate is that individuals believe bond prices are so high (because low interest rates mean high bond prices) that an investment in bonds is likely to turn out to be a bad deal. Individuals would rather hold all the additional money supply than use it to buy bonds, which, they believe, are priced so high that they have no place to go but down.

Q & A   **Q:** If interest rates and bond prices move in opposite directions, shouldn't people buy bonds when they expect interest rates to fall and sell bonds when they expect interest rates to rise?

A: That's correct. The objective is to buy low and sell high. Bond prices are at their lowest when interest rates are at their highest, so when interest rates appear to be at their highest, buy bonds. Bond prices are at their highest when interest rates are at their lowest, so when interest rates appear to be at their lowest, sell bonds. By the way, all this is easier said than done. Predicting interest rates is a tough business, and economic forecasters often miss the mark. However, they still do better than noneconomists (which, depending on how one looks at these things, might not be saying much).

THE MONETARIST TRANSMISSION MECHANISM: DIRECT

In monetarist theory, there is a direct link between the money market and the goods and services market. The monetarist transmission mechanism is short. Changes in the money market have a direct impact on aggregate demand, as illustrated in Exhibit 6. An increase in the money supply from S_1 to S_2 in part (a) leaves individuals with an excess supply of money. They increase their spending on a wide variety of goods. Households buy more refrigerators, personal computers,

exhibit 6

The Monetarist Transmission Mechanism

The monetarist transmission mechanism is short and direct. Changes in the money market directly affect aggregate demand in the goods and services market. For example, an increase in the money supply leaves individuals with an excess supply of money that they spend on a wide variety of goods.

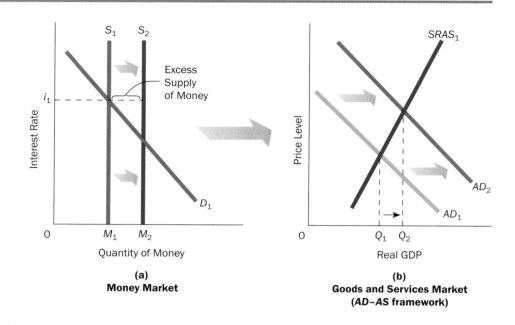

(a)
Money Market

(b)
Goods and Services Market
(AD–AS framework)

television sets, clothes, and vacations. Businesses purchase additional machinery. The aggregate demand curve in part (b) is directly affected. In the short run, Real GDP rises from Q_1 to Q_2 and unemployment falls. The process works in reverse for a decrease in the money supply.

$$\text{Money supply}\uparrow \rightarrow AD\uparrow \rightarrow Q\uparrow, P\uparrow, U\downarrow$$
$$\text{Money supply}\downarrow \rightarrow AD\downarrow \rightarrow Q\downarrow, P\downarrow, U\uparrow$$

The Keynesian transmission mechanism is indirect from the money market to the goods and services market; the monetarist transmission mechanism is direct.

Self-Test *(Answers to Self-Test questions are in the Self-Test Appendix.)*

1. Explain the inverse relationship between bond prices and interest rates.

2. "According to the Keynesian transmission mechanism, as the money supply rises, there is a direct impact on the goods and services market." Do you agree or disagree with this statement? Explain your answer.

3. Explain how the monetarist transmission mechanism works when the money supply rises.

MONETARY POLICY AND THE PROBLEM OF INFLATIONARY AND RECESSIONARY GAPS

An earlier chapter explains how expansionary and contractionary fiscal policies might be used to rid the economy of recessionary and inflationary gaps, respectively. Later in that chapter, the effectiveness of fiscal policy is questioned. In this section, we discuss how monetary policy might be used to eliminate both recessionary and inflationary gaps.

In Exhibit 7a, the economy is in a recessionary gap at point 1; aggregate demand is too low to bring the economy into equilibrium at its natural level of Real GDP. Economist *A* argues that, in time, the short-run aggregate supply curve will shift rightward to point 2 (see Exhibit 7b), so it is best to leave things alone.

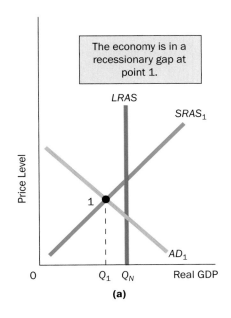

The economy is in a recessionary gap at point 1.

(a)

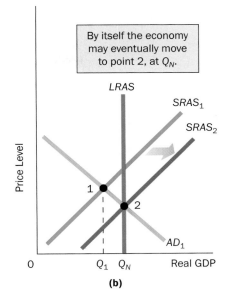

By itself the economy may eventually move to point 2, at Q_N.

(b)

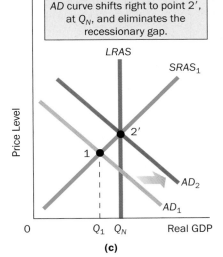

However, with an appropriate increase in the money supply the AD curve shifts right to point 2', at Q_N, and eliminates the recessionary gap.

(c)

exhibit 7

Monetary Policy and a Recessionary Gap

Expansionary Monetary Policy
The Fed increases the money supply.

Economist *B* says that the economy will take too long to get to point 2 on its own, and in the interim the economy is suffering the high cost of unemployment and a lower level of output.

Economist *C* maintains that the economy is stuck in the recessionary gap. Economists *B* and *C* propose **expansionary monetary policy** to move the economy to its Natural Real GDP level. An appropriate increase in the money supply will shift the aggregate demand curve rightward to AD_2, and the economy will be in long-run equilibrium at point 2' (see Exhibit 7c). The recessionary gap is eliminated through the use of expansionary monetary policy.[2]

In Exhibit 8a, the economy is in an inflationary gap at point 1. Economist *A* argues that, in time, the economy will move to point 2 (see Exhibit 8b), so it is best to leave things alone.

Economist *B* argues that it would be better to decrease the money supply so that aggregate demand shifts leftward to AD_2, and the economy moves to point 2' (see Exhibit 8c).

Economist *C* agrees with economist *B* and points out that the price level is lower at point 2' than at point 2 although Real GDP is the same at both points.

Most Keynesians believe that the natural forces of the market economy work much faster and more assuredly at eliminating an inflationary gap than a recessionary gap. In terms of Exhibits 7 and 8, they argue that it is much more likely that the short-run aggregate supply curve in Exhibit 8b will shift leftward to point 2, eliminating the inflationary gap, than that the short-run aggregate supply curve in Exhibit 7b will shift rightward to point 2, eliminating the recessionary gap. The reason is that wages and prices rise more quickly than they fall. (Recall that many Keynesians believe wages are inflexible in a downward direction.)

Go to *http://www.bankofengland.co.uk*, and select "Monetary Policy." What economic data does the Bank of England use when setting policy objectives? Which monetary tool(s) does the Bank of England use to meet its objectives? Does the Bank of England have policy objectives similar to the Fed's policy objectives?

---

2. In a static framework, expansionary monetary policy refers to an increase in the money supply and contractionary monetary policy refers to a decrease in the money supply. In a dynamic framework, expansionary monetary policy refers to an increase in the rate of growth of the money supply, while contractionary monetary policy refers to a decrease in the growth rate of the money supply. In the real world, where things are constantly changing, the growth rate of the money supply is more indicative of the direction of monetary policy.

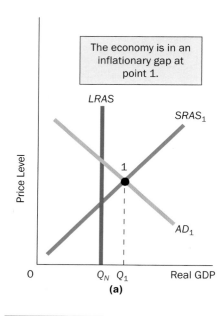

The economy is in an inflationary gap at point 1.

(a)

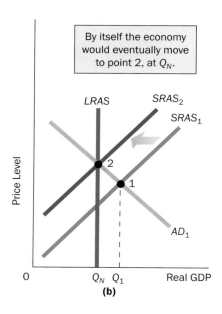

By itself the economy would eventually move to point 2, at Q_N.

(b)

However, with an appropriate decrease in the money supply the AD curve shifts left to point 2', at Q_N, and eliminates the inflationary gap.

(c)

exhibit 8

Monetary Policy and an Inflationary Gap

Contractionary Monetary Policy
The Fed decreases the money supply.

Activists
Persons who argue that monetary and fiscal policies should be deliberately used to smooth out the business cycle.

Fine-tuning
The (usually frequent) use of monetary and fiscal policies to counteract even small undesirable movements in economic activity.

Nonactivists
Persons who argue against the deliberate use of discretionary fiscal and monetary policies. They believe in a permanent, stable, rules-based monetary and fiscal framework.

Consequently, Keynesians are more likely to advocate expansionary monetary policy to eliminate a stubborn recessionary gap than **contractionary monetary policy** to eliminate a not-so-stubborn inflationary gap.

Q & A

Q: Would Keynesians advocate expansionary monetary policy to eliminate a recessionary gap if they believed that the money market was in a liquidity trap or that investment spending was interest insensitive?

A: No, they would not. In these two cases, Keynesians would say that expansionary monetary policy is ineffective at eliminating a recessionary gap. They would be likely to propose expansionary fiscal policy instead. Because Keynesians view monetary policy as sometimes ineffective and fiscal policy as always effective, they are sometimes called fiscalists.

MONETARY POLICY AND THE ACTIVIST-NONACTIVIST DEBATE

As an earlier chapter points out, some economists argue that fiscal policy is ineffective (owing to crowding out) or works in unintended and undesirable ways (owing to lags). Other economists, notably Keynesians, believe that neither is the case and that fiscal policy not only can but also should be used to smooth out the business cycle. This argument is part of the activist-nonactivist debate, which encompasses both fiscal and monetary policy. This chapter addresses only monetary policy within the activist-nonactivist debate.

Activists argue that monetary policy should be deliberately used to smooth out the business cycle. They are in favor of economic **fine-tuning,** which is the (usually frequent) use of monetary policy to counteract even small undesirable movements in economic activity. Sometimes the monetary policy they advocate is called *activist* or *discretionary monetary policy.*

Nonactivists argue *against* the use of activist or discretionary monetary policy. Instead, they propose a rules-based monetary policy. Sometimes the monetary policy they propose is called either *nonactivist* or *rules-based monetary policy.* An example of a rules-based monetary policy is a policy that is based on a predetermined steady growth rate in the money supply: in other words, putting the money supply on automatic pilot and allowing it to grow 3 percent a year, no matter what.

THE CASE FOR ACTIVIST (OR DISCRETIONARY) MONETARY POLICY

The case for activist (or discretionary) monetary policy rests on three major claims:

1. **The economy does not always equilibrate quickly enough at Natural Real GDP.** Consider the economy at point 1 in Exhibit 7a. Some economists maintain that, left to its own workings, the economy will eventually move to point 2 in part (b). Activists often argue that the economy takes too long to move from point 1 to point 2 and that too much lost output and too high an unemployment rate must be tolerated in the interim. They believe that an activist monetary policy speeds things along so that higher output and a lower unemployment rate can be achieved more quickly.

2. **Activist monetary policy works; it is effective at smoothing out the business cycle.** Activists are quick to point to the undesirable consequences of the constant monetary policy of the mid-1970s. In 1973, 1974, and 1975, the money supply growth rates were 5.5 percent, 4.3 percent, and 4.7 percent, respectively. These percentages represent a near constant growth rate in the money supply. The economy, however, went through a recession during this time (Real GDP fell between 1973 and 1974 and between 1974 and 1975). Activists argue that an activist and flexible monetary policy would have reduced the high cost the economy had to pay in terms of lost output and higher unemployment.

3. **Activist monetary policy is flexible; nonactivist (rules-based) monetary policy is not.** Activists argue that flexibility is a desirable quality in monetary policy; inflexibility is not. The implicit judgment of activists is that the more closely monetary policy can be designed to meet the particulars of a given economic environment, the better. For example, at certain times the economy requires a sharp increase in the money supply; at other times, a sharp decrease; at still other times, only a slight increase or decrease. Activists argue that activist (discretionary) monetary policy can change as the monetary needs of the economy change; nonactivist, rules-based, or "the-same-for-all-seasons" monetary policy cannot.

THE CASE FOR NONACTIVIST (OR RULES-BASED) MONETARY POLICY

The case for nonactivist (or rules-based) monetary policy also rests on three major claims:

1. **In modern economies, wages and prices are sufficiently flexible to allow the economy to equilibrate at reasonable speed at Natural Real GDP.** For example, nonactivists point to the sharp drop in union wages in 1982 in response to high unemployment. In addition, they argue that government policies largely determine the flexibility of wages and prices. For example, when government decides to cushion people's unemployment (such as through unemployment compensation), wages will not fall as quickly as when government does nothing. Nonactivists believe that a laissez-faire, hands-off approach by government promotes speedy wage and price adjustments and therefore a quick return to Natural Real GDP.

2. **Activist monetary policies may not work.** Some economists argue that there are really two types of monetary policy: (1) monetary policy that is anticipated by the public and (2) monetary policy that is unanticipated. Anticipated monetary policy may not be effective at changing Real GDP or the unemployment rate. We discuss this subject in detail in the next chapter, but here is a brief explanation.

If You're So Smart, Then Why Aren't You Rich?

Upon meeting a professional economist, the general member of the public will often ask some economics-related question, such as: "What stocks should I buy?" "Is this a good time to buy bonds?" "Are interest rates going up?" "Where do you think the economy is headed?"

The professional economist will often answer the question. Usually, the professional economist explains things well enough so that the general member of the public thinks, "Yes, but if you're so smart [about the economy], then why aren't you rich?"

Fact is, some economists are rich, but many are not. Still, the question is a good one, and it helps us to understand the public's perception of economists and the science of economics.

So, how can someone be smart about the economy and still not be rich? We use the inverse relationship between bond prices and interest rates to explain how this can be true. To become rich using the bond market, the rule to follow is simple: Buy bonds when you think interest rates are as high as they will go (because then bond prices will be low), and sell bonds when you think interest rates are as low as they will go (because then bond prices will be high). Buy low, sell high—that's the road to riches!

So, to walk down the road to riches, all you have to do is be able to predict interest rates. Now you may think it should be easy for economists to predict interest rates. It isn't. We illustrate just how difficult it is to predict interest rates by structuring our arguments in terms of the bond market.

We begin with the fundamentals. There is a demand for and supply of bonds in the bond market. The demand curve for bonds slopes downward: buyers of bonds will buy more bonds at lower prices than at higher prices. The supply curve of bonds slopes upward: suppliers of bonds will offer to sell more bonds at higher prices than at lower prices. In this regard, the demand for and supply of bonds is no different than the demand for and supply of any good (for example, cars, computers, CD players, and so on). Buyers will buy more bonds at lower prices and suppliers will offer to sell more bonds at higher prices.

Thus, we know that the demand for and supply of bonds must work together to determine the price of bonds. A rise in the demand for bonds will raise the price of bonds, *ceteris paribus*, in the same way that a rise in the demand for television sets will raise the price of television sets. Similarly, an increase in the supply of bonds will lower the price of bonds in the same way that an increase in the supply of houses will lower the price of houses.

Recall from an earlier chapter the factors that will change demand and supply. For example, a change in income, preferences, prices of substitutes, and so on, will change demand; a change in resource prices, (certain) taxes, and so on, will change supply.

The same holds for the demand and supply of bonds. It isn't necessary in this discussion to describe the details of all the factors that can change the demand for and supply of bonds. Let's just say that factors *A–F* can change the demand for bonds and factors *G–L* can change the supply of bonds. Another way to say this is: The demand for bonds depends on factors *A, B, C, D, E,* and *F;* and the supply of bonds depends on factors *G, H, I, J, K,* and *L.*

We can now enumerate the reasons why predicting interest rates is difficult:

1. We have to know how each of the factors *A–F* affects the demand for bonds. For example, does an increase in factor *B* increase or decrease the demand for bonds?

2. We have to know how each of the factors *G–L* affects the supply of bonds. Does a rise in factor *K* increase or decrease the supply of bonds?

3. If any of the factors *A–L* change, we have to know it. In other words, we need to know immediately which factors are changing. Suppose factor *C* changes, but we are unaware of it. A change in factor *C* changes the demand for bonds. A change in the demand for bonds changes the price of bonds. And, as we have shown, if bond prices change so do interest rates. Obviously, if we didn't know that factor *C* changed, there would be no way we could predict the change in interest rates.

4. Even if we know which factors are changing, we still have to determine the impact that each (relevant) factor will have on the demand for and supply of bonds. Suppose a rise in factor *A* increases the demand for bonds and a rise in factor *J* increases the supply of bonds. Now suppose *A* and *J* both rise. We can predict that the demand for bonds will rise and that the supply of bonds will rise, but we don't know how much each rises relative to the other.

If the demand for bonds rises by more than the supply of bonds, then the price of bonds will rise. (Can you show this graphically?) And if bond prices rise, interest rates fall.

But if the supply of bonds rises by more than the demand for bonds, the price of bonds will fall. (Can you show this graphically?) And if bond prices fall, interest rates rise.

Finally, if the supply of bonds rises by the same amount as the demand for bonds rises, the price of bonds will not change. And if bond prices don't change, neither do interest rates.

We conclude: In order to predict interest rates accurately, we need to know: (1) What factors affect the demand for and supply of bonds. Is it A, B, and C, or A, B, D, and E? (2) How those factors affect the demand for and supply of bonds. Does a rise in A increase or decrease the demand for bonds? (3) Which factors are changing? Did B just change? (4) How much bond demand and supply change given that some factors are changing. Did demand rise by more than supply, or did supply rise by more than demand?

Now do you see why not all economists are rich?

Suppose the public correctly anticipates that the Fed will soon increase the money supply by 10 percent. Consequently, the public reasons that aggregate demand will increase from AD_1 to AD_2 in Exhibit 9, and prices will rise.

Workers are particularly concerned about the expected higher price level because they know higher prices decrease the buying power of their wages. In an attempt to maintain their real wages, workers bargain for and receive higher money wage rates—which shifts the short-run aggregate supply curve from $SRAS_1$ to $SRAS_2$ in Exhibit 9.

Now if the $SRAS$ curve shifts leftward (owing to higher wage rates) to the same degree as the AD curve shifts rightward (owing to the increased money supply), Real GDP does not change. It stays constant at Q_1. Thus, *a correctly anticipated increase in the money supply will be ineffective at raising Real GDP.*

3. **Activist monetary policies are likely to be destabilizing rather than stabilizing; they are likely to make matters worse rather than better.** Nonactivists point to *lags* as the main reason that activist (or discretionary) monetary policies are likely to be destabilizing. For example, economist Robert Gordon has estimated that the total lag in monetary policy is 19.3 months. (The total lag consists of the data, wait-and-see, legislative, transmission, and effectiveness lags discussed in an earlier chapter.) To nonactivists, such a long lag makes it almost impossible to conduct effective activist monetary policy. They maintain that by the time the Fed's monetary stimulus arrives on the scene, the economy may not need any stimulus, and thus it will likely destabilize the economy. In this instance, the stimulus makes things worse rather than better.

Exhibit 10 illustrates this last point. Suppose the economy is currently in a recessionary gap at point 1. The recession is under way before Fed officials recognize it. After they are aware of the recession, however, the officials consider expanding the money supply in the hopes of shifting the AD curve from AD_1 to AD_2 so it will intersect the $SRAS$ curve at point 1′, at Natural Real GDP.

In the interim, however, unknown to everybody, the economy is regulating itself: The $SRAS$ curve is shifting to the right. Fed officials don't realize this shift is occurring because it takes time to collect and analyze data about the economy.

Thinking that the economy is not regulating itself, or not regulating itself quickly enough, Fed officials implement expansionary monetary policy. The AD curve shifts rightward. By the time the increased money supply is felt in the goods and services market, the AD curve intersects the $SRAS$ curve at point 2. In short, the Fed has moved the economy from point 1 to point 2, and not, as it had hoped, from point 1 to point 1′. The Fed has moved the economy into an inflationary gap. Instead of stabilizing and moderating the business cycle, the Fed has intensified it.

exhibit 9

Expansionary Monetary Policy and No Change in Real GDP
If expansionary monetary policy is anticipated (thus, a higher price level is anticipated), workers may bargain for and receive higher wage rates. It is possible that the $SRAS$ curve will shift leftward to the same degree that expansionary monetary policy shifts the AD curve rightward. Result: no change in Real GDP.

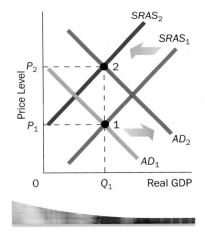

exhibit 10

Monetary Policy May Destabilize the Economy

In this scenario, the *SRAS* curve is shifting rightward (ridding the economy of its recessionary gap), but Fed officials do not realize this is happening. They implement expansionary monetary policy, and the *AD* curve ends up intersecting *SRAS*₂ at point 2 instead of intersecting *SRAS*₁ at point 1′. Fed officials end up moving the economy into an inflationary gap and thus destabilizing the economy.

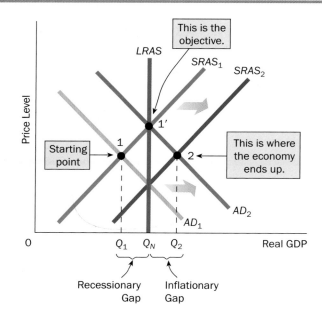

THINKING LIKE AN ECONOMIST

Ask an economist a question and you are likely to get a conditional answer. For example, if you ask an economist whether monetary policy stabilizes or destabilizes the economy, she may answer that it can do either—depending on conditions. For instance, starting in a recessionary gap, if expansionary monetary policy shifts the AD *curve rightward by just the right amount to intersect the* SRAS *curve and the* LRAS *curve at Natural Real GDP, then monetary policy stabilizes the economy. But if the monetary policy shifts the* AD *curve rightward by more than this amount, it may move the economy into an inflationary gap, thereby destabilizing the economy. If-then thinking is common in economics, as are if-then statements.*

Self-Test

1. Why are Keynesians more likely to advocate expansionary monetary policy to eliminate a recessionary gap than contractionary monetary policy to eliminate an inflationary gap?

2. How might monetary policy destabilize the economy?

3. If the economy is stuck in a recessionary gap, does this make the case for activist (expansionary) monetary policy stronger or weaker? Explain your answer.

NONACTIVIST MONETARY PROPOSALS

In this section, we outline four nonactivist (or rules-based) monetary proposals.

A CONSTANT-MONEY-GROWTH-RATE RULE

Many nonactivists argue that the sole objective of monetary policy is to stabilize the price level. To this end, they propose a *constant-money-growth-rate rule*. One version of the rule is:

The annual money supply growth rate will be constant at the average annual growth rate of Real GDP.

ECONOMICS IN...

How Far Does Monetary Policy Reach? Or, Monetary Policy and Blue Eyes

Two days before the beginning of the fall semester at a college in the Midwest, Suzanne, a student at the college, was waiting in line to register for classes. As she waited, she looked through the fall schedule. She had to take an economics principles course at 10 a.m.; two sections were listed at that time. The instructor in one section was Smith; Jones was the instructor for the other section. Suzanne, not knowing which section to take, asked the person behind her in line if he had ever taken a course from either instructor. The person said that he had taken a course with Smith and that he (Smith) was very good. That was enough for the Suzanne; she signed up for Smith's class.

While a student in Smith's class, Suzanne met the person whom she ended up marrying. His name is Bob. Suzanne often says to Bob, "You know, if that guy behind me in line that day had said that Smith wasn't a good teacher, or hadn't said anything at all, I might never have taken Professor Smith's class. I might have taken Jones's class instead, and I would never have met you. I'd probably be married to someone else right now."

While this story is untrue, still, it is representative of the many little things that happen every day. Little things can make big differences.

With this in mind, consider monetary policy (which is not really a little thing). Here is another story that is also not true, but is still representative of something that, if it hasn't happened, certainly can.

A few years ago, Real GDP was far below its natural level. The Fed decided to increase the money supply. As a result, the *AD* curve in the economy shifted to the right. One of the first places the new demand in the economy was felt was in Denver. Economic activity in Denver increased. Bob, who lived in Austin at the time, was out of work and looking for a job. He heard about the job prospects in Denver, and so one day, he got into his car and headed for Denver. Luckily for him, he got a job a few days after arriving in Denver. He rented an apartment near his job. He became a friend of Nick, who lived in the apartment across the hall.

Nick, knowing that Bob was new in town, asked Bob if he wanted a date with his girlfriend's friend Melanie. Bob said yes. Bob and Melanie ended up dating for two years; they've been married now for 10 years. They have three children, all of whom have blue eyes.

One day the youngest child asked her mother why she had blue eyes. Her mother told her it's because both she and her daddy have blue eyes. And that's not an incorrect explanation, as far as it goes.

But we can't help wondering if the youngest child has blue eyes because of an event that took place years ago, an event that has to do with the Fed and the money supply. After all, if the Fed hadn't increased the money supply when it did, maybe Denver's job prospects wouldn't have been so healthy, and maybe Bob wouldn't have left Austin. But, then, if Bob had not left Austin, he wouldn't have married Melanie and had three children, each with blue eyes. We're just speculating, of course.

For example, if the average annual Real GDP growth rate is approximately 3.3 percent, the money supply will be put on automatic pilot and will be permitted to grow at an annual rate of 3.3 percent. The money supply will grow at this rate regardless of the state of the economy.

Some economists predict that a constant-money-growth-rate rule will bring about a stable price level over time. This prediction is based on the equation of exchange ($MV \equiv PQ$). If the average annual growth rate in Real GDP (Q) is 3.3 percent and the money supply (M) grows at 3.3 percent, the price level should remain stable over time. Advocates of this rule argue that in some years the growth rate in Real GDP will be below its average rate, causing an increase in the price level, and in other years the growth rate in Real GDP will be above its average rate, causing a fall in the price level, but over time the price level will be stable.

A PREDETERMINED-MONEY-GROWTH-RATE RULE

Critics of the constant-money-growth-rate rule point out that it makes two assumptions: (1) Velocity is constant. (2) The money supply is defined correctly. These critics argue that there have been periods when velocity has not been constant. And it is not yet clear which definition of the money supply (M1, M2, or some broader monetary measure) is the proper one and therefore which money supply growth rate ought to be fixed.

Largely in response to the charge that velocity is not always constant, some nonactivists prefer the following rule:

> *The annual growth rate in the money supply will be equal to the average annual growth rate in Real GDP minus the growth rate in velocity.*

In other words,

$$\%\Delta M = \%\Delta Q - \%\Delta V$$

With this rule, the growth rate of the money supply is not fixed. It can vary from year to year, yet it is predetermined in that it is dependent on the growth rates of Real GDP and velocity. For this reason, we call it the *predetermined-money-growth-rate rule*. To illustrate the workings of this rule, consider the following extended version of the equation of exchange:

$$\%\Delta M + \%\Delta V = \%\Delta P + \%\Delta Q$$

Suppose $\%\Delta Q = 3$ percent and $\%\Delta V$ is 1 percent. The rule would specify that the growth rate in the money supply should be 2 percent. This would keep the price level stable; there would be a zero percent change in P:

$$\%\Delta M + \%\Delta V = \%\Delta P + \%\Delta Q$$
$$2\% + 1\% = 0\% + 3\%$$

A GOLD STANDARD

If a nation backs its paper money totally or partially with gold, the nation is said to be on a **gold standard.** A gold standard is a type of rules-based monetary policy. Most proponents of a gold standard maintain that it would stabilize the price level over time and restrain the money-creating activities of politicians, bureaucrats, and activist policymakers. Under a gold standard, the money supply would be tied to the stock of gold. Proponents of a gold standard and proponents of other rules-based monetary policies have the same objectives: to stabilize the price level over time and to reduce the amount of political and economic tinkering that can be applied to the money supply process.

The mechanics of a gold standard are as follows:

1. **The government sets the price of gold at some dollar amount.** Most proponents of the gold standard claim that the dollar amount should be the market price of gold. Let's pick a price of $300 an ounce. This, then, becomes the official price of gold. Initially, the free market price and the official price of gold are the same.

2. **The government promises to buy and sell gold at the official price.** Thus, if Schultz wants to buy gold from (or sell gold to) the government, the government will sell (or buy) gold at the price of $300 an ounce. It is this government action that maintains the official price of gold equal to the market price and, according to gold standard proponents, keeps the price level in the economy constant.

We explain the second point with the aid of Exhibit 11. In part (a), the demand and supply curves represent the demand for and supply of gold in the private market, where gold is used as a commodity (for jewelry and so on). Because of

Gold Standard
The monetary arrangement whereby a nation backs its paper money totally or partially with gold.

http://

Go to *http://www.federalreserve.gov/boarddocs/speeches/2001/*, and select "December 5, 2001" (Governor Laurence H. Meyer's speech). Read the "Evolution of Money" section. When did England officially adopt the gold standard? When did the United States move to a de facto gold standard? What period is known as "the international gold standard"? With the collapse of the gold standard, countries moved to what kind of monetary system?

(a)
Market Price > Official Price

(b)
Market Price < Official Price

inflation, the market price for gold rises to, say, $325 an ounce, which is above the official price of $300 an ounce, the price at which the government has agreed to buy and sell gold. This price discrepancy presents a profit opportunity: Individuals can buy gold from the government at the official price of $300 an ounce and sell the gold in the market at the market price of $325 an ounce, realizing a profit of $25 an ounce (not including exchange and transportation costs). In the private gold market, the policy increases the supply of gold. The supply curve shifts rightward from S_1 to S_2 until it intersects the demand curve at point 2. The market price of gold falls to the official price.

Do these transactions also have an impact on the money supply and ultimately the price level? As individuals buy gold from the government, they exchange their cash or checkable deposits (which are part of the money supply) for gold. The money supply in private hands is reduced, thus reducing aggregate demand and the inflationary forces that originally pushed up gold prices.

Market price of gold > Official price of gold →
Public buys gold from government →
Public exchanges money for gold → $M{\downarrow} \rightarrow P{\downarrow}$

Now consider the gold standard at work when the economy is in a recessionary gap and the price level is declining. In Exhibit 11b, the forces of supply and demand equilibrate at a market price for gold of $280 an ounce. The official gold price, $300 an ounce, is above the market price, so individuals have a monetary incentive to buy gold in the market at the lower price and sell it to the government at the higher price. In the private gold market, the policy reduces the supply of gold. The supply curve shifts leftward from S_1 to S_2 until it intersects the demand curve at point 2. The market price of gold increases to the official price.

Again, these transactions affect the money supply and the price level in the economy. Dollars received from government increase the privately held money supply. This increases aggregate demand and offsets deflationary tendencies in the economy.

Market price of gold < Official price of gold →
Public sells gold to government →
Public receives money for gold → $M{\uparrow} \rightarrow P{\uparrow}$

exhibit 11

The Market for Gold and the Workings of a Gold Standard
(a) The market price for gold is greater than the official price. This will cause individuals to buy gold from the government and sell it in the private market for $325 an ounce. This action will result in an increase in the supply of gold in the private market (from S_1 to S_2), a fall in the price of gold to the official level, a contraction in the money supply, and a lower price level. (b) The market price for gold is below the official price. This will cause individuals to buy gold in the private market for $280 an ounce and sell it to the government for $300 an ounce. This action will result in a decrease in the supply of gold in the private market (from S_1 to S_2), a rise in the price of gold to the official level, an expansion in the money supply, and a higher price level.

The result in both cases is a change in the money supply, in the market price of gold, and in the price level. A "too high" ("too low") price level, represented by a market price for gold higher (lower) than the official price, has been pushed downward (upward). The objective is to maintain the price level in the economy that is consistent with a constant market price for gold.

Critics charge that a gold standard is no guarantee against inflation. For example, if a cheap source of gold is discovered, the supply of gold on the market will increase, driving the market price down below the official price, which in turn will place upward pressure on the money supply and price level. This is what happened soon after the California gold rush of 1849.

Critics also charge that a reduction in national output and an increase in unemployment will result if prices do not fall in the same proportion when the gold-backed money supply is reduced. For example, if money wages do not fall as quickly as the prices of other goods and services, real wages will rise, reducing the quantity demanded of labor services and output production.

THE FED AND THE TAYLOR RULE

The economist John Taylor has argued that there may be a middle ground, of sorts, between activist and nonactivist monetary policy. He has proposed that monetary authorities use a rule to inform their discretionary decisions. There is some evidence that recent members of the Fed would agree. Laurence Meyer, a member of the Board of Governors, said:

> *Even if we cannot imagine policymakers turning over the conduct of policy to a rule, research on rules might provide guidance to policymakers that could improve their judgmental adjustments to policy. I strongly believe this is the case. No one would argue, after all, that good policy is whimsical. On the contrary, good policy should be systematic. Good discretionary policy therefore should be, in some meaningful way, rule-like, though it might be impossible to write down in a simple or even complicated equation all the complex considerations that underpin the conduct of such a systematic monetary policy.*[3]

The rule that John Taylor has proposed to inform monetary policy has come to be known as the *Taylor Rule*. The Taylor Rule specifies how policymakers should set the target for the (nominal) federal funds rate. (Recall from an earlier chapter that the federal funds rate is the interest rate banks charge one another for reserves.) The "economic thinking" implicit in the Taylor Rule is as follows: There is some federal funds rate target that is consistent with (1) stabilizing inflation around a rather low inflation rate and (2) stabilizing Real GDP around its full-employment level. Find this federal funds rate target, and then use the tools of the Fed to hit the target.

The Taylor Rule, which, according to John Taylor, will find the right federal funds rate target, is:

$$\text{Federal funds rate target} = \text{Inflation} + \text{Equilibrium real federal funds rate} + \tfrac{1}{2}(\text{Inflation gap}) + \tfrac{1}{2}(\text{Output gap})$$

Let's briefly discuss the four components of the rule:

- **Inflation.** This is the current inflation rate.
- **Equilibrium real federal funds rate.** The real federal funds rate is simply the nominal federal funds rate adjusted for inflation. Taylor assumes the equilibrium real federal funds rate is 2 percent.

---

3. Remarks by Governor Laurence H. Meyer at the Owen Graduate School of Management, Vanderbilt University, Nashville, Tennessee, 16 January 2002.

- **½ inflation gap.** The inflation gap is the difference between the actual inflation rate and the target for inflation. Taylor assumes that an appropriate target for inflation is about 2 percent. If this target were accepted by policymakers, they would effectively be saying that they would not want an inflation rate higher than 2 percent.
- **½ output gap.** The output gap is the percentage difference between actual Real GDP and its full-employment or natural level.

Let's now work through a problem. Suppose the current inflation rate is 1 percent, the equilibrium real federal funds rate is 2 percent, the inflation gap is 1 percent, and the output gap is 2 percent. What is the federal funds rate target?

$$\text{Federal funds rate target} = \text{Inflation} + \text{Equilibrium real federal funds rate}$$
$$+ \tfrac{1}{2}(\text{Inflation gap}) + \tfrac{1}{2}(\text{Output gap})$$
$$= 1\% + 2\% + \tfrac{1}{2}(1\%) + \tfrac{1}{2}(2\%)$$
$$= 4.5\%$$

Self-Test

1. Would a rules-based monetary policy produce price stability?
2. How would the gold standard (described in the text) work?

A Reader Asks...
Are There More Than Two Transmission Mechanisms?

A transmission mechanism describes "the routes or channels that ripples created in the money market travel to affect the goods and services market." We learned about the Keynesian and monetarist transmission mechanisms in this chapter. Are there other transmission mechanisms?

Yes, economists have put forth quite a few transmission mechanisms. We'll talk about a few.

One transmission mechanism focuses on monetary policy and stock prices. It says that when monetary policy is expansionary, the public finds itself with an excess of money. What does it do with the excess money? It buys stocks with the money. Greater demand for stocks drives up the price of stocks and increases the market value of firms. (The market value of a firm is the value investors believe a firm is worth; it is calculated by multiplying the number of shares outstanding by the current price per share.) As the market value of a firm rises, the firm decides to increase its investment spending. Higher investment, in turn, leads to greater aggregate demand and, in the short run, greater Real GDP.

Another transmission mechanism is similar to the one just described, except that it focuses on consumption spending instead of investment spending. Again, we start with an increase in the money supply. Initially, the public finds itself with excess money. They use the money to buy stocks and so the demand for and prices of stocks rise. Because stocks make up a part of a person's financial wealth, higher stock prices mean greater financial wealth for some people. What do people do with greater financial wealth? They spend some fraction of the increase in their financial wealth on consumer goods. As consumption rises, so does aggregate demand and, in the short run, Real GDP rises.

Another transmission mechanism looks at the effect of monetary policy on the exchange rate. According to this mechanism, an expansion in the money supply puts downward pressure on the interest rate (at least initially). As domestic interest rates fall, domestic dollar deposits become less attractive relative to deposits denominated in foreign currencies. As people move out of dollar-denominated deposits, the exchange-rate value of the dollar falls. In other words, the dollar depreciates relative to other currencies. Dollar depreciation and foreign currency appreciation makes U.S. exports less expensive for foreigners and foreign imports more expensive for Americans. Exports rise and imports fall, so net exports rise. As a result of net exports rising, aggregate demand rises and, at least in the short run, so does Real GDP.

The Keynesian Transmission Mechanism

- The Keynesian link between the money market and the goods and services market is indirect. Changes in the money market must affect the investment goods market before the goods and services market is affected. Assuming that no liquidity trap exists and that investment is not interest insensitive, the transmission mechanism works as follows for an increase in the money supply: An increase in the money supply lowers the interest rate and increases investment. This increases aggregate demand and thus shifts the *AD* curve rightward. Consequently, Real GDP rises and the unemployment rate falls. Under the same assumptions, the transmission mechanism works as follows for a decrease in the money supply: A decrease in the money supply raises the interest rate and decreases investment. This decreases aggregate demand and thus shifts the *AD* curve leftward. As a result, Real GDP falls and the unemployment rate rises.

- The Keynesian transmission mechanism may be short-circuited either by the liquidity trap or by interest-insensitive investment. Both are Keynesian notions. If either is present, Keynesians predict that expansionary monetary policy will be unable to change Real GDP or unemployment.

The Monetarist Transmission Mechanism

- The monetarist link between the money market and the goods and services market is direct. Changes in the money supply affect aggregate demand. An increase in the money supply causes individuals to increase their spending on a wide variety of goods.

Bond Prices and Interest Rates

- Interest rates and the price of old or existing bonds are inversely related.

The Activist-Nonactivist Debate

- Activists argue that monetary policy should be deliberately used to smooth out the business cycle; they are in favor of using activist, or discretionary, monetary policy to fine-tune the economy. Nonactivists argue against the use of discretionary monetary policy; they propose nonactivist, or rules-based, monetary policy.

- The case for discretionary monetary policy rests on three major claims: (1) The economy does not always equilibrate quickly enough at Natural Real GDP. (2) Activist monetary policy works. (3) Activist monetary policy is flexible, and flexibility is a desirable quality in monetary policy.

- The case for nonactivist monetary policy rests on three major claims: (1) There is sufficient flexibility in wages and prices in modern economies to allow the economy to equilibrate at reasonable speed at Natural Real GDP. (2) Activist monetary policies may not work. (3) Activist monetary policies are likely to make matters worse rather than better.

Nonactivist (or Rules-Based) Monetary Proposals

- The constant-money-growth-rate rule states that the annual money supply growth rate will be constant at the average annual growth rate of Real GDP.

- The predetermined-money-growth-rate rule states that the annual growth rate in the money supply will be equal to the average annual growth rate in Real GDP minus the growth rate in velocity.

- The Taylor Rule holds that the federal funds rate should be targeted according to the following: Federal funds rate target = Inflation + Equilibrium real federal funds rate + ½ (Inflation gap) + ½ (Output gap).

- A nation operates on a gold standard if it backs its paper money totally or partially with gold. The gold standard operates in the following way: If the market price of gold falls below the official price, individuals buy gold in the market and sell it to the government. In the process, the money supply expands; the predicted effect is a rise in the price level. If the market price of gold is above the official price, individuals buy gold from the government and sell it in the market. In the process, the money supply contracts; the predicted effect is a fall in the price level.

Monetary Policy	Expansionary Monetary Policy	Fine-tuning
Demand for Money (Balances)	Contractionary Monetary Policy	Nonactivists
Transmission Mechanism	Activists	Gold Standard
Liquidity Trap		

Economic facts, actions, and changes create ripples that move away from their point of origin. Eventually, these ripples can intersect your life and have an effect on you. Consider the following example.

What happens in the bond market—whether the demand for bonds rises or falls or the supply of bonds rises or falls—affects the price of bonds. Bond prices and interest rates are inversely related. Suppose bond

prices fall, causing interest rates to rise. The finance charges on the car you plan to buy will also rise, increasing the total cost of the car. Thus, there is a connection between the bond market and your costs to finance a car—an economic connection to you.

Based on the material in this chapter, identify other ways in which economic facts, actions, and changes create ripples that eventually affect you.

1. Consider the following: Two researchers, *A* and *B*, are trying to determine whether eating fatty foods leads to heart attacks. The two researchers proceed differently. Researcher *A* builds a model where fatty foods may first affect *X* in one's body, and if *X* is affected, then *Y* may be affected, and if *Y* is affected, then *Z* may be affected. Finally, if *Z* is affected, the heart is affected, and the individual has an increased probability of suffering a heart attack. Researcher *B* doesn't proceed in this step-by-step fashion. She conducts an experiment to see if people who eat many fatty foods have more, fewer, or the same number of heart attacks as people who eat few fatty foods. Which researcher's methods have more in common with the research methodology implicit in the Keynesian transmission mechanism? Which researcher's methods have more in common with the research methodology implicit in the monetarist transmission mechanism? Explain your answer.

2. If bond prices fall, will individuals want to hold more or less money? Explain your answer.

3. It has been suggested that nonactivists are not concerned with the level of Real GDP and unemployment because most (if not all) nonactivist monetary proposals set as their immediate objective the stabilization of the price level. Discuss.

4. Suppose the combination of more accurate data and better forecasting techniques made it easy for the Fed to predict a recession 10 to 16 months in advance. Would this strengthen the case for activism or nonactivism? Explain your answer.

5. Suppose it were proved that there is no liquidity trap and that investment is not interest insensitive. Would this be enough to disprove the Keynesian claim that expansionary monetary policy is not always effective at changing Real GDP? Why or why not?

6. Both activists and nonactivists make good points for their respective positions. Do you think there is anything an activist could say to a nonactivist to convince him or her to accept the activist position, and vice versa? If so, what is it? If not, why not?

7. The discussion of supply and demand in Chapter 3 noted that if two goods are substitutes, the price of one and the demand for the other are directly related. For example, if Pepsi-Cola and Coca-Cola are substitutes, an increase in the price of Pepsi-Cola will increase the demand for Coca-Cola. Suppose that bonds and stocks are substitutes. We know that interest rates and bond prices are inversely related. What do you predict is the relationship between stock prices and interest rates? Explain your answer.

8. Argue the case for and against a gold standard.

9. Conduct the following exercise. Pick any week of the year. Quickly read through all the issues of the *Wall Street Journal* for that week, and write down the number of articles in which the word *Fed* is used, along with a brief summary of each article. Usually, the article will have to do with monetary policy. Many articles will also present opinions about what the Fed has done, is doing, and will do. The chief economist at a major firm may say that he thinks the Fed is positioning itself to ease up on money supply growth in the upcoming months. An economic forecaster at a major bank may say she thinks the newest member of the Board of Governors will be persuasive in arguing for a slight tightening of the money supply because of his reputation as a fierce opponent of inflation.

   What is the point of this exercise? First, the large number of articles in which the Fed is mentioned will show you how important the Fed and monetary policy are to the economics, political, banking, and business communities. Second, the quotations from (supposedly) knowledgeable people will show you how much guessing and difference of opinion surrounds Fed monetary policy. Third, the factors cited as influencing Fed actions will give you a rough idea of how individuals think the Fed determines monetary policy.

After you conduct this exercise, sit down and reflect on the following questions:

a. Is the Fed implementing an activist monetary policy?
b. How does the Fed decide whether it should increase or decrease the rate of growth of the money supply?
c. Would the *Wall Street Journal* publish so many articles about monetary policy if the United States had a rules-based monetary policy? If not, why not?

d. Would I be better off or worse off if I could accurately predict monetary policy? What monetary institutions are needed for the accurate prediction of monetary policy?
e. Is the secrecy that surrounds Fed monetary policy needed to enable the Fed to stabilize the economy? Or does the secrecy—and the guessing by the markets that accompanies it—actually contribute to destabilizing the economy?

If answers to these questions are not easily forthcoming, do not be concerned. As long as you can ask or recognize questions relevant to monetary policy and have some idea of what the answers may be, you are ready to join the interesting and continuing debate on monetary policy. That is an important accomplishment.

Working with Numbers and Graphs

1. Bob bought a bond last year for $10,000 that promises to pay him $900 a year. This year it is possible to buy a bond for $10,000 that promises to pay $1,000 a year. If Bob wants to sell his (old) bond, what is its price likely to be?

2. Sally bought a bond last year for $10,000 that promises to pay her $1,000 a year. This year it is possible to buy a bond for $10,000 that promises to pay $800 a year. If Sally wants to sell her (old) bond, what is its price likely to be?

3. Suppose the annual average percentage change in Real GDP is 2.3 percent, and the annual average percentage change in velocity is 1.1 percent. Using the rule discussed in the text, what percentage change in the money supply will keep prices stable (on average)?

4. Graphically show that the more interest insensitive the investment demand curve, the less likely monetary policy is effective at changing Real GDP.

5. Which panel in the figure below best describes the situation in each of (a)–(d)?
    a. Expansionary monetary policy that effectively removes the economy from a recessionary gap
    b. Expansionary monetary policy that is destabilizing
    c. Contractionary monetary policy that effectively removes the economy from an inflationary gap
    d. Monetary policy that is ineffective at changing Real GDP

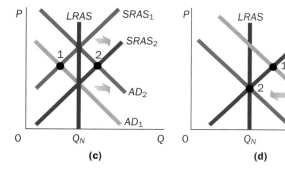

6. Graphically portray the Keynesian transmission mechanism under the following conditions: (1) a decrease in the money supply; (2) no liquidity trap; (3) investment demand curve is downward-sloping.
7. Graphically portray the monetarist transmission mechanism when the money supply declines.

8. According to the Taylor Rule, if inflation is 3 percent, the inflation gap is 5 percent, and the output gap is 2 percent, what does the federal funds rate target equal?

Internet Activities

Go to *http://www.federalreserve.gov/boarddocs/hh/*. Select the most recent testimony.

1. Who is delivering the testimony? Who is receiving the report?
2. Does the Fed chairman think the economy is performing well or poorly at this time? Does the Fed chairman cite any economic indicators to back up what he is saying? If so, which economic indicators?
3. What predictions (if any) does the Fed chairman make about changes in GDP in future years?

4. What predictions (if any) does the Fed chairman make about the inflation rate in future years?
5. What, if anything, does the Fed chairman say about the money supply, its growth rate, and Fed policy with respect to the money supply?
6. What, if anything, does the Fed chairman say about current and expected interest rates?
7. Does the Fed seem more concerned with inflation or unemployment?

Log on to the Arnold Xtra! Web site now (*http://arnoldxtra.swcollege.com*) for additional learning resources such as practice quizzes, help with graphing, video clips, and current event applications.

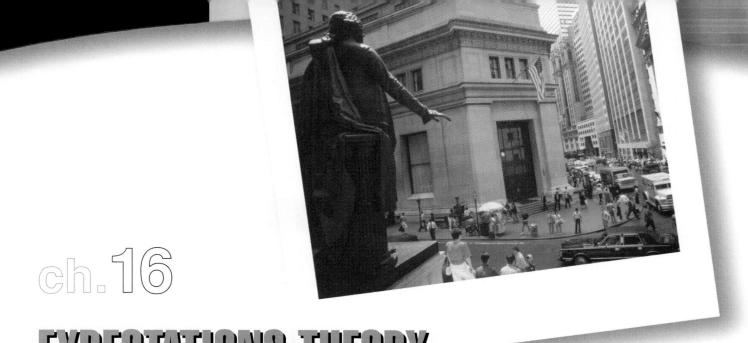

ch.16

EXPECTATIONS THEORY AND THE ECONOMY

A discussion of the economy often turns to a discussion of Congress, the President, or the Fed. For many of us these are the major economic players. Will Congress cut taxes? Will the President propose more spending? Will the Fed raise the discount rate? Most people, if they think about the economy at all, believe there is little they can do to influence the economic decisions made by these major economic players. In fact, most people would find it difficult to believe that their actions could affect the economy in any way. But they can. Just how they do this is an interesting story, as you will discover in this chapter.

Chapter Road Map

This chapter is about changes in Real GDP. Econo-
mists often argue that changes in Real GDP can originate on
either the demand side or the supply side of the economy. We discuss three
demand-side theories in this chapter: (1) the Friedman natural rate theory, (2) the new
classical theory, and (3) the New Keynesian theory. We also discuss one supply-side theory—
the real business cycle theory. As the flow chart below shows, you need to learn about Phillips curves
and adaptive and rational expectations before examining the demand-side theories.

As you read this chapter, look at the cast of characters, which includes many well-known economists. Also think
not only about how expectations are modeled but also about the effects of modeling expectations in different ways.

PHILLIPS CURVE ANALYSIS

The *Phillips curve* is used to analyze the relationship between inflation and unemployment. After an introduction to the Phillips curve, we bring expectations into the discussion and see how they affect the results.

We begin the discussion of the Phillips curve by focusing on the work of three economists, A. W. Phillips, Paul Samuelson, and Robert Solow.

THE PHILLIPS CURVE

In 1958, A. W. Phillips of the London School of Economics published a paper entitled "The Relation between Unemployment and the Rate of Change of Money Wages in the United Kingdom, 1861–1957" in the economics journal *Economica*. As the title suggests, Phillips collected data about the rate of change in money wages, sometimes referred to as wage inflation, and unemployment rates in the United Kingdom over a period of time. He then plotted the rate of change in money wages against the unemployment rate for each year. Finally, he fit a curve to the data points (Exhibit 1).

Phillips Curve
A curve that originally showed the relationship between wage inflation and unemployment. Now it more often shows the relationship between price inflation and unemployment.

An Inverse Relationship

The curve came to be known as the **Phillips curve.** Notice that the curve is downward-sloping, suggesting that the rate of change of money wage rates (wage inflation) and unemployment rates are *inversely related*. This inverse relationship suggests a tradeoff between wage inflation and unemployment. Higher wage inflation means lower unemployment; lower wage inflation means higher unemployment.

Policymakers concluded from the Phillips curve that it was impossible to lower both wage inflation and unemployment; one could do one or the other. So, the combination of low wage inflation and low unemployment was unlikely. This was the bad news.

The good news was that rising unemployment and rising wage inflation did not go together either. Thus, the combination of high unemployment and high wage inflation was unlikely.

The Theoretical Explanation for the Phillips Curve

What is the reason for the inverse relationship between wage inflation and unemployment? Early explanations focused on the state of the labor market given changes in aggregate demand. When aggregate demand is increasing, businesses expand production and hire more employees. As the unemployment rate falls, the

The Original Phillips Curve
This curve was constructed by A. W. Phillips, using data for the United Kingdom from 1861 to 1913. (The relationship here is also representative of the experience of the United Kingdom through 1957.) The original Phillips curve suggests an inverse relationship between wage inflation and unemployment; it represents a wage inflation–unemployment trade-off. (Note: Each dot represents a single year.)

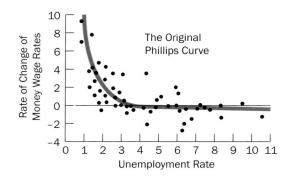

labor market becomes tighter and employers find it increasingly difficult to hire workers at old wages. Businesses must offer higher wages to obtain additional workers. Unemployment and money wage rates move in opposite directions.

SAMUELSON AND SOLOW: THE PHILLIPS CURVE IS AMERICANIZED

In 1960, two American economists, Paul Samuelson and Robert Solow, published an article in the *American Economic Review* in which they fit a Phillips curve to the U.S. economy from 1935 to 1959. Besides using American data instead of British data, they measured price inflation rates (instead of wage inflation rates) against unemployment rates. They found an inverse relationship between (price) inflation and unemployment (see Exhibit 2).[1]

Economists concluded from the Phillips curve that **stagflation,** or high inflation together with high unemployment, was extremely unlikely. The economy could register (a) high unemployment and low inflation or (b) low unemployment and high inflation. Also, economists noticed that the Phillips curve presented policymakers with a *menu of choices*. For example, policymakers could choose to move the economy to any of the points on the Phillips curve in Exhibit 2. If they decided that a point like *A,* with high unemployment and low inflation, was preferable to a point like *D,* with low unemployment and high inflation, then so be it. It was simply a matter of reaching the right level of aggregate demand. To Keynesian economists, who were gaining a reputation for advocating fine-tuning the economy, that is, using small-scale measures to counterbalance undesirable economic trends, this conclusion seemed to be consistent with their theories and policy proposals.

 Q: If the Phillips curve presents policymakers with a menu of choices (such as 5 percent inflation and 6 percent unemployment or 2 percent inflation and 8 percent unemployment, and so on), this implicitly assumes that the menu of choices does not change over time. The same combinations of inflation and unemployment rates exist year after year. Does the real world really work this way?

A: As we soon explain, the real world is not like this.

THE CONTROVERSY BEGINS: ARE THERE REALLY TWO PHILLIPS CURVES?

This section discusses the work of Milton Friedman and the hypothesis that there are two, not one, Phillips curves.

THINGS AREN'T ALWAYS AS WE THOUGHT

In the 1970s and early 1980s, economists began to question many of the conclusions about the Phillips curve. Their questions were largely prompted by events after 1969. Consider Exhibit 3, which shows U.S. inflation and unemployment rates for the years 1961–2001. The 1961–1969 period, which is shaded, depicts the original Phillips curve tradeoff between inflation and unemployment. The remaining period, 1970–2001, as a whole does not, although some subperiods, such as 1976–1979, do.

Focusing on the period 1970–2001, we note that stagflation—high unemployment and high inflation—is possible. For example, 1975, 1981, and 1982 are definitely years of stagflation. The existence of stagflation implies that a tradeoff between inflation and unemployment may not always exist.

Stagflation
The simultaneous occurrence of high rates of inflation and unemployment.

exhibit 2

The Phillips Curve and a Menu of Choices
Samuelson and Solow's early work using American data showed that the Phillips curve was downward-sloping. Economists reasoned that stagflation was extremely unlikely and that the Phillips curve presented policymakers with a menu of choices—point *A, B, C,* or *D.*

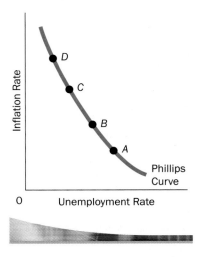

---

1. Today, when economists speak of the Phillips curve, they are usually referring to the relationship between price inflation rates and unemployment rates, instead of wage inflation rates and unemployment rates.

exhibit 3

The Diagram That Raises Questions: Inflation and Unemployment, 1961–2001

The period 1961–1969 clearly depicts the original Phillips curve tradeoff between inflation and unemployment. The later period, 1970–2001, as a whole, does not. However, some subperiods do, such as 1976–1979. The diagram presents empirical evidence that stagflation may exist; an inflation-unemployment tradeoff may not always hold.

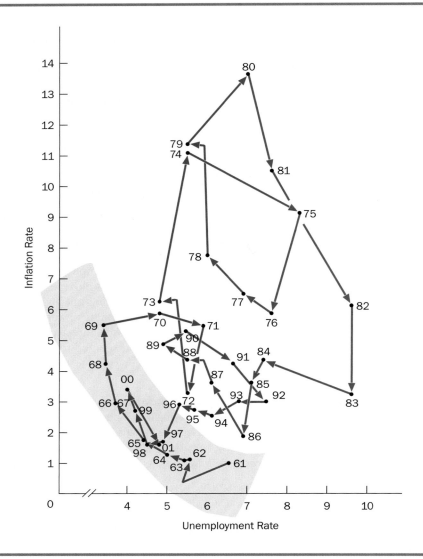

FRIEDMAN AND THE NATURAL RATE THEORY

Milton Friedman, in his presidential address to the American Economic Association in 1967 (published in the *American Economic Review*), attacked the idea of a permanent downward-sloping Phillips curve. Friedman's key point was that there are two, not one, Phillips curves: a short-run Phillips curve and a long-run Phillips curve. Friedman said, "There is always a temporary tradeoff between inflation and unemployment; there is no permanent tradeoff." In other words, *there is a tradeoff in the short run, but not in the long run.* Friedman's discussion not only introduced two types of Phillips curves to the analysis but also opened the macroeconomics door wide, once and for all, to expectations theory, that is, to the idea that people's expectations about economic events affect economic outcomes.

Exhibit 4 illustrates both the short-run and long-run Phillips curves. We start with the economy in long-run equilibrium, operating at Q_1, which is equal to Q_N. This is shown in Window 1. In the main diagram, the economy is at point 1 at the natural rate of unemployment. Further, and most important, *we assume that the expected inflation rate and the actual inflation rate are the same,* at 2 percent.

Now suppose government *unexpectedly* increases aggregate demand from AD_1 to AD_2, as shown in Window 2. As a result, the *actual* inflation rate increases (say, to 4 percent), but in the short run (immediately after the increase in aggre-

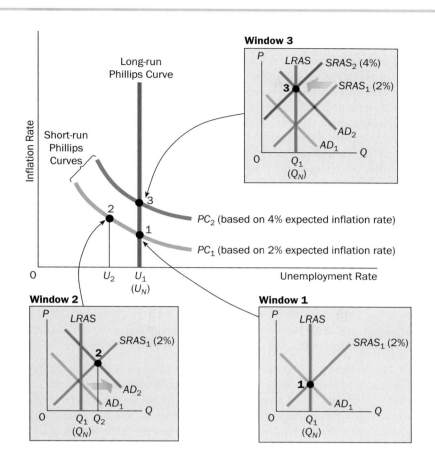

Window 3

Long-run
Phillips Curve

Short-run
Phillips
Curves

PC_2 (based on 4% expected inflation rate)

PC_1 (based on 2% expected inflation rate)

Unemployment Rate

Window 2

Window 1

exhibit 4

**Short-Run and Long-Run
Phillips Curves**
Starting at point 1 in the main diagram,
and assuming that the expected inflation rate stays constant as aggregate
demand increases, the economy
moves to point 2. As the expected
inflation rate changes and comes to
equal the actual inflation rate, the
economy moves to point 3. Points 1
and 2 lie on a short-run Phillips curve.
Points 1 and 3 lie on a long-run
Phillips curve. (Note: The percentage
in parentheses following the *SRAS*
curves in the windows refers to the
expected inflation rate.)

gate demand), individual decision makers do not know this. Consequently, the *expected* inflation rate remains at 2 percent. In short, aggregate demand increases at the same time that people's expected inflation rate remains constant. Because of this combination of events, certain things happen.

The higher aggregate demand causes temporary shortages and higher prices. Businesses then respond to higher prices and higher profits by increasing output. Higher output requires more employees, so businesses start hiring more workers. As job vacancies increase, many currently unemployed individuals find work. Furthermore, many of the newly unemployed persons accept the prevailing wage rate because they think the wages will have greater purchasing power (recall that they expect the inflation rate to be 2 percent) than, in fact, those wages will turn out to have.

So far, the results of an increase in aggregate demand with no change in the expected inflation rate are (1) an increase in Real GDP from Q_1 to Q_2 (see Window 2) and (2) a corresponding decrease in the unemployment rate from U_1 to U_2 (see the main diagram). Thus, the economy has moved from point 1 to point 2 in the main diagram.

This raises the question: Is point 2 a stable equilibrium? Friedman answered that it is not. He argued that *as long as the expected inflation rate is not equal to the actual inflation rate, the economy is not in long-run equilibrium.*

For Friedman, as for most economists today, the movement from point 1 to point 2 on PC_1 is a short-run movement. Economists refer to PC_1, along which short-run movements occur, as a short-run Phillips curve.

In time, inflation expectations begin to change. As prices continue to climb, wage earners realize that their real (inflation-adjusted) wages have fallen. In

Go to *http://www.frbsf.org/econrsrch/ wklyltr/wklyltr99/el99-09.html*, and read the article. Are economists still arguing over the nature of the Phillips curve? Why is it important that policymakers understand how the economy works? What does the article say about Sargent's work? What does it say about the economy of Ireland?

Friedman Natural Rate Theory
The idea that in the long run, unemployment is at its natural rate. Within the Phillips curve framework, the natural rate theory specifies that there is a long-run Phillips curve, which is vertical at the natural rate of unemployment.

hindsight, they realize that they accepted nominal (money) wages based on an expected inflation rate (2 percent) that was too low. They revise their inflation expectations upward.

At the same time, some wage earners quit their jobs because they choose not to continue working at such low *real wages*. Eventually, the combination of some workers quitting their jobs and most (if not all) workers revising their inflation expectations upward causes wage rates to move upward.

Higher wage rates shift the short-run aggregate supply curve from $SRAS_1$ to $SRAS_2$ (see Window 3), ultimately moving the economy back to Natural Real GDP and to the natural rate of unemployment at point 3 (see the main diagram). The curve that connects point 1, where the economy started, and point 3, where it ended, is called the long-run Phillips curve.

Thus, the short-run Phillips curve exhibits a tradeoff between inflation and unemployment, whereas the long-run Phillips curve does not. This is the idea implicit in what has come to be called the **Friedman natural rate theory** (or the *Friedman "fooling" theory*). According to this theory, in the long run, the economy returns to its natural rate of unemployment, and the only reason it moved away from the natural unemployment rate in the first place was because workers were "fooled" (in the short run) into thinking the inflation rate was lower than it was.

Q & A   **Q:** This chapter is about expectations theory. How, specifically, do people's expectations relate to the discussion of the short- and long-run Phillips curves?

A: Again, look at Exhibit 4. The economy starts out at point 1 in the main diagram. Then something happens in the economy: aggregate demand increases. This has the capacity to change the inflation rate, *but it takes some time before workers realize the change in the inflation rate.* In the interim, their expected inflation rate is "too low." And because their expected inflation rate is "too low," workers are willing to work at jobs (and produce output) that they wouldn't work at if they perceived the inflation rate realistically.

But in time, workers do perceive the inflation rate realistically. In other words, the expected inflation rate is no longer "too low"—it has risen to equal the actual inflation rate. There is a predicted response in the unemployment rate and output as a result: the unemployment rate rises and output falls.

In short: Because workers' expectations (of inflation) are, in the short run, inconsistent with reality, workers produce more output than they would have produced if those expectations were consistent with reality. Do you see how people's expectations can affect such real economic variables as Real GDP and the unemployment rate?

Exhibit 5 may also help explain the Friedman natural rate theory.

HOW DO PEOPLE FORM THEIR EXPECTATIONS?

Implicit in the Friedman natural rate theory is a theory of how individuals form their expectations. Essentially, the theory holds that individuals form their expected inflation rate by looking at past inflation rates. To illustrate, let's suppose that the actual inflation rates in years 1–4 are 5 percent, 3 percent, 2 percent, and 2 percent, respectively. What do you think the inflation rate will be next year, year 5? Friedman assumes that people weight past inflation rates to come up with their expected inflation rate. For example, John may assign the following weights to the inflation rates in the past four years.

Year	Inflation Rate	Weight
1	5 percent	10%
2	3 percent	20%
3	2 percent	30%
4	2 percent	40%

In other words, as the present approaches, the weight assigned to the year's inflation rate rises. Based on these weights, John forms his expected inflation

A Closer Look

The Friedman Natural Rate Theory

1. Wages and prices are flexible.
2. Expectations are formed adaptively.

AD increases **+** No change in expected inflation rate →

Economy moves from point 1 to 2, from Q_1 (Q_N) to Q_2. There is a short-run increase in Real GDP.

In time, workers revise their expected inflation rate upward in response to the higher prices brought on by the increase in aggregate demand. Wage rates begin to rise. →

SRAS curve begins to shift left, ultimately intersecting AD_2 at point 3. Economy has returned to Q_1 (Q_N).

rate (his "best guess" of the inflation rate in the upcoming year), by finding the weighted average of the inflation rates in the past four years.

Expected inflation rate = 0.10(5 percent) + 0.20(3 percent) + 0.30(2 percent)
            + 0.40(2 percent)
        = 2.5 percent

John's expected inflation rate is 2.5 percent.

Notice that in forming an expected inflation rate this way, the person is always looking to the past. He is, in a sense, looking over his shoulder to see what has happened, and then based on what has happened, "figuring out" what he thinks will happen. In economics, a person who forms an expected inflation rate this way is said to hold **adaptive expectations.** In short, the Friedman natural rate theory implicitly assumes that people hold adaptive expectations.

Some economists have argued this point. They believe that people do not form their expected inflation rate using adaptive expectations. Instead, they believe people hold *rational expectations*. We discuss this in the next section.

Adaptive Expectations
Expectations that individuals form from past experience and modify slowly as the present and the future become the past (as time passes).

Self-Test *(Answers to Self-Test Questions are in the Self-Test Appendix.)*

1. What condition must exist for the Phillips curve to present policymakers with a permanent menu of choices (between inflation and unemployment)?

2. Is there a tradeoff between inflation and unemployment? Explain your answer.

3. The Friedman natural rate theory is sometimes called the "fooling" theory. Who is being fooled and what are they being fooled about?

RATIONAL EXPECTATIONS AND NEW CLASSICAL THEORY

Rational expectations has played a major role in the Phillips curve controversy. The work of economists Robert Lucas, Robert Barro, Thomas Sargent, and Neil Wallace is relevant in this discussion.

RATIONAL EXPECTATIONS

In the early 1970s, a few economists, including Robert Lucas of the University of Chicago (winner of the 1995 Nobel Prize in Economics), began to question the short-run tradeoff between inflation and unemployment. Essentially, Lucas combined the natural rate theory with rational expectations.[2] (In this text, the natural rate theory that is built on adaptive expectations is called the *Friedman natural rate theory;* the natural rate theory built on rational expectations is called the *new classical theory.*)

Before presenting the new classical theory, we define and discuss **rational expectations.** Rational expectations holds that individuals form the expected inflation rate not only on the basis of their past experience with inflation (looking over their shoulders) but also on their predictions about the effects of present and future policy actions and events. In short, the expected inflation rate is formed by looking at the past, present, and future. To illustrate, suppose the inflation rate has been 5 percent for the past seven years. Then, the chairman of the Fed's Board of Governors speaks about "sharply stimulating the economy." Rational expectationists argue that the expected inflation rate might immediately jump upward, based on the current words of the chairman.

A major difference between adaptive and rational expectations is the *speed* at which the expected inflation rate changes. If the expected inflation rate is formed adaptively, then it is slow to change. It is based only on the past, so individuals will wait until the present and the future become the past before they change their expectations. If the expected inflation rate is formed rationally, it changes quickly because it is based on the past, present, and future. One implication of rational expectations is that people anticipate policy.

DO PEOPLE ANTICIPATE POLICY?

Suppose you chose people at random on the street and asked them this question: What do you think the Fed will do in the next few months? Do you think you would be more likely to receive (1) an intelligent answer or (2) the response, "What is the Fed"?

Most readers of this text will probably choose answer (2). There is a general feeling that the person on the street knows little about economics or economic institutions. The answer to our question "Do people anticipate policy?" seems to be no.

But suppose you chose people at random on Wall Street and asked the same question. This time you would likely receive an informed answer. In this case, the answer to our larger question "Do people anticipate policy?" is likely to be yes.

We suggest that not all persons need to anticipate policy. As long as some do, the consequences may be the same *as if* all persons do. For example, Juanita Estevez is anticipating policy if she decides to buy 100 shares of SKA because her best friend, Tammy Higgins, heard from her friend, Kenny Urich, that his broker, Roberta Gunter, told him that SKA's stock is expected to go up. Juanita is anticipating policy because it is likely that Roberta Gunter obtained her information from a researcher in the brokerage firm who makes it his business to "watch the Fed" and to anticipate its next move.

Of course, anticipating policy is not done just for the purpose of buying and selling stocks. Labor unions hire professional forecasters to predict future inflation rates, which is important information to have during wage contract negotiations. Banks hire professional forecasters to predict inflation rates, which they incorporate into the interest rate they charge. Export businesses hire professional forecasters to predict the future exchange-rate value of the dollar. The average

---

2. Rational expectations appeared on the economic scene in 1961 when John Muth published "Rational Expectations and the Theory of Price Movements" in the journal *Econometrica.* For about ten years, the article received little attention from the economics profession. Then, in the early 1970s, with the work of Robert Lucas, Thomas Sargent, Neil Wallace, Robert Barro, and others, the article began to be noticed.

investor may subscribe to a business or investment newsletter in order to predict interest rates, the price of gold, or next year's inflation rate more accurately. The person thinking of refinancing his or her mortgage watches one of the many financial news shows on television to find out about the government's most recent move and how it will affect interest rates in the next three months.

NEW CLASSICAL THEORY: THE EFFECTS OF UNANTICIPATED AND ANTICIPATED POLICY

New classical theory makes two major assumptions: (1) expectations are formed rationally; (2) wages and prices are flexible. With these in mind, we discuss new classical theory in two settings: where policy is unanticipated and where policy is anticipated.

Unanticipated Policy

Consider Exhibit 6a. The economy starts at point 1, where $Q_1 = Q_N$. Unexpectedly, the Fed begins to buy government securities, and the money supply and aggregate demand increase. The aggregate demand curve shifts rightward from AD_1 to AD_2. Because the policy action was unanticipated, individuals are caught off guard, so the anticipated price level (P_1), on which the short-run aggregate supply curve is based, is not likely to change immediately. (This is similar to saying, as we did in the discussion of the Friedman natural rate theory, that individuals' expected inflation rate is less than the actual inflation rate.)

In the short run, the economy moves from point 1 to point 2, from Q_1 to Q_2. (In Phillips-curve terms, the economy has moved up the short-run Phillips curve to a higher inflation rate and lower unemployment rate.) In the long run, workers correctly anticipate the higher price level and increase their wage demands accordingly. The short-run aggregate supply curve shifts leftward from $SRAS_1$ to $SRAS_2$ and the economy moves to point 3.

Anticipated Policy

Now consider what happens when policy is anticipated, in particular, when it is *correctly anticipated.* When individuals anticipate that the Fed will buy government securities and that the money supply, aggregate demand, and prices will

exhibit 6

Rational Expectations in an AD-AS Framework

The economy is in long-run equilibrium at point 1 in both (a) and (b). In (a), there is an unanticipated increase in aggregate demand. In the short run, the economy moves to point 2. In the long run, it moves to point 3. In (b), the increase in aggregate demand is correctly anticipated. Because the increase is anticipated, the short-run aggregate supply curve shifts from $SRAS_1$ to $SRAS_2$ at the same time the aggregate demand curves shifts from AD_1 to AD_2. The economy moves directly to point 2, which is comparable to point 3 in (a).

increase, they will adjust their present actions accordingly. For example, workers will bargain for higher wages so that their real wages will not fall when the price level rises. As a result, the short-run aggregate supply curve will shift leftward from $SRAS_1$ to $SRAS_2$ at the same time that the aggregate demand curve shifts rightward from AD_1 to AD_2 (see Exhibit 6b). The economy moves directly from point 1 to point 2. Real GDP does not change; throughout the adjustment period, it remains at its natural level. It follows that the unemployment rate does not change either. There is no short-run tradeoff between inflation and unemployment. The short-run Phillips curve and the long-run Phillips curve are the same; the curve is vertical.

POLICY INEFFECTIVENESS PROPOSITION (PIP)

Using rational expectations, we showed (see Exhibit 6) that *if the rise in aggregate demand is unanticipated, there is a short-run increase in Real GDP, but if the rise in aggregate demand is correctly anticipated, there is no change in Real GDP.* What are the implications of this result?

Let's consider the two types of macroeconomic policies—fiscal and monetary—that we have studied. Both of these policies can theoretically increase aggregate demand. For example, assuming there is no crowding out or incomplete crowding out, expansionary fiscal policy shifts the *AD* curve rightward. Expansionary monetary policy does the same. In both cases, expansionary policy is effective at increasing Real GDP and lowering the unemployment rate in the short run.

New classical economists question this scenario. They argue that if (1) the expansionary policy change is correctly anticipated, (2) individuals form their expectations rationally, and (3) wages and prices are flexible, then neither expansionary fiscal policy nor expansionary monetary policy will be able to increase Real GDP and lower the unemployment rate in the short run. This argument is called the **policy ineffectiveness proposition (PIP).**

Think what this means. If, under certain conditions, expansionary monetary and fiscal policy are not effective at increasing Real GDP and lowering the unemployment rate, the case for government fine-tuning the economy is questionable.

Q: Are new classical economists saying that monetary and fiscal policies are never effective?

A: No, they are saying that monetary and fiscal policies are not effective under certain conditions: When policy is correctly anticipated, people form their expectations rationally, and wages and prices are flexible.

Q: I know a number of people who do not anticipate policy and who do not seem to form their expectations by looking to the past, present, and future. Isn't this evidence that the new classical theory has incorrect assumptions and therefore is of little value?

A: Remember, we judge a theory by the accuracy of its predictions, not by its assumptions. Certainly, all of us can find people who do not anticipate policy and who do not form their expectations rationally. But the question is whether these people are great enough in number to upset the theory's predictions. If enough people form their expectations rationally and enough people anticipate policy, the effect may be the same *as if* everyone does. New classical theory does not purport to describe reality perfectly. All theories—classical, Keynesian, monetarist, and new classical—are abstractions from reality.

RATIONAL EXPECTATIONS AND INCORRECTLY ANTICIPATED POLICY

Suppose that wages and prices are flexible, people form their expectations rationally, and they anticipate policy—but this time they anticipate policy *incorrectly*. What happens?

To illustrate, consider Exhibit 7. The economy is in long-run equilibrium at point 1 where $Q_1 = Q_N$. People believe the Fed will increase aggregate demand

Policy Ineffectiveness Proposition (PIP)
If (1) a policy change is correctly anticipated, (2) individuals form their expectations rationally, and (3) wages and prices are flexible, then neither fiscal policy nor monetary policy is effective at meeting macroeconomic goals.

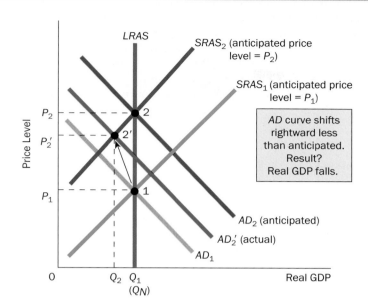

exhibit 7

The Short-Run Response to an Aggregate Demand-Increasing Policy That Is Less Expansionary Than Anticipated (in the New Classical Theory)
Starting at point 1, people anticipate an increase in aggregate demand from AD_1 to AD_2. Based on this, the short-run aggregate supply curve shifts leftward from $SRAS_1$ to $SRAS_2$. It turns out, however, that the aggregate demand curve only shifts rightward to AD_2' (less than anticipated). As a result, the economy moves to point 2', to a lower Real GDP and a higher unemployment rate.

by increasing the money supply, but they *incorrectly anticipate* the degree to which aggregate demand will be increased. Thinking aggregate demand will increase from AD_1 to AD_2, they immediately revise their anticipated price level to P_2 (the long-run equilibrium position of the AD_2 curve and the *LRAS* curve). As a result, the short-run aggregate supply curve shifts leftward from $SRAS_1$ to $SRAS_2$.

However, the actual increase in aggregate demand is less than anticipated, and the aggregate demand curve only shifts rightward from AD_1 to AD_2'. As a result, the economy moves to point 2', to a lower Real GDP and a higher unemployment rate. We conclude that a policy designed to increase Real GDP and lower unemployment can do just the opposite if the policy is less expansionary than anticipated.

Q & A   **Q:** In the example just given, people incorrectly anticipated policy in a particular direction, that is, they mistakenly believed that the aggregate demand curve was going to shift to the right more than it actually did. In other words, they *overestimated the increase in aggregate demand.* Can people incorrectly anticipate policy in the other direction, that is, can they *underestimate the increase in aggregate demand?*

A: Yes. This brings up an important point. When discussing rational expectations, we get different outcomes in the short run depending on whether policy is (1) unanticipated, (2) anticipated correctly, (3) anticipated incorrectly in one direction, or (4) anticipated incorrectly in the other direction.

HOW TO FALL INTO A RECESSION WITHOUT REALLY TRYING

Suppose the public witnesses the following series of events three times in three years. The federal government runs a budget deficit. It finances the deficit by borrowing from the public (issuing Treasury bills, notes, and bonds). The Fed conducts open market operations and buys many of the government securities. Aggregate demand increases and the price level rises. At the same time all this is going on, Congress says it will do whatever is necessary to bring inflation under control. The chairman of the Fed says the Fed will soon move against inflation. Congress, the President, and the Fed do *not* move against inflation.

ECONOMICS IN...

Everyday Life   Popular Culture   Technology   The World

Rational Expectations in the College Classroom

If people hold rational expectations, the outcome of a policy will be different if it is unanticipated than if it is anticipated. Specifically, unanticipated policy changes can move the economy away from the natural unemployment rate, but (correctly) anticipated policy changes cannot. Does something similar happen in a college classroom?

Suppose Ana's history class starts at 9:00 A.M. and it is "natural" for her to arrive one minute before class starts. In other words, her "natural waiting time" is one minute.

The first day of class, Ana arrives at 8:59, her instructor arrives at 8:59:30, and she starts class promptly at 9:00 A.M.

The second day of class, Ana arrives at 8:59, her instructor arrives at 9:01:30, and she starts class at 9:02. On this day, Ana has waited three minutes, which is above her natural waiting time of one minute.

The third, fourth, and fifth days of class are the same as the second. So, for the second through fifth days, Ana is operating at above her natural waiting time.

Rational expectations hold that people will not continue to make the same mistake.

In this case, Ana will take her professor's recent arrival time into account and adjust accordingly. On the sixth day of class, instead of arriving at 8:59, she arrives at 9:01. This day the instructor again arrives at 9:01:30 and begins class at 9:02. Ana has moved back to her natural waiting time of one minute.

Let's summarize our story so far: Ana had a natural waiting time which was met on the first day of class. On the second through fifth days of class, the professor obviously had a "change of policy" as to her arrival time. This change of policy was unanticipated by Ana, so she was fooled into waiting more than her natural waiting time. But Ana did not continue to make the same mistake. She adjusted to her professor's "policy change" and went back to her one-minute natural waiting time.

Now let's change things a bit. Suppose at the end of the first day of class the professor says, "I know I arrived to class at 8:59:30 today, but I won't do this again. From now on, I will arrive at 9:01:30."

In this situation, the professor has announced her policy change. Ana hears the announcement and therefore (correctly) anticipates what the professor will do from now on. With this information, she adjusts her behavior. Instead of arriving to class at 8:59, she changes her behavior and arrives at 9:01. Thus, she has correctly anticipated her professor's policy change, and she will remain at her natural waiting time (she will not move from it, even temporarily).

According to some economists, if the government says it will do *X* but continues to do *Y* instead, then people will see through the charade. They will equate "saying *X*" with "doing *Y*." In other words, the equation in their heads will read "Say *X* = Do *Y*." They will also always base their behavior on what they expect the government to do, not what it says it will do.[3]

Now, suppose the government changes; it says it will do *X* and actually does *X*. People will not know the government is telling the truth this time, and they will continue to think that saying *X* really means doing *Y*.

Some new classical economists say this is what happened in the early 1980s and that it goes a long way to explaining the 1981–1982 recession. They tell this story:

1. President Reagan proposed, and Congress approved, tax cuts in 1981.
2. Although some economists insisted that the tax cuts would stimulate so much economic activity that tax revenues would increase, the public believed that

---

3. Rational expectations has sometimes been reduced to this adage, "Fool me once, shame on you; fool me twice, shame on me."

the tax cuts would decrease tax revenues and increase the size of the budget deficit (that existed at the time).

3. People translated larger budget deficits into more government borrowing.
4. They anticipated greater money supply growth connected with the larger deficits because they had seen this happen before.
5. Greater money supply growth would mean an increase in aggregate demand and in the price level.
6. The Fed said it would not finance the deficits (buy government bonds), but it had said this before and it had acted contrarily, so few people believed the Fed this time.
7. The Fed actually did not increase the money supply as much as individuals thought it would.
8. This meant the monetary policy was not as expansionary as individuals had anticipated.
9. As a result, the economy moved to a point like 2′ in Exhibit 7. Real GDP fell and unemployment increased; a recession ensued.

The moral of the story, according to new classical economists, is that if the Fed says it is going to do X, then it had better do X because if it doesn't, then the next time it says it is going to do X, no one will believe it and the economy may fall into a recession as a consequence. The recession will be an unintended effect of the Fed saying one thing and doing another in the past.

Self-Test

1. Does the policy ineffectiveness proposition (PIP) always hold?

2. When policy is unanticipated, what difference is there between the natural rate theory built on adaptive expectations and the natural rate theory built on rational expectations?

3. If expectations are formed rationally, does it matter whether policy is unanticipated, anticipated correctly, or anticipated incorrectly? Explain your answer.

NEW KEYNESIANS AND RATIONAL EXPECTATIONS

New classical theory assumes complete flexibility of wages and prices. In this theory, an increase in the anticipated price level results in an immediate and equal rise in wages and prices, and the aggregate supply curve immediately shifts to the long-run equilibrium position.

In response to the assumption of flexible wages and prices, a few economists began to develop what has come to be known as the *New Keynesian rational expectations theory*. This theory assumes that rational expectations is a reasonable characterization of how expectations are formed, but drops the new classical assumption of complete wage and price flexibility. Economists who work with this theory argue that long-term labor contracts often prevent wages and prices from fully adjusting to changes in the anticipated price level. (Prices and wages are somewhat sticky, rigid, or inflexible.)

Consider the possible situation at the end of the first year of a three-year wage contract. Workers may realize that the anticipated price level is higher than they expected when they negotiated the contract, but will be unable to do much about it because their wages are locked in for the next two years. Price rigidity might also arise because firms often engage in fixed-price contracts with their suppliers. As discussed in an earlier chapter, Keynesian economists today put forth microeconomic-based reasons why long-term labor contracts and above-market wages are sometimes in the best interest of both employers and employees (efficiency wage theory).

exhibit 8

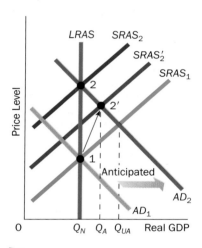

The Short-Run Response to Aggregate Demand-Increasing Policy (in the New Keynesian Theory)

Starting at point 1, an increase in aggregate demand is anticipated. As a result, this short-run aggregate supply curve shifts leftward, but not all the way to $SRAS_2$ (as would be the case in the new classical model). Instead it shifts only to $SRAS_2'$ because of some wage and price rigidities; the economy moves to point 2' (in the short run), and Real GDP increases from Q_N to Q_A. If the policy had been unanticipated, Real GDP would have increased from Q_N to Q_{UA}.

To see what the theory predicts, look at Exhibit 8. The economy is initially in long-run equilibrium at point 1. The public anticipates an increase in aggregate demand from AD_1 to AD_2. As a result, the anticipated price level changes. Because of some wage and price rigidities, however, the short-run aggregate supply curve does not shift all the way from $SRAS_1$ to $SRAS_2$, and the economy does not move from point 1 to point 2 (as in new classical theory). The short-run aggregate supply curve shifts instead to $SRAS_2'$ because rigidities prevent complete wage and price adjustments. In the short run, the economy moves from point 1 to point 2', from Q_N to Q_A. Note that had the policy been unanticipated, Real GDP would have increased from Q_N to Q_{UA} in the short run.

LOOKING AT THINGS FROM THE SUPPLY SIDE: REAL BUSINESS CYCLE THEORISTS

Throughout this chapter, changes in Real GDP have originated on the demand side of the economy. When discussing the Friedman natural rate theory, the new classical theory, and the New Keynesian theory, we begin our analysis by shifting the *AD* curve to the right. Then we explain what happens in the economy as a result.

From the discussions in this chapter, it is possible to believe that all changes in Real GDP (and unemployment) originate on the demand side of the economy. In fact, some economists believe this to be true. However, other economists do not. One group of such economists—called *real business cycle theorists*—believe that changes on the supply side of the economy can lead to changes in Real GDP and unemployment.

Real business cycle theorists argue that a decrease in Real GDP (which refers to the recessionary or contractionary part of a business cycle) can be brought about by a major supply-side change that reduces the capacity of the economy to produce. Moreover, they argue that what looks like a contraction in Real GDP originating on the demand side of the economy can be, in essence, the effect of what has happened on the supply side. Exhibit 9 helps explain the process.

We start with an adverse supply shock that reduces the capacity of the economy to produce. This is represented by a shift inward in the economy's production possibilities frontier or a leftward shift in the long-run aggregate supply

exhibit 9

Real Business Cycle Theory

We start with a supply-side change capable of reducing the capacity of the economy to produce. This is manifested by a leftward shift of the long-run aggregate supply curve from $LRAS_1$ to $LRAS_2$ and a fall in the Natural Real GDP level from Q_{N_1} to Q_{N_2}. A reduction in the productive capacity of the economy filters to the demand side of the economy and, in our example, reduces consumption, investment, and the money supply. The aggregate demand curve shifts leftward from AD_1 to AD_2.

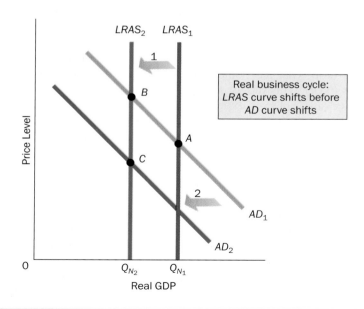

The Boy Who Cried Wolf (And the Townspeople with Rational Expectations)

You may know the fable about the boy and the wolf: There was a young boy who liked to play tricks on people. One day, the boy's father (a shepherd) had to go out of town. He asked his son to take care of the sheep while he was gone. While the boy was watching the sheep, he suddenly began yelling, "Wolf, wolf, wolf." The townspeople came running because they thought the boy needed help protecting the sheep from the wolf. When they arrived, they found the boy laughing at the trick he had played on them. The same thing happened two or three more times. Finally, one day, a real wolf appeared. The boy called, "Wolf, wolf, wolf," but no one came. The townspeople were not going to be fooled again. And so the wolf ate the sheep.

The fable about the boy and the wolf has something in common with what we have been discussing in this chapter—the unintended consequences of saying one thing and doing another.

In the new classical economic story of the 1981–1982 recession, the public incorrectly anticipated Fed policy and, as a result, the economy fell into a recession. But the reason the public incorrectly anticipated Fed policy was because, in the past, the Fed had said one thing and done another. It had said X but done Y.

It's the same with the boy and the wolf. The first few times the boy cried wolf, the townspeople found that there was no wolf and the boy was simply playing a trick on them. In their minds, "Crying Wolf = No Wolf." So, when the boy cried wolf the last time and actually meant it, no one from the town came to help him. And the wolf ate the sheep.

Just as the Fed might have learned that saying one thing and doing another can result in a recession, the boy learned that saying one thing and meaning another can result in sheep being killed. The moral of our story is that if you tell a lie again and again, people will no longer believe you when you tell the truth.

---

curve from $LRAS_1$ to $LRAS_2$, which moves the economy from point A to point B. As shown in Exhibit 9, a leftward shift in the long-run aggregate supply curve means that Natural Real GDP has fallen.

As a result of the leftward shift in the LRAS curve and the decline in Real GDP, firms reduce their demand for labor and scale back employment. Due to the lower demand for labor (which puts downward pressure on money wages) and the higher price level, real wages fall.

As real wages fall, workers choose to work less and unemployed persons choose to extend the length of their unemployment. Due to less work and lower real wages, workers have less income. Lower incomes soon lead workers to reduce consumption.

Because consumption has fallen, or because businesses have become pessimistic (prompted by the decline in the productive potential of the economy), or both, businesses have less reason to invest. As a result, firms borrow less from banks, the volume of outstanding loans falls, and therefore the money supply falls. A decrease in the money supply causes the aggregate demand curve to shift leftward, from AD_1 to AD_2 in Exhibit 9, and the economy moves to point C.

Real business cycle theorists sometimes point out how easy it is to confuse a demand-induced decline in Real GDP with a supply-induced decline in Real GDP. In our example, both the aggregate supply side and the aggregate demand side of the economy change, but the aggregate supply side changes first. If the change in aggregate supply is overlooked, and only the changes in aggregate demand are observed (or, specifically, a change in one of the variables that can change aggregate demand, such as the money supply), then the contraction in Real GDP will appear to be demand-induced. In terms of Exhibit 9, the leftward shift in the *LRAS* curve would be overlooked, but the leftward shift in the *AD* curve would be observed, giving the impression that the contraction is demand-induced.

If real business cycle theorists are correct, the cause-effect analysis of a contraction in Real GDP would be turned upside down. To take but one example, changes in the money supply may be an effect of a contraction in Real GDP (which originates on the supply side of the economy) and not its cause.

Self-Test

1. The *Wall Street Journal* reports that the money supply has recently declined. Is this consistent with a demand-induced or supply-induced business cycle, or both? Explain your answer.

2. How are New Keynesians who believe people hold rational expectations different from new classical economists who believe people hold rational expectations?

A Reader Asks...
Do Expectations Matter?

What insights, if any, does the introduction of expectations into macroeconomics provide?

Think of your study of macroeconomics in earlier chapters. You learned that changes in such things as taxes, government purchases, interest rates, the money supply and more could change Real GDP, the price level, and the unemployment rate. For example, starting at long-run equilibrium, a rise in the money supply will raise Real GDP and lower the unemployment rate in the short run and raise the price level in the long run. Or, consider that an increase in productivity can shift the *SRAS* curve to the right and thus bring about a change in Real GDP and the price level. In short, most of this text discusses how changes in real variables can affect the economy.

With the introduction of expectations theory, we move to a different level of analysis. Now we learn that what people think can also affect the economy. In other words, not only can a change in the world's oil supply affect the economy—almost everyone would expect that—but so can whether or not someone believes that the Fed will increase the money supply.

Think back to our discussion of rational expectations and incorrectly anticipated policy. The economy is in long-run equilibrium when the Fed undertakes an expansionary monetary policy move. The Fed expects to increase the money supply by, say, $100 billion, but somehow economic agents believe the increase in the money supply will be closer to $200 billion. In other words, economic agents think that the money supply will rise by more than it will rise. Does it matter that their thoughts are wrong? Expectations theory says that it does. As shown in Exhibit 7, wrong thoughts can lead to lower Real GDP and higher prices.

In conclusion, the insight that expectations theory provides is that what people think can affect Real GDP, unemployment, and prices. Who would have thought it?

Chapter Summary

The Phillips Curve
• A. W. Phillips plotted a curve to a set of data points that exhibited an inverse relationship between wage inflation and unemployment. This curve came to be known as the Phillips curve. From the Phillips curve relationship, economists concluded that neither the combination of low inflation and low unemployment nor the combination of high inflation and high unemployment was likely.

• Economists Samuelson and Solow fit a Phillips curve to the U.S. economy. Instead of measuring wage inflation against unemployment rates (as Phillips did), they measured price inflation against unemployment rates. They found an inverse relationship between inflation and unemployment rates.

• Based on the findings of Phillips and Samuelson and Solow, economists concluded the following: (1) Stagflation, or high inflation and high unemployment, is extremely unlikely. (2) The Phillips curve presents policymakers with a menu of choices between different combinations of inflation and unemployment rates.

Friedman Natural Rate Theory

- Milton Friedman pointed out that there are two types of Phillips curves: a short-run Phillips curve and a long-run Phillips curve. The short-run Phillips curve exhibits the inflation-unemployment tradeoff; the long-run Phillips curve does not. Consideration of both short-run and long-run Phillips curves opened macroeconomics to expectations theory.

- The Friedman natural rate theory holds that in the short run, a decrease (increase) in inflation is linked to an increase (decrease) in unemployment, but that in the long run, the economy returns to its natural rate of unemployment. In other words, there is a tradeoff between inflation and unemployment in the short run, but not in the long run.

- The Friedman natural rate theory was expressed in terms of adaptive expectations. Individuals formed their inflation expectations by considering past inflation rates. Later, some economists expressed the theory in terms of rational expectations. Rational expectations theory holds that individuals form their expected inflation rate by considering present and past inflation rates, as well as all other available and relevant information—in particular, the effects of present and future policy actions.

New Classical Theory

- Implicit in the new classical theory are two assumptions: (1) Individuals form their expectations rationally. (2) Wages and prices are completely flexible.

- In the new classical theory, policy has different effects (1) when it is unanticipated and (2) when it is anticipated. For example, if the public correctly anticipates an increase in aggregate demand, the short-run aggregate supply curve will likely shift leftward at the same time the aggregate demand curve shifts rightward. If the public does not anticipate an increase in aggregate demand (but one occurs), then the short-run aggregate supply curve will not shift leftward at the same time the aggregate demand curve shifts rightward; it will shift leftward sometime later. If policy is correctly anticipated, expectations are formed rationally, and wages and prices are completely flexible, then an increase or decrease in aggregate demand will change only the price level but not Real GDP or the unemployment rate. The

new classical theory casts doubt on the belief that the short-run Phillips curve is always downward-sloping. Under certain conditions, it may be vertical (as is the long-run Phillips curve).

- If policies are anticipated, but not credible, and rational expectations is a reasonable characterization of how individuals form their expectations, then certain policies may have unintended effects. For example, if the public believes that aggregate demand will increase by more than it (actually) increases (because policymakers have not done in the past what they said they would do), then anticipated inflation will be higher than it would have been, the short-run aggregate supply curve will shift leftward by more than it would have, and the (short-run) outcome of a policy that increases aggregate demand will be lower Real GDP and higher unemployment.

New Keynesian Theory

- Implicit in the New Keynesian theory are two assumptions: (1) Individuals form their expectations rationally. (2) Wages and prices are not completely flexible (in the short run).

- If policy is anticipated, the economic effects predicted by the new classical theory and the New Keynesian theory are not the same (in the short run). Because the New Keynesian theory assumes that wages and prices are not completely flexible in the short run, given an anticipated change in aggregate demand, the short-run aggregate supply curve cannot immediately shift to its long-run equilibrium position. The New Keynesian theory predicts that there is a short-run tradeoff between inflation and unemployment (in the Phillips curve framework).

Real Business Cycle Theory

- Real business cycle contractions (in Real GDP) originate on the supply side of the economy. A contraction in Real GDP might follow this pattern: (1) An adverse supply shock reduces the economy's ability to produce. (2) The *LRAS* curve shifts leftward. (3) As a result, Real GDP declines and the price level rises. (4) The number of persons employed falls, as do real wages, owing to a decrease in the demand for labor (which lowers money wages) and a higher price level. (5) Incomes decline. (6) Consumption and investment decline. (7) The volume of outstanding loans declines. (8) The money supply falls. (9) The *AD* curve shifts leftward.

Phillips Curve
Stagflation
Friedman Natural Rate Theory

Adaptive Expectations
Rational Expectations

Policy Ineffectiveness Proposition
(PIP)

Economic facts, actions, and changes create ripples that move away from their point of origin. Eventually, these ripples can intersect your life and have an effect on you. Consider the following example.

The world's supply of oil is reduced because of a major war in the Middle East. With less oil (an important resource in the production process), the productive capability of the U.S. economy declines—perhaps because the higher price of oil makes it too costly to use certain types of machinery. The LRAS curve in the United States shifts leftward. Conse- *quently, Real GDP falls and the unemployment rate rises. As a current college graduate looking for a job, your chances of finding suitable employment have diminished. Thus, there is a connection through economic channels between a war on the opposite side of the globe and your employment opportunities—an economic connection to you.*

Based on the material in this chapter, identify other ways in which economic facts, actions, and changes create ripples that eventually affect you.

1. What is a major difference between adaptive and rational expectations? Give an example.

2. It has been said that the policy ineffectiveness proposition (connected with new classical theory) does not eliminate policymakers' ability to reduce unemployment through aggregate demand-increasing policies because they can always increase aggregate demand by more than the public expects. What might be the weak point in this argument?

3. Why does the new classical theory have the word *classical* associated with it? Also, why has it been said that the classical theory failed where the new classical theory succeeds, as the former could not explain the business cycle ("the ups and downs of the economy"), but the latter can?

4. Suppose a permanent downward-sloping Phillips curve existed and offered a menu of choices of different combinations of inflation and unemployment rates to policymakers. How do you think society would go about deciding which point on the Phillips curve it wanted to occupy?

5. Suppose a short-run tradeoff between inflation and unemployment currently exists. How would you expect this tradeoff to be affected by a change in technology that permits the wider dispersion of economic policy news? Explain your answer.

6. New Keynesian theory holds that wages are not completely flexible because of such things as long-

term labor contracts. New classical economists often respond that experience teaches labor leaders to develop and bargain for contracts that allow for wage adjustments. Do you think the new classical economists have a good point? Why or why not?

7. What evidence can you point to that suggests individuals form their expectations adaptively? What evidence can you point to that suggests individuals form their expectations rationally?

8. Explain both the short-run and long-run movements of the Friedman natural rate theory, assuming expectations are formed adaptively.

9. Explain both the short-run and long-run movements of the natural rate theory, assuming expectations are formed rationally and policy is unanticipated.

10. "Even if some people do not form their expectations rationally, this does not necessarily mean that the new classical theory is of no value." Discuss.

11. In the real business cycle theory, why can't the change in the money supply prompted by a series of events catalyzed by an adverse supply shock be considered the "cause" of the business cycle?

12. The expected inflation rate is 5 percent and the actual inflation rate is 7 percent. According to Friedman, is the economy in long-run equilibrium? Explain your answer.

1. Illustrate graphically what would happen in the short run and long run if individuals hold rational expectations, prices and wages are flexible, and individuals underestimate the decrease in aggregate demand.
2. In each of the following figures, the starting point is point 1. Which part illustrates each of the following?
   a. Friedman natural rate theory (short run)

b. New classical theory (unanticipated policy, short run)
c. Real business cycle theory
d. New classical theory (incorrectly anticipated policy, overestimating increase in aggregate demand, short run)
e. Policy ineffectiveness proposition (PIP)

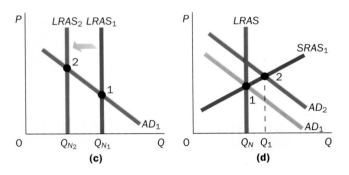

3. Illustrate graphically what would happen in the short run and the long run if individuals hold adaptive

expectations, prices and wages are flexible, and there is decrease in aggregate demand.

1. Go to *http://www.conference-board.org/*, and click on "ECONOMICS." Under "Economic Indicators," select "Consumer Confidence."
   a. How does the consumer confidence index today compare to the index last month?
   b. How does the Conference Board construct the index? How does the Conference Board interpret the new index number? Do you agree or disagree with the Board's interpretation?
2. Click on "Back" and select "Business Confidence."
   a. Are business leaders' expectations consistent with consumers' expectations? Are consumers more or less optimistic than business leaders about the future of the economy?

b. Do you think that (1) consumers' expectations affect business leaders' expectations, (2) business leaders' expectations affect consumers' expectations, (3) both, or (4) neither?
3. Go to *http://www.tcb-indicators.org/Us/LatestReleases/index.cfm*. The composite indexes are the key elements in an analytic system designed to signal peaks and troughs in the business cycle. The leading, coincident, and lagging indexes are essentially composite averages of between four and ten individual leading, coincident, or lagging indicators. Name the components of these composite indexes. Is the money supply (M2) a leading indicator?

Log on to the Arnold Xtra! Web site now (*http://arnoldxtra.swcollege.com*) for additional learning resources such as practice quizzes, help with graphing, video clips, and current event applications.

ECONOMIC GROWTH: RESOURCES, TECHNOLOGY, AND IDEAS

Rarely do we think of how we came to have the standard of living we enjoy. Most of us live in comfortable houses, drive nice cars, work on fast computers, enjoy exciting sporting events, attend entertaining jazz concerts, visit relaxing vacation spots, go to movies and restaurants, and so much more. To a large degree, our lives are what they are because we were born to parents who live in a country that in the last 100 years has experienced a relatively high rate of economic growth. How might your life be different if the U.S. economy had had a lower growth rate? To answer this question, you need to know the causes and effects of economic growth.

Chapter Road Map

In this chapter, we discuss an important topic in economics—
economic growth. We begin by looking at two types of growth: growth
that occurs starting at an inefficient level of production (below the production possi-
bilities frontier) and growth that occurs starting at an efficient level of production (on the pro-
duction possibilities frontier). We then examine the causes of economic growth and a few of the worries
about economic growth. Finally, we discuss new growth theory, an economic theory that has been referred to
as revolutionizing the way economists think about growth.

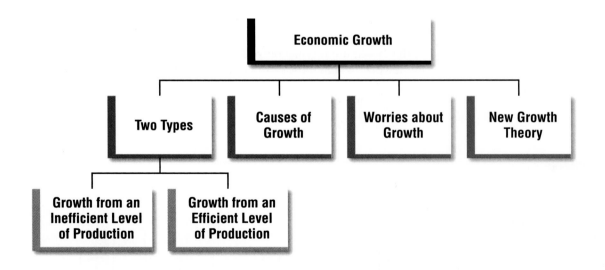

A FEW BASICS ABOUT ECONOMIC GROWTH

Absolute Real Economic Growth
An increase in Real GDP from one period to the next.

Per Capita Real Economic Growth
An increase from one period to the next in per capita Real GDP, which is Real GDP divided by population.

The term *economic growth* refers either to absolute real economic growth or to per capita real economic growth. **Absolute real economic growth** is an increase in Real GDP from one period to the next. Exhibit 1 shows absolute real economic growth (or the percentage change in Real GDP) for the United States for the period 1990–2000.

Per capita real economic growth is an increase from one period to the next in per capita Real GDP, which is Real GDP divided by population.

$$\text{Per capita Real GDP} = \frac{\text{Real GDP}}{\text{Population}}$$

DO ECONOMIC GROWTH RATES MATTER?

Suppose the (absolute) real economic growth rate is 4 percent in one country and 3 percent in another country. The difference in these growth rates may not seem very significant. But if these growth rates are sustained over a long period of time, the people who live in each country will see a real difference in their standard of living.

If a country's economic growth rate is 4 percent each year, Real GDP will take 18 years to double. If a country has a 3 percent annual growth rate, its Real GDP will take 24 years to double. In other words, a country with a 4 percent growth rate can double its Real GDP in 6 fewer years than a country with a 3 percent growth rate. (As an aside, to calculate the time required for any variable to double, simply divide its percentage growth rate into 72. This is called the *Rule of 72.*)

Let's look at things in a different way. Suppose two countries have the same populations. Real GDP is $300 billion in country *A* and $100 billion in country *B*. Relatively speaking, country *A* is three times richer than country *B*. Now suppose the annual economic growth rate is 3 percent in country *A* and 6 percent in country *B*. In just 15 years, country *B* will be the richer country.

TWO TYPES OF ECONOMIC GROWTH

Economic growth can be shown in two of the frameworks of analysis used so far in this book: the production possibilities frontier (PPF) framework and the *AD-AS* framework. Within these two frameworks, we speak about two types of economic growth: (1) economic growth that occurs from an inefficient level of production and (2) economic growth that occurs from an efficient level of production.

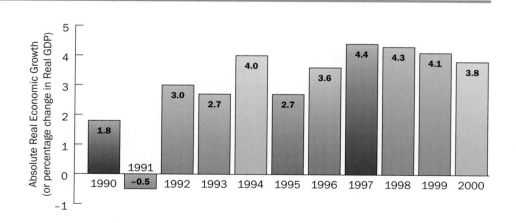

exhibit 1

Absolute Real Economic Growth Rates for the United States, 1990–2000

The exhibit shows the absolute real economic growth rates (or percentage change in Real GDP) in the United States for the period 1990–2000.

Source: Economic Report of the President, 2002.

Economic Growth from an Inefficient Level of Production

A production possibilities frontier is shown in Exhibit 2a. Suppose the economy is currently operating at point A, below the PPF. Obviously, the economy is not operating at its Natural Real GDP level. If it were, the economy would be located on the PPF instead of below it. Instead, the economy is at an inefficient point or at an inefficient level of production.

Point A in Exhibit 2a corresponds to point A' in Exhibit 2b. Here the economy is in a recessionary gap, operating below Natural Real GDP. Now suppose that through expansionary monetary or fiscal policy, the aggregate demand curve shifts rightward from AD_1 to AD_2. The economy is pulled out of its recessionary gap and is now producing Natural Real GDP at point B' in Exhibit 2b.

What does the situation look like now in Exhibit 2a? Obviously, if the economy is producing at its Natural Real GDP level, it is operating at full employment or at the natural unemployment rate. This means the economy has moved from point A (below the PPF) to point B (on the PPF). The economy has moved from operating at an inefficient level of production to operating at an efficient level.

Economic Growth from an Efficient Level of Production

How can the economy grow if it is on the PPF in Exhibit 2a—exhibiting efficiency—or producing at the Natural Real GDP level in Exhibit 2b? The answer is that the PPF must shift to the right (or outward) in (a), or the *LRAS* curve must shift to the right in (b). In other words, if the economy is at point B in Exhibit 3a, it can grow if the PPF shifts rightward from PPF_1 to PPF_2. Similarly, if the economy is at point B' in Exhibit 3b, the only way Real GDP can be raised beyond Q_{N_1} on a permanent basis is if the *LRAS* curve shifts to the right from $LRAS_1$ to $LRAS_2$.

Q & A **Q:** When economists talk about economic growth, are they describing the situation where the *AD* curve shifts rightward to move the economy from a point below its PPF to a point on it? Or are they talking about the situation where the PPF and the *LRAS* curve shift rightward?

A: Usually, it is the latter, where the PPF and the *LRAS* curve shift rightward.

ECONOMIC GROWTH AND THE PRICE LEVEL

Economic growth can occur with a falling price level, rising price level, or stable price level. To see this, look again at Exhibit 3b. The *LRAS* curve shifts from $LRAS_1$ to $LRAS_2$. Three possible aggregate demand curves may be consistent with this new *LRAS* curve: AD_1, AD_2, or AD_3.

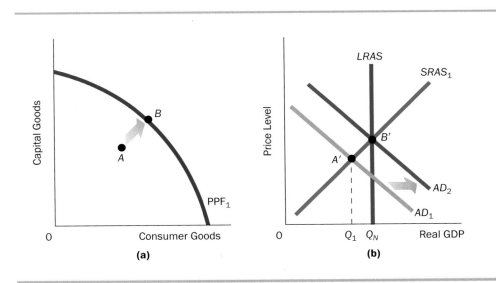

exhibit 2

Economic Growth from an Inefficient Level of Production
The economy is at point A in (a) and at point A' in (b). Currently, the economy is at an inefficient point, or below Natural Real GDP. Economic growth is evidenced as a movement from point A to B in (a), and as a movement from A' to B' in (b).

exhibit 3

Economic Growth from an Efficient Level of Production

The economy is at point B in (a) and at point B' in (b). Economic growth can only occur in (a) if the PPF shifts rightward from PPF₁ to PPF₂. It can only occur in (b) if the LRAS curve shifts from LRAS₁ to LRAS₂.

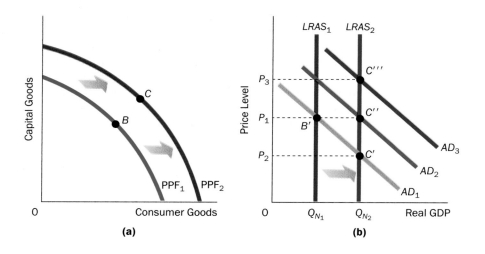

(a)

(b)

If AD_1 is the relevant AD curve, economic growth occurs with a declining price level. Before the LRAS curve shifted to the right, the price level was P_1; after the shift, it was lower, at P_2.

If AD_2 is the relevant AD curve, economic growth occurs with a stable price level. Before the LRAS curve shifted to the right, the price level was P_1; after the shift, it was the same, at P_1.

If AD_3 is the relevant AD curve, economic growth occurs with a rising price level. Before the LRAS curve shifted to the right, the price level was P_1; after the shift, it was higher, at P_3.

In recent decades, the U.S. economy has witnessed economic growth with a rising price level. This means the AD curve has been shifting to the right at a faster rate than the LRAS curve has been shifting to the right.

WHAT CAUSES ECONOMIC GROWTH?

This section looks at some of the determinants of economic growth, that is, the factors that can shift the PPF or the LRAS curve to the right. These factors include natural resources, labor, capital, technological advances, the property rights structure, and economic freedom. We then discuss some of the policies that promote economic growth.

NATURAL RESOURCES

People often think that countries that have a plentiful supply of natural resources experience economic growth, whereas countries that are short of natural resources do not. In fact, some countries with an abundant supply of natural resources have experienced rapid growth in the past (such as the United States), and some have experienced no growth or only slow growth. Also, some countries that are short of natural resources, such as Singapore, have grown very fast. It appears that natural resources are neither a sufficient nor a necessary factor for growth: Countries rich in natural resources are not guaranteed economic growth, and countries poor in natural resources may grow. Having said all this, it is still more likely for a nation rich in natural resources to experience growth, *ceteris paribus*. For example, if a place such as Hong Kong, which has few natural resources, had been blessed with much fertile soil, instead of only a little, and many raw materials, instead of almost none, it might have experienced more economic growth than it has.

LABOR

With more labor, it is possible to produce more output (more Real GDP), but whether or not the average productivity of labor rises, falls, or stays constant (as additional workers are added to the production process) depends on how productive the additional workers are relative to existing workers. If the additional workers are less productive than existing workers, labor productivity will decline. If they are more productive, labor productivity will rise. And if they are equally as productive, labor productivity will stay the same. (Note: average labor productivity is total output divided by total labor hours. For example, if $6 trillion of output is produced in 200 billion labor hours, then average labor productivity is $30 per hour.)

Both an increase in the labor force and an increase in labor productivity lead to increases in Real GDP, but only an increase in labor productivity tends to lead to an increase in per capita Real GDP.

How then do we achieve an increase in labor productivity? One way is through increased education, training, and experience. These are increases in what economists call *human capital*. Another way is through (physical) capital investment. Combining workers with more capital goods tends to increase the labor productivity of the workers. For example, a farmer with a tractor is more productive than a farmer without one.

CAPITAL

As just mentioned, capital investment can lead to increases in labor productivity and, therefore, not only to increases in Real GDP but also to increases in per capita Real GDP. But more capital goods do not fall from the sky. Recall that getting more of one thing often means forfeiting something else. To produce more capital goods, which are not directly consumable, present consumption must be reduced. Robinson Crusoe, alone on an island and fishing with a spear, must give up some of his present fish to weave a net (a physical capital good) with which he hopes to catch more fish.

If Crusoe gives up some of his present consumption—if he chooses not to consume now—he is, in fact, saving. There is a link between nonconsumption, or saving, and capital formation. As the saving rate increases, capital formation increases and so does economic growth.

Exhibit 4 shows that for the period 1970–1990, those countries with higher investment rates largely tended to have higher per capita Real GDP growth rates. For example, investment was a higher percentage of GDP in Austria, Norway, and Japan than it was in the United States. And these countries experienced a higher per capita Real GDP growth rate than the United States did.

TECHNOLOGICAL ADVANCES

Technological advances make it possible to obtain more output from the same amount of resources. Compare the amount of work that can be done by a business that uses computers with the amount accomplished by a business that does not.

Technological advances may be the result of new capital goods or of new ways of producing goods. The use of computers is an example of a technological advance that is the result of a new capital good. New and improved management techniques are an example of a new way of producing goods.

Technological advances usually come as the result of companies, and a country, investing in research and development (R&D). Research and development is a general term that encompasses such things as scientists working in a lab to develop a new product and managers figuring out, through experience, how to motivate workers to work to their potential.

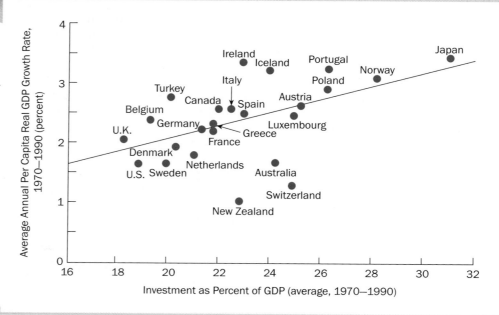

exhibit 4

Investment and Per Capita Real Economic Growth for Selected Countries, 1970–1990
Generally, but not always, those countries in which investment is a larger percentage of GDP have higher per capita Real GDP growth rates.

Source: Council of Economic Advisors, *Economic Report of the President,* 1997 (Washington, D.C.: U.S. Government Printing Office, 1997)

FREE TRADE AS TECHNOLOGY

Suppose someone in the United States has invented a machine that can turn wheat into cars.[1] The only problem with the machine is that it works only in Japan. So, people in the United States grow wheat and ship it to Japan. There, the machine turns the wheat into cars. The cars are then loaded on ships and brought to the United States.

Many economists say there is really no difference between a machine that can turn wheat into cars and free trade between countries. When there is free trade, people in the United States grow wheat and ship it to Japan. After awhile the ships come back loaded with cars. This is exactly what happened with our mythical machine. There is really no discernible difference between a machine turning wheat into cars and trading wheat for cars. In both cases, wheat is given up to get cars.

If the machine is a technological advancement, then so is free trade, as many economists point out. In that technological advancements can promote economic growth, so can free trade.

PROPERTY RIGHTS STRUCTURE

Some economists have argued that per capita real economic growth first appeared in areas that had developed a system of institutions and property rights that encouraged individuals to direct their energies to effective economic projects. Here property rights refers to the range of laws, rules, and regulations that define rights for the use and transfer of resources.

Consider two property rights structures. In one structure, people are allowed to keep the full monetary rewards of their labor. In the other, people are allowed to keep only half. Many economists would predict that the first property rights structure would stimulate more economic activity than the second, *ceteris paribus.* Individuals will invest more, take more risks, and work harder when the property rights structure allows them to keep more of the monetary rewards of their investing, risk taking, and labor.

---

1. The essence of this example comes from David Friedman, *Hidden Order* (New York: Harper Collins, 1996), 70.

ECONOMICS IN...

Technology   Popular Culture   Everyday Life   The World

How Economizing on Time Can Promote Economic Growth

If a society obtains more resources, its PPF will shift to the right, and economic growth is therefore possible. One way to obtain "more resources" is through a technological change or innovation that makes it possible to use fewer resources to produce a particular good. To illustrate, suppose there are 100 units of a given resource. Currently, 10 units of the resource are needed to produce 20 units of good X and 90 units of the resource are used to produce 900 units of other goods.

Now suppose a technological change or innovation makes it possible to produce 20 units of good X with only 5 units of the resource. This means 95 units of the resource can be used to produce other goods. With more resources going to produce other goods, more "other goods" can be produced. Perhaps with 95 units of the resource going to produce other goods, 950 units of other goods can be produced. In short, a technological advance or innovation that saves resources in the production of one good makes growth possible.

With this in mind, consider the resource *time*. Usually, when people think of resources, they think of labor, capital, and natural resources. But *time* is a resource because it takes time (in much the same way that it takes labor or capital) to produce goods. Any technological advance that economizes on time frees up some time that can be used to produce other goods.

To illustrate, consider a simple, everyday example. With today's computers, people can make calculations, write books, key reports, design buildings, and much more in less time than in the past. Thus, there is more time available to do other things. Having more time to produce other things promotes economic growth.

Let's consider something that is discussed in an earlier chapter—money. Does money economize on time? Before there was money, people made barter trades. In a barter economy, finding people to trade with takes time. Money economizes on this time. Because everyone accepts money, it is easier for people to acquire the goods and services they want. Money makes trading easier. It also makes it quicker. In other words, it saves time. Money is a "technology" that saves time and promotes economic growth.

ECONOMIC FREEDOM

Some economists believe that economic freedom leads to economic growth. Countries in which people enjoy a large degree of economic freedom develop and grow more quickly than countries in which people have little economic freedom. The Heritage Foundation and the *Wall Street Journal* have joined together to produce an "index of economic freedom." This index is based on 50 independent variables divided into 10 broad categories of economic freedom, such as trade policy, monetary policy, property rights structure, regulation, fiscal burden of government, and so on. For example, a country with few tariffs and quotas (trade policy) is considered to have more economic freedom than a country with many tariffs and quotas.

The index is a number between 1 and 5. A country with a great deal of economic freedom has a low index, and a country with little economic freedom has a high index. Thus, free countries have an index between 1.00 and 1.95; mostly free countries, between 2.00 and 2.95; mostly unfree countries, between 3.00 and 3.95; and repressed countries, between 4.00 and 5.00.

The data show that economic freedom and Real GDP per capita are correlated. For the most part, the more economic freedom the people of a country experience, the higher the Real GDP per capita. Some economists believe there is a "cause and effect" relationship: greater economic freedom causes greater economic wealth.

THINKING LIKE AN ECONOMIST

When looking at the causes of economic growth, economists think in terms of both tangibles and intangibles. The tangibles include natural resources, labor, capital, and technological advances. The intangibles include the property rights structure, which directly affects individuals' incentives to apply the tangibles to the production of goods and services. No amount of natural resources, labor, capital, and technological advances can do it alone. People must be motivated to put them all together. In addition, the degree of motivation affects the result. In a world where it is easy to think that only those things that occupy physical space matter, the economist is there to remind us that we often need to look further.

POLICIES TO PROMOTE ECONOMIC GROWTH

Recall from earlier in this chapter that economic growth can occur from either (1) an inefficient level of production or (2) an efficient level of production. When the economy is situated below its PPF, demand-inducing expansionary monetary or fiscal policy is often advocated. Its objective is to increase aggregate demand enough to raise Real GDP (and lower the unemployment rate). We refer to such policies as *demand-side policies*.

There are *supply-side policies* too. These policies are designed to shift the PPF and the *LRAS* curve to the right. The best way to understand the intent of these policies is to first recall the factors that cause economic growth. These factors include natural resources, labor, increases in human capital, increases in (physical) capital investment, technological advances, property rights structure, and economic freedom. Any policies that promote these factors tend to promote economic growth. Two supply-side policies that do this are lowering taxes and reducing regulation.

Tax Policy

Some economists propose cutting taxes on such activities as working and saving in order to increase the productive capacity of the economy. For example, some economists say that if the marginal income tax rate is cut, workers will work more. As they work more, output will increase.

Other economists argue that if the tax is lowered on income placed in saving accounts, the return from saving will increase and thus the amount of saving will rise. In turn, this will make more funds available for investment, which will lead to greater capital goods growth and higher labor productivity. Ultimately, per capita Real GDP will increase.

Regulatory Policy

Some economists say that some government regulations increase the cost of production for business and, consequently, reduce output. These economists are mainly referring to the costs of regulation, which may take the form of spending hours on required paperwork, adding safety features to a factory, or buying expensive equipment to reduce pollution emissions. On net, the benefits of these policies may be greater than, less than, or equal to the costs, but certainly, sometimes the costs are evidenced in the form of less output.

Economists who believe the benefits do not warrant the costs often argue for some form of deregulation. In addition, some economists are trying to make the costs of regulation more visible to policymakers so that regulatory policy will take into account all the benefits and all the costs.

What about Industrial Policy?

Industrial policy is a deliberate government policy of "watering the green spots," or aiding those industries that are most likely to be successful in the world marketplace.

The proponents of industrial policy argue that government needs to work with business firms in the private sector to help them compete in the world marketplace.

Industrial Policy
A deliberate policy by which government "waters the green spots," or aids those industries that are most likely to be successful in the world marketplace.

In particular, they argue that government needs to identify the industries of the future—microelectronics, biotechnology, telecommunications, robotics, and computers and software—and help these industries to grow and develop now. The United States will be disadvantaged in a relative sense, they argue, if governments of other countries aid some of their industries and the United States does not.

Critics maintain that however good the intentions, industrial policy does not always turn out the way its proponents would like for three reasons. First, in deciding which industries to help, government may favor the industries with the most political influence, not the industries that it makes economic sense to help. Critics argue that elected government officials are not beyond rewarding people who have helped them win elections. Thus, industrial policy may turn out to be more a way to reward friends and injure enemies than good economic policy.

Second, critics argue that the government officials who design and implement industrial policy aren't really smart enough to know which industries will be the industries of the future. Thus, they shouldn't try to impose their uninformed guesses about the future on the economy.

Finally, critics argue that government officials who design and implement industrial policy are likely to hamper economic growth if they provide protection to some industries. For example, suppose the United States institutes an industrial policy. U.S. government officials decide that the U.S. computer industry needs to be protected from foreign competition. In their effort to aid the computer industry, they impose tariffs and quotas on foreign competitors. This action might prompt foreign nations to retaliate by placing tariffs and quotas on U.S. computers. In the end, we might simply have less free trade in the world. This would hurt consumers because they would have to pay higher prices. It would hurt the people who work for export companies because many of them would lose their jobs. And, the reduction in trade would prevent the U.S. computer industry from selling in the world marketplace. The end result would be the opposite of what the policy wants to accomplish.

Self-Test *(Answers to Self-Test questions are in the Self-Test Appendix.)*

1. "Economic growth refers to an increase in GDP." Comment.
2. Country *A* has witnessed both economic growth and a rising price level during the past two decades. What does this imply about the *LRAS* and *AD* curves?
3. How can capital investment promote economic growth?

TWO WORRIES ABOUT FUTURE ECONOMIC GROWTH

Two worries commonly crop up in discussions of economic growth. One concerns the costs of growth. Some individuals argue that more economic growth comes with more pollution, more factories (and thus fewer open spaces), more crowded cities, more emphasis on material goods and getting ahead, more rushing around, more psychological problems, more people using drugs, more suicides, and so on. They argue for less growth instead of more.

Others maintain there is no evidence that economic growth (or faster as opposed to slower economic growth) causes any or all of these problems. They argue that growth brings many positive things: more wealth, less poverty, a society that is better able to support art projects and museums, less worry in people's lives (not having enough is a huge worry), and so forth. As for pollution and the like, such "undesirables" would be diminished if the courts were to establish and strictly enforce property rights—for example, in the rivers and the air (which are often the first to become polluted).

As you can see, the debate between those who favor more growth and those who favor less is not a simple one. Economists have joined in, as have psychologists, biologists, sociologists, and many others. The debate promises to continue for a long time.

Another worry concerns the relationship between economic growth and the future availability of resources. Some people believe that continued economic and population growth threatens the very survival of the human race because this growth will hasten the time when the world runs out of resources. Inevitably, a time will come when there will be no more natural resources, no more clean air, no more pure water, and no more land for people to live on comfortably. They urge social policies that will slow growth and preserve what we have.

Critics of this position often charge that such "doomsday forecasts," as they have come to be called, are based on unrealistic assumptions, oversights, and flimsy evidence. For example, economist Julian Simon pointed out that, contrary to the doomsday forecasts, there is not an inverse relationship between population growth and per capita income growth, the incidence of famine is decreasing, we are not running out of natural resources, and if and when scarcity of natural resources becomes a problem, rising relative prices of the resources will cause individuals to conserve them and stimulate economic activity to find substitutes.

Q & A

Q: It is easy to say that as oil reserves decline, for example, the relative price of oil will rise, causing individuals to buy less oil and to search for a substitute for oil. But how can anyone be sure a good substitute will be found? Aren't the critics of the doomsday forecasts doing what they charge the doomsdayers with doing: simply making a claim instead of proving it?

A: Probably some of them do this, and we need to watch out for it. But, then, the fact that someone hasn't come up with a substitute for X doesn't mean that a substitute won't one day be found. For example, it would have been hard for anyone living in eighteenth-century America to know that the car would one day be a substitute for the horse.

NEW GROWTH THEORY

Beginning in the 1980s, economists began discussing economic growth in ways different from the way it was discussed in previous decades. More attention was placed on technology, ideas, and education. The discussion takes place under the rubric, "new growth theory."

WHAT WAS WRONG WITH THE OLD THEORY? OR, WHAT'S NEW WITH NEW GROWTH THEORY?

To talk about *new growth theory* assumes there was a theory of economic growth that came before it. Before new growth theory there was *neoclassical growth theory*. Some economists believe that new growth theory came to exist to answer some of the questions that neoclassical growth theory could not, in much the same way that a new medical theory may arise to answer questions that an old medical theory can't answer.

Neoclassical growth theory emphasized two resources—labor and capital. Within neoclassical growth theory, technology was discussed, but only in a very shallow way. Technology, it was said, was exogenous; that is, it came from outside the economic system. Stated differently, technology was something that "fell out of the sky," that was outside of our control, that we simply accepted as a given.

New growth theory holds that technology is endogenous; it is a central part of the economic system. More importantly, the technology that is developed—both the amount and the quality—depends on the amount of resources we devote to it: The more resources that go to develop technology, the more and better technology that is developed.

Paul Romer, whose name is synonymous with new growth theory, asks us to think about technology the way we think about prospecting for gold. For one

Go to *http://www.newyorkfed.org/ rmaghome/economist/stiroh/ks_newec .pdf*, and read the article. What is the opinion of the author concerning the "New Economy" (or new growth theory)? How do conventional macroeconomic concepts like Okuns' Law and the Phillips curve relate to the "New Economy Theory"?

individual, the chances of finding gold are so small that if one did find gold, it would simply be viewed as good luck. However, if there are 10,000 individuals mining for gold across a wide geographical area, the chances of finding gold would greatly improve. As with gold, so with technological advances. If one person is trying to advance technology, his or her chances of success are much smaller than if hundreds or thousands of persons are trying.

New growth theory also places emphasis on the process of discovering and formulating ideas. According to Romer, discovering and implementing new ideas is what causes economic growth.

To explain, consider the difference between *objects* and *ideas*. Objects are material, tangible things—such as natural resources and capital goods. One of the arguments often made as to why some countries are poor is that they lack objects (natural resources and capital goods). The retort to this argument is that some countries that have had very few objects have been able to grow economically. For example, in the 1950s Japan had few natural resources and capital goods (it still doesn't have an abundance of natural resources), but still it grew economically. Some economists believe that Japan grew because it had access to ideas or knowledge.

DISCOVERY, IDEAS, AND INSTITUTIONS

If the process of discovering ideas is important to economic growth, then it behooves us to figure out ways to promote the discovery process. One way is for business firms not to get locked into doing things one way and one way only. They must let their employees—from the inventor in the lab to the worker on the assembly line—try new ways of doing things. Some might carry this further: Businesses need to create an environment that is receptive to new ideas. They need to encourage their employees to try new ways of doing things.

Employee flexibility, which is a part of the discovery process, is becoming a larger part of the U.S. economy. To some degree, this is seen in the amount of time and effort firms devote to discovery in contrast to the amount of time they devote to actually manufacturing goods. Consider the computer software business. Millions of dollars and hundreds of thousands of work hours are devoted to coming up with new and useful software, whereas only a tiny fraction of the work effort and hours go into making, copying, and shipping the disks or CDs that contain the software.

EXPANDING OUR HORIZONS

Let's return to Paul Romer. Romer has said that "economic growth occurs whenever people take resources and rearrange them in ways that are more valuable."[2] Let's focus on the word "rearrange." We can think of rearranging as in "rearranging the pieces of a puzzle," or in "changing the ingredients in a recipe," or in "rearranging the way a worker goes about his or her daily work." When we rearrange anything, we do that "thing" differently. Sometimes differently is better, and sometimes it is worse.

Think of the way you study for a test. Perhaps you read the book first, then go back and underline, then study the book, and then finally study your lecture notes. Would it be better to do things differently? Often we don't know until we try.

As with studying for a test, so it is with producing a car, computer software, or a shopping mall. We do not find the better ways of doing things unless we experiment. And with repeated experiments, we often discover new and better ideas, ideas that ultimately lead to economic growth.

Consider the research and development of new medicines. Sometimes what makes a mildly effective medicine into a strongly effective medicine is a change in one or two molecules of a certain chemical. In other words, small changes—

---

2. Paul Romer, *Economic Growth*, in *The Encyclopedia of Economics*, ed. David R. Henderson (New York: Warner Books, 1993), 184.

Professors, Students, and Ideas

Paul Romer, the founder of new growth theory, emphasizes ideas and knowledge as catalysts of economic growth. Ideas and knowledge don't fall from the sky, though; they need to be produced. According to Romer, one way to produce more ideas and knowledge is by investing in research and development (R&D).

But R&D can proceed in different ways. One way, the way Romer believes is currently in operation, is what he calls the linear model of science and discovery. In a business firm, this model is applied the following way: The firm has an R&D department that is responsible for coming up with new ideas and new knowledge. After the R&D department has done its job, the rest of the firm is responsible for turning the knowledge or idea into a product that will sell. In short, the process begins with an idea, gets turned into a product (or service), and is then marketed and distributed.

According to Romer, the linear model is the wrong way to proceed. Scientists and engineers (and others) can come up with new ideas and new knowledge, but it is not just new knowledge for knowledge's sake that is needed. We need new knowledge to solve the problems that we already have. Romer advocates the use of market-like mechanisms to focus research efforts.

Romer believes that one of the problems with the present system is that universities are not producing the kinds of scientists and engineers that the private sector needs. Universities are training and producing scientists and engi-neers who are copies of their professors and are not necessarily the scientists and engineers that are needed in the marketplace. He believes there are many areas in the private sector where the demand for scientists is not being met.

Why are colleges and universities producing the "wrong" kinds of scientists and engineers? One reason, Romer argues, is that the federal government gives research monies to professors (including monies for research assistants) and then the professors hire the assistants to do what the professors want them to do. In other words, people are trained in areas that professors want them to be trained in, areas that interest the professors. But what interests professors? They are interested in research grants, many of which are given out by the federal government. Thus, professors have an incentive to respond to the research priorities of the federal government. So the federal government indirectly controls much of the research.

Romer proposes a change: Give students and businesses some control over research funds. He says, "The approach I prefer is one where you give students more control over their own funds. Instead of giving the money for student fellowship positions to the research professor in the department, why not give it to the student? That way a student could take the fellowship and say, 'I've seen the numbers. I know I can't get a job if I get a math Ph.D., but if I go into bio-informatics, there is a huge demand for people right now.' If the students could control the funds, the universities would start to cater to their demands, which would be in line with the market and the private sector's needs."[3]

The same outcome, Romer believes, would be forthcoming if businesses had some control over (federal) research monies that go to universities. Businesses would direct the monies into financing research that could help answer questions and solve problems in the private sector.

changes perhaps no one would ever think would matter—can make a large difference. There is a policy prescription that follows from this knowledge: We ought to think of ways to make the process of discovering ideas, experimenting with different ways of doing things, and developing new technology more likely. Without this, we are likely to diminish our growth potential.

Stated differently, if we believe ideas are important to economic growth, then we need to have ideas as to how to generate more ideas. Paul Romer calls these meta-ideas: Ideas about how to support the production and transmission of other ideas.

---

3. See the interview with Paul Romer by Joel Kurtzman in *Strategy and Business* (first quarter 1997): 11.

Some ways have been proposed. Perhaps we need to invest more funds in education or research and development; or perhaps we need to find ways to better protect peoples' ideas (few people will invest the time, money, and effort to discover better ideas if those ideas can easily be stolen); and so on.

In the twenty-first century, those countries with the most natural resources and capital goods aren't likely to be the ones to grow the fastest. If new growth theory is correct, it will be those countries that have discovered how to encourage and develop the most and best ideas.

Self-Test

1. What are two worries about future economic growth?
2. If technology is endogenous, what are the implications for economic growth?
3. According to new growth theory, what countries will be the countries that grow the fastest in this century?

A Reader Asks...

Can an Understanding of How Economies Grow Help Me?

This chapter explains that economic growth is largely a function of, or dependent upon, such things as the amount of labor and capital an economy employs, technological advancements, the property rights structure, and so on. Are these factors translatable into personal income growth? For example, if my objective is to "grow" my income over time, will knowing how economies grow provide me with any information on how to cultivate the growth of my income?

Let's recall the factors that are important to economic growth: (1) natural resources, (2) labor, (3) capital, (4) technological advances, (5) the property rights structure, and (6) economic freedom. In terms of personal income growth, counterparts exist for some of these factors. For example, an individual's natural talent might be the counterpart of a country's natural resources. Just as a country might be "lucky" to have plentiful natural resources, so might an individual be lucky to be born with a natural talent, especially a talent that others value highly.

Two factors directly relevant to your income growth are labor and (human) capital. We know that more labor and greater labor productivity promote economic growth. Similarly, for an individual, more labor expended and greater labor productivity often lead to income growth. How can you "expend more labor"? The answer is by working more hours. How can you increase your labor productivity? As we said earlier in the chapter, "one way is through increased education, training, and experience." In other words, acquire more *human capital.* Simply put, one way to increase your income is to work more; another way is to work better.

Finally, consider the role the property rights structure and economic freedom play in income growth. We often observe people migrating to places where the property rights structure and level of economic freedom are conducive to their personal income growth. For example, very few people in the world migrate to North Korea, but many people migrate to the United States.

Chapter Summary

Economic Growth
- Absolute real economic growth refers to an increase in Real GDP from one period to the next.
- Per capita real economic growth refers to an increase from one period to the next in per capita Real GDP, which is Real GDP divided by population.

- Economic growth can occur starting from an inefficient level of production or from an efficient level of production.

Economic Growth and the Price Level
- Usually, economists talk about economic growth as a result of a shift rightward in the PPF or the *LRAS* curve.

- Economic growth can occur along with (1) an increase in the price level, (2) a decrease in the price level, or (3) no change in the price level.

Causes of Economic Growth

- Factors related to economic growth include natural resources, labor, capital, technological advances, the property rights structure, and economic freedom.
- Countries rich in natural resources are not guaranteed economic growth, and countries poor in natural resources may grow. Nevertheless, a country with more natural resources can evidence more economic growth, *ceteris paribus*.
- An increase in the amount of labor or in the quality of labor (as measured by increases in labor productivity) can lead to economic growth.
- More capital goods can lead to increases in economic growth. Capital formation, however, is related to saving: as the saving rate increases, capital formation increases.
- Technological advances may be the result of new capital goods or of new ways of producing goods. In either case, technological advances lead to economic growth.
- Economic growth is not unrelated to the property rights structure in the country. Individuals will invest more, take more risks, and work harder—thus there is likely to be greater economic growth—when the property rights structure allows them to keep more of the fruits of their investing, risk taking, and labor, *ceteris paribus*.
- For the most part, the more economic freedom the people of a country experience, the higher the Real GDP per capita.

Policies to Promote Economic Growth

- Both demand-side and supply-side policies can be used to promote economic growth. Demand-side policies focus on shifting the *AD* curve to the right. Supply-side policies focus on shifting the *LRAS* curve to the right.
- Some economists propose cutting taxes on such activities as saving and working in order to increase the productive capacity of the economy. Other economists argue that regulations on business should be relaxed in order to increase the productive capacity of the economy.

- Industrial policy is a deliberate government policy of "watering the green spots," or aiding those industries that are most likely to be successful in the world marketplace.
- Industrial policy has both proponents and opponents. The proponents argue that the government needs to identify the industries of the future and help these industries to grow and develop now. The United States will fall behind, they argue, if it does not adopt an industrial policy while some other countries do. The opponents of industrial policy argue that the government doesn't know which industries it makes economic sense to help and that industrial policy is likely to become protectionist and politically motivated.

Two Worries about Future Economic Growth

- Two worries are often mentioned concerning future economic growth. One concerns the costs of economic growth. Specifically, with more economic growth comes more pollution, more crowded cities, more rushing around, and so on. Critics of this position point out that with more economic growth comes more wealth, less poverty, a society that is better able to support the arts, and so on. The second worry concerns the future availability of resources. Specifically, some persons argue that with more economic growth (and population growth too), the world will run out of resources. Critics of this position point out that such "doomsday forecasts" rarely materialize. They argue that higher relative prices for resources will stimulate economic activity to find substitutes.

New Growth Theory

- New growth theory holds that technology is endogenous as opposed to neoclassical growth theory that holds technology to be exogenous. When something is endogenous, it is part of the economic system, under our control or influence. When something is exogenous, it is not part of the system; it is assumed to be given to us, often mysteriously through a process that we do not understand.
- According to Paul Romer, discovering and implementing new ideas is what causes economic growth.
- Certain institutions can promote the discovery of new ideas, and therefore promote economic growth.

Key Terms and Concepts

Absolute Real Economic Growth   Per Capita Real Economic Growth   Industrial Policy

Economic facts, actions, and changes create ripples that move away from their point of origin. Eventually, these ripples can intersect your life and have an effect on you. Consider the following example.

Suppose that, encouraged by the government's emphasis on new growth theory, an educator devises a new and better way to teach mathematics to elementary, junior, and high school students. Consequently, students learn more mathematics, which leads to a rise in overall education skills. Because workers are better educated, labor productivity rises. As a result of *higher labor productivity, Real GDP rises. Real GDP rises by a greater percentage than the growth in population, so per capita Real GDP rises too. Thus, the "average" person consumes more goods and services than previously. Thus, there is a connection between an economic theory and your consumption of goods and services—an economic connection to you.*

Based on the material in this chapter, identify other ways in which economic facts, actions, and changes create ripples that eventually affect you.

1. Why might per capita real economic growth be a more useful measurement than absolute real economic growth?
2. What does it mean to say "natural resources are neither a sufficient nor a necessary factor for growth"?
3. How do we compute (average) labor productivity?
4. Is it possible to have more workers working, producing a higher Real GDP, at the same time that labor productivity is declining? Explain your answer.
5. How does an increased saving rate relate to increased labor productivity?
6. Economic growth doesn't simply depend on having more natural resources, more or higher-quality labor, more capital, and so on; it depends on people's incentives to put these resources together to produce goods and services. Do you agree or disagree? Explain your answer.
7. It is possible to promote economic growth from either the demand side or the supply side. Do you agree or disagree? Explain your answer.
8. What is *new* about new growth theory?
9. How does discovering and implementing new ideas cause economic growth?
10. Explain how each of the following relates to economic growth: (a) technological advance, (b) labor productivity, (c) natural resources, (d) education.
11. Explain how free trade is a form of technology.
12. What does an understanding of relative prices have to do with doomsday forecasts?

1. The economy of country X is currently growing at 2 percent a year. How many years will it take to double the Real GDP of country X?
2. Diagrammatically represent each of the following: (a) economic growth from an inefficient level of production and (b) economic growth from an efficient level of production.
3. Diagrammatically represent each of the following: (a) economic growth with a stable price level, (b) economic growth with a rising price level, and (c) economic growth with a falling price level.

Go to *http://www.un.org/esa/*. Click on "Sustainable Development," then on "Agenda 21," and finally on "The Rio Declaration on Environment and Development."

1. Read Principles 2, 3, 4, and 5. What limits and requirements are put on a nation's plans for economic growth?
2. Read Principle 8. Is this goal consistent with the ideals and workings of a market-based economy? Do you think government should try to reduce "unsustainable" consumption? What is an example of a "demographic" policy?
3. Is there a principle that calls for industrial policy? If so, which principle(s)?

4. Can technology create a new future (See Principle 9)? To an economist, what incentives are needed for business to adopt new technology? Is there any recognition in the principles of these incentives?
5. Does the United Nations propose that environmental concerns take precedence over the economic benefits of free trade? Which principles relate to environmental concerns?
6. Find two principles that mention externalities.
7. Read Principles 24 and 25. Do you agree with the principles? Explain your answer.

Log on to the Arnold Xtra! Web site now (*http://arnoldxtra.swcollege.com*) for additional learning resources such as practice quizzes, help with graphing, video clips, and current event applications.

ch.18

INTERNATIONAL TRADE

Economics is about trade, and trade crosses boundaries. People do not trade exclusively with people who live in their city, state, or country. They trade with people in other countries, too. No doubt, many of the goods you consume are produced in other countries. This chapter examines international trade and the prohibitions that are sometimes placed on it.

Chapter Road Map

We state in an early chapter that economics is largely

about trade, and we have discussed the various aspects of trade and

its economic implications. But mainly, we have examined domestic trade—trade

between people who live within the United States. In this chapter, we extend our discussion

of trade to the rest of the world. We discuss international trade.

As shown in the chapter road map, we examine two main topics in international trade. First, we answer the question of why people in different countries trade, which leads us to the law of comparative advantage. Second, we discuss the effects of tariffs and quotas, two of the major restrictions sometimes placed on international trade.

INTERNATIONAL TRADE THEORY

International trade exists for the same reasons that trade at any level exists. Individuals trade to make themselves better off. Pat and Zach, both of whom live in Cincinnati, Ohio, trade because they both value something the other has more than they value some of their own possessions. On an international scale, Elaine in the United States trades with Cho in China because Cho has something that Elaine wants and Elaine has something that Cho wants.

Obviously, different countries have different terrains, climates, resources, skills, and so on. It follows that some countries will be able to produce some goods that other countries cannot produce or can produce only at extremely high costs.

For example, Hong Kong has no oil, and Saudi Arabia has a large supply. Bananas do not grow easily in the United States, but they flourish in Honduras. Americans could grow bananas if they used hothouses, but it is cheaper for Americans to buy bananas from Hondurans than to produce bananas themselves.

Major U.S. exports include automobiles, computers, aircraft, corn, wheat, soybeans, scientific instruments, coal, and plastic materials. Major imports include petroleum, automobiles, clothing, iron and steel, office machines, footwear, fish, coffee, and diamonds. Some of the countries of the world that are major exporters are the United States, Germany, Japan, France, and the United Kingdom. These same countries are some of the major importers in the world too.

HOW DO COUNTRIES KNOW WHAT TO TRADE?

To explain how countries know what to trade, we need to discuss the concept of *comparative advantage,* an economic concept first discussed in Chapter 2. Here is a simple model.

Comparative Advantage

Assume a two country–two good world. The countries are the United States and Japan, and the goods are food and clothing. Both countries can produce the two goods in the four different combinations listed in Exhibit 1. For example, the United States can produce 90 units of food and 0 units of clothing, or 60 units of food and 10 units of clothing, or another combination. Japan can produce 15 units of food and 0 units of clothing, or 10 units of food and 5 units of clothing, or another combination.

Suppose the United States is producing and consuming the two goods in the combination represented by point *B* on its production possibilities frontier, and Japan is producing and consuming the combination of the two goods represented by point *B'* on its production possibilities frontier. In other words, in this case, neither of the two countries is specializing in the production of one of the two goods, nor are the two countries trading with each other. We call this the *no specialization–no trade (NS-NT) case.* (See column 1 in Exhibit 2.)

Now suppose the United States and Japan decide to specialize in the production of a specific good and to trade with each other, called the *specialization-trade (S-T) case.* Will the two countries be made better off through specialization and trade? A numerical example will help answer this question. But, first, we need to find the answers to two other questions: What good should the United States specialize in producing? What good should Japan specialize in producing?

The general answer to both these questions is the same: *Countries specialize in the production of the good in which they have a comparative advantage.* A country has a **comparative advantage** in the production of a good when it can produce the good at lower opportunity cost than another country can.

For example, in the United States, the opportunity cost of producing 1 unit of clothing is 3 units of food (for every 10 units of clothing it produces, it forfeits 30 units of food). So the opportunity cost of producing 1 unit of food is $\frac{1}{3}$ unit of clothing. In Japan, the opportunity cost of producing 1 unit of clothing is 1 unit of food (for every 5 units of clothing it produces, it forfeits 5 units of food). To

Comparative Advantage
The situation where a country can produce a good at lower opportunity cost than another country can.

exhibit 1

Production Possibilities in Two Countries

The United States and Japan can produce the two goods in the combinations shown. Initially, the United States is at point B on its PPF and Japan is at point B' on its PPF. Both countries can be made better off by specializing in and trading the good in which each has a comparative advantage.

United States			Japan		
Points on Production Possibilities Frontier	Food	Clothing	Points on Production Possibilities Frontier	Food	Clothing
A	90	0	A'	15	0
B	60	10	B'	10	5
C	30	20	C'	5	10
D	0	30	D'	0	15

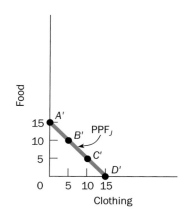

recap, in the United States, the situation is $1C = 3F$, or $1F = \frac{1}{3}C$; in Japan the situation is $1C = 1F$, or $1F = 1C$.

The United States can produce food at a lower opportunity cost ($\frac{1}{3}C$ as opposed to $1C$ in Japan), whereas Japan can produce clothing at a lower opportunity cost ($1F$ as opposed to $3F$ in the United States). Thus, the United States has a comparative advantage in food, and Japan has a comparative advantage in clothing.

Suppose the two countries specialize in the production of the good in which they have a comparative advantage. In other words, the United States specializes in the production of food (producing 90 units), and Japan specializes in the production of clothing (producing 15 units). In Exhibit 1, the United States locates at point A on its PPF, and Japan locates at point D' on its PPF. (See column 2 in Exhibit 2.)

Settling on the Terms of Trade

After they have determined which good to specialize in producing, the two countries must settle on the terms of trade, that is, how much food to trade for how much clothing. Recall that the United States faces the following situation: For every 30 units of food it does not produce, it can produce 10 units of clothing, as shown in Exhibit 1. Thus, 3 units of food have an opportunity cost of 1 unit of clothing ($3F = 1C$), or 1 unit of food has a cost of $\frac{1}{3}$ unit of clothing ($1F = \frac{1}{3}C$). Meanwhile, Japan faces the following situation: For every 5 units of food it does not produce, it can produce 5 units of clothing. Thus, 1 unit of food has an opportunity cost of 1 unit of clothing ($1F = 1C$). Recapping, for the United States, $3F = 1C$, and for Japan, $1F = 1C$.

With these cost ratios, it would seem likely that both countries could agree on terms of trade that specify $2F = 1C$. The United States would prefer to give up 2 units of food instead of 3 units for 1 unit of clothing, whereas Japan would prefer to give up 1 unit of clothing and get 2 units of food instead of only 1 unit.

Country	No Specialization– No Trade (NS-NT) Case		Specialization-Trade (S-T) Case			
	(1) Production and Consumption in the NS-NT Case		(2) Production in the S-T Case	(3) Exports (−) Imports (+) Terms of Trade Are $2F = 1C$	(4) Consumption in the S-T Case (2) + (3)	(5) Gains from Specialization and Trade (4) − (1)
United States						
Food	60 }	Point B in	90 }	−20	70	10
Clothing	10 }	Exhibit 1	0 }	+10	10	0
Japan						
Food	10 }	Point B' in	0 }	+20	20	10
Clothing	5 }	Exhibit 1	15 }	−10	5	0

(For US S-T Case: 90 / 0 = Point A in Exhibit 1. For Japan S-T Case: 0 / 15 = Point D' in Exhibit 1.)

Suppose the two countries agree to the terms of trade of $2F = 1C$ and trade, in absolute amounts, 20 units of food for 10 units of clothing. (See column 3 in Exhibit 2.)

Results of the Specialization-Trade (S-T) Case

Now the United States produces 90 units of food and trades 20 units to Japan, receiving 10 units of clothing in exchange. It consumes 70 units of food and 10 units of clothing. Japan produces 15 units of clothing and trades 10 to the United States, receiving 20 units of food in exchange. It consumes 5 units of clothing and 20 units of food. (See column 4 in Exhibit 2.)

Comparing the consumption levels in both countries in the two cases, the United States and Japan each consume 10 more units of food and no less clothing in the specialization-trade case than in the no specialization–no trade case (column 5 in Exhibit 2). We conclude that a country gains by specializing in producing and trading the good in which it has a comparative advantage.

Q & A

Q: Specialization and trade appear to allow a country's inhabitants to consume at a level beyond its production possibilities frontier. Is this correct?

A: Yes, that is correct. To see this, look at the PPF for the United States in Exhibit 1. In the NS-NT case, the United States consumes 60 units of food and 10 units of clothing—that is, the United States consumes at point B on its PPF. In the S-T case, however, it consumes 70 units of food and 10 units of clothing. A point that represents this combination of the two goods is beyond the country's PPF.

HOW DO COUNTRIES KNOW WHEN THEY HAVE A COMPARATIVE ADVANTAGE?

Government officials of a country do not analyze pages of cost data to determine what their country should specialize in producing and then trade. Countries do not plot production possibilities frontiers on graph paper or calculate opportunity costs. Instead, it is individuals' desire to earn a dollar, a peso, or a euro that determines the pattern of international trade. The desire to earn a profit determines what a country specializes in and trades.

Take the case of Henri, an enterprising Frenchman who visits the United States. Henri observes that beef is relatively cheap in the United States (compared with the price in France) and perfume is relatively expensive. Noticing the price differences for beef and perfume between his country and the United States, he decides to buy some perfume in France, bring it to the United States, and sell it for the relatively higher U.S. price. With his profits from the perfume transaction,

exhibit 2

Both Countries Gain from Specialization and Trade
Column 1: Both the United States and Japan operate independently of each other. The United States produces and consumes 60 units of food and 10 units of clothing. Japan produces and consumes 10 units of food and 5 units of clothing. Column 2: The United States specializes in the production of food; Japan specializes in the production of clothing. Column 3: The United States and Japan agree to the terms of trade of 2 units of food for 1 unit of clothing. They actually trade 20 units of food for 10 units of clothing. Column 4: Overall, the United States consumes 70 units of food and 10 units of clothing. Japan consumes 20 units of food and 5 units of clothing. Column 5: Consumption levels are higher for both the United States and Japan in the S-T case than in the NS-NT case.

ECONOMICS IN...

Dividing Up the Work

John and Veronica, husband and wife, have divided up their household tasks the following way: John usually does all the lawn work, fixes the cars, and does the dinner dishes, while Veronica cleans the house, cooks the meals, and does the laundry. Why have John and Veronica divided up the household tasks the way they have? Some sociologists might suggest that John and Veronica have divided up the tasks along gender lines—men have for years done the lawn work, fixed the cars, and so on, and women have for years cleaned the house, cooked the meals, and so on. In other words, John is doing "man's work," and Veronica is doing "woman's work."

Well, maybe, but that leaves unanswered the question of why certain work became "man's work" and other work became "woman's work." Moreover, it doesn't explain why John and Veronica don't split every task evenly. In other words, why doesn't John clean half the house and Veronica clean half the house? Why doesn't Veronica mow the lawn on the second and fourth week of every month and John mow the lawn every first and third week of the month?

The law of comparative advantage may be the answer to all our questions. To illustrate, suppose we consider two tasks, cleaning the house and mowing the lawn. The following table shows how long John and Veronica take to complete the two tasks individually.

	Time to Clean the House	Time to Mow the Lawn
John	120 minutes	50 minutes
Veronica	60 minutes	100 minutes

Here is the opportunity cost of each task for each person.

	Opportunity Cost of Cleaning the House	Opportunity Cost of Mowing the Lawn
John	2.40 mowed lawns	0.42 clean houses
Veronica	0.60 mowed lawns	1.67 clean houses

In other words, John has a comparative advantage in mowing the lawn and Veronica has a comparative advantage in cleaning the house.

Now let's compare two settings. In setting 1, John and Veronica each do half of each task. In setting 2, John only mows the lawn and Veronica only cleans the house.

In setting 1, John spends 60 minutes cleaning half of the house and 25 minutes mowing half of the lawn for a total of 85 minutes; Veronica spends 30 minutes cleaning half of the house and 50 minutes mowing half of the lawn for a total of 80 minutes. The total time spent by Veronica and John cleaning the house and mowing the lawn is 165 minutes.

In setting 2, John spends 50 minutes mowing the lawn and Veronica spends 60 minutes cleaning the house. The total time spent by Veronica and John cleaning the house and mowing the lawn is 110 minutes.

In which setting, 1 or 2, are Veronica and John better off? John works 85 minutes in setting 1 and 50 minutes in setting 2, so he is better off in setting 2. Veronica works 80 minutes in setting 1 and 60 minutes in setting 2, so Veronica is better off in setting 2. Together, John and Veronica spend 55 fewer minutes in setting 2 than in setting 1. Getting the job done in 55 fewer minutes is the benefit of specializing in various duties around the house. Given our numbers, we would expect that John will mow the lawn (and nothing else) and Veronica will clean the house (and nothing else).

he buys beef in the United States, ships it to France, and sells it for the relatively higher French price. Obviously, Henri is buying low and selling high. He buys a good in the country where it is cheap and sells it in the country where the good is expensive.

What are the consequences of Henri's activities? First, he is earning a profit. The larger the price differences in the two goods between the two countries and the more he reshuffles goods between countries, the more profit Henri earns.

Second, Henri's activities are moving each country toward its comparative advantage. The United States ends up exporting beef to France, and France ends up exporting perfume to the United States. Just as the pure theory predicts, individuals in the two countries specialize in and trade the good in which they have a comparative advantage. The outcome is brought about spontaneously through the actions of individuals trying to make themselves better off; they are simply trying to gain through trade.

Self-Test *(Answers to Self-Test questions are in the Self-Test Appendix.)*

1. Suppose the United States can produce 120 units of X at an opportunity cost of 20 units of Y, and Great Britain can produce 40 units of X at an opportunity cost of 80 units of Y. Identify favorable terms of trade for the two countries.

2. If a country can produce more of all goods than any other country, would it benefit from specializing and trading? Explain your answer.

3. Do government officials analyze data to determine what their country can produce at a comparative advantage?

TRADE RESTRICTIONS

International trade theory shows that countries gain from free international trade, that is, from specializing in the production of the goods in which they have a comparative advantage and trading these goods for other goods. In the real world, however, there are numerous types of trade restrictions, which raises the question: If countries gain from international trade, why are there trade restrictions?

WHY ARE THERE TRADE RESTRICTIONS IN THE REAL WORLD?

The previous section explains that specialization and international trade benefit individuals in different countries. But this benefit occurs on net. Every individual person may not gain. Suppose Pam Dickson lives and works in the United States making clock radios. She produces and sells 12,000 clock radios per year at a price of $40 each. As the situation stands, there is no international trade. Individuals in other countries who make clock radios do not sell their clock radios in the United States.

Then one day, the U.S. market is opened to clock radios from Japan. It appears that the Japanese manufacturers have a comparative advantage in the production of clock radios. They sell their clock radios in the United States for $25 each. Pam realizes that she cannot compete at this price. Her sales drop to such a degree that she goes out of business. Thus, the introduction of international trade in this instance has harmed Pam personally. This example raises the issue of the distributional effects of trade. Using the tools of supply and demand, we concentrate on two groups: U.S. consumers and U.S. producers. But first let's consider consumers' and producers' surplus.

CONSUMERS' AND PRODUCERS' SURPLUS

The concepts of consumers' and producers' surplus are first discussed in Chapter 2. These two concepts can help determine the effects of trade restrictions on consumers and producers. Let's start with a brief review.

Consumers' surplus is the difference between the maximum price a buyer is willing and able to pay for a good or service and the price actually paid.

Consumers' surplus = Maximum buying price − Price paid

Consumers' surplus is a dollar measure of the benefit gained by being able to purchase a unit of a good for less than one is willing to pay for it. For example, if Yakov would have paid $10 to see the movie at the Cinemax but paid only $4, his consumer surplus is $6. Consumers' surplus is the consumers' net gain from trade.

Producers' surplus (or sellers' surplus) is the difference between the price sellers receive for a good and the minimum or lowest price for which they would have sold the good.

$$\text{Producers' surplus} = \text{Price received} - \text{Minimum selling price}$$

Producers' surplus is a dollar measure of the benefit gained by being able to sell a unit of output for more than one is willing to sell it. For example, if Joan sold her knit sweaters for $24 each but would have sold them for as low as (but no lower than) $14 each, her producer surplus is $10 per sweater. Producers' surplus is the producers' net gain from trade.

Both consumers' and producers' surplus are represented in Exhibit 3. In part (a), consumers' surplus is represented by the shaded triangle. This triangle includes the area under the demand curve and above the equilibrium price. In part (b), producers' surplus is represented by the shaded triangle. This triangle includes the area above the supply curve and under the equilibrium price.

HOW IS TRADE RESTRICTED?

There are numerous ways to restrict free trade. Tariffs and quotas are two of the more commonly used methods.

Tariffs

Tariff
A tax on imports.

A **tariff** is a tax on imports. The primary effect of a tariff is to raise the price of the imported good for the domestic consumer. Exhibit 4 illustrates the effects of a tariff.

The world price for cars is P_W, as shown in Exhibit 4a. At this price in the domestic (U.S.) market, U.S. consumers buy Q_2 cars, as shown in part (b). They buy Q_1 from U.S. producers and the difference between Q_2 and Q_1 $(Q_2 - Q_1)$ from foreign producers. In other words, U.S. imports at P_W are $Q_2 - Q_1$.

What are consumers' and producers' surplus in this situation? Consumers' surplus is the area under the demand curve and above the world price, P_W. This is areas $1 + 2 + 3 + 4 + 5 + 6$. Producers' surplus is the area above the supply curve and below the world price, P_W. This is area 7. (See Exhibit 4b.)

Consumers' and Producers' Surplus
(a) Consumers' surplus. As the shaded area indicates, the difference between the maximum or highest amount consumers would be willing to pay and the price they actually pay is consumers' surplus. (b) Producers' surplus. As the shaded area indicates, the difference between the price sellers receive for the good and the minimum or lowest price they would be willing to sell the good for is producers' surplus.

(a)
Consumers' Surplus

(b)
Producers' Surplus

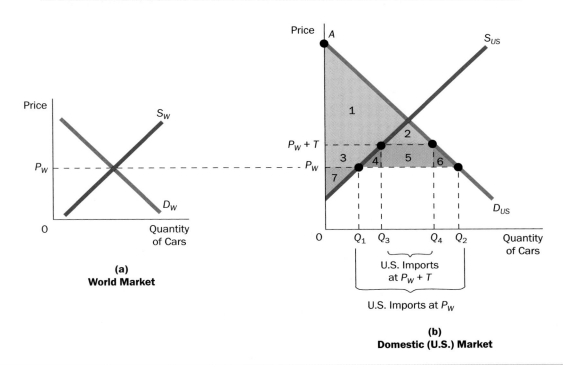

	Consumers' Surplus	Producers' Surplus	Government Tariff Revenue
Free Trade (No tariff)	$1 + 2 + 3 + 4 + 5 + 6$	7	None
Tariff	$1 + 2$	$3 + 7$	5
Loss or Gain	$-(3 + 4 + 5 + 6)$	$+3$	$+5$

Result of Tariff = Loss to consumers + Gain to producers + Tariff revenue
= $-(3 + 4 + 5 + 6)$ $+ 3$ $+ 5$
= $-(4 + 6)$

(a)
World Market

(b)
Domestic (U.S.) Market

exhibit 4

The Effects of a Tariff
A tariff raises the price of cars from P_W to $P_W + T$, decreases consumers' surplus, increases producers' surplus, and generates tariff revenue. Because consumers lose more than producers and government gain, there is a net loss due to the tariff.

Now suppose a tariff is imposed. The price for imported cars in the U.S. market rises to $P_W + T$ (the world price plus the tariff). At this price, U.S. consumers buy Q_4 cars: Q_3 from U.S. producers and $Q_4 - Q_3$ from foreign producers. U.S. imports are $Q_4 - Q_3$, which is a smaller number of imports than at the pretariff price. An effect of tariffs, then, is to reduce imports. What are consumers' and producers' surplus equal to after the tariff has been imposed? At price $P_W + T$, consumers' surplus is areas $1 + 2$ and producers' surplus is areas $3 + 7$.

Notice that consumers receive more consumers' surplus when tariffs do not exist and less when they do exist. In our example, consumers received areas $1 + 2 + 3 + 4 + 5 + 6$ in consumers' surplus when the tariff did not exist but only areas $1 + 2$ when the tariff did exist. Because of the tariff, consumers' surplus was reduced by an amount equal to areas $3 + 4 + 5 + 6$.

Producers, though, receive less producers' surplus when tariffs do not exist, and more when they do exist. In our example, producers received producers' surplus equal to area 7 when the tariff did not exist, but they received producers' surplus equal to areas $3 + 7$ with the tariff. Because of the tariff, producers' surplus increased by an amount equal to area 3.

The government collects tariff revenue equal to area 5. This area is obtained by multiplying the number of imports ($Q_4 - Q_3$) times the tariff, which is the difference between $P_W + T$ and P_W.[1]

---

1. For example, if the tariff is $100 and the number of imports is 50,000, then the tariff revenue is $5 million.

In conclusion, the effects of the tariff are a decrease in consumers' surplus, an increase in producers' surplus, and tariff revenue for government. Because the loss to consumers (areas $3 + 4 + 5 + 6$) is greater than the gain to producers (area 3) plus the gain to government (area 5), it follows that *a tariff results in a net loss.* The net loss is areas $4 + 6$.

Quotas

A **quota** is a legal limit on the amount of a good that may be imported. For example, the government may decide to allow no more than 100,000 foreign cars to be imported, or 10 million barrels of OPEC oil, or 30,000 Japanese television sets. A quota reduces the supply of a good and raises the price of imported goods for domestic consumers (Exhibit 5).

Once again, we consider the situation in the U.S. car market. At a price of P_W (established in the world market for cars), U.S. consumers buy Q_1 cars from U.S. producers and $Q_2 - Q_1$ cars from foreign producers. Consumers' surplus is equal to areas $1 + 2 + 3 + 4 + 5 + 6$. Producers' surplus is equal to area 7.

Suppose now that the U.S. government sets a quota equal to $Q_4 - Q_3$. Because this is the number of foreign cars U.S. consumers imported when the tariff was imposed (see Exhibit 4), the price of cars rises to P_Q in Exhibit 5 (which is equal to $P_W + T$ in Exhibit 4). At P_Q, consumers' surplus is equal to areas $1 + 2$

	Consumers' Surplus	Producers' Surplus	Revenue of Importers
Free Trade (No quota)	$1 + 2 + 3 + 4 + 5 + 6$	7	8
Quota	$1 + 2$	$3 + 7$	$5 + 8$
Loss or Gain	$-(3 + 4 + 5 + 6)$	$+3$	$+5$

Result of quota	=	Loss to consumers	+ Gain to producers	+ Gain to importers
	=	$-(3 + 4 + 5 + 6)$	$+3$	$+5$
	=	$-(4 + 6)$		

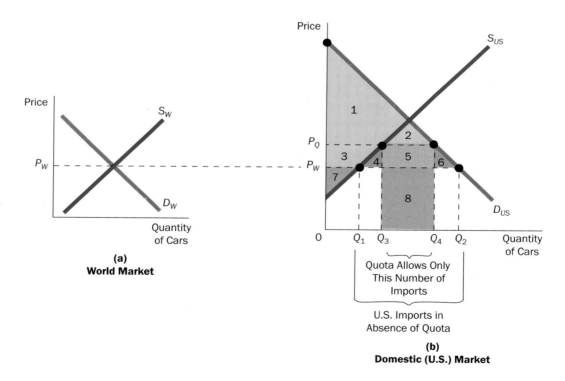

(a)
World Market

(b)
Domestic (U.S.) Market

and producers' surplus is areas 3 + 7. The decrease in consumers' surplus due to the quota is equal to areas 3 + 4 + 5 + 6; the increase in producers' surplus is equal to area 3.

But what about area 5? Is this area transferred to government, as was the case when a tariff was imposed? No, it isn't. This area represents the additional revenue earned by the importers (and sellers) of $Q_4 - Q_3$. Look at it this way: Before the quota, importers were importing $Q_2 - Q_1$, but only part of this total amount—$Q_4 - Q_3$—is relevant here. The reason only $Q_4 - Q_3$ is relevant is because this is the amount of imports now that the quota has been established. So, what dollar amount did the importers receive for $Q_4 - Q_3$ before the quota was established? The answer is $P_W \times (Q_4 - Q_3)$ or area 8. Because of the quota, the price rises to P_Q and they now receive $P_Q \times (Q_4 - Q_3)$ or areas 5 + 8. The difference between the total revenues on $Q_4 - Q_3$ with a quota and without a quota is area 5.

In conclusion, the effects of a quota are a decrease in consumers' surplus, an increase in producers' surplus, and an increase in total revenue for the importers who sell the allowed number of imported units. Because the loss to consumers (areas 3 + 4 + 5 + 6) is greater than the increase in producers' surplus (area 3) plus the gain to importers (area 5), there is a *net loss as a result of the quota*. The net loss is equal to areas 4 + 6.[2]

THINKING LIKE AN ECONOMIST

International trade often becomes a battleground between economics and politics. The simple tools of supply and demand and consumers' and producers' surplus show that there are net gains from free trade. On the whole, tariffs and quotas make living standards lower than they would be if free trade were permitted.

On the other side, though, are the realities of business and politics. Domestic producers may advocate quotas and tariffs to make themselves better off, giving little thought to the negative effects felt by foreign producers or domestic consumers.

Perhaps the battle over international trade comes down to this: Policies are largely advocated, argued, and lobbied for based more on their distributional effects than on their aggregate or overall effects. On an aggregate level, free trade produces a net gain for society, whereas restricted trade produces a net loss. But economists understand that just because free trade in the aggregate produces a net gain, it does not necessarily follow that every single person benefits more from free trade than from restricted trade. We have just shown how a subset of the population (producers) gains more, in a particular instance, from restricted trade than from free trade. In short, economists realize that the crucial question in determining real-world policies is more often "How does it affect me?" than "How does it affect us?"

IF FREE TRADE RESULTS IN NET GAIN, WHY DO NATIONS SOMETIMES RESTRICT TRADE?

Based on the analysis in this chapter so far, the case for free trade (no tariffs or quotas) appears to be a strong one. The case for free trade has not gone unchallenged, however. Some persons maintain that at certain times, free trade should be restricted or suspended. In almost all cases, they argue that it is in the best interest of the public or country as a whole to do so. In short, they advance a

---

2. It is perhaps incorrect to imply that government receives nothing from a quota. Although it receives nothing directly, it may gain indirectly. Economists generally argue that because government officials are likely to be the persons who will decide which importers will get to satisfy the quota, they will naturally be lobbied by importers. Thus, government officials will likely receive something, if only dinner at an expensive restaurant while the lobbyist makes his or her pitch. In short, in the course of the lobbying, resources will be spent by lobbyists as they curry favor with those government officials or politicians who have the power to decide who gets to sell the limited number of imported goods. In economics, lobbyists' activities geared toward obtaining a special privilege are referred to as rent seeking.

Go to *http://www.ustr.gov/*, and click on "About USTR." Select "USTR's Role." What is the official U.S. trade policy? Click on the "Back" button and then on "Press Releases." Select the most recent month and year. Find a press release that deals with a specific country and click the "HTML" link. Does the press release deal with a trade restriction? If so, what kind of trade restriction? What is the content of the press release?

public interest argument. Other persons contend that the public interest argument is only superficial; down deep, they say, it is a special interest argument clothed in pretty words. As you might guess, the debate between the two groups is often heated.

The following paragraphs describe some arguments that have been advanced for trade restrictions.

The National-Defense Argument

It is often stated that certain industries—such as aircraft, petroleum, chemicals, and weapons—are necessary to the national defense. Suppose the United States has a comparative advantage in the production of wheat and country X has a comparative advantage in the production of weapons. Should the United States specialize in the production of wheat and then trade wheat to country X in exchange for weapons? Many Americans would answer no. It is too dangerous, they maintain, to leave weapons production to another country.

The national-defense argument may have some validity. But even valid arguments may be abused. Industries that are not really necessary to the national defense may maintain otherwise. In the past, the national-defense argument has been used by some firms in the following industries: pens, pottery, peanuts, papers, candles, thumbtacks, tuna fishing, and pencils.

The Infant-Industry Argument

Alexander Hamilton, the first U.S. secretary of the treasury, argued that "infant" or new industries often need to be protected from older, established foreign competitors until they are mature enough to compete on an equal basis. Today, some persons voice the same argument. The infant-industry argument is clearly an argument for temporary protection. Critics charge, however, that after an industry is protected from foreign competition, removing the protection is almost impossible. The once infant industry will continue to maintain that it isn't old enough to go it alone. Critics of the infant-industry argument say that political realities make it unlikely that a benefit once bestowed will be removed.

Finally, the infant-industry argument, like the national-defense argument, may be abused. It may well be that all new industries, whether they could currently compete successfully with foreign producers or not, would argue for protection on infant-industry grounds.

The Antidumping Argument

Dumping is the sale of goods abroad at a price below their cost and below the price charged in the domestic market. If a French firm sells wine in the United States for a price below the cost of producing the wine and below the price charged in France, it is said to be dumping wine in the United States. Critics of dumping maintain that it is an unfair trade practice that puts domestic producers of substitute goods at a disadvantage.

In addition, critics charge that dumpers seek only to penetrate a market and drive out domestic competitors; then they will raise prices. However, some economists point to the infeasibility of this strategy. After the dumpers have driven out their competition and raised prices, their competition is likely to return. The dumpers, in turn, would have obtained only a string of losses (owing to their selling below cost) for their efforts. Opponents of the antidumping argument also point out that domestic consumers benefit from dumping because they pay lower prices.

The Foreign-Export-Subsidies Argument

Some governments subsidize the firms that export goods. If a country offers a below-market (interest rate) loan to a company, it is often argued that the government subsidizes the production of the good the firm produces. If, in turn, the

Dumping
The sale of goods abroad at a price below their cost and below the price charged in the domestic market.

firm exports the good to a foreign country, that country's producers of substitute goods call foul. They complain that the foreign firm has been given an unfair advantage that they should be protected against.[3]

Others say that one should not turn one's back on a gift (in the form of lower prices). If foreign governments want to subsidize their exports, and thus give a gift to foreign consumers at the expense of their own taxpayers, then the recipients should not complain. Of course, the recipients are usually not the ones who are complaining. Usually, the ones complaining are the domestic producers who can't sell their goods at as high a price because of the gift domestic consumers are receiving from foreign governments.

The Low-Foreign-Wages Argument

It is sometimes argued that American producers can't compete with foreign producers because American producers pay high wages to their workers and foreign producers pay low wages to their workers. The American producers insist that free trade must be restricted or they will be ruined. However, the argument overlooks the reason American wages are high and foreign wages are low in the first place: productivity. High productivity and high wages are usually linked, as are low productivity and low wages. If an American worker, who receives $20 per hour, can produce (on average) 100 units of X per hour, working with numerous capital goods, then the cost per unit may be lower than when a foreign worker, who receives $2 per hour, produces (on average) 5 units of X per hour, working by hand. In short, a country's high-wage disadvantage may be offset by its productivity advantage; a country's low-wage advantage may be offset by its productivity disadvantage. High wages do not necessarily mean high costs when productivity (and the costs of nonlabor resources) is included.

The Saving-Domestic-Jobs Argument

Sometimes the argument against completely free trade is made in terms of saving domestic jobs. Actually, we have already discussed this argument in its different guises. For example, the low-foreign-wages argument is one form of it. That argument continues along this line: If domestic producers cannot compete with foreign producers because foreign producers pay low wages and domestic producers pay high wages, domestic producers will go out of business and domestic jobs will be lost. The foreign-export-subsidies argument is another form of this argument. Its proponents generally state that if foreign-government subsidies give a competitive edge to foreign producers, not only will domestic producers fail but as a result of their failure, domestic jobs will be lost. Critics of the saving-domestic-jobs argument (in all its guises) often argue that if a domestic producer is being outcompeted by foreign producers and domestic jobs in a particular industry are being lost as a result, the world market is signaling that those labor resources could be put to better use in an industry in which the country holds a comparative advantage.

WHAT PRICE JOBS?

Suppose the U.S. government imposes a tariff on imported good X. As a result, the domestic producers of good X sell their goods for higher prices, receive higher producers' surplus, and are generally better off. Some of the domestic workers who produce good X are better off too. Perhaps without the tariff on imports of good X, some of them would have lost their jobs.

Such scenarios raise two important questions: How many domestic jobs in the firms that produce good X are saved because of the tariff? How much do

---

3. Words are important in this debate. For example, domestic producers who claim that foreign governments have subsidized foreign firms say that they are not asking for *economic protectionism*, but only for *retaliation*, or *reciprocity*, or simply *tit-for-tat*—words that have less negative connotation than the words their opponents use.

ECONOMICS IN...

Immigration and Wages

Many immigrants come to the United States each year. Immigrants who have the permission of the U.S. government to come to the country are officially referred to as documented immigrants. Immigrants who do not have the permission of the U.S. government are officially referred to as undocumented immigrants. During the 1990s, more than 9 million documented immigrants were admitted into the country and the undocumented immigrant population increased by about 5 million. Demographers expect the number of both documented and undocumented immigrants to the United States to rise in the near future.

Some residents of the United States argue that increased immigration will cause wages in the United States to decline. Their argument is based on simple supply and demand analysis: increased immigration leads to a greater supply of workers and lower wages.

There is little doubt that increased immigration will affect the supply of labor in the country. But it will affect the demand for labor too. The demand for labor is a derived demand— derived from the demand for the product that labor produces. With increased immigration, there will be more people living in the United States. A larger population translates into higher demand for food, housing, clothes, entertainment services, and so on. A higher demand for these goods translates into a higher demand for the workers who produce these goods.

In summary, increased immigration will affect both the supply of and demand for labor. What will be the effect on wages? It depends on whether the increase in the demand is greater than, less than, or equal to the increase in supply. If demand increases by more than supply, wages will rise; if supply increases by more than demand, wages will fall; if demand rises by the same amount as supply rises, wages will not change.

---

consumers have to pay in higher prices to save these jobs? Economists are interested in answering such questions. Here are a few answers for different industries at different times:

- In 1977, tariffs and quotas were imposed on imports of foreign footwear. An estimated 21,000 domestic jobs were protected in the domestic footwear industry as a result. The average worker in the industry earned $8,340 (in 1980 dollars). However, it cost domestic consumers $77,714 for each domestic footwear job protected.

- In 1981, **"voluntary" export restraints (VERs),** which work the way quotas do, were placed on Japanese car imports. The U.S. International Trade Commission estimated that 44,000 domestic jobs were protected—at a cost of $193,000 per job.

- In 1988, the consumer cost of VERs on machine tools was $48 million, while the gain to U.S. machine tool manufacturers was $11 million. The consumer cost per job saved turned out to be $120,000.

- In 1994, tariffs are said to have protected 190,000 jobs in 21 U.S. industries at a cost of $170,000 per job.

- In 1989, tariffs in Japan are said to have saved 180,000 jobs at a cost of $600,000 per job.

"Voluntary" Export Restraint (VER)
An agreement between two countries in which the exporting country "voluntarily" agrees to limit its exports to the importing country.

THE WORLD TRADE ORGANIZATION (WTO)

The international trade organization, the *World Trade Organization (WTO),* came into existence on January 1, 1995. It is the successor to the General Agreement on Tariffs and Trade (GATT), which was set up in 1947. In early 2002, 144 countries in the world were members of the WTO.

According to the WTO, its "overriding objective is to help trade flow smoothly, freely, fairly, and predictably." It does this by administering trade agreements, acting as a forum for trade negotiations, settling trade disputes, reviewing national trade policies, assisting developing countries in trade policy issues, and cooperating with other international organizations. Perhaps its most useful and controversial role is adjudicating trade disputes. For example, suppose the United States claims that the Canadian government is preventing U.S. producers from openly selling their goods in Canada. The WTO will look at the matter, consult with trade experts, and then decide the issue. A country that is found engaging in unfair trade can either desist from this practice or face appropriate retaliation from the injured country.

In theory, at least, the WTO is supposed to lead to freer international trade, and there is some evidence that it has done just this. The critics of the WTO often say that it has achieved this objective at some cost to a nation's sovereignty. For example, in the past, some of the trade disputes between the United States and other countries have been decided against the United States.

http://

Go to *http://www.wto.org/*, and select "TRADE TOPICS." Under "Dispute settlement," choose "Dispute settlement gateway page." Identify some of the current disputes. How does the WTO settle disputes?

Self-Test

1. Who benefits and who loses from tariffs? Explain your answer.

2. Identify the directional change in consumers' surplus and producers' surplus when we move from free trade to tariffs. Is the change in consumers' surplus greater than, less than, or equal to the change in producers' surplus?

3. What is a major difference between the effects of a quota and the effects of a tariff?

4. Outline the details of the infant-industry argument for trade restriction.

A Reader Asks...

Why Does the Government Impose Tariffs and Quotas?

If tariffs and quotas result in higher prices for U.S. consumers, then why does the government impose them?

The answer is that government is sometimes more responsive to producer interests than to consumer interests. But, then, we have to wonder why. To try to explain why, consider the following example.

Suppose there are 100 U.S. producers of good X and 20 million U.S. consumers of good X. The producers want to protect themselves from foreign competition, so they lobby for and receive a quota on foreign goods that compete with good X. As a result, consumers must pay higher prices. For simplicity's sake, let's say that consumers must pay $40 million more. Thus, producers receive $40 million more for good X than they would have if the quota had not been imposed.

If the $40 million received is divided equally among the 100 producers, each producer receives $400,000 more as a result of the quota. If the additional $40 million paid is divided equally among the 20 million consumers, each customer pays $2 more as a result of the quota.

A producer is likely to think, "I should lobby for the quota because if I'm effective, I'll receive $400,000." A consumer is likely to think, "Why should I lobby against the quota? If I'm effective, I'll only save $2. Saving $2 isn't worth the time and trouble my lobbying would take."

In short, the benefits of quotas are concentrated on relatively few producers, and the costs of quotas are spread out over relatively many consumers. This makes each producer's gain relatively large compared with each consumer's loss. We predict that producers will lobby government to obtain the relatively large gains from quotas but that consumers will not lobby government to keep from paying the small additional cost due to quotas.

Politicians are in the awkward position of hearing from those people who want the quotas but not hearing from those people who are against them. It is likely the politicians will respond to the vocal interests. Politicians may mistakenly assume that consumers' silence means that the consumers accept the quota policy, when in fact they may not. Consumers may simply not find it worthwhile to do anything to fight the policy.

Chapter Summary

Specialization and Trade

- A country has a comparative advantage in the production of a good if it can produce the good at a lower opportunity cost than another country can.
- Individuals in countries that specialize and trade have a higher standard of living than would be the case if their countries did not specialize and trade.
- Government officials do not analyze cost data to determine what their country should specialize in and trade. Instead, the desire to earn a dollar, peso, or euro guides individuals' actions and produces the unintended consequence that countries specialize in and trade the good(s) in which they have a comparative advantage. However, trade restrictions can change this outcome.

Tariffs and Quotas

- A tariff is a tax on imports. A quota is a legal limit on the amount of a good that may be imported.
- Both tariffs and quotas raise the price of imports.
- Tariffs lead to a decrease in consumers' surplus, an increase in producers' surplus, and tariff revenue for the government. Consumers lose more through tariffs than producers and government (together) gain.
- Quotas lead to a decrease in consumers' surplus, an increase in producers' surplus, and additional revenue for the importers that sell the quota. Consumers lose more through quotas than producers and importers (together) gain.

Arguments for Trade Restrictions

- The national-defense argument states that certain goods—such as aircraft, petroleum, chemicals, and weapons—are necessary to the national defense and should be produced domestically whether the country has a comparative advantage in their production or not.
- The infant-industry argument states that "infant" or new industries should be protected from free (foreign) trade so that they may have time to develop and compete on an equal basis with older, more established foreign industries.
- The antidumping argument states that domestic producers should not have to compete (on an unequal basis) with foreign producers that sell products below cost and below the prices they charge in their domestic markets.
- The foreign-export-subsidies argument states that domestic producers should not have to compete (on an unequal basis) with foreign producers that have been subsidized by their governments.
- The low-foreign-wages argument states that domestic producers cannot compete with foreign producers that pay low wages to their employees when domestic producers pay high wages to their employees. For high-paying domestic firms to survive, limits on free trade are proposed.
- The saving-domestic-jobs argument states that through low foreign wages or government subsidies (or dumping, and so forth), foreign producers will be able to outcompete domestic producers, and therefore domestic jobs will be lost. For domestic firms to survive and domestic jobs not be lost, limits on free trade are proposed.
- Everyone does not accept the arguments for trade restrictions as valid. Critics often maintain that the arguments can be and are abused and, in most cases, are motivated by self-interest.

Key Terms and Concepts

Comparative Advantage
Tariff

Quota
Dumping

"Voluntary" Export Restraint (VER)

Economic Connections to You

Economic facts, actions, and changes create ripples that move away from their point of origin. Eventually, these ripples can intersect your life and have an effect on you. Consider the following example.

The federal government, in response to protectionism policies in a foreign country, imposes a quota on cars imported from that country. Consequently, car prices rise in the United States. You must pay a higher price for your new car than you would have had the quota not been imposed. Thus, there is a connection between protectionism policies in a foreign country and in the United States and the price you pay for a car—an economic connection to you.

Based on the material in this chapter, identify other ways in which economic facts, actions, and changes create ripples that eventually affect you.

Questions and Problems

1. Although a production possibilities frontier is usually drawn for a country, one could be drawn for the world. Picture the world's production possibilities frontier. Is the world positioned at a point on the curve or below the frontier? Give a reason for your answer.

2. "Whatever can be done by a tariff can be done by a quota." Discuss.

3. Consider two groups of domestic producers: those that compete with imports and those that export goods. Suppose the domestic producers that compete with imports convince the legislature to impose a high tariff on imports, so high, in fact, that almost all imports are eliminated. Does this policy in any way adversely affect domestic producers that export goods? How?

4. Suppose the U.S. government wants to curtail imports; would it be likely to favor a tariff or a quota to accomplish its objective? Why?

5. Suppose the landmass known to you as the United States of America had been composed, since the nation's founding, of separate countries instead of separate states. Would you expect the standard of living of the people who inhabit this landmass to be higher, lower, or equal to what it is today? Why?

6. Even though Jeremy is a better gardener and novelist than Bill is, Jeremy still hires Bill as his gardener. Why?

7. Suppose that tomorrow, a constitutional convention were called and you were chosen as one of the delegates from your state. You and the other delegates must decide whether it will be constitutional or unconstitutional for the federal government to impose tariffs and quotas or restrict international trade in any way. What would be your position?

8. Some economists have argued that because domestic consumers gain more from free trade than domestic producers gain from (import) tariffs and quotas, consumers should buy out domestic producers and rid themselves of costly tariffs and quotas. For example, if consumers save $400 million from free trade (through paying lower prices) and producers gain $100 million from tariffs and quotas, consumers can pay producers something more than $100 million but less than $400 million and get producers to favor free trade too. Assuming this scheme were feasible, what do you think of it?

9. If there is a net loss to society from tariffs, why do tariffs exist?

Working with Numbers and Graphs

1. Using the data in the table, answer the following questions: (a) For which good does Canada have a comparative advantage? (b) For which good does Italy have a comparative advantage? (c) What might be a set of favorable terms of trade for the two countries? (d) Prove that both countries would be better off in the specialization-trade case than in the no specialization–no trade case.

Points on Production Possibilities Frontier	Canada		Italy	
	Good X	Good Y	Good X	Good Y
A	150	0	90	0
B	100	25	60	60
C	50	50	30	120
D	0	75	0	180

2. In the following figure, P_W is the world price and $P_W + T$ is the world price plus a tariff. Identify the following:
   a. The level of imports at P_W
   b. The level of imports at $P_W + T$
   c. The loss in consumers' surplus as a result of a tariff
   d. The gain in producers' surplus as a result of a tariff
   e. The tariff revenue as the result of a tariff
   f. The net loss to society as a result of a tariff
   g. The net benefit to society of moving from a tariff situation to a no-tariff situation

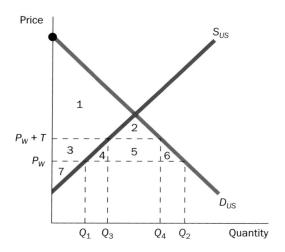

1. Go to *http://www.wto.org*, and select "What is the WTO?" Under "The WTO in Brief," click "Browse html version online." What is the objective of the WTO? How many countries are members of the WTO? Do you think the WTO is producer-oriented or consumer-oriented? Explain your answer.
2. Click on the "Back" button, and under "10 Benefits of the WTO Trading System," select "Browse html version online," and then select "Incomes." What evidence does the WTO present to prove that trade raises

incomes? Click on the "Back" button, and review the top 10 benefits of WTO trade. One of the benefits listed is "peace." Do you think that the WTO trading system promotes peace? Explain your answer.
3. Click on the "Back" button, and under "10 common misunderstandings about the WTO," select "Browse html version online." Select and read "Anti-Green" and "Small left out." What is the WTO position on both issues?

Log on to the Arnold Xtra! Web site now (*http://arnoldxtra.swcollege.com*) for additional learning resources such as practice quizzes, help with graphing, video clips, and current event applications.

ch.19

INTERNATIONAL FINANCE

When people travel to a foreign country, they buy various goods and services in the country. The prices of the goods and services are quoted in yen, euros, francs, pesos, or some other currency. For example, a tourist in Japan might want to buy a pair of shoes priced in yen. What would the shoes cost in U.S. currency? The answer depends on the current exchange rate between the dollar and the yen. But, what determines the exchange rate? This is just one of the many questions answered in this chapter.

Chapter Road Map

Our two major topics in international finance are the balance of payments and exchange rates. Think of the balance of payments as a statement of the money value of the transactions between residents of different countries. In other words, Americans buy things from and sell things to people all over the world. The balance of payments tells us how much buying and selling is going on, among other things.

An exchange rate is the price of one currency in terms of another currency—for example, the price of U.S. dollars in terms of Japanese yen. In this chapter, we explain why exchange rates are what they are (why is 1 dollar equal to 130 yen and not 120 yen?) and discuss two types of exchange rate structures—flexible and fixed.

THE BALANCE OF PAYMENTS

Countries keep track of their domestic level of production by calculating their gross domestic product (GDP). Similarly, they keep track of the flow of their international trade (receipts and expenditures) by calculating their balance of payments.

The **balance of payments** is a periodic statement (usually annual) of the money value of all transactions between residents of one country and residents of all other countries. The balance of payments provides information about a nation's imports and exports, domestic residents' earnings on assets located abroad, foreign earnings on domestic assets, gifts to and from foreign countries (including foreign aid), and official transactions by governments and central banks.

Balance of payments accounts record both debits and credits. A debit is indicated by a minus (−) sign, and a credit is indicated by a plus (+) sign. *Any transaction that supplies the country's currency in the foreign exchange market is recorded as a* **debit.** (The **foreign exchange market** is the market in which currencies of different countries are exchanged.) For example, suppose a U.S. retailer wants to buy Japanese television sets so that he can sell them in his stores in the United States. In order to buy the TV sets from the Japanese, the retailer first has to supply U.S. dollars (in the foreign exchange market) in return for Japanese yen. Then he will turn over the yen to the Japanese in exchange for the television sets.

Any transaction that creates a demand for the country's currency in the foreign exchange market is recorded as a **credit.** For example, suppose a Russian retailer wants to buy computers from U.S. computer producers. Can she pay the U.S. producers in Russian rubles? Probably not; U.S. producers want U.S. dollars. So the Russian retailer must supply rubles (in the foreign exchange market) in return for dollars. Then she will turn over the dollars to the U.S. producers in exchange for the computers. See Exhibit 1 for a summary of debits and credits.

The international transactions that occur, and that are summarized in the balance of payments, can be grouped into three categories, or three accounts—the current account, the capital account, and the official reserve account—and a statistical discrepancy. Exhibit 2 illustrates a U.S. balance of payments account for year Z. The data in the exhibit are hypothetical (to make the calculations simpler), but not unrealistic.

Q & A **Q:** When Americans buy Japanese goods, they supply dollars and demand yen. When the Japanese buy American goods, they supply yen and demand dollars. Thus, the first transaction is recorded as a debit (it supplies U.S. currency) and the second transaction is recorded as a credit (it increases demand for U.S. currency) in the U.S. balance of payments. Is this correct?

A: Yes, that is correct.

Balance of Payments
A periodic statement (usually annual) of the money value of all transactions between residents of one country and residents of all other countries.

Debit
In the balance of payments, any transaction that supplies the country's currency in the foreign exchange market.

Foreign Exchange Market
The market in which currencies of different countries are exchanged.

Credit
In the balance of payments, any transaction that creates a demand for the country's currency in the foreign exchange market.

Item	Definition	Example
Debit (−)	Any transaction that supplies the country's currency.	Jim, an American, supplies dollars in exchange for yen so that he can use the yen to buy Japanese goods.
Credit (+)	Any transaction that creates a demand for the country's currency.	Svetlana, who is Russian and living in Russia, supplies rubles in order to demand dollars so that she can use the dollars to buy U.S. goods.

exhibit 1

Debits and Credits

exhibit 2

U.S. Balance of Payments, Year *Z*
The data in this exhibit are hypothetical, but not unrealistic. All numbers are in billions of dollars. The plus and minus signs in the exhibit should be viewed as operational signs.

CURRENT ACCOUNT

1. EXPORTS OF GOODS AND SERVICES   +340
   a. Merchandise exports (including military sales)   +220
   b. Services   +30
   c. Income from U.S. assets abroad   +90

2. IMPORTS OF GOODS AND SERVICES   −390
   a. Merchandise imports (including military purchases)   −300
   b. Services   −40
   c. Income from foreign assets in U.S.   −50

Merchandise Trade Balance
Difference between value of merchandise exports (item 1a) and value of merchandise imports (item 2a): +220 − 300 = −80

3. NET UNILATERAL TRANSFERS ABROAD   −11

Current Account Balance
Items 1, 2, 3: +340 − 390 − 11 =   −61

CAPITAL ACCOUNT
4. OUTFLOW OF U.S. CAPITAL   −16
5. INFLOW OF FOREIGN CAPITAL   +60

Capital Account Balance
Items 4 and 5: −16 + 60 =   +44

OFFICIAL RESERVE ACCOUNT
6. INCREASE (−) IN U.S. OFFICIAL RESERVE ASSETS   −4
7. INCREASE (+) IN FOREIGN OFFICIAL ASSETS IN U.S.   +3

Official Reserve Balance
Items 6 and 7: −4 + 3 =   −1

STATISTICAL DISCREPANCY   +18

TOTAL $0 $0
(always zero)

Balance of Payments =

Summary statistic of all ◇ items (items 1 − 7 and the statistical discrepancy)

+$340 − $390 − $11 − $16 + $60 − $4 + $3 + $18 = $0

or

Summary statistic of all ▢ items (current account balance, capital account balance, official reserve balance, and the statistical discrepancy)

−$61 + $44 − $1 + $18 = $0

Note: The pluses (+) and the minuses (−) in the exhibit serve two purposes. First, they distinguish between credits and debits. A plus is always placed before a credit, and a minus is always placed before a debit. Second, in terms of the calculations, the pluses and minuses are viewed as operational signs. In other words, if a number has a plus in front of it, it is added to the total. If a number has a minus in front of it, it is subtracted from the total.

CURRENT ACCOUNT

Current Account
Includes all payments related to the purchase and sale of goods and services. Components of the account include exports, imports, and net unilateral transfers abroad.

The **current account** includes all payments related to the purchase and sale of goods and services. The current account has three major components: exports of goods and services, imports of goods and services, and net unilateral transfers abroad.

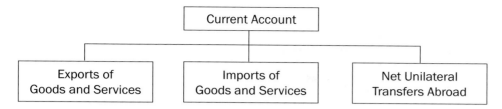

```
                    ┌─────────────────┐
                    │ Current Account │
                    └────────┬────────┘
        ┌────────────────────┼────────────────────┐
┌───────────────┐   ┌───────────────┐   ┌───────────────┐
│  Exports of   │   │  Imports of   │   │ Net Unilateral│
│Goods and      │   │Goods and      │   │Transfers      │
│Services       │   │Services       │   │Abroad         │
└───────────────┘   └───────────────┘   └───────────────┘
```

1. **Exports of goods and services.** Americans export goods (say, cars), they export services (such as insurance, banking, transportation, and tourism), and they receive income on assets they own abroad. All three activities increase the demand for U.S. dollars at the same time that they increase the supply of foreign currencies; thus, they are recorded as credits (+). For example, if a foreigner buys a U.S. computer, payment must ultimately be made in U.S. dollars. Thus, she is required to supply her country's currency when she demands U.S. dollars. (We use foreigner in this chapter to refer to a resident of a foreign country.)

2. **Imports of goods and services.** Americans import goods and services, and foreigners receive income on assets they own in the United States. These activities increase the demand for foreign currencies at the same time that they increase the supply of U.S. dollars to the foreign exchange market; thus, they are recorded as debits (−). For example, if an American buys a Japanese car, payment must ultimately be made in Japanese yen. Thus, he is required to supply U.S. dollars when he demands Japanese yen.

In Exhibit 2, exports of goods and services total +$340 billion in year *Z*, and imports of goods and services total −$390 billion.[1]

Before discussing the third component of the current account—net unilateral transfers abroad—we define some important relationships between exports and imports. Look at the difference between the *value of merchandise exports* (1a in Exhibit 2) and the *value of merchandise imports* (2a in the exhibit). This difference is the merchandise trade balance or the balance of trade. Specifically, the **merchandise trade balance** is the difference between the value of merchandise exports and the value of merchandise imports. In year *Z*, this is −$80 billion.

$$\text{Merchandise trade balance} = \frac{\text{Value of}}{\text{merchandise exports}} - \frac{\text{Value of}}{\text{merchandise imports}}$$

If the value of a country's merchandise exports is less than the value of its merchandise imports, it is said to have a **merchandise trade deficit.**

Merchandise trade deficit: Value of merchandise exports < Value of merchandise imports

If the value of a country's merchandise exports is greater than the value of its merchandise imports, it is said to have a **merchandise trade surplus.**

Merchandise trade surplus: Value of merchandise exports > Value of merchandise imports

Exhibit 3 shows the U.S. merchandise trade balance from 1990–2001. Notice that there has been a merchandise trade deficit in each of these years. As an aside, the merchandise trade deficit for the period January–June 2002 (not shown in the exhibit) was $229 billion.

Go to *http://www.bea.doc.gov/bea/di/ trans1.htm.* What are exports in the most recent quarter? What are imports in the most recent quarter?

Merchandise Trade Balance
The difference between the value of merchandise exports and the value of merchandise imports.

Merchandise Trade Deficit
The situation where the value of merchandise exports is less than the value of merchandise imports.

Merchandise Trade Surplus
The situation where the value of merchandise exports is greater than the value of merchandise imports.

---

1. In everyday language, people do not say, "Exports are a positive $*X* billion and imports are a negative $*Y* billion." Placing a plus sign (+) in front of exports and a minus sign (−) in front of imports simply reinforces the essential point that exports are credits and imports are debits. This will be useful later when we calculate certain account balances.

exhibit 3

U.S. Merchandise Trade Balance
In each of the years shown,
1990–2001, a merchandise trade
deficit has existed.

*Source: U.S. Department of Commerce,
Bureau of Economic Analysis*

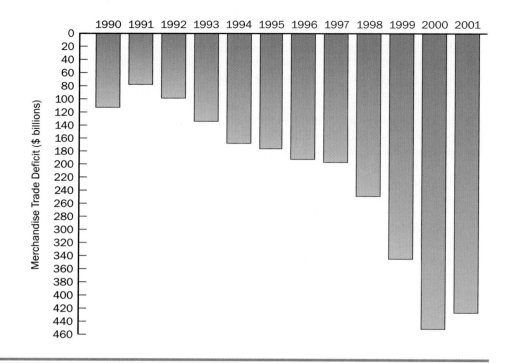

Q & A

Q: In Exhibit 2, merchandise exports are +$220 billion (item 1a) and merchandise imports are −$300 billion (item 2a). Can't the merchandise trade balance be calculated simply by subtracting the merchandise imports from the merchandise exports? Why does the definition use the "value of" exports and imports?

A: The merchandise trade balance can be calculated by subtracting merchandise imports from merchandise exports. But, you must be careful not to make the mistake of subtracting a negative $300 billion from a positive $220 billion. In other words, the merchandise trade balance does not equal $220 billion minus (negative $300 billion), or $520 billion. The merchandise trade balance is found by subtracting the *value of* the merchandise imports, $300 billion, from the *value of* the merchandise exports, $220 billion. In other words, balance of trade = $220 billion − $300 billion = −$80 billion.

In terms of calculations, the positive and negative signs in Exhibit 2 are operational signs. When a negative sign (−) appears in front of a number, subtract that number from the total. When a positive sign (+) appears in front of a number, add that number to the total.

3. **Net unilateral transfers abroad.** Unilateral transfers are one-way money payments. They can go from Americans or the U.S. government to foreigners or foreign governments. If an American sends money to a relative in a foreign country, or the U.S. government gives money to a foreign country as a gift or grant, or an American retires in a foreign country and receives a Social Security check there, all these transactions are referred to as unilateral transfers. If an American makes a unilateral transfer abroad, this gives rise to a demand for foreign currency and a supply of U.S. dollars; thus, it is entered as a debit item in the U.S. balance of payments accounts.

Unilateral transfers can also go from foreigners or foreign governments to Americans or to the U.S. government. If a foreign citizen sends money to a relative living in the United States, this is a unilateral transfer. If a foreigner makes a unilateral transfer to an American, this gives rise to a supply of foreign currency and a demand for U.S. dollars; thus, it is entered as a credit item in the U.S. balance of payments accounts.

Net unilateral transfers abroad include both types of transfers—from the United States to foreign countries and from foreign countries to the United States. The dollar amount of net unilateral transfers is negative if U.S. transfers are greater than foreign transfers. It is positive if foreign transfers are greater than U.S. transfers.

For year Z in Exhibit 2, we have assumed that unilateral transfers made by Americans to foreign citizens are greater than unilateral transfers made by foreign citizens to Americans. Thus, there is a *negative* net dollar amount, −$11 billion, in this case.

Items 1, 2, and 3 in Exhibit 2—exports of goods and services, imports of goods and services, and net unilateral transfers abroad—are known as the current account. The **current account balance** is the summary statistic for these three items. In year Z, it is −$61 billion. The news media sometimes call the current account balance the balance of payments. To an economist, this is incorrect; the balance of payments includes several more items.

CAPITAL ACCOUNT

The **capital account** includes all payments related to the purchase and sale of assets and to borrowing and lending activities. Its major components are outflow of U.S. capital and inflow of foreign capital.

1. **Outflow of U.S. capital.** American purchases of foreign assets and U.S. loans to foreigners are outflows of U.S. capital. As such, they give rise to a demand for foreign currency and a supply of U.S. dollars on the foreign exchange market. Hence, they are considered a debit. For example, if an American wants to buy land in Japan, U.S. dollars must be supplied to purchase (demand) Japanese yen.
2. **Inflow of foreign capital.** Foreign purchases of U.S. assets and foreign loans to Americans are inflows of foreign capital. As such, they give rise to a demand for U.S. dollars and to a supply of foreign currency on the foreign exchange market. Hence, they are considered a credit. For example, if a Japanese citizen buys a U.S. Treasury bill, Japanese yen must be supplied to purchase (demand) U.S. dollars.

Items 4 and 5 in Exhibit 2—outflow of U.S. capital and inflow of foreign capital—comprise the capital account. The **capital account balance** is the summary statistic for these two items. It is equal to the difference between the outflow of U.S. capital and the inflow of foreign capital. In year Z, it is $44 billion.

OFFICIAL RESERVE ACCOUNT

A government possesses official reserve balances in the form of foreign currencies, gold, its reserve position in the **International Monetary Fund,** and **special drawing rights (SDR).** Countries that have a deficit in their combined current and capital accounts can draw on their reserves. For example, if the United States

http://

Go to *http://www.bea.doc.gov/bea/di/ trans1.htm*. What is the current account balance in the most recent quarter? What are net unilateral transfers in the most recent quarter? What is the statistical discrepancy in the most recent quarter? What is the value of net exports?

Current Account Balance
The summary statistic for exports of goods and services, imports of goods and services, and net unilateral transfers abroad.

Capital Account
Includes all payments related to the purchase and sale of assets and to borrowing and lending activities. Components include outflow of U.S. capital and inflow of foreign capital.

Capital Account Balance
The summary statistic for the outflow of U.S. capital and the inflow of foreign capital. It is equal to the difference between the outflow of U.S. capital and the inflow of foreign capital.

International Monetary Fund (IMF)
An international organization created to oversee the international monetary system. The IMF does not control the world's money supply, but it does hold currency reserves for member nations and make loans to central banks.

Special Drawing Right (SDR)
An international money, created by the IMF, in the form of bookkeeping entries; like gold and currencies, they can be used by nations to settle international accounts.

has a combined deficit in its current and capital accounts of $5 billion, it can draw down its official reserves to meet this combined deficit.

Item 6 in Exhibit 2 shows that the United States increased its reserve assets by $4 billion in year Z. This is a debit item because if the United States acquires official reserves (say, through the purchase of a foreign currency), it has increased the demand for the foreign currency and supplied dollars. Thus, an increase in official reserves is like an outflow of capital in the capital account and appears as a payment with a negative sign. It follows that an increase in foreign official assets in the United States is a credit item.

STATISTICAL DISCREPANCY

If someone buys a U.S. dollar with, say, Japanese yen, someone must sell a U.S. dollar. Thus, dollars purchased = dollars sold.

In all the transactions discussed earlier—exporting goods, importing goods, sending money to relatives in foreign countries, buying land in foreign countries—dollars were bought and sold. The total number of dollars sold must always equal the total number of dollars purchased. However, balance of payments accountants do not have complete information; they can record only credits and debits that they observe. There may be more debits or credits than those observed in a given year.

Suppose in year Z, all debits are observed and recorded, but not all credits are observed and recorded—perhaps because of smuggling activities, secret bank accounts, people living in more than one country, and so on. To adjust for this, balance of payments accountants use the *statistical discrepancy,* which is that part of the balance of payments that adjusts for missing information. In Exhibit 2, the statistical discrepancy is +$18 billion. This means that $18 billion worth of credits (+) went unobserved in year Z. There may have been some hidden exports and unrecorded capital inflows that year.

WHAT THE BALANCE OF PAYMENTS EQUALS

The balance of payments is the summary statistic for the following:

- Exports of goods and services (item 1 in Exhibit 2)
- Imports of goods and services (item 2)
- Net unilateral transfers abroad (item 3)
- Outflow of U.S. capital (item 4)
- Inflow of foreign capital (item 5)
- Increase in U.S. official reserve assets (item 6)
- Increase in foreign official assets in the United States (item 7)
- Statistical discrepancy

Calculating the balance of payments using these items, we have (in billions of dollars) $+340 - 390 - 11 - 16 + 60 - 4 + 3 + 18 = 0$.

Alternatively, the balance of payments is the summary statistic for the following:

- Current account balance
- Capital account balance
- Official reserve balance
- Statistical discrepancy

Calculating the balance of payments using these items, we have (in billions of dollars) $-61 + 44 - 1 + 18 = 0$. The balance of payments for the United States in year Z equals zero. The balance of payments *always* equals zero.

 Q: Why does the balance of payments always equal zero?

A: The reason the balance of payments always equals zero is that the three accounts that comprise the balance of payments, when taken together, plus the statistical discrepancy, include all of the *sources* and all of the *uses* of dollars in international transactions. And because every dollar used must have a source, adding the sources (+) to the uses (−) necessarily gives us zero.

Self-Test *(Answers to Self-Test questions are in the Self-Test Appendix.)*

1. If an American retailer buys Japanese cars from a Japanese manufacturer, is this transaction recorded as a debit or a credit? Explain your answer.

2. Exports of goods and services equal $200 billion and imports of goods and services equal $300 billion. What is the merchandise trade balance?

3. What is the difference between the merchandise trade balance and the current account balance?

4. A newspaper reports that the U.S. balance of payments is −$100 billion. Can this be correct?

FLEXIBLE EXCHANGE RATES

If a U.S. buyer wants to purchase a good from a U.S. seller, the buyer simply gives the required number of U.S. dollars to the seller. If, however, a U.S. buyer wants to purchase a good from a seller in Mexico, the U.S. buyer must first exchange her U.S. dollars for Mexican pesos. Then, with the pesos, she buys the good from the Mexican seller.

As mentioned earlier, the market in which currencies of different countries are exchanged is the foreign exchange market. In the foreign exchange market, currencies are bought and sold for a price; an **exchange rate** exists. For instance, it might take 96 cents to buy a euro, 10 cents to buy a Mexican peso, and 13 cents to buy a Danish krone.

In this section, we discuss how exchange rates are determined in the foreign exchange market when the forces of supply and demand are allowed to rule. Economists refer to this as a **flexible exchange rate system.** In the next section, we discuss how exchange rates are determined under a fixed exchange rate system.

Exchange Rate
The price of one currency in terms of another currency.

Flexible Exchange Rate System
The system whereby exchange rates are determined by the forces of supply and demand for a currency.

THE DEMAND AND SUPPLY OF CURRENCIES

To simplify our analysis, we assume that there are only two countries in the world, the United States and Mexico. This, then, means there are only two currencies in the world, the U.S. dollar (USD) and the Mexican peso (MXP).[2] We want to answer the following two questions:

1. What creates the demand for and supply of dollars on the foreign exchange market?
2. What creates the demand for and supply of pesos on the foreign exchange market?

Suppose an American wants to buy a couch from a Mexican producer. Before he can purchase the couch, the American must buy Mexican pesos—hence, Mexican pesos are demanded. But the American buys Mexican pesos with U.S. dollars; that is, he supplies U.S. dollars to the foreign exchange market in order to demand Mexican pesos. We conclude that *the U.S. demand for Mexican goods leads to (1) a demand for Mexican pesos and (2) a supply of U.S. dollars on the foreign exchange market* (see Exhibit 4a). Thus, the demand for pounds and the supply of dollars are linked:

Demand for pesos ↔ Supply of dollars

---

2. Sometimes the abbreviation MXN instead of MXP is used for the Mexican peso.

exhibit 4

The Demand for Goods and the Supply of Currencies

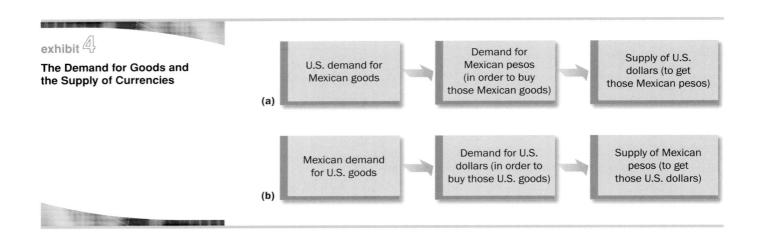

(a)

(b)

The result is similar for a Mexican who wants to buy a computer from a U.S. producer. Before she can purchase the computer, the Mexican must buy U.S. dollars—hence, U.S. dollars are demanded. The Mexican buys the U.S. dollars with Mexican pesos. We conclude that *the Mexican demand for U.S. goods leads to (1) a demand for U.S. dollars and (2) a supply of Mexican pesos on the foreign exchange market* (see Exhibit 4b). Thus, the demand for dollars and the supply of pesos are linked:

Demand for dollars ↔ Supply of pesos

Now let's look at Exhibit 5 to see the markets for pesos and dollars. Part (a) shows the market for Mexican pesos. The quantity of pesos is on the horizontal axis, and the exchange rate—stated in terms of the dollar price per peso—is on the vertical axis. Exhibit 5b shows the market for U.S. dollars, which mirrors what is happening in the market for Mexican pesos. Notice that the exchange rates in (a) and (b) are reciprocals of each other. If 0.10 USD = 1 MXP, then 10 MXP = 1 USD.

In Exhibit 5a, the demand curve for pesos is downward-sloping, indicating that as the dollar price per peso increases, Americans buy fewer pesos, and as the dollar price per peso decreases, Americans buy more pesos.

Dollar price per peso↑   Americans buy fewer pesos
Dollar price per peso↓   Americans buy more pesos

For example, if it takes 0.10 dollars to buy a peso, Americans will buy more pesos than they would if it takes 0.20 dollars to buy a peso. (It is analogous to buyers purchasing more soft drinks at 3 dollars a six-pack than at 5 dollars a six-pack.) Simply put, the higher the dollar price per peso, the more expensive Mexican goods are for Americans and the fewer Mexican goods Americans will buy. Thus, a smaller quantity of pesos are demanded.

The supply curve for pesos in Exhibit 5a is upward-sloping. It is easy to understand why if we recall that the supply of Mexican pesos is linked to the Mexican demand for U.S. goods and U.S. dollars. Consider a price of 0.20 dollars for 1 peso compared with a price of 0.10 dollars for 1 peso. At 0.10 USD = 1 MXP, a Mexican buyer gives up 1 peso and receives 10 cents in return. But at 0.20 USD = 1 MXP, a Mexican buyer gives up 1 peso and receives 20 cents in return. At which exchange rate are U.S. goods cheaper for Mexicans? The answer is at the exchange rate of 0.20 USD = 1 MXP.

To illustrate, suppose a U.S. computer has a price tag of 1,000 dollars. At an exchange rate of 0.20 USD = 1 MXP, a Mexican will have to pay 5,000 pesos to buy the American computer (1,000 USD/0.20 USD = 5,000 MXP). But at an

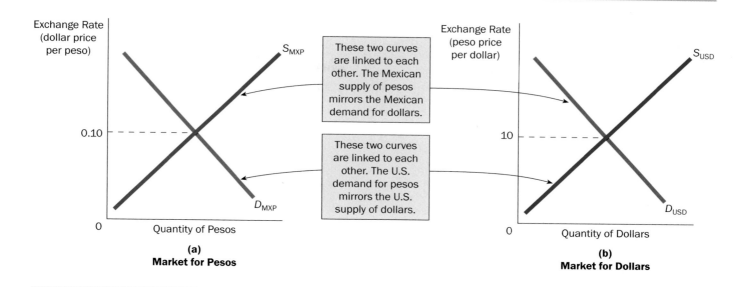

Exchange Rate (dollar price per peso)

S_{MXP}

0.10

D_{MXP}

0

Quantity of Pesos

(a)
Market for Pesos

These two curves are linked to each other. The Mexican supply of pesos mirrors the Mexican demand for dollars.

These two curves are linked to each other. The U.S. demand for pesos mirrors the U.S. supply of dollars.

Exchange Rate (peso price per dollar)

S_{USD}

10

D_{USD}

0

Quantity of Dollars

(b)
Market for Dollars

exchange rate of 0.10 USD = 1 MXP, a Mexican will have to pay 10,000 pesos for the computer (1,000 USD/0.10 USD = 10,000 MXP). To a Mexican buyer, the American computer is cheaper at the exchange rate of 0.20 dollars per peso than at 0.10 dollars per peso.

Exchange Rate	Dollar Price	Peso Price
0.20 USD = 1 MXP	1,000 USD	5,000 MXP (1,000 USD/0.20 USD)
0.10 USD = 1 MXP	1,000 USD	10,000 MXP (1,000 USD/0.10 USD)

It follows, then, that the higher the dollar price per peso, the greater the quantity demanded of dollars by Mexicans (because U.S. goods will be cheaper), and therefore the greater the quantity supplied of pesos to the foreign exchange market. The upward-sloping supply curve for pesos illustrates this.

THINKING LIKE AN ECONOMIST

The demand for dollars is linked to the supply of pesos and the demand for pesos is linked to the supply of dollars. Economists often think in terms of one activity being linked to another because economics, after all, is about exchange. In an exchange, one gives (supply) and gets (demand): John "supplies" $25 in order to demand the new book from the shopkeeper; the shopkeeper supplies the new book in order that he may "demand" the $25. In such a transaction, we usually diagrammatically represent the demand for and supply of the new book—but we could also diagrammatically represent the demand for and supply of money. Of course, in international exchange, where monies are bought and sold before goods are bought and sold, this is exactly what we do.

THE EQUILIBRIUM EXCHANGE RATE

In a completely flexible exchange rate system, the forces of supply and demand are allowed to rule. Suppose in this situation that the equilibrium exchange rate (dollar price per peso) is 0.10 USD = 1 MXP, as shown in Exhibit 6. At this dollar price per peso, the quantity demanded of pesos equals the quantity supplied of pesos. There are no shortages or surpluses of pesos. At any other exchange rate, however, either an excess demand for pesos or an excess supply of pesos exists.

Let's look at the exchange rate of 0.12 USD = 1 MXP. At this exchange rate, a surplus of pesos exists. As a result, downward pressure will be placed on the

exhibit 5

Translating U.S. Demand for Pesos into U.S. Supply of Dollars and Mexican Demand for Dollars into Mexican Supply of Pesos

(a) The market for pesos. (b) The market for dollars. The demand for pesos in (a) is linked to the supply of dollars in (b): When Americans demand pesos, they supply dollars. The supply of pesos in (a) is linked to the demand for dollars in (b): When Mexicans demand dollars, they supply pesos. In (a), the exchange rate is $0.10 USD = 1 MXP, which is equal to 10 MXP = 1 USD in (b). Exchange rates are reciprocals of each other.

exhibit 6

The Foreign Exchange Market

The demand curve for pesos is downward-sloping. The higher the dollar price for pesos, the fewer pesos will be demanded; the lower the dollar price for pesos, the more pesos will be demanded. At 0.12 USD = 1 MXP, there is a surplus of pesos, placing downward pressure on the exchange rate. At 0.08 USD = 1 MXP, there is a shortage of pesos, placing upward pressure on the exchange rate. At the equilibrium exchange rate, 0.10 USD = 1 MXP, the quantity demanded of pesos equals the quantity supplied of pesos.

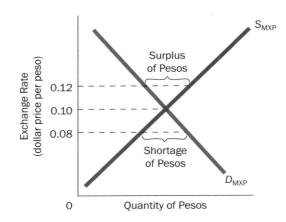

dollar price of a peso (just as downward pressure will be placed on the dollar price of an apple if there is a surplus of apples). At the exchange rate of 0.08 USD = 1 MXP, there is a shortage of pesos, and upward pressure will be placed on the dollar price of a peso.

Q & A

Q: Are the demand and supply curves in Exhibit 6 related in any way to the U.S. balance of payments in Exhibit 2?

A: Yes, they are. For example, U.S. exports represent a demand for U.S. dollars by foreigners (and therefore constitute the supply of foreign currencies), while U.S. imports represent the U.S. demand for foreign currencies (and therefore constitute the supply of U.S. dollars). In fact, any dollar amount with a plus sign (+) in front of it in Exhibit 2 represents a demand for U.S. dollars and a supply of foreign currencies, and any dollar amount with a minus sign (−) in front of it represents a demand for foreign currencies and a supply of U.S. dollars.

CHANGES IN THE EQUILIBRIUM EXCHANGE RATE

Chapter 3 explains that a change in the demand for a good, or in the supply of a good, or in both will change the equilibrium price of the good. The same holds true for the price of currencies. A change in the demand for pesos, or in the supply of pesos, or in both will change the equilibrium dollar price per peso. If the dollar price per peso rises—say, from 0.10 USD = 1 MXP to 0.12 USD = 1 MXP—the peso is said to have **appreciated** and the dollar to have **depreciated.**

Appreciation
An increase in the value of one currency relative to other currencies.

Depreciation
A decrease in the value of one currency relative to other currencies.

A currency has appreciated in value if it takes more of a foreign currency to buy it. A currency has depreciated in value if it takes more of it to buy a foreign currency. For example, a movement in the exchange rate from 0.10 USD = 1 MXP to 0.12 USD = 1 MXP means that it now takes 12 cents instead of 10 cents to buy a peso, so the dollar has depreciated. The other side of the "coin," so to speak, is that it takes fewer pesos to buy a dollar, so the peso has appreciated. That is, at an exchange rate of 0.10 USD = 1 MXP it takes 10 pesos to buy 1 dollar, but at an exchange rate of 0.12 USD = 1 MXP, it takes only 8.33 pesos to buy 1 dollar.

If the equilibrium exchange rate can change owing to a change in the demand for and supply of a currency, then it is important to understand what factors can change the demand for and supply of a currency. Three are presented here.

A Difference in Income Growth Rates

An increase in a nation's income will usually cause the nation's residents to buy more of both domestic and foreign goods. The increased demand for imports will result in an increased demand for foreign currency.

Suppose U.S. residents experience an increase in income, but Mexican residents do not. As a result, the demand curve for pesos shifts rightward, as illustrated in Exhibit 7. This causes the equilibrium exchange rate to rise from 0.10 USD = 1 MXP to 0.12 USD = 1 MXP. *Ceteris paribus,* if one nation's income grows and another's lags behind, the currency of the higher-growth-rate country *depreciates* and the currency of the lower-growth-rate country *appreciates.* To many persons this seems paradoxical; nevertheless, it is true.

Differences in Relative Inflation Rates

Suppose the U.S. price level rises 10 percent at a time when Mexico experiences stable prices. An increase in the U.S. price level will make Mexican goods relatively less expensive for Americans and U.S. goods relatively more expensive for Mexicans. As a result, the U.S. demand for Mexican goods will increase and the Mexican demand for U.S. goods will decrease.

How will this affect the demand for and supply of Mexican pesos? As shown in Exhibit 8, the demand for Mexican pesos will increase (Mexican goods are relatively cheaper than they were before the U.S. price level rose), and the supply of Mexican pesos will decrease (American goods are relatively more expensive, so Mexicans will buy fewer American goods; thus, they demand fewer U.S. dollars and supply fewer Mexican pesos).

As Exhibit 8 shows, the result of an increase in the demand for Mexican pesos and a decrease in the supply of Mexican pesos is an *appreciation* in the peso and a *depreciation* in the dollar. It takes 11 cents instead of 10 cents to buy 1 peso (dollar depreciation); it takes 9.09 pesos instead of 10 pesos to buy 1 dollar (peso appreciation).

An important question is: How much will the U.S. dollar depreciate as a result of the 10 percent rise in the U.S. price level? (Recall that there is no change in Mexico's price level.) The **purchasing power parity (PPP) theory** predicts that the U.S. dollar will depreciate by 10 percent. This requires the dollar price of a peso to rise to 11 cents (10 percent of 10 cents is 1 cent, and 10 cents + 1 cent = 11 cents). A 10 percent depreciation in the dollar restores the *original relative prices of American goods to Mexican customers.*

Go to *http://research.stlouisfed.org/ fred/data/exchange.html.* Under "Exchange Rates," find "U.S. Dollars to One Euro," and click "Monthly." What was the dollar-euro exchange rate in the earliest month and year specified? the most recent month and year specified? Has the dollar appreciated or depreciated (relative to the euro) over the time period reported?

Purchasing Power Parity (PPP) Theory
States that exchange rates between any two currencies will adjust to reflect changes in the relative price levels of the two countries.

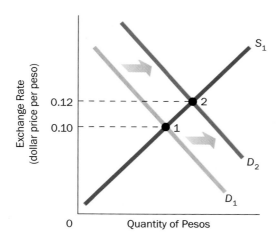

exhibit 7

The Growth Rate of Income and the Exchange Rate
If U.S. residents experience a growth in income but Mexican residents do not, U.S. demand for Mexican goods will increase, and with it, the demand for pesos. As a result, the exchange rate will change; the dollar price of pesos will rise. The dollar depreciates, the peso appreciates.

exhibit 8

Inflation, Exchange Rates, and Purchasing Power Parity (PPP)
If the price level in the United States increases by 10 percent while the price level in Mexico remains constant, then the U.S. demand for Mexican goods (and therefore pesos) will increase and the supply of pesos will decrease. As a result, the exchange rate will change; the dollar price of pesos will rise. The dollar depreciates, and the peso appreciates. PPP theory predicts that the dollar will depreciate in the foreign exchange market until the original price (in pesos) of American goods to Mexican customers is restored. In this example, this requires the dollar to depreciate 10 percent.

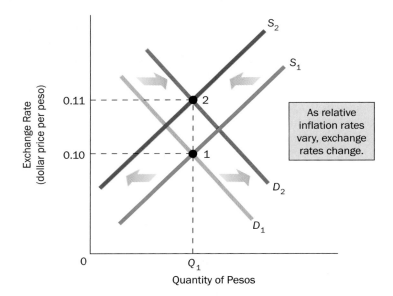

As relative inflation rates vary, exchange rates change.

Consider a U.S. car with a price tag of 20,000 dollars. If the exchange rate is 0.10 USD = 1 MXP, a Mexican buyer of the car will pay 200,000 pesos. If the car price increases by 10 percent to 22,000 dollars and the dollar depreciates 10 percent (to 0.11 USD = 1 MXP), the Mexican buyer of the car will still pay only 200,000 pesos.

Exchange Rate	Dollar Price	Peso Price
0.10 USD = 1 MXP	20,000 USD	200,000 MXP (20,000 USD/0.10 USD)
0.11 USD = 1 MXP	22,000 USD	200,000 MXP (22,000 USD/0.11 USD)

In short, the PPP theory predicts that *changes in the relative price levels of two countries will affect the exchange rate in such a way that one unit of a country's currency will continue to buy the same amount of foreign goods* as it did before the change in the relative price levels. In our example, the higher U.S. inflation rate causes a change in the equilibrium exchange rate and leads to a depreciated dollar, but one peso continues to have the same purchasing power it previously did.

On some occasions, the PPP theory of exchange rates has predicted accurately, but on others, it has not. Many economists suggest that the theory does not always predict accurately because the demand for and supply of a currency are affected *by more than the difference in inflation rates between countries.* For example, we have already noted that different income growth rates affect the demand for a currency and therefore the exchange rate. In the *long run*, however, and in particular, when there is a *large difference in inflation rates across countries,* the PPP theory does predict exchange rates accurately.

Changes in Real Interest Rates

As shown in the U.S. balance of payments in Exhibit 2, more than goods flow between countries. Financial capital also moves between countries. The flow of financial capital depends on different countries' *real interest rates*—interest rates adjusted for inflation. To illustrate, suppose, initially, that the real interest rate is 3 percent in both the United States and Mexico. Then the real interest rate in the

United States increases to 4.5 percent. What will happen? Mexicans will want to purchase financial assets in the United States that pay a higher real interest rate than financial assets in Mexico. The Mexican demand for dollars will increase, and therefore Mexicans will supply more pesos. As the supply of pesos increases on the foreign exchange market, the exchange rate (dollar price per peso) will change; fewer dollars will be needed to buy pesos. In short, the dollar will appreciate and the peso will depreciate.

Self-Test

1. In the foreign exchange market, how is the demand for dollars linked to the supply of pesos?

2. What could cause the U.S. dollar to appreciate against the Mexican peso on the foreign exchange market?

3. Suppose the U.S. economy grows while the Swiss economy does not. How will this affect the exchange rate between the dollar and the Swiss franc? Why?

4. What does the purchasing power parity theory say? Give an example to illustrate your answer.

FIXED EXCHANGE RATES

The major alternative to the flexible exchange rate system is the **fixed exchange rate system.** This system works the way it sounds. Exchange rates are fixed; they are not allowed to fluctuate freely in response to the forces of supply and demand. Central banks buy and sell currencies to maintain agreed-on exchange rates. The workings of the fixed exchange rate system are described in this section.

FIXED EXCHANGE RATES AND OVERVALUED/UNDERVALUED CURRENCY

Once again, we assume a two country–two currency world. Suppose this time, the United States and Mexico agree to fix the exchange rate of their currencies. Instead of letting the dollar depreciate or appreciate relative to the peso, the two countries agree to set the price of 1 peso at 0.12 dollars; that is, they agree to the exchange rate of 0.12 USD = 1 MXP. Generally, we call this the fixed exchange rate or the *official price* of a peso.[3] We will be dealing with more than one official price in our discussion, so we refer to 0.12 USD = 1 MXP as official price 1 (Exhibit 9).

If the dollar price of pesos is above its equilibrium level (which is the case at official price 1), a surplus of pesos exists. Also, the peso is said to be **overvalued.** This means that the peso is fetching more dollars than it would at equilibrium. For example, if in equilibrium, 1 peso trades for 0.10 dollars but at the official exchange rate, 1 peso trades for 0.12 dollars, then the peso is said to be overvalued.

It follows that if the peso is overvalued, the dollar is undervalued, which means it is fetching fewer pesos than it would at equilibrium. For example if in equilibrium, 1 dollar trades for 10 pesos but at the official exchange rate, 1 dollar trades for 8.33 pesos, then the dollar is undervalued.

Similarly, if the dollar price of pesos is below its equilibrium level (which is the case at official price 2 in Exhibit 9), a shortage of pesos exists. Also, the peso is **undervalued.** This means that the peso is not fetching as many dollars as it would at equilibrium. It follows that if the peso is undervalued, the dollar must be overvalued.

Overvalued peso ↔ Undervalued dollar

Undervalued peso ↔ Overvalued dollar

Fixed Exchange Rate System
The system where a nation's currency is set at a fixed rate relative to all other currencies, and central banks intervene in the foreign exchange market to maintain the fixed rate.

Overvaluation
A currency is overvalued if its price in terms of other currencies is above the equilibrium price.

Undervaluation
A currency is undervalued if its price in terms of other currencies is below the equilibrium price.

---

3. If the price of 1 peso is 0.12 dollars, it follows that the price of 1 dollar is approximately 8.33 pesos. Thus setting the official price of a peso in terms of dollars automatically sets the official price of a dollar in terms of pesos.

exhibit 9

A Fixed Exchange Rate System
In a fixed exchange rate system, the exchange rate is fixed—and it may not be fixed at the equilibrium exchange rate. The exhibit shows two cases. (1) If the exchange rate is fixed at official price 1, the peso is overvalued, the dollar is undervalued, and a surplus of pesos exists. (2) If the exchange rate is fixed at official price 2, the peso is undervalued, the dollar is overvalued, and a shortage of pesos exists.

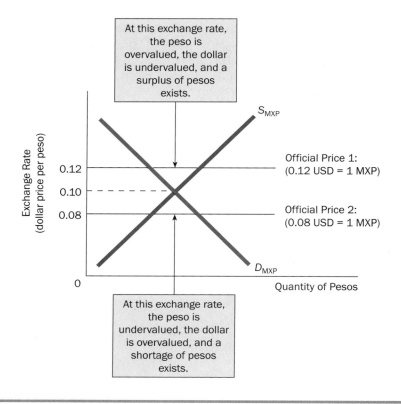

At this exchange rate, the peso is overvalued, the dollar is undervalued, and a surplus of pesos exists.

S_{MXP}

Official Price 1:
(0.12 USD = 1 MXP)

Official Price 2:
(0.08 USD = 1 MXP)

D_{MXP}

Exchange Rate (dollar price per peso)

0.12

0.10

0.08

0

Quantity of Pesos

At this exchange rate, the peso is undervalued, the dollar is overvalued, and a shortage of pesos exists.

WHAT IS SO BAD ABOUT AN OVERVALUED DOLLAR?

Suppose you read in the newspaper that the dollar is overvalued. You also read that economists are concerned about the overvalued dollar. "But why are economists concerned?" you ask.

They are concerned because the exchange rate—and hence the value of the dollar in terms of other currencies—affects the amount of U.S. exports and imports. Because it affects exports and imports, it naturally affects the merchandise trade balance. To illustrate, suppose the demand for and supply of pesos are represented by D_1 and S_1 in Exhibit 10. With this demand curve and supply curve, the equilibrium exchange rate is 0.10 USD = 1 MXP. Let's also suppose the exchange rate is fixed at this exchange rate. In other words, the equilibrium exchange rate and the fixed exchange rate are initially the same.

Time passes and eventually the demand curve for pesos shifts to the right, from D_1 to D_2. Under a flexible exchange rate system, the exchange rate would rise to 0.12 USD = 1 MXP. But a flexible exchange rate is not operating here—a fixed one is. In other words, the exchange rate stays fixed at 0.10 USD = 1 MXP. This means the fixed exchange rate (0.10 USD = 1 MXP) is below the new equilibrium exchange rate (0.12 USD = 1 MXP).

Recall that if the dollar price per peso is below its equilibrium level (which is the case here), the peso is undervalued and the dollar is overvalued. In other words, in equilibrium (at point 2 in Exhibit 10), 1 peso would trade for 0.12 dollars but at its fixed rate (at point 1), it trades for only 0.10 dollars—so the peso is undervalued. In equilibrium (at point 2), 1 dollar would trade for 8.33 pesos but at its fixed rate (at point 1), it trades for 10 pesos—so the dollar is overvalued.

But what is so bad about the dollar being overvalued? The answer is that it makes U.S. goods more expensive (for foreigners to buy), which in turn can affect the U.S. merchandise trade balance.

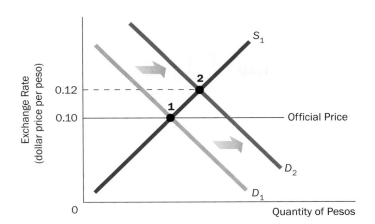

exhibit 10

Fixed Exchange Rates and an Overvalued Dollar
Initially, the demand for and supply of pesos are represented by D_1 and S_1, respectively. The equilibrium exchange rate is 0.10 USD = 1 MXP, which also happens to be the official (fixed) exchange rate. In time, the demand for pesos rises to D_2, and the equilibrium exchange rate rises to 0.12 USD = 1 MXP. The official exchange rate is fixed, however, so the dollar will be overvalued. As explained in the text, this can lead to a trade deficit.

For example, suppose a U.S. good costs 100 dollars. At the equilibrium exchange rate (0.12 USD = 1 MXP), a Mexican would pay 833 pesos for the good; but at the fixed exchange rate (0.10 USD = 1 MXP), he will pay 1,000 pesos.

Exchange Rate	Dollar Price	Peso Price
0.12 USD = 1 MXP (equilibrium)	100 USD	833 MXP (100 USD/0.12 USD)
0.10 USD = 1 MXP (fixed)	100 USD	1,000 MXP (100 USD/0.10 USD)

The higher the prices of U.S. goods (exports), the fewer of those goods Mexicans will buy, and, as just shown, an overvalued dollar makes U.S. export goods higher in price.

Ultimately, an overvalued dollar can affect the U.S. merchandise trade balance. As U.S. exports become more expensive for Mexicans, they buy fewer U.S. exports. If exports fall below imports, the result is a U.S. trade deficit.[4]

GOVERNMENT INVOLVEMENT IN A FIXED EXCHANGE RATE SYSTEM

Look back at Exhibit 9. Suppose the governments of Mexico and the United States agree to fix the exchange rate at 0.12 USD = 1 MXP. At this exchange rate, a surplus of pesos exists. What becomes of the surplus of pesos?

To maintain the exchange rate at 0.12 USD = 1 MXP, the Federal Reserve System (the Fed) could buy the surplus of pesos. But what would it use to buy the pesos? The Fed would buy the surplus of pesos with dollars. Consequently, the demand for pesos will increase and the demand curve will shift to the right, one hopes by enough to raise the equilibrium rate to the current fixed exchange rate.

Alternatively, instead of the Fed buying pesos (to mop up the excess supply of pesos), the Banco de Mexico (the central bank of Mexico) could buy pesos with some of its reserve dollars. (Why doesn't it buy pesos with pesos? Using pesos would not reduce the surplus of pesos on the market.) This action by the Banco de Mexico will also increase the demand for pesos and raise the equilibrium rate.

---

4. The other side of the coin, so to speak, is that if the dollar is overvalued, the peso must be undervalued. An undervalued peso makes Mexican goods cheaper for Americans. So while the overvalued dollar is causing Mexicans to buy fewer U.S. exports, the undervalued peso is causing Americans to import more goods from Mexico. In conclusion, U.S. exports fall, U.S. imports rise, and we move closer to a trade deficit, or if one already exists, it becomes larger.

ECONOMICS IN...

Everyday Life   Popular Culture   Technology   The World

The Nobel Prize in Economics and Foreign Exchange Markets

Do winners of the Nobel Prize in Economics care what is happening on foreign exchange markets? Because the prize money they win is paid in Swedish kronor, should they care?[5]

Consider the case of Robert Mundell, the 1999 winner of the prize. Mundell received a prize of 7.9 million Swedish kronor. In mid-October, when he was informed that he had won the prize, the prize money was worth nearly 1 million dollars. Mundell, however, decided not to take the prize money in kronor and then exchange it for dollars. Instead, he asked the Nobel Foundation to deposit the funds in his bank account in euros because he expected that over the next few months the euro would appreciate relative to the dollar.

Gary Becker was the 1992 winner of the Nobel Prize in Economics. Like all winners, he was notified of his winning the coveted prize in mid-October. He would not actually collect the prize money, however, until late December. In mid-October, the prize money (at current exchange rates) was worth 1.2 million dollars. Becker thought that the Swedish kronor was likely to depreciate in the near future, and so intended to buy dollars on the futures market. He never got around to it, though. Two weeks after he had been notified that he had won the Nobel Prize, there was a currency crisis in Sweden. As a result, his prize money shrank to 900,000 dollars.

Ronald Coase, who won the Nobel Prize in Economics in 1991, was to be paid his prize money at the end of 1991. Coase suspected that the kronor was about to appreciate in value relative to the dollar, so he asked the Foundation to pay him part of his prize money in January, 1992, to which the Foundation agreed. In January, the kronor appreciated in value, giving Coase more dollars per kronor.

Finally, the two actions could be combined; that is, both the Fed and the Banco de Mexico could buy pesos.

Q & A

Q: Why does the Fed play a much larger role under a fixed exchange rate system than under a flexible exchange rate system?

A: To support or maintain a fixed exchange rate, someone or something has to do the supporting or the maintaining. Central banks play this role. Under a flexible exchange rate system, there is no exchange rate to support or maintain; exchange rates simply respond to the forces of supply and demand.

OPTIONS UNDER A FIXED EXCHANGE RATE SYSTEM

Suppose there is a surplus of pesos in the foreign exchange market—indicating that the peso is overvalued and the dollar is undervalued. The Fed and the Banco de Mexico each attempt to rectify this situation by buying pesos. But suppose this combined action is not successful. The surplus of pesos persists for weeks, along with an overvalued peso and an undervalued dollar. What is there left to do? There are a few options.

Devaluation and Revaluation

Devaluation
A government act that changes the exchange rate by lowering the official price of a currency.

Revaluation
A government act that changes the exchange rate by raising the official price of a currency.

Mexico and the United States could agree to reset the official price of the dollar and the peso. This entails *devaluation* and *revaluation*.

A **devaluation** occurs when the official price of a currency is lowered. A **revaluation** occurs when the official price of a currency is raised. For example, suppose the first official price of a peso is 0.10 USD = 1 MXP. It follows that the first official price of 1 dollar is 10 pesos.

---

5. This feature is based on Sylvia Nasar, "Nobel Economics: Spending the Check," *New York Times*, 5 December 1999.

Now suppose Mexico and the U.S. agree to change the official price of their currencies. The second official price is 0.12 USD = 1 MXP. This means, then, that the second official price of 1 dollar is 8.33 pesos.

Moving from the first official price to the second, the peso has been revalued. That's because it takes *more dollars to buy a peso* (12 cents instead of 10 cents). Of course, moving from the first official price to the second means the dollar has been devalued. That's because it takes *fewer pesos to buy a dollar* (8.33 pesos instead of 10 pesos).

Might one country want to devalue its currency but another country not want to revalue its currency? For example, suppose Mexico wants to devalue its currency relative to the U.S. dollar. Would U.S. authorities always willingly comply? Not necessarily.

To see why, we have to understand that the United States will not sell as many goods to Mexico if the dollar is revalued. That's because, as we stated earlier, revaluing the dollar means Mexicans have to pay more for it—instead of paying, say, 8.33 pesos for 1 dollar, Mexicans might have to pay 10 pesos for 1 dollar. At a revalued dollar (higher peso price for a dollar), Mexicans will find U.S. goods more expensive and not want to buy as many. Americans who produce goods to sell to Mexico may see that a revalued dollar will hurt their pocketbooks and so they will argue against it.

Protectionist Trade Policy (Quotas and Tariffs)

Recall that an overvalued dollar can bring on or widen a trade deficit. How can a country deal with both the trade deficit and the overvalued dollar at once? Some say it can impose quotas and tariffs to reduce domestic consumption of foreign goods. (The previous chapter explains how both tariffs and quotas meet this objective.) A drop in the domestic consumption of foreign goods goes hand in hand with a decrease in the demand for foreign currencies. In turn, this can affect the value of the country's currency on the foreign exchange market. In this case, it can get rid of an overvalued dollar.

Economists are quick to point out, though, that trade deficits and overvalued currencies are sometimes used as an excuse to promote trade restrictions—many of which simply benefit special interests (such as U.S. producers that compete for sales with foreign producers in the U.S. market).

Changes in Monetary Policy

Sometimes a nation can use monetary policy to support the exchange rate or the official price of its currency. Suppose the United States is continually running a merchandise trade deficit; year after year, imports are outstripping exports. To remedy this, the United States might enact a tight monetary policy to retard inflation and drive up interest rates (at least in the short run). The tight monetary policy will reduce the U.S. rate of inflation and thereby lower U.S. prices relative to prices in other nations. This will make U.S. goods relatively cheaper than they were before (assuming other nations didn't also enact a tight monetary policy) and promote U.S. exports and discourage foreign imports, as well as generate a flow of investment funds into the United States in search of higher real interest rates.

Some economists argue against fixed exchange rates because they think it unwise for a nation to adopt a particular monetary policy simply to maintain an international exchange rate. Instead, they believe domestic monetary policies should be used to meet domestic economic goals—such as price stability, low unemployment, low and stable interest rates, and so forth.

THE GOLD STANDARD

If nations adopt the gold standard, they *automatically fix* their exchange rates. Suppose the United States defines a dollar as equal to 1/10 of an ounce of gold and Mexico defines a peso as equal to 1/100 of an ounce of gold. This means that one ounce of gold could be bought with either 10 dollars or 100 pesos. What, then, is the exchange rate between dollars and pesos? It is 10 MXP = 1 USD or 0.10 USD = 1 MXP. This is the fixed exchange rate between dollars and pesos.

To have an international gold standard, countries must do the following:

1. Define their currencies in terms of gold.
2. Stand ready and willing to convert gold into paper money and paper money into gold at the rate specified (for example, the United States would buy and sell gold at 10 dollars an ounce).
3. Link their money supplies to their holdings of gold.

With this last point in mind, consider how a gold standard would work. Let's again look at Mexico and the United States, and initially assume that the gold-standard (fixed) exchange rate of 0.10 USD = 1 MXP is the equilibrium exchange rate. Then, a change occurs: Inflation in Mexico raises prices there by 100 percent. A Mexican table that was priced at 2,000 pesos before the inflation is now priced at 4,000 pesos. At the gold-standard (fixed) exchange rate, Americans now have to pay 400 dollars (4,000 pesos/10 pesos per dollar) to buy the table, whereas before the inflation Americans had to pay only 200 dollars (2,000 pesos/ 10 pesos per dollar) for the table. As a result, Americans buy fewer Mexican tables; Americans import less from Mexico.

At the same time, Mexicans import more from the U.S. because American prices are now relatively lower than before inflation hit Mexico. A quick example illustrates our point. Suppose that before inflation hit Mexico, an American pair of shoes cost 200 dollars and, as before, a Mexican table cost 2,000 pesos. At 0.10 USD = 1 MXP, the 200-dollar American shoes cost 2,000 pesos and the 2,000-peso Mexican table cost 200 dollars. In other words, 1 pair of American shoes traded for (or equaled) 1 Mexican table.

Now look at things after inflation has raised the price of the Mexican table to 4,000 pesos, or 400 dollars. Because the American shoes are still 200 dollars (there has been no inflation in the United States), and the exchange rate is still fixed at 0.10 USD = 1 MXP, 1 pair of American shoes no longer equals 1 Mexican table; instead, it equals 1/2 of a Mexican table. In short, the inflation in Mexico has made U.S. goods *relatively cheaper* for Mexicans. As a result, Mexicans buy more U.S. goods; Mexicans import more from the United States.

To summarize: The inflation in Mexico has caused Americans to buy fewer goods from Mexico and Mexicans to buy more goods from the United States. What does this mean in terms of the merchandise trade balance for each country? In the United States, imports decline (Americans are buying less from Mexico) and exports rise (Mexicans are buying more from the United States), so the U.S. trade balance is likely to move into surplus. Contrarily, in Mexico, exports decline (Americans are buying less from Mexico) and imports rise (Mexicans are buying more from the United States), so Mexico's trade balance is likely to move into deficit.

On a gold standard, Mexicans have to pay for the difference between their imports and exports with gold. Gold is therefore shipped to the United States. An increase in the supply of gold in the United States expands the U.S. money supply. A decrease in the supply of gold in Mexico contracts the Mexican money supply. Prices are affected in both countries. In the United States, prices begin to rise; in Mexico, prices begin to fall.

As U.S. prices go up and Mexican prices go down, the earlier situation begins to reverse itself. American goods look more expensive to Mexicans, and they begin to buy less, whereas Mexican goods look cheaper to Americans, and they begin to buy more. Consequently, American imports begin to rise and exports begin to fall; Mexican imports begin to fall and exports begin to rise. Thus, by changing domestic money supplies and price levels, the gold standard begins to correct the initial trade balance disequilibrium.

The change in the money supply that the gold standard sometimes requires has prompted some economists to voice the same argument against the gold standard that is often heard against the fixed exchange rate system; that is, it subjects domestic monetary policy to international instead of domestic considerations. In fact, many economists cite this as part of the reason many nations abandoned the gold standard in the 1930s. At a time when unemployment was unusually high, many nations with trade deficits felt that matters would only get worse if they contracted their money supplies to live by the edicts of the gold standard. We explore this question in greater detail in a later section.

Self-Test

1. Under a fixed exchange rate system, if one currency is overvalued, then another currency must be undervalued. Explain why this is true.

2. How does an overvalued dollar affect U.S. exports and imports?

3. In each case, identify whether the U.S. dollar is overvalued or undervalued.
   a. The fixed exchange rate is 2 dollars = 1 pound and the equilibrium exchange rate is 3 dollars = 1 pound.
   b. The fixed exchange rate is 1.25 dollars = 1 euro and the equilibrium exchange rate is 1.10 dollars = 1 euro.
   c. The fixed exchange rate is 1 dollar = 10 pesos and the equilibrium exchange rate is 1 dollar = 14 pesos.

4. Under a fixed exchange rate system, why might the United States want to devalue its currency?

FIXED EXCHANGE RATES VERSUS FLEXIBLE EXCHANGE RATES

As is the case in many economic situations, there are both costs and benefits to any exchange rate system. This section discusses some of the arguments and issues surrounding fixed exchange rates and flexible exchange rates.

PROMOTING INTERNATIONAL TRADE

Which are better at promoting international trade, fixed or flexible exchange rates? This section presents the case for each.

The Case for Fixed Exchange Rates

Proponents of a fixed exchange rate system often argue that fixed exchange rates promote international trade, whereas flexible exchange rates stifle it. A major advantage of fixed exchange rates is certainty. Individuals in different countries know from day to day the value of their nation's currency. With flexible exchange rates, individuals are less likely to engage in international trade because of the added risk of not knowing from one day to the next how many dollars or euros or yen they will have to trade for other currencies. Certainty is a necessary ingredient in international trade; flexible exchange rates promote uncertainty, which hampers international trade.

Economist Charles Kindleberger, a proponent of fixed exchange rates, believes that having fixed exchange rates is analogous to having a single currency for the entire United States instead of having a different currency for each of the 50 states. One currency in the United States promotes trade, whereas 50 different currencies would hamper it. In Kindleberger's view:

> *The main case against flexible exchange rates is that they break up the world market. . . . Imagine trying to conduct interstate trade in the USA if there were fifty different state monies, none of which was dominant. This is akin to barter, the inefficiency of which is explained time and again by textbooks.*[6]

---

6. Charles Kindleberger, *International Money* (London: Allen and Unwin, 1981), p. 174.

The Case for Flexible Exchange Rates

Advocates of flexible exchange rates, as we have noted, maintain that it is better for a nation to adopt policies to meet domestic economic goals than to sacrifice domestic economic goals to maintain an exchange rate. They also say that there is too great a chance that the fixed exchange rate will diverge greatly from the equilibrium exchange rate, creating persistent balance of trade problems. This leads deficit nations to impose trade restrictions (tariffs and quotas) that hinder international trade.

OPTIMAL CURRENCY AREAS

As of 2002, the European Union (EU) consists of 15 member states—Austria, Belgium, Denmark, Finland, France, Germany, Greece, Ireland, Italy, Luxembourg, The Netherlands, Portugal, Spain, Sweden, and the United Kingdom. According to the European Union, its ultimate goal is "an ever close union among the peoples of Europe, in which decisions are taken as closely as possible to the citizen." As part of meeting this goal, the EU established its own currency—the euro—on January 1, 1999.[7] Although euro notes and coins were not issued until January 1, 2002, certain business transactions were made in euros beginning in January 1, 1999.

The issue of the European Union and the euro is relevant to a discussion of an **optimal currency area.** An optimal currency area is a geographic area in which exchange rates can be fixed or a *common currency* used without sacrificing domestic economic goals—such as low unemployment. The concept of an optimal currency area originated in the debate over whether fixed or flexible exchange rates are better. Most of the pioneering work on optimal currency areas was done by Robert Mundell, the winner of the 1999 Nobel Prize in Economics.

Before discussing an optimal currency area, we need to look at the relationships among labor mobility, trade, and exchange rates. Labor mobility means that it is easy for the residents of one country to move to another country.

> **Optimal Currency Area**
> A geographic area in which exchange rates can be fixed or a common currency used without sacrificing domestic economic goals—such as low unemployment.

Trade and Labor Mobility

Suppose there are only two countries, the United States and Canada. The United States produces calculators and soft drinks and Canada produces bread and muffins. Currently, the two countries trade with each other and there is complete labor mobility between the two countries.

One day, the residents of both countries reduce their demand for bread and muffins and increase their demand for calculators and soft drinks. In other words, there is a change in relative demand. Demand increases for U.S. goods and falls for Canadian goods. Business firms in Canada lay off employees because their sales have plummeted. Incomes in Canada begin to fall and the unemployment rate begins to rise. In the United States, prices initially rise because of the increased demand for calculators and soft drinks. In response to the higher demand for their products, U.S. business firms begin to hire more workers and increase their production. Their efforts to hire more workers drive wages up and reduce the unemployment rate.

Because labor is mobile, some of the newly unemployed Canadian workers move to the United States to find work. This will ease the economic situation in both countries. It will reduce some of the unemployment problems in Canada, and with more workers in the United States, more output will be produced, thus dampening upward price pressures on calculators and soft drinks. Thus, changes in relative demand pose no major economic problems for either country if labor is mobile.

---

7. So far, only 11 of the 15 member states have adopted the euro as their official currency.

ECONOMICS IN...

Back to the Futures

Meet (the fictional) Bill Whatley, owner of a Toyota dealership in Tulsa, Oklahoma. It is currently May, and Bill is thinking about a shipment of Toyotas he plans to buy in August. He knows that he must buy the Toyotas from Japan with yen, but he has a problem. At the present time, the price of 1 yen is 0.008 dollars. Bill wonders what the dollar price of a yen will be in August when he plans to make his purchase. Suppose the price of 1 yen rises to 0.010 dollars. If this happens, then instead of paying 20,000 dollars for a Toyota priced at 2.5 million yen, he would have to pay 25,000 dollars.[8] This difference of 5,000 dollars may be enough to erase his profit on the sale of the Toyotas.

What is Bill to do? He could purchase a futures contract today for the needed quantity of yen in August. A futures contract is a contract in which the seller agrees to provide a particular good (in this example, a particular currency) to the buyer on a specified future date at an agreed-on price. In short, Bill can buy yen today at a specified dollar price and take delivery of the yen at a later date (in August).

But suppose the price of 1 yen falls to 0.007 dollars in August. If this happens, Bill would have to pay only 17,500 dollars (instead of 20,000 dollars) for a Toyota priced at 2.5 million yen. Although he could increase his profit in this case, Bill, like other car dealers, might not be interested in assuming the risk associated with changes in exchange rates. He may prefer to lock in a sure thing.

Who would sell yen to Bill? The answer is someone who is willing to assume the risk of changes in the value of currencies—for example, Julie Jackson. Julie thinks to herself, "I think the dollar price of a yen will go down between now and August. Therefore, I'll enter into a contract with Bill stating that I'll give him 2.5 million yen in August for 20,000 dollars—the exchange rate specified in the contract being 1 JPY = 0.008 USD. If I'm right, and the actual exchange rate in August is 1 JPY = 0.007 USD, then I can purchase the 2.5 million yen for 17,500 dollars, and fulfill my contract with Bill by turning the yen over to him for 20,000 dollars. I walk away with 2,500 dollars in profit."

Many economists argue that futures contracts offer people a way of dealing with the risk associated with a flexible exchange rate system. If a person doesn't know what next month's exchange rate will be and doesn't want to take the risk of waiting to see, then he or she can enter into a futures contract and effectively shift the risk to someone who voluntarily assumes it.

Trade and Labor Immobility

Now let's change things. Suppose that relative demand has changed but this time labor is not mobile between the United States and Canada (labor immobility). There are either political or cultural barriers to people moving between the two countries. What happens in the economics of the two countries if people cannot move? The answer depends largely on whether exchange rates are fixed or flexible.

If exchange rates are flexible, the value of U.S. currency changes vis-à-vis Canadian currency. If Canadians want to buy more U.S. goods, they will have to exchange their domestic currency for U.S. currency. This increases the demand for U.S. currency on the foreign exchange market at the same time that it increases the supply of Canadian currency. Consequently, U.S. currency appreciates and Canadian currency depreciates. Because Canadian currency depreciates, U.S. goods become relatively more expensive for Canadians, so they buy fewer. And because U.S. currency appreciates, Canadian goods become relatively cheaper for Americans, so they buy more. Canadian business firms begin to sell more goods, so they

---

8. If 1 yen equals 0.008 dollars, then a Toyota with a price of 2.5 million yen costs 20,000 dollars because 2.5 million × 0.008 dollars = 20,000 dollars. If 1 yen equals 0.010 dollars, then a Toyota with a price of 2.5 million yen costs 25,000 dollars because 2.5 million × 0.010 dollars equals 25,000 dollars.

hire more workers, the unemployment rate drops, and the bad economic times in Canada begin to disappear.

If exchange rates are fixed, however, U.S. goods will not become relatively more expensive for Canadians and Canadian goods will not become relatively cheaper for Americans. Consequently, the bad economic times in Canada (high unemployment) might last for a long time indeed instead of beginning to reverse. Thus, if labor is immobile, changes in relative demand may pose major economic problems when exchange rates are fixed but not when they are flexible.

Costs, Benefits, and Optimal Currency Areas

There are both costs and benefits to flexible exchange rates. The benefits we have just discussed. The costs include the cost of exchanging one currency for another (there is a charge to exchange, say, U.S. dollars for Canadian dollars or U.S. dollars for Japanese yen) and the added risk of not knowing what the value of one's currency will be on the foreign exchange market on any given day. For many countries, the benefits outweigh the costs, and so they have flexible exchange rate regimes.

Suppose some of the costs of flexible exchange rates could be eliminated, while the benefits were maintained. Under what conditions could two countries have a fixed exchange rate or adopt a common currency and retain the benefits of flexible exchange rates? The answer is when labor is mobile between the two countries. Then, there is no reason to have separate currencies that float against each other because resources (labor) can move easily and quickly in response to changes in relative demand. There is no reason why the two countries cannot fix exchange rates or adopt the same currency.

When labor in countries within a certain geographic area is mobile enough to move easily and quickly in response to changes in relative demand, the countries are said to constitute an *optimal currency area*. Countries in an optimal currency area can either fix their currencies or adopt the same currency and thus keep all the benefits of flexible exchange rates without any of the costs.

It is commonly argued that the states within the United States constitute an optimal currency area. Labor can move easily and quickly between, say, North Carolina and South Carolina in response to relative demand changes. Some economists argue that the countries that compose the European Union are within an optimal currency area and that adopting a common currency—the euro—will benefit these countries. Other economists disagree. They argue that while labor is somewhat more mobile in Europe today than in the past, there are still certain language and cultural differences that make labor mobility less than sufficient to truly constitute an optimal currency area.

THE CURRENT INTERNATIONAL MONETARY SYSTEM

Managed Float
A managed flexible exchange rate system, under which nations now and then intervene to adjust their official reserve holdings to moderate major swings in exchange rates.

Today's international monetary system is best described as a managed flexible exchange rate system, sometimes referred to more casually as a **managed float.** In a way, this system is a rough compromise between the fixed and flexible exchange rate systems. The current system operates under flexible exchange rates, but not completely. Nations now and then intervene to adjust their official reserve holdings to moderate major swings in exchange rates.

Proponents of the managed float system stress the following advantages:

1. **It allows nations to pursue independent monetary policies.** Under a (strictly) fixed exchange rate system, fixed either by agreement or by gold, a nation with a merchandise trade deficit might have to enact a tight monetary policy in order to retard inflation and promote its exports. This would not be the case with the managed float. Its proponents argue that it is better to adjust one price—the exchange rate—than to adjust the price level to solve trade imbalances.

2. **It solves trade problems without trade restrictions.** As stated earlier, under a fixed exchange rate system, nations sometimes impose tariffs and quotas to solve trade imbalances. For example, a deficit nation might impose import quotas so that exports and imports of goods will be more in line. Under the current system, trade imbalances are usually solved through changes in exchange rates.

3. **It is flexible and therefore can easily adjust to shocks.** In 1973–1974, the OPEC nations dramatically raised the price of oil, which resulted in many oil-importing nations running trade deficits. A fixed exchange rate system would have had a hard time accommodating such a major change in oil prices. The current system had little trouble, however. Exchange rates took much of the shock (there were large changes in exchange rates) and thus allowed most nations' economies to weather the storm with a minimum of difficulty.

Opponents of the current international monetary system stress the following disadvantages:

1. **It promotes exchange rate volatility and uncertainty and results in less international trade than would be the case under fixed exchange rates.** Under a flexible exchange rate system, volatile exchange rates make it riskier for importers and exporters to conduct business. As a result, there is less international trade than there would be under a fixed exchange rate system.

   Proponents respond that the futures market in currencies allows importers and exporters to shift the risk of fluctuations in exchange rates to others. For example, if an American company wants to buy a certain quantity of a good from a Japanese company three months from today, it can contract today for the desired quantity of yen it will need, at a specified price. It will not have to worry about a change in the dollar price of yen during the next three months. There is, of course, a cost to purchasing a futures contract, but it is usually modest.

2. **It promotes inflation.** As we have seen, the monetary policies of different nations are not independent of one another under a fixed exchange rate system. For example, a nation with a merchandise trade deficit is somewhat restrained from inflating its currency because this will worsen the deficit problem. It will make the nation's goods more expensive relative to foreign goods and promote the purchase of imports. In its attempt to maintain the exchange rate, a nation with a merchandise trade deficit would have to enact a tight monetary policy.

   Under the current system, a nation with a merchandise trade deficit does not have to maintain exchange rates or try to solve its deficit problem through changes in its money supply. Opponents of the current system argue that this frees nations to inflate. They predict more inflation will result than would occur under a fixed exchange rate system.

3. **Changes in exchange rates alter trade balances in the desired direction only after a long time; in the short run, a depreciation in a currency can make the situation worse instead of better.** It is often argued that soon after a depreciation in a trade-deficit nation's currency, the trade deficit will increase (not decrease, as was hoped). The reason is that import demand is inelastic in the short run: Imports are not very responsive to a change in price.

   Suppose Mexico is running a trade deficit with the United States at the present exchange rate of 0.12 USD = 1 MXP. At this exchange rate, the peso is overvalued. Mexico buys 2,000 television sets from the United States, each with a price tag of 500 dollars. Assume Mexico therefore spends 8.33 million pesos on imports of American television sets.

   Now suppose the overvalued peso begins to depreciate, say, to 0.11 USD = 1 MXP. Furthermore, in the short run, Mexican customers buy only 100 fewer American television sets; that is, they import 1,900 television sets. At a price of 500 dollars each and an exchange rate of 0.11 USD = 1 MXP, Mexicans now spend 8.63 million pesos on imports of American television sets.

In the short run, then, a depreciation in the peso has widened the trade deficit because imports fell by only 5 percent while the price of imports (in terms of pesos) increased by 9.09 percent. As time passes, imports will fall off more (it takes time for Mexican buyers to shift from higher-priced American goods to lower-priced Mexican goods), and the deficit will shrink.

Q & A

Q: Does the discussion here imply that a system of flexible exchange rates is undesirable?

A: Some economists say yes. They argue that if import demand is inelastic, then changes in exchange rates are a rather crude way of solving a trade imbalance because in the short run they make things worse.

Self-Test

1. What is an optimal currency area?

2. Country 1 produces good *X* and country 2 produces good *Y*. People in both countries begin to demand more of good *X* and less of good *Y*. Assume there is no labor mobility between the two countries and that a flexible exchange rate system exists. What will happen to the unemployment rate in country 2? Explain your answer.

3. How important is labor mobility in determining whether or not an area is an optimal currency area?

A Reader Asks...

How Do I Convert Currencies?

I plan to travel to several different countries in the summer. How do I convert prices of products in other countries into dollars?

Here is the general formula you would use:

Price of   Price of   Price of the
the product = the product in × foreign currency
in dollars foreign currency in dollars

For example, suppose you travel to Mexico and see something priced at 100 pesos. You'd change the general formula into a specific one:

Price of   Price of Price of
the product = the product × a peso
in dollars in pesos in dollars

If the dollar price of a peso is, say, 0.12 dollars, then the dollar price of the product is 12 dollars. Here is the calculation:

Price of the product in dollars = 100 × 0.12
= 12

Or suppose you are in Tokyo and you see a product for 10,000 yen. What is the price in dollars? At the exchange rate of 0.008 USD = 1 JPY, it is 80 dollars.

Price of the product in dollars = 10,000 × 0.008
= 80

Now let's suppose you are in Russia and you don't know what the exchange rate is between dollars and rubles. You pick up a newspaper to find out (often exchange rates are quoted in the newspaper). But instead of finding the exchange rate quoted in terms of the dollar price of a ruble (for example, 0.0318 dollars for 1 ruble), you find the ruble price of a dollar (31.4190 rubles for 1 dollar). What do you do now?

Perhaps the easiest thing to do is first convert rubles per dollar into dollars per ruble, and then use the earlier formula to find the price of the Russian product in dollars. Recall that exchange rates are reciprocals, so:

$$\text{Dollars per ruble} = \frac{1}{\text{Rubles per dollar}}$$

To illustrate, if it takes 31.4190 rubles to purchase 1 dollar, then it takes 0.0318 dollars to buy 1 ruble. Here is the computation:

$$\text{Dollars per ruble} = \frac{1}{31.4190}$$
$$= 0.0318$$

Now because you know that 0.0318 dollars = 1 ruble, it follows that, say, a Russian coat that costs 10,000 rubles costs 318 dollars:

$$\text{Price of the product in dollars} = 10{,}000 \times 0.0318$$
$$= 318$$

Chapter Summary

Balance of Payments

- The balance of payments provides information about a nation's imports and exports, domestic residents' earnings on assets located abroad, foreign earnings on domestic assets, gifts to and from foreign countries, and official transactions by governments and central banks.
- In a nation's balance of payments, any transaction that supplies the country's currency in the foreign exchange market is recorded as a debit (−). Any transaction that creates a demand for the country's currency is recorded as a credit (+).
- The three main accounts of the balance of payments are the current account, capital account, and official reserve account.
- The current account includes all payments related to the purchase and sale of goods and services. The three major components of the account are exports of goods and services, imports of goods and services, and net unilateral transfers abroad.
- The capital account includes all payments related to the purchase and sale of assets and to borrowing and lending activities. The major components are outflow of U.S. capital and inflow of foreign capital.
- The official reserve account includes transactions by the central banks of various countries.
- The merchandise trade balance is the difference between the value of merchandise exports and the value of merchandise imports. If exports are greater than imports, a nation has a trade surplus; if imports are greater than exports, a nation has a trade deficit. The balance of payments equals current account balance + capital account balance + official reserve balance + statistical discrepancy.

The Foreign Exchange Market and Flexible and Fixed Exchange Rates

- The market in which currencies of different countries are exchanged is called the foreign exchange market. In this market, currencies are bought and sold for a price; an exchange rate exists.
- If Americans demand Mexican goods, they also demand Mexican pesos and supply U.S. dollars. If

Mexicans demand American goods, they also demand U.S. dollars and supply Mexican pesos. When the residents of a nation demand a foreign currency, they must supply their own currency.
- Under flexible exchange rates, the foreign exchange market will equilibrate at the exchange rate where the quantity demanded of a currency equals the quantity supplied of the currency; for example, the quantity demanded of U.S. dollars equals the quantity supplied of U.S. dollars.
- If the price of a nation's currency increases relative to a foreign currency, the nation's currency is said to have appreciated. For example, if the price of a peso rises from 0.10 USD = 1 MXP to 0.15 USD = 1 MXP, the peso has appreciated. If the price of a nation's currency decreases relative to a foreign currency, the nation's currency is said to have depreciated. For example, if the price of a dollar falls from 10 MXP = 1 USD to 8 MXP = 1 USD, the dollar has depreciated.
- Under a flexible exchange rate system, the equilibrium exchange rate is affected by a difference in income growth rates between countries, a difference in inflation rates between countries, and a change in (real) interest rates between countries.
- Under a fixed exchange rate system, countries agree to fix the price of their currencies. The central banks of the countries must then buy and sell currencies to maintain the agreed-on exchange rate. If a persistent deficit or surplus in a nation's combined current and capital account exists at a fixed exchange rate, the nation has a few options to deal with the problem: devalue or revalue its currency, enact protectionist trade policies (in the case of a deficit), or change its monetary policy.

The Gold Standard

- To have an international gold standard, nations must do the following: (1) define their currencies in terms of gold; (2) stand ready and willing to convert gold into paper money and paper money into gold at a specified rate; and (3) link their money supplies to their holdings of gold. The change in the money supply that the gold standard sometimes requires has prompted some economists to voice the same argument against the gold standard that is often heard against the fixed exchange rate system: It subjects domestic monetary policy to international instead of domestic considerations.

The Current International Monetary System

- Today's international monetary system is described as a managed flexible exchange rate system, or managed float. For the most part, the exchange rate system is flexible, although nations do periodically intervene in the foreign exchange market to adjust exchange rates. Because it is a managed float system, it is difficult to tell if nations will emphasize the "float" part or the "managed" part in the future.

- Proponents of the managed flexible exchange rate system believe it offers several advantages: (1) It allows nations to pursue independent monetary policies. (2) It solves trade problems without trade restrictions. (3) It is flexible and therefore can easily adjust to shocks. Opponents of the managed flexible exchange rate system believe it has several disadvantages: (1) It promotes exchange rate volatility and uncertainty and results in less international trade than would be the case under fixed exchange rates. (2) It promotes inflation. (3) It corrects trade deficits only a long time after a depreciation in the currency; in the interim, it can make matters worse.

Key Terms and Concepts

Balance of Payments
Debit
Foreign Exchange Market
Credit
Current Account
Merchandise Trade Balance
Merchandise Trade Deficit
Merchandise Trade Surplus
Current Account Balance

Capital Account
Capital Account Balance
Exchange Rate
Flexible Exchange Rate System
Appreciation
Depreciation
Purchasing Power Parity (PPP)
 Theory
Fixed Exchange Rate System

Overvaluation
Undervaluation
Devaluation
Revaluation
Optimal Currency Area
International Monetary Fund
 (IMF)
Special Drawing Right (SDR)
Managed Float

Economic Connections to You

Economic facts, actions, and changes create ripples that move away from their point of origin. Eventually, these ripples can intersect your life and have an effect on you. Consider the following example.

The Fed increases the money supply in the United States by a larger percentage than Banco de Mexico (the central bank of Mexico) increases the money supply in Mexico. As a result, the inflation rate in the United States rises relative to the inflation rate in Mexico. This changes the demand for and supply of dollars and pesos on foreign exchange markets. Con-

sequently, the dollar depreciates and the peso appreciates. Just as the dollar is depreciating and the peso is appreciating, you take a trip to Mexico. You must pay higher prices for the goods and services you buy in Mexico. Thus, there is a connection between a change in the money supply and the prices you pay on a trip abroad—an economic connection to you.

Based on the material in this chapter, identify other ways in which economic facts, actions, and changes create ripples that eventually affect you.

1. Suppose the United States and Japan have a flexible exchange rate system. Explain whether each of the following events will lead to an appreciation or depreciation in the U.S. dollar and Japanese yen. (a) U.S. real interest rates rise above Japanese real interest rates. (b) The Japanese inflation rate rises relative to the U.S. inflation rate. (c) Japan imposes a quota on imports of American radios.

2. Give an example that illustrates how a change in the exchange rate changes the relative price of domestic goods in terms of foreign goods.

3. Suppose the media report that the United States has a deficit in its current account. What does this imply about the U.S. capital account balance and official reserve account balance?

4. Suppose Canada has a merchandise trade deficit and Mexico has a merchandise trade surplus. The two countries have a flexible exchange rate system, so the Mexican peso appreciates and the Canadian dollar depreciates. It is noticed, however, that soon after the depreciation of the Canadian dollar, Canada's trade deficit grows instead of shrinks. Why might this occur?

5. What are the strong and weak points of the flexible exchange rate system? What are the strong and weak points of the fixed exchange rate system?

6. Individuals do not keep a written account of their balance of trade with other individuals. For example, John doesn't keep an account of how much he sells to Alice and how much he buys from her. In addition, neither cities nor any of the 50 states calculate their balance of trade with all other cities and states. However, nations do calculate their merchandise trade balance with other nations. If nations do it, should individuals, cities, and states do it? Why or why not?

7. Every nation's balance of payments equals zero. Does it follow that each nation is on an equal footing in international trade and finance with every other nation? Explain your answer.

8. Suppose your objective is to predict whether the euro (the currency of the European Union) and the U.S. dollar will appreciate or depreciate on the foreign exchange market in the next two months. What information would you need to help you make your prediction? Specifically, how would this information help you predict the direction of the foreign exchange value of the euro and dollar? Next, explain how a person who could accurately predict exchange rates could become extremely rich in a short time.

9. Suppose the price of a Big Mac always rises by the percentage rise in the price level of the country in which it is sold. According to the purchasing power parity (PPP) theory, we would expect the price of a Big Mac to be the same everywhere in the world. Why?

10. If everyone in the world spoke the same language, would the world be closer to or further from being an optimal currency area? Explain your answer.

1. The following foreign exchange information appeared in a newspaper:

	U.S. Dollar Equivalent		Currency per U.S. Dollar	
	THURS.	FRI.	THURS.	FRI.
Russia (ruble)	0.0318	0.0317	31.4190	31.5290
Brazil (real)	0.3569	0.3623	2.8020	2.7601
India (rupee)	0.0204	0.0208	48.9100	47.8521

a. Between Thursday and Friday, did the U.S. dollar appreciate or depreciate against the Russian ruble?
b. Between Thursday and Friday, did the U.S. dollar appreciate or depreciate against the Brazilian real?
c. Between Thursday and Friday, did the U.S. dollar appreciate or depreciate against the Indian rupee?

2. If 1 dollar equals 0.0093 yen, then what does 1 yen equal?

3. If 1 dollar equals 7.7 krone (Danish), then what does 1 krone equal?

4. If 1 dollar equals 31 rubles, then what does 1 ruble equal?

5. If the current account is −$45 billion, the capital account is +$55 billion, and the official reserve balance is −$1 billion, what does the statistical discrepancy equal?

6. Why does the balance of payments always equal zero?

1. Go to *http://www.imf.org*, click on "About the IMF," and then select "IMF at a Glance." How many countries are members of the IMF? When did the IMF come into existence? What are the objectives of the IMF? What is the most recent amount of loans outstanding (in billions of SDRs)?

2. Click on the "Back" button to return to the "About the IMF" page. Click on "Frequently asked questions," and select "Where does the IMF get its money?" Where does the IMF get its money? Which country is the largest contributor to the IMF?

3. Click on the "Back" button to return to the home page. Click on "Country Information," and select "Latvia." Read one of the notices, press releases, or statements about Latvia and the IMF. What is the extent of IMF involvement in Latvia?

4. Go to *http://www.worldbank.org/*, and choose "Countries & Regions." Scroll down the Web page, and select "El Salvador." Under "Our Work in El Salvador," select "IFC in El Salvador." Read the Web page.

   a. What does IFC stand for? What does it do? What is its relationship with the World Bank?

   b. What is the World Bank Group's current strategy for El Salvador's economic development?

   c. Is El Salvador's current account balance positive or negative? What could explain this fact?

Log on to the Arnold Xtra! Web site now (*http://arnoldxtra.swcollege.com*) for additional learning resources such as practice quizzes, help with graphing, video clips, and current event applications.

CHAPTER 1

Chapter 1, page 5

1. False. It takes two things for scarcity to exist: finite resources and infinite wants. If peoples' wants were equal to or less than the finite resources available to satisfy their wants, there would be no scarcity. Scarcity exists only because peoples' wants are greater than the resources available to satisfy their wants. Scarcity is the condition of infinite wants clashing with finite resources.

2. Both define economics as having to do with ends and means, which implicitly brings up the concept of scarcity. In short, both Friedman and Robbins emphasize the concept of scarcity in their definitions.

3. Positive economics deals with what is; normative economics, with what should be. Macroeconomics deals with human behavior and choices as they relate to an entire economy. Microeconomics deals with human behavior and choices as they relate to relatively small units—an individual, a firm, an industry, a single market.

Chapter 1, page 15

1. Because of scarcity, there is a need for a rationing device. People will compete for the rationing device. For example, if dollar price is the rationing device, people will compete for dollars.

2. Every time a person is late to history class, the instructor subtracts one-tenth of a point from the person's final grade. If the instructor raised the opportunity cost of being late to class—by subtracting one point from the person's final grade—economists predict there would be fewer persons late to class. In summary, the higher the opportunity cost of being late to class, the less likely people will be late to class.

3. Yes. To illustrate, suppose the marginal benefits and marginal costs (in dollars) are as follows for various hours of studying.

Hours	Marginal Benefits	Marginal Costs
First hour	$20.00	$10.00
Second hour	$14.00	$11.00
Third hour	$13.00	$12.00
Fourth hour	$12.10	$12.09
Fifth hour	$11.00	$13.00

   Clearly you will study the first hour because the marginal benefits are greater than the marginal costs. Stated differently, there is a net benefit of $10 (the difference between the marginal benefits of $20 and the marginal costs of $10) for studying the first hour. If you stop studying after the first hour and do not proceed to the second, then you will forfeit the net benefit of $3 for the second hour. To maximize your net benefits of studying, you must proceed until the marginal benefits are as close to equal to the marginal costs as possible. (In the extreme, this is an epsilon away from equality. However, economists simply speak of "equality" between the two for convenience.) In this case, you will study through the fourth hour. You will not study the fifth hour because it is not worth it; the marginal benefits of studying the fifth hour are less than the marginal costs. In short, there is a net cost to studying the fifth hour.

4. An example is a politician who says: "My opponent has been in office for the past two years and during this time, interest rates have gone up and bankruptcies have gone up. We don't need any more bad economics. Don't cast your vote for my opponent. Vote for me." The politician implies that his opponent caused the dismal economic record when this is probably not the case.

5. Unless stated otherwise, when economics instructors identify the relationship between two variables they implicitly make the *ceteris paribus* assumption. In other words, the instructor is really saying, "If the price of going to the movies goes down, people will go to the movies more often—assuming that nothing else changes, such as the quality of movies, etc." Instructors don't always state *"ceteris paribus"* because if they did, they would be using the term every minute of a lecture. So the instructor is right, although a student new to economics might not know what the instructor is assuming but not saying.

Chapter 1, page 20

1. The purpose of building a theory is to explain something that is not obvious. For example, the cause of

changes in the unemployment rate is not obvious, and so the economist would build a theory to explain changes in the unemployment rate.

2. A theory of the economy would seek to explain why certain things in the economy happen. For example, a theory of the economy might try to explain why prices rise or why output falls. A description of the economy is simply a statement of what exists in the economy. For example, we could say the economy is growing, or the economy is contracting, or more jobs are available this month than last month. A description doesn't answer questions; it simply tells us what is. A theory tries to answer a "why" question, such as: Why are more jobs available this month than last month?

3. If you do not test a theory, you will never know if you have accomplished your objective in building the theory in the first place. That is, you will not know if you have accurately explained something. We do not simply accept a theory if it "sounds right" because what sounds right may actually be wrong. For example, no doubt during the time of Columbus, the theory that the earth was flat sounded right to many people and the theory that the earth was round sounded ridiculous. The right-sounding theory turned out to be wrong, though, and the ridiculous-sounding theory turned out to be right.

CHAPTER 2

Chapter 2, page 48

1. A straight-line PPF represents constant opportunity costs between two goods. For example, for every unit of X produced, one unit of Y is forfeited. A bowed-outward PPF represents increasing opportunity costs. For example, we may have to forfeit 1 unit of X to produce the eleventh unit of Y, but we have to forfeit 2 units of X to produce the one hundredth unit of Y.

2. Political battles are most often waged when one political party can have more of what it wants only if another political party gets less of what it wants. This condition exists when the economy is on its PPF and stagnant (not growing). More of X means less of Y. In a growing economy, it is possible to get more of X without getting any less of Y, or to get more of both X and Y.

3. The first condition is that the economy is currently operating *below* the PPF. It is possible to move from a point below the PPF to a point on the PPF and get more of all goods. The second condition is that the economy's PPF shifts outward.

4. False. Take a look at Exhibit 5. There are numerous efficient points, all of which lie on the PPF.

Chapter 2, page 54

1. The producers' surplus is $3,000; the consumers' surplus is $8,000.

2. Transaction costs are the costs associated with the time and effort needed to search out, negotiate, and consummate a trade. The transaction costs are likely to be higher for buying a house than for buying a car because buying a house is a more detailed and complex process.

3. Not necessarily. Cynthia may simply be expressing her discontent over the terms of trade. Stated differently, she may wish she could have obtained more consumers' surplus than she obtained.

4. Answers will vary. Sample answer: John buys a magazine and reads it. There is no third-party effect. Sally asks a rock band to play at a party. Sally's next-door neighbor (a third party) is disturbed by the loud music.

Chapter 2, page 56

1. If George goes from producing $5X$ to $10X$, he gives up $5Y$. This means the opportunity cost of 5 more X is 5 fewer Y. It follows that the opportunity cost of $1X$ is $1Y$. Conclusion: the opportunity cost of $1X$ is $1Y$.

2. If Harriet produces 10 more X she gives up $15Y$. It follows that the opportunity cost of $1X$ is $1.5Y$ and the opportunity cost of $1Y$ is $0.67X$. If Bill produces 10 more X he gives up $20Y$. It follows that the opportunity cost of $1X$ is $2Y$ and the opportunity cost of $1Y$ is $0.5X$. Harriet is the lower-cost producer of X and Bill is the lower-cost producer of Y. In short, Harriet has the comparative advantage in the production of X; Bill has the comparative advantage in the production of Y.

Chapter 2, page 60

1. What goods will be produced? How will the goods be produced? For whom will the goods be produced?

2. Trade benefits the traders. If George buys a book for $40, both George and the bookseller have been made better off. George would not have traded $40 for the book unless he expected to be made better off. Similarly, the seller would not have sold the book unless she expected to be made better off.

3. One of the questions every society must answer is *What goods will be produced?* In a way, this is no different than *Where on its PPF will an economy operate?* In other words, what combination of goods will be produced? Under capitalism, where on its PPF the economy operates is largely decided by the market (buyers and sellers). Under socialism, where on its PPF the economy operates is largely decided by government.

CHAPTER 3

Chapter 3, page 76

1. Popcorn is a normal good for Sandi. Prepaid telephone cards are an inferior good for Mark.

2. Asking why demand curves are downward-sloping is the same as asking why price and quantity demanded are inversely related (as one rises, the

other falls). There are two reasons mentioned in this section: (1) As price rises, people substitute lower-priced goods for higher-priced goods. (2) Because individuals receive less utility from an additional unit of a good they consume, they are only willing to pay less for the additional unit. The second reason is a reflection of the law of diminishing marginal utility.

3. Suppose only two people, Bob and Alice, have a demand for good *X*. At a price of $7, Bob buys 10 units and Alice buys 3 units; at a price of $6, Bob buys 12 units and Alice buys 5 units. One point on the market demand curve represents a price of $7 and a quantity demanded of 13 units; another point represents $6 and 17 units. A market demand curve is derived by adding the quantities demanded at each price.

4. A change in income, preferences, prices of related goods, number of buyers, and expectations of future price can change demand. A change in the price of the good changes the quantity demanded of the good. For example, a change in *income* can change the *demand* for oranges, but only a change in the *price* of oranges can directly change the *quantity demanded* of oranges.

Chapter 3, page 81

1. It would be difficult to increase the quantity supplied of houses over the next 10 hours, so the supply curve in (a) is vertical, as in Exhibit 8. It is possible to increase the quantity supplied of houses over the next 3 months, however, so the supply curve in (b) is upward-sloping.
2. **a.** The supply curve shifts to the left.
   b. The supply curve shifts to the left.
   c. The supply curve shifts to the right.
3. The upward-sloping supply curve illustrates that a rising price of a good brings about an increase in the quantity supplied of the good. This occurs because in most instances, a higher price acts as an incentive for producers to produce more of the good.

Chapter 3, page 88

1. Disagree. In the text, we plainly saw how supply and demand work at an auction. Supply and demand are at work in the grocery store, too, although there is no auctioneer present. The essence of the auction example is the auctioneer raising the price when there was a shortage and lowering the price when there was a surplus. The same thing happens at the grocery store. For example, if there is a surplus of corn flakes, the manager of the store is likely to have a sale (lower prices) on corn flakes. Many markets without auctioneers act as if there are auctioneers raising and lowering prices in response to shortages and surpluses.
2. No. It could be the result of a higher supply of computers. Either a decrease in demand or an increase in supply will lower price.
3. **a.** Lower price and quantity
   b. Lower price and higher quantity

c. Higher price and lower quantity
d. Lower price and quantity

Chapter 3, page 91

1. Yes, if nothing else changes—that is, yes, *ceteris paribus*. If some other things change, though, they may not. For example, if the government imposes an effective price ceiling on gasoline, Jamie may pay lower gas prices at the pump but have to wait in line to buy the gas (due to first-come-first-served trying to ration the shortage). It is not clear if Jamie is better off paying a higher price and not waiting in line or paying a lower price and having to wait in line. The point, however, is that buyers don't necessarily prefer lower prices to higher prices unless everything else (quality, wait, service, etc.) stays the same.
2. Disagree. Both long-lasting shortages and long lines are caused by price ceilings. First the price ceiling is imposed, creating the shortage; then the rationing device first-come-first-served (FCFS) emerges because price isn't permitted to fully ration the good. There are shortages every day that don't cause long lines to form. Instead, buyers bid up price, output and price move to equilibrium, and there is no shortage.
3. Buyers might argue for price ceilings on the goods they buy—especially if they don't know that price ceilings have some effects they may not like (such as fewer exchanges, FCFS used as a rationing device, and so on.) Sellers might argue for price floors on the goods they sell—especially if they expect their profits to rise. Employees might argue for a wage floor on the labor services they sell—especially if they don't know that they may lose their jobs or have their hours cut back as a result.

CHAPTER 4

Chapter 4, page 99

1. If supply and tuition are constant and demand rises, the shortage of openings at the university will become greater. The university will continue to use its non-price rationing devices (GPA, SAT scores, ACT scores) but will have to raise the standards of admission. Instead of requiring a GPA of, say, 3.5 for admission, it may raise the requirement to 3.8.
2. Not likely. A university that didn't make admission easier in the face of a surplus of openings might not be around much longer. When tuition cannot be adjusted directly—in other words, when the rationing device of price cannot be adjusted—it is likely that the nonprice rationing device (standards) will be.

Chapter 4, page 100

1. In the section, we say "Because the workers in groups *B* and *C* are equally productive and because employers show no preference for hiring one group of workers over the other, the demand for group *B* workers is the same as the demand for group *C* workers." It follows, then, that if some workers are

more productive than other workers or if employers show a preference for hiring one group of workers over the other (and that preference is unrelated to differences in productivity), then the demand for workers will be different. Bottom line: If *B* workers are more productive than *C* workers, the demand for *B* workers will be higher than the demand for *C* workers, *ceteris paribus*.

2. If two groups of people are equally productive and a discriminator employer decides not to hire one group, the demand for that group's services is less. Lower demand translates into lower wages and lower costs for nondiscriminator employers. In turn, lower costs will give nondiscriminator employers the ability to underprice their discriminator competitors.

Chapter 4, pages 100–101
1. Price will fall.
2. Quantity will rise.

Chapter 4, page 102
1. Yes. At the equilibrium wage rate, the quantity demanded of labor equals the quantity supplied. At a higher wage (the minimum wage), the quantity supplied stays constant (given the vertical supply curve) but the quantity demanded falls. Thus, a surplus results.
2. The person is assuming that the labor demand curve is vertical (no matter what the wage rate is, the quantity demanded of labor is always the same).

Chapter 4, page 104
1. Agree. At any price below equilibrium price, a shortage exists: the quantity demanded of kidneys is greater than the quantity supplied of kidneys. As price rises toward its equilibrium level, quantity supplied rises and quantity demanded falls until the two are equal.
2. It depends on whether or not $0 is the equilibrium price of kidneys. If it is—that is, if the kidney demand and supply curves intersect at $0—then there is no shortage of kidneys. But if, at $0, the quantity demanded of kidneys is greater than the quantity supplied, then a shortage exists.

Chapter 4, page 106
1. The wholesale price of electricity rises. Because of this, the supply curve of electricity in the retail market shifts leftward. The retail price is prevented from rising, so there is now a shortage of electricity in the retail market.
2. No, not if, say, demand for electricity had risen in the retail market. Specifically, if demand had risen in the retail market and price was prevented from rising, there would still be a shortage of electricity and blackouts in the retail market. There would also be shortages in the wholesale market. Higher demand in the wholesale market and no change in price would result in a shortage.

Chapter 4, page 107
1. The answer can be either "the shifting supply of gold" or "the attempt to earn profit." Consider the first answer. If the price of gold is higher in one location than another, the supply of gold shifts from the lower-priced location to the higher-priced location. In the process, the gold prices in the two locations converge. Now, if we want to know what causes the shifting supply of gold, the answer is the attempt to earn profit. Specifically, it is the attempt to earn profit that prompts people to buy gold in the lower-priced location and sell it in the higher-priced location.
2. You can move a Camry from one place to another in response to a rising price. What holds for gold holds for Camrys too.

Chapter 4, page 108
1. Prices go up at some times, down at other times. If greed explains higher prices, does altruism explain lower prices? Is the person who is greedy in June and raises prices the same person who is altruistic in July and lowers prices? If so, what caused him to be greedy one month and altruistic the next? The greed explanation of higher prices seems incapable of answering this question. Economists do not assume that people are greedy one month and not greedy the next month. They assume that sellers are always greedy and want to receive the highest price possible for what they sell, and they assume that buyers are always greedy and want to pay the lowest price possible for what they buy.
2. Expectations of future price. To illustrate, suppose there is an earthquake in southern California. Consequently, some people, rightly or wrongly, think that the price of bottled water will rise due to interruption or contamination of piped water. Because they expect a higher price for bottled water in the future, their current demand for bottled water rises. When the current demand for bottled water rises, the current price of bottled water rises, *ceteris paribus*.

Chapter 4, page 110
1. Moving from a system where patients cannot sue their HMOs to one where they can gives patients something they didn't have before (the right to sue) at a higher price (higher charges for health care coverage). The "free lunch"—the right to sue—isn't free after all.
2. If the students get the extra week and nothing else changes, then the students will probably say they are better off. In other words, more of one thing (time) and no less of anything else makes one better off. But if because of the extra week, the professor grades their papers harder than she would have otherwise, then some or all of the students may say that they weren't made better off by the extra week.

Chapter 4, page 111
1. One possible answer is: There are two cities, one with clean air and the other with dirty air. The

demand to live in the clean-air city is higher than the demand to live in the dirty-air city. As a result, housing prices are higher in the clean-air city than in the dirty-air city.

2. Ultimately, the person who owns the land in the good-weather city receives the payment. Look at it this way: People have a higher demand for houses in good-weather cities than in bad-weather cities. As a result, house builders receive higher prices for houses built and sold in good-weather cities. Because of the higher house prices in good-weather cities, house builders have a higher demand for land in good-weather cities. In the end, higher demand for land translates into higher land prices or land rents for landowners.

Chapter 4, page 112

1. The shortage is greater in computer science. If supply in each field is the same, the wage rate is the same, and demand is greater in computer science than in biology, then the horizontal difference (which measures the degree of shortage) between the demand curve and supply curve in computer science is greater than in biology. Draw this and see.

2. Under the condition that demand and supply are the same in all fields. Stated differently, under the condition that the equilibrium wage in each field is the same.

Chapter 4, page 113

1. They may not. Because of the tax, the demand for the new houses may be lower than it would be if there were no special tax. As a result of lower demand, the price of the houses may be lower than it would be without the tax. This is similar to the new car–used car example. Because people can resell the cars they buy, their demand for new cars is higher than it would be if they couldn't resell their old cars. Similarly, because people who buy the new houses dislike the tax, their demand for the houses is lower than it would be without the tax.

2. Yes, being able to sell your old car is like getting a rebate. You pay a certain price for a new car (say, $15,000), use the car for a few years, and then sell it on the used car market (for, say, $10,000). The price you paid for the car, some would say, was $5,000, not $15,000.

Chapter 4, page 114

1. Any price above 70 cents.
2. Assuming that tolls are not used, freeway congestion will worsen. An increase in driving population simply shifts the demand curve for driving to the right.

Chapter 4, page 115

1. A person's time is worth something. For example, if a person spends one hour doing something instead of working and has a wage rate of $10 an hour, then one hour of her time is worth $10. When we know a person's wage rate, we can convert "time spent" into "dollars forfeited."

2. If demand rises more than supply and price is held constant, there will be a shortage of parking. Some nonprice rationing device will emerge to allocate parking spaces along with dollar price. It will probably be first-come-first-served (whoever gets to an empty parking spot first gets to park).

Chapter 4, page 116

1. All other things equal—such as the number of people on a flight, and so on—lines will be longer for a Southwest flight because all seats are rationed on a first-come-first-served basis on the day of the flight. On other airlines, seats are rationed on a first-come-first-served basis starting one month before the flight. Lines are shorter on the day of the flight because many seats have already been rationed.

2. On flight *A*. The shortage of aisle seats is greater on flight *A* than flight *B*, which means that more seats must be rationed by first-come-first-served on that flight.

3. In both cases there are submarkets within markets. Specifically, demand and supply intersect at a different equilibrium price for some airline seats than for other airline seats just as demand and supply intersect at a different equilibrium wage for professors in some fields than for professors in other fields. Equilibrium price (or wage) in one submarket is likely to be different than equilibrium price (or wage) in another submarket.

Chapter 4, page 117

1. Answers will vary. Students sometimes say that it is "fairer" if everyone is charged the same price. Is it unfair then that moviegoers pay less if they go to the 2 P.M. movie than if they go to the 8 P.M. movie?

2. Both analyses deal with an equilibrium price being charged in one submarket and a disequilibrium price being charged in another submarket. Both deal with the effects of a disequilibrium price.

Chapter 4, page 119

1. Broadway doesn't have any need to have people line up early for the show. There are no slot machines in the playhouse.

2. It depends on two things: the equilibrium price for a good seat and the price that is charged for a good seat. The higher the equilibrium price, all other things equal, the greater the tip. The lower the price charged, all other things equal, the greater the tip. We would expect that those persons who do the seating and receive the tips would argue to keep show prices down.

Chapter 4, page 120

1. Disagree. The demand for romance novels may be greater than the demand for classic novels, but this is not necessarily the case. In fact, the demand for classic novels may be greater than the demand for romance novels, but if the price of romance novels is lower than the price of classic novels, the quantity demanded of romance novels may be greater.

2. This is really the same question as number 1. If popularity is equated with "quantity demanded," then popularity is a function of both demand and price. The greater the demand, for a given price, the greater the quantity demanded; the lower the price, for a given demand, the greater the quantity demanded.

Chapter 4, page 122

1. If there is a "speed trap," the probability of being apprehended for speeding rises, and, for a given speeding ticket price, the price of speeding rises. If you slow down, you are responding to a change in the price of speeding the way that the law of demand predicts you will respond.

2. As police officers earn more, the costs (to taxpayers) of a police force increase. Taxpayers (or the public) may want to reduce the number of police officers, but not at the expense of more speeders. To prevent people from speeding more often with fewer officers working, the price of a speeding ticket will have to increase.

Chapter 4, page 123

1. Oil that is owned is more likely to be conserved than oil that is not owned. If it is not owned, then the first person to the oil gets to sell it. Leaving it in the ground (conserving it) increases the probability that someone will get to it before you do. Individuals will rush to get to the oil first and sell it immediately (before someone else does). Conclusion: Private property is critical to conservation.

2. If he expects to die, and he has no children (no heirs), then Tex is less likely to conserve oil for the future because he won't be around to receive payment for the oil. He may think that it is better to sell the oil now. If Tex has children, he may conserve the oil and not sell it now. He may benefit by leaving a more valuable resource to his children.

CHAPTER 5

Chapter 5, page 138

1. The CPI is calculated as follows: (1) Define a market basket. (2) Determine how much it would cost to purchase the market basket in the current year and in the base year. (3) Divide the dollar cost of purchasing the market basket in the current year by the dollar cost of purchasing the market basket in the base year. (4) Multiply the quotient times 100. For a review of this process, see Exhibit 1.

2. Approximately 8.08 percent.

3. Annual (nominal) income has risen by 13.85 percent while prices have risen by 4.94 percent. We conclude that because (nominal) income has risen more than prices, real income has increased. Alternatively, you can look at it this way: Real income in year 1 is $31,337 and real income in year 2 is $33,996.

4. Suppose in year 1 a person buys 10 apples and 15 oranges—this is his market basket. We see that he buys 1.5 oranges for every 1 apple he buys. The next year, in response to a change in apple and orange prices, he buys 1.4 oranges for every 1 apple he buys. A fixed-weighted price index would measure prices between the two years based on the dollar cost of buying the same weighted market basket each year—the market basket where the ratio of oranges to apples is 1.5 to 1. A chain-weighted price index would not. It would measure the dollar cost of buying the 1.5-to-1 market basket in year 1 and the dollar cost of buying the 1.4-to-1 market basket in year 2.

Chapter 5, page 143

1. The frictionally unemployed person has readily transferable skills and the structurally unemployed person does not.

2. It implies that the (actual, measured) unemployment rate in the economy is greater than the natural unemployment rate. For example, if the unemployment rate is 8 percent and the natural unemployment rate is 6 percent, the cyclical unemployment rate is 2 percent.

Chapter 5, page 148

1. As unemployment benefits increase, the reservation wage curve shifts to the right. This raises the search time. As the optimal search time rises, the unemployment rate rises.

2. Searching for a job for as long as it takes to get a job is not necessarily contrary to considering the costs and benefits of job search. It depends on what the person means by the statement. If he means that he will search for only as long as it takes to get *any* job at *any* wage rate, then probably he is right that he doesn't consider costs and benefits. But if he means he will search for as long as it takes to find a job that he thinks is right for him (and "right for him" takes into account the duties of his job, the wage the job pays, and so on), then he has implicitly considered the costs and benefits of searching for a job. As long as there is some job at some wage rate that he would turn down, the costs and benefits of (continued) search are being considered.

CHAPTER 6

Chapter 6, page 158

1. Roberto, a Mexican, lives and works in the United States producing telephones. Jennifer, an American, lives and works in France producing radios. U.S. GDP is the total market value of all final goods and services produced annually within the borders of the United States. So GDP includes Roberto's productive contributions but not Jennifer's. U.S. GNP is the total market value of all final goods and services produced annually by the citizens of the United States. So GNP includes Jennifer's productive contributions but not Roberto's.

2. No. GDP doesn't account for all productive activity (e.g., it omits the production of nonmarket goods and services). Even if GDP is $0, it doesn't necessarily follow that there was no production in the economy.

Chapter 6, page 167

1. In the expenditure approach, GDP is computed by finding the sum of consumption, investment, government purchases, and net exports. (Net exports is equal to exports minus imports.)
2. Yes. To illustrate, suppose consumption is $200, investment is $80, and government purchases are $70. The sum of these three spending components of GDP is $350. Now suppose exports are $0 but imports are $100, which means that net exports are −$100. Since GDP = $C + I + G + (EX − IM)$, it follows that GDP is $250.
3. No. Each individual would have $40,000 worth of goods and services only if the entire GDP were equally distributed across the country. There is no indication that this is the case. The $40,000 (per capita GDP) says that the "average" person in the country has access to $40,000 worth of goods and services, but in reality there may not be any "average" person. Example: If Smith earns $10,000, and Jones earns $20,000, then the average person earns $15,000. But neither Smith nor Jones earns $15,000, so neither is average.

Chapter 6, page 172

1. We can't know for sure; we can say what might have caused the rise in GDP. It could be: (a) a rise in prices, no change in output, or (b) a rise in output, no change in prices, or (c) rises in both prices and output, or (d) a percentage increase in prices that is greater than the percentage decrease in output, or some other situation.
2. More output was produced in year 2 than in year 1.
3. Yes. Business cycles—ups and downs in Real GDP—don't prevent Real GDP from growing over time. Exhibit 8 shows Real GDP higher at the second peak than at the first even though there is a business cycle in between.

CHAPTER 7

Chapter 7, page 187

1. Real balance effect: a rise (fall) in the price level causes purchasing power to fall (rise), which decreases (increases) a person's monetary wealth. As people become less (more) wealthy, the quantity demanded of Real GDP falls (rises).
2. If the dollar appreciates, it takes more foreign currency to buy a dollar and fewer dollars and cents to buy foreign currency. This makes U.S. goods (denominated in dollars) more expensive for foreigners and foreign goods cheaper for Americans. In turn, foreigners buy fewer U.S. exports and Americans buy more foreign imports. As exports fall and imports rise, net exports fall. If net exports fall, total expenditures fall, *ceteris paribus*. As total expenditures fall, the *AD* curve shifts to the left.
3. If personal income taxes decline, disposable incomes rise. As disposable incomes rise, consumption rises. As consumption rises, total expenditures rise, *ceteris paribus*. As total expenditures rise, the *AD* curve shifts to the right.

Chapter 7, page 193

1. As wage rates decline, the cost per unit of production falls. In the short run (assuming that prices are constant), profit per unit rises. Higher profit causes producers to produce more units of their goods and services. In short, the *SRAS* curve shifts to the right.
2. Last year, ten workers produced 100 units of good X in one hour. This year, ten workers produced 120 units of good X in one hour.

Chapter 7, page 198

1. a. Real GDP rises, price level falls
   b. Real GDP falls, price level rises
   c. Real GDP rises, price level rises
   d. Real GDP falls, price level falls
   e. Real GDP rises, price level rises
   f. Real GDP falls, price level rises
2. To identify the change in short-run equilibrium, first identify the factor that has changed. Next determine whether the factor affects *AD, SRAS,* or neither. If it affects *AD* or *SRAS*, decide whether the factor causes *AD* or *SRAS* to rise or fall. Then note how the price level, Real GDP, and the unemployment rate are affected. For example, suppose there is an increase in the money supply. This affects *AD*. Specifically, it causes *AD* to increase and the *AD* curve to shift to the right. As a result, Real GDP and the price level rise and the unemployment rate falls in the short run.

Chapter 7, page 201

1. In long-run equilibrium, the economy is producing Natural Real GDP. In short-run equilibrium, the economy is not producing Natural Real GDP, although the quantity demanded of Real GDP equals the quantity supplied of Real GDP.
2. The diagram should show the price level in the economy at P_1 and Real GDP at Q_1, but the intersection of the *AD* curve and the *SRAS* curve at some point other than (P_1, Q_1). In addition, the *LRAS* curve should not be at Q_1 or at the intersection of the *AD* and *SRAS* curves.

CHAPTER 8

Chapter 8, page 212

1. Say's Law states that supply creates its own demand. In a barter economy, Jones supplies good X only so that he can use it to demand some other good, say good Y. The act of supplying is motivated by the desire to demand. Supply and demand are opposite sides of the same coin.

2. No, total spending will not decrease. For classical economists, an increase in saving (reflected in a decrease in consumption) will lower the interest rate and stimulate investment spending. So, one spending component goes down (consumption) and another spending component goes up (investment). Moreover, according to classical economists, the decrease in one spending component will be completely offset by an increase in another spending component so that overall spending does not change.
3. They are flexible; they move up and down in response to market conditions.

Chapter 8, page 217
1. A recessionary gap exists if the economy is producing a Real GDP level that is less than Natural Real GDP. An inflationary gap exists if the economy is producing a Real GDP level that is more than Natural Real GDP.
2. There is a surplus in the labor market when the economy is in a recessionary gap. There is a shortage in the labor market when the economy is in an inflationary gap.
3. The economy is somewhere above the institutional PPF and below the physical PPF.

Chapter 8, page 223
1. In a recessionary gap, the existing unemployment rate is greater than the natural unemployment rate. This implies that unemployment is relatively high. When old wage contracts expire, business firms negotiate contracts that pay workers lower wage rates. As a result, the *SRAS* curve shifts rightward. As this happens, the price level begins to fall. The economy moves down the *AD* curve—eventually moving to the point where it intersects the *LRAS* curve. At this point, the economy is in long-run equilibrium.
2. In an inflationary gap, the existing unemployment rate is less than the natural unemployment rate. This implies that unemployment is relatively low. When old wage contracts expire, business firms negotiate contracts that pay workers higher wage rates. As a result the *SRAS* curve shifts leftward. As this happens, the price level begins to rise. The economy moves up the *AD* curve—eventually moving to the point where it intersects the *LRAS* curve. At this point, the economy is in long-run equilibrium.
3. Any changes in aggregate demand will affect—in the long run—only the price level and not the Real GDP level or the unemployment rate. Stated differently, changes in *AD* in an economy will have no long-run effect on the Real GDP that a country produces or on its unemployment rate; changes in *AD* will only change the price level in the long run.

CHAPTER 9

Chapter 9, page 233
1. They mean that an economy may not self-regulate at Natural Real GDP (Q_N). Instead, an economy can get stuck in a recessionary gap.

2. To say that the economy is self-regulating is the same as saying that prices and wages are flexible and adjust quickly. This is just two ways of describing the same thing.
3. The main reason is because Say's law may not hold in a money economy. This raises the question, Why *doesn't* Say's law hold in a money economy? Keynes argued that an increase in saving (which leads to a decline in demand) does not necessarily bring about an equal amount of additional investment (which would lead to an increase in demand) because neither saving nor investment is exclusively affected by changes in the interest rate. See Exhibit 1 for the way Keynes might have used numbers to explain his position.

Chapter 9, page 241
1. Autonomous consumption is one of the components of overall consumption. To illustrate, look at the consumption function: $C = C_0 + (MPC)(Y_d)$. The part of overall consumption (C) that is autonomous is C_0. This part of consumption does not depend on disposable income. The part of consumption that does depend on disposable income (that is, changes as disposable income changes) is the "$(MPC)(Y_d)$" part. For example, assume $MPC = 0.8$. If Y_d rises by $1,000, then consumption goes up by $800.
2. When $TP > TE$, firms are producing and offering for sale more units of goods and services than households and government want to buy. As a result, business inventories rise above optimal levels. In reaction, firms cut back on their production of goods and services. This leads in decline in Real GDP. Real GDP stops falling when $TP = TE$.

Chapter 9, page 248
1. If there are no idle resources, increased spending cannot increase Real GDP because additional resources are needed to produce additional output, *ceteris paribus*. Increased spending can, however, increase GDP because GDP = $P \times Q$. The additional spending will simply raise prices, thus raising GDP in the face of constant output.
2. The multiplier equals $1/(1 - MPC)$. The denominator is the same as the MPS, so the multiplier equals $1/0.23$, or 4.35.
3. There is a direct relationship: the larger the MPC, the larger the multiplier, and the larger the change in Real GDP.

CHAPTER 10

Chapter 10, page 266
1. If there is no crowding out, expansionary fiscal policy is predicted to increase aggregate demand and, if the economy is in a recessionary gap, either reduce or eliminate the gap. However, if there is, say, complete crowding out, expansionary fiscal policy will not meet its objective. The following example illustrates complete crowding out: If government pur-

chases rise by $100 million, private spending will decrease by $100 million so that there is no net effect on aggregate demand.

2. They can, but there is no guarantee. Ultimately, it depends on how much the demand for credit rises as a result of the deficit and how much the supply of credit rises due to the higher taxes implied by the deficit. If demand rises by more than supply, then bigger deficits do lead to higher interest rates. If demand rises by the same amount as supply, then bigger deficits leave the interest rate unchanged.

3. Let's say that the budget deficit rises due to increased government spending in the face of constant tax revenues. As a result of the deficit, U.S. Treasury borrowing (in credit markets) increases, driving up the interest rate. Higher U.S. interest rates cause foreign lenders to increase their demand for U.S. dollars in order to buy dollar-denominated securities. As a result of the increased demand for dollars, the dollar appreciates (relative to other currencies), making American goods more expensive for foreigners and foreign imports cheaper for Americans. Export spending falls and import spending rises, thus widening the trade deficit.

Chapter 10, page 271

1. Let's suppose that a person's taxable income rises by $1,000 to $45,000 and that her taxes rise from $10,000 to $10,390 as a result. Her marginal tax rate—the percentage of her additional taxable income she pays in taxes—is 39 percent. Her average tax rate—the percentage of her (total) income she pays in taxes—is 23 percent.

2. Not necessarily. It depends on whether the percentage rise in tax rates is greater than or less than the percentage fall in the tax base. Here's a simple example: Suppose the average tax rate is 10 percent and the tax base is $100. Tax revenues then equal $10. If the tax rate rises to 12 percent (a 20 percent rise) and the tax base falls to $90 (a 10 percent fall), tax revenues rise to $10.80. In other words, if the tax rate rises by a greater percentage than the tax base falls, tax revenues rise. But, then, let's suppose that the tax base falls to $70 (a 30 percent fall) instead of to $90. Now tax revenues are $8.40. In other words, if the tax rate rises by a smaller percentage than the tax base falls, tax revenues fall.

CHAPTER 11

Chapter 11, page 280

1. With a proportional income tax, the tax rate is constant as one's income rises. With a progressive income tax, the tax rate rises as one's income rises (up to some point). With a regressive income tax, one's tax rate falls as one's income rises.

2. The top 5 percent of income earners received 34.0 percent of all income and paid 55.5 percent of all income taxes.

3. Personal income, corporate income, and Social Security taxes.

Chapter 11, page 284

1. Because after a nonexcludable public good is produced, the individual or firm that produced it wouldn't be able to collect payment for it. When a nonexcludable public good is provided to one person, it is provided to everyone. Because an individual can consume the good without paying for it, he is likely to take a free ride. Another way of answering this question is to simply say, "The market won't produce nonexcludable public goods because of the free rider problem."

2. (a) A personal computer is a private good. It is rivalrous in consumption; if one person is using it, someone else cannot. (b) A Broadway play is an excludable public good. It is nonrivalrous in consumption (everyone in the theater can see the play), but excludable (a person must pay to get into the theater). (c) It could be a private good or an excludable public good. It is nonrivalrous in that more than one person can look at it at a time (this argues that it is a public good), but it is rivalrous in that not everyone can sit under it (this argues that it is a private good). In either case, people can be prevented from consuming it. The tree can either be fenced in (thus preventing people from sitting under it) or have a high wall built around it (so no one can see it). (d) A telephone is a private good. One person using the phone (in, say, your house) prevents someone else from using it. (e) Sunshine is a nonexcludable public good. It is nonrivalrous in consumption (one person's consumption of it doesn't reduce its consumption by others) and nonexcludable (it is impossible to exclude free people from consuming the sunshine).

3. A concert is an example. If one person consumes the concert, this does not take away from others consuming it to the same degree. However, people can be excluded from consuming it.

4. Suppose there are 100 members in group A and 100 members in group B. If group A proposes redistributing $100 from group B to itself, then the average member of group A receives $1 and the average member of group B loses $1. Average benefits equal average costs. In this setting, it is likely that group B has as much incentive to fight against the redistribution as group A has to fight for it. Now suppose group A has 100 members, group B has 1,000 members, and group A again proposes redistributing $100 to itself from group B. The average member of group A receives $1 and the average member of group B loses 10 cents. In this case, the average member of group B has less incentive to fight against the redistribution than the average member of group A has to fight for it. Conclusion: Special interest legislation (of the type discussed) has a higher probability of passing when benefits are concentrated on a few and the costs are dispersed over many.

Chapter 11, page 288

1. Economists estimate what the deficit would equal if the economy were operating at full employment. This is identified as the structural deficit. Then, economists subtract the structural deficit from the existing (total) deficit to find the cyclical deficit.
2. $60 billion
3. Suppose the federal government decides to spend $30 billion more than it has budgeted in order to increase the country's infrastructure. It doesn't have the tax revenue to pay for the spending, so it borrows the $30 billion. As a result, the public debt rises by $30 billion. The government borrowing redirects some resources that would have gone into producing computers, television sets, and so on, into producing more bridges and roads. Because the current generation has to give up some computers, television sets, and more for the infrastructure, it bears the burden of the debt.
4. The unified budget takes into account both on-budget and off-budget items.

CHAPTER 12

Chapter 12, page 301

1. Money evolved because individuals wanted to make trading easier (less time-consuming). It was this that motivated individuals to accept that good (in a barter economy) that had relatively greater acceptability than all other goods. In time, the effect snowballed and finally the good that (initially) had relatively greater acceptability emerged into a good that was widely accepted for purposes of exchange. At this point, the good became money.
2. No. M1 will fall, but M2 will not rise—it will remain constant. To illustrate, suppose M1 = $400 and M2 = $600. If people remove $100 from checkable deposits, M1 will decline to $300. For purposes of illustration, think of M2 as equal to M1 + money market accounts. The M1 component of M2 falls by $100, but the money market accounts component rises by $100, so there is no net effect on M2. In conclusion, M1 falls and M2 remains constant.
3. In a barter (moneyless) economy, a double coincidence of wants will not occur for every transaction. When it does not occur, the cost of the transaction increases because more time must be spent to complete the trade. In a money economy, money is acceptable for every transaction, so a double coincidence of wants is not necessary. All buyers offer money for what they want to buy and all sellers accept money for what they want to sell.

Chapter 12, page 310

1. $55 million
2. $6 billion
3. $0. Bank A was required to hold only $1 million in reserves, but held $1.2 million instead. Therefore, its loss of $200,000 in reserves does not cause it to be reserve deficient.

CHAPTER 13

Chapter 13, page 318

1. Federal Reserve Bank of New York.
2. Control the money supply.
3. It means the Fed stands ready to lend funds to banks that are suffering cash management or liquidity problems.

Chapter 13, page 324

1. a. Money supply falls
   b. Money supply rises
   c. Money supply falls
2. The federal funds rate is the interest rate one bank charges another bank for a loan. The discount rate is the interest rate the Fed charges a bank for a loan.
3. Reserves in bank A rise; reserves in the banking system remain the same (bank B lost the reserves that bank A borrowed).
4. Reserves in bank A rise; reserves in the banking system rise because there is no offset in reserves for any other bank.

CHAPTER 14

Chapter 14, page 336

1. If M times V increases, total expenditures increase. In other words, people spend more. For example, instead of spending $3 billion on goods and services, they spend $4 billion on goods and services. But if there is more spending (greater total expenditures), it follows that there must be greater total sales. P times Q represents this total dollar value of sales.
2. The equation of exchange is a truism: MV necessarily equals PQ. This is similar to saying that $2 + 2$ necessarily equals 4. It cannot be otherwise. The simple quantity theory, which is built on the equation of exchange, can be tested against real-world events. That is, the simple quantity theory of money assumes that both velocity and Real GDP are constant and then based on these assumptions, predicts that changes in the money supply will be strictly proportional to changes in the price level. This prediction can be measured against real-world data, so the simple quantity theory of money may offer insights into the way the economy works. The equation of exchange does not do this.
3. a. AD curve shifts rightward.
   b. AD curve shifts leftward.
   c. AD curve shifts rightward.
   d. AD curve shifts leftward.

Chapter 14, pages 339–340

1. a. As velocity rises, the AD curve shifts to the right. In the short run, P rises and Q rises. In the long

run, Q will return to its original level and P will be higher than it was in the short run.

b. As velocity falls, the AD curve shifts to the left. In the short run, P falls and Q falls. In the long run, Q will return to its original level and P will be lower than it was in the short run.

c. As the money supply rises, the AD curves shifts to the right. In the short run, P rises and Q rises. In the long run, Q will return to its original level and P will be higher than it was in the short run.

d. As the money supply falls, the AD curve shifts to the left. In the short run, P falls and Q falls. In the long run, Q will return to its original level and P will be lower than it was in the short run.

2. Yes, a change in velocity can offset a change in the money supply (on aggregate demand). Suppose that the money supply rises and velocity falls. A rise in the money supply shifts the AD curve to the right and a fall in velocity shifts the AD curve to the left. If the strength of each change is the same, there is no change in AD.

Chapter 14, page 346

1. We cannot answer this question based on the information given. We know only that three prices have gone up; we don't know if other prices (in the economy) have gone up, if other prices have gone down, or if some have gone up and some have gone down. To determine whether inflation has occurred, we have to know what has happened to the price level, not simply to three prices.

2. No. For continued inflation (continued increases in the price level) to be the result of continued decreases in $SRAS$, workers would have to continually ask for and receive higher wages while output was dropping and the unemployment rate rising. This is not likely.

3. Continued inflation.

Chapter 14, page 352

1. 3 percent.

2. Yes, it is possible. This would occur if the expectations effect immediately set in and outweighed the liquidity effect.

3. Certainly the Fed directly affects the supply of loanable funds and the interest rate through an open market operation. But it works as a catalyst to indirectly affect the loanable funds market and the interest rate via the changes in Real GDP, the price level, and the expected inflation rate. We can say this: The Fed directly affects the interest rate via the liquidity effect, and it indirectly affects the interest rate via the income, price-level, and expectations effects.

CHAPTER 15

Chapter 15, page 364

1. Smith buys a bond for a face value of $10,000 that promises to pay a 10 percent interest rate each year

for 10 years. In one year, though, bonds are being offered for a face value of $10,000 that pay an 11 percent interest rate each year for 10 years. If Smith wants to sell his bond, he won't be able to sell it for $10,000 because no one today will pay $10,000 for a bond that pays a 10 percent interest rate when he or she can pay $10,000 for a bond that pays an 11 percent interest rate. Smith will have to lower the price of his bond if he wants to sell it. Thus, as interest rates rise, bond prices decrease (for old or existing bonds).

2. We disagree for two reasons. First, if the money market is in the liquidity trap, a rise in the money supply will not affect interest rates and therefore will not affect investment or the goods and services market. Second, even if the money market is not in the liquidity trap, a rise in the money supply does not affect the goods and services market directly. It affects it indirectly: The rise in the money supply lowers the interest rate, causing investment to rise (assuming investment is not interest-insensitive). As investment rises, the AD curve shifts rightward, affecting the goods and services market. In other words, there is an important intermediate market between the money market and the goods and services market in the Keynesian transmission mechanism. Thus the money market can affect the goods and services market only indirectly.

3. A rise in the money supply brings about an excess supply of money in the money market that flows to the goods and services market, stimulating aggregate demand.

Chapter 15, page 370

1. Because they believe that prices and wages are inflexible downward, but not upward. They believe it is more likely that natural forces will move an economy out of an inflationary gap than out of a recessionary gap.

2. Suppose the economy is regulating itself out of a recessionary gap, but this is not known to Fed officials. Thinking that the economy is stuck in a recessionary gap, the Fed increases the money supply. When the money supply is felt in the goods and services market, the AD curve intersects with the $SRAS$ curve (that has been moving rightward, unbeknownst to officials) at a point that represents an inflationary gap. In other words, the Fed has moved the economy from a recessionary gap to an inflationary gap instead of from a recessionary gap to long-run equilibrium at the Natural Real GDP level.

3. It makes it stronger, *ceteris paribus*. If the economy can't get itself out of a recessionary gap, then the case is stronger that the Fed should. This does not mean to imply that expansionary monetary policy will work ideally. There may still be problems with the correct implementation of the policy.

Chapter 15, page 375

1. This is an open-ended question and depends on many factors. First, it depends on what the rule specifies because not all rules are alike. Second, it depends on the stability and predictability of velocity. For example, suppose the rule specifies that each year the money supply will rise by the average annual growth rate in Real GDP. If velocity is constant, this will produce price stability. But suppose velocity is extremely volatile. In this case, changes in velocity might offset changes in the money supply, leading to deflation instead of price stability. (For example, suppose Real GDP rises by 3 percent and the money supply increases by 3 percent, but velocity decreases by 3 percent. The change in velocity offsets the change in the money supply, leaving a net effect of a 3 percent rise in Real GDP. This, then, would lead to a 3 percent decline in the price level.)

2. The government would set the price of gold at some dollar amount and would be willing to buy and sell gold at the official price. If the market price is above the official price, then people will buy gold from the government and sell it in the market. When people buy gold from the government, they exchange their money for gold. This action reduces the money supply and, ultimately, puts downward pressure on the price level. Also, the increased supply of gold in the market brings down the price of gold. On the other hand, if the market price of gold is below the official price, people will sell gold to the government. In exchange, they receive money. This increase in the money supply puts upward pressure on prices. Also, the reduction of the gold supply in the market puts upward pressure on the price of gold. The hope is that by stabilizing the price of gold (that is, buying and selling gold to maintain the official price of gold equal to the market price of gold), the price level in the economy is stabilized too.

CHAPTER 16

Chapter 16, page 387

1. A given Phillips curve identifies different combinations of inflation and unemployment; for example, 4 percent inflation with 5 percent unemployment and 2 percent inflation with 7 percent unemployment. For these combinations of inflation and unemployment to be permanent, there must be only one (downward-sloping) Phillips curve that never changes.

2. Sometimes there is and sometimes there is not. Look at Exhibit 3. Unemployment is higher and inflation is lower in 1964 than in 1965, so there is a tradeoff between these two years. But both unemployment and inflation are higher in 1980 than in 1979—that is, between these two years there is not a tradeoff between inflation and unemployment.

3. Workers are fooled into thinking that the inflation rate is lower than it is. In other words, they underes-

timate the inflation rate and, therefore, overestimate the purchasing power of their wages.

Chapter 16, page 393

1. No. PIP says that, under certain conditions, neither expansionary fiscal policy nor expansionary monetary policy will be able to increase Real GDP and lower the unemployment rate in the short run. The conditions are that the policy change is anticipated correctly, individuals form their expectations rationally, and wages and prices are flexible.

2. None. When there is an unanticipated increase in aggregate demand, the economy moves from point 1 to 2 (in Exhibit 6a) in the short run, and then to point 3. This occurs whether people are holding rational or adaptive expectations.

3. Yes. To illustrate, suppose the economy is initially in long-run equilibrium at point 1 in Exhibit 6a. As a result of an unanticipated rise in aggregate demand, the economy will move from point 1 to point 2, and then to point 3. If there is a correctly anticipated rise in aggregate demand, the economy will simply move from point 1 to point 2, as in Exhibit 6b. If there is an incorrectly anticipated rise in aggregate demand—and furthermore, the anticipated rise overestimates the actual rise—then the economy will move from point 1 to point 2′ in Exhibit 7. In conclusion, Real GDP may initially increase, may remain constant, or may decline depending on whether the rise in aggregate demand is unanticipated, correctly anticipated, or overestimated, respectively.

Chapter 16, page 396

1. Both. The relevant question is, Was the decline in the money supply caused by a change on the supply side of the economy? If the answer is no, then the decline in the money supply is consistent with a demand-induced business cycle. If the answer is yes, then it is consistent with a supply-induced (real) business cycle.

2. New Keynesians believe that prices and wages are somewhat inflexible; new classical economists believe that prices and wages are flexible.

CHAPTER 17

Chapter 17, page 409

1. An increase in GDP does not constitute economic growth because GDP can rise from one year to the next if prices rise and output stays constant. Economic growth refers to an increase either in Real GDP or in per capita Real GDP. The emphasis here is on "real" as opposed to nominal (or money) GDP.

2. If the *AD* curve remains constant, a shift rightward in the *LRAS* curve (which is indicative of economic growth) will bring about falling prices. If the *AD* curve shifts to the right by the same amount as the *LRAS* curve, prices will remain stable. Only if the *AD* curve shifts to the right by more than the *LRAS* curve

shifts to the right could we witness economic growth and rising prices.

3. Labor is more productive when there are more capital goods. Furthermore, a rise in labor productivity promotes economic growth (an increase in labor productivity is defined as an increase in output relative to total labor hours). So, increases in capital investment can lead to increases in labor productivity and, therefore, to economic growth.

Chapter 17, page 413

1. One worry concerns the costs of economic growth. Some persons argue that with more economic growth come more "bads"—such as pollution, crowded cities, greater emphasis on material goods, more psychological problems, and so on. The other worry concerns the relationship between economic growth and the future availability of resources. Specifically, some persons argue that continued economic (and population) growth threatens the survival of the human race because this growth will hasten the time when the world runs out of resources. Both these worries (and the arguments put forth relevant to these worries) have their critics.

2. If technology is endogenous, then we can promote advances in technology. Technology does not simply "fall out of the sky"; we can promote technology, not simply wait for it to "rain down" on us. This means we can actively promote economic growth (because advances in technology can promote economic growth).

3. In new growth theory, ideas are important to economic growth. Those countries that discover how to encourage and develop new and better ideas will likely grow faster than those that do not. New growth theory, in essence, places greater emphasis on the intangibles (such as ideas) in the growth process than on the tangibles (natural resources, capital, and so on).

CHAPTER 18

Chapter 18, page 423

1. For the United States, $1X = 1/6Y$ or $1Y = 6X$. For England, $1X = 2Y$ or $1Y = 1/2X$. Let's focus on the opportunity cost of $1X$ in each country. In the United States $1X = 1/6Y$ and in Great Britain $1X = 2Y$. Terms of trade that are between these two endpoints would be favorable for the two countries. For example, suppose we choose $1X=1Y$. This is good for the United States because it would prefer to give up $1X$ and get $1Y$ in trade than to give up $1X$ and only get $1/6Y$ (without trade). Similarly, Great Britain would prefer to give up $1Y$ and get $1X$ in trade than to give up $1Y$ and get only $1/2X$ (without trade). Any terms of trade between $1X = 1/6Y$ and $1X = 2Y$ will be favorable to the two countries.

2. Yes; this is what the theory of comparative advantage shows. Exhibit 1 shows that the United States could produce more of both food and clothing than Japan. Still, the United States benefits from specialization and trade, as shown in Exhibit 2. In column 5 of this exhibit, the United States can consume 10 more units of food by specializing and trading.

3. No. It is the desire to buy low and sell high (earn a profit) that pushes countries into producing and trading at a comparative advantage. Government officials do not collect cost data and then issue orders to firms in the country to produce X, Y, or Z. We have not drawn the PPFs in this chapter and identified the cost differences between countries to show what countries actually do in the real world. We described things technically to simply show how countries benefit from specialization and trade.

Chapter 18, page 431

1. Domestic producers benefit because producers' surplus rises; domestic consumers lose because consumers' surplus falls. Also, government benefits in that it receives the tariff revenue. Moreover, consumers lose more than producers and government gain, so that there is a net loss resulting from tariffs.

2. Consumers' surplus falls by more than producers' surplus rises.

3. With a tariff, the government receives tariff revenue. With a quota, it does not. In the latter case, the revenue that would have gone to government goes, instead, to the importers who get to satisfy the quota.

4. Infant or new domestic industries need to be protected from older, more established competitors until they are mature enough to compete on an equal basis. Tariffs and quotas provide these infant industries the time they need.

CHAPTER 19

Chapter 19, page 443

1. A debit. When an American enters into a transaction in which he has to supply U.S. dollars in the foreign exchange market (in order to demand a foreign currency), the transaction is recorded as a debit.

2. We do not have enough information to answer this question. The merchandise trade balance is the difference between the value of merchandise exports and merchandise imports. The question gives only the value of exports and imports. Exports is a more inclusive term than merchandise exports. Exports include (a) merchandise exports, (b) services, and (c) income from U.S. assets abroad. See Exhibit 2. Similarly, imports is a more inclusive term than merchandise imports. It includes (a) merchandise imports, (b) services, and (c) income from foreign assets in the United States.

3. The merchandise trade balance includes fewer transactions than are included in the current account balance. The merchandise trade balance is the summary statistic for merchandise exports and merchandise imports. The current account balance is the summary

statistic for exports of goods and services (which includes merchandise exports), imports of goods and services (which includes merchandise imports), and net unilateral transfers abroad. See Exhibit 2.

4. No. The balance of payments always equals zero. It is possible that the journalist who wrote the story is reporting something other than the balance of payments (although he or she uses this term). Often, the news media use the term *balance of payments* when they are actually referring to the current account balance.

Chapter 19, page 449

1. As the demand for dollars increases, the supply of pesos increases. For example, suppose someone in Mexico wants to buy something produced in the United States. The American wants to be paid in dollars, but the Mexican doesn't have any dollars—she has pesos. So, she has to buy dollars with pesos; in other words, she has to supply pesos to buy dollars. Thus, as she demands more dollars, she will necessarily have to supply more pesos.

2. The dollar is said to have appreciated (against the peso) when it takes more pesos to buy a dollar and fewer dollars to buy a peso. For this to occur, either the demand for dollars must increase (which means the supply of pesos increases) or the supply of dollars must decrease (which means the demand for pesos decreases). To see this graphically, look at Exhibit 5b. The only way for the peso price per dollar to rise (on the vertical axis) is for either the demand curve for dollars to shift to the right or the supply curve of dollars to shift to the left. Each of these occurrences is mirrored in the market for pesos in part (a) of the exhibit.

3. *Ceteris paribus,* the dollar will depreciate relative to the franc. As incomes for Americans rise, the demand for Swiss goods rises. This increases the demand for francs and the supply of dollars on the foreign exchange market. In turn, this leads to a depreciated dollar and an appreciated franc.

4. The theory states that the exchange rate between any two currencies will adjust to reflect changes in the relative price levels of the two countries. For example, suppose the U.S. price level rises 5 percent and Mexico's price level remains constant. According to the PPP theory, the U.S. dollar will depreciate 5 percent relative to the Mexican peso.

Chapter 19, page 455

1. The terms *overvalued* and *undervalued* refer to the equilibrium exchange rate: the exchange rate at which the quantity demanded and quantity supplied of a currency are the same in the foreign exchange market. Let's suppose the equilibrium exchange rate is 0.10 USD = 1 MXP. This is the same as saying that 10 pesos = 1 dollar. If the exchange rate is fixed at 0.12 USD = 1 MXP (which is the same as 8.33 pesos = 1 dollar), the peso is overvalued and the dollar is undervalued. Specifically, a currency is overvalued if 1 unit of it fetches more of another currency than it would in equilibrium; a currency is undervalued if 1 unit of it fetches less of another currency than it would in equilibrium. In equilibrium, 1 peso would fetch 0.10 dollars and at the current exchange rate it fetches 0.12 dollars—so the peso is overvalued. In equilibrium, 1 dollar would fetch 10 pesos and at the current exchange rate it fetches only 8.33 pesos—so the dollar is undervalued.

2. An overvalued dollar means some other currency is undervalued—let's say it is the Japanese yen. An overvalued dollar makes U.S. goods more expensive for the Japanese, so they buy fewer U.S. goods. This reduces U.S. exports. On the other hand, an undervalued yen makes Japanese goods cheaper for Americans, so they buy more Japanese goods; the U.S. imports more. Thus, an overvalued dollar reduces U.S. exports and raises U.S. imports.

3. a. Dollar is overvalued.
   b. Dollar is undervalued
   c. Dollar is undervalued.

4. When a country devalues its currency, it makes it cheaper for foreigners to buy its products.

Chapter 19, page 460

1. An optimal currency area is a geographic area in which exchange rates can be fixed or a common currency used without sacrificing any domestic economic goals.

2. As the demand for good Y falls, the unemployment rate in country 2 will rise. This increase in the unemployment rate is likely to be temporary, though. The increased demand for good X (produced by country 1) will increase the demand for country 1's currency, leading to an appreciation in country 1's currency and a depreciation in country 2's currency. Country 1's good (good X) will become more expensive for the residents of country 2, and they will buy less. Country 2's good (good Y) will become less expensive for the residents of country 1, and they will buy more. As a result of the additional purchases of good Y, country 2's unemployment rate will begin to decline.

3. Labor mobility is very important to determining whether or not an area is an optimal currency area. If there is little or no labor mobility, an area is not likely to be an optimal currency area. If there is labor mobility, an area is likely to be an optimal currency area.

Glossary

Absolute (Money) Price The price of a good in money terms. (Chapter 3)

Absolute Real Economic Growth An increase in Real GDP from one period to the next. (Chapter 17)

Abstract The process (used in building a theory) of focusing on a limited number of variables to explain or predict an event. (Chapter 1)

Activists Persons who argue that monetary and fiscal policies should be deliberately used to smooth out the business cycle. (Chapter 15)

Adaptive Expectations Expectations that individuals form from past experience and modify slowly as the present and the future become the past (as time passes). (Chapter 16)

Aggregate Demand The quantity demanded of all goods and services (Real GDP) at different price levels, *ceteris paribus.* (Chapter 7)

Aggregate Demand (*AD*) Curve A curve that shows the quantity demanded of all goods and services (Real GDP) at different price levels, *ceteris paribus.* (Chapter 7)

Aggregate Supply The quantity supplied of all goods and services (Real GDP) at different price levels, *ceteris paribus.* (Chapter 7)

Appreciation An increase in the value of one currency relative to other currencies. (Chapters 7, 19)

Automatic Fiscal Policy Changes in government expenditures and/or taxes that occur automatically without (additional) congressional action. (Chapter 10)

Autonomous Consumption The part of consumption that is independent of disposable income. (Chapter 9)

Average Propensity to Consume (*APC*) Consumption divided by disposable income: $APC = C/Y_d$. (Chapter 9)

Average Propensity to Save (*APS*) Saving divided by disposable income: $APC = S/Y_d$. (Chapter 9)

Bad Anything from which individuals receive disutility or dissatisfaction. (Chapter 1)

Balance of Payments A periodic statement (usually annual) of the money value of all transactions between residents of one country and residents of all other countries. (Chapter 19)

Balanced Budget Government expenditures equal to tax revenues. (Chapter 10)

Barter Exchanging goods and services for other goods and services without the use of money. (Chapter 12)

Base Year The year chosen as a point of reference or basis of comparison for prices in other years; a benchmark year. (Chapter 5)

Board of Governors The governing body of the Federal Reserve System. (Chapter 13)

Budget Deficit Government expenditures greater than tax revenues. (Chapter 10)

Budget Surplus Tax revenues greater than government expenditures. (Chapter 10)

Business Cycle Recurrent swings (up and down) in Real GDP. (Chapter 6)

Capital Produced goods that can be used as inputs for further production, such as factories, machinery, tools, computers, and buildings. (Chapter 1)

Capital Account Includes all payments related to the purchase and sale of assets and to borrowing and lending activities. Components include outflow of U.S. capital and inflow of foreign capital. (Chapter 19)

Capital Account Balance The summary statistic for the outflow of U.S. capital and the inflow of foreign capital. It is equal to the difference between the outflow of U.S. capital and the inflow of foreign capital. (Chapter 19)

Capital Consumption Allowance (Depreciation) The estimated amount of capital goods used up in production through natural wear, obsolescence, and accidental destruction. (Chapter 6)

Cash Leakage Occurs when funds are held as currency instead of being deposited into a checking account. (Chapter 12)

Ceteris Paribus A Latin term meaning "all other things held constant." (Chapter 1)

Checkable Deposits Deposits on which checks can be written. (Chapter 12)

Comparative Advantage The situation where an individual or country can produce a good at lower opportunity cost than another individual or country can. (Chapters 2, 18)

Complements Two goods that are used jointly in consumption. If two goods are complements, the demand for one rises as the price of the other falls (or the demand for one falls as the price of the other rises). (Chapter 3)

Complete Crowding Out A decrease in one or more components of private spending completely offsets the increase in government spending. (Chapter 10)

Consumer Price Index (CPI) A widely cited index number for the price level; the weighted average of prices of a specific set of goods and services purchased by a typical household. (Chapter 5)

Consumers' Surplus (*CS*) The difference between the maximum price a buyer is willing and able to pay for a good or service and the price actually paid. CS = Maximum buying price − Price paid. (Chapter 2)

Consumption The sum of spending on durable goods, nondurable goods, and services. (Chapter 6)

Consumption Function The relationship between consumption and disposable income. In the consumption function used here, consumption is directly related to disposable income and is positive even at zero disposable income: $C = C_0 + (MPC)(Y_d)$. (Chapter 9)

Continued Inflation A continued increase in the price level. (Chapter 14)

Contractionary Fiscal Policy Decreases in government expenditures and/or increases in taxes to achieve particular economic goals. (Chapter 10)

Contractionary Monetary Policy The Fed decreases the money supply. (Chapter 15)

Credit In the balance of payments, any transaction that creates a demand for the country's currency in the foreign exchange market. (Chapter 19)

Crowding Out The decrease in private expenditures that occurs as a consequence of increased government spending or the financing needs of a budget deficit. (Chapter 10)

Currency Coins and paper money. (Chapter 12)

Current Account Includes all payments related to the purchase and sale of goods and services. Components of the account include exports, imports, and net unilateral transfers abroad. (Chapter 19)

Current Account Balance The summary statistic for exports of goods and services, imports of goods and services, and net unilateral transfers abroad. (Chapter 19)

Cyclical Deficit The part of the budget deficit that is a result of a downturn in economic activity. (Chapter 11)

Cyclical Unemployment Rate The difference between the unemployment

rate and the natural unemployment rate. (Chapter 5)

Debit In the balance of payments, any transaction that supplies the country's currency in the foreign exchange market. (Chapter 19)

Decisions at the Margin Decision making characterized by weighing additional (marginal) benefits of a change against the additional (marginal) costs of a change with respect to current conditions. (Chapter 1)

Demand The willingness and ability of buyers to purchase different quantities of a good at different prices during a specific time period. (Chapter 3)

Demand for Money (Balances) Represents the inverse relationship between the quantity demanded of money balances and the price of holding money balances. (Chapter 15)

Demand Schedule The numerical tabulation of the quantity demanded of a good at different prices. (Chapter 3)

Depreciation A decrease in the value of one currency relative to other currencies. (Chapters 7, 19)

Devaluation A government act that changes the exchange rate by lowering the official price of a currency. (Chapter 19)

Directly Related Two variables are directly related if they change in the same way. (Chapter 1 Appendix)

Discount Rate The interest rate the Fed charges depository institutions that borrow reserves from it. (Chapter 13)

Discretionary Fiscal Policy Deliberate changes of government expenditures and/or taxes to achieve particular economic goals. (Chapter 10)

Disequilibrium A state of either surplus or shortage in a market. (Chapter 3)

Disequilibrium Price A price other than equilibrium price. A price at which quantity demanded does not equal quantity supplied. (Chapter 3)

Disposable Income The portion of personal income that can be used for consumption or saving. It is equal to personal income minus personal taxes (especially income taxes). (Chapter 6)

Disutility The dissatisfaction one receives from a bad. (Chapter 1)

Double Coincidence of Wants In a barter economy, a requirement that must be met before a trade can be made. It specifies that a trader must find another trader who is willing to trade what the first trader wants and at the same time wants what the first trader has. (Chapter 12)

Double Counting Counting a good more than once when computing GDP. (Chapter 6)

(Downward-Sloping) Demand Curve The graphical representation of the law of demand. (Chapter 3)

Dumping The sale of goods abroad at a price below their cost and below the price charged in the domestic market. (Chapter 18)

Economic Growth Increases in Real GDP. (Chapter 6)

Economic System The way in which society decides to answer key economic questions—in particular those questions that relate to production and trade. (Chapter 2)

Economics The science of scarcity: the science of how individuals and societies deal with the fact that wants are greater than the limited resources available to satisfy those wants. (Chapter 1)

Efficiency Exists when marginal benefits equal marginal costs. In terms of production, the condition where the maximum output is produced with given resources and technology. Efficiency implies the impossibility of gains in one area without losses in another. (Chapters 1, 2)

Efficiency Wage Models These models hold that it is sometimes in the best interest of business firms to pay their employees higher-than-equilibrium wage rates. (Chapter 9)

Employment Rate The percentage of the civilian noninstitutional population that is employed: Employment rate = Number of employed persons/Civilian noninstitutional population. (Chapter 5)

Entrepreneurship The particular talent that some people have for organizing the resources of land, labor, and capital to produce goods, seek new business opportunities, and develop new ways of doing things. (Chapter 1)

Equation of Exchange An identity stating that the money supply times velocity must be equal to the price level times Real GDP. (Chapter 14)

Equilibrium Equilibrium means "at rest"; it is descriptive of a natural resting place. Equilibrium in a market is the price-quantity combination from which there is no tendency for buyers or sellers to move away. Graphically, equilibrium is the intersection point of the supply and demand curves. (Chapters 1, 3)

Equilibrium Price (Market-Clearing Price) The price at which quantity demanded of the good equals quantity supplied. (Chapter 3)

Equilibrium Quantity The quantity that corresponds to equilibrium price. The quantity at which the amount of the good that buyers are willing and able to buy equals the amount that sellers are willing and able to sell, and both equal the amount actually bought and sold. (Chapter 3)

Ex Ante Phrase that means "before," as in before a trade. (Chapter 2)

Ex Post Phrase that means "after," as in after a trade. (Chapter 2)

Excess Reserves Any reserves held beyond the required amount. The difference between (total) reserves and required reserves. (Chapter 12)

Exchange Rate The price of one currency in terms of another currency. (Chapters 7, 19)

Excludability A good is excludable if it is possible, or not prohibitively costly, to exclude someone from receiving the benefits of the good after it has been produced. (Chapter 11)

Expansionary Fiscal Policy Increases in government expenditures and/or decreases in taxes to achieve particular economic goals. (Chapter 10)

Expansionary Monetary Policy The Fed increases the money supply. (Chapter 15)

Expectations Effect The change in the interest rate due to a change in the expected inflation rate. (Chapter 14)

Exports Total foreign spending on domestic (U.S.) goods. (Chapter 6)

Fallacy of Composition The erroneous view that what is good or true for the individual is necessarily good or true for the group. (Chapter 1)

Federal Funds Market A market where banks lend reserves to one another, usually for short periods. (Chapter 13)

Federal Funds Rate The interest rate in the federal funds market; the interest rate banks charge one another to borrow reserves. (Chapter 13)

Federal Open Market Committee (FOMC) The 12-member policymaking group within the Fed. This committee has the authority to conduct open market operations. (Chapter 13)

Federal Reserve Notes Paper money issued by the Fed. (Chapter 12)

Federal Reserve System (the Fed) The central bank of the United States. (Chapter 12)

Final Good A good in the hands of its final user. (Chapter 6)

Fine-Tuning The (usually frequent) use of monetary and fiscal policies to counteract even small undesirable movements in economic activity. (Chapter 15)

Fiscal Policy Changes in government expenditures and/or taxes to achieve particular economic goals, such as low unemployment, stable prices, and economic growth. (Chapter 10)

Fixed Exchange Rate System The system where a nation's currency is set at a fixed rate relative to all other currencies, and central banks intervene in the foreign exchange market to maintain the fixed rate. (Chapter 19)

Fixed Investment Business purchases of capital goods, such as machinery and factories, and purchases of new residential housing. (Chapter 6)

Flexible Exchange Rate System The system whereby exchange rates are determined by the forces of supply and demand for a currency. (Chapter 19)

Foreign Exchange Market The market in which currencies of different countries are exchanged. (Chapter 19)

Fractional Reserve Banking A banking arrangement that allows banks to hold reserves equal to only a fraction of their deposit liabilities. (Chapter 12)

Free Rider Anyone who receives the benefits of a good without paying for it. (Chapter 11)

Frictional Unemployment Unemployment due to the natural "frictions" of the economy, which is caused by

changing market conditions and is represented by qualified individuals with transferable skills who change jobs. (Chapter 5)

Friedman Natural Rate Theory The idea that in the long run, unemployment is at its natural rate. Within the Phillips curve framework, the natural rate theory specifies that there is a long-run Phillips curve, which is vertical at the natural rate of unemployment. (Chapter 16)

Full Employment The condition that exists when the unemployment rate is equal to the natural unemployment rate. (Chapter 5)

Gold Standard The monetary arrangement whereby a nation backs its paper money totally or partially with gold. (Chapter 15)

Good Anything from which individuals receive utility or satisfaction. (Chapter 1)

Government Purchases Federal, state, and local government purchases of goods and services and gross investment in highways, bridges, and so on. (Chapter 6)

Government Transfer Payments Payments to persons that are not made in return for goods and services currently supplied. (Chapter 6)

Gross Domestic Product (GDP) The total market value of all final goods and services produced annually within a country's borders. (Chapters 1 Appendix, 6)

Gross National Product (GNP) The total market value of all final goods and services produced annually by the citizens of a country. (Chapter 6)

Imports Total domestic (U.S.) spending on foreign goods. (Chapter 6)

Income Effect In macroeconomics, the change in the interest rate due to a change in Real GDP. In microeconomics, the portion of the change in the quantity demanded of a good that is attributable to a change in real income (brought about by a change in absolute price). (Chapter 14)

Incomplete Crowding Out The decrease in one or more components of private spending only partially offsets the increase in government spending. (Chapter 10)

Independent Two variables are independent if as one changes, the other does not. (Chapter 1 Appendix)

Industrial Policy A deliberate policy by which government "waters the green spots," or aids those industries that are most likely to be successful in the world marketplace. (Chapter 17)

Inefficiency In terms of production, the condition where less than the maximum output is produced with given resources and technology. Inefficiency implies the possibility of gains in one area without losses in another. (Chapter 2)

Inferior Good A good the demand for which falls (rises) as income rises (falls). (Chapter 3)

Inflation An increase in the price level. (Chapter 5)

Inflationary Gap The condition where the Real GDP the economy is producing is greater than the Natural Real GDP and the unemployment rate is less than the natural unemployment rate. (Chapter 8)

Interest Rate Effect The changes in household and business buying as the interest rate changes (which, in turn, is a reflection of a change in the demand for, or supply of, credit brought on by price level changes). (Chapter 7)

Intermediate Good A good that is an input in the production of a final good. (Chapter 6)

International Monetary Fund (IMF) An international organization created to oversee the international monetary system. The IMF does not control the world's money supply, but it does hold currency reserves for member nations and make loans to central banks. (Chapter 19)

International Trade Effect The change in foreign sector spending as the price level changes. (Chapter 7)

Inventory Investment Changes in the stock of unsold goods. (Chapter 6)

Inversely Related Two variables are inversely related if they change in opposite ways. (Chapter 1 Appendix)

Investment The sum of all purchases of newly produced capital goods, changes in business inventories, and purchases of new residential housing. (Chapter 6)

Labor The physical and mental talents people contribute to the production process. (Chapter 1)

Labor Force Participation Rate The percentage of the civilian noninstitutional population that is in the civilian labor force: Labor force participation rate = Civilian labor force/Civilian non-institutional population. (Chapter 5)

Laffer Curve The curve, named after Arthur Laffer, that shows the relationship between tax rates and tax revenues. According to the Laffer curve, as tax rates rise from zero, tax revenues rise, reach a maximum at some point, and then fall with further increases in tax rates. (Chapter 10)

Laissez-faire A public policy of not interfering with market activities in the economy. (Chapter 8)

Land All natural resources, such as minerals, forests, water, and unimproved land. (Chapter 1)

Law of Demand As the price of a good rises, the quantity demanded of the good falls, and as the price of a good falls, the quantity demanded of the good rises, *ceteris paribus*. (Chapter 3)

Law of Diminishing Marginal Utility For a given time period, the marginal (additional) utility or satisfaction gained by consuming equal successive units of a good will decline as the amount consumed increases. (Chapter 3)

Law of Increasing Opportunity Costs As more of a good is produced, the opportunity costs of producing that good increase. (Chapter 2)

Law of Supply As the price of a good rises, the quantity supplied of the good rises, and as the price of a good falls, the quantity supplied of the good falls, *ceteris paribus*. (Chapter 3)

Liquidity Effect The change in the interest rate due to a change in the supply of loanable funds. (Chapter 14)

Liquidity Trap The horizontal portion of the demand curve for money. (Chapter 15)

Long-Run Aggregate Supply (LRAS) Curve The *LRAS* curve is a vertical line at the level of Natural Real GDP. It represents the output the economy produces when wages and prices have adjusted to their (final) equilibrium levels and neither producers nor workers have any relevant misperceptions. (Chapter 7)

Long-Run Equilibrium The condition that exists in the economy when wages and prices have adjusted to their (final) equilibrium levels and neither producers nor workers have any relevant misperceptions. Graphically, long-run equilibrium occurs at the intersection of the *AD* and *LRAS* curves. (Chapter 7)

M1 Includes currency held outside banks + checkable deposits + traveler's checks. (Chapter 12)

M2 Includes M1 + savings deposits (including money market deposit accounts) + small-denomination time deposits + money market mutual funds (noninstitutional). (Chapter 12)

Macroeconomics The branch of economics that deals with human behavior and choices as they relate to highly aggregate markets (such as the goods and services market) or to the entire economy. (Chapter 1)

Managed Float A managed flexible exchange rate system, under which nations now and then intervene to adjust their official reserve holdings to moderate major swings in exchange rates. (Chapter 19)

Marginal (Income) Tax Rate The change in a person's tax payment divided by the change in the person's taxable income: ΔTax payment/ΔTaxable income. (Chapter 10)

Marginal Propensity to Consume (MPC) The ratio of the change in consumption to the change in disposable income: $MPC = \Delta C/\Delta Y_d$. (Chapter 9)

Marginal Propensity to Save (MPS) The ratio of the change in saving to the change in disposable income: $MPS = \Delta S/\Delta Y_d$. (Chapter 9)

Medium of Exchange Anything that is generally acceptable in exchange for goods and services. A function of money. (Chapter 12)

Menu Costs The costs of changing prices. (Chapter 7)

Merchandise Trade Balance The difference between the value of merchandise exports and the value of merchandise imports. (Chapter 19)

Merchandise Trade Deficit The situation where the value of merchandise exports is less than the value of merchandise imports. (Chapter 19)

Merchandise Trade Surplus The situation where the value of merchandise exports is greater than the value of merchandise imports. (Chapter 19)

Microeconomics The branch of economics that deals with human behavior and choices as they relate to relatively small units—an individual, a firm, an industry, a single market. (Chapter 1)

Mixed Capitalism An economic system characterized by largely private ownership of the factors of production, market allocation of resources, and decentralized decision making. Most economic activities take place in the private sector in this system, but government plays a substantial economic and regulatory role. (Chapter 2)

Monetary Policy Changes in the money supply, or in the rate of change of the money supply, to achieve particular macroeconomic goals. (Chapter 15)

Monetary Wealth The value of a person's monetary assets. Wealth, as distinguished from monetary wealth, refers to the value of all assets owned, both monetary and nonmonetary. In short, a person's wealth equals his or her monetary wealth (such as $1,000 cash) plus nonmonetary wealth (a car or a house). (Chapter 7)

Money Any good that is widely accepted for purposes of exchange and in the repayment of debts. (Chapter 12)

Money Market Deposit Account An interest-earning account at a bank or thrift institution. Usually a minimum balance is required for an MMDA. Most MMDAs offer limited check-writing privileges. (Chapter 12)

Money Market Mutual Fund An interest-earning account at a mutual fund company. Usually a minimum balance is required for an MMMF account. Most MMMF accounts offer limited check-writing privileges. Only noninstitutional MMMFs are part of M2. (Chapter 12)

Multiplier The number that is multiplied by the change in autonomous spending to obtain the change in Real GDP: $m = 1/(1 - MPC)$. (Chapter 9)

National Income Total income earned by U.S. citizens and businesses, no matter where they reside or are located. National income is the sum of the payments to resources (land, labor, capital, and entrepreneurship). National income = compensation of employees + proprietors' income + corporate profits + rental income of persons + net interest. (Chapter 6)

Natural Real GDP The Real GDP that is produced at the natural unemployment rate. The Real GDP that is produced when the economy is in long-run equilibrium. (Chapter 7)

Natural Unemployment Unemployment caused by frictional and structural factors in the economy. Natural unemployment rate = Frictional unemployment rate + Structural unemployment rate. (Chapter 5)

Net Domestic Product (NDP) GDP minus the capital consumption allowance. (Chapter 6)

Net Exports Exports minus imports. (Chapter 6)

Neutral Good A good the demand for which does not change as income rises or falls. (Chapter 3)

Nominal Income The current-dollar amount of a person's income. (Chapter 5)

Nominal Interest Rate The interest rate actually charged (or paid) in the market; the market interest rate. The nominal interest rate = Real interest rate + Expected inflation rate. The interest rate determined by the forces of supply and demand in the loanable funds market. (Chapter 14)

Nonactivists Persons who argue against the deliberate use of discretionary fiscal and monetary policies. They believe in a permanent, stable, rules-based monetary and fiscal framework. (Chapter 15)

Nonexcludability A good is nonexcludable if it is impossible, or prohibitively costly, to exclude someone from receiving the benefits of the good after it has been produced. (Chapter 11)

Nonrivalrous in Consumption A good is nonrivalrous in consumption if its consumption by one person does not reduce its consumption by others. (Chapter 11)

Normal Good A good the demand for which rises (falls) as income rises (falls). (Chapter 3)

Normative Economics The study of "what should be" in economic matters. (Chapter 1)

One-Shot Inflation A one-time increase in the price level. An increase in the price level that does not continue. (Chapter 14)

Open Market Operations The buying and selling of government securities by the Fed. (Chapter 13)

Open Market Purchase The buying of government securities by the Fed. (Chapter 13)

Open Market Sale The selling of government securities by the Fed. (Chapter 13)

Opportunity Cost The most highly valued opportunity or alternative forfeited when a choice is made. (Chapter 1)

Optimal Currency Area A geographic area in which exchange rates can be fixed or a common currency used without sacrificing domestic economic goals—such as low unemployment. (Chapter 19)

Overvaluation A currency is overvalued if its price in terms of other currencies is above the equilibrium price. (Chapter 19)

Own Price The price of a good. For example, if the price of oranges is $1, this is (its) own price. (Chapter 3)

Per Capita Real Economic Growth An increase from one period to the next in per capita Real GDP, which is Real GDP divided by population. (Chapter 17)

Personal Income The amount of income that individuals actually receive. It is equal to national income minus undistributed corporate profits, social insurance taxes, and corporate profits taxes, plus transfer payments. (Chapter 6)

Phillips Curve A curve that originally showed the relationship between wage inflation and unemployment. Now it more often shows the relationship between price inflation and unemployment. (Chapter 16)

Policy Ineffectiveness Proposition (PIP) If (1) a policy change is correctly anticipated, (2) individuals form their expectations rationally, and (3) wages and prices are flexible, then neither fiscal policy nor monetary policy is effective at meeting macroeconomic goals. (Chapter 16)

Positive Economics The study of "what is" in economic matters. (Chapter 1)

Price Ceiling A government-mandated maximum price above which legal trades cannot be made. (Chapter 3)

Price Floor A government-mandated minimum price below which legal trades cannot be made. (Chapter 3)

Price Index A measure of the price level. (Chapter 5)

Price Level The weighted average of the prices of all goods and services. (Chapter 5)

Price-Level Effect The change in the interest rate due to a change in the price level. (Chapter 14)

Producers' (Sellers') Surplus (PS) The difference between the price sellers receive for a good and the minimum or lowest price for which they would have sold the good. PS = Price received − Minimum selling price. (Chapter 2)

Production Possibilities Frontier (PPF) Represents the possible combinations of two goods that can be produced in a certain period of time, under the conditions of a given state of technology and fully employed resources. (Chapter 2)

(Production) Subsidy A monetary payment by government to a producer of a good or service. (Chapter 3)

Profit The difference between total revenue and total cost. (Chapter 1)

Progressive Income Tax An income tax system in which one's tax rate rises as one's taxable income rises (up to some point). (Chapter 11)

Proportional Income Tax An income tax system in which one's tax rate is the same no matter what one's taxable income is. (Chapter 11)

Public Debt The total amount the federal government owes its creditors. (Chapter 11)

Public Good A good the consumption of which by one person does not reduce the consumption by another person— that is, a public good is characterized by nonrivalry in consumption. There are both excludable and nonexcludable public goods. An excludable public good is a good that while nonrivalrous in consumption can be denied to a person who does not pay for it. A nonexcludable public good is a good that is nonrivalrous in consumption and that cannot be denied to a person who does not pay for it. (Chapter 11)

Purchasing Power The quantity of goods and services that can be purchased with a unit of money. Purchasing power and the price level are inversely related: As the price level goes up (down), purchasing power goes down (up). (Chapter 7)

Purchasing Power Parity (PPP) Theory States that exchange rates between any two currencies will adjust to reflect changes in the relative price levels of the two countries. (Chapter 19)

Quota A legal limit on the amount of a good that may be imported. (Chapter 18)

Rational Expectations Expectations that individuals form based on past experience and also on their predictions about the effects of present and future policy actions and events. (Chapter 16)

Rationing Device A means for deciding who gets what of available resources and goods. (Chapter 1)

Real Balance Effect The change in the purchasing power of dollar-denominated assets that results from a change in the price level. (Chapter 7)

Real GDP The value of the entire output produced annually within a country's borders, adjusted for price changes. (Chapter 6)

Real Income Nominal income adjusted for price changes. A person has more (less) real income as the price of a good falls (rises), *ceteris paribus*. (Chapter 5)

Real Interest Rate The nominal interest rate adjusted for expected inflation; that is, the nominal interest rate minus the expected inflation rate. When the expected inflation rate is zero, the real interest rate equals the nominal interest rate. (Chapter 14)

Recessionary Gap The condition where the Real GDP the economy is producing is less than the Natural Real GDP and the unemployment rate is greater than the natural unemployment rate. (Chapter 8)

Regressive Income Tax An income tax system in which one's tax rate declines as one's taxable income rises. (Chapter 11)

Relative Price The price of a good in terms of another good. (Chapter 3)

Required Reserve Ratio (r) A percentage of each dollar deposited that must be held on reserve (at the Fed or in the bank's vault). (Chapter 12)

Required Reserves The minimum amount of reserves a bank must hold against its checkable deposits as mandated by the Fed. (Chapter 12)

Reservation Wage The lowest wage a person will accept at any time in the job search process. (Chapter 5)

Reserve Requirement The rule that specifies the amount of reserves a bank must hold to back up deposits. (Chapter 13)

Reserves The sum of bank deposits at the Fed and vault cash. (Chapter 12)

Revaluation A government act that changes the exchange rate by raising the official price of a currency. (Chapter 19)

Rivalrous in Consumption A good is rivalrous in consumption if its consumption by one person reduces its consumption by others. (Chapter 11)

Savings Deposit An interest-earning account at a commercial bank or thrift institution. Normally, checks cannot be written on savings deposits and the funds in a savings deposit can be withdrawn (at any time) without a penalty payment. (Chapter 12)

Say's Law Supply creates its own demand. Production creates demand sufficient to purchase all goods and services produced. (Chapter 8)

Scarcity The condition in which our wants are greater than the limited resources available to satisfy those wants. (Chapter 1)

Short-Run Aggregate Supply (SRAS) Curve A curve that shows the quantity supplied of all goods and services (Real GDP) at different price levels, *ceteris paribus*. (Chapter 7)

Short-Run Equilibrium The condition that exists in the economy when the quantity demanded of Real GDP equals the (short-run) quantity supplied of Real GDP. This condition is met where the aggregate demand curve intersects the short-run aggregate supply curve. (Chapter 7)

Shortage (Excess Demand) A condition in which quantity demanded is greater than quantity supplied. Shortages occur only at prices below equilibrium price. (Chapter 3)

Simple Deposit Multiplier The reciprocal of the required reserve ratio, $1/r$. (Chapter 12)

Simple Quantity Theory of Money The theory that assumes that velocity (V) and Real GDP (Q) are constant and predicts that changes in the money supply (M) lead to strictly proportional changes in the price level (P). (Chapter 14)

Slope The ratio of the change in the variable on the vertical axis to the change in the variable on the horizontal axis. (Chapter 1 Appendix)

Special Drawing Right (SDR) An international money, created by the IMF, in the form of bookkeeping entries; like gold and currencies, they can be used by nations to settle international accounts. (Chapter 19)

Special Interest Group A subset of the general population that holds (usually) intense preferences for or against a particular government service, activity, or policy. Often special interest groups gain from public policies that may not be in accord with the interests of the general public. (Chapter 11)

Stagflation The simultaneous occurrence of high rates of inflation and unemployment. (Chapter 16)

Store of Value The ability of an item to hold value over time. A function of money. (Chapter 12)

Structural Deficit The part of the budget deficit that would exist even if the economy were operating at full employment. (Chapter 11)

Structural Unemployment Unemployment due to structural changes in the economy that eliminate some jobs and create others for which the unemployed are unqualified. (Chapter 5)

Substitutes Two goods that satisfy similar needs or desires. If two goods are substitutes, the demand for one rises as the price of the other rises (or the demand for one falls as the price of the other falls). (Chapter 3)

Supply The willingness and ability of sellers to produce and offer to sell different quantities of a good at different prices during a specific time period. (Chapter 3)

Supply Schedule The numerical tabulation of the quantity supplied of a good at different prices. (Chapter 3)

Surplus (Excess Supply) A condition in which quantity supplied is greater than quantity demanded. Surpluses occur only at prices above equilibrium price. (Chapter 3)

T-Account A simplified balance sheet that shows the changes in a bank's assets and liabilities. (Chapter 12)

Tariff A tax on imports. (Chapter 18)

Tax Base When referring to income taxes, the total amount of taxable income. Tax revenue = Tax base × (average) Tax rate. (Chapter 10)

Technology The body of skills and knowledge concerning the use of resources in production. An advance in technology commonly refers to the ability to produce more output with a fixed amount of resources or the ability to produce the same output with fewer resources. (Chapter 2)

Terms of Trade How much of one thing is given up for how much of something else. (Chapter 2)

Theory An abstract representation of the real world designed with the intent to better understand that world. (Chapter 1)

Tie-in Sale A sale whereby one good can be purchased only if another good is also purchased. (Chapter 3)

Time Deposit An interest-earning deposit with a specified maturity date. Time deposits are subject to penalties for early withdrawal. Small-denomination time deposits are deposits of less than $100,000. (Chapter 12)

Trade (Exchange) The process of giving up one thing for something else. (Chapter 2)

Trade Deficit The situation where the value of exports is less than the value of imports. (Chapter 10)

Tradeoff More of one good means less of another good. (Chapter 2)

Transaction Costs The costs associated with the time and effort needed to search out, negotiate, and consummate an exchange. (Chapter 2)

Transfer Payment A payment to a person that is not made in return for goods and services currently supplied. (Chapter 6)

Transmission Mechanism The routes or channels that ripple effects created in the money market travel to affect the goods and services market (represented by the aggregate demand and aggregate supply curves in the *AD-AS* framework). (Chapter 15)

U.S. Treasury Securities Bonds and bondlike securities issued by the U.S. Treasury when it borrows. (Chapter 13)

Undervaluation A currency is undervalued if its price in terms of other currencies is below the equilibrium price. (Chapter 19)

Unemployment Rate The percentage of the civilian labor force that is unemployed: Unemployment rate = Number of unemployed persons/Civilian labor force. (Chapter 5)

Unit of Account A common measure in which relative values are expressed. A function of money. (Chapter 12)

(Upward-Sloping) Supply Curve The graphical representation of the law of supply. (Chapter 3)

Utility A measure of the satisfaction, happiness, or benefit that results from the consumption of a good. (Chapter 1)

Value Added The dollar value contributed to a final good at each stage of production. (Chapter 6)

Velocity The average number of times a dollar is spent to buy final goods and services in a year. (Chapter 14)

"Voluntary" Export Restraint (VER) An agreement between two countries in which the exporting country "voluntarily" agrees to limit its exports to the importing country. (Chapter 18)

Wealth The value of all assets owned, both monetary and nonmonetary. (Chapter 7)

Photo Credits

Index